Tell It All

by

MRS. T. B. H. STENHOUSE

with an Introductory Preface by
Harriet Beecher Stowe

APPLEWOOD BOOKS
Carlisle, Massachusetts

Tell It All
was originally published in 1875

ISBN: 978-1-4290-1902-6

For a free copy of our current print catalog featuring our bestselling books, write to:

APPLEWOOD BOOKS
P.O. Box 27
Carlisle, MA 01741

For more complete listings,
visit us on the web at:
awb.com

Prepared for publishing by HP

Eng⁴ by Geo E Perine, New York

Faithfully Yours
Fanny Stenhouse

A D WORTHINGTON & Cº
Hartford.

"TELL IT ALL":

THE STORY OF A LIFE'S EXPERIENCE

IN

MORMONISM.

An Autobiography:

BY

Mrs. T. B. H. STENHOUSE,

OF SALT LAKE CITY,

FOR MORE THAN TWENTY YEARS THE WIFE OF A MORMON MISSIONARY AND ELDER.

WITH INTRODUCTORY PREFACE BY MRS. HARRIET BEECHER STOWE.

Full-page Illustrations, and steel-plate Portrait of the Author.

[PUBLISHED BY SUBSCRIPTION ONLY.]

———

HARTFORD, CONN.:
A. D. WORTHINGTON & CO., PUBLISHERS.
QUEEN CITY PUBLISHING CO., CINCINNATI. EXCELSIOR PUBLISHING CO., ST. LOUIS.
LOUIS LLOYD & CO., CHICAGO. A. L. BANCROFT & CO., SAN FRANCISCO.
1875.

TO

MY CHILDREN;

WITH

ALL A MOTHER'S LOVE AND TENDERNESS,

THIS VOLUME,

THE

STORY OF MY LIFE'S EXPERIENCE,

IS

AFFECTIONATELY INSCRIBED.

List of Illustrations

CHAS. SPIEGLE, OF NEW YORK.

PUBLISHERS' NOTICE.

————•◦•————

By the merest accident, a few months ago, in New York City, the Publishers became personally acquainted with Mr. T. B. H. Stenhouse, of Salt Lake City, the husband of the Author of the present volume, and before they separated, preliminary steps were taken for its publication.

Almost a year before that time, Mrs. Harriet Beecher Stowe, the talented author of "Uncle Tom's Cabin," had addressed a kind note to Mrs. Stenhouse, congratulating her upon the appeal which she had made on behalf of the women of Utah, in a little work which she had then just published. Some correspondence subsequently ensued between the two ladies who had so successfully attacked "the twin relics of barbarism"—polygamy and slavery. They afterwards became personally acquainted ; and when Mrs. Stenhouse requested Mrs. Stowe to write the preface for her new work, that gifted author unhesitatingly replied : "I am happy to be able to do the least thing which can show how heartily I sympathise with the effort you are making. May God bless both it and you, is the prayer of yours ever truly,—H. B. Stowe."

PREFACE

MRS. HARRIET BEECHER STOWE.

————•♦•————

In these pages, a woman, a wife and mother, speaks the sorrows and oppressions of which she has been the witness and the victim.

It is because her sorrows and her oppressions are those of thousands, who, suffering like her, cannot or dare not speak for themselves, that she thus gives this history to the public.

It is no sensational story, but a plain, unvarnished tale of truth, stranger and sadder than fiction.

Our day has seen a glorious breaking of fetters. The slave-pens of the South have become a nightmare of the past ; the auction-block and whipping-post have given place to the church and school-house ; and the songs of emancipated millions are heard through our land.

Shall we not then hope that the hour is come to loose the bonds of a cruel slavery whose chains have cut into the very hearts of thousands of our sisters—a slavery which debases and degrades womanhood, motherhood, and the family?

Let every happy wife and mother who reads these lines give her sympathy, prayers, and efforts to free her sisters from this degrading bondage. Let all the womanhood of the country stand united for them. There is a power in combined enlightened sentiment and sympathy before which every form of injustice and cruelty *must* finally go down.

May He who came to break every yoke hasten this deliverance.

HARRIET BEECHER STOWE.

PREFACE.

In the fall of the year 1869, a few earnest, thinking men, members of the Mormon Church, and living in Salt Lake City, inaugurated what was regarded at the time as a grand schism. Those who had watched with anxiety the progress of Mormonism, hailed the "New Movement" as the harbinger of the work of disintegration so long anticipated by the thoughtful-minded Saints, and believed that the opposition to Theocracy then begun, would continue until the extraordinary assumptions of the Mormon priesthood were exploded, and Mormonism itself should lose its political *status* and find its place only among the singular sects of the day.

It was freely predicted that Woman, in her turn, would accept her part in the work of reformation, take up the marriage question among the Saints, and make an end of polygamy.

Little did I imagine at that period, that any such mission as that which I have since realised as mine, was in the Providence of Time awaiting me, or that I should ever have the boldness, either with tongue or pen, to plead the cause of the Women of Utah. But, impelled by those unseen influences which shape our destinies, I took my stand with the "heretics;" and, as it happened, my own was the first woman's name enrolled in their cause.

The circumstances which wrought a change in my own life produced a corresponding revolution in the life of my husband.

In withdrawing from the Mormon Church, we laid ourselves, our associations and the labors of over twenty years, upon the altar, and took up the burden of life anew. We had sacrificed everything in obedience to the "counsel" of Brigham Young; and my husband, to give a new direction to his mind, and also to form some plan for our future life, thought it advisable that he should visit New York. He did so; and shortly after employed himself in writing a history of the Mormon Church, which has since been published.

In course of time, the burden of providing for a large family, and the anxiety and care of conducting successfully a business among a people who make it a religious duty to sternly set their faces against those who dissent from their faith, exhausted my physical and mental strength. Considering, therefore, that change might be beneficial to me, and my own personal affairs urgently calling me to New York City, I followed my husband thither.

On my way East, I met a highly-valued friend of my family, who, in the course of our journey together over the Pacific Railroad, enthusiastically urged me to tell the story of my life, and to give to the world what I knew about Polygamy. I had been repeatedly advised to do so by friends at home, but up to that time no plan had been arranged for carrying out the suggestion.

I had hardly arrived in New York, before the electric messenger announced that a severe snow-storm was raging on the vast plains between the Rocky Mountains and the Missouri River, and for several weeks all traffic over the Union Pacific Railroad was interrupted, and I could not return to my home in the distant West.

That unlooked-for snow-blockade became seriously annoying; for not only was I most anxious to return to my children, but also, never having known an idle hour, I could not live without something to do. At that moment of unsettled feeling, a lady-friend, with whom I was visiting, suggested again " *the book*;" and she would not permit me to leave her house, until she had exacted from me a promise that it should be written.

Next morning, I began my task in earnest. I faithfully kept my room and labored unremittingly; and in three weeks the manuscript of my little work on "Polygamy in Utah," was completed.

It was issued in pamphlet form, and was very kindly welcomed by the press — both secular and religious — and for this I was sincerely grateful. I had not, up to that time, thought of much else than its effect upon the people of Utah; but the voluminous notices which that little book received, showed the deep interest which the people of the United States had taken in "the Mormon question," and how ardently they desired to see the extinction of the polygamic institution among the Saints.

In Salt Lake City, I was so situated that I was daily—I might almost say hourly—brought in contact with visitors to the Modern Zion; for, during the summer, thousands of travellers pass over the Pacific Railroad. Not a few of these called to see me; and I received from ladies and gentlemen—whose kind interest in my welfare I felt very deeply—many personal attentions, many words of sympathy and encouragement, and many intelligent and useful suggestions in respect to my future life. Indeed, I saw myself quite unexpectedly, and, I may truthfully say, without my own desire, become an object of interest.

By the earnest suggestions of friends and strangers, and by the widely published opinions of the press, I was made to feel that I had but *begun* my work—that I had but partly drawn aside the veil that covered the worst oppression and degradation of woman ever known in a civilised country. Nearly all who spoke to me expressed their surprise that intelligent men and women should be found in communion with the Mormon Church, in which it was so clearly evident that the teachings of Christianity had been supplanted by an attempt to imitate the barbarism of Oriental nations in a long past age, and the sweet influences of the religion of Jesus were superseded by the most objectionable practices of the ancient Jews. How persons of education and refinement could ever

have embraced a faith that prostrated them at the feet of
the Mormon Prophet, and his successor Brigham Young, was
to the enquiring mind a perfect mystery.

The numerous questions which I had to answer, and the
explanations which I had to give, shewed me that my little
book had only whetted the appetite of the intelligent investi-
gator, and that there was a general call for *a woman's book*
on Mormonism, a book that should reveal *the inner life* of
the Saints,—exhibit the influences which had contributed to
draw Christian people away from Christian Churches to the
standard of the American Prophet, Joseph Smith, and subject
them to the power of that organisation which has, since his
death, subjugated the mass of the Mormon people in Utah
to the will and wickedness of the Priesthood under the leadership of Brother Brigham.

There have from time to time appeared many works on
Mormonism which professed to give an insight into the "inner
life" of the Saints. Some of those books were written by
women; some by visitors to Utah, or persons who had resided
for a longer or shorter period in the Territory; and more than
one at least was published under the name of women who
claimed to be members of the Mormon Church. How untrustworthy the accounts of visitors and Gentiles are, and the
reason why such should be the case, I shall hereafter, in the
course of this volume, have occasion to explain;—and that
the autobiographies of supposed Mormon women were equally
unreliable, the following facts will clearly demonstrate.

A French Lady—a Countess and a woman of the world—
Madame Olympe Odouard—came to see me in Salt Lake City.
She was a woman of intelligence and quick perception, with
whom to spend an hour was a perfect pleasure. After her
return to France, she, of course, wrote a book, entitled *Le Far
West.* And in that book, (page 335,) she said:

"Il y a deux grands journaux à Salt Lake City: le *New Descret* et le *New
Telegraph.* Mr. Stenhouse, le redacteur en chef du premier, est un homme
éminemment instruit. Allemand d'origine, il parle le Français tres purement.
Sa femme, née Française, est une femme du monde, bonne, charmante, tres-
instruite, bonne musicienne, et mère de treize beaux enfants. C'est une ex-Sœur

de Charité et la seule femme Catholique et Française què soit parmi les Mormones."

Some of my readers may perhaps have forgotten their French lessons : I, therefore, translate :

There are two principal journals in Salt Lake City—the *New Deseret* and the *New Telegraph*. Mr. Stenhouse is editor-in-chief of the first. He is a well-taught man of German origin, and speaks the French language with the greatest purity. His wife, a French lady, is a woman of the world—good looking, charming, well educated, a good musician, and the mother of thirteen fine children. She is an ex-Sister of Charity, and the only French Catholic who has joined the "Mormon Church."

Now here is an example in type. Let us judge of its truthfulness. In the first place there never was such a paper as the *New Deseret* or the *New Telegraph*. The *Deseret News* has been in existence for some years. My husband assisted on its staff, but he was never editor-in-chief. The *Daily Telegraph* was my husband's own paper, but it never appeared under any other name. Little items may seem of small importance, but in a case where truthfulness is called in question, they are worth mentioning. Mr. Stenhouse is a Scotchman by birth, and I am an Englishwoman. His acquaintance with the French tongue is, of course, limited ; while I, for my part, never was, or will be, either a Roman Catholic or a Sister of Charity. Ten, and not thirteen "fine" children are all who call me mother; and at the time when Madame Olympe wrote there were only eight. Here I state the whole case briefly. Let the reader judge of the truthfulness of "travellers' stories."

That comprehensive and truthful works on this subject have appeared, I readily admit, but most of them are mere sketches :—such, for example, as that by Secretary Ferris—a Gentile, but a fair and impartial author ;—or else were published—as that, for instance, by John Hyde, a good man and a vigorous writer—so many years ago that they are now, to a great extent, out of date. Mrs. Waite is the best Gentile lady-writer; but for obvious reasons, although she was a woman of intelligence and penetration, her knowledge of the inner life of Mormonism was necessarily circumscribed.

Two books appeared, each claiming to be written by genu-

ine Mormon women. They were, however, originally published fifteen or twenty years ago ; and although they are still
on sale, they are, as a matter of course, silent concerning
recent events. The first of these two volumes was really
written by a gentleman who was himself neither a Mormon
nor had any intimate acquaintance with the system and doctrines of that people. He obtained from the lady—the supposed author—all the information which she was capable of
imparting, and then worked it up in a startling and sensational
manner, mingling facts and fiction in such a way that the
Mormons have always declared that the whole volume was a
scandalous libel.

The other volume was first published nearly twenty years
ago. It was professedly written by the wife of a Mormon elder ;
but it was really the production of an old lady in New Jersey,
who had never even been out to Utah, and who drew entirely
upon her own imagination for all that she could not adapt
from other sensational writers on Mormonism. This book
was first published by a New York firm, and being supposed
by the innocent public to be genuine, it had an extraordinary
circulation—forty or fifty thousand being sold. The publishers, however, failed, and the stereotype plates passed into other
hands. Subsequently the work having come under the notice
of a subscription firm at Hartford, they negotiated for the use
of the plates. One word of the heading of each page was
cut out, a new title was selected, some old illustrations and a
few new ones were added, and an ancient steel-plate portrait, which had once done duty in some book of poetry or
illustrated volume of fashionable beauties of years ago, was
vamped up, and the supposed signature of the fictitious author
was engraved beneath it. This book, now re-christened, and
apparently a new volume, was launched upon the market. It
is at the present moment advertised in many local newspapers,
and the confiding public cheerfully buy it under the impression that it is the genuine production of a Mormon woman.
Such is the history of some of the so-called autobiographies
which have appeared.

I mention these facts to show that the demand for a *true* history by *a real Mormon woman* has never yet been supplied. It was this knowledge which induced me to publish my former little work, and encourages me to hope that the present volume may meet with acceptance.

A few months after the publication of my first book, I was invited to lecture upon "Polygamy in Utah," and wherever I spoke I observed the same spirit of enquiry and met with a renewed demand for more of circumstance and narrative—which I had, from a sense of personal delicacy, withheld in my former work.

I saw no way of satisfying myself and others than by accepting the rather spiteful invitation of a certain Mormon paper to " TELL IT ALL," and this, in a narrative of my own personal experience, which I now present to the reader, I have endeavored to do. Myself not in any sense a literary woman, or making any pretensions as a writer, I hope to escape severe criticism from the public and the press. I had a simple story to tell—the story of my life and of the wrongs of women in Utah. Startling and terrible facts have fallen under my observation. These also I have related ; but my constant effort has been to tell my story in the plainest, simplest way, and to avoid exaggeration, but never shrink from a straightforward statement of facts. I have disguised nothing, and palliated nothing ; and I feel assured that those who from their actual and intimate acquaintance with Mormonism in Utah as it really is, are capable of passing a just and impartial judgment upon my story, will pronounce without hesitation that I have told " *the truth, the whole truth, and nothing but the truth.*"

FANNY STENHOUSE.

SALT LAKE CITY, UTAH.

CONTENTS.

—o—

CHAPTER I.

MY EARLY LIFE.

CHAPTER II.

MY FIRST INTRODUCTION TO MORMONISM.

CHAPTER VI.

THE FIRST WHISPERINGS OF POLYGAMY.

CHAPTER VII.

MY HUSBAND'S MISSION :—I AM LEFT ALONE.

2

CHAPTER XVII.

WE FORSAKE ALL, AND SET OUT FOR ZION—OUR JOURNEY ACROSS THE PLAINS.

CHAPTER XVIII.

MY FIRST IMPRESSIONS OF THE CITY OF THE SAINTS.

CHAPTER XIX.

BRIGHAM YOUNG AT HOME:—WE VISIT THE PROPHET AND HIS WIVES.

CHAPTER XX.

THE WIVES OF BRIGHAM YOUNG:—THEIR HISTORY AND THEIR DAILY LIFE.

CHAPTER XXI.

THE ORIGIN OF "THE REFORMATION": EXTRAORDINARY DOINGS OF THE SAINTS.

CHAPTER XXII.

THE "REIGN OF TERROR" IN UTAH:—THE REFORMATION OF THE SAINTS.

CHAPTER XXIII.

THE MOUNTAIN MEADOWS' MASSACRE:—"I WILL REPAY, SAITH THE LORD."

CHAPTER XXIV.

CHAPTER XXV.

CHAPTER XXVI.

CHAPTER XXVII.

CHAPTER XXVIII.

CHAPTER XXIX.

CHAPTER XXXVI.

MY DAUGHTER BECOMES THE FOURTH WIFE OF BRIGHAM YOUNG'S SON— THE SECOND ENDOWMENTS.

CHAPTER XXXVII.

REALITIES OF POLYGAMIC LIFE :—ORSON PRATT : THE STORY OF HIS YOUNG ENGLISH WIFE.

CHAPTER XXXVIII.

CHAPTER XXXIX.

CHAPTER XL.

CHAPTER XLI.

MY HUSBAND DISFELLOWSHIPPED—WE APOSTATISE—BRUTAL OUTRAGE UPON MY HUSBAND AND MYSELF.

CHAPTER XLII.'

AMUSING TROUBLES OF MY TALKATIVE FRIEND—CHARLOTTE WITH THE GOLDEN HAIR!

CHAPTER XLIII.

CHAPTER I.

MY EARLY LIFE.

The Memory of my Youthful Days—Early Religious Impressions—I become a Church-Member—My Pious Admirer—A brief Homily on Feminine Vanities —My first Start in Life—Faithful Counsels of a Friend—Life in a French School—The Maison-Martin—Preparing my Lessons—Objecting to a Protestant—"Assisting" at Service—My Ghostly Adviser—The "instructions" of a Handsome Young Priest—Flirtation and Apostolic Succession—The Blind Leading the Blind—The Scene of Labor Changed—Domestic life at St. Brieux— An indifferent Young Gentleman—The Presence of an "Icicle"—Quiet Attentions to "Mademoiselle-Miss"—The Man who waits Wins—My Affianced Lover—Reasons why a French girl Marries—Views of Marriage among the French—Traces of Early Teachings—Mental Struggles and Doubts—I Resolve to Visit England—The Crisis of my Life.

THE story which I propose to tell in these pages is a plain, unexaggerated record of facts which have come immediately under my own notice, or which I have myself personally experienced.

Much that to the reader may seem altogether incredible, would to a Mormon mind appear simply a matter of ordinary every-day occurrence with which everyone in Utah is supposed to be perfectly familiar. The reader must please remember that I am not telling—as so many writers have told in newspaper correspondence and sensational stories—the hasty and incorrect statements and opinions gleaned during a short visit to Salt Lake City ; but my own experience—the story of a faith, strange, wild, and terrible it may be, but which was once so intimately enwoven with all my associations that it became a part of my very existence itself ; and facts, the too true reality of which there are living witnesses by hundreds and even thousands who could attest if only they would.

With the reader's permission I shall briefly sketch my experience from the very beginning.

I was born in the year 1829, in St. Heliers, Jersey—one of the islands of the English Channel.

From my earliest recollection I was favorably disposed to religious influences, and when only fourteen years of age I became a member of the Baptist Church, of which my father and mother were also members. With the simplicity and enthusiasm of youth I was devoted to the religious faith of the denomination to which I had attached myself, and sought to live in a manner which should be acceptable to God.

My childhood passed away without the occurrence of any events which would be worthy of mention, although, of course, my mind was even then receiving that religious bias which afterwards led me to adopt the faith of the Latter-day Saints. Like most girls in their teens I had a natural love of dress— a weakness, if such it be, of the sex generally. I was not extravagant, for that I could not be; but thirty years ago members of dissenting churches were more staid in their dress and demeanor and were less of the world, I think, than they are to-day. In plainness of dress the Methodists and Baptists much resembled the Quakers. My girlish weakness caused me to be the subject of many a reprimand from older church-members, who were rather strict in their views. I well remember one smooth-faced, pious, corpulent brother who was old enough to be my father, saying to me one day: "My dear young sister, were it not for your love of dress, I have seriously thought that I would some day make you my wife." I wickedly resolved that if a few bright colored ribbons would disgust my pious admirer, it should not be my fault if he still continued to think of me. But many of our other church-members were more lenient. Our good minister in particular bore with my childish imperfections, as he said, on account of my youth and inexperience; and later still, when I was ready to leave my native island, an extra ribbon or a fashionable dress had not affected my standing in the Baptist denomination.

I mention these trifles, not because I attach any importance to them in themselves, but because similar religious tendencies and a devotional feeling were almost universally found to be the causes which induced men and women to join the Mormon Church. From among Roman Catholics, who place unquestioning confidence in their priesthood, and also from among persons predisposed to infidelity, came few, if any, converts to Mormonism. But it was from among the religiously inclined—the Evangelical Protestants of the Old World that the greater number of proselytes came.

But to return to my story. I was one of the younger members of a large family; and when I thought of the future I readily saw that if I desired a position in life I should have to make it for myself; and this I resolved to do. I began by consulting all my friends who I thought would be able to counsel or assist me in carrying out my determination; and before long I found the opportunity which I sought. An English lady, the wife of a captain in the British army, to whom I had confided my aspirations, proposed—although I was not yet fifteen years of age—to take me with her to France, in the temporary capacity of governess to her children, assuring me at the same time that she would advance my interests in every possible way after our arrival.

This lady and her husband were as kind to me as my own parents could have been; and soon after our arrival in France they procured for me a situation in one of the best schools in St. Brieux, called the Maison-Martin, where, young as I was, I engaged myself to teach the young ladies fancy-needlework and embroidery, as well as to give lessons in English. Some of the elder girls, I soon found, were further advanced in fancy-needlework and some other matters than I was myself. This, of course, I did not tell them; but to supply my deficiency I spent many a midnight hour in study and in preparing myself to give the advanced instructions which would be required by my pupils on the following day. For some time after I began my work as teacher in that school, I spent the whole of my salary in paying for private lessons to keep me in advance of

3

my pupils. It was for awhile a severe task and a strain upon my youthful energies; but I have never since regretted it, as it gave an impulse to my mind that has remained with me through life.

I had not been more than six months in my situation when the parents of one of the pupils objected to the school retaining a Protestant teacher, and I was consequently given to understand that unless I consented to be instructed, if nothing more, in the Roman Catholic faith, I could not remain in my present position. This was my first experience of that religious intolerance of which I afterwards saw so much. The principal of the establishment, however, being very kindly disposed towards me, advised me to submit, and it was finally agreed that I should be allowed twelve months for instruction and consideration.

During this probationary year I attended mass every morning from seven to eight o'clock, and was present at vespers at least three times a week. Every Saturday morning I accompanied my pupils to the confessional, where I had to remain from seven o'clock till noon; after which we returned to breakfast. On Sundays there was the usual morning mass, and after that high mass; and in the afternoon, from two to four, we listened to a sermon. In addition to all these services, at which I was expected to "assist," a very good-looking, interesting young priest was appointed to attend to the spiritual instruction of the young Protestant, as they called me, after school hours. He saw me frequently, but he was ill-qualified to instruct me in the Catholic faith or to remove my doubts, for he was not himself too happy in the sacerdotal robe. At first he aimed at convincing me that the apostolic priesthood vested in the Fishermen of Galilee had descended in unbroken succession in the Church of Rome; but he seemed to me much more inclined for a flirtation than for argument; I thought I could at times discover something of regret on his own part at having taken holy orders; and in after years I heard that he had abandoned his profession.

To the numerous stories of Catholic oppression and artifice in undermining Protestants and seducing them from their faith, I cannot add my own testimony. Those among whom I lived very naturally desired that I should be instructed in their religion and join the church to which they belonged; but their bearing towards me was ever kind and respectful; although when the twelve months of probation had expired, I found myself as much attached to the religion of my childhood as ever, and had in consequence to resign my situation. I had made many warm friends in the school, and none were kinder to me than the principal, who proved her attachment by finding for me a lucrative situation in a wealthy private family.

My new position was a decided advance in social life. The family consisted of husband and wife, two children, the husband's brother, and an elderly uncle. The husband was a wealthy commoner. The lady by birth was of the *noblesse*, but poor. The guardians of the titled lady had formed a matrimonial alliance for her by advertisement, and, fortunately for them, when the husband and wife first saw each other, they loved—an experience not too common in France. The fruits of this marriage were happiness and two sweet little girls, who were, when I first knew them, of the ages of five and seven years respectively. The young gentleman alluded to—the husband's brother—had been educated for the church, but when the proper time came had refused to take orders; the uncle was a fine old gentleman, a retired general in the French army and a bachelor. Altogether they formed as happy a domestic circle as I had ever known. The position which I occupied among them was that of governess and English teacher to the two little girls.

My young charges during the first year made rapid progress, which was very gratifying to the family and secured for me their good-will and interest. Had I been their nearest relative I could not have received more respect and consideration from them. One member of the circle alone seemed to be entirely indifferent to my presence; this was the brother of Monsieur De Bosque. Though I had lived in the same house with him a whole year, and had sat at the same table every day, scarcely a word had ever passed between us beyond a formal salutation.

The young gentleman was very handsome, and when conversing with others his manner was extremely fascinating. I did not believe that I particularly desired his attentions, but his indifference annoyed me—for I had never before been treated with such coldness, and I determined to become as frigid and formal as he could possibly be himself. This formal acquaintanceship continued for two years, and I persuaded myself that I had become altogether indifferent to the presence of my icicle, while at the same time all the other members of the family increased in their manifestations of attachment to me.

But trifles often possess a great significance. It was the custom of the family to get up a little lottery once a week for the children, if my report of their deportment and progress was favorable. In this lottery were presents of books, toys, gloves, and a variety of fancy articles, and among them there was sure to be a *bouquet* of choice flowers for "Mademoiselle-Miss," as they familiarly called me. I knew not positively whom to thank, although I instinctively felt from whom they came, for the other members of the family always made me more useful presents. In time one little attention led to another, until at the end of three years I found myself the *fiancée* of the wealthy Constant De Bosque. Then—or rather shortly before—he avowed that he had been silently watching me all those years.

Madame De Bosque was opposed to my marriage with her brother-in-law, as she desired that he should marry one of her own wealthy cousins of the old *noblesse* of France. She treated me, notwithstanding, with great kindness and confined her opposition to persuading me not to listen to her brother's suit ; but finding opposition to ·his wishes ineffectual, she finally consented to our engagement, which took place in the following winter.

From what I observed of the relations which existed between husbands and wives in France, I did not feel perfectly happy in the thought of becoming the wife of a Frenchman, although I dearly loved the French people. Several of my young lady acquaintances, I knew, had married because it was fashionable, and especially because it was an emancipation from what ladies in the higher ranks of society regarded as a severe social restraint. It was considered shocking for any young lady to be seen talking to a young gentleman in the street; indeed it was hardly proper for any unmarried girl to be seen in the street at all without a *bonne* or some married lady to accompany her. But immediately she was married she was at liberty to flirt and promenade with all the gentlemen of her acquaintance, while her husband enjoyed the same liberty among the ladies. This state of affairs did not at all coincide with my English ideas, for to me the very thought of marriage was invested with the most sacred obligations, and I knew I should never be able to bring my mind to accept less from my husband than I should feel it my duty to render to him.

I loved the French people, and was pleased with their polite mannerism, but I was not French in character; and though the prospect before me of an alliance with a wealthy and noble family was certainly pleasant, and I was greatly attached to my *fiancée*, my mind was considerably agitated upon the subject of marriage, as it had before been occupied with religion.

During my sojourn in France I had frequently questioned myself whether I had not done wrong in remaining absent for so many years from my home and from communion with the church of my childhood, and I had always looked forward to the time when I should return to them again. To this occasional self-examination was now added another cause of anxiety, produced by the thought of marriage with a person of a different faith. Marriage, to me, was the all-important event in a woman's life, and some mysterious presentiment seemed to forewarn me that marriage in *my* life was to be more than an ordinary episode—though little did I then dream that it would have a polygamic shaping.

My young ambition alone had led me to France. I had aspired to an honorable social position, and had found both it and also devoted friends. Sometimes I felt that I could not relinquish what I had gained; at other times I yearned for the associations of my childhood and the guiding hand of earlier friends. The conflict in my mind was often painful. My early prejudices and the teachings of those around me induced me to believe that the Roman Catholic religion was entirely wrong; yet, notwithstanding, while living among Catholics I saw nothing to condemn in their personal lives, but much to the contrary. In fact, Romanism fascinated me, while it failed to convince my judgment.

While laboring under these conflicting sentiments, I resolved to visit my native land, to consult with my parents about my contemplated marriage; and for that purpose I asked and obtained two months' vacation. Surely some mysterious destiny must have been drawing me to England at that particular crisis, and before the fulfilling of my engagement, which would have changed so entirely the whole current of my existence.

CHAPTER II.

MY FIRST INTRODUCTION TO MORMONISM.

Returning Home—" *Au Revoir* "—A visit to Jersey—The Home of my Child-
hood—My First Introduction to Mormonism—An " Apostate's " View of the
Saints—Revelation and Roguery—A Matter of Personal Interest—A Lady's
Logic—A Warning against the New Religion—First Visit to a Mormon Meet-
ing—Catching the " Mormon Fever "—Snubbing an Elder—A Polite Saint—
Fighting a Delusion—Among Dear Friends—" Full of the Spirit"—Religion
in Practical Life—Preparing Comforts for the Missionary Elders—Emotional
Religion—The Testimony of the Spirit—Sunday Service among the Saints—
Contagious Enthusiasm—The Story of a Too-confiding Convert—How He
Went out to Zion—Terrible Fate of an Apostate—Killed by " the Indians "—
Preaching under Difficulties—My First Introduction to my Future Husband—
" The Other Daughter from France "—The Eloquence of Elder Stenhouse—
Creating an Impression—A Memorable Era in My Life.

DURING my residence in France, my parents had left St.
Heliers and returned to Southampton, England. To
visit them now I had to take a sailing vessel from Portrieux
to the Isle of Jersey, and thence I could take the steamer to
Southampton.

Monsieur and Madame De Bosque, together with the two
little girls, accompanied me in their private carriage to Portrieux, a distance of forty miles, in order to confide me safely
to the captain's care. As they wished me " *bon voyage* " and
embraced me affectionately, Mons. De Bosque handed me a
valuable purse for pocket-money during my absence, and they
all exhibited great anxiety for my welfare, saying over and
over again *au revoir*, as they entered their carriage to return
to their happy home ;—thereby implying that this was not a
final *adieu*, but that we should soon meet again.

I cannot tell why it was, but I experienced at that moment a
painful feeling of mental indecision about the future. I had no

real reason to doubt my return to France and the certainty of a warm welcome when I should again greet those dear ones who were now leaving me in tears ; but my mind was troubled by a vague feeling of uncertainty which made me anything but happy.   Filial affection and a sense of duty drew me towards my parents in England ; while a feeling of gratitude, and, I think, another and more tender sentiment, turned the current of my thoughts towards the happy home at St. Brieux.

It was not necessary for me to stop in Jersey for more than a few hours, but I wanted to revisit the scenes of my childhood's happy days and to speak again with those whom I had known and loved in early life.   In later years the scenes and memories of childhood seem like the imaginings of a pleasant dream.   A sweet charm is thrown around all that we then said and did ; and the men and women who then were known to us are pictured in our recollection as beings possessing charms and graces such as never belonged to the common-place children of earth.   The glamour of a fairy wand is over all the past history of mankind ; but upon nothing does it cast so potent a spell as upon the personal reminiscences of our own infant years.   To me that little island had charms which no stranger could ever have discovered ; and even now after the lapse of so many long, eventful years I often feel an earnest wish to visit again those rock-bound shores, to listen to the everlasting murmur of the wild, wild waves, to watch the distant speck-like vessels far away upon the swelling ocean, and to drink in the invigorating breezes which seem to give life and energy to every pulsation of the living soul.

But I must not theorise : life has been to me too earnest and too painful to admit of much sentiment or fancy as I recall the past.   Little as I thought it, during the short visit which I paid to my birthplace, the web of destiny was being woven for me in a way which I could not then have conjectured even in a dream.

At St. Heliers I heard for the first time of the Latter-day Saints, or Mormonites, as they were more familiarly called ; but I cannot express how perfectly astonished I was when I learned that my father, mother, sisters, and one of my brothers nad been converted to the new faith.

It was my own brother-in-law who told me this. He himself, with my sister, were " Apostate " Mormons. They had been baptized into the Mormon Church, but became dissatisfied and abandoned it. The St. Heliers' branch of the Latter-day Saints had had a turbulent experience. Their first teachings had been a mixture of Bible texts about the last days, and arguments about the millennium, the return of the Jews to Palestine, the resurrection of the dead, and a new revelation and a new prophet ; but the improper conduct of some of the elders had disgusted the people with their doctrines, and the tales of wickedness which I heard were, if true, certainly sufficient to justify them in rejecting such instructors.

The more I heard of this strange religion the more I was troubled ; yet, as I knew my parents were devoted Christians, I could hardly believe that Mormonism was such a vile delusion and imposture as it had been represented to me, or they would never have accepted it : still it was possible that they had been led astray by the fascinations of a new religion.

In this state of mind I met in the street the wife of the Baptist minister whom I have already mentioned. She greeted me affectionately and then began at once to warn me against the Latter-day Saints. I enquired what she knew of them, and she replied that personally she knew nothing, but she believed them to be servants of the Evil One, adding, " There is a strange power with them that fascinates the people and draws them into their meshes in spite of themselves. Let me entreat you not to go near them. Do not trust yourself at one of their meetings, or the delusion will take hold of *you* too."

" I cannot ignore Mormonism in this way," I said, " or pass it by with indifference, for my parents whom I tenderly love have been blinded by this delusion, and I can do no less than investigate its teachings thoroughly, and expose its errors, and, if possible, save my father's family from ruin."

She was not convinced that this was the wisest course for me to pursue, but I resolved at once to attend a meeting of the Saints and judge for myself. My brother-in-law, when he heard of my intentions, tried to dissuade me, but, finding me determined, finally offered to escort me to the meeting-place.

What I heard on this occasion made a great impression on my mind, and set me thinking as I had never thought before. On returning to my sister's house she asked me what opinion I had now formed of the Latter-day Saints. I replied that I had not yet formed any conclusion, but that what I had heard had given me serious cause for reflection. " Oh," she said, " You have caught the Mormon fever, I see."

I felt a disposition to resent this implication, but I was half afraid that, after all, my sister was right. Much that I had heard could, I knew, be proved true from Scripture ; and the rest seemed to me to be capable of demonstration from the same authority. I resolved, however, to fortify myself against a too easy credulity, and thought that probably if I heard more of these doctrines I might be able to discover their falsity.

On the following day, the elder who had preached at the meeting, and who, by the way, is one of the present proprietors of the Salt Lake *Herald*, called to see me, as he had been intimate with my parents before they left the island. I hardly knew how to be civil to him, though he had done nothing to offend me, nor had he been the cause of my parents entering the Mormon Church ; but I disliked him solely on account of the stories which I had heard about the Mormons. Intending only to be kind to me, he told me that on the following day he proposed to take the steamer for Southampton, as he was going to attend a conference of the Saints in London, and that he should be pleased to shew me any attentions while crossing the Channel, and would see me safe home in England. I confess I really felt insulted at a Mormon Elder offering to be my escort ; and although my trunks were ready packed for my departure by the same steamer, and Mr.

Dunbar knew it, I thanked him politely but said I would not go by that boat. He tried to persuade me to change my mind and said that I should have to wait a whole week for another vessel ; and at last I frankly told him the abhorrence I felt at the things I had heard about the Mormons, and that I should be afraid to travel in the same steamer with him or any of the Mormon Elders who I regarded as no better than so many whited sepulchres. He, however, very kindly took no offence for he knew that I had been listening to those who disliked the Saints. I felt ashamed at having been betrayed into such unladylike rudeness, but, notwithstanding, tried to persuade myself that his civility was, after all, an insult ; for I had conceived a detestation of every Mormon, on account of the deception which I felt sure had been practiced upon my family.

This feeling was not lessened by the consciousness that an impression had been made upon my own mind. The more in accordance with Scripture the teaching of the Elders appeared, the more firmly I believed it must be a powerful delusion. Here, I said, Satan has indeed taken the form of an angel of light to deceive, if possible, the very elect.

Elder Dunbar finding me unyielding, left by the next steamer and had a pleasant passage across the Channel, and I remained on the island another week. During that interval my mind was haunted with what I had heard of this new gospel dispensation, as it was called. That angels had again descended from heaven to teach men upon earth ; that a prophet had been raised up to speak again the mind of the Lord to the children of men ; that the Saints were partakers of the gifts of the Spirit, as in the Early Christian Church,—all these assumed facts took the form of reality, and came back into my mind with greater force every time I strove to drive them away ; just as our thoughts do when we desire to sleep, and cannot—our very efforts to dismiss them bring them back with greater force to torment us.

We had an unusually bad passage across the Channel, which annoyed me all the more when I remembered my scornful refusal to go in the same boat with Elder Dunbar.

On my arrival in Southampton I soon discovered that my father, mother, and sisters were full of the spirit of Mormonism. They were rejoicing in it, ardently believing that it was the fulness of the everlasting gospel, as the elders styled it ; and whatever I might think of the new religion I was forced to confess that it brought into my father's house peace, love, kindness, and charity such as were seldom seen in many households of religious people. My sisters were completely changed in their manner of life. They cared nothing for the amusements which girls of their age usually crave and enjoy. Their whole thoughts seemed to be occupied with the Church, attending the meetings of the saints, and employing every leisure hour in preparing comforts for the Elders who were travelling and preaching without purse and scrip. And in all this they were as happy as children.

Of my parents I might say the same. My dear mother rejoiced in the belief that she had been peculiarly blessed in being privileged to live at a time when "the last dispensation" was revealed ; and my father, though an invalid, rejoiced that he had entered into the kingdom by baptism. Such was the condition of my father's house ; and who can wonder that, accustomed as I was to listen with respect to the opinions of my parents, I was more than ever troubled about the new religion which they had adopted.

The first Sunday morning that I was in England, my parents asked me to accompany them to meeting, and I readily complied, as I wanted to hear more of the strange doctrines which in some mysterious way had made our family so happy, but which in other quarters had provoked such bitter hostility. I know now that this joyousness of heart is not peculiar to new converts to Mormonism, but may be found among the newly-converted of every sect which allows the emotional feelings to come into play. To me, at the time, however, it was a mystery, but I must confess that the change which had taken place in those nearest and dearest to me, affecting me personally, and being so evidently in accordance with the teachings of the Saviour, led me to regard Mormonism with less antipathy. The bright side alone of the new faith was presented to the world abroad ; we had yet to go to Utah and witness the effects of Brigham Young's teachings at home before we could know what Mormonism really was.

I shall never forget the trial it was to my pride to enter the dirty, mean-looking room where the Saints assembled at that time. No one would rent a respectable hall to them, and they were glad to obtain the use of any place which was large enough for their meetings. On the present occasion there was a very fair gathering of people, who had come together influenced by the most varied motives. The Presiding Elder —I should here remark that the word " Elder" has among the Mormons no reference whatever to age, but is simply a rank in the priesthood—called the meeting to order, and read the following hymn :

> The morning breaks, the shadows flee ;
>   Lo ! Zion's standard is unfurled !
> The dawning of a brighter day
>   Majestic rises on the world.
>
> The clouds of error.disappear
>   Before the rays of truth divine ;
> The glory bursting from afar,
>   Wide o'er the nations soon will shine !
>
> The Gentile fulness now comes in,
>   And Israel's blessings are at hand ;
> Lo ! Judah's remnant, cleansed from sin,
>   Shall in the promised Canaan stand.
>
> Angels from heaven and truth from earth
>   Have met, and both have record borne ;
> Thus Zion's light is bursting forth
>   To bring her ransomed children home.

Every word of this hymn had a meaning peculiar to itself, relating to the distinctive doctrines of the Saints. The congregation sang with an energy and enthusiasm which made the room shake again. Self and the outer world were alike forgotten, and an ecstacy of rapture seemed to possess the souls of all present. Then all kneeled down, and prayer was offered for the Prophet, the apostles, high-priests, "seventies," elders, priests, teachers, and deacons; blessings were invoked upon the Saints, and power to convert the Gentiles; and as the earnest words of supplication left the speaker's lips, the congregation shouted a loud "Amen."

There was no prepared sermon. There never is at a Mormon meeting. The people are taught that the Holy Ghost is "mouth, matter, and wisdom." Whatever the preaching elder may say is supposed to come directly by inspiration from heaven, and the Saints listening, as they believe, not to his utterances but to the words of God Himself, have nothing to do but to hear and obey.

The first speaker on this occasion was a young gentleman of respectable family, who had been recently baptized and ordained. He, too, was from St. Heliers, and I had known him from childhood. His address impressed me very much. He had been a member of the Baptist church, and he related his experience, told how often he had wondered why there were not inspired men to preach the glad tidings of salvation to the world to-day, as there were eighteen centuries ago. He spoke of the joy which he had experienced in being baptized into the Mormon Church and realising that he had received the "gift of the Holy Ghost." The simplicity with which he spoke, his evident honesty, and the sacrifice he had made in leaving the respectable Baptists and joining the despised Mormons, were, I thought, so many evidences of his sincerity.

Alas! how little could that young preacher conjecture how different the practical Mormonism in Utah was from the theoretical Mormonism which he had learned to believe in Europe, before polygamy was known among the Saints. A short time afterwards he gave up his business, married an accomplished young lady, and went with her to Salt Lake City. There they were soon utterly disgusted with what they witnessed, apostatized, and set out for England. When they had gone three-fourths of their way back to the Missouri river, the young man, his wife, child, and another apostate and his wife, were killed by "Indians:"—such, at least, was the report; but dissenting Mormons have always charged their "taking off" to the order of the leaders of the Mormon Church.

But to return to the meeting. The reader must please forgive me if I dwell a little upon the events of that particular morning, for naturally they made a deep impression upon my own mind—it was there that I saw for the first time my husband who was to be.

I had heard a good deal about a certain elder, from my family and from the Saints who visited at our house. They spoke with great enthusiasm of the earnestness with which he preached, of the influence which his addresses produced, and of his confidence in the final triumph of "the kingdom."

At that time—the summer of 1849—although the branch of the Mormon Church in Britain was in a most flourishing condition, there were not in England more than two or three American elders preaching the faith, for when—two years before the period of which I speak—the Saints left Nauvoo and undertook that most extraordinary exodus across the plains to the Rocky Mountains, the missionary elders were all called home, and the work of proselytizing in Europe was left entirely to the native elders. To direct their labors there was placed over them an American elder named Orson Spencer, a graduate of Dartmouth University, a scholar and a gentleman—a man well calculated from his previous Christian education to give an elevated tone to the teachings of the young English missionaries.

Mormonism in England, then, had no resemblance to the Mormonism of Utah to-day. The Mormons were then simply an earnest religious people, in many respects like the Methodists, especially in their missionary zeal and fervor of spirit. The Mormon Church abroad was purely a religious institution, and Mormonism was preached by the elders as the gospel of Christianity restored. The church had no political shaping nor the remotest antagonism to the civil power. The name of Joseph Smith was seldom spoken, and still more seldom was heard the name of Brigham Young, and then only so far as they had reference to the Church of the Saints.

About eighteen months before I visited Southampton, one of these missionaries had come into that town, "without purse or scrip." He was quite a young man and almost penniless, but he was rich in faith and overflowing with zeal. He knew no one there, and homeless, and frequently hungry, he continued his labors. Of fasting he knew much, of feasting nothing. He first preached under the branches of a spreading beech tree in a public park, and when more favored he held forth in a school-room or public hall. He had come to convert the people to Mormonism or he was going to die among them, and before such zeal and determination, discouragements, of course, soon vanished away. He troubled the ministers of other dissenting churches when they found him distributing tracts and talking to their people. He was sowing broadcast dissatisfaction and discontent wherever he could get any one to listen to him, and thus he drew down upon himself the eloquence of the dissenting pulpits and the derision of the local press. But the more they attacked him the more zealously did he labor, and defied his opponents to public discussion. Mormonism was bold then in Europe—it had no American history to meet in those days.

This, and a great deal more, I had heard discussed in glowing language by my relatives and friends ; and thus the young missionary—Elder Stenhouse—was, by name, no stranger to me.

It was Elder Stenhouse who now addressed the meeting, and I listened to him with attention. The reader must remember that at that time polygamy was unheard of as a doctrine of the Saints, and the blood-atonement, the doctrine that Adam is God, together with the polytheism and priestly theocracy of after years were things undreamed of. The saving love of Christ, the glory and fulness of the everlasting Gospel, the gifts and graces of the Spirit, together with repentance, baptism, and faith, were the points upon which the Mormon teachers touched; and who can wonder that with such topics as these, and fortifying every statement with powerful and numerous texts of Scripture, they should captivate the minds of religiously inclined people? However this may be, I can only confess that as I listened to Elder Stenhouse's earnest discourse, I felt my antipathy to Mormonism rapidly melting away.

At the close of the service, when he left the platform, he was warmly received by the brethren and sisters, for so the Saints speak of one another, and they came about him to shake hands, or it might be to seize the opportunity of slipping a trifle into his hand to help him in his work. Young and old, the poor and their more wealthy neighbors mingled together like one happy family. It was altogether a most pleasing scene, and, whatever explanation may yet be given to Mormonism in America, one thing I know—the facts of its early history in Europe are among the most pleasant reminiscences of my life.

Elder Stenhouse came up in a familiar and open-hearted way to my mother and sisters, and I was introduced to him as "the other daughter from France." He kindly welcomed me, and when I frankly told him the state of my mind, he made, I must admit, a successful attempt to solve my doubts, and when I left the meeting it was with sentiments towards the saints and their religion far different from those which I entertained when I entered.

This meeting was a memorable era in my life.

4

CHAPTER III.

IN the afternoon I attended a meeting of a still more interesting character. These Sunday afternoon meetings were
held for the purpose of receiving the sacrament, and the confirmation of those who had been baptized during the week;
they were intended exclusively for the Saints, but for certain
reasons I was permitted to be present.

The meeting was opened with singing and prayer, and then
the presiding Elder—Brother Cowdy—arose, and invited all
those who had been baptized during the week to come to the
front seats. Several ladies and gentlemen came forward, and
also three little children. Upon inquiry I found that children
of eight years of age were admitted members of the Church
by baptism—which is administered by immersion. At that
age they are supposed to understand what they are doing; but
before that, if of Mormon parents, they are considered members of the Church by virtue of the blessing which they re-

ceived in infancy. Brother Cowdy—the presiding elder—then called upon two other elders to assist him in the confirmation.

One of the ladies took off her bonnet but retained her seat, when all three of the Elders placed their hands upon her head, and one of them said :—

"Martha; by virtue of the authority vested in us, we confirm you a member of the Church of Jesus Christ of Latter-day Saints; and as you have been obedient to the teachings of the Elders, and have gone down into the waters of baptism for the remission of your sins, we confer upon you the Gift of the Holy Ghost, that it may abide with you for ever, and be a lamp unto your feet and a light upon your pathway, leading and guiding you into all truth. This blessing we confirm upon your head, in the name of the Father, and of the Son, and of the Holy Ghost. Amen."

Then, before they took their hands off her head, the presiding Elder asked the other two if they wished to say anything. Whereupon one of them began to invoke a blessing upon the newly-confirmed sister. He spoke for some time with extreme earnestness, when suddenly he was seized with a nervous trembling which was quite perceptible, and which evidently betokened intense mental or physical excitement. He began to prophesy great things for this sister in the future, and in solemn and mysterious language proclaimed the wonders which God would perform for her sake. When we consider the excited state of her mind, and—if the statements of psychologists be true—the magnetic currents which were being transmitted from the sensitive nature of the man into the excited brain of the new convert, together with the pressure of half a dozen human hands upon her head, it is not at all astonishing that when the hands were lifted off she should firmly believe that she had been blessed indeed. She had been told that she should receive the Gift of the Holy Ghost; and she did not for an instant doubt that her expectations had been realized.

Each of the newly baptized went through the same ceremony, and then they all partook of the sacrament, when, after another hymn, the meeting was closed with prayer.

In the evening I returned to listen to a lecture upon "the character, spirit, and genius" of the new church, delivered by

Elder Stenhouse; and I was captivated by the picture which he drew of the marvellous latter-day work which he affirmed had already begun. The visions of by-gone ages were again vouchsafed to men; angels had visibly descended to earth; God had raised up in a mighty way a Prophet, as of old, to preach the dispensation of the last days; gifts of prophecy, healing, and the working of miracles were now, as in the days of the Apostles, witnesses to the power of God. The long-lost tribes of Israel were about to be gathered into the one great fold of Christ; and the fulness of the Gentiles being come, they, too, were to be taken under the care of the Good Shepherd. All were freely invited to come and cast away their sins, ere it was too late; and the fullest offers of pardon, grace, sanctification and blessing, in this world and in the next, were presented to every repentant soul.

Surely, I thought, these are the selfsame doctrines which my mother taught me when I knelt beside her in childhood, and which I have so often heard—only in colder and less persuasive language—urged from the pulpits of those whom I have ever regarded in the light of true disciples of Jesus. Who can wonder that I listened with rapt attention, and that my heart was even then half won to the new faith? The days passed; and as I pondered over these things it appeared to me that I had at last found that which I had so long earnestly desired and prayed for—a knowledge of that true religion for which the Saviour presented Himself a Holy Sacrifice, and which the Apostles preached at peril of their lives—the *only* faith, in which I might find joy and peace in believing.

But why should I dwell upon those moments, soul-absorbing as was their interest to me *then*—sadly-pleasing as is their memory *now!* The reader can see the drift of my thoughts at that time; and I feel sure, although I have but hastily sketched the causes which brought about these great changes in my religious belief and in my life, that he will not hastily accuse me of fickleness and love of change, if he himself has fought the battles of the soul and has learned even in a slight measure to realize the mystery of his inner-being.

Each day the finger of destiny drew me nearer to the final step. The young Elder, whose words I had listened to with such strange and, to me, momentous results, was intimate with my father's family and called frequently to see us, and before long he convinced me that it was my duty to test for myself whether the work was of God, or not. In the agitated state of my mind at that time, I could not withstand the earnest appeals which were made to my affections and hopes; and within two weeks after my arrival in England, I became formally a member of the Church of Jesus Christ of Latter-day Saints; or in more popular language—I became a Mormon.

The day was fixed for my baptism. Several others were to be baptized at the same time; for scarcely a week passed without quite a number of persons joining the church. For this purpose we all repaired to a bath-house on the banks of the Southampton river. This place was not perhaps the most convenient, and it certainly was devoid of the slightest tinge of romance; but it was the only one available to the saints at that time.

When we were all assembled and had united in singing and prayer, Elder Stenhouse went down into the water first, and then two men went down and were baptized, and came up again. Now came my turn. I was greatly agitated, for I felt all the solemnity of the occasion. I had dressed myself very neatly and purely, for I believed that angel eyes were upon me; I wished to give myself—a perfect and acceptable offering—to my God, and I was filled with the determination henceforth to devote my whole life to his service.

As I went down into the waters of baptism, how thankful I felt that it had been my privilege to hear the gospel in my youth, for now I could give my heart in all its freshness to the Lord, before it had been chilled by the cold, hard experience of life.

I descended the steps, and Elder Stenhouse came forward and led me out into the water; then taking both my hands in one of his, he raised his other hand towards heaven, and in a solemn and impressive voice he said:

"Fanny; by virtue of the authority vested in me, I baptize you for the remission of your sins; in the name of the Father, and of the Son, and of the Holy Ghost. Amen."

Then he immersed me in the water; and as I reäscended the steps, I really felt like another being: all my past was buried in the deep—the waters of baptism had washed away my sins; and a new life lay open before me, in which my footsteps would be guided by the inspired servants of God. All now would be peace and joy within me, for I had obeyed the commands of God, and I doubted not that I should receive the promised blessing, and that now I could indeed go on my way rejoicing.

My baptism took place one Saturday afternoon, and the afternoon following I was confirmed a member of the church. Elder Stenhouse presided at the meeting, and he, with Elder Cowdy and two other elders, confirmed me. As the "blessing" which I then myself received differs somewhat from the one which I have already given, and as it is a very fair specimen of those effusions, I present it to the reader in full.

Elder Stenhouse, Elder Cowdy, and the two other elders, placed their hands solemnly upon my head, and Elder Stenhouse said :—

"Fanny; by virtue of the authority   vested in me, I confirm you a member of the Church of Jesus Christ of Latter-day Saints ; and inasmuch as you have been obedient to the command of God, through his servants, and have been baptized for the remission of your sins, I say unto you that those sins are remitted. And in the name of God I bless you, and say unto you, that inasmuch as you are faithful and obedient to teachings of the priesthood, and seek the advancement of the kingdom, there is no good thing that your heart can desire that the Lord will not give unto you. You shall have visions and dreams, and angels shall visit you by day and by night. You shall stand in the tèmple in Zion, and administer to the Saints of the Most High God. You shall speak in tongues, and prophesy ; and the Lord shall bless you abundantly, both temporally and spiritually. These blessings I seal upon your head, inasmuch as you shall be faithful ; and I pray heaven to bless you ; and say unto you—*Be thou blessed*, in the name of the Father, and of the Son, and of the Holy Ghost. Amen."

After the meeting, I received the congratulations of all the Saints present, and more particularly those of my own family. My dear mother and father were overjoyed, and I now learned how anxious they had been, and how they had feared that I should return to France and reject the faith of the new dispensation. Altogether we were very happy.

Elder Stenhouse and Elder Cowdy returned home with us to tea, and afterwards we all attended the usual evening lecture. In this way was passed one of the happiest days of my life—one which I shall ever remember;—and yet that memory will always be mingled with regret that so much love and devotion as I then felt were not enlisted in a better cause.

Thus began a new era in my life. All my former friends and associations were now to be remembered no more: my lot was cast among the Saints; and in the state of my mind at that time, I believed that I should be happy in my new position, and resolved to give evidence of the sincerity of my faith.

The untiring energy and restless activity of Elder Stenhouse was ever before our eyes, and inspired all who associated with him with a similar enthusiasm. There were no drones in that hive. The brethren, at a word from him, would roam the country, teaching and preaching in the open air, while the sisters would go from house to house in the city, distributing tracts about the new faith. I caught the enthusiasm of the rest, and was soon in the ranks with the other sisters, as devoted in my endeavors as a young, ambitious heart could be. I was indeed like one born again from an old existence into a new life. I felt grateful and happy—I began to dream of the eternal honor which crowns a faithful missionary life; and I soon found an ample field for testing my fitness for that vocation.

At the time of which I speak, the Primitive Methodists in England were doing a great work in the way of converting sinners. Their missionaries were zealous and devoted men, though generally poor and uneducated. They resembled very closely the Mormon elders in their labors; and, in fact, a very large number of the leading Mormons had been Methodist local-preachers and exhorters; and the greater number of the new-born Saints had come from that denomination with their former teachers, or else had followed them soon after.

The change from Methodist to Mormon was, in course of time, very strongly marked ; but for a considerable period the same, or what seemed the same, influences were at work among the people. Remarkable scenes of excitement were often witnessed at the " love feasts ; " and from the " anxious seats," as they were called, might be heard, the entreaties of self-accusing souls, frightened by a multitude of sins, crying earnestly, nay, wildly, for grace, mercy, and the Holy Ghost, while many of the supplicants would fall upon the ground, completely overcome by nervous excitement. Then they would have visions, and beheld great and unutterable things ; received the forgiveness of their sins ; and, coming back to consciousness, believed themselves now to be the children of God, and new creatures ; doubting not that they would ever after be happy in the Lord.

The experience of the Saints at their meetings, when Mormonism was first preached, was exactly similar to this. Into the psychological, moral, or religious causes of these scenes of excitement I cannot here enter ;—I simply mention facts as they came under my own observation.

The Mormon Missionary often came upon whole communities in the rural districts of England, where this " good time " was in full operation ; and being a man of texts he would follow up the revival, preaching that the spirit of the prophet was subject to the prophet, and not the prophet subject to the spirit. Controversy would arise, and his appeal to Scripture, literally interpreted, was almost invariably triumphant. Even in this country, especially in New York and Ohio, the same causes produced the same effects. It was after his mind was excited by a general revival near his native place, that Joseph Smith, the founder of Mormonism, received his first religious impression, and saw, as he asserted, his first angelic vision. His followers, even in the early days of the church, had revival-meetings and meetings at which the most extraordinary excitement was manifested,—when the Saints fell into ecstatic trances, saw heaven opened, and spake with tongues. But Joseph, shrewd man as he was, albeit " a prophet," when he found too many rival seers were coming into the field, announced by "special revelation," that these too-gifted persons were possessed by devils, and that their visions and prophecyings must be at once suppressed. And he did suppress them.

Not long after my own baptism I was present at a meeting of this description, in Southampton. It was called a "testimony meeting," and was held in a large upper room situated, if I rightly remember, in Chandos street. No one from the outside would have supposed that it was the place of assembly of the Saints, for it was generally used for ordinary secular meetings, and I have heard that great objections were at first raised as to the propriety of letting it to the Mormons.

As we entered the door, we were saluted by Brother Williams, who expressed great pleasure at seeing us. There was a full attendance of the Saints, and every face wore an expression of peaceful earnestness. A person who has never attended a Mormon meeting can form no idea of the joyous spirit which seemed to animate every one present. I am not, of course, speaking of modern meetings, but of meetings as they used to be. Whence and whatever that "spirit" might be which moved the sisters and brethren when they met in early times, I cannot tell; but I, and with me, ten thousand Mormons and seceding Mormons in Utah, can, from our own experience, testify that *that* spirit no longer visits the Tabernacle services over which Brigham Young presides, or the meetings of the Saints since they adopted the accursed doctrine of polygamy, and forsook the gentle leadings of their first love.

Often have I heard Mormons of good standing and high position in the church, lament the "good old times" as they called them, when the outpouring of the Spirit was so abundant, and mourn over the cold, barren services of the present day. But the elders explain this away. It is, they say, the fault of the people themselves, and because their own hearts have become cold.

At the meeting of which I speak, that happy spirit was

peculiarly marked. An encouraging smile, or a kind word, greeted me on every side, and, as a newly converted sister, I received the most cordial welcome. The brethren were seated on forms and chairs and any other convenient article which came to hand, while at the further end of the room was Brother Bench, who was to preside, and with him several other leading elders. Brother Bench gave out a suitable hymn.

The whole congregation joined in the singing, and every heart seemed lifted up with devotion. Then another elder rose and offered a spirit-moving prayer ; and then the brother who presided stated that for the time he withdrew his control of the proceedings, and, as the phrase was, he "put the meeting in the hands of the Saints," exhorting them not to let the time pass by unimproved.

There was at first a momentary hesitation, but Brother Burton got up and fixed the hearts of the Saints by relating what the Lord had done for him. He told us of his zeal for the faith, and how, during the week, he had had a terrible discussion with an unbeliever—a clever and learned man, too, and well skilled in dialectics—how he trembled at first at the idea of contesting with such an antagonist, but that the Lord had helped him, until argument after argument had been overthrown and he had come off victor in the fight. Then appealing to every one present he exhorted them to similar zeal, and promised them abundant help from on high to achieve a like result.

Then arose Brother Edwards, a well-tried champion of the faith, and to him every one listened with profound attention, eagerly drinking in his every utterance. I could almost, even now, imagine that he was really inspired. *Then* I firmly believed he was. His voice thrilled with an earnestness which seemed to us something more than the mere excitement of the soul. A burning fire seemed to flash from his large, expressive eyes ; his features were lighted up with that animation which gives a saint-like halo to the earnest face when fired with indignation or pleading soul-felt truths ; while his whole frame seemed to glow with the glory of a land beyond this earth, as in the most impressive and convincing language he reminded us that our sins had been washed away by the waters of baptism, that upon us had been poured the gifts and graces of the Spirit, and that it was our sacred privilege to testify of these things.

The effect of this exhortation was magical. We forgot all our outward surroundings, in the realisation that the great work of the Lord was so gloriously begun and that it would surely go on, conquering and to conquer. One sister—an elderly woman—who was present, unable to control her emotion, burst out with that Mormon hymn which I have heard some old Nauvoo Saints declare produced upon the people in those days an enthusiasm similar to that which moves the heart of every true Frenchman when he listens to the soul-stirring notes of the Marseillaise:

> The Spirit of God like a fire is burning!
> The latter-day glory begins to come forth;
> The visions and blessings of old are returning,
> The angels are coming to visit the earth.
> We'll sing and we'll shout with the armies of heaven
> Hosannah! Hosannah, to God and the Lamb!
> All glory to them in the highest be given,
> Henceforth and for ever: Amen, and Amen!

I have often heard in magnificent cathedrals, hoary with the dust of time, and in vast places of amusement dedicated specially to music and to song, the outpouring of that glorious vocal flood, which a chorus of a thousand well-trained singers can alone send forth. I have felt sometimes that entrancing state of ecstacy which thrilled the soul of the seer in Patmos, as he listened to the melody of the angelic throng—"the voice of many waters, and the peal of mighty thunders, and the notes of harpers harping upon their harps;" but never, even when surrounded by all that was best calculated to produce a sentiment of devotion in my mind—never did I experience so rapt a feeling of communion with "the armies of heaven"—as I felt in that unadorned meeting-room surrounded by those plain but earnest and united people.

Nor was I alone in this. The feeling was contagious. There was not one present who did not sympathise. And thus, I suppose, melody has always played a prominent part in all religious revivals, whether of divine or human origin. The Apostles had their psalms, and hymns, and spiritual songs ; the Martyrs their *Te Deum ;* the Waldenses made the hills and vales of Piedmont vocal with their singing; the Lollards and Hussites had their melodies ; and in more modern days the followers of Luther, Wesley, and (may I add ?) Joseph Smith, have poured out the fulness of their souls after the same fashion.

The last notes of the hymn had scarcely died away when another, and then another brother arose and bore testimony to the great work, told what the Lord had done for them personally, told of their zeal for the faith, and fervently exhorted all present to persevere unto the end. Again prayer was offered, another hymn sung, and the Saints were dismissed with a solemn benediction.

CHAPTER IV.

LIFE AMONG THE SAINTS :—MY NEW ENGAGEMENTS.

Beginning Life as a Mormon—Breaking Way from the Past—My Friends in France—Placed in a Difficult Position—I Remember my Betrothed—Exclusiveness of my New Faith—An "Apostle" lays down the Law—How to Keep aloof from the Gentiles—Woman's Duty—"The Foundation of a Little Family Kingdom"—The "Gift of Tongues" in Modern Days—An Extraordinary Meeting—Sister Ellis exercises her "Gift,"—Need of an Interpreter—Emotional Religion—How Brother Brigham once "Spake in Tongues"—A "High time" at Kirtland in the days of Joseph—A Scene in the Lion House—One of the Prophet's Wives "Speaks"—Another Wife Interprets—I Receive a Blessing—Brother Young Discountenances the "Gift"—Only half Convinced—"To Doubt is Sin"—I Arrive at an Important Conclusion—I instruct Elder Stenhouse in the French Language—An Interesting Pupil—Declining the verb *J'Aime*—Studies in the Back Parlor—A Persevering Young Man—Why I listened to Elder Stenhouse's Suit—I am Engaged to Him—I become a Missionary's Wife—I write to my Friends in France—A Free Confession—Pleasant Memories of the Past.

I WAS now a Mormon in every sense of the word, although entirely ignorant of Utah politics and polygamy.

My dreams were of a life of happiness spent in seeking to convert the whole world to the religion of Jesus, which I believed had been restored again to earth by the ministry of holy angels. It is easy to say that such an ambition was ill-directed when associated with Mormonism, but no one can deny that, in itself, it was the noblest and purest that could inspire the heart of man. There was no sacrifice too great for me to make ; there was no object too dear for me to resign, if it stood in the way of my sacred calling. The whole current of my thoughts and plans was now changed. It was henceforth my duty to be entirely forgetful of self, and to devote my energies—my all—to the advancement of the King-

dom of God. My life was to be identified with the Saints,—
my faith required it, and I was willing that it should be so.

But what of my beloved-France, all this time ; and my betrothed husband ?

This reflection aroused within me a most painful train of
thought. How many fond and endearing memories entwined
themselves around my heart at that moment, when most I
needed to banish them for ever ! With what lingering love
did I look back to those dear ones from whom I had parted
but a few short weeks before, and who I might perhaps never
see again ! To return would be to desert my newly-adopted
friends and faith—to violate the covenant which I had made
at baptism to " be ever afterwards governed by the servants
of God."

No ; it was too late—I could not now return ;—I tried to
persuade myself that I did not even wish to ;—in a word,
affection, and what I thought duty, were at war together in
my heart. All my former ties and associations must now be
severed, however terrible the cost might be ; and I was bound
not only to submit, but even to glory in the sacrifice.
Thus I argued away the regrets which would at times agitate
my very soul itself, and caused me so much painful thought.

The trial of my profession in the new faith came swiftly to
my door. My marriage-engagement must be broken off,
though I knew not how that could honorably and conscientiously be done. Of myself I had no wish to draw back from
anything that I had promised of my own free will ; and much
less did I desire to be faithless to my solemnly plighted
word.

I now first realised the all-absorbing influence of an earnest
religious faith. I was brought face to face with the fact that
I could not marry out of the Mormon Church. The teaching
of the elders was against it, and I saw that in this they were
consistent. Great as was the trial, and painful as was the
sacrifice, I resolved to be true to my religion. How very
earnestly the elders insisted upon such sacrifices, may be seen
from an appeal made at a later date by the " Apostle " Orson

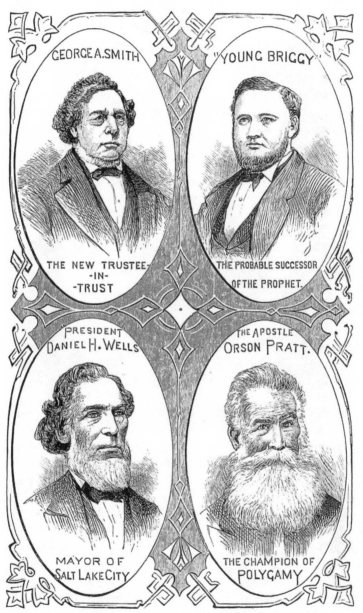

GEORGE A. SMITH

"YOUNG BRIGGY"

THE NEW TRUSTEE
-IN-
-TRUST

THE PROBABLE SUCCESSOR
OF THE PROPHET.

PRESIDENT
DANIEL H. WELLS

THE APOSTLE
ORSON PRATT.

MAYOR OF
SALT LAKE CITY

THE CHAMPION OF
POLYGAMY

PILLARS OF THE MORMON CHURCH.

Pratt. Brother Orson was in Europe, and, speaking author-
itatively, he set forth the duties of mothers and daughters in
" Babylon," as he graciously styled the rest of the world, in
the following terms which unmistakably show the purposes
of the leaders relative to marriage :

" Many of you have daughters, some of whom are grown to womanhood;
others are now young. Would you have them gather with you to a land where
virtue and peace dwell, where God has promised to protect and bless the right-
eous ? If so, teach them, as they love their parents, and the Saints, and the
truth, not to throw themselves away by marrying Gentiles ; teach them to *keep
themselves entirely aloof from Gentile* courtships and associations. Scores of
women who once were counselled as you are now, are mourning in wretchedness,
in bondage to Gentile husbands, cut off from all privilege of gathering with their
fathers, mothers, brethren, and sisters ; and, in some instances, cut off from
even attending the Saints' meetings. But this is not all. They are raising up
children in these lands to perish with themselves in the general desolations coming upon Babylon. But what is still more aggravating and heart-rending, they
are raising up children not only destined for temporal judgments, but who must
for ever be cut off from the presence of God and the glory of the celestial kingdom * * * * * What fearful responsibility for any young sister to volun-
tarily take upon herself, after all the warnings she has received. See to it,
then, parents, that you not only do not give your consent, but actually forbid all
such marriages.

   *   *   *   *   *   *

Let them marry according to the holy order of God, and begin to lay the
foundation of a little family kingdom which shall no more be scattered upon the
face of the earth, but dwell in one country, keeping their genealogies from generation to generation, until each man's house shall be multiplied as the stars of
heaven."

These were the influences which were brought to bear upon
my mind at a time when it was peculiarly sensitive and open
to impressions from without.

While in this uncertain state a little incident occurred
which, though in itself of the most trifling nature, assisted in
forming my ultimate decision.

It was a beautiful evening in early summer, and my mother
and sister asked me to accompany them to one of the testi-
mony-meetings which I have already described. This meeting was very similar to the others, with one notable exception:—it was here that I saw and heard, for the first time in
my own experience, the " gift of tongues " exercised.

I had, of course, heard a great deal about this " gift," much of which was anything but satisfactory, as I think the reader will agree with me, when I explain myself.

I had read in Scripture that the Apostles of Jesus Christ tarried in Jerusalem until the day of Pentecost, when power was given them from on high. Being all together in one place, engaged in earnest supplication and the praise of God, suddenly the building in which they were, shook to its very foundation, and the sound of a mighty, rushing wind was heard, and the Spirit of the Eternal One, who, ere the dawning of creation moved upon the waters of chaos, descended in visible shape, palpable to their eyes in the form of a cloven tongue, an emblem of the gift of eloquence and diversity of speech which was henceforth to be theirs.

Then arose Peter, that disciple so full of zeal. Henceforth he was no longer to be called a disciple, but an " Apostle," which by interpretation is one " sent forth ;"—for now he had received his commission, and, in the power of the Highest, he, with the other Ambassadors of Jesus, could go forth upon their glorious work. But newly pardoned for his great transgression, and still remembering the Saviour's pitying look, and the thrice-repeated question—" Lovest thou Me more than these ?"—burning, also, with zeal to give evidence of his love —the Leader of the Apostles addressed the multitude gathered from every clime to keep the feast.

Lo, then, a miracle! The Jew of Jerusalem wondered at the wisdom of the unlettered Fisherman. The magi from the still more distant Orient were amazed to hear so strange a story. The Greek paused at the utterances of this new philosophy. But strangest of all was the fact that, though utterly unable to comprehend each other's speech, they all, listening at the same time, could understand the words of the untaught fisherman.

Long before I had even heard of Mormonism, I had frequently thought how wonderfully useful this gift must have been to the Apostles. One of the great difficulties encountered by the missionary is learning the language of the people among whom he works and lives. To be able to dispense with all this labor, and to be understood wherever he went, must have lightened the mind of the holy man of half its load ; and naturally, when I heard that the Mormons had "the Gift of Tongues," I supposed it was the self-same power of diverse speech as that exercised by the Apostles ; and I presume the reader will conjecture with me that it was the same "gift," or, at least, some imitation of it. How surprised I was when I first discovered the meaning of the term "speaking in tongues," among the Mormons, may perhaps be imagined when I explain what happened at that testimony-meeting.

After prayer, and singing, and listening to several very fervent addresses from some of the elders, Brother Seely had delivered a most impassioned speech, and had hardly concluded, when Sister Ellis, who was sitting near me, gave evidence of being in an abnormal condition of mind, which to me was painful in the extreme. Her hands were clenched, and her eyes had that wild and supernatural glare which is never seen, save in cases of lunacy or intense feverish excitement. Every one waited breathlessly, listening to catch what she might say ;—you might have heard a pin drop.

Then in oracular language and with all the impassioned dignity of one inspired of heaven, she began to speak.

I say "speak," as that term is generally applied to the utterances of the human voice ; but she did not *speak* in the sense in which we always employ that word ; she simply emitted a series of sounds. They seemed to me chiefly the repetition of the same syllables—something like a child repeating, *la, la, la, le, lo ; ma, ma, ma, mi, ma ; dele, dele, dele, hela*—followed, perhaps, by a number of sounds strung together, which could not be rendered in *any* shape by the pen. Sometimes in the Far West, in later years, I have heard old Indian women, crooning wierdly monotonous and outlandish ditties in their native tongue. These wild dirges, more nearly than anything else I ever heard, resembled the prophetic utterances of Sister Ellis; save only, that the appearance of the latter was far too solemn to admit of even a smile at what she said.

Ridiculous as this appears when I now write it down on paper, and strange as even then it was to me, there was something so commanding, so earnest, so "inspirational," if I may be allowed the term, in Sister Ellis's manner, that I could not wonder at the attention which the brethren and sisters paid to this gifted speaker in tongues.

I now know that these extraordinary displays are by no means confined to Mormonism. People of a certain temperament, excited to frenzy—generally by religious enthusiasm—have in all ages given painful illustrations of this mental disease; as the student who remembers the *Convulsionnaires* of the middle ages, the Munster Anabaptists of Luther's time, and the various emotional sects of more modern days, will abundantly bear me witness. But at that time, new in the faith, and believing as I did, that, as the elders said, it was the manifestation of the power of God, as foretold by the prophet Joel, though I secretly felt a sense of repugnance, I tried to combat my better sentiments.

Overcome by the excitement of the moment, Sister Ellis suddenly paused, not so much intentionally as from sheer inability to proceed; and the leading elders looked round from one to another to see if any one was present who could interpret. The gift of interpretation is very rarely possessed by the same person who has the gift of tongues, and you may often hear one after another arise and "speak," but there is no one to "interpret," and the Saints go away unedified. Even when an interpreter is present, there is no authority to determine whether he gives the proper rendering of the sounds uttered, and I have over and over again heard the most ludicrous stories of the comical interpretation placed by some half witty or half-witted expounder upon these oracles.

When Brother Brigham—then a man who was lowly in his own eyes—first met the prophet Joseph Smith, at Kirtland, Ohio, there was a scene somewhat like the one I have described; and the future leader of "this people," as he calls the Saints, himself spake with tongues and uttered wonderful things. But even supposing his words at that time to have been of the wisest, we all know from the example of Balaam's *reprover*, that it does not require a very high order of intellect to speak in unaccustomed language—and that, too, to some purpose. In later days the exercise of this gift has been discouraged by the elders, and especially by Brigham Young. Going one day, some years after, to the Lion-House to see a certain member of the Prophet's little family concerning a subject which lay very near to my heart at that time, we prayed together earnestly and anxiously; when suddenly the lady's face was lighted up with a supernatural glow, and placing her hand on my head she, sibyl-like, poured forth a flood of eloquence which—although I did not understand a single word that was uttered—I confess sent through me a magnetic thrill as if I had been listening to an inspired seeress. Another of Brigham's wives who was present interpreted the words of blessing to me, but added: "Do not speak of this, Sister Stenhouse, for Brother Young does not like to hear of these things." Thus we see that one inspired prophet in the presence of another "prophet, seer, and revelator," could himself take part at one time in a miraculous manifestation, which in later years he "would not like to hear of," if it was only one of his many wives who enacted the prophet's *rôle*.

But my meeting! I have wandered far away from that. Let me proceed.

After more testimony, more "speaking," and much enthusiasm, the Saints separated. My sister was talking with a young-lady friend, and regretting that no one present had been able to interpret; and I stood by, but did not join in the conversation. Suddenly the young lady turned to me and said: "Sister Fanny, do you not see in all this, more and more, the convincing power of God?"

Rather hesitatingly I replied, "Yes, I think I do."

"*Think!* sister?" said she, with warmth. "Oh, yes, I see by your looks that you are only half convinced; your faith is not strong enough yet; but remember, whatsoever is of doubt *is sin!*"

"But," I answered, "I do not see clearly what good we receive from these manifestations when no one can understand them."

"That is your want of faith—nothing else; you have the evidence of the truth before you, and you see how these miraculous powers build up the belief of God's people; and yet you doubt. *To doubt is sin:* whatsoever is not of faith is sin. You must pray and strive, sister, to be strengthened against temptation."

All this was not very logical, and it certainly did not help to dispel my doubts. But, twice in the course of a few short sentences, she had used a certain expression which, though trifling in itself, was recalled to my mind very forcibly before many days had passed.

This was my first experience of speaking in tongues.

But there were every-day matters of much more real importance to me than those strange speculations which had recently employed so much of my time and attention. It was now necessary that I should either return to France and fulfill my engagement with Monsieur De Bosque, or else resolve, once and for ever, to renounce all those ties which had become so dear to me.

Meanwhile, religious theories were not the only influences brought to bear upon my mind.

While day by day I began to be still more doubtful whether it would not after all be sinful in God's sight for me to leave my friends in the new faith and go back to France and my betrothed, who I knew neither was nor ever could become a Saint, other thoughts began to intrude themselves, and to shake my determination.

Elder Stenhouse's visits to my father's house began to be more frequent than ever, but as he desired to become familiar with the French language, and would bring his French grammar with him "to get a lesson," as he said, no particular notice was taken of his frequent coming. He was always welcomed with pleasure by the whole family, and, of course, by myself, who was his teacher. After awhile he took so much delight in his studies that he could not endure to let an evening pass without a lesson; and somehow or other, I must confess, it was the first time since I had been a teacher that I felt such a peculiar pleasure in imparting instruction. I suppose it was the interest which all teachers experience when their pupils are studiously inclined. My pupil was particularly studious—so much so that he told my father and mother that he could not study very well in the parlor where every one was conversing, and begged the privilege of having the folding doors thrown partly open, that we might sit in the back parlor and be more quiet.

This was granted. But after a few evenings my pupil took a notion to partly close the folding doors after him, and as mothers' eyes are ever watchful, one of my sisters was sent in with her sewing to keep us company. But my pupil by this time had made rapid progress in the French language, and while my sister was innocently sewing, he was repeating his lesson to me; and it was not our fault if in those French phrase-books there were passages expressive of love and devotion. Unconsciously to us both, he formed the habit of repeating those phrases to me at all times, and I formed the equally bad habit of blushing whenever he made use of them.

This my sister observed, and communicated the fact to my mother, who immediately said that we had better discontinue our French for awhile, as it was monopolizing too much of our time, and keeping both of us from attending to other and more important duties. But the discontinuation of the French lessons did not put an end to the visits of Elder Stenhouse. He was a persevering young man; but the secret of the great interest taken in the French lessons was soon discovered.

Then it was that arguments of all kinds, and strong reasons were brought forward to shake my purpose of returning to France. I was "in doubt":—when one day, discussing the point, Elder Stenhouse made use of the very same expression which had fallen from the sister's lips at the testimony-meet-

ing—" Whatsoever is not of faith is sin." My mind unsettled,
with all the strength of argument and religion on the one
side, and on the other no one to plead for reason and for my
return to France, who can wonder that I—at best only a
weak and inexperienced girl—listened to the entreaties of my
friends, and resolved to stay.

In the course of a few months I was engaged to be married to Elder Stenhouse. It may, perhaps, seem strange that
I could so soon forget the past, with all its pleasant memories,
and renouncing my betrothed husband, accept the attentions
of another; but it should be remembered that I now firmly
believed it was my duty—a duty which I dared not neglect—
to blot out for ever all past associations, however dear to my
heart they might be. Besides which, I, in common with all
around me, had learned to look upon Elder Stenhouse as
almost an angel, on account of what he had endured for the
Gospel's sake; and I thought that any girl might consider
herself honored by an offer of marriage from a man in his
position in the church. My marriage in France would, I
feared, have been but doubtful happiness in this world, and
certain ruin in the next; but heaven itself would bless my
union with one of its own ordained and tried servants.

Thus it came to pass that on the 6th of February, 1850—
eight months after my arrival in Southampton—I was married to the young Mormon missionary, Elder Stenhouse. I
entered upon my new sphere as a missionary's wife, feeling
that there were no obstacles so great that I could not overcome them for the Gospel's sake. How little could I then
imagine the life that was before me.

I wrote to my friends in France. I told them frankly *all*.
In return they wrote to me—especially Monsieur De Bosque
entreating me to alter my determination. Kind, and very
gentle, were those letters. Dear, very dear, has been the
memory of them, and of their writers, in later days. But,
at the time, I felt that the influence which they still retained
over me was in itself a sin.

I told all to my friends at home—showed them the letters

and everything—and, both before and after my marriage with Elder Stenhouse, I never hid from myself and from him the fact that until my dying day I should cherish with an unchanging affection the memory of those friends whose tender love was the charm of my early life.

CHAPTER V.

MORMON WONDERS:—ANOINTINGS AND MIRACLES.

How a "Miracle" was Performed—The Evidence of One's Senses—Successful use of Scripture Arguments—Mormon *versus* Local Preacher—A lively Discussion—A little "Personal" Matter—A Man who Never saw a Miracle—Success Dependent upon Faith—"I Hardly know What to Think of It"—A New Convert—How Sister Armstrong was Healed—A Genuine Case—Five Years of Helplessness—Testing the Claims :—A fair Proposal—The Faithful Accept the Offer—The Magnetic Principle—A good Dose of Oil—How the Anointing was performed :—Aaron Outdone—Making the Passes—An Exhausting Labor —"Give me your hand, Brother"—"Have faith, Sister Armstrong!"—"We Thought that She was Dead"—My first Introduction to Mary Burton—A Wilful Lassie—We become Fast Friends—Seeing is sometimes Believing—Elder Stenhouse Works a Miracle :—Cures a man of the Cholera—How a "regular battle" was Fought—A Wife's unprofitable Faith—How the Miraculous Power was All Used Up—How my Husband made Himself useful Again.

NOT long after my marriage I saw a miracle performed— a real, true miracle.

Let not the reader smile, or think that I am only jesting, for I am quite in earnest, and mean what I say. I saw a sick person who for years had been confined to her bed, her limbs distorted and her back bent; I was present when, after her conversion, the elders visited her; I saw them anoint her, and lay hands on her, and pray most fervently; and I saw the same decrepit old woman walking and singing and praising God. If that was not a miracle, I should like to know what is?

The Mormon leaders preached everywhere that their religion was not really a new one—it was only the *fulness* of the Gospel—the dispensation of the last days. Just—they said—as Jesus Christ fulfilled and completed the old Jewish law, so the modern prophet preached the perfection of Christ's Gospel;— nothing new; only the perfection of the old. This it was that made them so very successful when arguing with people who were well-taught in the letter of the Bible, but otherwise had received very little educational training.

The following attempt at an argument, which was once carried on between a Mormon Missionary and a Methodist local preacher, in my presence will serve to explain what I mean:—

Local Preacher: But, sir, I deny *in toto* that your elders ever do work miracles. The age of miracles is past.

Mormon: Statement is not proof. You say, sir, that the age of miracles is past.—Do you believe in the Bible?

L. P.: Certainly.

M.: Well then, sir,—do you consider that the Bible asserts that miracles can be, and have been worked,—do you believe that, or not?

L. P.: Certainly I do. Christ and His Apostles worked miracles, and the Bible speaks of many others besides.

M.: We agree on that point. But did Christ anywhere say that miracles should ever cease? Did His Apostles?

L. P.: Yes—No—Yes,—that is to say, I don't remember.

M.: Let me try to refresh your memory. Have not all the sacred writers foretold that ultimately this globe should be destroyed by fire, that the heavens should pass away, and the earth melt, and the sun, and the stars, and the moon be blotted out?

L. P.: Yes, of course, we all know that.

M.: Then let me ask you, Is such a terrible convulsion a common matter of fact. Is it not out of all calculation, out of all order of nature? Is it not *a miracle*—and a miracle *yet to be* performed.—Have then miracles ceased?

L. P.: Oh yes; but that's not a personal matter like healing the sick.

M.: Tell me then, does the Bible teach, or does it not teach, that bone shall come to bone and sinew to sinew and earth and sea shall give up their dead, at the last trump? Is not *that* a miracle, and don't you think it's a little "personal" to you and to me?

L. P.: Well, of course I admit that.

M.: But I have not done yet. Did, or did not Christ say, "These signs shall follow them that believe; in my name they shall cast out devils; they shall speak with new tongues; they shall take up serpents; and if they drink any deadly thing, it shall not hurt them; they shall lay hands on the sick and they shall recover?" Now tell me—Are not miracles promised there, and nothing said about *when* they should cease. Is it not just as fair for the infidel to say that one of Christ's promises was of no avail as for you to say that He has broken His word? Solemnly He makes a promise to be with them to the end of the world and to confirm their miracles. You, because of your want of faith, see and work no miracles, and so you virtually say Christ broke His word on *that* point. The rest of the promise you don't deny, because you can say it is fulfilled without bringing forth any visible proofs.

L. P.: Well, I hardly know what to say to all this.

M.: Let me ask you one more question sir—Have *you* ever seen a miracle of any kind performed?

L. P.: No sir. Certainly not!

M.: And are you a teacher in Israel and know not these things? Have you been preaching the Gospel, as I think you said you had, for over eighteen years, and never yet saw a miracle performed: been preaching Christ and yet never saw Him discover His power in proof of what you taught?

L. P.: I'm afraid not, sir:—you trouble me.

M.: No, sir, it is not I who trouble you: it is *He* troubles you whose word you have doubted. Only last week Mr. Sterne—a minister of your own persuasion—but not far, I trust, from the kingdom of God—visited Bill Wright, the murderer, in prison. Bill had lived a life of infamy—the vilest of the vile—and he wound up his horrible crimes by cutting the throat of his wife. That brute in human form refused at first to speak with any one. Day after day and night after night the good man went to see him, but long in vain. At length one day he chanced to mention the words of Jesus: "Him that cometh unto me, I will in no wise cast out." A little boy, by his mother's knee, the murderer had listened to those words which have brought peace to so many broken hearts. The appeals of the good minister had fallen dead upon his ears. But now was the time of the Spirit's influence, and the strong man wept. I have seen that fiendish man, whose very face betrays the depths of degradation to which his nature has fallen—I have seen him listening meekly and humbly to the word of God—without hope for earth, but with a changed soul within. Tell me, was not *that* a miracle if ever there was one?

L. P.: Sir, I admit that what you say is very forcible. I admit that these things are miraculous; but what I deny is that, in these days, men,—whether Catholic priests, or Mormon Missionaries,—can like St. Paul, or St. Peter, go about with power to heal the sick or raise the dead.

M.: And what I assert, sir, is, that God in these last days has raised up a holy priesthood to preach the *fulness* of the everlasting Gospel. Peter quoted the prophecy of Joel, and said that it was *now* fulfilled, and that "your young men should see visions, and your old men dream dreams, and I will pour out my Spirit upon all flesh, saith the Lord." Now if those were the last days—what are *these? That* was the beginning of the end; *this is* the end. I do not deny that much imposture has been practiced; but the existence of a counterfeit only proves that the real thing must be somewhere. In many instances, too, some of our holiest men have failed, and the world has scoffed at what it called their imposture. But even the disciples of Christ, you remember, once tried to work a miracle, and were not able to do so. What did Christ say, but that it was their want of faith, and bade them fast and pray more?

L. P.: Well, sir, I am willing to allow this, but if you yourself could perform a miracle before my eyes—if, for instance, you'd cure some man or woman who I *knew* really and truly was a confirmed invalid—then, sir, I'd accept all you say—I'd become a Mormon at once; but you'd decline that test, I suppose?

M.: No, sir! I would *not* decline! Brother Sturges, a new convert of ours, has been ill for years. You know him well, for he used to go to your meeting, years ago before he fell from a ladder and the doctors pronounced him incurably deaf. Your religion didn't help him, and the doctors didn't;—but if that man has only faith—faith as a little child—he shall hear as well as you or I hear to-day. We are going to pray over him; will you go with me?

L. P.: Yes. I'll go, but—but I hardly know what to think of it.

So saying, the two disputants walked off together. What ocular demonstration of miracle-working was presented to the Methodist minister, I do not know; I can only say that a fortnight after, I was present at a meeting of the Saints when he was admitted into the Church by immersion. He was followed by a goodly number of his flock; he became a very earnest missionary, and, years after, died in the full odor of sanctity and was buried in Zion, clothed in the full canonicals of a high-priest.

At the time of which I speak, such arguments as those I have briefly sketched from memory, and many which were much more forcibly put, had great weight with me. The Holy Scriptures I implicitly believed; and taking them quite literally I found that the reasoning employed by the Mormons, was, at least to me, altogether unanswerable.

But, for all that, I always liked my believing to be mixed with a little seeing and judging for myself; and on this account it was that I went, with a good deal of pleasure, to the house of Sister Armstrong upon whom the elders were going to lay hands and pray. St. James had said: "Is any sick among you? Let him call for the Elders of the Church; and let them pray over him, anointing him with oil in the name of the Lord: and the prayer of faith shall save the sick, and the Lord shall raise him up; and if he have committed sins, they shall be forgiven him." I wanted to see this command obeyed in *these* days, and to note results.

Sister Armstrong lived in a by-street not very far from the place where our meetings were held. She had lived in Southampton nearly all her life, and probably even now, although in the course of nature she must long since have gone to her rest, there must be many persons living who could remember her and her sudden recovery from illness ; for at the time, as might be expected, it produced no small sensation in the immediate locality in which she resided. She had been the wife of a master-builder, who meeting with an accident while engaged in business, was for a long time confined helplessly to the house, and then to his bed, from which he never arose.

His wife was a faithful and good woman. She nursed him tenderly, and by dint of great exertions on her part, was able to provide all the necessaries and decencies of life for her afflicted husband, herself, and their two little girls, besides paying for suitable medical attendance. In course of time the girls were sent to school—it was the mother's pride that they should not go to a free-school, or as schools of that class are called in England, a "charity-school"—and, night and day, she would toil with her needle in order to carry out this praiseworthy determination. When their father died, the girls were a great comfort to their mother. They were now almost grown up to womanhood, and were able by their own exertions to add very considerably to the family income. Thus happily and contentedly they lived together for several years, until one of the girls married very suitably a good, hard-working mechanic who had known her from childhood ; but the other remained at home with her mother.

Not long after the marriage of her elder daughter, Mrs. Armstrong was troubled with a severe cold which confined her for some weeks to the house. She grew alarmingly worse, and finally took to her bed. One morning her daughter found her speechless, and a doctor being called in, he pronounced her condition desperate. She was subject to convulsive fits which were at first of very frequent occurrence. After a time they came only at intervals, but their effect upon her was terrible ; her limbs were drawn up towards her body and her spine was completely curved, while all one side of her face was permanently distorted;—and this continued for over five years.

Sarah, the younger daughter, watched her mother tenderly; earning meanwhile a modest living by her needle, and from the proceeds of a little miscellaneous shop which she was able to tend without leaving the invalid for more than a few minutes at a time. Thus they lived together contentedly and happy until the arrival of the Mormon Missionaries in Southampton.

The married daughter and her husband being rather better in education and position than people of that class usually are in England, had made it a rule to go regularly every Sunday to their own parish church, and their children were baptized by the regular clergyman. This latter gentleman, however, died, and his successor who, of course, was appointed without consulting the wishes of the people, was, although a scholar and a gentleman, utterly without the slightest tinge of religious enthusiasm. The Methodists at that time had a grand-revival, and the young couple being induced to attend one of their meetings, liked what they heard, and, not long after, left off their attendance at the Anglican Church and joined the denomination to which they had become attached. This change, as might be expected, somewhat unsettled them, and when the Mormon Missionaries came, Bible in hand, and quoting chapter and verse for everything they said, they found ready listeners; and in a very short time the whole family was admitted into the Mormon Church by baptism.

The affliction of the old lady was naturally the subject of conversation among these newly-made Saints and their neighbors. As we have seen, the Mormon Missionaries not only asserted their power to work miracles, but appealed to them as proofs of their mission. People suggested that if this was really true, here was an opportunity of the best kind for putting these pretensions to the test; for every one knew that there was no deception about the malady of Sister Armstrong.

Themselves firmly believing in what they taught, the

Elders desired nothing more than to be able to prove the truth of their assertions, and declared their readiness to do what was required of them. A proper time was appointed when the relations and friends of the sick person should meet together to intercede for her in solemn prayer, after which they would anoint her with oil, as the Apostle James had directed, and lay their hands upon her, that the prayer of faith might save the sick, and God should raise her up.

The room was full of people. There were several of the leading elders present, and also a goodly number of the Saints, who naturally felt a deep interest in the result of these proceedings; besides these, the neighbors who, of course, had heard what was going on, came and filled up the room quite inconveniently.

A stranger would at once have been struck with the prevalence of that peculiar magnetic feeling which evidently influenced all present. Even those who, as the poet says, came to scoff, felt the same influence, as many afterwards acknowledged. The elders surrounded the bed, and after a brief but most earnest address from one of them, we all engaged in prayer. The subject of the prayer can readily be supposed; but the earnestness—the intense, anxious pleading of the supplicants—no one could comprehend who had never been present at such a scene.

A bottle of oil was now brought out by the eldest daughter of the invalid; and three of the elders took it in their hands. It was an Italian flask of very thin glass, covered with wicker, and holding somewhat more than a pint. In taking hold of it, the elders placed their fingers quite round it; though, where many assist in the consecration, I have seen them simply touch it with their fingers. Then one of the elders said:

"By virtue of the holy priesthood, and in the name of Jesus Christ; we consecrate this oil to the healing of all those who are sick and afflicted; that it may remove all infirmities and impurities of the system. And may this oil, which we dedicate especially to the healing of our afflicted sister, penetrate her to the afflicted parts, and give them new life and vigor, that she may be strengthened and healed by the power of faith, and the laying on of hands, as commanded by

thy servants in the last days;—for this especial purpose do we bless and consecrate this oil; in the name of Jesus Christ.—Amen."

After this a large tablespoon was brought forth and filled
with the consecrated oil, which latter was poured down the
throat of the patient. She was then thoroughly anointed—
the oil not being applied by the tip of the finger as in
"extreme unction," but *poured upon her* much after the fashion
described by King David when he says the precious fluid ran
down the beard of Aaron and saturated all his clothing.

The patient, however, was *patient* indeed. To her it was
no idle form. She was newly converted and her heart was
burning with zeal and faith. Perhaps the reader may think
that this had much to do with the success of the operation,
as probably it had. However this might be, the elders, who
while they anointed her had mingled prayers and benedic-
tions above her head, now once more united in fervent supplication, and then laid their hands upon her, according to the
letter of the Scripture.

There was something peculiar about this laying on of
hands. It was not a mere gentle touching, but a thorough
manipulation. The two hands were placed firmly on the top
of the head and then drawn energetically down the body
while vigorous "passes"—as magnetizers call the action—
were made repeatedly over the affected parts. These prayers
and manipulations were made for very nearly three hours,
when the elders engaged in the work—for *work* it was—were
thoroughly exhausted. One of them then placing his right
hand on the head of the sufferer suddenly blessed her in the
name of the Lord, told her that her sins were forgiven her;
that the evil spirits who had afflicted her were cast out; that
the infirmity and disease which for five long years had kept her
bound upon the bed of sickness was rebuked, and would
torment her no more; and bade her be strong in the faith and
be of good cheer, for God would raise her up.

Watching all this, as I was; believing all this, as I did;
my heart filled with joy at the manifestation of heavenly
power which I expected to witness,—I must nevertheless

acknowledge that a feeling of wonder pervaded my mind when I saw Sister Armstrong, who for so many years had been unable even to turn in the bed by herself, stretch forth her poor, bony arm, all unassisted, and say to one of the elders—" Give me your hand, brother."

One of the brethren put forth his hand, and took hers, saying as he did so: " Have faith ; have faith Sister Armstrong ;"—while the brother who had recently blessed her repeated : " The prayer of faith shall save the sick, and God shall raise him up !"

Sister Armstrong, who an hour before could not, unaided, have changed her position, now grasping the elder's hand, raised herself up in the bed. She looked upon us with a smile of triumph for a moment—faith was triumphant. But nature asserted her immutable laws and the next instant the poor sister sank gently back upon the pillows and closed her eyes. We thought that she was dead.

The room was cleared of all but those immediately connected with the sufferer, and I, on account of my new position as Elder Stenhouse's wife, was allowed to remain. Sarah and her younger sister applied such simple restoratives as came conveniently to hand, and we were soon satisfied that Sister Armstrong had only fainted ; and who could wonder at it?

I sat there, not far from the bed, lost in astonishment at what I had seen, and wondering whether what Elder Bronson had said was true—that in a day or two, at furthest, she would be quite well. To me it was all a mystery. I knew then nothing of the miraculous power of faith—not religious faith, but often just the reverse, which has so often relieved and cured diseases and infirmities which have baffled the power of the most skilful physicians. Moreover I knew nothing then of that peculiar magnetic power which scientific men now have proved belongs to certain constitutions and can be used for curative purposes. So, in the childlike simplicity of my heart, I knelt down and thankfully poured forth my gratitude to God that he had permitted me to witness this wonderful manifestation of his power and love.

6

As I rose from my knees, I saw standing just by me and intently watching my movements, a young girl—little more than a child—who was destined in after years to cross my path more than once, and whose sisterly affection I shall ever cherish among the treasures of my heart. She wore a light summer dress, with little or no ornament, and indeed she needed none ; while on her head was a little coquettish hât of the prettiest and most becoming style. Her hair was bright and golden—such hair as I have never seen, except in pictures and on one or two extremely rare occasions—and her eyes, I could not tell the deep, deep love—the charming, engaging beauty which beamed from them.

The reader may perhaps think I am romancing a little, but I do assure him that when I first saw that young girl in all the heavenly beauty of budding maidenhood, I could hardly persuade myself for a moment that I was not dreaming after the fashion of some fairy story. Years passed away—years of anxious cruel trial to us both, and now how changed we are ! She then a pretty, gentle faërie queen ; I, a new-made bride, hardly out of my teens. What are we both now ?

She came right up to me, and said, " Mrs. Stenhouse, you don't know me, but I have seen you often, and I like you very much—yes, and I want to talk to you."

" Yes, dear," I said, and I kissed her on both cheeks and she looked pleased,—in her simplicity she thought it was a great honor to be noticed by a missionary's wife.

Then we sat down together and she told me all about herself :—how her father was a wealthy man, a doctor in good practice and with property beside ; how he had accidentally met with a Mormon gentleman—a man of education and position ; for many such joined the Church before the blighting doctrine of polygamy was promulgated ;—how that his arguments and Bible-proofs had been so convincing that her father had been baptized and had cast in his lot among the Saints ;—how that he, being called away on business, had left her with a maiden aunt who did not belong to the Mormon Church, and who would not let her come to see

Sister Armstrong anointed ; and how she had quietly crept out unnoticed, and would now have to return quite alone."

" No," I said, " I will go with you and see you safe home, but you must not come out all by yourself in this way again."

She kissed me, with a comical little smile dancing on her lips, as much as to intimate that whatever I might sagely suggest, she would, after all, be pretty certain to have her own way.

I saw my young friend safely to her father's house, and then I went home myself, thinking of her childish beauty and winning ways, and pondering over what I had witnessed.

The next morning Sarah called in to see us. She told us that her mother had had a calm and peaceful night, and had been much refreshed ; that when she awoke she insisted upon being washed and dressed and was now sitting up, with my new acquaintance—Mary Burton—talking to her. I could hardly believe this could be true, so I put on my bonnet and went to see.

There, sure enough, wás Sister Armstrong, very pale, and evidently very weak, but quite another woman. No one could have recognised her. The muscles of her face were no longer contracted, and she sat there straight enough for a woman of her age. I could scarcely believe my eyes. The poor old lady seemed glad to see me, and it did my heart good to hear her talk of the mercies of God.

As we talked, Mary came near and put her hand in mine. I stooped down and touched her cheek gently, and kissed her. " You did not even tell me what your other name was, dear ?" I asked.

"No, Sister Stenhouse ; but I told you everything else. My name is Mary *Burton*," she replied, " but *you* must call me only Mary."

I stooped down and kissed her again. That was my only answer.

Then she arose from the stool on which she was sitting,

and said : "I must leave you for a few minutes, please ; I promised to go back directly I'd seen how Mrs. Armstrong was ; but I'll return soon." And with a little whimsical nod and an imperative wave of the hand, she tripped away.

After this I saw plenty of the gift of healing and the working of miracles. Some cases were not quite so success-ful as that which I have described. Then we were told the fault was in our want of faith. That cures were really affected, no one who has been present on such occasions could possibly doubt. That they were miracles in the sense in which we generally use that term, I do not for a moment believe ; but I think that in cases where the efforts of the elders were suc-cessful, scientific enquiry would readily show that the effects were only natural results of natural causes.

One 'brother—a deacon in the church—was suddenly at-tacked with cholera. He sent immediately for Elder Sten-house. It matters not what the disease may be, 'the same means are employed. Young and old, of both sexes, are treated alike ;—from measles to cholera morbus, from tooth-ache to blindness, from whooping-cough to deafness ; and from headache to " possession by devils "—the same prescrip-tion serves for every one. And so satisfied are the Saints that this is the only right way to effect a cure, that, until very recently, to send for a physician would have been accounted a sin—doubting the promises of God—want of faith.

In the case of the deacon to whom I have just alluded, the experiment was successful. Another missionary happened to be in Southampton at that time, and he was with Elder Sten-house when the messenger arrived. They were both much surprised, for they had seen the sick man only an hour and a half before, but they set off at once, and found him in such a state that he could hardly be recognised.

They immediately anointed him with oil, administering a good dose internally ; then laid hands on him and prayed for him ; but the cholera maintained its hold. The two Mission-aries were full of zeal and were determined not to yield to the terrible disease ; from early evening to the following morning at daybreak they continued to anoint the brother and to lay hands on him, praying for his recovery probably thirty times during the night. In their rough but expressive language, they " had a regular battle."

Victory at length crowned their efforts :—the disease was mastered; but they themselves were utterly prostrated by the physical and mental exertions of the night.

The Saints regarded this as a great miracle ; but unbelievers would doubtless wonder why, if it was done by " the power of God "—as the Elders asserted—it had cost so much exertion on the part of man. I, however, simply state the facts as they fell under my own observation ; and I may add that, during that same night, in the same block of low tenement buildings,. five persons died of that dreadful scourge.

On the following day, an enthusiastic sister came running to Elder Stenhouse for him to come and lay hands upon her husband who had also been attacked by the cholera. She was a woman of great faith, or thought she was, and she had no doubt that a wonderful miracle would be wrought. Even in the midst of the affliction at home she was perfectly jubilant over the idea that the power of the priesthood would be demonstrated. She had called in several of her neighbors before the elders arrived, and they stood round the bed of the sick man.

When the elders reached the house, the livid countenance of the sufferer told plainly that he was very far gone. Elder Stenhouse laid his hands upon him in the usual way, but instead of commanding the disease to depart, as it was expected he would, he prayed that the afflicted brother himself might pass away in peace. The head of the dying man instantly fell back upon his pillow, and all was over.

The bereaved woman was almost petrified with surprise and disappointment, and the unexpected change which had made her a widow. Elder Stenhouse could only answer that there was " no virtue in him ;" he had no faith at that moment to heal any one ; the former exercise of the gift had exhausted him. There was, perhaps, more truth in his answer than he himself imagined.

The poor woman of whom I have spoken must have been greatly distressed when she saw the promise of miraculous assistance upon which she had so confidently relied fail her in such an unexpected manner. But she was not alone in her disappointment. Many a man and woman who believed that the laws of nature would be reversed and the decrees of the Almighty set aside because their faith was strong and they "expected" God to act in such and such a way, made shipwreck of their hopes as this poor woman did, upon the quicksands of a false expectation.

My husband and myself were invited to take tea at the house of a brother in Southampton. The brother's name was Isles, and he and his wife had a child who had been very seriously ill for nearly three weeks. Mr. Stenhouse had frequently "administered" to him by the laying on of hands. On the evening to which I allude the child appeared to be much better, and he even sat up to the tea-table, perched, child-like, upon his high chair and in accordance with his own earnest request. We all thought that he was doing very nicely.

After tea, and just when we were about to leave, Sister Isles said : " Brother Stenhouse, please lay your hands upon my babe, and ask the Lord to bless him, that he may have a refreshing sleep to-night. My husband complied, and began by praying that the child might rest well,—when, suddenly, as if by an irresistible impulse he implored that the child might die easily and without pain. I instinctively glanced at the mother, and our eyes met. She looked as if frozen to the heart ; and in a moment we knew that the child was dying,— not painfully, but calmly and peacefully, as if he were going to sleep. The poor mother wept piteously ; but my husband bade her not trouble the last moments of the dying child.

In a few moments all was over ; and I—and probably the mother, too—asked mentally ;—if this also is the age of miracles—" is the Lord's hand shortened that He cannot save, or His ear heavy that He will not hear ?" We had yet to learn that the thoughts of God are beyond the comprehension of man.

Since those times when the spirit of enthusiasm and religious zeal animated the Mormon missionaries and teachers, and stirred up the Saints who listened to them to emulate in faithfulness the Christians of the Early Church, a great change has come over everything connected with the doctrines which were then taught and practiced.

Several years after the occurrence of the events which I have just narrated, when we had been for a considerable time resident in Salt Lake City, our faith in the miraculous gift of healing was still so strong that we suffered one of our children to lie almost at the door of death before we would dare to call in medical assistance, and when, at length, love for our suffering child overcame, to a certain extent, our scruples, it was under protest and with many an effort to silence the voice of a falsely-accusing conscience, that my husband reluctantly went for the physician.

Now—so great are the changes which the influx of Gentiles and more intimate contact with the advanced civilisation of the age have produced—there is not one of the most pious leaders of the Church—including Brother Brigham (who but a very little while ago denounced such a course as the first step towards rank apostasy)—who would not call in, if it appeared needful, the very best medical assistance—whether Mormon or Gentile—which could be procured. And yet Brigham, despite his notorious inconsistencies, lays claim to an " Infallible Priesthood !"

The Saints, in theory, still cling to the first teachings of the Church ; but, if the truth must be told, not only does " iniquity abound," but " the love of *many* has waxed cold."

CHAPTER VI.

THE FIRST WHISPERINGS OF POLYGAMY.

ABOUT three months after our marriage it was rumored
that four of the Twelve Apostles had been appointed to
foreign missions, and were then on their way to England.

The Saints in Britain had been for several years without
any missionaries direct from the body of the church, and the
announcement of this foreign mission was hailed with joy.

I confess to experiencing much pleasure at the thought of
becoming acquainted with a living Apostle. How often in my
girlhood I had wished that I had lived when men inspired of
God walked the earth. What a joy, I thought, it would have
been to have listened to the wisdom of such teachers. Now
the time was near when I should realise all the happiness of
my day-dreams—when I should really have the privilege of
conversing with those chosen men of God. The invitation,
therefore, to meet the conference in London on the first of
June, was very welcome intelligence.

It must not, however, be supposed that I expected to find in them anything which would place them out of the ordinary pale of humanity. I knew that the Apostles of our Lord were very ordinary men, who in their day pursued the common avocations of life. Their charm and glory consisted only in the fact that the spirit of God rested upon them, guiding them in all their ways. These men who now were coming to England were, I firmly believed, as true Apostles as any who ever saw Christ in the flesh ; but they, like the chosen ones of old, had also the gift of inspiration, and were consecrated and set apart specially, by direct revelation from on high, to perform a great and glorious work. But though I did not expect to find them differ, either in appearance or in ordinary conversation, much from their brethren, I expected to find in them grave and very earnest men, and I certainly did experience a sense of disappointment when, in all their conversation and, in all their doings, I found that American Prophets and Apostles were, after all, very much like other men.

We went to the London Conference—my husband and I— and there for the first time I met with Apostles, who were also Prophets, and Priests, and High-priests, and Teachers, and Elders, and Deacons—all assembled in solemn convocation.

The four Apostles whom I met at that time were John Taylor, Lorenzo Snow, Erastus Snow, and Franklin D. Richards —pleasant and agreeable men, and withal very fair specimens of Mormon missionaries, who had found favor in the eyes of Brigham Young and of the leaders in Zion, and who had been promoted accordingly. They lived comfortably, wore the finest broadcloth, fashionably cut, and were not averse to gold chains, and charms, and signet-rings, and other personal adornments. They put on no particular airs, were as polite and attentive to ladies as gentlemen always are, and could go to a theatre or any other place of amusement without hesitation. I afterwards discovered that in one particular, at least, if not in all, they resembled the early Apostles, for they too could, like St. Paul, "lead about a sister" without any compunctions of conscience.

At that time I had not become acquainted with the Mormon "mystery of godliness," and was far from suspecting these pleasant American Apostles of having even the slightest inclination to imitate King Solomon or the patriarchs in their domestic habits. That was to be a discovery of later date.

I do not care to describe this London Conference, as it was very much like any other meeting of the same kind. It had been specially called for the purpose of welcoming the four newly-arrived Apostles. Saints from every part of Britain were assembled, and a good deal of enthusiasm was manifested. Hymns and prayers were interspersed with speeches, and business details of all kinds were fully entered into.

The Southampton Saints had hitherto formed only a branch of the London Conference, but did not form a conference of their own. It was now resolved that since so large a number had recently been baptized in Hampshire, the several branches of the church there should be organised into a special conference at Southampton, with Elder Stenhouse as its president; and the Sunday following was appointed for that purpose, when the Apostle Snow, *en route* to Italy—to which country he had just been appointed missionary—would honor the occasion with his presence.

As we returned, some gentlemen in the same railway carriage, to while away the time, I suppose, entered into a religious discussion. What the subject was I do not now remember, but I can recollect that a good deal was said as to which of all the numerous Christian sects really possessed divine authority. Elder Stenhouse took an active part in the argument, and being, like all the Mormon missionaries at that time, very well posted in Scriptural discussions, he attracted considerable attention, and was much complimented by several persons present.

The Apostle Lorenzo Snow was silent all the time, but he took note of all that passed. Elder Stenhouse was a man of great zeal and untiring energy—qualities in which perhaps Brother Snow felt himself a little deficient; and he was going on a mission which required unflagging devotion and perseverance. We had not been an hour at home, before he told my husband that the Lord had *thrice* revealed to him that he should accompany him to Italy! How often—even while I still clung to Mormonism—did it appear strange to me that the "revelations" of distinguished Saints should so frequently coincide with their own personal wishes, and come at such convenient times.

I had laid aside my travelling dress, and was hastening to provide some refreshment for the Apostle, when my husband came and told me of the revelation which had been so opportunely received. I was at that time as much an enthusiast as Elder Stenhouse himself, and I felt honored that my husband should be the first English elder appointed to a foreign mission. Here was the fulfilment of my ambition that we should be in the forefront of the battle, and should obtain distinction as zealous servants of God. But at what a cost was this ambition purchased! My poor, weak heart sickened at the thought—I had been but four months married.

When the Apostle asked me if I were willing that Elder Stenhouse should go to Italy, I answered "Yes," though I felt that my heart would break. I remembered that in my first transport of joy and gratitude after being baptized, I had made a covenant with the Lord that I would do anything which he might require of me, and I dared not rebel or break that vow. Oh, the agony that fell upon my young heart; it seemed that the weight of a mountain rested upon it when I was told that my husband might be five years absent. He had already been five years a travelling elder, without a home, trusting for daily bread to the voluntary kindness of the Saints. He had labored faithfully, and looked forward to the day when his "conference" should be established, and he could count upon an improvement in his temporal position, and an early call to emigrate to Zion. In the few months that I had been his wife, it was only natural that I should share his hopes; but just at the moment when they were about to be realised, hopes and expectations were scattered to the winds.

On the following day the Saints assembled, the Southam
ton Conference was organised, and Elder Stenhouse elect
its president.   Ten minutes later he was publicly appoint
by the Apostle on a mission to Italy.

In one short year what changes I had seen.   I had rel
quished a happy home in France and forsaken the friends
my youth ; I had set aside an alliance that promised wea:
and honor, to embrace a faith that was everywhere ridicul
and to cast in my lot among a people universally regarded
dupes and fools ; I had married a missionary elder who cou
offer me nothing but toil and privation ; and now to comple
the changes of an eventful year, my husband was about
leave me—probably for five years, and in fact it was very po
sible that I might never see him again.   All this for faith—
faith no doubt mistaken, but certainly sincere.

During the few days which intervened between the tir
when Elder Stenhouse received his appointment, to the ho
of his departure, I enjoyed but little of his society.   Arrar
ing the affairs of the conference which he was leaving, a
preparation for his mission, fully occupied his attention.
do not think we either of us uttered a word, when alo
together, respecting the future that was before us.   It w
probably better that we did not.   There are moments of o
life when silence is better than speech, and it is safer to tru
in the mercy of God than try to shape our own destiny.

The Saints are noted for the fraternal spirit which exis
among them.   There are, of course, exceptions; but, as a ru
every Mormon is willing to help his brother in the faith, a
ing upon the principle, " One is your Master, even Chris
and all ye are brethren."   The Southampton Saints were 1
exception to this rule, but showed their kindness both to m
husband and myself in a thousand little ways.   I have spok
of my unhappiness during that week of preparation, but
must not forget that there were gleams of hope in the dar
ness.   One occasion I shall never forget—a pic-nic which o
friends held as a kind of valedictory feast in honor of tl
missionaries—of Elder Stenhouse in particular.

Right up the Southampton River, not far from Netley Abbey, is a pleasant and picturesque spot named Bittern, which I need not too particularly describe, although the memory of its beauty recalls recollections of mingled sadness and pleasure to my mind. There my parents now lived, and thither it was proposed our friends should go. They could obtain all they needed for the pic-nic at my father's house, and we could take our good things into the woods and enjoy ourselves as we pleased. We had a very happy time—for the moment, even *I* forgot the cloud that was hanging over me, and our dear friends not only enjoyed themselves to the utmost, but seemed bent upon making the time pass pleasantly to everyone else.

I had been talking to Sister White about the recent doings of the Saints, the establishment of the conference and the sending away of Elder Stenhouse. I wanted Sister White, as in fact I wanted everyone else, to think that I was perfectly happy in the separation, and that I counted my feelings as a wife as nothing when placed in the balance against my duty as a missionary, and I tried to impress upon her how proud I was that my husband should be the first English Elder entrusted with a foreign mission. We talked together a great deal. She was still quite a young woman, though married, and the mother of four darling little children; but probably she had a better experience than I had and could see through my attempts to stifle my natural feelings, while at the same time she sympathised with me. She spoke very kindly to me; and as we talked, we wandered inadvertently away from the rest of the party. Suddenly she thought of her little boy, and, mother-like, thinking he might be in danger, ran off to find where he was, promising to come back immediately.

I sat down upon the grass to await her return. I was somewhat excited by the conversation which had passed between us; but as I sat musing my agitation began to cool down and I was soon lost in thought and did not notice that I was not alone.

I did not hear the light footsteps near me, and did not see

my fairy friend, as I called her, pass between me and the sun. But a tiny hand was laid gently on my shoulder, and looking up I saw the loving eyes of Mary Burton looking straight down into mine.

"Where have you been, dear?" I asked, "Why, I have hardly seen you all the day."

"But I knew you were here," she said, "and I thought you were alone—and I wanted to see you and talk with you."

"Come and sit down beside me, Mary," I said, "and let us have a little chat together." Then I drew her gently towards me, and she sat down by my side. For a few moments we said nothing, but I was watching her, and waiting to hear what she would say. She seemed such a pretty, such a sweet and gentle girl—more like one of those little birds of glorious plumage and thrilling song that we see glittering among the dew-drops and the dancing leaves, than a child of earth. And I pitied her for her beauty, for such beauty is a snare; and I wondered whether her innocent soul was as fair and glorious before God as her face was sweet to me; and I asked whether, in years to come, when the glory of her childish radiance had passed away, the brightness of a soul pure and serene would lend a new beauty to her features—the beauty not of childish innocence but of a noble womanhood.

I took her hand in mine, and asked her some trifling question; but she did not answer. Suddenly she looked up full into my face and said, "Sister Stenhouse; I'm very, very sorry for you."

"Sorry for *me*, dear?" I said, "*Why* should you be sorry? I am not sad."

"You shouldn't say so," she replied, "you know in your heart you *are* sad, although you don't say so. It's a fine thing, no doubt, for Elder Stenhouse to go away, though for my part I'd rather stop at home if I loved any one there, and at-any-rate, you must feel sorry that he is going away so far, if you love him."

"But Mary," I said, "you know it is his duty to go, and he has been called to it by the Apostle, and it is a great honor."

"Oh yes, I know that," she replied—"I know that." Then we relapsed into silence for some few moments. Presently drawing nearer to me, she said again quite suddenly, "Sister Stenhouse, do you know the meaning of the word *Polygamy!*"

"Why, what a funny question to ask me, child!" I exclaimed.

"Child, you call me, Sister Stenhouse, but I'm not a child—at least not quite a child—I shall be fifteen next birthday."

"Well dear," I said, "I did not mean to offend you; and I call you ' child' because I love you; but you asked me such a strange question and used such a strange word."

This was quite true, for at that time the word Polygamy was as seldom used as the word 'polyandry,' or any other word signifying a state of things with which we have nothing to do.

"I'm not offended," she said, "only people have a way of treating me as if I were only such a *very* little girl:—I suppose I look so."

She certainly did look so, and I suppose she read my thoughts. Womanhood, by and by, brought to her more of reality both in face and figure as well as in the terrible facts of life; but at that time the term "little fairy," which I have so often used respecting her, seemed the most appropriate. The meaning of that terrible word " Polygamy" she understood, in later years, fully as well as I did.

"Well dear," I said, "Why did you ask me that strange question?"

"You must promise not to be angry with me if I tell you," she answered, "and yet I think you ought to know."

I readily promised—what could I have refused her?—and she said:

"The other day two of the Sisters were at our house—I may not tell you their names for fear of making mischief—and they were talking together between themselves and did not notice that I was present—or else they didn't care. And I heard one of them tell the other that she had heard secretly that in Zion men were allowed to have many wives, and she

used that word "Polygamy" very often, and said that was
what the people of the world called it."

"Well, Mary dear," I replied, "that is no great secret.   We
have all heard that said before.   Wicked people who hate the
Gospel say that, and a great deal more, in order to bring
scandal upon the Church ; but of course it isn't true."

"Ah, but I haven't told you all," she said, "the sisters had
a long talk about it and they explained who they heard it
from, and it was from no one outside the Church ; and then
one of them said that Elder Stenhouse had heard all about it
and knew it was true, only of course he did not talk about
such things yet ; but that the time would come when everyone would acknowledge it, and all the Saints would have
many wives.   I was frightened when I heard this, and very
angry—for I thought of you—and I spoke to her and said it
was all untrue and I'd ask Elder Stenhouse ; and they
scolded me very much for saying so, and said it was very
wicked for a child to listen, and that was why I did not like
you to call me ' child.' "

"Well darling," I said, " I'll not offend you any more in
that way—and it was very good of you to tell me anything
you thought I ought to know."   Then I kissed her, and continued : "But, after all, I don't think it's of any consequence.
It's the old scandal, just as in the early days they said wicked
things of Christ and His apostles.   Elder Stenhouse knows all
that people say, but he has told me again and again that there
is not a word of truth in it, and I believe him."

"You think so, Sister Stenhouse," she replied, "and I suppose I ought to think so too, but if it's all false how did
people first begin to think of it ?   People don't say that the
Mormons are murderers or thieves, because we have given
them no reason to think so.   Then why should they think of
such an unheard-of thing as Polygamy—surely there must
have been *some* reason.   Don't you think so ? "

"No, dear," I answered, "Elder Stenhouse says that some
very wicked men have sometimes joined the Church, and
have done all manner of shocking things, so that they had to

be cut off, and then they went about trying to make other people believe that the Mormons were as wicked as they were. There was John C. Bennett who lived a frightful life at Nauvoo, and then tried to make out that Joseph Smith was as bad as he was. And Marsh, the president of the twelve apostles, and Orson Hyde, when they apostatised not only said bad things of Joseph, but took affidavit and swore solemnly before the magistrates that the prophet had been guilty of the most fearful crimes."

I kissed her again, and she said, "Well, perhaps you are right"; but I could see that in her heart she was not convinced.

Then we talked of ourselves and all that interested us, and she told me all her childish hopes and ambitions; and to me—young as I was myself—it was pleasant to listen to her innocent prattle. She promised to come and see me when Elder Stenhouse had gone and I should be left alone; and when we got back to the rest of the party we were as firm friends as if we had known each other a lifetime.

At midnight, Saturday, June 15th, 1850, the steamer left Southampton for Havre-de-Grace, bearing on board the first two Mormon Missionaries to Italy—one of them was my husband.

The Saints had called in the evening to bid Elder Stenhouse good-bye, and as he was, of course, to travel "without purse or scrip," they vied with each other in showing their appreciation of his position and his devotion to the faith. The poorest among them would not be denied the privilege of contributing their mites to aid in the conversion of the Italians, and none of the brethren felt that they could show too much kindness to the departing missionary. Just in this way have all the foreign missions of the Mormon Church been projected and sustained ; the elements of success were always present—devotion and self-abnegation on the part of the missionaries, and an earnest, self-sacrificing disposition on the part of the people, commanding respect, however erroneous or foolish the foundation of their faith.

In the bustle of departure, Mr. Stenhouse seemed never to have thought about himself, and certainly he made no preparation for me. I had full confidence in him, however, and loved him devotedly, and knew that my love was returned. But men who look for miracles, and count upon special providences for daily bread, are not generally very prudent or far-seeing in their domestic arrangements. Elder Stenhouse had been told that "the Lord would provide," and it therefore seemed to him superfluous that he should interfere; it would have been a lack of faith to have shown too much interest in what might become of me. He left me with only £1.

I now realised the loneliness of my position,—there was no earthly friend to whom I could turn for sympathy at a time like this. Before my Heavenly Father alone I could pour out the bitterness of my soul and all my griefs, and in His presence weep and pray.

CHAPTER VII.

MY HUSBAND'S MISSION:—I AM LEFT ALONE.

WHEN the Apostle Snow called upon Mr. Stenhouse to go to Italy, the Saints willingly accepted the responsibility of providing for me during his absence.

They thought it was more an honor than a burden to have this charge committed to them; but it was very humiliating to me to be placed in such a position, however anxious they might be to assist me and to serve the general cause. To face opposition or to give my all for my religion, I was willing indeed; but to depend upon others for my daily bread was utterly repugnant to my feelings, although, of course, if the Church sent away my husband, whose proper place and duty it was to support his family, it was only right that the members of that Church should undertake the responsibility. But

then, and at many other times during my life, I have learned
the truth of Christ's precept " It is more blessed to give than
to receive."

The American Apostle was not without worldly wisdom
when he proposed that an unmarried man should be appointed
to preside over the Southampton conference, as his wants
would be few. But Mr. Stenhouse had been solicited by a
friend who had a wife and children, to secure his appointment, and with ready confidence in that friend, he overlooked
his own interests and my welfare, and I was left to pass
through trials and privations which I can never forget.

The Saints were very kind, and took pleasure in doing all
they could for me ; but the mistake which my husband committed in leaving his friend to succeed him as president of the
conference was soon apparent. The 'friend' thought of his
own family first, and the family required all that the Saints
could reasonably be expected to contribute, and even then
they had not enough. I therefore received only such little
sums as could be withheld from them, and to make the
matter worse those who had any property or estate were
counselled to sell all and "gather to Zion." The more wealthy Saints were soon gone, and the current expenses of the
church fell heavily upon those who were hardly able to support their own families.

They tried to send me something every week, and I have
no doubt they did send me all that they could. When their
contributions reached four or five shillings (about $1) I
thought myself fortunate ; more often I did not receive the
value of fifty cents in the whole week, at times less, and sometimes nothing at all. That unfailing comfort to respectable
English poverty—a cup of tea—was my greatest luxury, but
at times for weeks together I had not even that ; I had nothing but bread—but I never complained.

Whenever it was possible I concealed my true situation
from every one, and in my almost daily letters to my husband
not a shadow of a hint was ever dropped relative to my own
privations. I wanted him to be successful in his mission,

and I feared that his energy would desert him if he knew of my difficulties.   I was in extreme poverty, certainly, but for myself I was not in trouble.   God would provide for me, I felt, and it was glorious to suffer in a sacred cause.

But darker days—days of severer trial, were creeping slowly near me.   Up to this time I had worshipped God and loved my husband with a perfect heart.   Now the dark shadow of an accursed thing was looming in the distance, but approaching surely if slowly.   The strange suggestions made by darling little Mary Burton at the pic-nic, were not the first whisperings that I had heard of a probable change in our faith and practice respecting marriage, though I did not care to tell her so.   Others had spoken in my presence of the same subject, but I had not believed them.   I had questioned my husband, and his answers had reassured me.

Although Polygamy was utterly denied by the Missionaries in Europe, yet long before it was openly avowed a great deal was written and said on the subject.   Joseph Smith, whatever he said and did in private, always denied it in public, and after his death the leaders of the Church followed his example. In some way, however, an idea had got abroad that the Mormons were somewhat unsound respecting the marriage question.   Still the elders stoutly denied the charge, and the more they were accused the more strenuous became their denials.

At a public discussion at Boulogne-sur-mer in France, the Apostle John Taylor, in reply to the accusations of Polygamy which were brought against him, said :

" We are accused here of actions the most indelicate and disgusting, such as none but a corrupt and depraved heart could have contrived.   These things were too outrageous to admit of belief. . . . . . I shall content myself with quoting our views of chastity and marriage from a work published by us, containing some of our articles of faith—Doctrine and Covenants."

He then proceeded to quote from the Book of Doctrine and Covenants " such passages as the following :—

" Marriage is ordained by God unto man ; wherefore it is lawful that he should have *one* wife, and they *twain* should be *one* flesh.   [p. 218].

He quoted many other things also, among which might be enumerated the following :

"Thou shalt love thy wife with all thy heart, and shalt cleave unto her, and none else."

He quoted also many other passages of Scripture which had reference to the subject;—each powerful to put aside even the idea of polygamy; and each equally powerful as an argument against polygamy itself.

Let the reader here note the value of what Mormons say when their faith is called in question :—See and judge :—

Brother Taylor, who spoke at that meeting, and utterly denied polygamy, had himself—at that very moment when he so atrociously perjured himself and when he swore that no Mormon had more than one wife—*five wives* living in Salt Lake City : One of his friends there present had two wives ; and the other was married to a mother and her own daughter !

Any conclusion, any expression of disgust at these abominations and deliberate perjuries, I leave to the reader.

Among those who came to see Mr. Stenhouse before he left for Italy, was Elder Margetts, an English elder of some prominence in the British mission. At the pic-nic, of which I have already spoken, I noticed that this elder was more than usually attentive to a pretty young sister who was also present. There was always an affectionate familiarity among the Saints ; as I previously mentioned, they were like brothers and sisters, and addressed each other as such. But the attentions of the elder I speak of pointed a little beyond all this. He could not, perhaps, be accused of any open impropriety, but he certainly looked much more like the girl's lover than an ordinary friend or her spiritual adviser.

I knew this Elder's family in London, and his conduct pained me a good deal. So I drew the attention of my husband to the circumstance, and he said the Elder was foolish but he would speak to them both ; and this he did.

After the departure of the missionaries, this elder remained for several days. He then returned to London, but it was not long before he was again in Southampton, and he still paid marked attention to the same young sister. This caused unpleasant remarks among the Saints, who at this time certainly did not believe that polygamy was practiced in Utah.

At a later date this Elder, with some others, was again in Southampton, and I was invited to take tea with them at the house of one of the Saints. In the course of the evening there was a general conversation on " the work of the Lord," in which I, of course, was greatly interested.

Whenever any of the missionaries were visiting, the Saints would seek their society just like children who were glad to meet again their parents after a long absence ; and at such times they were at liberty to ask what questions they pleased. On the evening I speak of, I well remember that the general subject of conversation was the apostasy of the Christian Church from the true order of God's salvation. Prominence was given to the history of Abraham and his descendants, and occasional allusion was made to their marital relations ; but nothing directly was spoken. It was very evident that these elders only wanted to drop a word or two here and there to suit those who wanted it, but nevertheless they spoke so obscurely and mysteriously that they could easily have retracted what was said if any one had accused them of teaching a doctrine which they were unwilling openly to avow.

When I returned home that night I was fully satisfied that the Elder I have spoken of had a reason for his frequent visits to Southampton, and shortly after, the young sister went to London. Whether Polygamy was ever to be a doctrine of the Church or not, it was very clear to me that the London Elder was a polygamist at heart. The more my mind dwelt on these things, the more sick at heart did I become, and faint and weary.

I had, however, personal cares and trials enough to engage my attention. I found that I could not depend upon the Saints to provide me with even the barest necessaries of life, so I looked about me and made enquiries for some light em-

ployment by which I might support myself. My health at
that time would not have allowed me to do much, but for a
long time I could not get anything at all to do. I had, of
course, been used to teaching, but employment of that kind it
was just then impossible for me to take, even if I could have
got it ; the only resource which seemed left to me was to
find occupation for my needle, and it was a long and weary
time before I could obtain even this.

At length I got a little plain sewing to do, and out of the
miserable pittance thus earned I contrived to pay my rent and
provide a few necessaries; but at times that too was beyond
my power, and I have gone a fortnight at a time with nothing
to eat but dry bread. Still my faith never failed. And thus
the weary days passed by.

Now, however, a new interest began to gather round my life,
for I expected before the end of the year the arrival of a little
stranger to share my affections and my care. This certainly
was a sad beginning of domestic bliss, but still the thought
was pleasant to me. I had at that time no one to aid me or
comfort me. The Saints were very kind, but they could not
supply the place of an absent husband. My dearest friend,
Mary Burton, used to come as often as she could to see me,
and her presence was like a gleam of sunshine; but she was
so young, and innocent, and happy that I had not the heart to
trouble her with my sorrows. All my jewelry and trinkets
and the greater part of my wardrobe had gone in providing for
my daily wants and in preparing those necessary trifles upon
which a young mother bestows so much loving care. My
health was daily failing, and sometimes I doubted if I should
ever be well and strong again. But all that I suffered was for
the Church, and that thought sustained me.

Often I would sit alone and think—think of the past and
all my early day-dreams of love, and hope, and bliss; think of
my husband in a far-off land devoting his life and all his energies to the preaching of the latter-day glory; think of those
whisperings of that accursed doctrine which has since brought
desolation and anguish to the hearts of so many weary women;

think of my future life, dark as its promise even then appeared.

Sometimes I heard from Italy, heard how my husband was progressing with his work, and with wifely love I sympathised with him in all his difficulties, for he told me how arduous the task was in which he was engaged.

It was not the expectation of the Mormon Apostles that the missionaries would do much in Catholic Italy. The same causes were in operation there as affected the work in France. Few, if any, really good Roman Catholics have ever joined the Saints. The Irish Mission was never successful, and the same may be said of the French and Italian Missions. In France and Italy by far the greater part of the people might be classed under two heads—Roman Catholics, and infidels. The first had already an infallible guide in which they trusted, and as for the infidels, they ridiculed the idea of any guide at all. Both classes were utterly devoid of that acquaintance with Scripture of which the Mormon Missionaries understood so well how to take advantage, and which rendered them so susceptible to religious influences which took the Bible as their basis. The Missionaries in Italy soon experienced the difficulties presented by these facts.

After their arrival in Genoa, Mr. Stenhouse was directed to carry the gospel to the Waldenses—those brave old Protestants of the dark ages, who so manfully suffered, even unto death, for conscience sake; and some time after he had begun his labors among them, the Apostle Snow joined him.

Whatever they might believe or teach theoretically, there can be no doubt that the American Apostles were largely endowed with the "organ" of caution. Preaching without purse or scrip among people who either detest you as a heretic or else regard you with profound indifference is not a pleasant task, and the Mormon Apostles very prudently "took up" liberal collections in England before they started. Had it not been for this common-sense proceeding I am at a loss to say what would have become of the Missionaries in Italy; and as it was, their lot was not a very enviable one.

Besides the scarcity of money, the other great difficulty experienced by the Missionaries was learning the language of their destined converts. For many years, it was supposed among the Saints that the "Gift of Tongues" would be all-sufficient for this purpose. The two distinguished Apostles, Orson and Parley P. Pratt, whose writings did so much for Mormonism, had both of them eloquently discussed the subject in print; but the Missionaries soon discovered that for practical purposes the "gift" was not of much service; and the two Pratts themselves afterwards experienced—the one in South America and the other in Austria—the fallacy of their theories. Without the "gift" in any shape the work in Italy was necessarily very slow, and an Elder who could speak a little French was sent out from London to assist them. They had at last come to the conclusion that if the Lord would not bestow the "gift" upon them, they must try to acquire it themselves.

The Apostle Snow now thought of sending the Gospel to the Swiss, and Mr. Stenhouse was selected for the work. But before he went it was determined that the Church in Italy should be "organised," and about a week later, I received a long account of how this was done. I heard how, one pleasant November morning, the Apostle Snow, Elders Stenhouse and Woodward, together with several Waldenses whom they had converted, ascended the mountain-side contiguous to La Tour, and overlooking the fertile valley of Pinerello. There they sang praises and prayed:—they christened the place "Mount Brigham;" and the stone upon which the three elders stood and offered up a written prayer, they named "The Rock of Prophecy"; and there they organised the church—dedicating the soil of Italy to the Lord. Moreover, then and there, my husband was solemnly consecrated a "High-Priest, after the Order of the Son of God."

All this I heard, and much more; and in confiding faith that this was indeed a great and glorious work, I rejoiced that I had been accounted worthy to suffer patiently at home, if only my husband might successfully fulfil his task abroad.

After that I heard that he had left Italy and had arrived in

Geneva, believing that he would be more successful among the Swiss than the Italians.

A few days after the arrival of the Missionary in Geneva, an event occurred which interested my own self personally— my little Clara was born. Very happy was I when I looked upon her tiny little face for the first time and kissed her for being the prettiest baby in the world: very happy was I when I folded her in my arms and talked to her as if she could understand all that I said—very happy indeed, as I looked at her again and again, and marvelled whether she really could be indeed and certainly my own baby girl. It seemed as if baby's papa would never come back again, but I had a companion now in my child; and weak and weary as I was, with new responsibilities and less power to help myself, I found comfort in my new care, and realised the truth of the old Scotch song:

> "Muckle lichter is the load,
> When luve bears up the creel."

I was not now alone.

Then, too, came round to see me, Mary Burton. She was as fond and tender to me as ever, and tripped quietly about the room, and tried to wait upon me, and sat by the bed, playing with baby, calling her all the pretty things she could think of, and I felt that her presence brought new light and life to my room. She brought me another letter from my husband, and I found that he was now acquiring for himself the " gift" of the French tongue, unable to do much else, as he and everybody didn't understand each other. He could not yet talk to the French-speaking Genevese; and the English-speaking residents would not listen to him; they had only heard of Mormonism as a clumsy fraud, and looked upon the prophet Joseph Smith as an impostor. So, for a whole winter, he sat shut up in his own room poring over a French grammar, and deploring his hard fate in being denied the gift of tongues.

In the spring of the new year I received a distinguished visitor who kindly interested himself in my welfare. The Apostle Lorenzo Snow left Piedmont for England and passed through Geneva *en route*. On his way to London he called

upon me at Southampton, and expressed much sympathy for
me :—he noticed the change in my appearance, and immediately
sent for Mr. Stenhouse to return to England. He acted very
kindly by me at that time ; did all that he could to assist me,
and said that he never again would ask any man to make such
a sacrifice. I fully appreciated all his kindness ; but much as I
wanted to, I did not venture to ask him about the truth or
falsity of those terrible suggestions which I had heard whispered of late.

My husband hastened home, coming by way of Calais, in
order to meet his president and receive his instructions. The
Apostle showed much sympathy for him, and very early in the
morning accompanied him some miles to the railway station ;
but he never once mentioned how I had been situated in
Southampton until he left him, and then he exacted from him
a promise not to open his lips whatever he might learn.

I need not say that I was happy to see my husband once
again, and to present to him his little daughter who was now
five months old. He was, of course, soon busy in visiting the
Saints, and he received from them many tokens of attachment.

In the beginning of June a General Conference of the
branches of the Church in Britain was held in London. The
Apostles and foreign Missionaries were present, and my husband and I were also there. We had speeches and prayers.
The business of the Conference occupied but very few minutes,
for no measure was questioned. Among the Mormons there
are no opinions, no discussion. The presiding head has made
out his programme before he comes to the conference; he
knows what he wants to do, and no one ever questions him.
He may perhaps for form's sake invite the brethren to speak
on any point he introduces; but when he has furnished the
clew to his wishes, the Elders who speak only spend their time
in arguments in favor of his measures. At the Conference of
which I speak the reports of the native elders were very cheering to us. Throughout England and Wales they had been
most successful in adding members to the Church. Mormonism was then most successfully preached in Britain. There

were more Mormons there than in all Utah Territory : there
were fifty Conferences, with over seven hundred organised
" Branches," and more than six thousand men ordained to
the priesthood.   That peculiar influence which the Mormons
call " the Spirit," of which I have spoken, elsewhere, was
spoken of by the Elders as being a common experience everywhere.

During all that Conference, I listened carefully for a word
from the lips of any of the speakers which might indicate in
any way that Polygamy was part of the Mormon faith ; but
not a whisper, not a hint was uttered.   I naturally concluded
that the Elders, whose doubtful expressions at Southampton
had so troubled my mind, were misinformed or unsafe men.
Still I could not altogether banish my apprehension of coming
evil ; but so bound to secresy were those who did know of
Polygamy being practiced in Utah, that there was not one
who would admit it, and even my own husband's lips were
sealed to me.   He did not deny it, but he would not talk
about it, and did everything he could to banish the thought
from my mind.

At that Conference the Apostle Snow spoke very strongly
of the way in which I had been neglected ; and it was
arranged that Elder Stenhouse should return to Switzerland,
and that I should accompany him.   My knowledge of French
was expected to be very serviceable.

We now made preparations for an early departure, and prepared to leave our friends.   To the reader it may seem strange
for a man, his wife, and babe, to be sent out in this way on a
mission without any proper arrangement for their mainten-
ance, but to my mind, at the time, it seemed to me not only
perfectly proper, but altogether in accordance with God's word
and commandment.

My young friend, Mary Burton, came round to bid me good-
bye ; and the poor girl wept, and I wept with her, and we
kissed one another tenderly as our tears mingled.   We had
become very dear to each other, and the thought of separation for years, or perhaps for ever, was very painful to us.

She hung about my neck at the last moment, kissing me and begging me not to forget to write to her very, very often, and this I gladly promised her, asking the same in return. Then with a fond embrace we parted, and it was years before I saw her dear face again.

Thus it was that we three—my husband, my babe, and myself—set forth on our pilgrimage to convert the Swiss.

It was with no ordinary feelings that I entered the ancient city of Geneva. I was not ignorant of its history and the struggles of its inhabitants for civil and religious liberty. It had been the refuge for the English Protestants during the fiery days of Queen Mary, just as in the time of the French Revolution it was the refuge of infidel and Papist, royalist and republican alike;—there Calvin lived in gloomy austerity, battling with Rome; there Servitus, the Unitarian, was condemned to be roasted alive as a heretic; and there we expected in our own humble way to be able to testify, by our suffering and patience, to what we firmly believed was the truth.

In free countries like England and the United States—free from the surveillance of a military police, it is easy, if he wishes it, for the Missionary to mount a chair at a street corner, or hold forth under a tree, and such has often been done. But all over continental Europe there is hardly a place where this would be possible. In the various grand duchies, kingdoms, and empires, paternal governments look too closely after the morals and religion of their subjects; while under the ephemeral republics, as long as they happen to last, there is often to be found, under the name of liberty, a despotism more despotic than under the rule of royalty. It is the *colporteur*, the man of books and tracts, who makes the converts there, and in this slow way we soon found that we were destined to proceed.

During my husband's former stay in Geneva he had had neither Mormon books nor Mormon papers, with the exception of a paper published at Boulogne, containing a letter by the apostle Taylor, in French and English. This single copy he

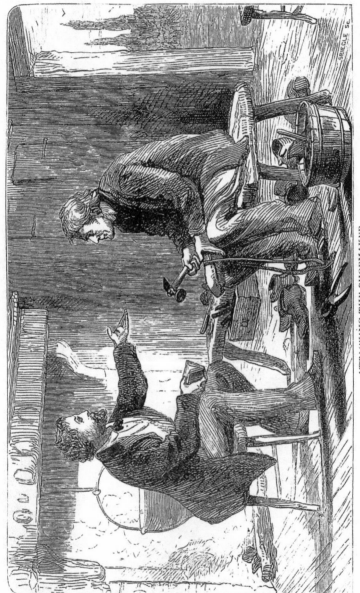

ATTACKING THE SHOEMAKER.

lent to a Genevese to read, and never saw it again ; and yet in a short time, even before he could properly speak French, he converted and baptized two men in the Rhone, one of whom is to-day a devoted Mormon in Southern Utah.

His first attack was upon a shoemaker whom he visited for the purpose of repairs. While the shoemaker worked, Elder Stenhouse talked ; and as the English are all reputed wealthy on the Continent, the friendly overtures of the Mormon Missionary were graciously received. As they grew intimate, Elder Stenhouse would sit down on the bench beside the man as he worked, and taking from his pocket a French Testament, which he always carried about with him, would try to read it aloud—the good-natured shoemaker undertaking to correct his pronunciation. In this way he kept his auditor's attention constantly fixed upon certain passages, more especially those which spoke of baptism for the remission of sins, and the laying on of hands for the gift of the Holy Ghost. So persistent was he that at last the shoemaker's curiosity was awakened, and finally he was baptized ; but unfortunately, not long after, a small pamphlet upon the mission of Joseph Smith fell into his hands and made shipwreck of his faith.

With his second convert he was much more successful. This time it was his landlord who was to be the subject of attack. He was a tailor, and, fortunately for the Missionary, somewhat talkative. The same arrangement was made about reading and correction, and with a like result—the tailor was baptized. Just at this time came the Apostle Snow's letter telling my husband to return to England ; and as he might not leave the country without a representative, he ordained the tailor a Priest in the Mormon Church.

When we arrived in Geneva, *Monsieur le tailleur* was all that constituted the Church of Jesus Christ of Latter-Day Saints in Switzerland.

Soon a few personal friends began to gather to hear the English Missionary tell about the new religion, and my husband being very much in earnest, interest before long began to be excited. I remember well our first meetings among the

Swiss :—half-a-dozen people sitting round a table with open Bibles before them, passages from which Mr. Stenhouse was trying in very bad French to make them understand. I pitied him very much, but those who were present made as if they did not notice his embarrassment, and listened with marked attention. Among the Mormons it is a woman's duty to keep silence; I therefore remained a listener only. But at the close of the service—for such it was regarded—when I might speak, my missionary labors began, I was aroused to elo- quence, and our parting was longer than our meeting.

The warmth with which the few who were present responded to our efforts satisfied me that they had come under the same mysterious influence which I had observed in England. I was then convinced that Mormonism could awaken the Chris- tian soul more to a realisation of what it already possessed, than impart to it any new moral or religious qualities. Mor- monism of itself never made Christians, but Christianity built up Mormonism. It was an awakening to the teachings of Christ and his Apostles that begat confidence in the mis- sion of the Mormon Prophet.

Although we observed the very strictest economy, it did not take long for us to exhaust what little money we brought from England. This placed us in a very awkward position. It is inconvenient enough to be without money in one's own country, where one understands and is understood by every- body ; but to be in a strange land, especially in a country like Switzerland, where every Englishman is supposed to be a "milor" and the bounteous dispenser of unlimited wealth, it is more than inconvenient.

We left our first quarters, where we had had so many visitors, and rented a room from a widow woman, who fortunately was not inquisitive. She had a family of children to support, and as we paid our rent monthly in advance, she had no occasion to know whether or not we kept a bank account, and we were thankful that it was so, for, had it been so ordained, we could there have starved to death without attracting the notice of any one.—A nice thing to be thankful for.

We were not hopeless, though we were heavy-hearted ; but we had expected trial, and could not complain, for we knew from the beginning that thus it would probably be.

One day my husband received a letter from an infidel gentleman who lived in Lausanne—a neighboring canton—requesting him to come and see him, that they might talk together over Mormonism, for he had heard of us and of our doctrine, and my husband resolved to visit him before our money was all gone.

When Mr. Stenhouse reached Lausanne, he visited first a Protestant minister with whom he had some slight acquaintance, and who was also interested in Mormonism, and told him that he was going to call upon the Governeur de l'Hopital. The minister was greatly opposed to my husband visiting such a man. "He is a socialist," he said—"a revolutionist; he fought at the barricades ; he is a *mauvais sujet*, and anything but a fit person to be spoken to about religion."

This only increased the interest which Mr. Stenhouse felt in the Governor, and made him more than ever determined to see him ; and he did see him, although the good minister had represented him *"aussi noir que le diable."* So they met; and my husband began the work for which he had come. They had long talks together, and my husband—as did the Elders ever in such cases—spoke to the Governor of redemption through Christ, and baptism for the remission of sins. Faith is not an act of the will. Like the unseen wind, it comes, and we see the power thereof, but know not whence it proceeds. Thus at first the unbelieving Governor found it—he might find himself no match for the arguments of his opponent, but he could not force his heart to believe, and he was by no means a willing convert. My husband, however, remained with him, and before he left, the Governor had been baptized into the Church.

Our new convert proved to be a most excellent and worthy man, notwithstanding his former infidelity, and he was subsequently a great aid to us in our mission. We felt satisfied

8

that the expenses of that journey had been well spent, although a few francs at that time could ill be spared.

But our circumstances seemed to be getting worse and worse, and my health began to fail. For several months neither of us had had sufficient nourishment, and my anxieties increased my physical weakness; I was dispirited, yet I feared to complain, or even to let my husband know what I felt. At length I was really ill, and could not leave my bed. I well remember the solemn silence that reigned in our home one day. I had risen from my bed, weak, and Oh, so faint-hearted, that I had scarcely any desire to live; and I was sitting with my little daughter in my arms. She had cried herself to sleep, cold and hungry, and much as I loved her—nay, idolised her—I confess that for an instant, I harbored in my soul the impious, the unnatural wish, that rather than see my darling awake again to cold and hunger, she might sleep her sweet young life away. For *me* to yield to such a thought—to wish my child to wake no more—I, who would have given gladly the last drop of my life-blood to save her—for *me* to look upon her innocent little face with such a thought! I can hardly now believe that such a thing was possible, even for a moment. But I was desperate, and bold, and cowardly—all at the same time—or my heart was humiliated by poverty, and my faith was rousing bitter thoughts in my mind.

My husband was pacing the room; I knew too well all that was passing in his mind, although we had long been silent. At length I said to him: "Take courage, dear, for we are the servants of the great God, and surely He will find a means of escape for us. We were sent here; we came because the Lord wanted us to come, and surely He will provide for us!"

He turned to me in reply, and said kindly, "We can at least have some water," and he went for some water, and then with as reverential feeling in his soul as ever inspired a grace before dinner, he blessed it, and we drank.

We had scarcely done so when the mail-courier brought a letter to our door.

Governor Stoudeman, with a feeling of delicacy, had hesitated, when my husband visited him at Lausanne, to offer him any assistance; but, he said in his letter, he had been "impressed" to do so, and hoped that we should not be offended. As the letter was opened, a piece of gold fell upon the table. We could hardly believe that God had so soon answered our prayers and sent us relief, and our emotions of gratitude for this timely aid, found expression in tears.

All this time our landlady knew nothing of our distress; she was as ignorant of our situation as if she had never seen us. So long as I was able to walk about, I used at regular hours to go to the kitchen, get the cooking utensils, and go through the routine of cooking as if we had had a well-filled larder all the time. I set the table with punctilious care, and the good old widow never suspected but that we had plenty. Thus supposing that we wanted nothing, she and her children were more than ordinarily kind to us and to our little girl, who was now old enough to toddle round and go from room to room. Very often they would get her into their room at meal-time and give her little things to please her; and while they felt honored in being permitted to do so, we were silently thankful for our child's sake, for her sufferings were more than we could endure.

The temporary aid from Lausanne was very welcome to us, though it only served to make us feel more keenly our dependent position. I might relate stories—alas, too true—of cold and want; of days, and even almost an entire week passed at one time without food—stories which for painful detail would eclipse romance. It was a weary waiting for Providence! Such things are better forgotten. And yet I feel that in after years my temper was more subdued and my mind more patient under affliction than it would have been had I not experienced this preparatory discipline.

People who have heard, with a sneer, of Mormon Missionaries and their work, would perhaps have realised that faith may be sincere, although mistaken, if they could have seen us at that time. The first teachers of a doctrine, whether it be.

good or evil, if only it stems the current opinions of the hour, have ever found that at the end of a rocky way there was waiting for them a crown of thorns.

Many a time since then I have felt the weight of anxious care in providing for my family—the trial of our faith has not been light or seldom repeated ; but those days of trouble in Switzerland were, I think, the darkest that I ever experienced. We realised literally the necessity of trusting to God's daily mercies for our daily bread ; and the assurance that the Lord would provide was our only hope.   To say that we practiced the strictest economy would be to give but a faint idea of the way in which we had to consider and contrive in order to exist at all.   For years we kept "The Word of Wisdom"— a "Revelation of Joseph Smith," which enjoined abstinence from wine, coffee, tea, or, in fact, warm drinks of any kind ; and trifling as such self-denial may at first appear, it was not really so when other privations were added thereto.   For months at a time we existed,—for I dare not say lived,— without what are considered, even by the poorest, the most common necessaries.   I can even recall to mind one trying week in Switzerland, when, for the whole seven long days, we had less than a pint of corn-flour to live upon, and that was chiefly reserved for our poor child.

As I look back to those dark, painful times I feel that it was by little short of a miracle that our lives were spared.— our faith alone saved us.

CHAPTER VIII.

OUR MISSION IN SWITZERLAND :—MUTTERINGS OF THE
COMING STORM.

An Apostle Comes to Help Me—How the Wives of Missionaries were Sup-
ported—I Meet with Friends—My Attempts at Proselytizing—Madame Balif
Rejects the Revelation—Primitive Meetings of the Saints—Certain Bashful
Men—A Lady Weak in the Faith—How My Faith was Tried—"If You
Could Get that Child Healed"—Wanted: The Gift of Healing—What
Governor Stoudeman Did—The Fate of a Little Child—Madame Balif Makes
a Suggestion—An Effort of Faith—My Doubts and Fears—An Anxious
Night—Mary Burton's Letter—Elder Shrewsbury Manifests Himself—A
Girl's Opinion of Her Lover—Fears of Polygamy—Certain Imprudent Elders
—The American Brethren—Learning a Business—Jealous of Her Husband—
"My Elder"—An Unsettled Mind—Obtaining Information—Nothing Deter-
mined.

VERY. soon after this we were notified that the Apostle
Snow was on his way to Switzerland, and that we might
shortly expect him.

This to me was joyful news, for he had relieved me of my
trouble once before, and I almost looked upon him as my
good angel. He came, and remained with us a few days, and
before he left he instructed Mr. Stenhouse to repair to England to raise funds to aid the mission. He also gave me a
few pounds to procure what I needed for an event which I
expected shortly to take place. This kindness on his part
brought to my mind such a sense of relief, and renewed my
energy, so that I felt ready for my missionary labors again.

When my second child was about two months old, I went
to Lausanne, to reside, while my husband was absent in
England. Apartments were engaged for me at the house of
a gentleman who had recently been baptized. I was made

very comfortable there, and for the first time since my husband was sent on a mission, I experienced a feeling of repose,
so that I now had some hopes of regaining mental and
physical strength. No provision had been made by the Saints
for my support; but even without that, I thought, living
among those who were themselves happy, and one with us in
the faith, I should myself find more tranquillity of mind.

Madame and Monsieur Balif, in whose house I resided, were
persons of good social position. The husband was one of
nature's gentlemen, and as good a man as I ever knew. He
received the Mormonism taught by Mr. Stenhouse with all
his heart, and never seemed weary of showing his gratitude
by his good deeds. Madame Balif did not at once join the
Church, and probably never would have done so but for the
love which she bore to her husband; she was not however
hostile to the new faith, as some other wives were, and she
did all that she could to render pleasant my stay with them,
and tried to make me forget what I had suffered in Geneva.

Madame Balif was a high-spirited, impulsive woman, and
devotedly attached to her husband; I never saw a woman
more so. She impressed me as being one of the happiest of
wives ; he one of the best of husbands. After I had lived in
the house a few weeks, she was baptized; but she never was
satisfied with Mormonism. Poor, dear lady! How often
have I bitterly regretted that I was instrumental in leading
her into the Mormon Church, in which, as years later, in
Utah, she told me, she endured such cruel humiliation and
martyrdom. I knew well indeed then what all that meant.

While I lived with them, it was agreed that I should pay
for my apartments monthly ; but after I had paid for the first
month, Monsieur Balif told me that I should do so no more;
and knowing that he meant it as an expression of kindness
and gratitude on his part, I felt relieved of all anxiety on that
account. All that I had, even then, for the support of myself
and my two little ones was about five francs ($1) a week, but
my wants were few, for I had taught myself to require nothing
but what was absolutely necessary to keep me alive.

During Mr. Stenhouse's absence, the meetings were held in
my parlor, and as the brethren who had joined the Church
had not previously been religious men, though they were persons of the best moral character, they were very diffident
about conducting the meetings, and for a time could not
think of praying before others.   It devolved upon me—of
sheer necessity, for I disliked prominence as much as they
did—to lead the singing, to pray,. to preach, in fact, to do
everything.   Had I not done so, they would have sat looking
at each other, for they were all too timid to speak.   I encouraged them in every way to try, and finally we got along
very well.   A "good spirit" prevailed, and we were like a
little band of brothers and sisters.

The only person, now, who gave me any anxiety was
Madame Balif, who was very weak in the faith.   Her doubts
and fears troubled me much, for I had conceived a very great
regard for her.   I feared that with a heart so proud and rebellious as hers, she would never get salvation, and I trembled
for her happiness.   How slight a hold the new faith had taken
of her mind I was forcibly reminded by an incident which
was at the time a great trial to me.

My little daughter fell sick of intermittent fever, and I
dared not call in a physician ; it would not do for me—a missionary's wife, to show lack of faith.   Such was our zeal in
those days ; but now, as I once before stated, even the most
orthodox Mormons, including Brigham Young, do not think
of relying upon God and the ordinances of the Church, as
they used to in former years, but call in the best physician
they can get.

I was much troubled about my little girl, for she was evidently failing fast.   She had been " administered to " by one
the native Elders who had anointed her with oil and prayed
over her, but yet she did not get better.   Madame Balif, in
the midst of my affliction taunted me about the child not recovering, and asked where was the power of God, of which I
had talked so much : " Now," said she, " if you could get that
child healed, it would be some proof, to my mind, that the

power you speak of is still in the Church." I felt ashamed
that I had not exercised more faith ; I was certain that the
gift of healing *was* in the Church, and I believed it was my
own fault that the child was not even now well.   In my zeal
I replied rather warmly : " My child *will* be healed, and you
shall see it."   But I had no sooner uttered these words than
I began to fear I had promised too much.

I determined, however, that nothing on my part should be
left undone.   I sent for Governor Stoudeman—our new convert—as he was the President of the branch and an Elder.   I
told him that this child *must* be healed by the power of God.
We had not witnessed any manifestation of the healing power
among the Saints in Switzerland, up to that time, and I earnestly desired that now for the first time this gift might be
proved among us, for the sake of the Church as well as for my
own.   So I told the Governor that it was his duty, as well as
mine, to fast and pray that the Lord might grant us this blessing, that it might be a testimony that it was His work and that
we were His servants.

He became as enthusiastic as I was myself, and we fasted
and prayed for nearly two days.   At the end of that time he
came to see me, and by the bedside we knelt and prayed, and
he laid his hands upon the child and blessed her in the name
of the Lord.

That night the child was very low, and though I strove to
show my faith, I dreaded that she would have her usual attack of fever about midnight.   After the departure of the
elder, Madame Balif came into the room and said : " Your
child is very ill ; if your God cannot help her, why do not you
send for a physician ?"   This appeared to me so profane and
such an insult to my God and my faith, that I replied indig-
nantly : " Madame ; she *will* and *shall* be healed this very
night ; for I know that power is in the Church.   The reason
why the child was not healed before is because I have not
been earnest enough in seeking the Lord."

When I was left alone I sat down by the bedside, trembling
lest I had been too rash in declaring that the child would be

healed that same night. Much and fondly as I loved my little treasure, I confess that I suffered more at the thought of God's name suffering reproach than I did from fear of my darling's death ; and I tried earnestly to banish my doubts with the remembrance that all things are possible to them that believe.

Kneeling there in the dark and lonesome midnight, I poured out my soul fervently to God, beseeching Him for His kingdom's sake and for the glory of His great name to answer, and not to suffer my unworthiness to stand in the way. I watched hour after hour beside my darling's bed, and the child slept on peacefully, without any symptoms of returning fever ; and, Oh, how anxiously I waited for her awaking.

At last, worn out with fatigue and watching, I laid myself down on the bed beside her, and soon fell asleep; and when I awoke it was daylight, and my little one was peacefully sleeping on still—the fever had left her. No tongue could tell the gratitude which filled my heart ; I could only weep tears of joy and sing aloud my praise to God.

Madame Bailif entered the room early in the morning to see what kind of a night we had passed. Then I drew her to the bedside, and told her how tranquilly the child had slept all night, and showed her how much better she looked, and asked her if she did not see in all this the providence of God. But she simply said : "Ah, well! I suppose the disease had run its course." This grieved me, for I had trusted that such a direct answer to my prayers would have helped to increase her faith in our religion, but Mormonism had not touched her heart, and I believe it is much more the devotion of the heart than it is the mental acquiescence in doctrine which gives us the power to hope, and endure and believe.

When, by-and-by, my little Clara awoke, she was evidently very much better, and not only free from the fever, but bright and cheerful, like her former self, and she never relapsed. In the course of a week she was running about as well as ever, and the Saints were greatly confirmed in their faith.

One morning not long after this, Madame Balif brought me a letter which, as it bore the English post-mark, she supposed came from my husband. The writing, however, was strange to me; and dreading that some terrible thing might have happened, I tore it open. There, at the bottom of the last page— for the letter was very long—in neat, clear characters, was the signature of my fairy friend, as I called her, Mary Burton. I read the letter through with the deepest interest. It was addressed " to darling Sister Stenhouse," and was overflowing with affection. Used as I was to all her endearing ways, I could almost fancy that while I read I heard her speaking the words. After a great outpouring of love, she said :—

.   .   .   .   Since you left Southampton, we have had many changes. We remained there until nearly all our old friends had left us and emigrated to Zion ; and although my father could not possibly go at that time, and I was much too young to travel alone, the President actually scolded me for not being willing to emigrate with the others. When I told him that I was too young to act for myself he said a good deal about Elder Shrewsbury. I do not know whether you will remember Elder Shrewsbury but I will try to bring him to your mind. Do you not remember a gentleman who came several times to the meeting with me, and who was at the pic-nic just before you left England ? He was very young, with dark hair and beautiful dark eyes to match. He came with Papa first to the meeting, and then he contrived to make friends with me, and I used to see him very often, and he paid me much attention.

I suppose I ought to tell you all that I think about him, and how we have had such pleasant times together,—and so I would, too, if you were here so that I might be kissed first, as you used to do ; but it seems so formal to write such things on paper ; I'm afraid almost that *he* might see. No ! I never told him yet that I cared for him a bit, and I am not sure myself whether I do. I think he's very nice, but I know he's a good Mormon, and if I thought there was any truth in those things which we used to talk about, I'd die before I'd marry him, or go to Salt Lake either.

I remember you talked to him on the day of the pic-nic, and I thought you seemed to like him; in fact you could not help doing so, for he is so clever and so intellectual. That was a happy time we had then ; the brethren and sisters all seemed to have cast dull care to the winds, and to have given themselves up to full and free enjoyment, with the exception of one solitary pair of married lovers—you know *who* I mean—but now you are again united, I suppose, and, of course happy.

I told the President that I had not the " spirit of gathering," and that if my father agreed, I would perhaps go next season; but, *entre nous*, I did not tell him that I had another reason besides. What would you think, dear, if I were to go out as a bride ? But I am very naughty I suppose to think of such a thing.

Since you went, I have grown quite an old woman. You used to call me "little fairy," but, Sister Stenhouse, I am much bigger now. I am now a good deal over fifteen, and people say that I am getting to be quite a woman. I might tell you some other pretty things that are said about me, but I'm afraid you'd say it was all vanity of vanities. If you stay away much longer you won't recognise me when we meet again.

And now I want to tell you something that interests you as much as me. I have not been able to discover anything more with certainty about those hateful things of which I told you, although the word Polygamy seems to me to become every day much more familiar in people's conversation. Elder Shrewsbury tells me that there is not a word of truth in it, and he has had a good deal of conversation upon that subject with the apostles who are here, and also with a man named Curtis E. Bolton—an Elder from the Salt Lake ; and they all positively declare that it is a foul slander upon the Saints of the Most High. So you see that all our unhappiness was for nought. Our Saviour said we should be blessed when all men spoke evil of us falsely for His name's sake ; and the wicked scandal which has been raised against our religion has had a tendency to strengthen my faith, which you know was rather wavering.

And yet do you know, Sister Stenhouse, that even while I am writing to you in this strain, I am weak enough to allow doubts and fears to creep into my heart when I think of the conduct of some of the American brethren.

They appear to me, for married men, to act *so very* imprudently ; and to call their conduct 'imprudent' is really treating it with the greatest leniency, for I have often been quite shocked at the way in which some of the brethren and sisters acted. But I will tell you a little about it, and you shall judge for yourself.

When I found out, as I had long suspected, that dear Papa was going to marry again, I at once resolved that I would no longer be a burden to him, but would find some employment and support myself. I was induced to do this partly because, as you know, step-mothers and daughters do not always love each other quite as much as they might. So I communicated my wishes to Papa, and told him that I had been introduced to a very nice lady, who has a large dress-making establishment at the west end of London ; she is a member of the Church, and has always been very highly spoken of. I told him that she employed a number of highly respectable young girls, and that four, at least, of them were members of the Church, and that in consideration of my lonely situation, and at the earnest request of Elder Shrewsbury, she was willing to take me into her house to board and lodge me, and teach me the business thoroughly, if my father would pay her a premium of fifty pounds.

This Papa readily agreed to do, as I expected he would, for he is so taken up with my step-mama—that is to be—and besides which he has, I know, been unfortunate lately in some railway speculations, and has lost a great deal of money, and therefore wishes to economise. In this way I went to London, and became a member of Mrs. Elsworth's family—and here I am still.

Now you have been in London, Sister Stenhouse, and must remember " the office " in Jewin Street—the head-quarters where all the elders congregate, and where the American elders board, and Church-business is managed. Well, the very first week I was at Mrs. Elsworth's I noticed that the four young sisters who were working there were constantly talking of Jewin Street and the dear American brethren who were stopping there. One of them in particular was always talking about dear Elder Snow; and another girl whispered to me that she went to Jewin Street every evening, and frequently remained there to tea with him, and went afterwards to the theatre with him, or to a meeting, as the case might be; and, the young lady added, " She does make such a fuss over him, toying with him and brushing and combing his hair. I know that she does it, for I have been there with her, and have seen her do it; and he appears to enjoy it quite as much as she does, and, I believe, if Polygamy was true he would marry her."

" But," I said, " it is not true, and therefore it is very wrong for her to act in that way, for he is a married man."

" Oh, but you know," she answered, " that we are all brothers and sisters, and the brethren tell us that those little attentions make them feel that they are not so far from home, and they are thus enabled to perform their mission better; and if that is so, it is the duty of the young sisters to encourage them. These *little attentions* cost nothing, and I'm sure it's quite a pleasure to me."

" Then *you* go to Jewin Street ?" I asked.

" Yes," she said, " sometimes, but not very often, for *my* elder calls here frequently, as he is acquainted with Mrs. Elsworth; and then I take my work up into the parlor sometimes and have a long talk with him. Mrs. Elsworth does not like it, I know, but she does not care to oppose the Elders;—in fact her husband will not allow any such thing—he has dared her to do so. After all, she is very silly, for we ought to love each other and be free and friendly. My Elder—I call him *my* elder, you know, simply because I like him better than the others—calls Mrs. Elsworth ' Gentilish,' and says she'll get over when she goes to Zion. But she says she won't. She is awfully jealous of her husband and a certain Miss Caroline somebody, though she doesn't care for him."

" But what difference can it make to him," I asked her ; " he has a wife and ought not to pay attention to other women."

" Ah, you silly child," she said, " it is only brotherly love, after all, and men often have wives who do not make them happy and that makes them seek the society of the young sisters, for those who are far from home are lonely. My own elder's wife is here in London, but he isn't much with her. He spends nearly all his time in Jewin Street ; he is a travelling Elder, and when he is going anywhere to preach he always calls for me, as he does not like going alone, he is such a genial soul. If Polygamy were true I'd promise to marry him when we reached the valley."

Then I asked why his wife didn't go with him, and she said: " Oh, poor man ! he has no pleasure in *her* society. She is always moping and unhappy ; you know, some women are naturally so. I do all I can to make him feel well, for it must be awful to be married to a woman who is always sad."

I asked her *why* his wife should be so unhappy, and she said : " He tells me that she has got it into her head that somehow or other Polygamy is practiced in Zion ; and I'm sure I, for one, wish it was so, for then we could marry whoever we pleased."

" Oh, for shame !" I said, " I'm sure I'd never go there if I thought so."

Then I asked her whether she did not think it was wrong for her to encourage the attentions of *her* elder ; and she said : " He wishes it just as much as I do, and his wife had better behave herself, or I'll marry him whether Polygamy exists or not in Zion ; and he does not know, though we both suspect, that there *is* something in the rumors which we have heard." Then I told her I thought it was very wicked to encourage the visits of that man, for I believe that if he paid a little more attention to his wife she would be less unhappy—for I supposed she knew of his attentions to her.

She said the wife knew nothing about it ; that he was obliged to be out late at night, preaching, or at Jewin Street, which I knew meant flirting with the sisters and going to the theatre, and I fancy he does more of that than preaching. But she seemed to think it was all the wife's fault, and blamed her. I asked her if she would like to be treated so, if she were an Elder's wife, and had to work as hard and endure as much as all the Missionaries' wives do; but she said she never could be in such a position, and told me that I was not a good Mormon or I would not set myself up as the accuser of the brethren. But I ask you, Sister Stenhouse, if that is the Mormonism which the elders used to teach us ?

And now I have told you all our long talk together and so you can judge for yourself what a change has taken place since you left.

The same day, after dinner, Brother Snow called, in company with two other elders, to see Mrs. Elsworth, and to ask her and the girls to a tea-party the next day. Mrs. Elsworth declined; but one young lady would go with Brother Snow, and Miss Caroline went with another Elder ; and my light-hearted friend waited till *her* Elder came also to ask *her*. After that, came Elder Shrewsbury, and I, of course, was to go with him.

With all my faith, I am very much troubled about these things. They are not right, I think. Why, scarcely a day passes but some of those Elders, who appear to have very little to do, call here and send for one or two of these young sisters, and detain them from their work, much to the annoyance of poor Mrs. Elsworth, who I believe will apostatise over it eventually.

See what a long letter I have written to you ! I am afraid it will tire you. I often long to have you here, that I might come to you and tell you all my troubles. But perhaps, after all, I am wrong, and ought to see things in a different light. Have not the Elders and Apostles positively denied that Polygamy or any other sin was practiced in Utah, or formed any part of the Mormon religion; and we know that these men of God would not lie to us.

Be sure, dear, to write a nice long letter to me *very soon;* and with fondest love remember your own

MARY BURTON."

I read this letter carefully through, and I sat down and thought of dear Mary Burton, and felt deeply sorry that she should be placed in a situation surrounded by so many temptations. To myself the letter brought a sad confirmation of all my fears. There was something painful in the thought. Had polygamy been openly avowed as a Mormon doctrine I should never have joined the Church. But now, what could I do ?

After three months' absence, Mr. Stenhouse was to return home, and I went to Geneva to meet him, feeling very happy when I saw him once again. Numbers of persons, both in Geneva and Lausanne had been converted while he was away and were waiting for him to baptize them ;—among them was a retired Protestant minister, Monsieur Petitpierre, of whom I have something yet to mention. We began at last to rejoice in our success and to be thankful that the Lord had answered our prayers.

I was now more than ever anxious about Polygamy. From much thinking on that subject, it had become the haunting spectre of my existence, and I dreaded what every day might bring forth. The news which my husband brought with him by no means reassured me. He told me that he had heard in England from the American Elders that there was a general expectation among the Saints in Utah that at the October Conference in Salt Lake City, Brigham Young would publish to the world that Polygamy was a doctrine of the Mormon Church.

After all the prevarications and denials then of the Apostles and Elders, Polygamy among the Saints was really a fact. As the truth became clearer to my mind, I thought I should lose my senses ;—the very foundations of my faith were shaken, and not only did I feel a personal repugnance to the unholy doctrine, but I began to realise that the men to whom I had listened with such profound respect and had regarded as the representatives of God, had been guilty of the most deliberate and unblushing falsehood, and I began to ask myself whether if they could do this in order to carry out their purpose in one particular, might they not be guilty of deception upon other points? *Who* could I trust now? For ten years the Mormon Prophets and Apostles had been living in Polygamy at home, while abroad they vehemently denied it and spoke of it as a deadly sin. This was a painful awakening to me ; we had all of us been betrayed ; I lost confidence in man, and even began to question within myself whether I could even trust in God.

There was no argument between Mr. Stenhouse and myself. It would have been worse than useless, for it was not his doing, and he assured me that he had as great a repugnance to the doctrine as I had. He had at first only hinted that it *might* eventually be acknowledged by the leaders of the Church, but it was a matter of too deeply a personal character for me to keep silence, and I did not rest until he had told me all. He had not seen the revelation, but the information which he had received was beyond a question; and singularly enough Elder Margetts, the London Elder, of whose flirtation in Southampton I have already spoken, was at that time on a visit to Switzerland, and confirmed all that my husband had said. Thus the very man who, two years before, first excited my suspicions, now confirmed my fears, and openly stated as a fact, that which he then was ashamed almost to suggest.

Elder Margetts had been in Utah from the time I saw him in England, and was now on a mission to Italy. He knew, therefore, very well what was said and done among the Saints in Zion. I, and those like me, whose faith was not too strong, were spoken of as 'babes' to whom milk only must be given; and in this way any deception necessary to quiet our tender consciences was allowable; but Elder Margetts was one of the 'strong men' to whom meat was necessary:—in other words, they were initiated into all the mysteries of the faith.

My husband enjoined me not to speak of what I had heard, and I felt very little inclination to do so—my heart was too full. The pleasant dreams and hopes of life were ended now to me—what could I look forward to? Henceforth the stern realities of a lonely and weary existence were all the future that should be mine.

Still, the "Revelation" sanctioning a change in the doctrines and practice of the Church, was not yet published; and until Polygamy was openly avowed I felt that the doom of my happiness was not yet sealed, and like many another heart-broken woman, I hoped against hope.

CHAPTER IX.

THE REVELATION ON "CELESTIAL MARRIAGE."

AND time flew by; and at length the dreaded Revelation came.

One very pleasant morning, early in January, 1853, two Elders of the Italian Mission, Jabez Woodward and Thomas Margetts, took breakfast with us; and with them also was Mons. Petitpierre from Geneva, the Protestant minister of whom I have already spoken. While I was busy preparing the meal, Mr. Stenhouse and the two English Elders went to the post-office to get their letters, for at that time they were expecting important news. When they returned, breakfast was quite ready, and they took their seats at the table. I asked if there were any letters from England, and my husband said: "No; no letters, but there is a *Star*, and it contains the Revelation on Polygamy."

He handed me a copy of the *Millennial Star*—a Mormon paper published in Liverpool—and as I took it, I felt as if I

were receiving my death-warrant :—it was indeed the death-warrant to all my hopes of happiness. I rose from the table, asking them to excuse me ; and overcome with agitation and conflicting emotions, I retired to my own chamber. There, for the first time, I read that document which has since brought such sorrow and misery to so many wronged and heart-broken women. The reader may perhaps like to see the only foundation and authority for the practice of Polygamy, ever produced by the Mormon leaders. So I copy *exactly* from the *Millennial Star*, what I then read, leaving out only a few lines here and there, which had no special reference to the subject, but helped to swell the size of the "revelation :"

CELESTIAL MARRIAGE:

A REVELATION ON THE PATRIARCHAL ORDER OF MATRIMONY, OR
PLURALITY OF WIVES.

Given to Joseph Smith, the Seer, in Nauvoo, July 12th, 1843.

1. Verily, thus saith the Lord, unto you, my servant Joseph, that inasmuch as you have inquired of my hand, to know and understand wherein I, the Lord, justified my servants, Abraham, Isaac, and Jacob; as also Moses, David, and Solomon, my servants, as touching the principle and doctrine of their having many wives and concubines : Behold ! and lo, I am the Lord thy God, and will answer thee as touching this matter : Therefore prepare thy heart to receive and obey the instructions which I am about to give unto you; for all those who have this law revealed unto them must obey the same ; for behold ! I reveal unto you a new and everlasting covenant, and if ye abide not that covenant, then are ye damned ; for no one can reject this covenant, and be permitted to enter into my glory ; for all who will have a blessing at my hands shall abide the law which was appointed for that blessing, and the conditions thereof, as was instituted from before the foundations of the world : and as pertaining to the new and everlasting covenant, it was instituted for the fulness of my glory; and he that receiveth a fulness thereof, must and shall abide the law, or he shall be damned, saith the Lord God.

2. And verily I say unto you, that the conditions of this law are these : All covenants, contracts, bonds, obligations, oaths, vows, performances, connections, associations, or expectations, that are not made or entered into, and sealed, by the Holy Spirit of promise, of him who is annointed both as well for time and for all eternity, and that too most holy, by revelation and commandment, through the medium of mine anointed, whom I have appointed on the earth to hold this power, (and I have appointed unto my servant Joseph to hold this power in the last days, and there is never but one on the earth at a time; on whom this power and the keys of the priesthood are conferred), are of no efficacy, virtue, or force,

9

in and after the resurrection from the dead : for all contracts that are not made unto this end, have an end when men are dead.

*   *   *   *   *   *   *   *   *

4. Therefore, if a man marry him a wife in the world, and he marry her not by me, nor by my word ; and he covenant with her so long as he is in the world, and she with him, their covenant and marriage is not of force when they are dead, and when they are out of the world ; therefore they are not bound by any law when they are out of the world ; therefore, when they are out of the world, they neither marry, nor are given in marriage, but are appointed angels in heaven, which *angels are ministering servants,* to minister for those who are worthy of a far more, and an exceeding, and an eternal weight of glory; for these angels did not abide my law, therefore they cannot be enlarged, but remain separately and singly, without exaltation, in their saved condition, to all eternity, and from henceforth are not gods, but are angels of God for ever and ever.

5. And again, verily I say unto you, if a man marry a wife, and make a covenant with her for time, and for all eternity, if that covenant is not by me, or by my word, which is my law, and is not sealed by the Holy Spirit of promise, through him whom I have anointed and appointed unto this power, then it is not valid, neither of force, when they are out of the world, because they are not joined by me, saith the Lord, neither by my word; when they are out of the world, it cannot be received there, because the angels and the gods are appointed there, by whom they cannot pass; they cannot, therefore, inherit my glory, for my house is a house of order, saith the Lord God.

6. And again, verily I say unto you, if a man marry a wife by my word, which is my law, and by the new and everlasting covenant, and it is sealed unto them by the Holy Spirit of promise, by him who is anointed, unto whom I have appointed this power, and the keys of this priesthood, and it shall be said unto them, Ye shall come forth in the first resurrection ; and if it be after the first resurrection, in the next resurrection; and shall inherit thrones, kingdoms, principalities, and powers, dominions, all heights and depths—then shall it be written in the Lamb's Book of Life, that he shall commit no murder whereby to shed innocent blood; and if ye abide in my covenant, and commit no murder whereby to shed *innocent blood,* it shall be done unto them in all things whatsoever my servant hath put upon them, in time, and through all eternity, and shall be of full force when they are out of the world ; and they shall pass by the angels, and the gods, which are set there, to their exaltation and glory in all things, as hath been sealed upon their heads, which glory shall be a fulness and a continuation of the seeds for ever and ever.

7. Then shall they be gods, because they have no end ; therefore shall they be from everlasting to everlasting, because they continue ; then shall they be above all, because all things are subject unto them. Then shall they be gods, because they have all power, and the angels are subject unto them.

*   *   *   *   *   *   *   *   *

9. Verily, verily I say unto you, if a man marry a wife according to my word, and they are sealed by the Holy Spirit of promise, according to mine appointment, and he or she shall commit any sin or transgression of the new and everlasting covenant whatever, and all manner of blasphemies, and if they commit no murder, *wherein they shed innocent blood*—yet they shall come forth in the

first resurrection, and enter into their exaltation, but *they shall be destroyed in the flesh*, and shall be delivered unto the buffetings of Satan, unto the day of redemption, saith the Lord God.

10. The blasphemy against the Holy Ghost, which shall not be forgiven in this world, nor out of the world, is in that ye commit murder, wherein ye shed innocent blood, and assent unto my death, after ye have received my new and everlasting covenant, saith the Lord God; and he that abideth not this law can in no wise enter into my glory, but shall be damned, saith the Lord.

*　　*　　*　　*　　*　　*　　*　　*　　*

13. God commanded Abraham, and Sarah gave Hagar to Abraham, to wife. And why did she do it? Because this was the law, and from Hagar sprang many people. This, therefore, was fulfilling, among other things, the promises. Was Abraham, therefore, under condemnation? Verily, I say unto you, *Nay;* for I, the Lord, commanded it. Abraham was commanded to offer his son Isaac; nevertheless, it was written, Thou shalt not kill. Abraham, however, did not refuse, and it was accounted to him for righteousness.

14. Abraham received concubines, and they bare him children, and it was accounted unto him for righteousness, because they were given unto him, and he abode in my law: as Isaac also, and Jacob did none other things than that which they were commanded, they have entered into their exaltation, according to the promises, and sit upon thrones; and are not angels, but are gods. David also received many wives and concubines, as also Solomon, and Moses my servant; as also many others of my servants, from the beginning of creation until this time; and in nothing did they sin, save in those things which they received not of me.

15. David's wives and concubines were given unto him of me, by the hand of Nathan, my servant, and others of the prophets who had the keys of this power; and in none of these things did he sin against me, save in the case of Uriah and his wife; and therefore, he hath fallen from his exaltation, and received his portion; and he shall not inherit them out of the world; for I gave them unto another, saith the Lord.

16. I am the Lord thy God, and I gave unto thee, my servant Joseph, an appointment, and restore all things; . . . . I have conferred upon you the keys and power of the Priesthood, wherein I restore all things, and make known unto you all things, in due time.

17. And verily, verily I say unto you, that whatsoever you seal on earth shall be sealed in heaven; and whatsoever you bind on earth, in my name, and by my word, saith the Lord, it shall be eternally bound in the heavens; and whosesoever sins you remit on earth shall be remitted eternally in the heavens; and whosesoever sins you retain on earth shall be retained in heaven.

18. And again, verily I say, whomsoever you bless I will bless, and whomsoever you curse I will curse, saith the Lord; for I, the Lord, am thy God.

19. And again, verily I say unto you, my servant Joseph, that whatsoever you give on earth, and to whomsoever you give any one on earth, by my word, and according to my law, it shall be visited with blessings.

*　　*　　*　　*　　*　　*　　*　　*　　*

20. Verily I say unto you, a commandment I give unto mine handmaid Emma Smith your wife . . . . let mine handmaid, Emma Smith, receive all those

that have been given unto my servant Joseph, and who are virtuous and pure before me; and those who are not pure, and have said they were pure, shall be destroyed, saith the Lord God ! . . . . I give unto my servant Joseph, that he shall be made ruler over many things, for he hath been faithful over a few things, and from henceforth I will strengthen him.

21. And I command mine handmaid, Emma Smith, to abide and cleave unto my servant Joseph, and to none else. But if she will not abide this commandment, she shall be destroyed, saith the Lord ; for I am the Lord thy God, and will destroy her if she abide not in my law ; but if she will not abide this commandment, then shall my servant Joseph do all things for her, even as he hath said ; and I will bless him, and multiply him, and give unto him a hundred fold in this world, of fathers and mothers, brothers and sisters, houses and lands, wives and children, and crowns of eternal lives in the eternal worlds. And again, verily I say, let mine handmaid forgive my servant Joseph his trespasses, and then shall she be forgiven her trespasses, wherein she has trespassed against me ; and I, the Lord thy God, will bless her, and multiply her, and make her heart to rejoice.

*   *   *   *   *   *   *   *   *

24. And again, as pertaining to the law of the priesthood : If any man espouse a virgin, and desire to espouse another, and the first give her consent ; and if he espouse the second, and they are virgins, and have vowed to no other man, then is he justified ; he cannot commit adultery, for they are given him ; for he cannot commit adultery with that that belongeth unto him, and to none else ; and if he have ten virgins given unto him by this law, he cannot commit adultery, for they belong to him ; and they are given unto him—therefore is he justified. But if one or either of the ten virgins, after she is espoused, shall be with another man, she has committed adultery, and shall be destroyed ; for they are given unto him to multiply and replenish the earth, according to my commandment, and to fulfil the promise which was given by my Father before the foundation of the world ; and for their exaltation in the eternal worlds, that they may bear the souls of men ; for herein is the work of my Father continued, that He may be glorified.

25. And again, verily, verily I say unto you, if any man have a wife who holds the keys of this power, and he teaches unto her the law of my priesthood, as pertaining to these things ; then shall she believe and administer unto him, or she shall be destroyed, saith the Lord your God ; for I will destroy her; for I will magnify my name upon all those who receive and abide in my law. Therefore, it shall be lawful in me, if she receive not this law, for him to receive all things whatsoever I, the Lord his God, will give unto him, because she did not believe and administer unto him, according to my word ; and she then becomes the transgressor, and he is exempt from the law of Sarah, who administered unto Abraham according to the law, when I commanded Abraham to take Hagar to wife. And now, as pertaining to this law : Verily, verily I say unto you, I will reveal more unto you, hereafter ; therefore, let this suffice for the present. Behold, I am Alpha and Omega. Amen.

And this was the "revelation !"—this mass of confusion, cunning absurdity, falsehood, and bad grammar ! *This* was the celebrated document which was henceforth to be law to the confiding men and women who had embraced Mormonism! Looking at it now; noting its inconsistencies and its flagrant outrage upon common decency and morality, I can hardly credit that I should ever have been such a silly dupe as to give it a second thought. And yet, what *could* I do? I was bound hand and foot, as it were, and my very vision itself was distorted. Unquestioning obedience, we had been taught, was the highest virtue; rebellion was as the sin of witchcraft. I had been convinced of the truth of some of the tenets of the Mormon faith, and confident in them, I accepted without question all the rest. Never, till the possibility that polygamy might some day be acknowledged by the Church, began to be whispered among the Saints—never did a solitary doubt respecting my religion intrude itself upon my mind; and after my apprehensions were fairly aroused by those rumors, whenever I felt the faintest shadow of unbelief or suspicion arising in my heart, I banished it as an unholy thing. The time had not yet come when I could judge dispassionately: the "revelation" aroused within me feelings of horror and dismay, but I did not dare to question its authenticity. It brought bitterness to my soul, but I believed it was from God, and that I must learn to bear the cross patiently.

I did not at that time read the document through from beginning to end. No; my indignation was such that before I had read half of it I threw it from me in anger. Perhaps if I had read it all, and considered it carefully, my own judgment and my sense of right and wrong might have pointed out its absurdity and wickedness. But I was far from being tranquil enough to think calmly. I felt bitterly that this new doctrine was a degradation to woman, and I wondered why God should see fit to humiliate my sex in this way. I was willing to devote myself, my life, my all to His service, but wherefore should He doom me to everlasting sorrow.

What now was to be a woman's lot among the Mormons? A life without hope! Who can express the terrible meaning of those words—*without hope!* Yet so it was. Hereafter

our hearts were to be daily and hourly trampled upon ; the
most sacred feelings of our sex were to be outraged, our affections were to be crushed ;—henceforth we were to be nothing
by ourselves ; without a husband, we were told, we could not
even enter heaven ! But had our trials been limited to this
life we might have borne them, as many a weary soul has
done, waiting for the relief of death. But death was to bring
no hope to us: we were told that in the other world Polygamy
should be the only order of marriage, and that without it none
could be exalted in glory. We were told these things by men
who we believed were true and holy men of God; and we
trusted in them.

Rebellious I felt, indeed, as I paced the room after I had
thrown the Revelation on the ground : I almost felt as if I
should lose my reason. A woman in the time of trouble
always looks to some one in whom she can confide ; but to
whom could I turn for one kind or cheering word—*who* would
comfort me ? I had neither relation or friend to whom I
could speak of *this* trial ; there was no one who could understand me. I could not turn to my husband in *this* sorrow, and
I dared not even kneel to my God to implore His aid. It was
He, they said, who had declared this revelation was His will ;
how then could I turn to Him ? No ; my heart sank within
me ; henceforth there was to be no hope, no peace for me !

There was a knock at my chamber door, and my husband
came in. He knew how acutely I must feel, and he came to
comfort me. I was almost choked with emotion and tears,
but he threw his arms round me tenderly and spoke to me as
if I had been a child that needed consolation. He tried to
persuade me that God as a loving Father could never have
intended the pain or misery of his children, and that when we
came to understand the doctrine better, we should find that
all would be well. He spoke also of his own unchanging
attachment, and appealed to me whether I thought he could
ever love me less or place his affections on another.

I tried to believe, and when I felt a little better I went with
him to the breakfast room where the others were waiting for us.

We were not a very entertaining party that morning. The Elders present, of course knew what had kept me in my room, and their attempt at cheerfulness was not very successful. My husband was in sympathy with me, and I have no doubt that I looked sad enough. There was only one person present who did not appreciate the situation—Monsieur Petitpierre, the Protestant minister—and they handed the Revelation to him. Mr. Stenhouse and the other Elders had some misgivings as to how he would receive it, and they were afraid it might disgust him with Mormonism. But the old gentleman stood the test bravely, and I saw then, as I have seen since, that men can be easily satisfied that the Revelation on Polygamy, or *any other* revelation, is divine, if they desire it to be so.

Here was old Monsieur Petitpierre, a man of more than three score years, and childless. To him the example of Abraham and Solomon appeared most instructive—an example which might be followed with advantage. His wife, like Sarah of old, had never been called by a mother's name; and now although, thus far, he had no idea who might act the part of a second Hagar, there seemed a fair chance that a little Ishmael might perpetuate the race of Petitpierres on earth, if only the Revelation was acted upon by the faithful.

"It ought to be prayerfully thought of," he said.

Prayerfully thought of! Poor, silly old man! Before then I had respect for his years and learning; but now—what could I think of a man who talked such nonsense? Had the revelation told him that the wife of his youth, now tottering in step, and with hair silvered by age, was commanded to take two or a dozen young husbands—I wondered whether he would have added with such satisfaction: "It ought to be prayerfully thought of!"

From that day I learned to regard polygamy as an essential part of the Mormon faith, and such for many years the world has considered it; but when I first joined the Church, such an innovation would have appeared to the European Saints beyond the wildest fancies of a dream

CHAPTER X.

MISSIONARY WORK:—TEACHING POLYGAMY.

Preaching Polygamy—A Phase of Missionary Life—An Embarrassing Position
—Bearing the Cross—One Ever-Present Thought—The Haunting Spectre of
My Life—My Little Daughter Clara—The Work of Repentance—Why Men
are Sent on Mission—Working in the Dark—Days and Nights of Prayer and
Fasting—Preparing for Work—Breaking the News—My First Convert—The
Victim Chosen—The "Beauties" of "Celestial Matrimony"—Introducing a
Pleasant Subject—" Came Down Stairs Singing "—A Cruel Task—" Does
My Serge Believe This ? "—" I Tried to Comfort Her"—Not Wisely, but Too
Well—How the Swiss Women Received the Revelation—A Companion in
Misery—A Letter from Mary Burton—Polygamy in England—Elder Shrews-
bury in Difficulties—Love and Religion—How Polygamy Was Denied—
Looking Most Miserable—"He Kissed My Hand Sorrowfully."

I NOW entered upon a new phase of my Missionary life ;
the Elders assured me that it was my duty to teach
Polygamy to the women of Switzerland.

Hitherto, although I had suffered much from poverty and
privation, my work as a Missionary had been very pleasant.
I believed with my whole heart all that I taught, and my best
wishes for the people around me were that they might
become altogether such as I was, except in my sufferings.

Now, however, all this was changed. It was no longer salvation through faith in Christ, or repentance, or baptism ; it
was no longer love and peace for this world and the promise
of everlasting joy in the world to come, that I was called upon
to teach. My task hitherto had been a labor of love ; now
it was to be a weary work of pain. How could I teach
the sisters, the affection of whose guileless hearts I had
won to myself—how could I teach them that which my own

heart abhorred, a doctrine which I hated with my whole soul!

How I strove against my rebellious nature: how I battled with myself! That God had sent the Revelation I never questioned, and all rebellion to His will I knew must be sinful. I had no thought of evading the responsibility: my heart must be subdued. It might be subdued; it might be crushed and broken, but I could never again, I felt, be truly happy. I tried to reason with myself and to persuade myself that it was I who was to blame and not the Revelation. If the Lord required me to submit, it must be for some good purpose, and I must not refuse the cross that He called upon me to bear. Sometimes for a few moments something would attract my attention and divert my thoughts; but the terrible reality—Polygamy, refused to be ignored, and I felt all the more bitterly afterwards. I never was happy, for life had lost its charm to me. Ere I slept at night one dreadful thought was haunting my pillow,—it disturbed my very dreams,—and when I awoke in the morning, it was with a feverish apprehension of coming evil hanging over me. All through the long, weary day it haunted my footsteps like a spectre, and like a fearful blight that had fallen upon me it seemed to be withering my soul. One thought was ever present in my mind—that thought, Polygamy!

It can be no wonder that I lost all interest in life, and that I should almost wish to die rather than live that life of degradation which I dreaded would be mine. But death flies from those who woo her; the wretched, the weary, the hopeless, they find her not. I felt that there was no rest for me. My only comfort was in my children; no revelation, I felt, could change *their* relationship to me. But over my little daughter Clara I mourned, for I thought if this revelation were acted upon by the Saints, as doubtless it would be, she would some day be called upon to suffer as I did. How little did I then, however, anticipate in what way my fears would be realised! My Clara is now the daughter-in-law of Brigham Young, having married his eldest son, Joseph A. Young.

I am afraid at that time I was somewhat of a trial to my husband, for my heart was not yet quite subdued. I grew impatient at the wrong which I felt had been done to me, and I often said bitter things against the Prophet of the Lord and all his sex, including my husband, who was then, and for years after, a devoted Mormon, and was quite horrified at what I said. He often told me that I was a great hindrance to him, and that it was impossible for any one who lived with me to enjoy the Spirit of God,—and I was afraid that he only spoke the truth.

Then I repented, and sought to chasten myself; and I fasted and prayed and asked forgiveness of God and my husband. But even when most subdued I was as unhappy as ever, and some one was sure to say something which reminded me of my trouble, and whenever the Elders came to the house they were sure to discuss the one painful topic. Then my indignant feelings all came back again, and I felt the spirit of rebellion stirring within me. I could not help it, for I felt that woman's nature itself was insulted by the degrading doctrine, and any mention of it excited my anger.

My husband and the Elders had anticipated that I would not readily submit, and they bore with me as patiently as they could, losing no opportunity of strengthening me in the faith, ever keeping before me the obligation that rested upon me in particular to explain the doctrine to the Swiss sisters. They knew very well that nothing tends more to confirm the faith of the wavering than setting them to teach others. Brigham Young has always acted on this principle, and whenever any of the brethren have evinced signs of doubt or disaffection they have been at once despatched on Mission. Their efforts to convert others, established their own faith.

Among the Swiss we had never spoken on Polygamy or any kindred subject, and we were therefore spared the humiliation which the British Elders experienced in having to retract their own teachings. Nevertheless, Mr. Stenhouse and the other Elders felt great anxiety as to how the new doctrine would be received. My husband did not at once openly tell them that such a Revelation had been sent from Zion; but whenever an opportunity presented he took them aside singly and spoke to them about the ancient patriarchs who practiced Polygamy; and so great was his influence with the converts that he soon won them over to the new teaching, and made them feel that they would not be justified in rejecting the Revelation. Many of the Swiss Saints before their conversion had been more Socialists than Christians, and they probably thought that this change in the marriage institution was a sign of advancing intellectual supremacy; but their wives were very far from sharing these opinions with them.

After many days and nights of prayer and fasting I prepared myself for my work. To a certain extent I had brought my own self under control, or I thought I had, and I almost felt anxious to begin, so that I might get over the painful scenes which I fully anticipated. It was agreed that Madame Baliff, of whom I have already spoken as being rather sceptical when my child recovered from her critical condition, should be the first to whom the intelligence should be imparted, for it was thought that if she accepted the Revelation without much difficulty, the other sisters would be more easily won over. She was a well-educated and intelligent woman, and had seen a good deal of the world. She had met her husband while travelling in Russia, had married him, and they had returned to their native land. She was in every respect a lady, but she was a spoilt child and had her whims; and she possessed a great influence over the minds of the other sisters. On this account it was that she was selected as the victim to whom should first be imparted the mysteries of the Revelation, for it was thought that whatever reception she might give to Polygamy, her views would greatly influence the conduct of the rest.

As I before mentioned, Madame Baliff and her husband were models of affection to one another, and it seemed to me quite a sin that I should introduce into such a household a doctrine which could only produce disunion and misery. I had, however, schooled my heart to what I thought was my duty, and I strove to smother the rebellion rising within me. But, after all it seemed to me hardly fair that I should be selected for this painful task. These husbands had not courage enough, or were ashamed, to tell their own wives about this wonderful Revelation; and so I, a weak woman, hating in my heart the doctrine as much as a woman could hate—*I* was chosen to introduce this pleasant subject, and to persuade those I loved to their own ruin. I had had it all fully explained to me, and I thoroughly understood the *beauties* of the system in the sight of the Elders, and what they considered the strong points in the Revelation;—but it is miserable work to try to convince others of a thing that you yourself detest.

One day, quite unexpectedly to her, they had told Madame Baliff that a new Revelation had been sent from Zion, and that I would explain it to her; then Monsieur Baliff left the house and remained absent until the wife whom he so devotedly loved should have heard this new thing.

Madame Baliff came down stairs singing, in her usual gay spirits, little expecting what she was going to hear; and when she came to me I felt so unfitted for my task that I dared not look her straight in the face, although she was my dearest friend and I had such an affection for her. I stood there, pale and trembling, and she thought that I was not well;—I was not indeed well—I was sick at heart. Never before had the face of a friend been so unwelcome.

She asked me what it was that I had to tell her; and when I hesitatingly denied having wanted to speak to her at all, she said she knew there must be something, as her husband had told her so.

I hesitated still; but at last found courage, and told her all. It was a cruel task to impose upon me. Day after day I had observed her and her husband, I had noticed their deep affection; had seen her watching at the window for his return; and he would come with a little offering of choice fruit or flowers: and I thought no woman could be happier than Madame Baliff. And now for me to so cruelly awaken them from their dream of bliss!

She sat and listened eagerly as I told my story; and when

at length she began to understand what was meant by it, she thought that I must be playing some unseasonable joke upon her, and showed as much in her countenance. But when she saw that I really was in earnest, she sprang up and cried out : "Oh, my God! what a beastly religion! How dared your husband and you come to us Swiss with such a religion as that?" My eyes sank before her as she turned on me with mingled rage and disgust, as if she would wither me with her contemptuous looks. I felt as humbled as if I myself had been the author of the Revelation.

"And does my Serge believe this?" she cried.

I assured her that he did believe it, and she paced the room, to and fro, as if she would go crazy; my heart ached for her. She gave way to a perfect storm of rage, and then sobbed and cried like a child who had lost its mother. I was silent, for I knew how she must feel, and I felt that she would be relieved by tears. I had gone through the trial all alone, without one word from a woman's heart that could reach my own. And I tried to comfort her. I remembered how I had felt myself, and I believed that thus it was now with her. In an instant, when I first realised that Polygamy had anything to do with me, just as I have heard it said of dying men, all my past life rushed to my remembrance, and every word or deed of love therein, stood out in brightest reality. Thus I doubted not it was with my friend. Every tender word which her husband had ever uttered; every loving deed he had ever done, came to her recollection with a ten-fold dearness as she realised the horrors which awaited her in the future.

How little did we either of us imagine the story she would afterwards tell me in Utah!

I tried to soothe her, and she threw her arms passionately round me, and pressed me to her throbbing heart, and wept again. She thought of her husband and her little girls. But with all her fears she dreamed not how miserable was the life before her in poverty and Polygamy. She was herself handsome in form and fair in feature, and, in the full enjoyment of all that could be desired in her sphere of life, she was as happy as a youthful wife could be. She pictured to herself a time—not now, her Serge loved her too truly *now*—when her husband might cast his eyes upon some blooming damsel, younger than she was *then*, and might begin to take a nearer interest in Polygamy. She pictured him bestowing on the youthful beauty the love and tenderness which he had always bestowed on *her;*—how his affections would die out towards her; how her heart would be desolate and alone!

I took her hand in mine and spoke very gently to her, and when she was calmer, I talked to her more freely. We found now, as we tried to look our common enemy in the face, how strong a hold Mormonism had taken of us; and it is in this that persons unacquainted with the Saints have so greatly misjudged the women of Utah; they know how small a hold such a religion—now they look upon Mormonism and Polygamy as identical—would have upon them; and they forget how all-absorbing was our faith in Mormonism *without* Polygamy. We confided not wisely, but too well.

Had Polygamy been an invention of our husbands, or a system which they capriciously adopted, we might have been grieved, but we should have known how to act, for we were in a Christian country where women had rights as well as men; —it was our own hearts which were traitors to us. We had been taught to regard Abraham and Jacob, and David and Solomon as types of holiness, as men who were fit objects for imitation; and now it was proved to us, from Scripture, that these men were Polygamists, and yet were blessed by God; and we were called upon to follow their example. Thus we tried to crush out the remembrance of our own womanhood. Had we but followed the light of reason which God had given for our guide, we should have trampled in the dust that vile burlesque upon the holy religion of Jesus, called a "Revelation upon Celestial Marriage." As it was, the religious teachings which we had received both before and after we embraced Mormonism alike combined to blind us to the truth.

In this state of mind we knelt and prayed for the Lord to increase our faith in that very doctrine which in our hearts we cursed and hated; and on our knees we wept again; and natural feelings of repugnance mingled with an earnest struggle to submit to the will of God. Madame Baliff had not so much faith in Mormonism as I had, and she had consequently less to trouble her in that respect; but she loved her husband, and she knew that he was determined to go to Zion as soon as he could, and then not only would all the luxuries of a happy home be sacrificed, but all her anticipations of the future were overshadowed by a terrible apprehension. Thus we were equally troubled, though I had to endure most, as the task of teaching fell upon me. I did at last manage to persuade her not to offer any active opposition to the revelation, but I could not satisfy her that all was right. She even went so far as to promise to try to overcome her own feelings, for if it was really true she did not wish to be found fighting against the Lord. She had, however, hardly ceased speaking when the thought of her little daughters crossed her mind and once more she paced the room like an enraged tigress, declaring angrily that "no vile Polygamist should ever possess either of her sweet girls." I had felt like this for my own darling Clara.

I had now a companion in misery—some one who could sympathise with me. Even had my husband detested the doctrine, as I did, he could not have comforted me as a woman and a mother could. My poor friend could feel as I felt, and her sympathy was very dear to me—misery loves companionship—we were sisters in affliction. Not only so—Madame Baliff declared that this painful task should not rest on me alone; she would help me in speaking to the sisters. Thus we helped each other in the time of our trouble.

It must have been about this time that I received another letter from Mary Burton. The postmark is quite indistinct, but a week or two one way or the other does not signify much. In her usual quick and impulsive way she gave me *her* views of the "beauties" of Polygamy, and perhaps the reader would like to hear what she said.

. . . . . . I am very miserable, Sister Stenhouse, and furiously indignant. I little thought when I last wrote to you that I should have such news to tell ; but I suppose you know it all without my saying a word. How we all felt when we first learned that Polygamy was true, no words of mine can describe ; we hardly dared look one another in the face. Let me tell you how it was.

One night, quite late, Elder Shrewsbury came round in a hurry, and asked to see me. I went down into the parlour to meet him, and Mrs. Elsworth came down also, and remained until he went away. Elder Shrewsbury looked very strange that night, just like a man who had been doing something wrong and was ashamed of it—and well he might feel so. He began by talking to Mrs. Elsworth about the weather, and when they had both said all they could think of on that interesting and original subject, we all three sat silent for some time. Elder Shrewsbury at last spoke.

He excused himself for coming so late, but he said he had only just received some important news, and could not rest until he had seen us. He had been round at the Conference-house, and had there seen a good many of the Elders. They were all talking earnestly upon the same subject, for that day they had received not only letters from the Apostle at Liverpool, but also copies of the *Millennial Star*, with the Revelation in it, which I suppose you have seen. Of course it was impossible for them to doubt any longer, but most of them felt it was a cruel blow. Elder Shrewsbury said they looked at one another, but did not dare to speak. Nearly all of them had been anxiously trying to get rid of the false scandal, as they supposed the accusation of Polygamy to be ; and in public in their sermons, and in private to all the weak brethren, they had over and over again solemnly declared that Polygamy was unheard of among the Saints, that it was a Gentile lie ; and they had proved from the Bible, and from the Book of Mormon, that a doctrine so sinful could never be believed or practiced by God's people.

Now, all this would be thrown in their teeth. Those who hated Mormonism would revile them for it, and, worse still, the Saints themselves would despise and doubt them for the lies which many of them had innocently told. Who could tell where all this would end? When they were found to have been deceived in a matter like Polygamy, about which it was so easy to arrive at facts and certainty, who would trust them concerning other doctrines which depended upon their veracity and testimony alone ?

Then, too, there was worse to be said about the American Elders and Apostles. Who could believe that Orson Pratt or Lorenzo Snow knew nothing of Polygamy ? And yet they denied it in the most solemn way. And, oh, Sister Stenhouse, think of the Apostle Taylor calling God to witness his truth when he proved from the Book of Covenants that there was no such thing as Polygamy : and all the while he had himself *five* wives in Salt Lake City ! Oh, my ! This is dreadful. Whether the doctrine is true or not, I can never believe that God would forgive all that abominable lying about it.

But I was telling you of that evening.

Elder Shrewsbury told us all this, but he spoke slowly and disjointedly, like a man whose mind is troubled. He said he hardly knew what he was doing. Then he gave Mrs. Elsworth a copy of the *Star*, and he asked me, too, to read the Revelation carefully before I condemned it.

" If the Revelation, as you call it, allows Polygamy," I exclaimed, "it is a lie, and I hate and despise it, and you, and Mormonism, and all !" I was quite in a fury, and I *did* feel as if I hated him then.

He did not answer me; he seemed too cut up to utter a word, but I did not pity him. I felt that men who would write such a revelation as that for their own wicked purposes deserved all the hatred which the cruellest heart could muster up—they were loathesome to any pure-minded woman. Then we went down stairs, for I generally go to see him out. He took my hand in his to shake it, and he held it there, although I tried to take it away, and he said mournfully, "Sister Mary, I know you have good cause for anger; but be just. I have been just as much deceived as ever you have been. It has unsettled all my faith; even our best and most tried Missionaries are shrinking from it. Do not blame me for what I have not done. I never deceived you about it."

"How can I tell that?" I said. "If the Apostles thought nothing of deceiving us and perjuring themselves, how can I trust *any* one? If they had only held their tongues, I should have thought it wrong for them to passively let us be deceived; but you yourself know how solemnly they affirmed that it was all false. I tell you fairly, I hate them."

The Apostles, he said, *had* told some who were strong enough in the faith to bear it, all the truth, but they gave us milk, as the Bible says, because we were babes and our faith was weak.

"Nonsense!" I said, "to tell me such stuff as that! As if the Bible called lies and perjury 'milk!' Nice food for babes, indeed! Why, it's blasphemy even to talk so!"

"I cannot help it, Sister Mary," he said:—"I am more sorry than I can tell you—but what can I do?"

I did not answer him, and after a few moments, during which he still held my hand in his, he said:—"Mary, I want to speak to you *alone* about these things; I have much that I want to say, and I don't want Mrs. Elsworth to be with us. Can I see you, to-morrow evening, if I call? Can I speak with you for half an hour by ourselves?"

"I wish you would not call me 'Mary,' any more, Elder Shrewsbury," I said; "it is too familiar *now*. We have been far too friendly, but, thank God, I have found out in time, and know how to act. I hardly think I ought to let you call me Sister Mary even;—there can be no brotherhood or sisterhood with Polygamy; but I don't want to be unkind to you." Then I told him that he might come as he said, and that I would ask Mrs. Elsworth to let me see him.

He went away looking most miserable, and Mrs. Elsworth scolded me for being so long at the door. I suppose she thought we were love-making, but she was greatly mistaken. She did not seem much pleased or vexed about the Revelation, and she told me that she knew quite well before that it would come some day; and as she said that there was a peculiar look of determination about her mouth that I had never noticed before. I felt sure at once that she had formed a plan of some kind, that she would carry it out if it cost her her life.

Then I went to my own room, and tried to think the matter out. If I were married, as you are, Sister Stenhouse, and if my husband believed in the Revelation, I think I should go crazy. As it was, I felt it terribly. You know, dear, I told you that I *liked* Elder Shrewsbury very well, but nothing more. Well, that was very true *then*, but now I know that it was not all the truth. I take care that he shall **never** know what I think of him, but, *entre nous*, I know that he is **not** the same to me as other people. I do not think I love him; no, I'm sure I don't *now*; but I do feel a great deal of interest in him. That night, however, I felt very bad at him. That he had been deceived, I knew, and also that he must have felt sorry for having deceived me ; and, if he cares for me, he must have felt uneasy for what I might say or do, now the doctrine was proclaimed. But I thought that as a man he ought to have shown more courage, and not to have appeared so thoroughly frightened before a girl like me.

Well, the more I thought of it, the more angry I became, and I couldn't sleep all night. The next morning I wrote a little note to Elder Shrewsbury, saying that after all that had happened, I had fully resolved not to see him again. Many of my friends, I said, were married and could not help themselves, but I both could and would. The Mormon sisters I should ever pity and love; but as for the Mormon men, I would never have anything to do with one of them as long as I lived. I did not want to be unkind to him personally, but I really could not trust any one now.

Then I showed this note to Mrs. Elsworth, and asked her to give it to Elder Shrewsbury that night when he came.

He came, of course, and he came again and again ; but I would not see him; and I did not even go to the meetings for fear of coming across him there. He had long talks with Mrs. Elsworth, and tried to get her to interfere, and at last he sent me a long letter, entreating me not to refuse him. I was cooler now, and when Mrs. Elsworth said I ought at least to see him, even if I dismissed him then, I agreed to do so, and the next night he came.

He was very humble that night. You know what torrents of eloquence he pours forth about anything that interests him, and how earnest he is. But then all his eloquence had fled. He hesitated and blundered until I really quite pitied him. He came and sat by me, and would have taken my hand, but I would not let him. He did not tell me that he loved me, but he spoke as if I were conscious of the fact, and you know, of course, I couldn't help feeling that he cared for me, whether he spoke about it or not. He assured me over and over again that though he had often heard the scandal—as I had done—he did not for a moment believe it ; he said that he should *never* himself act up to the Revelation ; that if he loved it should be an undivided and all-absorbing love ; that he would rather have less glory in eternity, with *one* whom he could idolize, than obey the Revelation on Polygamy, and obtain a higher position.

All this time he hardly once looked at me, but when I did see his eyes they seemed very sorrowful and very earnest. I confess to you that what he said made me feel very differently for him. For a man of his ability and talents, who has such an influence, and wins so much respect from every one he meets, to be sitting there all bashful, like a naughty child, before a young girl like me, and all because he loved me, made me feel for him a pity which was very near to love.

But it was not love quite ; and I did not let him read my thoughts. I asked him to tell me all he knew, and to explain to me the meaning of different parts of the Revelation which were rather obscure to me ; and he did so. Then he tried to shake my resolution, and so anxious and troubled did he seem, that I really do think that if I had asked him to give up Mormonism altogether, he would have done so for my sake. I told him that I had quite resolved, now that Polygamy was acknowledged, never to see him again, except as I might see the other Elders at meeting.   I said I believed I was still a good Mormon, as Mormons used to be, but I would never receive Polygamy, or be more than an ordinary friend to any one who did believe it.   We talked together a good deal, and we sat silently together a long while ; and at last he rose to go.   He kissed my hand sorrowfully—and I didn't like to be vexed with him for doing so, he looked so doleful—and he said he'd wait and wait, ever so long, if I wanted him to do so ; but that he would hope on, trusting that *some* day I might change.   I told him I thought—I *knew* I should *never* change.

After that I only saw him at meeting.   And, oh dear ! you should see what meetings we have now !   Half the people don't attend, and everything is so cold and lifeless.   Some of our most earnest Elders never come ; and it is said among the brethren, that Polygamy will produce the greatest apostasy which the Church has ever seen.   Every one seems ashamed of it.

And now, dear, I have written you a terrible long letter, but you must please forgive me, for I have no one to whom I can open my heart except to you.   I wish I had some keepsake to remember you by.   Well, I don't mean that, but I should so like to have your portrait.   Did you not once tell me that Elder Stenhouse talked of learning photography ?   Does he ever practice it now ?   And if so, couldn't you get him to take a shadow of yourself ?   I should *so* like to have one.   Mine I will send you as soon as it is taken.   I mean to write again to you in the course of a day or two, and then I'll tell you what Elder Shrewsbury said about the Revelation itself.   Meanwhile, dear, kiss both the babies, please, for me ; and write soon to your most affectionately loving,

MARY BURTON."

Poor girl ! I said, as I folded up her letter ; but it is better for her to suffer a little now than for her to have been married first, as I was, and then, when too late to go back, to have Polygamy announced as an article of faith.

CHAPTER XI.

MORMONISM IN ENGLAND:—PREPARING TO EMIGRATE.

A Blissful State of Ignorance—The Opinions of Monsieur Petitpierre—Strong
Arguments—How He Became an Apostate—"He Shall Rule over Her"—The
Nobler Sex—How Women were Sufficiently Honored—Looking Anxiously
for a Chang?—Establishing a Mormon Paper—Denouncing the Gentiles—
Terrible Expectations—Hastening to Zion—A Journey of Many Days—The
Swiss Pilgrims—Death by the Way—Disobeying Counsel—The "Judg-
ments" of the Lord—The Love of Many Waxes Cold—The President of the
London Conference—Distinguished Apostates—Strange News from Zion—
An "Object of Interest"—Great Success of Mormonism in Britain—How
Saints were Re-baptized—Poor Elder Marsden!—The Emigration Season—
My Little Daughter Minnie—Saintly Treatment—A Visit from Mary Burton
—How Love Affairs Progressed—Pacifying a Lover—The Meaning of the
Word "Patience."

IT was fortunate for the Swiss Mission that the new converts in general could not read any language but their
own, and thus were ignorant of the deceptions which the
American Elders had practiced upon the people.

Monsieur Petitpierre, the Protestant minister, who thought
that the Revelation ought to be "prayerfully considered," was
the only one who understood English, and his knowledge was
very limited. His wife did not at all coincide with him about
the prayerful consideration of Polygamy; she disposed of the
subject without any prayer at all, and it is to be regretted that
in this respect the whole body of the Mormon women did not
follow her example.

What arguments she used I do not know; but that they
were very much to the point no one can doubt, for they banished for ever all thoughts of Polygamy from her husband's

mind. It was said among the Saints that she was very ener-
getic in her private discussions with her husband. But however this might be, it is certain that Monsieur Petitpierre
resisted as long as he could, for the revelation quite fascinated
the childless old man, and it is possible that he might have
held fast to the faith; but, unfortunately, just then certain
documents and publications of the Apostles, and a very large
amount of evidence respecting them and their doings,
attracted his attention. He was in the main a good and
truthful man, although of small mental calibre, and the
deceptions and contradictions which he discovered quite disgusted him. His wife's strong personal arguments gave the
finishing blow to his faith, and the spell was broken. The
vision of a modern Hagar and a little Ishmael vanished from
his mind; he apostatised—and Mr. Stenhouse lost the services
of a very useful translator.

When I heard that he had left the Church, how I wished
that I could have followed in his footsteps. But apostasy
from Mormonism is only possible to two classes—the young
disciple, who has embraced the faith more from enthusiasm
than from conviction, whose experience is limited, and the
old disciple who has entirely outgrown it, and has become disgusted with it all.

I was neither of these. My faith was too firmly grounded
to admit of my giving it up. Though I hated Polygamy, I
did not dare to question the divinity of its origin. I only
pitied myself and my sex for the burden which God had seen
fit to place upon us. I never for a moment supposed that
any man would have been so wicked as to fabricate a "Revelation," or so blasphemous as to palm it off in the name of
the Lord.

Oh yes, I hated Polygamy in my heart. And my efforts in
teaching it only increased my hatred; for when I was gravely
told by the Elders that woman had been cursed in the Garden of Eden, and that Polygamy was one of the results of
that curse—"her desire shall be unto her husband, and *he
shall rule over her*!"—I must confess that my heart within me

was rebellious. From my earliest childhood I had thought of God as a father and a friend, to whom I might go and tell all my griefs and cares; but now He was presented to me as a hard taskmaster, not as a father or a friend.

I met with much kindness, but I did not meet with much sympathy from the brethren. They could not understand that opposition to Polygamy was anything else than selfishness on the part of the sisters; they did not comprehend the feelings of a woman's heart—its craving for some object upon which to devote its whole wealth of love. They were taught that theirs was a nobler position than that of the sisters, and that women might consider themselves sufficiently honored in being allowed to become the mothers of their children and to help in building up *their* " kingdom."

Of my Missionary work in Switzerland subsequent to the introduction of Polygamy I will say but little, except that it was too successful. The same sorrow and indignation which Madame Baliff had so forcibly expressed, were shown by almost every new convert, and I had to bear the blame of teaching such a doctrine. The sisters became unhappy, and wished that they had died in ignorance of Mormonism; and I felt humbled to the dust to think that I should be the innocent cause of so much misery to others. I looked anxiously for a change, but the only change which seemed probable was that we might be permitted to emigrate to Utah, and there was no comfort for me in that prospect.

We remained in Switzerland until the close of the year 1854, and through the unremitting efforts of my husband, Mormonism was introduced into six cantons of the Confederation. Monsieur Baliff became an indefatigable Missionary, as was also Governor Stoudeman; and to their liberality and zeal Mr. Stenhouse was greatly indebted. With the aid of Monsieur Baliff, he established in Geneva a monthly periodical in the French language, for the edification of the Saints, beside a volume in reply to the attacks of the clergy, and many minor effusions.

At that time there was great excitement among the Saints

in Utah.   Brigham Young and his Apostles were denouncing
the Gentiles in the most unmeasured language.   As I write,
a volume of sermons delivered at that time is before me, and
I really can hardly credit that so much ridiculous nonsense,
bad grammar, and blasphemy, could ever have been uttered
in a public place of worship ;—yet it was so.   The Saints
were told that in these last times all the Vials of the Wrath of
God were about to be poured upon the earth; wars and desolations, anarchy and persecution, fire, pestilence, and unheard
of horrors, were to desolate all the world, until men should
call upon the rocks to hide them, and in the bitterness of
their souls curse the day in which they were born; death was
to be sought for, but not found.   Believing, as they did, that
all this was true, it is no wonder that the Saints in Europe
were alarmed, and became anxious to emigrate to Utah, where
they were told they would be safe.   A seven years' famine
was said to be at the door, when a sack of wheat should be
sold for a sack of gold, and Gentile Kings and Princes were
to come and crouch to the Saints for a morsel of bread.   The
very women in Zion were counselled to sell the ribbons from
their bonnets, to buy flour with the proceeds, and to hide it
away against the day of wrath.

The brethren and sisters in Switzerland who could dispose
of their property hastened to " flee to Zion."   Some did so at
a ruinous sacrifice.   One gentleman—a Monsieur Robella—I
knew, who was part proprietor of a newspaper and printing
establishment.   In a very short time it would have been
entirely in his own hands ; but he sold out at a great loss,
dreading that the storm might overtake him before he reached
the "Chambers of the Lord in the Mountains," as the Elders
called Salt Lake City.

The journey from Europe to Utah at that time occupied
six or eight months ; it was a very tedious pilgrimage.   My
Swiss friends had first to travel to Liverpool ; thence by sailing vessel to New Orleans ; by steamer up the Mississippi as
far as St. Louis ; up the Missouri to the frontiers ; and then
across the Plains by ox-teams.   Much of this distance had to

be travelled during the worst part of the year. They left
their homes while the Jura Mountains were still draped in
snow, and those who escaped the ravages of cholera and the
perils of the way, reached their destination just as the frosts
of winter were beginning to whiten the hoary heads of the
hills which stand about Zion.

All the Swiss pilgrims travelled together until they arrived
at St. Louis ; there they separated, one party going up the
river, and the other making the journey overland. The
cholera attacked the latter party and cut off the greater number of them, and their bones now whiten the prairie.

The news of their death soon arrived in Switzerland, and
the people at Lausanne were exasperated against the Mormon
Missionaries, and when my husband visited that place he
found it prudent not to remain long. At the same time those
of the Saints whose relations had perished in the emigration
were pained to hear that it was because they "had not obeyed
counsel," and gone up the river with the other party, that they
fell by the way. And, as if in mockery of this statement, the
next news that we received was that a Missouri steamer, on
board of which were many Mormon Missionaries—all most
obedient to counsel—had been blown to atoms. Many of the
Saints began to consider these things, and their love waxed
cold.

Through all this our position was anything but pleasant,
and my husband applied for permission to be released from
the Presidency of the Swiss and Italian Missions, in order
that he might "gather to Zion." His request was granted;
and in the autumn of 1854, we bade a final adieu to Switzerland.

We might now be said to have *begun* our journey to Zion,
although we tarried long by the way,. and several years
elapsed before we reached our destination.

When we arrived in London we obtained apartments in the
house of the President of the London Conference, and there
I had opportunities of observing the effects of the system
upon the English Saints. Elder Marsden, the President, was

a thorough Mormon, and a man who was very highly thought
of.   He had been acquainted with all the Apostles and High-
priests who had resided in Liverpool—the great *rendezvous* of
the Saints in England; had been President of the Conference there, and now occupied the highest position of the
European mission.   He was a pleasant, intelligent man, who
in his day had done much to build up the Church; but like
his two predecessors, John Banks and Thomas Margetts, he
also apostatised from the Mormonism of later years.   At the
time, however, of which I speak, he was considered to be of
good standing among the Saints.

Up to this time I had never seriously doubted my religion,
and I probably never should have done so had it not been for
the introduction of Polygamy.   But what I saw in London at
that time sadly shook my faith, and the stories which I heard
from Utah quite frightened me.   Nothing, of course, was
openly said, and at first I disbelieved every evil report, until
at last it was impossible for me altogether to reject what was
told me.   The testimony of an Apostate or of a Gentile would
have been dismissed with contempt; but when we saw letters
from mothers to their children, and husbands to their wives—
all people of unquestioned faith, setting forth the troubled
state of men's minds in Utah, expressing fears for their own
safety, and hinting at "cutting off" the transgressor, and the
doings of "Avenging Angels," we could not cast them aside
with contempt.   My views of the glories of Zion were changing;—henceforth I was never firm in the faith—I felt that
there was *something* wrong.

Perhaps the reader may think that now I might have left
the Church, and thus have avoided all those troubles which
awaited me in Utah.   But let him remember that, although
my faith was shaken, it was not wholly destroyed.   All that I
clung to on earth—my husband, whom I truly loved, and my
darling children—were part and parcel of Mormonism.   I
could not tear myself from them, and isolate my soul from all
that made life worth having.

My unsettled state of mind, however, did not long remain

a secret. It was spoken of among the Saints, and I became
an object of interest. The Pastor over the London and
adjoining Conferences was the son of one of the chief Apostles in Utah—a young man, whose good nature was far better
than his religion. He visited us very frequently, and used to
bring with him the distinguished American Elders who might
be visiting the metropolis. I have no doubt that they were
sincere in their desire to do me good, but it was not kind
attentions that I then needed, it was the removal of the cause
of my sorrows.

They tried to persuade me that it was all "the work of the
Lord;" but I could not see it in that light, and very often in
reply to their consolations I said very hard things of Polygamy and the leaders of the Church, whose conduct I considered sinful. And in this I did not stand alone, for I soon
found that the President of the Conference—Elder Marsden
—had been in the same position for years, and his wife was
"quite through" with Mormonism. In fact, so great had been
the distrust occasioned by Polygamy, that in the report ending June 30th, 1853, it was stated that from the whole British
Church—which then numbered very nearly thirty-one thous-
and souls—seventeen hundred and seventy-six had been ex-
communicated for apostasy!

Of those who remained faithful I cannot give a much more
cheering account. The Elders who visited President Marsden made as damaging reports of the condition of the Saints
as their worst enemies could desire. All that my young
friend, Mary Burton, had told me did not equal the truth of
what I saw for myself. No one had any confidence *now* in
what the Elders said;—how could they be trusted after so
many years of deception?

The Elders who visited me and reasoned with me about my
want of faith, tried to persuade me to be baptized again.
Among the Mormons it is the privilege of the faithful to be
baptized over and over again, as often as may be needed, for
the remission of their sins, which are thus washed away, and
the penitent is enabled to start afresh. At that time of fear-

ful excitement in Utah, called by the Mormons "The Reformation," when people were being exhorted under terrible penalties to confess their sins, many were so frightened that they
acknowledged themselves guilty of crimes of which they had
never dreamed, while at the same time many horrible and
detestable sins were brought to light. Brigham and the leaders found that they were confessing too much—the sinners
were far more numerous than the godly. Brigham, with his
usual craft, soon found a way of escape; the people were told
to be baptized again, as then, their sins being washed away,
they could truly say they were not guilty of such crimes of
which they might be accused.

I was not convinced, and did not see that I had anything
to repent of, but I was quite willing to be re-baptized if it was
thought proper. At the same time I stipulated that the President of the Conference—Elder Marsden—should be baptized
with me. I felt that if I required re-baptizing, how much
more necessary was it for Elder Marsden to have *his* sins
washed away also. I partly believed in the fearful stories
that I had heard from Zion, but it was *he* who had shown
them to me. The Pastor of the Conference gave no sign that
he suspected my meaning in wishing Elder Marsden to be
baptized at the same time as I was, though I believe he must
have formed a pretty shrewd guess. And so we two went
down into the water, but I am afraid that little of our sins
was washed away. Not long after, President Marsden apostatised, and my heart remained as hard as ever. At least I
was frequently told so.

Poor Elder Marsden! He was branded with the most
opprobrious titles which Mormon ingenuity or malice could
fling against him :—and yet I know of *many* men—not one
nor two—associated most intimately with Brigham Young,
to-day, whose faith is not a whit stronger than that apostate's,
who serve the Prophet because it is their interest to do so,
but who in their hearts no more believe in his high pretensions than did James Marsden, the President of the London
Conference.

Meanwhile, the season for emigration had again arrived, and we were directed to hold ourselves in readiness to start. Although by no means unexpected, this "counsel" to emigrate came very painfully to me, for every step we took toward Utah seemed to bring me nearer to the realisation of my worst apprehensions. I had lost my affection for Mormonism, and my enthusiasm had now quite melted away. But to refuse to go was altogether out of the question.

Two little ones had been added to our family in Geneva, and a fourth was born in London, the Christmas day after our return from the Continent. The foggy atmosphere of the metropolis did not agree with them at all—accustomed, as they had been, to the pure and bracing air of Switzerland—and I soon had serious illness in my family. My second little girl, Minnie, was so sick that we almost despaired of her life, and the others required constant attention, while the little baby boy only a few weeks old, was seldom out of my arms. Just then it was, when so very awkwardly situated, that the notification came for us to set our faces Zionward.

They chided us for our want of faith, because we did not take our poor little sick child from her bed at the risk of life ; but I thank God now that nature was stronger than our fanaticism, and that our little girl was spared to grow up a blessing of which we shall ever be proud.

One day, President Marsden came to me confidentially and told me that the brethren were determined that I should leave England, and had counted upon my yielding in a moment of despair. My husband was to be counselled to go without me to Utah, if I persisted in my refusal. After he had left London, Elder Marsden was to give me notice to leave his house; and left destitute, and entirely among strangers, it was thought that I should be only too glad to follow.

I cannot tell how indignant I was ; I could not find words sufficiently contemptuous to express what I felt, but I reproached Elder Marsden with cowardice for agreeing to such an inhuman proposition, and I declared that I would not risk the life of my child if an eternity of suffering awaited me.

My husband was absent when this took place; but when he returned he approved of what I had done, and Elder Marsden was consequently "counselled" to send us away. The doctor warned us against the danger of exposing my little daughter to the cold in removing her, but we had no choice, for we were obliged to leave. Those were very painful times. Constant watching and anxiety had undermined my own health, and I fell ill. Even then, had we been left alone, we might have escaped much of our trouble, but the incessant meddling of "counsel" was a perpetual irritation, and we were completely worn out with annoyance.

A pleasant apartment at the west end of the town was taken for me, by the advice of the medical man, and I was removed thither with my baby. I was not equal even to the task of taking care of that little thing, and had to procure the assistance of a nurse; the other children were cared for by friends. All that I needed was rest and tranquility of mind, and I soon began to recover strength, though far from well. But this state of quietude was soon to be disturbed. Again we were notified that the last emigrant ship of the season was about to leave, and we must sail in her, and again we were obliged to refuse. My husband telegraphed to the Apostle at Liverpool that I was not well enough to travel, and he was told to "bring me along, and I should get better." The Apostle(!) cared nothing for individual suffering, providing the ambitious plans of the priesthood in Salt Lake City were carried out. But my husband, anxious though he was to set out for Utah, and obedient, as he ever was to "counsel," was not such a slave as they thought him, and he positively refused to go. For this he was very much blamed, and it was said that his own faith must be wavering.

Since my arrival in London I had several times seen my young friend, Mary Burton, but some one was always present at the time. She had, as she told me in her letters, very greatly changed, for she had now become quite a young lady. Still she retained most of her winning ways, though her childish prettiness had given place to the more mature beauty

of womanhood, and when I saw her I was not surprised that
she should be an object of attention, or that Elder Shrewsbury should have felt so deeply her rejection of him. She
was as loving to me as ever, and when she found that we
could not have one of our old quiet chats together, on account
of the people who were present, she promised to call on me
some afternoon when we should be quite alone.

Before she came, however, I had a visit from another person, whom I little expected to see. This was no other than
Elder Shrewsbury himself, who, I had been informed, had left
London some months before. This, after the usual saluta-
tions, he told me was quite true ;—he had left London and
gone to work as a Missionary hundreds of miles away ; trying
to forget his disappointment, but to no purpose. His was
one of those natures which, though kind and considerate to
every one, are not ready to form hasty attachments, but
which, when once they do meet with an object upon which to
lavish their affections, become devoted in friendship and
unchanging in love. Their affections flow more deeply than
those of most people.

Such was Elder Shrewsbury, and such I thought he would
always be ; but what disposition, however good, can be relied
upon when influenced by religious fanaticism ? He stood
before me, *then*, manly and upright in his bearing, truthful and
honest, a man who would have scorned evasion or deceit, and
his every thought of Mary was replete with tenderness and
love. And yet I lived to see that man again, in Utah—alas,
how changed a man !

Before we first left England I was acquainted with Elder
Shrewsbury, but not very intimately. We had had one or
two interesting conversations together, but I remembered
him chiefly in connection with Mary Burton. It was about
her that he now came to see me ;—he wanted me to talk to her
and intercede with her in his behalf. But I was no match-
maker, and all my thoughts respecting love and marriage had
recently been anything but pleasant. I told him plainly that
I thought Mary had done quite right in refusing to see him,

and, in fact, declining to receive the attentions of *any* Mormon man. I did not doubt his love for her at present, I said, but no one could any longer rely upon a Mormon Elder's word. Years to come, when they had a little family growing up around them, and when it would be too late for Mary to repent of trusting him, he might suddenly be convinced of the necessity of obeying the Revelation, and then, what could she do? No! Even supposing that she loved him, which, I said, was very questionable, it was better that she should suffer a disappointment now than have her heart wrung with cruelty and neglect in after years.

"What!" he cried, his eyes flashing with indignation; "do you take me for a dog that I should treat *her* so?"

"No, no," I said, and tried to pacify him; "I do not think anything bad of you, but I look upon you as a man who is in love, and therefore blind. You think of nothing now but Mary, and are willing to sacrifice everything, and to promise anything, providing you can win her. But when she has become your wife, if she ever does, and you have time to cool down, you'll begin to see things in another light. You'll find that she is a real ordinary woman, made of flesh and blood, like all the other daughters of Eve, and with, I daresay, quite as many whims, and fancies, and perverse ways as any ot them; and then, when she ceases to be 'an angel' in your eyes, and becomes merely a woman, you'll begin to assert your right to think and judge for yourself, and very probably all your former devotion to your religion will return."

"Sister Stenhouse," he replied, "you do not seem to have a very high opinion of my constancy; but I can assure you that I have given this matter my most earnest, prayerful thought. My love for Mary I need not mention; my devotion to my religion you only partly know. While we were told that Polygamy was not true, no one could be more steadfast in the faith than I was; and when the Revelation came, I looked upon it as a blight and a curse to the Church of God, and how well-founded my fears were you can see from this terrible apostasy which has come upon us. I almost myself

left the Church.   Then I went to the Apostle, and I told him
how I was situated.   I told him all about Mary, and my devotion to her ; that I wished to win her for my wife, but that I
knew she would not marry me if she thought there was the
shadow of a chance that I should live up to the Revelation.   I
told him that I myself should be perfectly wretched in Polygamy, and that it was impossible that I should love more than
one.   The Apostle said that I was quite right in all this.   We
had no proof, he said, in the Bible, that Isaac had more than
one wife, and he was accepted by God.   He counselled me
to do all I could to win Mary, and told me that I might truthfully promise her that I would never enter into Polygamy.
But Mary would not so much as listen to me—in fact, since
then she never would see me alone."

"I am not sure," I answered, "whether I am doing right;
but I don't mind saying to you that I think, from what I have
seen of Mary, that she does not dislike you; but she is a sensible girl, and does not choose to risk the happiness of her
whole life."

He was vexed with me for saying this.   How could I suppose that *he* would wreck her happiness?   Was he not willing to die if it would give her a moment's pleasure?   And
much more lovers' nonsense he talked.   He had met her at
the meetings sometimes, but she had very coldly said good-
morning, or evening, as the case might be ; but whenever he
had ventured a word more than that, she had made some
excuse to leave him.   What he wanted me to do was to invite
Mary to meet him with me, and to use my influence with her
in his favor.   I answered him very kindly, and did my best to
reassure him, but I told him that I never would try to influence the conduct or affections of any one in a matter of the
heart; such things should take their own course; and if he
waited patiently no doubt all would be well.

"Patience !" he said ; "Sister Stenhouse, do you think a
man in love knows the meaning of that word?   Patience,
indeed !"

CHAPTER XII.

EMIGRATING TO ZION:—WE ARRIVE IN NEW YORK.

Mary Burton Tells her Story—A Persevering Lover—A Long Conversation—
Some "Strong Points" of the Revelation—A Trifling Circumstance—Terrible
Doings in Zion—How Orson Hyde became an Apostate—He Bears Witness
Against Joseph Smith—"Danites" and "Avenging Angels"—Murders Commit-
ted by "Indians!"—Emigration in the Old Times—A Journey of Nine Months
—How the Mormon Emigration was Managed—A Favored Apostle—How
the Profits were Pocketed—On Board Ship—We Suffer Loss—How we were
Deceived—An Untruthful Apostle—How Poor Mr. Tennant was Robbed—
Brigham Young Acts his Accustomed Part—Love and Marriage at Sea—
Cooking Under Difficulties—"Harry and the Rats"—A Smart Lad—An An-
cient Scotch Sister—Working "for a Consideration"—Christmas on Board
Ship—Cruel Treatment of Seamen—A New Year in the New World.

THE afternoon following, Mary herself came to see me,
her face all flushed with excitement, and eager to tell me
something.

"Who do you think I've been talking to, Sister Stenhouse?" she exclaimed, "You'd never guess."

"I don't think there's much need for guessing," I said,
"Your face betrays the secret, Mary."

"Well," she said, "perhaps it does, but you wouldn't wonder
at it, if you only knew how very anxious I have been. All this
time I have kept my word, and I did not see him or speak to
him once, except at meetings, and not much then, and I have
been *very* unhappy. This afternoon I came round about an
hour ago to see you, and there on the step was Elder Shrewsbury. He said he was here yesterday, and was just going to
call on you again, and then he asked me to go a little way with

him, as he had something very important to say to me. At
first I refused to go, but he wouldn't listen to it for a moment.
So I went with him, and we have been talking ever since; or
rather he has been talking, and I have been listening to him.
I can't tell you, Sister Stenhouse, all he said—you can guess
better than I can tell you. But I'm afraid I shall not be able
to keep my resolution much longer, for when we came back to
the door again he said he wouldn't come in to see you now, and
when he begged me to let him call at Mrs. Elsworth's to-morrow night, I did not feel it in my heart to refuse him;—was it
very wrong of me to do so?"

Said I—"I'm afraid, Mary, my opinion would not matter
much either way; Elder Shrewsbury's eloquence is the music
which you like best to listen to."

She blushed, and came and sat down beside me, and we
talked together until the sun went down and my little room
was quite dark. I told her of my troubles in Switzerland and
of the miserable effects of introducing Polygamy there; and
she in return told me all her love affairs with Elder Shrewsbury and of her resolution not to listen to him unless he solemnly promised never to have anything to do with the hated
Revelation. Her faith in Mormonism itself had, as I expected,
been very severely shaken, and I think that had it not been
for my efforts to re-assure her, she would have left the Church
at that time. Would, to God, she had.

After tea, she said—"Have you a copy of the Revelation
here, Sister Stenhouse? I want to show you some strong
points in it which I think will astonish you. I learned all
about it from Elder Shrewsbury that night when he came to
see me, and it was that that disgusted me with the whole
affair." We searched through my trunk but could not find
the document, and I told her that I had not patience to read
it quite through when it was given to me, and that since
then I was not sure that I had even seen it. "Never
mind," she said, "I'll bring it with me when I come again."

How often have I thought since how much depended upon
that trifling circumstance. Had we then together read over

the Revelation and noticed the "strong points," of which she spoke, I believe my eyes would have been opened and I never should have submitted to the misery which I afterwards endured in Utah.

By and by she asked me whether I had heard anything of the terrible doings out in Zion, and I, in return, asked her what doings she alluded to.

"Well," she said, "I hardly like to tell you, if you have heard nothing about the matter, for I'm not quite sure whether it all is true ; but we have had some strange reports floating about here, just like the reports of Polygamy, before it was acknowledged. It is said that in the time of Joseph Smith a band of men was organised who put to death any one who was troublesome to the Church or offended the Elders. Some people say that it was one or perhaps more of this band who fired at Governor Boggs, of Missouri, and who killed many other Gentiles. Dr. Avard and Sidney Rigdon are said to have been mixed up in the matter, and that wretched man, John C. Bennett, tells a frightful story about it. But that is not the worst, for Elder Shrewsbury himself told me long ago that Thomas B. Marsh, the then President of the Twelve, when he apostatised, took oath that the Saints had formed a "Destruction Company," as he called it, for the purpose of avenging themselves, and Orson Hyde, in a solemn affidavit swore that all that Marsh had said was true."

"Well dear," I said, "I've heard all that before, but no doubt it is all scandal."

"I'm afraid not," she replied; "for I have heard from people who ought to know, that since the Saints have been in Salt Lake Valley the same things have been done; only now they speak of those men as "Danites" and "Avenging Angels." People say that those who are dissatisfied and want to leave Zion, almost always are killed after they set out, *by the Indians*, and they dare not say boldly who they believe those "Indians" are. Then, too, one lady told me that she had heard from her sister that not only were apostates killed in a mysterious way by Indians or some one else, but that many people were "missing," or else found murdered, who were only *suspected* of being very weak in the faith. These things are horrible, and sometimes I think I will never go out to Zion."

I had heard these very same stories, and told her so; and I tried to make her believe that they were without foundation; but I could see that what she had heard had made a great impression on her mind. So I turned the conversation to other topics, and we talked over our plans and prospects for the future. Neither of us were very hopeful—she because she was undecided what course to pursue ; I because of the shadow of coming sorrow which already began to darken my way. We tried, however, to comfort each other; and when she left I certainly felt more assured and hopeful.

At this time I was left much alone, for my husband having no business in which to employ himself was sent by the Pastor of the London Conference to travel among the Saints ; domestic comfort or the claims of a wife were never for a moment thought worthy of consideration. Then it was that I felt how lonely one may be in the midst of that Great City.

Towards the end of the year 1855, it was determined that a company of Mormon emigrants, numbering several hundreds, should leave Liverpool *en route* for Salt Lake City; and for that purpose a vessel was chartered early in November. This was not the ordinary season for emigration, but there were then in England numbers of the Saints, anxious to go to Zion, but too poor to pay their passage all the way. It was thought that when they arrived in New York they would have time to earn sufficient to carry them on, and it was then supposed they could join those who came over by the ordinary spring emigration. My husband and myself were counselled to join these emigrants in Liverpool and proceed at once to New York.

I was now strong enough to travel, and though far from well, and the prospect of such a journey in the middle of winter, was anything but cheering. My husband, however, who was anxious to go, smoothed away every difficulty, and it was resolved that this time we should " obey " counsel.

The reader may perhaps think me somewhat unreasonable
in regarding such a journey as more than an ordinary annoyance; but he should remember that I am speaking
of eighteen years ago. The passage across the Atlantic
Ocean in mid-winter is anything but inviting even under
the best of circumstances, but in the old days of sailing-ves-
sels it was infinitely worse. The ocean-steamers now make the
passage in from ten to fourteen days; but then a month was considered a good, quick passage for a sailing boat. Then too the
modern accommodations—even for steerage passengers—bear
no comparison with the frightful disorder and utter lack of comfort experienced in former times. All this ought to be taken
into consideration when speaking of the early Mormon emigrants and the sacrifices which that people then made
for their faith. There was the same difference between them
and the snug little party which a year ago crossed the ocean
under the guidance of the councillor Apostle G. A. Smith, and
the childless versifier Eliza R. Snow, as there was between
St. Paul braving the perils of shipwreck with the tempestuous
Euroclydon, and the modern orthodox missionary with well-
filled purse and comfortable outfit on board the magnificent
steamers of the Mediterranean.

The Mormon emigration has always been a well-managed
business; and, forming a united body, under the guidance of
inspired leaders, the Mormons have never given so much trouble
as ordinary passengers. At the time of which I speak, the emigration was on a much larger scale than at present; although
even now several thousand converts arrive every summer in
New York on their way to Utah. Now the journey from
Liverpool to Salt Lake City is accomplished easily in less
than a month;—then it required *nine*. The Saints used then
to speak of Zion as being "a thousand miles from everywhere;" and when they went East they used to talk of "going
to the States" as if they belonged to another nation:—but
now the Great Pacific Railway has knit together the utmost
limits of this vast country, and a journey to the Far West is
only a pleasant summer tour.

Every presiding Elder in Britain is a Mormon Emigration-Agent:—unpaid, but no less effective. It is a part of his mission. The Elder presiding over "the office" at Liverpool—generally some favored Apostle—pockets all *the profits* of the transaction, and has but little trouble in return. The Saints are notified through the *Star* of the day when the vessel will sail, and are told to forward their emigration-money, or at least a portion of it;—as the Church risks nothing. The Apostle, being thus secured by the deposits, arranges with the shipping agent for the passage of a specified number of persons, and receives a very nice commission upon each emigrant—which commission is one of the chief perquisites of his office.

The Mormons in London were very kind to us before we left and did all they could to help us in preparing for our journey. A kinder people than the Saints in Europe could nowhere be found. My husband had been directed to take charge of the emigrants in the transit from London to Liverpool, and consequently I received no assistance from him. It seemed to me a very cruel arrangement for the Elders to take away from me and my helpless little ones the very person to whom we ought naturally to have turned for protection; but what were the feelings of a weak woman when they came in conflict with the "counsel" of inspired Apostles?

We arrived in Liverpool the same evening, and there my husband was relieved of the charge of the company, and some of the brethren were appointed to see that the baggage was safely transferred from the railway to the ship. Early the next morning we went on board, and it was not long before we began to experience the pleasures (?) of an emigrant life.

Before we set out for Liverpool, I had been told that on board ship I should be able to obtain all the help that I might desire; and anxious to provide for the comfort of the children, I engaged the services of two young girls to look after them and assist me generally. This was an imprudent step, as I afterwards found to my cost ; but at the time I thought that

I had made a very sensible arrangement. Help being secured, my next thought was to get our berths fixed, so that all
might bè ready before the rolling of the ship began. My first
enquiries were for our bedding; but it was no where to be
found. Now this was very annoying, for we were all tired and
the children, poor things, were fidgetty; and anticipating a
long and unpleasant voyage I wanted to have everything in
readiness. Besides which I had made special preparations in
the shape of many additional comforts which I knew on board
ship would be absolutely necessary, and had even sold my
watch and jewelry for that purpose.

I enquired of the proper authorities, but could obtain no
information, and nothing remained but for me to wait until the
Apostle came on board to bid a final adieu to the emigrants.
I felt this annoyance all the more as I considered that we had
no right to expect such mismanagement. We would naturally have preferred to make our own arrangements and to
go alone, had we been permitted to do so ; but we had, over
and over again, been instructed not to go by any other vessel
but that chartered by the Apostle Richards, that so we
might escape the perils which were sure to overtake the Gentiles. Imagine our disgust when we found that as there
were not enough of the Saints to occupy the whole ship, the
lower deck was filled with Irish emigrants of the most barbarous type, and that their luggage and ours had been thrown
together indiscriminately into the hold. Most of the Mormon
emigrants recovered their property when they arrived at New
York, but as for our own, personally, we never saw it
again, and all the voyage through we were left utterly destitute.

The Apostle Richards and Pastor Kimball came on board
before the vessel sailed and I told them all about it. We
could not possibly put to sea in that condition, I said, and I
wanted to leave the ship. He promised that the things should
be looked after, and assured me that on no account should we
be permitted to sail without being properly provided for. I
not only trusted their word as gentlemen but I believed in

them as favored servants of God ; and when subsequently I found that they had wilfully deceived me I became conscious that there was as little of the true and truthful gentleman about some of the modern Apostles, as there was of the apostle about ordinary gentlemen.

Thus in the cold, foggy days of an English November we set out, bereft of the commonest necessaries, and deceived by our own leaders, to begin a new life in a new world.

I would not for my own sake mention these unpleasant reminiscences were it not that so many mean and cruel deceptions—and, were it not that I do not care to use harsh words, I might call downright "*swindles*"—had come beneath my observation in connection with the Mormon emigration in past years. I will mention one alone which ought not to be passed by unnoticed.

In the year 1854, Brigham Young and the leading Elders were most anxious to draw to Zion the converts from every part of the globe; and for this purpose the faithful were called upon to bring in freely their contributions to the Perpetual Emigration Fund. To set them an example, Brother Brigham himself stated that he would present as a free-gift his own property—a valuable city house and lot, if any purchaser could be found wealthy enough to purchase it. An English gentleman named Tenant, a new convert, accepted the offer and advanced the money—thirty thousand dollars—and set out for Salt Lake City, expecting there to be put in possession of the property. He was one of the unfortunate Hand-Cart Emigrants, of whom I shall presently have occasion to speak more fully; and he died on the plains. His wife and children, when they arrived in the Valley, were told that the transaction was not made with them but with Mr. Tenant, and all their efforts to obtain the property, which in common justice was theirs, were unavailing. At the present moment Mr. Tenant's wife lives in miserable poverty in Salt Lake City, while there is no one to bring the honest Prophet to account.

The vessel sailed, and we heard no more of our property. Whether it ever left London, or whether some obliging brother took charge of it on his own account, I cannot say, but I could form a pretty good guess. I frequently see that man in Salt Lake City, and I aways think of my bedding when I see him. Nothing, however, remained but for me to put the best face I could upon matters. I took my wearing apparel and other articles out of the trunks and put them into pillow slips, and extemporised as well as I could a rough substitute for beds. These served for the children, and I covered them with my cloaks and shawls ; and for our own berths and bed-covering I had only a few pieces of carpet which I had put aside for the cabin floor, together with a worn-out blanket which an old lady on board was good enough to lend me.

We had not been long at sea when the young sisters whom I had engaged to help me, fell sick, and some of the brethren were very anxious to nurse them. This appeared to be quite the established order of things, for I then found that it was very seldom that a Mormon emigrant ship crossed the ocean without one or more marriages on board. It was, no doubt, very interesting to them, but to me it was extremely inconvenient, especially considering that my husband had now taken to his berth, which he did not leave during the remainder of the voyage, and myself and the children were not much better off.

Sick as I was, I had to prepare our food, and manage everything, for in those times emigrants either took out their own provisions or were allowanced in raw material, and in either case had to do their own cooking. My chief difficulty was in getting what I had prepared to the fire-galley, for I could not leave the children, and I was afraid to venture myself upon deck. So I got any of the brethren who chanced to be passing to take it up, and of course they were willing to oblige me; but the galley was so crowded—every one having his or her own interests to attend to—that I very rarely, if ever, had my provisions decently cooked, and on more than one occasion I never saw them again. This was an inconvenience which modern emigrants do not suffer at the present day.

Unsuccessful with the young sisters, I thought I would try if I could not get one of the brethren to help me, and fortune at first appeared to favor me. There was on board a young man—Harry, they called him,—and he was so situated that I found it easy to open a negotiation with him. He had been a saddler's apprentice in a country town in England, and having listened to some itinerant preacher, had been converted, joined the Church, and begun to think for himself. So hearing that terrible judgments were quickly coming upon the Old World, he resolved to flee to the New, and in his hurry to get there he forgot to inform his master that he was about to leave. This accounted for his being so badly provided for.

Now, Harry had those two great blessings—a splendid appetite and unimpeachable powers of digestion. I will not say that he enjoyed these two blessings, for that he did not, on account of lacking a third blessing, namely, the wherewithal to make the first two blessings a pleasure, and not an inconvenience. The ship's allowance was altogether insufficient for him, and he, therefore, gladly engaged to do what few things I required upon condition that I should add a little to his own private commissariat.

Harry was a smart lad and at first very useful, and he soon convinced me that he had told the truth when he said that he had not had enough to eat ever since he came on board— it seemed to me very questionable whether he ever had before. He had, however, nothing to complain of in that respect while in our employment, for although the children were able to eat whenever we had anything fit for them, my husband and myself could seldom touch our rations, and as everything that was not used fell to Harry's share, he fared pretty well.

Harry was not the lad to neglect his own interests, and as our interests appeared just then to be his also, matters worked very harmoniously. Our bread was never now brought back to us half raw or burnt to a cinder. It must be properly cooked for our eating or it would not do for Harry's, and as for it being lost or delayed on its way to or from the galley that was, of course, quite out of the question. But the strangest thing of all connected with Harry was that immediately after his coming we were incessantly annoyed by *the rats.* I had brought for the children's use a small supply of preserves and other little delicacies ; but these mysteriously disappeared with alarming rapidity, and whenever I saved any trifle for the children to eat between meals, that also was gone when it was wanted, and in every instance Harry suggested that it was "the rats," though I never could find any traces of those interesting animals. I was sorry to part with Harry, for he used to tell funny stories to the children, and amused them a great deal, but "the rats" and Harry were so closely associated in my mind that I thought if Harry left, the rats might perhaps also cease their visits. So Harry went, and I was once more left alone to do the best I could.

The weather was very cold, and though we wore our clothing day and night, we felt its severity very much. The rigging of the ship was hung with icicles, and without fire or warmth of any sort, it is no wonder that we all were soon hardly able to move from cold and sickness. I have heard emigrants who came over in steam-vessels say that even in mid-winter the heat in their berths was almost unendurable ; but in a sailing-vessel there were, of course, no engine fires to warm the ship, and the passengers suffered accordingly.

In the midst of my trouble I was told of an ancient Scotch sister—a maiden lady, sharp and shrewd,—who, like the miser in Scott's "Fortunes of Nigel," was willing to help us "for a consideration." So we talked the matter over, and it was agreed that she should give me her services for the remainder of the voyage ; and the "consideration" was to be two pounds English. Small as was our stock of money, and much as I knew we should need it upon our arrival, I felt that I could do no better than engage her. There was no saying upon whom *she* might chance to set her maiden fancy, but there was not the remotest chance of any of the brethren falling in love *with her* ; so I considered her a safe investment, and, besides, I must have *somebody*—there was no alternative.

It was now Christmas time—a season which in England was always sacred to joyous memories and festivities; but to us, exiles and wanderers, seeking a land of which we knew nothing, and which to us was a new and untried world, it was far from being a happy time. In the midst of the wild, dreary ocean there was nothing to recall the pleasant reminiscences of the past, or to inspire us with hope and courage as we thought of the future.

The Captain told us that we might prepare to eat our Christmas dinner in New York; but he was mistaken. I can form no opinion of the captain as a seaman, but as a man I detested him for his cruel treatment of two unfortunate men who were under him. These men—one a Spaniard, and the other a Hungarian—had agreed to work out their passage to New York, but they were quite unfit for sea life. One of them when he refused or was unable to go up into the shrouds, was dragged aloft by main force, and there they tied him, and there they kept him until he was nearly frozen to death. On another occasion they beat both of these men with spikes, and I feared they would kill them, and their cries and groans right above my head were most painful to listen to. In fact, so badly were they treated that on their arrival they had to be carried to the hospital. Such was the "discipline" on board that ship.

The Captain was mistaken in his calculations. We did not eat our Christmas dinner in New York, as he had promised. A storm came on, which compelled us to stand out to sea again, and then a dead calm followed, and it was not until New Year's eve that we set foot upon the shore of the New World.

We were now three thousand miles nearer to Zion; but my heart misgave me as I thought of the future, and the first New Year's day that I spent in the United States was anything but a day of pleasure to me.

CHAPTER XIII.

LIFE IN NEW YORK:—CONDUCTING A MORMON PAPER.

An Introduction to a New World—The New York Saints—How Certain Elders Disappeared—An Uncomfortable Week—Left all Alone—Love Waxing Cold —Mental Slavery—The School-House at Williamsburgh—Miserable Condition of the Emigrants—Suffering for Their Faith—The Apostle Taylor Lec· tures the Saints—Some Smart "Counsel"—Buying Shovels—An Unprofitable Speculation—The "Mean Yankee Gentiles"—Days and Nights of Trial —How the "*Mormon*" was Edited—A Rather Small Salary—The Doings of High-Priests and "Seventies"—An Amiable Connecticut Girl—Half-a-dozen Wives—Permission from Brigham Young—Certain Elders who had "Disease of the Heart"—The Course of True Love—A Young Widow Who Looked Well in Weeds—Arranging the Affairs of the Heart—The True Source of Modern Revelations.

VERY cold, and dark, and dreary, were the first days which we spent in the New World. That faith which once had led me to hope, and believe, and endure all things, was now powerless to nerve me to any new course of action for my religion's sake; for the dark shadow of Polygamy had come across my way; hope had fled, and my love, with the love of many other faithful Saints, had waxed cold.

To my husband and children I was, of course, devotedly attached, and was willing to combat any difficulty or endure any trial with them, or for their sake; and it was not long before my constancy was put to the test.

The Mormon emigrants have always a Captain and two "Counsellors" to every company. The Captain on board the *Emerald Isle*—the vessel in which we came—was a returning Utah Elder;—one of his Counsellors was also a returning Elder, and my husband was the other. As soon as the Mor-

mon Captain had come on shore, aud had reported to the
Apostle in charge of the New York Saints, he left to visit his
friends. The Utah Counsellor had a young lady in the company to whom he had become very much attached, and who
afterward became one of his wives. I was not, therefore,
surprised that, as soon as he could get his baggage, he also
should disappear ; but my husband—the other Counsellor—
being encumbered with a wife and family, was obliged to
remain, and the whole charge of seeing to the company
devolved upon him.

We had, therefore, to remain in Castle Gardens until the
whole company of emigrants was provided for ; and during all
the next week I, with my four children, remained in that public place, sick and weary, and as destitute of bedding and
covering as we had been on board ship. The weather was
intensely cold, and, unaccustomed as we were to the severity
of an American winter, we suffered not a little. The other
unfortunate victims to faith were in the same condition, with,
the exception that they had something to sleep on at nights,
while I had nothing but the bare boards for my bed since
we left Liverpool ;—all that I could gather together had been
reserved for my babes. How we lived through that journey
I know not, but I am certain that, could I have forseen what
we should have to endure, I would never have left England,
whatever my refusal might have cost me.

I could not refrain from contrasting my life before and
since I knew Mormonism. Before, I scarcely knew what suffering was, so little had I been called upon to endure; I never
knew what it was to be without money, or to want for anything ; but now I was in a strange land, in the depth of winter, without a home, without a pillow to rest my weary head
upon, and with a future before me so dark that not a single
ray of light gave to it the promise of hope. Could any
slavery be more complete than mine ? My fanaticism and
zeal were all gone—I had nothing to sustain me. Certainly,
I was still held by the fear that Mormonism, after all, *might*
be of God, and that all this suffering *might* be necessary for

my salvation—but if at that time I had only had a friend whose mind was clear from all the nonsense of Mormonism, and who had felt sufficient interest in me to advise me for my good, I think even then I might have freed myself from the mental slavery in which I was bound. But I had no intercourse with any but Mormons ; and, indeed, a wish to form Gentile friendships I should then have considered a sin.

A week after our arrival, my husband found time to seek for apartments for his family, and I was thankful to leave our miserable quarters at Castle Gardens.

The Mormon authorities had, meanwhile, given instructions to the other emigrants how to act, and they did little more than this. Those who had not found work or places to go to were ordered to leave the Gardens, and received permission to occupy an old dilapidated school-room in Williamsburgh, which had been used for preaching. I went there almost daily to see them, and therefore state what I saw as an eye-witness, and neither exaggerate nor misrepresent. There they huddled together about one hundred and fifty men, women and children. Most of the men had been respectable mechanics in their own country ; many of them I had known personally and had visited in their cosy English homes ; and their wives and families had been decently brought up. What they must have suffered under this change of circumstances I leave the reader to guess.

In that miserable place they lived day and night—the poor, dispirited mothers—many of them very sick—having to cook, and wash, and perform all the necessary domestic duties, round two small sheet-iron stoves. It was not long before the place became like a pest-house from so many being confined in so small a place, and breathing the same fetid and pestilential atmosphere, and many of the young children died of an epidemic which was raging among them.

They had saved some of their ship's provisions, and that was all they had to eat, and it did not last long. To me it was most distressing to witness so much misery without being able to render any assistance, particularly to see the poor little children shivering and crying with hunger and cold, while many of their mothers were in such a miserable state of apathy that they paid little or no attention to them. I often tried to awaken in them feelings of human sympathy, but I was met with a murmur of discontent—the people, men and women alike—seemed to be utterly demoralised. Nor can this be a matter of wonder; for in England the men had been told that—while at home they could only earn four or five shillings a day, and would never be able to put by enough to carry them all the way to Utah—in New York they would be able to earn two-and-a-half to three, and even four dollars a day—equal to from ten to sixteen shillings English—and that employers would even come on board ship anxious to engage them. Thus they had by false statements been allured from their homes and plunged into the most abject poverty. Day by day they went out seeking work, but finding none, willing to do anything to provide bread for their families, but returning nightly, unsuccessful, to their starving wives and children.

My own resources were gone. I could do nothing. When we left Castle Garden I think we only had about five dollars left, while the heavy snow which covered the ground and the intense cold promised many weeks of unusual severity. Needing so greatly pity myself, how I sympathised with those poor sufferers, how I pitied them!

In the midst of all this, the Apostle John Taylor learned that some of these poor souls had been seen begging. So he came from his comfortable boarding-house in Brooklyn, well wrapped up in a handsome overcoat, and scolded these poor, starving creatures, and harangued them concerning the meanness of begging. With great swelling words he spoke of the dignity of the Saints of the Most High, and told them that he despised a Mormon who could fall to the level of a common street beggar.

Could he have heard the unspoken curses of the poor, wounded hearts of those who listened to him, as they thought of his brother "Apostle" in England, and of how he had deceived them and sent them into a strange country, in the

MOCKED WITH WORDS.

depth of winter, to beg, to starve, or to steal, he would have learned that though the victim of a delusive faith may mentally submit to man-made creeds and priesthoods, in his heart he will judge, not so much the words he hears as the man who utters them.

The wisdom of the Apostle found out a remedy. He "counselled" the men and boys to buy shovels, and go forth into the streets and clean away the snow from the fronts of the doors and from the side-walks, and told them that they would thus get plenty of money to keep them until winter was over. One elderly brother, who had a little money left, bought a stock of shovels; but the emigrants found that there were plenty of others who were as eager as they for work, and who were much better acquainted with the way of obtaining it. The shovel experiment was a failure, and the poor old brother lost his money in the investment.

For whatever the Apostle Taylor may have contributed to these unfortunate persons—whether in "counsel," money, or provisions—he will doubtless have his reward; and, for aught I know, he may have been unable to give anything more than counsel; but, at the same time, my opinion of the value of counsel remains unchanged. There has been no lack of "counsel" or counsellors in the Mormon Church. "Counsel" has been given in abundance to all, and by no means always for the benefit of those who received it. It was not, however, because he failed to assist them practically that the people hated the Apostle Taylor, and have hated him ever since, but it was for his pride and arrogance, and the way in which he dared to talk to free-born Englishmen and Englishwomen about the dignity of the Priesthood, and the contempt in which he held them in the hour of their humiliation and distress—for that they hated him.

I do not, of course, wish to justify the people in begging; such conduct would have been despicable if they could have found employment of any sort. But when I saw the starving condition of those men and their helpless families, in that wretched school-house, in my heart I almost honored them for

12

having the courage to beg; and I thanked God that the
"mean Yankee Gentiles"—as the Elders taught the Saints
to call American citizens who did not believe in Mormonism
—were able and willing to assist them.

One of those emigrants very recently related to me some
of the painful circumstances through which he passed at that
time. He told me that he walked the streets of Williamsburgh for three days and three nights without a mouthful of
anything to eat, or a place to lay his head;—he could obtain
no work, and at length, in sheer desperation, he was *forced* to
beg. The Church authorities knew well the misery of the
people, but took no adequate steps to alleviate it.

During the first weeks after our arrival in New York city
we had nothing to depend upon but the provisions which we
had saved from the ship's rations. I had known what it was
to be in a foreign country without money and without food;
and on board ship I took care of our rations when they were
not consumed by Harry or "the rats;" for I thought that if I
did not need them—which, indeed, I sincerely hoped might
be the case—I could certainly find some one who would be
thankful for them. These rations consisted chiefly of sugar
that was almost black; very bad black tea, which when made
looked like dye; the poorest kind of sea-biscuit; and other
things accordingly. The provisions for the Mormon emigrants were purchased in bulk by the Church authorities, who
made their own profits out of them, and the Apostle at Liverpool had the benefit of all that could be saved out of them
during the voyage. It was commonly said among the people
that the sight of them alone was quite sufficient for any one
who was not half-starved; and yet they had paid the price of
the best.

We had been in New York several weeks when one day my
husband called at the office of a paper called *The Mormon*,
and there met with the Apostle Taylor who conducted that
paper. The Apostle expressed great regret that Mr. Stenhouse should be without occupation at that season of the year,
and with a family of children upon his hands. This sympathy

coming from a brother Missionary was, I thought, very tardy, for my husband had then devoted over ten years of his life to the cause, and his record in the Church had been untarnished. The Apostle was living in an elegant house surrounded by every comfort and luxury, while he knew that we had not so much as a chair, or even a bed to lie upon. What had he done for the Church more than my husband had done? Indeed, I firmly believe that he had not endured half as much, but—he was an Apostle! His unhelping sympathy appeared to me a little more than questionable.

He told my husband that he might come into the office of *The Mormon*, and write the addresses on the wrappers, and that he would give him a few dollars a week "to help things along," until something better presented itself. My husband thought this a disinterested action on the part of the Apostle John Taylor, but my experience in Mormonism led me to be distrustful and suspicious of everything that an Elder or Apostle said or did. This offer, however, came when we really had nothing to look to, and dared not refuse any assistance that was offered, however small it might be. But I must allow that my ideas of Apostolic liberality were very much shocked when at the end of the week Mr. Stenhouse informed me that he had been allowed four dollars for his services, and that out of that magnificent sum the Apostle John Taylor had deducted twenty-five cents which sheer necessity had compelled him to borrow for the week's ferriage.

The Apostle-editor had two assistants from Utah with him in the "*Mormon*" office—the one a "Seventy," and the other a "High-Priest"—terms and titles which I shall presently explain. A few weeks after my husband entered the office, the "Seventy" who had charge of getting out the paper was allowed to return to Zion. The High-Priest remained in the Eastern States visiting alternately the various branches of the Church, and doing some very zealous courting with a young English girl who lived in Williamsburgh, while his two unsuspecting wives at home in Salt Lake City were earnestly praying the Lord to bless him in his "mission."

Whatever the Apostle may have thought of his associate, he could not very well remonstrate with him, for he himself was, and had been for some time, doing a good deal in that line with an amiable Connecticut girl, and was only waiting for special permission from Brigham Young, to add her to the half-dozen wives he already had in Utah.

There was, moreover, another High-Priest attached to that office, but no one seemed to understand his exact position. To all appearance his principal occupation was travelling from New York to Connecticut and from Connecticut back again to New York. He was a very robust-looking man, but it was reported that he was troubled with heart-disease, and that the purer air of Connecticut was a great relief to him. This I fully believed when, some time after, I discovered that the young lady engaged to the Apostle had a charming sister, for I thought it very probable that she rendered no small assistance to the Connecticut air in giving relief to his diseased heart.

My husband not being at that particular time under the influence of "heart-disease," soon became very useful on the editorial staff. In fact, pretty well everything was left to him, and not unfrequently for two or three days he saw nothing of the Apostle or either of his associates, and the whole responsibility of getting out the paper—at the magnificent salary of four dollars a week!—rested upon him. He was told that he must regard it as a mission and be prepared to act accordingly.

In course of time, however, the visits to Connecticut came to an end. The Apostle obtained Brother Brigham's permission to practice a little Polygamy among the Gentiles, and Miss Young made him an excellent housekeeper in a handsomely furnished house in Brooklyn. The poor High-Priest and the Seventy did not fare so well: they were expected to wait until they reached Zion. The two young ladies to whom they were engaged were amiable and good girls who would without doubt have met with excellent husbands either in or out of the Church; but the name of an Apostle or High-Priest—when the men themselves were away from home—

carried with it many charms, and won the hearts of the young ladies and their friends. The Apostle was, of course, well used to the training of wives in the "celestial order," and when he returned home with his youngest bride he suffered no particular inconvenience. But the High-Priests realised the truth of the adage "the course of true love never did run smooth." The first wife of one of them refused to have anything to do with his new bride, and kept him at a respectful distance from herself then and ever afterwards; while the first wife of the other declined to acknowledge the claims of her youthful rival. The first High-Priest has gone to heaven; the other, in the course of time, gave a bill of divorce to his young wife. What happiness either of these three girls found in Polygamy, they best know, but the young widow appears decidedly the happiest of the three.

I had heard so much while in London about men taking wives "from principle" and that, after the first wife, they made no open display of their love, but I could not see that they differed in the slightest from their Gentile brethren in that respect; the Utah Elders, of whom I have spoken, always seemed to me very human. In all Polygamic courtships that I have since witnessed, the brethren have appeared to think that the "Lord's" revelation was a trifle too slow in arranging affairs of the heart, and they have very zealously prepared for its coming. In some instances the revelation has come too late, and in many others it would have been very disastrous if it had not come at all. In all cases it may be safely asserted that all that has been said about getting the consent of the first wife and obtaining a revelation from the Lord as to whether it is pleasing in His sight for a man to take another wife, or not—is purely folly and nonsense. Brigham Young is the only "lord" who has ever been consulted on that question. If he acknowledged this to the people and they chose to abide by it, they alone would be to blame; but it is the grossest of frauds for men claiming to be the representatives of Jesus Christ to play upon the credulity of an honest people, trifling with the most sacred subjects, and tell-

ing them that God answers by special revelation and declares
whether or not it is His will that each of these plural marriages should take place. The Apostles and Elders themselves are not deceived. They know well enough that there is
no truth in all this mockery ; they know that the only
source of all their revelations is the man Brigham Young.

CHAPTER XIV.

SAINTLY PILGRIMS ON THE WAY—THE "DIVINE" HAND-CART SCHEME.

The Eastern Saints—Service in Williamsburgh—"The "Prophet of the Lord" Tries an Experiment—The Pilgrims Cross the Plains—The Hand-Cart Scheme—The Poor Emigrants—A "Divine" Plan—The Great Gathering to Zion—An Interesting Letter from Mary Burton—How Elder Shrewsbury Won his Bride—A Solemn Oath Against Polygamy—Mary Burton's Marriage—Arrival of the Hand-Cart Emigrants—Scene at Castle Gardens—Meeting with Mary Burton and her Husband—The Story of her Courtship—Her Trustful Enthusiasm—Proposing to make Brigham Young a *King!*—Anticipations of War—How the Prophet Defrauded Brother Tenant of Sixty Thousand Dollars—The Pilgrims Leave for the West—The Story of a Truant Wife—Second Thoughts are Sometimes Best—The *Mormon* Paper Comes to Grief—A New Trial of Faith—Literary Work—Waiting for Permission to Journey Zionward.

O NE Sunday morning in early spring, I attended a meeting of the Saints in Williamsburgh.

My husband was there and took part in the service, and so did the Apostle Taylor, and one or two other Utah Elders. I went to that meeting in a very desponding state of mind, for our prospects since the day of our arrival had not brightened very much, and I felt the need of some comforting and cheering words.

Whether it was the influence of the clear spring morning, or that the Elders had noticed the depression of spirit among the Saints, I cannot tell, but I know that on that particular occasion their words seemed to me more earnest and encouraging than they had been for a long time past.

As we came out from the meeting, Brother Benton, one of the Elders, stepped up to my husband and said: " Brother Stenhouse, *they* are expected to arrive to-night or to-morrow ; I suppose you will be down at the " Gardens " to meet them."

I knew well enough who " they " were who were expected to arrive, and so did Mr. Stenhouse. " Yes," he said, " of course I shall be there, but most likely we shall have to wait a few days before they come." Then he stopped and talked over the matter with Elder Benton.

Now it chanced that at that time Brigham Young was trying an experiment. The " Prophet of the Lord " sometimes finds it necessary—notwithstanding the "revelations" which he is supposed to receive—to try experiments like other men before he can feel sure that his plans are likely to succeed. The only difference between him and other men is, that he—knowing himself that his plans are his own inventions, or the inventions of the leaders—gives out that they come direct from God, thereby deceiving the ignorant, innocent, and confiding people ; and when his plans fail, as they often do, he never confesses that he is wrong or mistaken, but lays all the blame on some other person, or, failing that, on " the Lord " or the devil. Other men, as a rule, say nothing about the "Lord" or devil, but when their experiments fail, they frankly confess that they themselves were not inspired, but were liable to err. That is all the difference.

In the present instance Brigham Young tried an experiment upon a rather large scale.

Up to the year 1856, the Mormon emigrants made the journey from the Frontiers across the Plains by ox-teams, as I have already described, and every season some of the wealthier Mormons formed themselves into an independent company, paid their own expenses, and travelled with more comfort. The expense to the poorer emigrants was very small, for they performed the greater part of the journey on foot—the ox-teams being used for transporting provisions and baggage—one hundred pounds of the latter being allowed to each emigrant.

This "plan" was, so far, a success, and the settlements of the Saints increased thereby slowly but surely, in population and wealth. There were, however, at that time thousands of Saints in Europe anxious to emigrate, but who were too poor to provide the small sum requisite for that purpose. During the winter of 1855, this difficulty was discussed in Conference by Brigham and the leading men in Salt Lake, and some one suggested what was afterwards known as the "Hand-Cart Scheme." The idea of this "scheme" was to transfer the people from Liverpool to the Frontiers in the cheapest possible way, and for them then to cross the Plains with light-made hand-carts, just strong enough to carry the fewest possible necessary articles, but sufficiently light for the men, women, and even young girls, to draw them.

This "plan" would not perhaps have been a bad one if it had been properly carried out, and if Brigham Young had seen, as he might have done, that suitable preparations were made beforehand. But the Hand-Cart Emigration Scheme began with a lie and ended in ruin.

The confiding Saints were told that "God" had specially inspired His servant Brigham for this purpose, and the scheme was a revelation direct from on high. No proper measures were taken to provide for the emigrants—all was done upon faith—faith on the part of the people in their—as they supposed—inspired leaders ; deception on the part of those leaders towards the people, whose only fault was that they trusted them too well.

The *Millennial Star* proclaimed the "plan" to the Saints in Europe, and so great was the response to this special summons that in that year—1856—it was roughly estimated that no fewer than five or six thousand Mormon emigrants travelled from Liverpool to Salt Lake City. It was the first company of these emigrants that Brother Benton alluded to when he told Mr. Stenhouse that "*they*" were expected that night or the next ; but in those days emigrant vessels were frequently delayed by adverse winds and other circumstances, and no one could calculate upon the exact time of their arrival in port.

The following morning, my husband when he returned from the *Mormon* office, brought with him a letter bearing the English postmark and addressed to me in the neat unmistakeable handwriting of Mary Burton. I had been waiting and watching for a letter from her ever since our arrival; I was anxious to hear from her, and I hastily tore it open, so impatient was I to know how she was getting on. What I read interested me deeply, though it did not surprise me. I had seen Mary many times after the interview which I have already related, and our conversations and discussions were to us of all-absorbing interest; but as they were mostly personal, I have not cared to record them in this narrative. To tell the truth, her love affairs with Elder Shrewsbury occupied more and more the most prominent place in all our discussions. His enthusiasm was perfectly infectious. As long as Mary absolutely refused to see him, her love for him and her faith in Mormonism were anything but overpowering. But Elder Shrewsbury was one of those peculiar persons who have a sort of magnetic charm about them, who without our knowing it, or even, in some instances, contrary to our will and reason, enlist all our sympathies and leave behind them an impression that we vainly try to efface. He only wanted *opportunity* and his success was sure.

Opportunity he had had for pressing his suit with Mary and making an impression upon her heart, ever since the day when they had met at my door, and had taken that walk together, as Mary said, for the purpose of discussing important matters.

Now the letter which I received opened to me another chapter in Mary's life which, without the gift of prophecy, I might have easily predicated. Elder Shrewsbury's patience and perseverance met with their due reward, and Mary at length promised to become his wife;—but fascinated though she was, and herself almost as deeply in love as he was, she nevertheless made one condition which showed that she had not entirely lost that prudence and determination which she had shown in the early days of their courtship:—

"When he spoke to me in *that* way,—you know *how*, Sister Stenhouse "—she said in her impulsive way :—" How could I persist in saying *No* to him ?" It wasn't in my heart to do so. I didn't say " Yes " in so many words, but I simply said nothing, and he took my silence for consent. Then————but no, I won't even tell *you* everything . . . . I know he thought he was going to have it all his own way ; but I didn't think so. I told him then that I had firmly resolved upon one thing—that I never would marry him unless he made a solemn vow and promise before God that he would never enter into Polygamy. I could not hide from him that I loved him—he knew it and could see it ; but I said I *never* would go to Utah alone, and I certainly never would marry at the risk of my husband taking another wife. No; I was willing to give him my heart, my all—it was only fair for him to do the same by me. . . . . . He was very near me then; and my hand was in his; and he was looking up into my eyes. Then he whispered the promise I had asked of him, and, dear Sister Stenhouse, I *know* I can depend upon *his* word. We shall be happier in this world *by ourselves*, and we feel quite sure that God will not ask us to do anything in heaven that would make us miserable. Perhaps I oughtn't to say this, but I'm so happy that I cannot allow myself one single wretched doubt about the future or *my* husband, such as I used to have. . . . .

We were married on the 27th of January.

. . . .

"And now we are getting ready for Zion, and are busy day and night. Of course you have heard of the " Divine Plan "—the Hand-Cart Scheme. Oh, Sister Stenhouse, I am so very, *very* much ashamed of myself for all the wicked things that I used to say about the Apostles and the Elders. Since our marriage, Elder Shrewsbury has explained everything to me and set things in their right light. It is a glorious privilege for us to be permitted to gather to Zion, and now that I know my dear husband will never even think of another besides myself, I glory in the thought of leaving the Gentile world and all its wickedness.

. . . .

We go with the first company this season.

I will tell you all the rest of the news when I meet you, dear "

So Mary Burton was married, and coming with the Hand-Cart Company. " Why," I said, turning to my husband " they'll be here in a day or two now."

" Perhaps to-day," he replied.

They did not, however, arrive either that day or the next; but towards the end of the week we were told that their vessel was in the river, and I accompanied my husband to Castle Gardens to see them.

A strange spectacle was presented to our view. More than six hundred Mormon emigrants were gathered there, all on their way to Zion, and burning with zeal and enthusiasm worthy of a better cause. There were aged men and women, whose heads were hoary with the snows of many a winter, and whose tottering steps had borne them to the verge of three score years and ten; there were stout-hearted fathers of families, and matrons with sons and daughters growing up around them ; there were young men in the pride and strength of manhood; and maidens in the modest blush of womanly beauty; and little toddling children, and babes in their mother's arms—all obedient to what they thought was the command of God Himself—all with their faces set steadfastly and anxiously Zionward.

Let not the reader smile at the blind infatuation of those poor emigrants. Would he or she have suffered so confidingly—so faithfully—for his or her religion ? They might be mistaken; but truly theirs was a faith which "hoped all things, believed all things, endured all things." Surely, in His sight— who judges the heart—the blind obedience of those men and women who were ready to suffer and to endure unto the bitter end, because in their child-like faith they thought it was His holy will—such practical devotion was more truly acceptable than the formal professions of an untested faith which orthodox professors are so ready to make.

I met at Castle Gardens many whom I had known in the old country; but it was one particular face which I was anxious to see. A man wrapped in a thick great-coat, and with a fur cap upon his head, brushed against me; and before I had time to raise my eyes, my hand was grasped in his, and I heard Mary's husband say " Oh Sister Stenhouse, I'm so glad to see you : I knew we should meet you in New York. Come and see Mary. She's *my* Mary now!"

I went with Elder Shrewsbury and I saw Mary. But oh, how greatly was she changed! When I returned from our Swiss mission and saw her, after an interval of several years, I was, of course, struck with the alteration which had then transformed her from a pretty little fairy-like girl into a decorous young lady contemplating matrimony ; but although I had now been absent from England only a few months, I observed a much more striking alteration in her than on the previous occasion. It was not now, I thought, so much an outward and personal change, as a new development of her inner consciousness—her soul itself. Her form was as graceful, and her eyes as bright as ever; but from those eyes there now shone forth another light than that which I had thought so charming in the by-gone time.

Her affection for me was as warm and demonstrative as when we first met :—She recognised me in a moment, before her husband had time to say a word ; and, throwing both her arms round me, she kissed me again and again with all the effusion of her childish days. Taking my hand she led me gently into a quiet corner and seated me beside her upon a big trunk, and then she began to talk. It was the same soft sweet voice again, which used to be so dear to me when I was left all alone in Southampton, soon after my marriage, while my husband was on mission in Italy.

She told me all the story of her courtship—all, and much more than she had told me in her letter. But it was when she came to speak of her marriage, of her husband, and especially of their pilgrimage to Utah that I observed more especially the change which had taken place in her. She was no longer the light-hearted girl, half-doubting her strange religion, and rejecting it altogether when it did not coincide with her own ideas and wishes. No :. Elder Shrewsbury—had he been ten times a Mormon Elder—could not have wished for a more obedient, a more earnest, I might say—a more fanatical believer than was now to be found in his young and beautiful wife. Her eyes really glowed with enthusiasm as she spoke of "the work of the Lord" and of "gathering to Zion;" and her voice, though soft and sweet as ever, had in it, now and then, a tinge of sternness which told of a determination and spirit which the casual observer would never have suspected.

I expressed some surprise that she and her husband, not being without funds, should have gone with the Hand-Cart Company when they might have waited and have gone with so much more comfort with one of the independent companies.

"Why, Sister Stenhouse," she said, "We have done it as a matter of faith. Certainly we could have afforded to go in any way we chose, but my husband said we ought to be an example to the poorer saints ; so we gave away nearly all our money to help the emigration fund, and then we came, just as you see us, along with the rest."

"But the danger and discomfort is so great," I suggested. "Surely the Lord does not want us to sacrifice ourselves when no one is benefitted by it ?"

"Not a bit," said she, "there's no danger, Sister Stenhouse, and if there were it would only please me all the more. As for discomfort, why we should have had that any way, and we both glory in making sacrifices. Besides which, we have been told by the Apostle that this will be the most pleasant and successful journey across the plains that has ever been made."

"I am a little doubtful of the promises of Apostles and Elders," I said, "and I remember, Mary, when you used to agree with me."

"I know I did," she answered, "but Brother Shrewsbury has shown me how wrong I was—I never doubt *now*. But I think you have a wrong notion about this hand-cart scheme. It is not an ordinary plan such as any man might have made. God Himself revealed this plan to Brigham, and in fact we call it 'the divine plan' in our songs. Oh, you should hear our songs! They're a little rough, but the singing is so earnest and the voices of the men and girls blend so well together that I know you'd like them. There's only one thing that I don't like about this plan, and that I daresay is all right if only I knew it."

"I think, Mary," I said, "I could tell you a good deal that you wouldn't like if you knew it."

"No, dear," she replied hastily, as if afraid to hear me, "don't tell me unpleasant matters. I'll tell you all I meant. The Prophet and Heber C. Kimball, and Jedediah Grant counselled the richer emigrants to give as much as they could —all their property, if they had faith enough—to help the poor brethren to emigrate; but the American Elders had private instructions—so Brother Shrewsbury told me—to use the money to help out all the unmarried girls who are willing to go. I confess that this troubled me not a little; but my husband says that when we get to Zion we shall find all will be right, and of course I believe him."

Mary's conversation puzzled me a good deal at the time. She had formerly-been so clear-sighted and so unbiassed by prejudice, and now she seemed ready to believe anything. All her husband's enthusiasm was now her own; she saw with his eyes, and in the intensity of her love for him she believed all that he accepted as true. Long after, when I thought of that short interview, I called to mind her impulsive earnestness, and I felt that a secret misgiving, unconsciously to herself, was partly the cause of it. Unknown to herself her excess of zeal was the offspring of doubt.

Life in the future was in anticipation to my poor friend one long day of hope and happiness. She could not see the shadow of a cloud—no coming sorrow darkened her way. Zion, to her excited imagination, was the abode of peace, and sanctity, and unchanging joy.

I asked her whether the Saints in England had heard any of those strange reports about Brigham Young defying the Government, which had attracted so much attention in this country.

"Certainly," she said, "it is because the day is so very near when all intercourse between God's people and the Gentile world shall be cut off for ever that these great efforts are being made to gather the Saints to Zion. Of course you know this, but I don't think you know all. Why, at the last general conference in Liverpool, the president had instructions from Salt Lake to propose Brigham Young as 'prophet, seer, revelator, and *King!*'"

"*King?*" I said, "How can President Young ever be 'king?' Utah is part of the territory of the States, and under their jurisdiction ; it is not even a State itself yet, and Congress has refused to sanction the name of *Deseret*. This country will never suffer a kingdom to be set up in Utah ; you must be misinformed, Sister Mary."

"No, Sister Stenhouse," she exclaimed, "I am under no mistake. My husband assured me that the conference accepted the proposition, and that it was received unanimously. The Saints are gathering in from all parts of the world, and when war is declared they will not be found unprepared. Why, here on board with us, the American Elders are all provided with swords and revolvers of the very best make that could be got for love or money, and I myself have heard them say that Brigham Young intends shortly to declare his independence of the United States. We didn't know this before we left England, but we felt sure that he had some great purpose in view which had been revealed to him."

"Before we left," I said, "the Saints were all eager to emigrate."

"Yes, dear," she answered, "but nothing like they are now. You have no idea how excited and anxious everybody is. Some of the people, in order to obey counsel, sold their watches and jewelry, and even their best clothes, scarcely keeping enough for the journey, and every one who had any money gave it away. Brigham Young set a noble example in that ; even the Gentiles would admire him if they knew all. Why, we had on board ship with us Brother Tenant, the rich, new convert who paid thirty thousand dollars for the property which Brigham Young so generously gave to help the Emigration Fund. He hardly had enough left to carry him and his family to Zion ; and now he is going to cross the Plains with us, to settle in Salt Lake City. He is somewhere here among the emigrants, I believe, at the present moment, and you could ask him all about it if you liked. The brethren assure him that Brother Brigham is so liberal that he will get vastly more than the value of his thirty thousand dollars when he reaches Zion, and I hope he will, for I like both him and his wife."

All this was thus far true, but it was with some misgivings that I heard Mary talk about it. Still I tried to persuade myself that it was a sin to doubt. How little did either of us imagine that after poor Mr. Tenant's miserable death upon the Plains we should live to see his wife—destitute and defrauded of her property by generous-hearted Brigham—dragging out a miserable existence in Zion, and dependent even for a crust of bread upon the kindness of the brethren. And yet, as I previously stated in another place, this was how the Prophet, under the mask of liberality, contrived, for his own purposes, to cheat this unfortunate and too-confiding Saint.

Then we talked of what more nearly interested ourselves, and Mary asked me when Mr. Stenhouse and myself were coming out. I told her that it was quite uncertain, but that we expected to before long. "At any rate you will come out before the season is over," she said.

"Most likely so," I replied, "but you will be safely there and settled before we arrive."

How little did she imagine the fearful scenes she was to witness—the terrible sufferings she was to endure before the season she spoke of had passed away. Could I at that time have known all, I would have prayed that sooner than set out on that fearful journey she might find refuge in the grave from the horrors which, unknown to her, were brooding over her way.

We talked long, and then my husband joined us—Elder Shrewsbury was called away by some necessary duty—and when we parted it was with many promises to write frequently to each other of our common religious interests, as well as the welfare of ourselves and those we loved. Then I spoke with several other old friends, and we exchanged greetings with all sorts of people, for my husband wherever he goes is always sure to be upon speaking terms with almost everybody he meets.

The Hand-Cart Company left New York for Utah—a long and formidable journey at best—but in that instance, through

13

mismanagement and neglect, one of the most fatal expeditions that imprudent man has ever undertaken ; and it was not until months and months had passed away, and another season had come round that we heard anything of their fate.

And time went on, but my troubles did not lighten. My husband still continued to work at the *Mormon* office, and after a while his salary was slightly increased from time to time ; but still his earnings were altogether inadequate for the support of a family, and I found it absolutely necessary to obtain some employment for myself. It cost me many a long and weary day of search and enquiry, and many a battle with my pride before I could get anything to do, but at last I was successful, and although my little ones required constant attention, I contrived to add a very decent quota to the scanty family purse.

And thus matters continued until the following year—our life of uncertainty and care unchanged. Little in my life at that time is worth recording : to me it was one long, painful struggle, and any change which could come, I felt must be for the better. My experience of Mormonism was of course enlarged as new facts presented themselves to my observation, and by nothing was my faith so much shaken as by the discrepancies between the written and spoken Mormonism which was presented with fair face to the European Saints and the world at large, and the actual conduct of the Elders.

From the first moment when Polygamy was announced, the leaders had strictly forbidden the missionaries to enter into any alliances with the sisters abroad, or to make any proposals of marriage to them, or to enter into any matrimonial covenants. In the language of Heber C. Kimball— Brigham's first counsellor—they were "not to pick out from the flock the young, fair, and tender lambs," but were to bring them all safely home to Zion.

This counsel was all very well, for it tended to keep the Elders out of mischief, and afforded an opportunity to the brethren at home to select more, and more youthful wives from the fair converts who were gathered in to Zion. But the missionaries found it very irksome to obey this counsel, and in point of fact, those who did so formed a very small minority.

One of the Missionaries who had just returned from Europe came one day to our house in New York, and brought a youthful sister with him. He was by no means a handsome man or prepossessing in his appearance, but I saw at once that he had succeeded in obtaining considerable influence over the young sister's mind. He said she was not very happy, and he wanted her to stay with some respectable family for a week or two until they set out for Utah, and I agreed that she should stay with us.

She began to play with the children, and took one of them in her arms in a way which attracted my attention, for I noticed that tears were in her eyes, and she excited my sympathy. I asked her as gently and as delicately as I could what was the matter with her, and what her sorrow was, and she told me that she herself had two little ones at home and was wretched at being parted from them. She had obeyed counsel, and had left her husband and a happy home to go to Zion. She loved them all dearly, but deluded by false teachings, and promises that she should soon have her children again, she had stolen away and left them all.

I reasoned with her, tried to make her see how wrongly she had acted, and persuaded her to return to her husband and seek his forgiveness. No; it was all in vain. The salvation of her soul she thought was beyond all earthly considerations; she must stifle the suggestions of her heart within her; she must hasten to Zion. Thus she left me, and like many another victim, I never expected to see her again.

One morning, a few months later, I was astonished to receive a visit from her. After expressing my pleasure at seeing her once more, she told me that what I said had so impressed her that when the emigrants had arrived at St. Louis she had refused to proceed any further on the journey, had written to her husband, had made all right with him, and was now on her way back to her home in England.

My story is so full of painful reminiscences, that it is with pleasure that I record this incident—one of the rare cases in which folly was not succeeded by utter ruin and misery. Alas, how many instances I might mention, which fell beneath my own personal observation, of wives and mothers led away by the delusive doctrines which they mistook for inspiration, and who sought vainly, through years of misery, for peace and rest, until at length they found it in the darkness of the tomb.

Towards the end of the year 1857, the difficulties in Utah, and a financial panic in New York, resulted in the discontinuance of the *Mormon*. My husband was thus thrown out of employment, and to add to our difficulties, the people for whom I worked suspended operations. This new trial of our faith, however, was not long; out of apparent evil, good came. Released from his obligations to the Apostle and the Mormon paper, my husband now set earnestly to work to obtain a living without the crippling influences of "counsel" or the dictates of those whom his religion taught him to respect.

I had always believed that if suffered to act for himself, his energy was such that he would certainly carve his way to a respectable position in the world. In this I was not deceived, either at the time of which I speak or at a later period when in Salt Lake City he engaged in active business on his own account. In New York, where he had been, by this time, appointed President of the Eastern Mission, and was actively engaged in advocating the claims of the Mormon Church, he sought and found employment on the staff of the *Herald*, and in connection with other daily papers; and such was his success, that from a condition of misery and poverty we were very soon raised to a position of comfort, and surrounded by every luxury suitable to our station in life; and this position we enjoyed until called upon to leave all and journey across the Plains to Zion.

Our own journey to Zion was postponed for a while; but not long before we set forth, I received the long-expected letter which Mary Burton had promised me; and as it contains a vivid picture of a mode of transit—the only mode which could *then* be used—across the Plains; and shows what people were forced to endure so recently as a few short years ago, I shall give extracts from it in the following chapter ; for I feel sure that if the reader did not peruse the story in the exact words of my unfortunate friend, he never would believe that in this country and in our own times such a terrible tragedy could have been enacted.

CHAPTER XV.

" I PROMISED to write and tell you all about our journey
across the Plains, but I little expected to have such a
terrible tale to tell.

" You have heard so much of the journey to Salt Lake Valley that you know pretty well how we must have travelled to
Iowa City where it was necessary that we should wait until
the whole company was quite ready for the long journey which
lay before us.

" Our life up to a certain point was much the same, and we
met with the same difficulties as all other emigrants who had
gone before us. But there the comparison ends. Privation,

and toil, and weariness, and not infrequently sickness and
death, wore out many of the companies that went before us,
but they never suffered as we did. It is utterly impossible
for me to tell you all that we went through. And when I
finish this letter and lay down my pen, and even when you
read the fearful story of my own experience during that journey, you will still have but the faintest idea of the horrors and
sufferings which we endured.

"At Iowa City we found nothing prepared for us. When
we left Liverpool we were told that hand-carts, provisions, and
all that we needed should be provided before we arrived. If
this had been done we should have had just fairly time
enough to travel over the Plains and reach Salt Lake before
the terrible cold of winter set in. As it was, everything went
wrong. The Elders who had been sent out before us to buy
tents and carts and all that we wanted, had either been
unfortunate or very careless, for, as I said, when we arrived in Iowa City not the slightest preparation had been
made.

"You know how strong my faith was when we left New
York and how Brother Shrewsbury and myself were ready to
sacrifice everything. I can assure you that we were fully
tested, and I do think that but for our strong faith, not a
single soul of all that company would have survived that
journey.

"Three companies had, after a long delay, been sent out
before we reached Iowa City. As it was then early in the
season they completed their journey before the cold of winter
set in. I afterwards heard that Brigham Young and the Elders, when they saw those companies arrive safely in Salt Lake
City, spoke of the scheme as *a successful experiment.* We have
been taught that the scheme came directly from heaven and
was neither speculation nor experiment, and when I heard
that, after all, the Prophet himself spoke of it as a matter
of doubtful issue, I asked myself—*Who* then can we believe ?

"We waited three weeks in Iowa Camp while they were

making the hand-carts. They were very lightly made and I think not at all suitable for such a long and wearisome journey; and being so hastily put together and most of the wood unseasoned, they were utterly unfit for the rough work for which they were constructed. Twenty of these carts—one to every five—were allowed to every hundred persons, who were also allowed five good-sized tents, and one Chicago wagon, with three yoke of oxen to transport the baggage and provisions. We were only allowed seventeen pounds of bedding and clothing each, which, with cooking utensils, &c., made up about one hundred pounds to each cart, and that was quite as much as the cart (itself only sixty pounds in weight) could carry. You can see, Sister Stenhouse, how difficult it must have been out of every hundred persons—men, women, and children—to find twenty who were strong enough to pull even such frail things as those hand-carts were. The married men and the young men and boys did the best they could, but they could do no more, and some of the carts were drawn by young girls alone.

"The girls and women who had no husbands used to occupy a tent by themselves at night, but in the other tents, whole families, without respect to age or sex, together with the young men who assisted them during the day, used to find shelter. This you will see at once was exceedingly inconvenient, but we had no choice, and we had been so long associated and had suffered so much together that we did not feel it as much as we otherwise must have done.

"What weary days we spent! Hour after hour went by, mile after mile we walked, and never, never seemed to be a step the further on our way. Sometimes I recalled to mind a hymn which we used to sing at Sunday School, when I was a child—an evening hymn in which we returned thanks that we were—

'A day's march nearer home.'

"But day after day went by—wearily, hopelessly—and

when each night came on, and, tired and footsore, we lay down to rest we seemed no nearer to our home in Zion.

"Do not think, Sister Stenhouse, that we gave way to despondency. What we felt, God alone knows ; but our poor weary hearts were full of confiding faith in Him, and we placed undoubting confidence in the promises and prophecies which we had received through His chosen servants. The young folks were light-hearted and gay, and with all the enthusiasm of youth they pressed on, thinking not of the way but only of the end ; and their example was most encouraging.

"My husband was one of the bravest and truest of all that band. He drew the cart which we shared with another Elder and his wife and their grown-up daughter. They were old people—I mean the Elder and his wife—and the daughter was an old maid, unpleasant, thin, and sour, and too feeble to do anything. There were reasons why I was excused from taking any share in hard work ; but I felt as zealous as the rest, and day after day walked beside my husband thinking that, if nothing more, my companionship might cheer him. The old folks walked behind, and so did the children, but sometimes, when the little ones were very weary indeed, the parents would place them on the top of the bedding in the hand-cart and give them a lift. But some of the elderly people who were unused to walking far, and whom it was impossible to carry, suffered a great deal ; and sometimes mothers with children at their breasts would trudge on mile after mile in all the heat and dust without a murmur or complaint until they almost dropped down with fatigue. What some of those poor creatures suffered, no words could tell.

"The sun shone down upon us with intense heat as we travelled through Iowa, and the people from the farm-houses and villages came out to see us and wondered at our rashness in undertaking such a journey. They were very kind to us and came and visited us in our camps and offered some of the men work and good wages if they would wait there instead of going on to Zion. A few of the people accepted these offers, but the Elders, as you may suppose, watched carefully every company and every man ; and in the evening, when meetings for prayer and preaching were held, we were earnestly exhorted to obedience, and the sin of acting upon our own judgments was set forth in the very plainest terms. The kindness of the Iowa people, however, encouraged us, and they freely gave to those who most needed whatever they could to help us on our way.

" And we needed help and sympathy.

" Of course, with only one wagon to carry all the provisions for a hundred persons, besides five tents, our supply of food was very limited. At that period of the journey the grown-up people were allowed ten ounces of flour a day and a little— and but a very little—coffee, sugar, rice, and bacon. This was a very scanty allowance for people who all day long had to draw the hand-carts or to trudge mile after mile in all that burning heat and dust—but we never complained. Some of the men ate all their rations at breakfast, and went without anything more until the next morning, unless they were able to beg a little of some friendly farmer by the way. The little children received just half as much as the others. With a very small amount of management this inconvenience might certainly have been avoided, for provisions of all sorts were very cheap in the districts through which we passed. Some of the more thoughtful Saints, I know, felt very bitterly the injustice of this, for, as you are aware, we had paid *all* our expenses *in full*—even to the uttermost farthing ; and we had been promised in return a safe and sufficient outfit with plenty of provisions, and in fact all that was necessary. Had we been left to ourselves we should of course have provided for every contingency ; but we came in obedience to counsel under the direction of the Church, and after we had paid for everything ; the Church even " took care " of our money, so that we therefore could not procure necessaries by the way, as otherwise we might have done.

" Thus wearily, and suffering not a little privation, we travelled all through Iowa until we came to the Missouri river and encamped at Florence, a place about six miles north of Omaha, and there we remained about a week preparing for our journey across the Plains.

"It was the middle of August when we arrived at Florence, and we had been delayed so much on the way that it appeared to many of the more experienced that it would now be the height of imprudence for us to cross the Plains at that season. With old people, delicate women, and little children, and without carriages of any sort—except the frail hand-carts that carried our bedding—it would be a weary long time, before we could reach Salt Lake. Every step must be trudged on foot, and it was quite impossible that we could walk many miles a day, while there was before us a journey of over a thousand. Some of the Elders proposed that we should settle where we were, or somewhere near by until the following spring, and then go on to Zion; but others who were more confident urged that we should proceed at once. The Elders called a great meeting to settle the matter, at which we were all present.

"I should tell you that when we first started, our whole company was placed under the guidance of Elder James G. Willie as captain; and we were again sub-divided into five parties of about one hundred each, and over every hundred was placed an Elder or sub-captain. The first hundred was headed by Elder Atwood, the second by Levi Savage, the third by William Woodward, the fourth by John Chislett, and the fifth by Elder Ahmensen. About two hundred of the people were Scotch and Scandinavians; nearly all the rest were English. All were assembled at the meeting. You know, Sister Stenhouse, how meetings were held at home. Well, it was just the same there. We, of course, had nothing really to say—we had only to obey counsel and sanction the decision of the leading Elders. I used to feel annoyed rather at that sort of thing in London, as you may remember, but now when life and death depended upon the wisdom of our decision, with all my faith, I felt worse than annoyed, wicked as I have no doubt it was for me to feel so. My husband never uttered a word, but I know he felt much as I did, and in that he was not alone among the Elders.

"We had neither vote nor influence—the elders held our destiny in their hands. In all our company there were only three or four men who had been out to Salt Lake before, and of course they could not be overlooked, so they gave their opinion at the meeting. They must have fully known the dangers and difficulties of the way, and what hardships *must* overtake a company so scantily provided for as was ours, if we continued our journey. But, for all that, they not only spoke slightingly of the danger which threatened us, but prophesied in the name of the Lord, that we should pass through triumphantly and suffer neither loss nor harm.

"One man alone—Levi Savage—dared to tell the truth. People well-mounted, or even with good ox-teams, could safely and easily make the journey, he said, but for a band of people like ourselves, with aged folks, and women, and little children, to attempt it so late was little short of madness. He strongly urged that we should take up our quarters there for the Winter, when, he said, as soon as Spring came on, we could safely and successfully perform the remainder of our journey.

"The other Elders thought that he was weak in the faith, and plainly told him so; and one of them even said he'd eat all the snow that fell between Florence and Salt Lake City. The people, of course, believed without question what they were told to believe, for they had long ago made up their minds that the leaders were inspired, and therefore they dared not doubt them, and the prudent counsel of Brother Savage was rejected accordingly. I was not near enough to hear his words, but I was afterward told that he said: 'What I have said, I know is the truth; but as you are counseled to go forward, I will go with you; I will work, and rest, and suffer with you, and, if God wills it so, I will also die with you.' Never was man more faithful to his word than was Brother Savage, and often after that, when sickness, and weariness, and cold, and hunger, and death, overtook us—as he had fore-

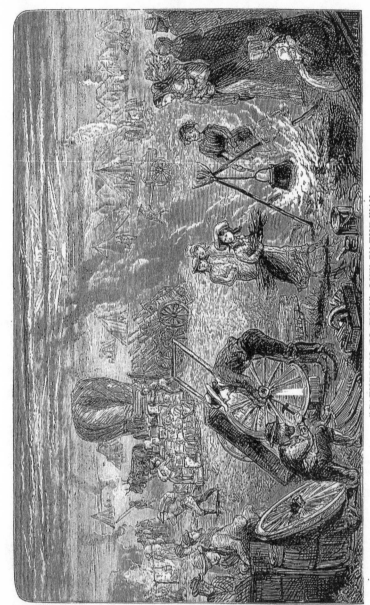

"GATHERING TO ZION."—LIFE BY THE WAY.

seen—he never for one moment forgot the promise which he had so solemnly made.

"Then—the middle of August being passed—we left Florence behind us, and began our weary journey across the Plains in much the same fashion as we had already travelled through Iowa. We had, however, taken in fresh provisions to last us until we reached Utah, and as the oxen could not draw so much extra weight, one sack, weighing about a hundred pounds, was placed on each of the hand-carts, in addition to the other baggage. This was a severe task upon the endurance of the people, but most of them bore it without a murmur. On the other hand, we fared a little better in the matter of provisions, for we were allowed a pound of flour a day each, and also, occasionally, a little fresh beef, and, besides that, each hundred had three or four milch cows. As we continued our journey, and the provisions were consumed, the burdens on the carts, of course, grew lighter.

"But this was only the beginning of our pilgrimage :—the end we could not foresee. Every evening, when we pitched our tents, we endeavored by songs, and jests, and interesting stories, to beguile the tediousness of the way. The days were not quite so warm now, and the nights were more chilly ; but altogether it was much more pleasant travelling than it was in the earlier part of the journey, and no one seemed to remember the almost prophetic remonstrance of Brother Savage.

"Still we travelled very slowly, for the carts were always breaking down ; the wheels came off, and we had nothing to grease them with. The boxes of the wheels were made of unseasoned wood, and the heavy pressure upon them, and the dust that got into them, soon wore them out. Some of the people cut off the tops of their boots and wrapped them round the axles, and others cut up their tin plates and kettles for the same purpose, and for grease they used soap, and even their pitiful allowance of bacon. But as the days passed, and the flour began to be used up, these accidents became less frequent.

"Upon an average, they said, we travelled about fifteen miles a day, which I think was very good. Some few days we even made a little over twenty miles, but they were balanced by the shortcomings. We tried to feel happy and hopeful, and even the aged and infirm tried to make light of their toil and privations, for we did not yet see that heavy cloud which was looming across our way. I frequently talked with the old and weakly among the people, to whom both my husband and myself were able to offer little kindnesses, and they all spoke cheerfully of our prospects. Such faith had they in the promises of the Elders.

"Just before we reached Wood river, vast herds of buffaloes appeared in our vicinity, and one evening all our cattle stampeded, and the men had to go in search of them. About thirty were lost, and after hunting after them for three days, we gave them up. We had only one yoke of oxen now for each wagon, and as the wagons were loaded each with three thousand pounds of flour, the teams could not move them. So they yoked up the beef-cattle, and cows, and heifers, but they were unmanageable—and at last we were obliged again to place a sack of flour upon each hand-cart.

"This sorely tried us all. Some of the people even complained, but the greater part of us bore up bravely, believing that it was the will of the Lord. We still had faith that all would yet be well. This was, however, a hard blow. Our milch cows were useless to us, our beef-rations were stopped, and the burdens which we drew were doubled. Every one did his or her best, but many of us began to be disheartened, and could hardly get along.

"One evening there was quite a commotion in the camp. We had pitched our tents for the night on the banks of the Platte River, I think, when suddenly quite a grand turn-out of carriages and light wagons came up from the east and joined us. Each carriage was drawn by four horses, and the outfits were in first-class style. Nothing could be too good for Apostles and other "distinguished" servants of the Lord. I was anxious to know who they were, but was not long in

finding out.   There was the Apostle Franklin Richards, and
Elders Webb and Felt, and Joseph A. Young, the son of the
Prophet, and Elders Dunbar, and Kimball, and Grant—all
returning Missionaries.   They stayed with us all night, and
in the morning called a great meeting, and the Apostle Richards delivered a speech, which troubled me not a little, and
made me very sorrowful.

   " He had heard of what Brother Savage had said, and then
and there, before us all, he rebuked him.   He then exhorted
us to remember the hope set before us, and told us to pray
and work on, and especially to be obedient to counsel; and he
finished by solemnly prophesying, in the name of the God of
Israel, that the Almighty would make a way for us to Zion,
and that though the snow might fall and the storm rage on
the right hand and on the left, not a hair of our heads should
perish.

   " Some of the people wept with joy as they heard these
words.   My own heart was full.   To me, this was the voice
of inspiration—the voice of God—how could I doubt again ?

   " Sister Stenhouse ; before a month was over, I saw with
my own eyes that prophecy, those promises, falsified to the
very letter ; and yet at the time they came to me and to all
else as the word of the Lord from heaven.   Tell me, if men
can thus deceive themselves—for I do not doubt for a moment
that the Apostle believed his own prophecy—and if we could
be so sadly deluded as to believe that what was said was
divine, what surety have we for our religion at all ?   I strive
against these sinful doubts, but they *will* sometimes creep
into my heart unbidden.

   " The Apostle and the Elders with him told Captain Willie
that they wanted some fresh meat, and the Elders killed and
gave them of our very best.   What could be denied to the
Servants of the Lord ?   We were then more than four
hundred in number—aged men and feeble women, with babes
and poor little children too young to walk ; many of them
infirm and sick, all of them footsore and weary.   We were far
away from home, travelling slowly hundreds and hundreds of

miles, worn out and without sufficient provisions for the way or the remotest chance of obtaining any: And yet, Oh God! I shame to tell it; these servants of Heaven—our leaders, our guides, our example—these chosen vessels who came to us, riding comfortably and at ease in their well-appointed carriages, took of our poverty—took the very best we had!

"As they left the camp, I looked up into my husband's face and our eyes met. We said not a word, but in our hearts there was the same thought. Sister Stenhouse, there must have been that selfsame thought in the mind of many another poor soul who watched those Elders depart after they had lectured us on faith and patience and obedience!

"They crossed the river pleasantly enough, and pointed out the best fording-place and then they watched us wade through —the water there being nearly a mile in width, and in some places two and even three feet in depth—and though many of the heavy-laden carts were drawn by women and girls, they never so much as offered to lend us the aid of their handsome teams. One sister told me that they watched the poor people crossing, through glasses, as if it were an entertainment, but I did not see that, and can hardly believe it was true. All that they did, however, was to promise that when we reached Laramie we should find provisions and bedding and other necessaries ready for us, and that they would send help from Salt Lake Valley to meet us."

CHAPTER XVI.

"IT was early in September when we reached Laramie, but
we found nothing awaiting us there. We were all very
much discouraged at this, and Captain Willie called another
meeting for consultation. We knew, of course, beforehand,
that our position was very bad, but figures when stated plainly
become startling facts. We now learned that if we continued
at the same rate as that which we had previously been travelling, and received each the same allowance daily, we should
be left utterly destitute of provisions when we were yet three
hundred and fifty miles from the end of our journey. Nothing

remained but to reduce our allowance; so, instead of one pound, we were rationed at three-quarters of a pound a day, and, at the same time, were forced to make incredible exertions to travel faster.

"Not long after this, Captain Willie received a message from the Apostle Richards. It is the custom, you know, for people who want to send messages to emigrants who come after them, to write a note on a scrap of paper and tie it to a stone or a piece of wood and leave it on the way. No one disturbs it, as no one but the emigrants travel along that road, and they are sure to find it. It was from a rough post-office like this that Captain Willie got his letter. In it the Apostle told him that we should receive supplies from Salt Lake when we reached the South Pass; but that we knew would be too late. So our allowance was again reduced, and after that we were rationed at an average of ten ounces for every person over ten years of age. The men who drew the carts received twelve ounces, the women and aged men, nine ounces, and the children from four to eight ounces according to age. Before this, the men with families had done better than the single men, as they had been able to save a little from the children's rations, and of course they did not like this new arrangement so well.

"Picture to yourself these men—in the cool air of September, drawing after them each one a loaded cart, with one or more children most frequently superadded to its weight, trudging wearily every day, ten, fifteen, or twenty miles over the rough desert, wading across streams with the women and children, setting up tents at night, working as they never worked before in all their lives, and withal keeping soul and body together upon twelve ounces of flour a day. This is but one side of the picture—the physical toil and endurance of the working men. Think what the feeble and aged, the sick, the women and children must have endured!

"By this time many of those who had hitherto held out bravely began to fail, and the people in general were greatly discouraged. Captain Willie and the Elders who assisted him did their best to keep up the spirits of the people and to get them over as much ground as they could each day. The captains over the hundreds had also no little work to perform in distributing provisions, helping the sick and infirm, and, in fact, superintending everything.

"For some time the nights had been getting colder and colder, and by the time we arrived at the Sweetwater river we suffered considerably from that cause ; we felt that winter was fast approaching. In fact, it came on earlier and more severely last year than at any time before, since the Saints settled in Utah. Does it not seem strange that at the very time when they were offering up special prayers for us in Zion, that we might be defended from cold and storm, the terrors of a more than ordinary winter overtook us and proved fatal to so many of our company! The mountains were covered with snow, and it was soon quite evident, even to those who had prophesied most loudly that the Lord would work a special miracle in our behalf, that the storm-clouds of winter would soon burst upon us.

"You have never seen the Sweetwater river, so I may as well tell you that it is a very irregular stream, and we had to cross it again and again upon our way. As usual we had to wade through the water each time, and though the men helped over the women and children as well as they could, many of us got very wet indeed, and quite chilled, and we were all cold and miserable. Still, our faith never gave way— some, I know, began to doubt a little, but they had not yet lost all faith, and discouraged and wretched, as indeed we were, the greater number bore up with heroic resolution. I noticed, however, on the faces of some poor souls—men and women—a peculiar expression which it is quite impossible for me to describe. Later on I was led to believe that at that time they, perhaps unconsciously, felt the presentiment of that fearful death which so soon overtook them.

"We suffered much at night. You may remember that I told you we were only allowed seventeen pounds of clothing and bedding, and that, of course, was of little use. Sleeping

in a tent, under any circumstances, is not generally pleasant
to those who are accustomed to the shelter of a house, but
sleeping in a tent, exposed to the keen night air of the wilder-
ness, and with scarcely a rag of covering, was almost sufficient to prove fatal to the stoutest and strongest. During
the summer time, although our fare was scanty and our labor
incessant, we rose each morning refreshed and strengthened
and ready for the toils of the day. But now we crept out of
our tents cramped and miserable, half-frozen, and with our
eyes red and tearful with the cold. We seemed to have no
life left in us.

"These things soon began to tell upon the health of every
one of us, especially upon the aged and those who were sickly.
Hope at last died out in their poor weary hearts. One by
one they fell off—utterly worn out. Poor things! how they
had longed to see the promised Zion, and now all expectation
of peaceful rest on earth was over—the bitter end had come.

"We dug graves for them by the wayside in the desert, and
there we laid them with many tears, scarcely daring to look
one another in the face, for we felt that our own time might
perhaps be nearer than we thought.

"One by one at first they fell off, but before long the
deaths became so frequent that it was seldom that we left a
camp-ground without burying one or more. This was, however, only the beginning of evil.

"Soon it was no longer the aged and the sickly who were
taken off, but the young and strong, who under other circumstances would have set disease and death at defiance. Cold,
hunger, and excessive toil brought on dysentery, and when
once attacked by that, there was little hope for the sufferer,
for we had no medicine, and it was quite out of our power to
give them relief in any other way. I now began to fear for
my husband, for I had noticed for some time an expression of
extreme weariness in his face. Our trials had not hardened
our hearts; on the contrary, I think, as death seemed to be
drawing near, our affection for each other grew more pure and
devoted, and in my heart I often prayed, that if it were His

will, God would let us die together and rest in the same
grave. We never spoke a word to each other on this subject,
but we felt the more. I exerted all my strength, and day
after day toiled along at his side, helping him all I could ;
but although he never complained, I saw in his eyes a dull
and heavy look which, more than any words, told of failing
strength and the approach of disease, and my heart sank
within me.

"But my own troubles did not alone engross my attention ;
there was too much wretchedness around us to allow anyone
to be absorbed entirely in his own griefs. Acts of devotion
on the part of both parents and children came before me daily
such as would have put to shame the stories of filial and
parental piety which we used to be taught at school.

"I saw one poor man whose health had evidently never
been strong, draw the cart with his two little ones in it, as
well as the baggage, mile after mile, until he could hardly
drag his weary limbs a step further ; his wife carried a little
five months old baby in her bosom. This they did day after
day, until disease attacked the husband, and it was evident
that he could bear up no longer. The next morning I saw
him, pale as a corpse, bowed down, and shivering in every
limb, but still stumbling on as best he could. Before the day
was half over, the poor wife lagged behind with her babe, and
the husband did not seem to notice her. This was not the
result of heartlessness on his part ; I believe that even then
he had lost all consciousness. He did not know it, but he
was dying. Still he stumbled on, until the short wintry day
came to a close, and we pitched our camp, and then I missed
him. There was no time to enquire, and a chill came over
my heart as I thought of what might be his fate. Presently
my husband came to the tent and told me all. The poor man
had dragged the cart up to the last moment, and, when the
company halted for the night, he had turned aside, and sitting
down he bowed his head between his knees and never spoke
again. Later still, the poor wife reached the camp, and I saw
her then. There was no tear in her eyes, and she uttered

neither cry nor moan, but there was upon her features a terrible expression of fixed despair which I dared not even look upon.

A few days after this, one morning as we were almost ready to start, I saw that poor mother in her tent, just as they had found her. She was cold and still—frozen to death— her sorrows were over at last, and her poor weary spirit was at rest; but on her bosom, still clasped in her arms, and still living, was her little child, unconscious of its mother's fate.

"Most of those who died, as far as I could tell, seemed to pass away quietly and with little pain, as if every feeling of the heart were numbed and dead. But my own sufferings and fears at that time were so great that I could not be a very close observer. Strange as it may seem, the fear of death did not so much appear to terrify these poor victims as the thought that their bodies would be buried by the way-side in the desert, instead of in the sacred ground of Zion. Poor souls! the absorbing passion of their life was strong in death.

"As death thinned our ranks, the labors of those who survived were increased, until at last there were hardly enough left with strength sufficient to pitch our tents at night. A great deal devolved upon the captain of our hundred, Elder Chislett. He is a very good man, and a devoted Saint; and I am glad to say that both he and a lady to whom he was betrothed, and who was also with our company, escaped with their lives. I have often seen him, when we stopped for the night, carrying the sick and feeble on his back from the wagon to the fire, and then working harder than a slave would work in putting things straight for the night. He showed a great many kindnesses to my husband and myself.

"But individual efforts availed nothing against fatigue and hunger, and the fearful cold. To the minds of all of us, the end was fast approaching. Nothing but our faith sustained us; and foolish as many people would think that faith, I am quite sure, that but for it, no living soul of all our company would have ever reached Salt Lake.

OVER AT LAST.

" At last the storm came, and the snow fell—I think it must have been at least five or six inches deep within half an hour. The wind was very keen and cutting, and it drifted the snow right into our faces ; and thus blinded by the storm, and scarcely able to stand, we stumbled on that day for fully sixteen miles. What we suffered it would be useless for me to attempt to describe. The scenes we witnessed were too terrible to describe.

" There was a young girl, with whom I was very well acquainted, and who I saw struggling in the snow, clinging to one of the hand-carts, and vainly trying to help in pushing it on, but really doing just the contrary. She is now in Salt Lake City, and you can see her wandering about any day upon the stumps of her knees, her limbs downwards having been frozen during that storm, and subsequently amputated. A poor old woman, too, who I think you must have known in London, lingered behind later in the day. When night came on it was impossible for any one to go back to search for her, but, in the morning, not very far from the camp, some torn rags—the remains of her dress—were found, a few bones, a quantity of hair, and at a little distance a female skull, well gnawed. and with the marks of the wolf fangs still wet upon it ;—the snow all round was crimsoned with blood.

" We halted for a little while in the middle of that day, and to our surprise and joy, Joseph A. Young and Elder Stephen Taylor drove into the camp. We found that when the returning missionaries, of whom I have already told you, left us by the Platte river, they made their way as speedily as they could to Salt Lake City. Joseph A., who felt deeply for our sufferings, although he had been away from home for two whole years, hastened to his father and reported to him the condition in which we were. Brigham Young was of course anxious to undo the mischief which had resulted from the people following his inspired counsel, and at his son's earnest entreaty allowed him to return with provisions and clothing to meet us. Joseph A. lost no time, but pressed on to the rescue, and having told us that assistance was on the way, hastened eastward to meet the company that was following us.

"I cannot tell you what a relief this intelligence was to the minds of all, and how much the poor people felt encouraged by it. But as for me, at that time my heart was sad enough. For some time my husband's strength had evidently been failing, and for the last two days I had felt very serious apprehensions on his behalf. He had been overtasked, and like the rest of us he was starving with cold and hunger, and I saw that he could not hold out much longer. My worst fears were speedily realised. We had not journeyed half a mile from the place where we rested at noon, when, blinded by the snow, and completely broken down, he dropped the rail of the cart, and I saw that he could go no further. How I felt, you, as a wife and mother, only can guess. In a moment my own weakness was forgotten; my love for my husband made me strong again. To leave him there or to delay would have been death to one if not all of us. So I called to those who shared the cart with us, and they helped me as well as they could to lift my husband up and put him under part of the bedding. It was the only chance of saving his life, for, as I before mentioned, some, previous to this, who had been overcome, and had lingered by the way, had been frozen to death or devoured by the wolves.

"I then took hold of the cross-bar or handle of the cart, and numbed with the cold, and trembling in every limb, it was as much as I could do to raise it from the ground. To move the cart was impossible, so I appealed to the old folks again, and they exerted all their strength to push it from behind, and our combined efforts at length succeeded; but the chief weight fell upon me. How gladly I bore it; how gladly I would have borne anything for the mere chance of saving my dear husband's life, your own heart can tell.

"The snow drifted wildly around us, and beat in our faces so blindingly that we could hardly proceed. The greater part of the train had passed on while we delayed on account of my husband, and now every one was making the most desperate efforts to keep up with the rest ; to be left behind was death. Had I been asked whether under any circumstances I could have dragged that heavy cart along in all that storm, I should certainly have replied that it would be utterly impossible ; but until we are tried we do not know what we can bear. It was not until the night came on, and we pitched our tents, that I realised what I had passed through.

" They helped me to carry my husband to the tent, and there we laid him, and I tried to make him as easy as was possible under the circumstances, but comfort or rest was altogether out of the question. All that night I sat beside him, sometimes watching, sometimes falling into a fitful sleep. I did not believe that he would live through the night. In the morning he was by no means improved, and then I felt too truly the abject misery of our position. It is a painful thing to watch at the bedside of those we love when hope for their recovery is gone, but think what it must be to sit upon the cold earth in a tent, upon the open desert, with the piercing wind of winter penetrating to the very bones, and there before you, the dear one—your life, your all on earth—dying, and you without a drop of medicine, or even a morsel of the coarsest nourishment, to give him. Oh, the bitterness of my soul at that moment! I tried to pray, but my heart was full of cursing ; it seemed to me as if even God Himself had forgotten us. The fearful misery of that dark hour has left on my soul itself a record as ineffaceable as the imprint of a burning iron upon the flesh.

" The morning broke at last, dark and dreary, and a thick heavy mantle of snow covered all the camp, but we contrived to communicate with each other, and soon it was whispered that five poor creatures had been found dead in the tents. Want, and weariness, and the bitter cold had done their work, and we did not weep for them—they were at rest ; but for ourselves we wept that we were left behind—and we looked at one another, wistfully, wondering which of us would be taken next.

We buried those five poor frozen corpses in one grave,

wrapped in the clothing in which they died, and then we comforted each other as best we might, and left the dead who
were now beyond our reach, that we might do what we could
for those who were fast following them to the grave. A
meeting of the leaders was held, and it was resolved that we
should remain where we were until the promised supplies
reached us. We could not, in fact, do otherwise, for the snow
was so deep that it was impossible for us to proceed, and the
sick and dying demanded immediate attention. That morning, for the first time, no flour was distributed—there was
none. All that remained, besides our miserable cattle, was a
small quantity of hard biscuit which Captain Willie bought at
Laramie, and a few pounds of rice and dried apples. Nearly
all the biscuit was at once divided among the whole company,
and the few pounds which remained, together with the rice and
apples, were given to Elder Chislett for the use of the sick
and the very little children. They also killed two of the cattle and divided the beef. Most of the people got through
their miserable allowance that very morning, and then they
had to fast.

"Captain Willie set out that morning with another Elder to
meet the coming supplies and hasten them on, and as we saw
them disappear in the distant west we almost felt as if our last
hope departed with them, so many chances there were that we
should never see them again.

"The whole of that long, long day I sat beside my husband
in the tent—and I might almost say I did no more. There
was nothing that I could do. The little bedding that was allowed for both of us I made up into a couch for him; but
what a wretched make-shift it was! And I got from Elder
Chislett a few of the dried apples which had been reserved for
the sick; but it was not until nightfall that my husband was
capable of swallowing anything—and then, what nourishment
to give to a sick man! The day was freezingly cold, and I
had hardly anything on me, and had eaten nothing since the
day before; for my mind was so agitated that I do not think
the most delicate food would have tempted me. God alone

knows the bitterness of my heart as I sat there during all that weary day. I never expected to see my husband open his eyes again, and I thought that when evening came I would lie down beside him and we would take our last long sleep on earth together.

"When night came on and all was dark I still sat there; I dreaded to move lest I should learn the terrible truth—my husband dead! I looked towards the place where I knew he was lying, but I could see nothing. I listened, and I fancied that I heard a gentle breathing—but it was only fancy. Then, louder than the incessant moaning of the wind, I could hear in the distance a fearful cry—a cry which had often chilled our hearts at midnight on the plains—it was the wolves! The darkness grew darker still—so thick that one could almost feel it; the horror of death seemed stealing over all my senses. Oh that there might be one long eternal night to blot out for ever our miseries and our existence. I threw my hands wildly above me and cried bitterly: 'Oh God, my God, *let me die !*'"

"God was nearer to me than I thought. As my hand dropped lifelessly to the ground it touched some moving thing—it was my husband's hand—the same hand which I had watched in the twilight, stiffening, as I thought, in death. The long, thin fingers grasped my own, and though they were very, very cold, I felt that life was in them; and as I stooped down to kiss them I heard my husband's voice, very weak and feeble, saying in a whisper—"Mary." I threw myself upon his bosom. In a moment the fear of death—the longing for death—the wild and terrible thoughts, all had gone;—the sound of that voice was life to me, and forgetful of his weakness, forgetful of everything but him, I threw myself upon his bosom and wept tears of joy.

"Very carefully and gently I raised him up, and, in the darkness, every whispered word conveyed more meaning to my mind than all his eloquence in by-gone times. After some time I persuaded him to take a little nourishment—miserable stuff that it was—and presently he fell asleep again. I laid his

dear head upon the best pillow that I could make of some of
my own clothes, and then I slept a little myself—not much,
but it was more refreshing than any sleep that had visited my
eyes for long time past—hope had come again.

"The next morning my husband was evidently better, and
I knelt down beside him and thanked God for the miracle that
He had wrought; for was it not a miracle thus to raise my
dead to life again? How many stronger, stouter men than he
had I seen fall sick and die; but to me God had shown mercy
in my utmost need.

"We waited three long days for the return of Captain Willie. My heart was so full of thankfulness that my husband
had been spared that I certainly did not feel so acutely the
misery with which I was surrounded as I otherwise should
have done; I was like the prisoner who feels happy in a reprieve from death, but whose situation is nevertheless such as
would appear to any other person the most wretched in which
he could be placed. The misery that was suffered in that
camp was beyond the power of words to describe. On the
second day they gave us some more beef-rations, but they did
us little good. The beef was, of course, of the poorest, and,
eaten alone, it did not seem to satisfy hunger, and those who
were prostrated by dysentery, although they ate it ravenously,
suffered much in consequence afterwards.

"The number of the sick rapidly increased, and not a few
died from exhaustion; and really those seemed happiest who
were thus taken from the horrors which surrounded them.
Had it not been for the intense frost, we should all probably
have fallen victims to the intolerable atmosphere of the camp.
I would not even allow my mind to recall some of the scenes
which I witnessed at that time: scenes, the disgusting and
filthy horrors of which, no decent words could describe.
When you consider the frightful condition in which we were,
the hunger and cold which we endured, you may perhaps be
able in a small degree to conjecture—as far as a person can
conjecture who has not himself suffered such things—what we
then passed through. I saw poor miserable creatures, utterly

worn out, dying in the arms of other forlorn and hopeless creatures as wretched as themselves; I saw strong and honest, honorable men, or who had once been such, begging of the captain for the miserable scraps which had been saved for the sick and the helpless children; I saw poor heart-broken mothers freezing to death, but clasping as they died, in an agony of loving woe, the torn and wretched remnants of clothing which they still retained, around the emaciated forms of their innocent babes—the mother-instinct strong in death; and sometimes at night when, all unbidden, I see again in dreams the awful sufferings of those poor God-forsaken wretches, I start in horror and pray the Almighty rather to blot out from my mind the memory of *all* the past, than to let me ever recollect, if but in fancy, that fearful time.

"The third day came, and still no relief. There are mysterious powers of endurance in human nature, weak as we often deem it, but there is a point beyond which the bow, however flexible, will not bend. It was evident that if no help arrived speedily, the end was not far off.

"The sun was sinking behind the distant western hills, in all the glory of the clear frosty atmosphere of the desert, and many who gazed upon its beauty did so with a mournful interest, believing that they would never again behold the light of day. But at that moment some who were anxiously watching with a last hope—watching for what they hardly dared expect to see—raised a shout of joy. We knew what it was! Men, women, and children rushed from their tents to welcome the approaching wagons and our friends in time of need. Captain Willie and the other Elder had found the rescue from Salt Lake overtaken by the storm just as we were, but he had told them of our terrible situation, and they had hastened on without a moment's delay. It was he and they, convoying good supplies, who now approached us. The poor creatures shouted wildly for joy, even the strong men shed tears, and the sisters, overcome with the sudden change from death to life, flung themselves into the arms of the brethren as they came into

the camp and covered them with kisses. Such happiness you
never saw—everyone shaking hands and speaking joyfully—
everyone saying ' God bless you ' with a meaning such as is
seldom attached to those words.

" The supplies were to us more than food and clothing—
they were life itself. Elder John Chislett was appointed to
distribute the provisions and clothing, and everything was
placed in his hands. He gave out to us all what was immediately necessary, but strongly cautioned us to be very moderate in what we ate, as it was dangerous to go from the
extreme of fasting to a full meal. After supper, the clothing
and bedding was fairly divided, and we felt more thankful for
those little comforts than a person, who had never endured as
we had, would have felt had he become suddenly the recipient
of boundless luxury.

" Two of the Elders who had held forth such delusive hopes
to the company, not long before, as I have already told you,
were with the brethren who came to our relief. I have never
ventured to ask how it was that they could hold out to us in
God's name such promises, when they must have known, after
a moment's reflection, that they were utterly baseless, but I
think that probably they left their comfortable homes in Salt
Lake City and came across the stormy desert with supplies to
meet us, only to show practically how anxious they were to
atone for having led us astray. Next morning Elder Grant
went on east to meet the company following us, but Elder
W. H. Kimball took command of our company for the rest of
the way.

" We could now journey but very slowly, for the road was
bad, the sick and weakly were, however, able to ride, and
altogether we suffered less. To some this change for the
better arrived too late—the mental and physical sufferings
which they had endured were too much for them. Poor souls!
they alone and their Father in heaven knew what they had
passed through. They seemed to have lost all consciousness,
as if their faculties had been numbed and stultified. We
talked to them of the past, but they looked at us with unmean-

ing eyes, as if we spoke of something in which they had no interest ; we tried to lead their thoughts to Zion, and the promises of the Lord ; but it was all in vain.   They turned from
us with a look of terrible apathy ; and one or two, who partly
seemed to understand, only replied with an indifference painful to witness—" too late, too late !"

"As we journeyed, the weather every day grew colder :
Many of the unfortunate people lost their fingers and toes,
others their ears ; one poor woman lost her sight, and I was
told of a poor sick man who held on to the wagon-bars to save
himself from jolting and had all his fingers frozen off.   Few,
if any, of the people recovered from the effects of that frost.
One morning they found a poor old man who had vainly tried
the evening before to keep up with the rest.   His corpse was
not far from the camp, but it had been sadly mangled by the
wolves.   Then there came another snow-storm, only worse in
proportion as the weather was colder, and it was with the utmost difficulty that we could be kept from freezing.   We
wrapped blankets and anything else we could get around us,
but the cold wind penetrated to our very bones.   I was told
that some of the people, even women and children who lagged
behind were whipped so as to make them keep up, and to keep
life in them.   I did not see this myself, but I believe, if the
story was true, it was an act of mercy and not of cruelty, for to
delay a moment was fatal.   The captain of our hundred, more
than once stayed behind the company to bury some unfortunate person who died on the road : how he ever got up with us
again I cannot tell, but he seemed to be as indefatigable in his
labors as he was wonderfully preserved.

"Sometimes the carts came to a dead stand-still, and
several had to be fastened together and drawn by a united
effort, and in more than one instance the poor people gave up
altogether ;—they were carried on, while they lived, as well as
we could ; but their carts were abandoned.   The stragglers
came in slowly to camp the night of the storm ;—the people
from the Valley even went back to fetch some in ; and it was
nearly six o'clock in the morning before the last arrived

"The next day we remained in camp, for there were so many sick and dying that we could not proceed. Early in the morning Elder Chislett and three other Elders went round to see who was dead, that they might be buried. They found in the tents fifteen corpses—all stiff and frozen. Two more died during the day. A large square hole was dug and they were buried in it three abreast, and then they were covered with leaves and earth, every precaution being taken to keep them from the wolves. Few of the relatives of those who were dead came to the burial—they did not seem to care —death had become familiar to them, and personal misery precluded sorrow for the dead.

"As we drew nearer to Salt Lake Valley we met more of the brethren coming to our assistance. They supplied us with all we needed, and then hastened on to meet those who followed us. The atmosphere seemed to become sensibly warmer, and our sufferings were proportionately less as we approached Zion.

"What the feelings of others might have been when they first saw the goal of our hopes—Zion of our prayers and songs—I cannot tell. Weary, Oh, *so* weary I felt, but thankful, more than thankful that my husband's life had been spared. He was pale and sick, but he was with me still.

"I have written too much already, Sister Stenhouse. I cannot tell you more now, but I may as well add that when we left Iowa City we were about five hundred in all. Some left us on the way. When we left Florence and began the journey across the Plains we were over four hundred and twenty, of which number we buried sixty-seven—a sixth of the whole. The company which followed us, and to which I have frequently alluded, fared worse than we. They numbered six hundred when they started, but they buried one hundred and fifty on the journey—one in every four. May God grant that I may never again see such a sight as was presented by the miserable remnant of that last company as they came on slowly through the Cañon towards Salt Lake Valley."

CHAPTER XVII.

WE FORSAKE ALL, AND SET OUT FOR ZION:—OUR JOURNEY ACROSS THE PLAINS.

Considering Our Position—Doubts and Fears—A Visit from the Apostle Geo. Q. Cannon—We are "Counselled" to Emigrate—Giving up All for the Church—Taking Charge of the Emigrants—The Insignificance of Women—Wives are Never to Follow their own Judgment—"Be Obedient"—We Begin our Pilgrimage—The Perpetual Emigration Fund—How Mormon Emigration is Managed—Settling the Debts of a Lady-Love—How Certain Imprudent Englishmen Have Suffered—The "Emigration" of Miss Blank—An Ancient "Sister" who was Forced to Wait—Living Contradictions—First Glimpse of Salt Lake City—A Glorious Panorama—The Spectre of My Existence—The Prison-Walls of the Mountains—Without Hope—Life in the Wagons—Search for a House—"Roughing It" in Zion—First Impressions—A Cheerless Prospect for Winter—Daniel H. Wells Promises Assistance—A Woful Spectacle of Tallow Candles—Odorous Illumination—"*L'Eglise c'est moi*"—"An Ugly Man With a Cast in His Eye"—An Awkward Mistake—Beginning Life in Zion.

IT was with strange feelings of doubt and unrest that I read that painful story; but I folded up Mary Burton's letter and stored it carefully away in my desk, and then I began to think.

Certainly I was still a Mormon—at least I was nothing else—but I was not now so firmly grounded in my faith as once I was, and these terrible stories completely unsettled my mind. Then, too, I was well aware that, before long, my husband and myself would be called upon to cross the Plains to Zion, and I felt that if our experience were anything like that of Mary Burton, I and my children would never reach Salt Lake. The prospect was not very cheering.

15

One morning we were surprised to receive a visit from the Apostle George Q. Cannon who informed us that he had received letters from Utah and had come to take the place of Mr. Stenhouse as President of the Mission in the Eastern States, and that we might now prepare to travel with the next company of emigrants.

To me this was most unpleasant intelligence. Polygamy,— the knowledge that before long I should be brought personally within its degrading influence,—had now for years been the curse of my life, and I had welcomed every reprieve from immediate contact with it in Utah. But the time had come at last when I was to realise my worst apprehensions, and I think at that time, had I been permitted to choose, I would have preferred to die rather than journey to Zion. Besides this, ever since my husband had been engaged with the secular papers, we had been getting along very comfortably. We had now a pleasant home and many comforts and little luxuries which we had not enjoyed since we left Switzerland, and I was beginning to hope that we should be allowed to remain in New York for a few years at least. We had also by this time six children—the youngest only a few days old— and I leave it to any mother to determine whether I had not good cause for vexation when I was told that we were expected to leave New York within two weeks with the emigrants who were then *en route* from England. My husband also was to take charge of the company, and therefore everything would depend upon me—all the preparations for our long and perilous journey, the disposal of our furniture, and, in fact, the thousand and one little necessary duties which must attend the packing up and departure of a family.

In the course of a few days the emigrants arrived, and then my husband was compelled to devote all his time to them. When I told the Elders that it was almost impossible for me, in the delicate state of health in which I was, and with a babe only two weeks old, to undertake such a journey, they told me that I had no faith in the power of God, and that if I would arise and begin my preparations, the Lord would give me strength according to my day. Thinking that probably my husband believed as they did, I made the effort, but it cost me much. In the Mormon Church the feelings or sufferings of women are never considered. If an order is given to any man to take a journey or perform any given task, his wife or wives are never thought of. They are his property just as much as his horses, mules, or oxen, and if one wife should die, it is of little consequence, if he has others, and if he has not he can easily get them ; and if he is not young or fascinating enough to win his way with the young ladies, he has only to keep on good terms with Brigham Young, or even with his bishop, and every difficulty will be smoothed away, and they will be " counselled" to marry him.

It is never expected, nor would it be tolerated in any Mormon woman that she should exercise her own judgment in opposition to her husband, no matter how much she might feel that he was in the wrong : I have frequently seen intelligent women subjected to the grossest tyranny on the part of ignorant and fanatical husbands who were influenced by the absurd teachings of the Tabernacle. One of the greatest Mormon writers has said :

"*The wife should never follow her own judgment in preference to that of her husband;* for if her husband desires to do right, but errs in judgment, the Lord will bless her in endeavoring to carry out his counsels ; for *God has placed him at the head*, and though he may err in judgment, yet God will not justify the wife in disregarding his instructions and counsels ; far greater is the sin of rebellion, than the errors which arise from the want of judgment ; therefore *she would be condemned for suffering her will to arise against his. Be obedient*, and God will cause all things to work for good."

The trouble and annoyance occasioned by leaving a comfortable position in New York to travel to such an unknown region as Utah was then, was not a trifle ; but we hastened our preparations, sacrificing all that we possessed, in the most reckless manner, and in due time set out.

When we reached Florence—the starting-point on the Frontiers—we were detained on account of some mismanagement on the part of the Church Agents, and remained for three weeks in camp. Ours was what was called "an independent company"; by which I mean that we were able to defray our own expenses without borrowing from the Church: the poorer emigrants were assisted from a fund provided for that purpose—the Perpetual Emigration Fund. More than twenty years ago contributions were levied on the more wealthy Saints for the purpose of providing the passage, outfit, &c., of those who could not otherwise have "gathered to Zion." It was not, however, intended that a free passage should be provided; those who had a little money were *assisted*, and then, after all, they had to make good to the last farthing, with interest, what they had borrowed from the fund. I have known many people who contributed very largely, and it was represented constantly as the duty of all to do so.

Men who contemplate entering into the patriarchal order of matrimony, if they are Americans, generally try to discover whether the "emigration" of their lady-love has been "settled for," and if their investigations end unfavorably the result very frequently is that their devotion is turned into another channel and some other maiden whose expenses have been fully paid bears off the palm. Englishmen have not always been quite so prudent, and some have married according to their own sweet fancy without asking a question, and to their dismay, not long after the wedding, an account has been sent in for the emigration of Miss Blank. Others, again, have not been allowed to marry the lady of their choice until she was first paid for, and if the old man was very much in love, this was a quick way of getting the account settled. The Mormon Church never gives, it only lends to the poor. Many a man and woman has given enough to have emigrated himself or herself over and over again. This was because they were old people, and it was the young girls and young people generally who received the benefits of the fund. Many years ago a poor old widow woman in England said to me: "I have nearly starved myself to contribute all that I could to the emigration fund, in hopes that I should have the privilege of going to Zion and mingling with the chosen people of God, but every season the young girls are all picked out of our branch, and I am told to wait. I cannot think that this is right, but I don't wish to judge the actions of God's servants. I suppose I must wait."

She did wait, and died waiting.

Our company was in an infinitely better position than that of those emigrants of whose sad fate my friend Mary Burton had told me; for our journey was made at the proper season, and as far as was possible under the circumstances, convenience and comfort had been attended to. The incidents which befell us were few, and although, of course, every one of us felt weary and worn out, we were not called upon to pass through the miseries and sufferings endured by the hand-cart emigrants. Looking back to our primitive mode of travelling, it appears to me almost as if I must be making some mistake about my own age, and that it must have been several centuries, instead of a few years ago, since we crossed the plains. The ox-team and wagon, the walk on foot in the day and the camp life at night have been pleasantly exchanged for the swift travel of a few days in a Pullman palace-car.

What living contradictions we were as we crossed the Plains—singing in a circle, night and morning, the songs of Zion and listening to prayers and thanksgivings for having been permitted to gather out of Babylon, and then during the day as we trudged along in twos and threes expressing to each other all our misgivings, and doubts, and fears, and the bitterness of our thoughts against Polygamy; while each wife, confiding in her husband's honor and faithfulness, solaced herself with the hope that all might yet be well. How little sometimes do the songs of gladness reflect the real sentiments of the heart. How often have I heard many a poor heart-broken woman singing the chorus:

> " I never knew what joy was
> Till I became a Mormon."

I never could sing that song, for my experience had been exactly the reverse.

It was the month of September—the beginning of our beautiful Indian summer—when we emerged from the cañon, and caught sight of Salt Lake City. Everything looked green and lovely, and in spite of all my sad forebodings while crossing the Plains, I involuntarily exclaimed, " Ah, what a glorious spot !" It looked like a beautiful garden—another Eden—in the midst of a desert valley. We had a glimpse of the Great Salt Lake far away in the distance, stretching out like a placid sheet of molten silver, while everywhere around were the lonely-looking snow-capped mountains, encircling us like mighty prison-walls.

It would be impossible for me to describe my feelings at that time. Even while I was enchanted with the glorious prospect before me, there arose again in my mind that haunting spectre of my existence—Polygamy. I believed that this little earthly paradise would probably be to me and my daughters after me, a prison-house, and with a mother's instinct I shuddered as I thought of what they might be destined to suffer there. Lovely as the scene was, there was a fatal shadow overhanging it all. Then, too, there was no escape : if the sad forebodings of my heart were realised, it would be utterly impossible for us ever to get away. The idea of a railway being constructed across those desert plains and rocky mountains never for a moment entered my mind, and even had I thought it possible, I should have supposed that it would take a life-time to complete. No, there was no help for me, even if it came to the worst. I felt that my doom was sealed ; and there were many women in our company who thought just the same as I did and who were troubled at heart with fears as sad as mine.

My first impressions of Salt Lake City when we began life there were anything but pleasant—we had to " rough it." For nearly two weeks we were obliged to remain in our wagons, as it was quite impossible to obtain house-room. At that time each family built their own little hut, and there were no vacant houses to let.

The weather was now growing very cold and wintry, and it

was absolutely necessary that we should have some better shelter than the wagons afforded. One day my husband told me, when he came home, that he had been offered a house which belonged to the Church. It was in a very dilapidated condition, he said, but that if I would go and look at it with him, we could then decide about taking it. No time was to be lost, for companies of emigrants were coming in almost daily, and if we neglected this chance we might not find another.

When we arrived at the house I was much discouraged at seeing the condition it was in : the window panes were all cracked or broken out, the floors and walls looked as if they had never known soap or paint, and the upper rooms had no ceilings ; in fact it was not fit for any civilised Christian to live in. In point of size there was nothing to complain of, but of comfort or convenience there was none,—the wind whistled through every door and every cracked window ; and altogether it presented anything but a cheering prospect for winter.

My husband told me that Daniel H. Wells, who was superintendent of Church property and also one of the First Presidency of the Church, had promised him that if we took the house it should be repaired and made fit for living in, before winter fully set in ; and under the circumstances we thought we could do no better than accept his offer.

Thus we began housekeeping in Utah, and we unpacked our trunks and tried to give the place as home-like an appearance as we possibly could. I had known what it was to be in a strange country and destitute ; and, therefore, benefiting by experience, when I left New York, regardless of the teachings of the Elders and of my own husband's directions to the contrary, I had secretly stowed away many little necessaries towards housekeeping. Indeed, had I not done so, we should have been as badly off when we reached Zion as when we arrived in New York. Besides which, I have no doubt that our wagons would have been filled with the trunks of those very brethren who counselled us not to take more than was abso-

lutely necessary.   The brethren who gave this counsel were,
I noticed, constantly purchasing while they advised everyone else to sell, and I thought it wiser to follow their example
than their precepts.

Among my treasures was some carpet, and when that was
laid down and the stove put up we began to feel almost at
home.   The wind, however, soon drove away all thoughts of
comfort, for it came whistling in through a thousand undetected crevices, and the tallow candles which we were obliged to
burn presented a woful spectacle.   Even the most wealthy,
then, had no other light but candles, and every family had to
make their own : I have often seen people burning a little
melted grease with a bit of cotton-rag stuck in the middle
for a wick—how pleasant the smell, and how brilliant the light
thus produced can be imagined.   Everything was upon the
same scale—and to keep house in any fashion was really a
formidable undertaking, especially to those who had been accustomed to the conveniences of large towns.   I believe that
many women consented to their husbands taking other wives
for the sake of getting some assistance in their home duties.

We spent nearly all the first evening in our new house in
trying to discover some means of keeping out the storm,
but to little purpose.   Nearly a fortnight passed before any one
came to see about repairing the house, but as it belonged to the
Church my husband seemed to think it must all be right.
The Mormon men are always very lenient towards "the
Church"—very much more so than the Mormon women, for
the latter have somehow got mixed up in their minds the idea
that Brigham Young and "the Church" are synonymous
terms.   I remember one day a good young sister—a daughter
of one of the twelve Apostles—saying to me, "I have just seen
the Church," and when I asked her what she meant, she said:
"I have just met Brigham Young and Hyram Clawson, and
are they not the Church ?"   It was evident to me that others
besides myself sometimes gave way to wicked thoughts.
Nevertheless I was still of opinion that "the Church" had
plenty of money and ought to have repaired the house.

One day a man whom I had never seen before, called upon me and asked what repairs I should like done. I was not feeling very well, and had been annoyed at the delay, and I answered rather ungraciously that I should like anything done, if only it were done at once, for I thought we had waited long enough. He answered me very politely and said that he would see to it immediately. When Mr. Stenhouse returned home in the evening he said : " So you have had a visit from President Wells." " No," I said, " there has been no one here but a carpenter—an ugly man with a cast in his eye, and I told him that I wanted the house fixed right away."

" Why, that was President Wells," he said, very much shocked, and I think I felt as bad as he did when I realised that I had treated one of the " First Presidency " so unceremoniously.

This Daniel H. Wells, besides being an Apostle, a Counsellor of Brigham Young, and one of the three " Presidents " who share with Brigham the first position in the Church, and are associated with him in all his official acts, was Lieutenant-General of the Nauvoo Legion, and at the present time and for some years past, Mayor of Salt Lake City. It was a shocking indiscretion, to say the least, to speak slightingly of such a high and mighty personage.

The repairs, however, were seen to, and the house rendered a little more habitable. We had now to begin the struggle of life afresh and could not afford to be too particular about trifles ;—to obtain shelter was something—for the rest we must still continue to hope and trust.

CHAPTER XVIII.

MY FIRST IMPRESSIONS OF THE CITY OF THE SAINTS.

Some Personal Observations—An Innocent Prophet—Living Witnesses of the Truth—How Salt Lake City was Laid Out and Built—The Houses of Many-Wived Men—My First Sunday in the Tabernacle—Curious Millinery of Lady-Saints—Two Remarkable Young Ladies—A Doubtful Experiment—How Service is Conducted in the Tabernacle—Extraordinary Sermons—Deceitful Dealings of the Original Prophet—Why Joseph, the "Seer," Married Miss Snow—Another of the Prophet's Wives—A Shameful Story—Aunty Shearer, and her Funny Ways—Spiritual Wives and Proxy Wives—How the Saints are Married for Time and for Eternity—Concerning Certain Generous Elders —How Wives are Secretly "Sealed"—Extraordinary Request of One of Brigham's Wives—"The Next Best Thing"—Mormon Ideas of the Marriage at Cana—The "Fixins" of a Mormon Husband—How "The Kingdom" is Built Up—Women Only to be Saved by Their Husbands—A Painful Story— A Very Cautious Woman—A Woman Who Wanted to be "Queen"—A Deceitful Lover—A Strange Home-Picture—"These Constitute My Kingdom"—Forebodings.

WITH the eager observation of a woman who has a great personal interest at stake, I took note of everything in Zion which was new to me, and especially all that related to the system of plural marriages, and all my worst fears were abundantly realised.

Although I had looked at the dark side of Mormonism and had pictured with horror the life of women in Polygamy, there were nevertheless some truths which broke upon my mind with painful effect. In England we had heard so frequently from the lips of the Apostles and Elders that not only was Polygamy contrary to the teachings of Joseph Smith, but that it was utterly unknown in Nauvoo during the Prophet's life-time. Directly the Revelation was published, we, of course, knew that if it really proceeded from Joseph he could not have been so innocent of Polygamy as we had been taught; but I was hardly prepared to meet several of his wives out in Utah; and yet almost the first thing that I heard was that there were living in Salt Lake City, ladies well-known and respected, who had been sealed to the Prophet. This I afterwards found was true.

The Mormon Colony in Salt Lake City had at first to contend with all those difficulties and submit to all those privations which beset the path of all new settlers in a strange country. Until very recently the greater number of the dwellings were small and low, like so many little huts, and not infrequently you might see a row of these huts, with one window and a door to each, and, inside, a wife, a bedstead, two chairs and a table—with poverty to crown the whole. But even then might be seen in the laying out of the streets, and in the other arrangements, the germs of a great city. The roadways were broad and the sidewalks convenient, and provision was made—more with an eye to the future than to present necessity—for a great depth in the measurement of the houses and blocks. Down the sides of the streets flowed a sparkling stream—the water of which was brought from the mountains for the purpose of irrigating the gardens in the city; and, as far as they possibly could, the settlers marked out and planned a capital worthy of that name for the Mormon people.

When I arrived in Salt Lake City, a great many improvements had been effected; and expecting, as I did, that this would be our future home for many years, perhaps for life, I was interested in everything that I saw. But even then, in merely taking a walk about the city, I met with evidences of the degrading teachings of Polygamy—I saw that little deference was paid to the women, they were rudely jostled at the crossings, and seemed to be generally uncared for. Since the completion of the railway and the consequent influx of Gentiles, this, of course, has not been noticeable.

The city is built on a slope formed by a bend in the mountain-range. Brigham Young's house is on the northern side, and has a commanding prospect. The Tabernacle and tithing-office are in the same street. The Tabernacle is a plain-looking building entirely devoid of any architectural beauty. It stands in the block where the Temple, which has been building for the last quarter of a century, and is now only a few feet above ground, is waiting to be finished. Nearly twenty-six years ago Brigham wrote to Orson Spencer, the President of the Mormon Church in England, urging him to "gather up as much tithing as he possibly could, for glass, nails, paint, &c., to assist in building up the Temple of the Lord in the Valley of the Great Salt Lake." A large sum of money was collected, and millions have been raised by tithing and by other means, but there has been no one hitherto with courage and authority sufficient to demand of the Prophet an account of those funds, and the interest and compound interest which should be accruing thereunto.

The first Sunday I went to the Tabernacle I was greatly amused at the way in which some of the sisters were dressed. Quite a number wore sun-bonnets, but the majority wore curious and diverse specimens of the milliner's art—relics of former days. Some wore a little tuft of gauze and feathers on the top of the head, while others had helmets of extraordinary size. There were little bonnets, half-grown bonnets, and "grandmother bonnets" with steeple crowns and fronts so large that it was difficult to get a peep at the faces which they concealed. As for the dresses, they were as diversified as the bonnets. Some of them presented a rather curious spectacle. I noticed two young women who sat near me: they were dressed alike in green calico sun-bonnets, green calico skirts, and pink calico sacks. On enquiring who they were, I was told that they were the wives of one man and had both been married to him on the same day, so that neither could claim precedence of the other. Outside of Utah such a thing would seem impossible, but so many of the young girls at that time came out to Zion without father or

VIEW OF MAIN STREET, SALT LAKE CITY.
[From a Photograph.]

mother or any one else to guide them, and left to their own inexperience and afraid to disobey "counsel" it is no wonder that they soon yielded to the universal custom.

The two young women whom I have mentioned, did not appear to me to be overburdened with intelligence; they looked like girls who could be made to believe anything; but after that I met with two well-educated women who, like these foolish girls, thoughtlessly tried the experiment of two or more marrying the same man on the same day,—agreeing with their "lord" that that would be the best way to preserve peace in their household. But they were terribly mistaken, and even before the marriage-day was over, the poor bewildered husband had to fly to brother Brigham for counsel.

The Tabernacle services seemed to me as strange as the women. There was no regular order in conducting the proceedings, but the prominent brethren made prayers, or " sermons" as they were called upon to do so. The "sermons" would be more properly called speeches—they were nothing but a rambling, disconnected glorification of the Saints, interspersed with fearful denunciations of the Gentiles, and not infrequently a good sprinkling of words and expressions such as are never used in decent society. More unedifying discourses could hardly be imagined. As for the spirituality and devotional feeling which characterised our meetings in England, they were only conspicuous by their absence, and many devout Saints have told me that when they first went there— before the erection of the great organ—the free-and-easy manners of the speakers and the brass band which was then stationed in front of the platform, made them feel as if they had come to witness a puppet-show, rather than to attend a religious meeting.

There was one lady at the Tabernacle service whom I regarded with considerable interest. This was no other than Eliza R. Snow, one of the Prophet's wives. I was told that she was the first woman married in Polygamy after Joseph Smith received the Revelation, and I believe it was so. People who lived in Nauvoo, respectable people, and not one or two either, have assured me that for four years before Joseph is said to have received the Revelation, he was practicing Polygamy, or something worse, and that the Revelation was given to justify what was already done. After it was given, or said to be given, Joseph and his brother Hyrum cut off from the Church more than one person for preaching it, and nine years more passed away during which the Mormon Elders everywhere most emphatically and solemnly denied it, before it was publicly avowed. However this might be, it is generally understood that Eliza Snow was the first plural wife of the Prophet, and I was told by a lady from Nauvoo that Joseph did not care much for her, but that she was getting to be quite a querulous old maid, and he married her to keep her tongue quiet. If that is true she has entirely changed her tactics since she left Nauvoo, for her principal occupation at the present time is converting rebellious wives to obedience to their husbands and convincing young girls that it is their duty to enter into Polygamy. Unhappy husbands derive great consolation from her counsels. In matters of religion she is a perfect fanatic, and in connection with the Female Relief Society she reigns supreme ; but otherwise there are many excellent *traits* in her character, and I could tell of many acts of loving-kindness and self-denial which she has performed, and which will surely have their reward. She is said to have been tolerably good-looking when young, but in appearance there is nothing now to distinguish her. As the chief poet of the Mormon Church, and as the representative of Eve in the mysteries of the Endowment House, she enjoys a reputation such as would be impossible to any other woman among the Saints.

Another of the late Joseph's wives is a Mrs. Doctor Jacobs, who was actually married to the Prophet while she was still living with her original husband, Jacobs. Under the same circumstances she married Brigham Young, after Joseph's death. For some time her husband knew nothing of the whole affair, but Brigham very soon gave him to understand that his company was not wanted. The sister of Mrs. Jacobs

—a Mrs. Buel—was another of Joseph's wives, and she married the Apostle Heber C. Kimball, but does not appear to have made a very good bargain.

Besides these there is another lady, a Mrs. Shearer—or as she is familiarly called—"Aunty Shearer." She is in every respect a unique specimen of womanhood, tall and angular, with cold yet eager grey eyes, a woman of great volubility, and altogether grim-looking and strong-minded. She was an early disciple and is said to have sacrificed everything for Mormonism. She lived in Joseph Smith's family, and, of course, saw and heard a great deal about Polygamy, and at first it was a great stumbling-block to her. She was, however, instructed by the immaculate Joseph, and so far managed to overcome her feelings as to be married to him for eternity. Like the others she is called " Mrs.," and I suppose there is a *Mr.* Shearer somewhere, but upon that point she is very reticent. Her little lonely hut is filled with innumerable curiosities and little nick-nacks which some people are for ever hoarding away in the belief that they will come into use some day. She is a woman that one could not easily forget. She wears a muslin cap with a very wide border flapping in the wind under a comical-looking hood, and is easily recognised by her old yellow marten-fur cape and enormous muff: her dress, which is of her own spinning and weaving, is but just wide enough, and its length could never inconvenience her. Add to these personal ornaments a stout pair of brogues, and you will see before you " Aunty Shearer," one of the Prophet's spiritual wives.

I may as well explain what is meant by "spiritual" wives and " proxy " wives.

Marriages contracted by the Gentiles, or by Mormons in accordance with Gentile institutions, are not considered binding by the Saints. That was partly the cause of my indignation and the indignation of many another wife and mother— we were told that we had never been married at all, and that our husbands and our children were not lawfully ours : surely that was enough to excite the indignation of any wife, whatever her faith might be. For a marriage to be valid it must be solemnized in the Endowment House in Salt Lake City, or the persons contracting it can never expect to be husband and wife in eternity. Should the husband die before he reaches Zion, and if the wife loves him sufficiently well to wish to be his in eternity—when she arrives in Salt Lake City, if she receives an offer of marriage from one of the brethren, and does not object to him as a second husband in this world, she will make an agreement with him that she will be his wife *for time*, but that in eternity she and all her children shall be handed over to the first husband. A woman thus married is called a "proxy" wife. It can well be understood that if the lady had lost her youth and good looks there would be very little chance of her husband seeing her again in eternity, as there would not be too many willing to stand proxy for him, and in that case he would have to depend upon the generosity of friends.

Now "spiritual" wives are of two classes. The one consists of old ladies who have plenty of money or property which of course needs looking after; and generous Elders marry them, and accordingly "look after" that same property, and the owner of it becomes the Elder's *spiritual* wife. She will only be his *real* wife in eternity when she is rejuvenated —the prospect of which rejuvenation is, I suppose, very fascinating to some men, for I have known quite youthful Elders who displayed their self-sacrificing spirit by marrying "spiritually" very old, but very wealthy, ladies.

The other kind of "spiritual" wife is one who is married already, but who does not think that her husband can "exalt" her to so high a position in the celestial world as she deserves; —perhaps some kind brother who takes a great interest in her welfare has told her so—she then is *secretly* "*sealed*" to one of the brethren who is better able to exalt her—perhaps to this same brother; and in the resurrection she will pass from him who was her husband on earth to him who is to be her husband in heaven—*if she has not done so before.*

This is what is meant by "proxy" and "spiritual" wives.

I think it will be evident even to the dullest comprehension that under such a system, "the world, the flesh, and the devil" are far more likely to play a prominent part than anything heavenly or spiritual.

All this is so repugnant to the instincts and feelings of a true woman, that I feel quite ashamed to write about it. And yet the working out of this system has produced results which would be perfectly grotesque were it not that they outrage every ordinary sense of propriety. Let me give an example. One of the wives of Brigham Young—Mrs. Augusta Cobb Young—a highly educated and intelligent Boston lady with whom I am intimately acquainted, requested of her Prophet-husband a favor of a most extraordinary description. She had forsaken her lawful husband and family and a happy and luxurious home to join the Saints, under the impression that Brigham Young would make her his queen in heaven. She was a handsome woman—a woman of many gifts and graces, and Brigham thoroughly appreciated her; but she made a slight miscalculation in respect to the Prophet. He cares little enough for his first wife, poor lady, and few people who know him doubt for a moment that he would un-queen her and cut her adrift for time and eternity too, if his avaricious soul saw the slightest prospect of gain by doing so—he did not care for her, but he never would allow himself to be dictated to by any woman. So when the lady of whom I speak asked him to place her at the head of his household, he refused: she begged hard, but he would not relent. Then finding that she could not be Brigham's "queen," and having been taught by the highest Mormon Authorities that our Saviour had, and has, many wives, she requested to be "sealed" to Him! Brigham Young told her (for what reason I do not know) that it really was out of his power to do that, but that he would do "the next best thing" for her—he would "seal" her to Joseph Smith. So she was sealed to Joseph Smith, and though Brigham still supports her and she is called by his name on earth, in the resurrection she will leave him and go over to the original Prophet.

16

The reader will certainly be shocked at this terrible burlesque of sacred things, but I felt it my duty to state the truth
and place facts in their right light.   It is not generally known
that the Mormons are taught that the marriage at Cana of
Galilee was Christ's own nuptial feast, that Mary and Martha
were his plural wives, and that those women who in various
parts of the New Testament are spoken of as ministering to
him stood to him in the same relation.

Malicious first wives, especially if they are rather elderly
themselves, frequently call the proxy wives "fixins;" and the
tone in which some of them utter the word is in the last degree contemptuous.   These poor "fixins" are seldom treated
as real wives by the husband himself.   He may think sufficiently well of the "proxy" wife to make her his for time and
to raise up children to his friend, as the Elders say, but he
never forgets that in eternity she will be handed over to the
man for whom he has stood proxy, and he expects that she'
also will bear that in mind, and do all she can for her own
support, and never complain of his want of attention to her.
Some men, after having married a young proxy wife, have become so enamored that they grew jealous of the dead husband,
and have tried to get the wife to break faith with him, and be
married to them for eternity as well as time.   This was certainly rather mean.   Very few Gentile husbands would fret
themselves about possibilities in the world to come, if in this
world they had the certainty of enjoying the undivided affections of their wives.

Mormon husbands are so influenced by their religion that
they neither act nor think like other men.   I am thinking of
one wretched family that I knew soon after I went to Utah.
There was a man and his wife and four children, all living
together in a miserable, poverty-stricken hut.   I had heard
that the man was paying attentions to a young girl with a view
to making her his second wife, and I frequently watched the
first wife as she went in and out, doing her chores, and wondered how she felt about it.   The poverty of the man, of
course, was of no consequence; living in the primitive style

in which necessity then compelled the Saints to live, one or
even half-a-dozen extra wives, made very little difference, and
Brigham and the leading Elders have always represented it as
a meritorious act, for the young especially, to " build up the
kingdom," without regard to consequences, or the misery of
bringing up a family in a destitute condition.   I never can see
children without loving them, and in this case it was not long
before I contrived to make acquaintance with the little ones.
One day, while I was talking to them, the mother came out.
She seemed pleased to see me, for she had heard of me that I
was not too strong in the faith, and she told me that her husband had said, in speaking of such women as myself, who did
not like the celestial order of marriage, that their husbands
ought to force them right into it, and that would show what
they were made of : if they were true-hearted women seeking
their husband's glory and " exaltation " in the world to come,
they would bear it well enough ; and, if not, the sooner it
killed them the better ; for if they were dead their husbands
could save them in the resurrection, but if they lived they
would only be an incumbrance.

    This, I found, was the general opinion among the Mormon
men.   Even in England, the American Elders had taught us
that the man was the head and "saviour" of the woman, and that
the woman was only responsible to her husband.   It was necessary, we were told, that the woman should keep in favor
with her lord, otherwise he might withdraw his protection and
refuse to take her into the celestial kingdom ; in which case
when she got to heaven she would only be an angel !   To be
an angel is not considered by the Saints to be by any means
the highest state of glory.   Those who do not obey the " Celestial Order of Marriage" will, like the angels, neither marry nor
be given in marriage ; they will be located, the men in one
place, and the women in another, and will serve as slaves, lack-
eys, and boot-blacks to the Saints.   Brigham Young once
publicly said of a certain President of the United States, that
he would clean the boots of the Mormon leaders in heaven.
He did not say this as a figure of speech, but meant it liter-

ally. Those who have obeyed the Gospel of the new dispensation, but who have failed to enter into Polygamy will be as upper servants, but the rebellious—the " vile apostates," and the " wicked Gentiles" will join the angels and do all the drudgery for the men of many wives. Thus I learned in Zion that my youthful notions about the glory of the cherubim were quite a mistake, and that it was not such a fine thing to be an angel, after all.

But I have run away from my story, and had almost forgotten my poor acquaintance. She was a woman who was likely to preserve a painful place in the memory of any one who once saw her. Her face was pale as death, and her jet-black eyes glistened with an unearthly lustre ; it was easy to perceive that she was very unhappy, although she tried hard to exhibit a cheerful disposition, and when our conversation turned to that subject which to women here is all-absorbing, the nervous twitching of her pale face showed how deeply painful such thoughts were to her. She told me that her husband was soon to be married to a young girl about fourteen years of age. " Do you see," she said, " that he is building for her ?" And sure enough he was, at odd hours, adding another hut to the miserable hovel in which they already lived; and thither, when it was finished, he intended to take his bride. As I looked at the poor wife, I felt little doubt, that ere that time came, her troubles on earth would have ended and her little ones would be motherless.

The Mormon women, as well as the Mormon men, are noted for attending to their own business—they do not care to tell their sorrows and trials to strangers or to people who are not of their own faith. In this way visitors to Salt Lake who have gone there with the intention of "writing-up" the Saints in the newspapers or in a book, have generally been misled. My own experience as a Mormon woman leads me to form anything but a flattering opinion of the Mormon stories told by Gentile pens. The following instance will show that the sisters are not quite so free in giving their experience as some writers would suggest.

One day, while passing through the city, I saw a young woman running across the road with a little child in her arms. The child was crying piteously, for the water was running from its clothing, and I saw in a moment that it had fallen into the stream which ran in front of the house. I followed, to see if I could be of any assistance, but fortunately found that the little creature was not seriously hurt, but would soon recover from the fright and cold. I helped the mother to change its clothing, and while she was lulling her baby to sleep, we entered into conversation. At first she appeared to be very shy of me, and avoided speaking of anything in the slightest degree personal ; but growing more interested, she said at last :

" Are you a Mormon ?"

" Certainly," I answered, " but why do you ask me ?"

" Because," she said, " We have had one or two Gentile women among us, and they go round among our people and question the women, and get them to tell their troubles, which God knows are heavy enough, and then they go and write about it, and Brigham Young finds it out, and their husbands are called to account for allowing their wives to speak to the Gentiles. You are sure you are a Mormon?" she added, " and you are not deceiving me ?"

" I'm sorry you should think such a thing," I said, " but if you suppose I would deceive you, I will not trouble you with my company." And I rose up to leave.

" Do not go yet," she said, " and pray forgive me if I have wounded your feelings ; it is simply the fear I have of getting into trouble. Brigham Young and the Elders have frequently told us to have nothing to do with the Gentiles, for they are enemies to the kingdom of God, and are seeking our overthrow—and I suppose it is true."

" How long have you been here ?" I asked.

" Over two years," she replied, " and it seems almost twenty —time has passed so slowly. I left father and mother, sisters and brother for the Gospel's sake, and I do not regret it, because it is right, but it was a very great sacrifice to make.

Yet I believe that God blesses us for the sacrifices we make, and I shall get my reward."

"You have it already," I said, " in that pretty child on your knee, and your husband, I hope, is a good man and kind to you."

"Yes," she anwered, "my child is a very great source of happiness to me, and I love my husband very much but—" (hesitatingly) "are *you* in Polygamy ?"

" No, not yet, but I do not know how soon my husband may take it into his head to get another wife."

" Are you first wife ?" she asked.

" Yes," I replied, " and I suppose you are also ?"

" No, I am third wife," she said, " I wish I were first wife."

" But why," I suggested, " do you wish that ?   If Polygamy is the true order of marriage, I do not see that it makes much difference whether one is the first or the twentieth wife ?"

" Oh dear, yes," she replied, " it *does* make a great deal of difference ; for the first wife will be queen over all the others, and reign with her husband.   If I had known that before I was married, I should have made my husband promise to place me first.   Men can do that if they like."

" But do you think you would be doing right in trying to gain the position of first wife in that way ?"

" Why not ?" she said, " Didn't Jacob obtain his brother's birthright by deception—and was he ever punished for it ?   Do you think that Brother Brigham, notwithstanding that he is the inspired servant of God, could have obtained his position, and all his money, by simple honest dealing ?   If you think so, I don't ; and it is just as proper and right for us women to secure a position for ourselves by such means as it is for Brigham Young—the end justifies the means."

" If that is so," I said, " it is a wonder to me that any woman should consent to become second, third, or fourth wife —seeing they cannot be queens."

" I can see that you have not yet had your ' Endowments,' " she said, " or you would understand more about these things,. but as you are a good Mormon I can speak freely to you.

You see it is not always those who are first wives in this world who will be first in the celestial kingdom. It all depends upon the amount of sacrifice the wife is capable of making for her husband, her faithfulness to him, and the number of children she has borne him. If she pleases him in every particular and is good, patient, and above all things obedient to all his wishes and commands, then she is almost certain to be made queen, unless the first wife is just as good, and then I don't know how they would fix that. And so you see it is safer to be first wife at once."

" Well but," I asked, " knowing all this, I am surprised that you consented to be third wife !"

" But I did not know it then," she continued. " My husband told me that *all* the wives were queens—all equal—and he says so still when I talk to him about it. But he can't deceive me. I have spoken to some of the old Nauvoo women who know all about it, and they tell me that all the Polygamic wives will be subject to the first wife; but the first wife, having suffered most, will be the one who has gone through the fire and been purified, and found worthy."

" But do you think that your husband would wish to deceive you about such an important matter ?" I said.

" Wait till you have lived a little longer here," she replied, " and you will be able to answer that question yourself, or else your experience will be very different from that of the rest of the people here."

Just then the husband made his appearance, and put an end to the conversation. He was a tall, dark-looking man, with grey hair, old enough to be her father. He appeared to be well educated and to have seen better days, though everything about their home indicated poverty—the room in which we were sitting had no carpet on the floor, there was a plain white-pine table in the middle, a small sheet-iron stove, four wooden chairs, a small looking-glass, and some cheap pictures. This was the sitting-room for the whole family—three wives, eleven children, one husband. He asked me if I had seen the rest of the family.

I replied negatively, and he said he would see if any of them were about. Presently he returned accompanied by an elderly woman whom he introduced as Mrs. Simpson. Then came another, not quite as good-looking as the first, but a great deal younger, and he introduced her as " My wife Ellen. And this one," he said, turning to the one with whom I had been conversing, "is my wife Sarah. Don't you think I have got three fine-looking women ?" Then, after a pause, he added : " And they are just as good as they are good-looking —good, obedient wives. I have no trouble with them : my wishes are law in this house. Here you have a family in which the Spirit of God reigns. We are not rich in worldly goods, as you see, but we are laying up treasure in heaven. We all live in this little home of four rooms. My wife Ellen, here, has given up her room for a parlor for us all to meet together in, and she sleeps in a wagon-box ; it is not the most comfortable, but she never grumbles. Then, here is our Sarah ; we are obliged to humor her a little, and give her a room all to herself. She is young and inexperienced, and doesn't like to put up with the inconveniences that the Saints have to bear with ; while old mother here has got to have half-a-dozen children in her room, but she never complains."

" Why did you not wait," I said, "until you had a larger house ?"

" Then where would my kingdom be ?" he answered, " Young men may wait, but old men must improve their time."

There came in now a troop of children of all ages. They had been playing in the lot, were miserably clad, barefooted, and some looked gaunt and hungry:—manners to match. "These," he said, with all a father's fondness— " these constitute my kingdom, and I am proud of them."

I felt thankful that I was not destined to be queen over such a kingdom, wished them good-bye, and with a sad heart, went home to my own darling little ones not knowing what might be *their* fate.

CHAPTER XIX.

BRIGHAM YOUNG AT HOME:—WE VISIT THE PROPHET AND
HIS WIVES.

SHORTLY after our arrival in Salt Lake City we visited
President Young, who received us very graciously and
appointed an early day for us to dine with him.

On that occasion he invited some of the Apostles and leading men to meet us at his table, and we passed an exceedingly
pleasant evening. The Prophet made himself very affable;
talked with us about our missionary life and other subjects of
personal and general interest ; and expressed a high opinion
of the energy and ability which my husband had displayed.
His wives, too,—who I found, as far as I could judge from
such a casual acquaintance, to be amiable and kind-hearted
ladies,—made every effort to render our visit agreeable.

I was much pleased with the manner and appearance of

Brigham Young, and felt greatly re-assured; for he did not seem to me like a man who would preach and practice such things as I had heard of him while I was in London. This I was glad to see, for it encouraged me to think that, perhaps, after all, matters might not be so bad as I had anticipated. We were, in fact, very kindly received in Salt Lake City by every one with whom we came in contact; for having been Missionaries for so many years, we were, of course, well known by name, and had a wide circle of acquaintances among the chief Elders and emigrants.

Fifteen years have, of course, worked a great change in the appearance of Brigham Young; but though he is now nearly seventy-three years of age, he is still a portly-looking—I might almost say handsome man. His good looks are not of the poetic or romantic kind at all; he is very common-place and practical in his appearance, but long and habitual exercise of despotic authority has stamped itself upon his features, and is seen even in the way he carries himself:—he might without any stretch of the imagination be mistaken for a retired sea-captain.

When I first knew him in appearance he was little over fifty years of age, was of medium height, well built, upright, and, as I just stated, with the air of one accustomed to be obeyed. His hair was light,—sandy, I suppose I ought to call it,—with eyes to match; and the expression of his countenance was pleasant and manly. I, of course, regarded him from a woman's stand-point; but there were others who were accustomed to study physiognomy, and they detected—or thought they detected—in the cold expression of his eye and the stern, hard lines of his lips, evidences of cruelty, selfishness, and dogged determination which, it is only fair to say, I myself never saw.

The lines on his face have deepened of late years, as what little of gentleness his heart ever knew has died out within him; but still he presents the appearance of a man who would afford a deep study to the observer of human nature. In early life he had to work hard for a living, and according to

Brigham Young

his own statement he had a rough time of it. He was, by trade, a painter and glazier, and has frequently said in public that in those times he was glad to work for "six bits" a day, and to keep his hands busy from morning to night to get even that. Whether or not the privations of early years fostered in him that avaricious and grasping spirit which of late years has been so conspicuous in him, I cannot say, but it is certain that it cropped out very early in his career as a Saint. An old Nauvoo Missionary,—a Mormon of the Mormons once, but now, alas! a "vile apostate" as Brigham would politely call him,—once told me that when the Prophet Joseph Smith sent the Apostle Young on Mission, a good deal of discontent was shown that the said Apostle did not account properly for the collections and tithings which passed through his hands. Brother Joseph who was *then* "the Church" suggested in a pleasant way—for the Prophet Smith was a big, jovial fellow, six feet two or three inches in height, and withal somewhat of a humorist—that the said Apostle Brigham would appear in his eyes a better Saint if he displayed a little less love for filthy lucre. Thereupon the Apostle, like somebody else who shall be nameless, quoted Scripture and reminded the Prophet that Moses had said "Thou shalt not muzzle the mouth of the ox that treadeth out the corn." "True, Brother Brigham," said Joseph, "but Moses did not say the ox was to eat up *all* the corn." Brother Brigham made no reply, but is said to have "sulked" for two or three days.

I have not the slightest doubt that, but for Mormonism, the Prophet would have remained all his life a journeyman painter, and his "sweetness," as the poet says, would have been wasted "on the desert air." But he was born just at the right time, and he fitted into the right groove; and thus, while, the original Prophet of the new faith—Joseph Smith—a man of ten times the intellect of his successor, a man ignorant and deluded, it is true, but, at the same time, a man in whom was the material for one of those natural giants who from age to age have left the impress of their individuality upon the history of the world;—while, I say, this man's name and doings

have ceased to interest any but persons of studious mind—
Brigham Young, whose narrow soul could never look beyond
the little circle in which he lived; whose selfishness and
heartlessness have been only equalled by his cruelty and
degrading avarice, has, by the force of circumstances alone,
obtained a place in the recognition of the world, to which by
nature or by grace he had not the shadow of a claim.

I have often heard intelligent Gentiles remark " Well, Brigham Young may be a wicked man and an impostor, but there
must be a great deal of talent in him, to manage those people
for so many years."

From this opinion I altogether dissent ; and those who
know Brigham best, think with me, though many of them
would not dare to say so. I do not think Brigham Young a
wicked man or an impostor in the sense in which those words
are ordinarily used ; and experience, and a careful study of his
life and doings, have convinced me that he is certainly not a
great man or a man of genius in *any* sense of the word.
There can be no doubt that he has been guilty of many and
great crimes, but I believe that in the early part of his career
he was so blinded by fanaticism that those crimes appeared to
him actually virtues :—the force of habit and the daily associations of his life have so completely taken from him all sense of
right and wrong ; while the devotion of his people has made
the idea that *he* could possibly do the slightest wrong so
utterly inconceivable to him and to them ; that his perceptions of justice, truth, honor, honesty, and upright dealing are
as utterly stultified as they ever were in the mind of the
wildest savage who prowled among the cliffs and cañons of
the Rocky Mountains.

People think that Brigham Young attained to his present
position by the exercise of ability, such as has been displayed,
only on a greater scale, by all those men, who, not being born
to power, nor having it thrust upon them, have by the force of
their genius seized it and held it—unlawfully it might be, but,
nevertheless, with talent and moral energy.

Nothing could be more untrue. The fact that he was of a

certain age at a certain time, and only that, was the cause of Brother Brigham's first step up the ladder of ambition. Joseph Smith endeavored, in organising his newly-invented religion, to make it resemble as much as was possible both the old and new dispensations of Christianity, and among other institutions he appointed "Twelve Apostles" who were to assist in governing the Church. He associated with himself his elder brother, Hyrum, and also Sidney Rigdon, who had so greatly assisted in every way to establish the new faith and define its principles. This Rigdon is the same who has always been suspected of the authorship of the Book of Mormon, though it must be admitted that nothing more than circumstantial evidence can be adduced in support of this statement. However that might be, the two Smiths, Joseph and Hyrum, and Sidney Rigdon formed what was called the "First Presidency" —in other words they were "the Church." Next in order to them came the "Twelve Apostles," and after them the "Seventies," and the other grades of the Priesthood, of which I shall say more presently. The "Twelve Apostles" were first appointed according to a plan of Joseph's own—Lyman Johnson was placed first, Brigham Young came next, and the others followed. Not long after, however, Joseph made a new arrangement, and placed the Twelve according to their age, and this plan was always followed subsequently. Thomas B. Marsh now stood first, and next to him came David Patten, and then Brigham Young.

I am obliged to give these little details, in order that the reader may understand Brigham's position after the death of Joseph Smith.

When Joseph was murdered in Carthage Jail, with his brother Hyrum, Sidney Rigdon alone remained of the First Presidency.

At that time Thomas B. Marsh, the first of the Apostles, had apostatised ; David Patten had been killed in a fight with the mob ; and, consequently, Brigham Young was now President of the Twelve—he being the next in age. Thus it will be seen that even had he been (which he was not) the most stupid and least fitted of all the Apostles to preside over the Church, his years would nevertheless have given him the leadership.

Up to this time there is no evidence that any idea of becoming head of the Church had ever entered into Brigham's mind.   Indeed it is reported that Joseph on one occasion, reproving him, said ironically that if ever the Church had the misfortune to be led by Brother Brigham, he would lead it to ——well, a place which is understood to be uncomfortably warm.   But Joseph was now dead, and Rigdon alone remained between the Apostle Young and the headship of the Church. Then it was that his eyes appear for the first time to have been fully opened to the advantages of his position.

Now when the ancients took the fox as an emblem of craftiness, it was because they had never known Brigham.   Brigham worked cautiously and prudently, for he probably is one of the greatest cowards in existence, both morally and physically, and like all cowards he was perfectly *au fait* in working in the dark.   In accomplishing the removal of Rigdon, Rigdon himself was Brigham's best assistant.   A man of prudence, or even of common sense, might have safely held his position against all the Brighams in the world, but prudence and common sense were qualities utterly unknown to Rigdon.   He began to have wonderful visions and revelations, announced the immediate ending of the world, and stated that he would forthwith lead out the armies of the Lord to the battle of Armageddon, in Palestine, and then return in triumph, calling by the way, as he said, " to pull the nose of little Vic. !" " Little Vic." was the English Queen—then a young woman —but how she incurred Rigdon's wrath, I do not know.   In addition to all this absurd nonsense, he ordained some of his particular friends to be prophets, priests, and kings, and otherwise showed that he intended to carry matters with a high hand.

Brigham watched his chance, and when he considered that matters were ripe for a change, by dint of secret manœuvering, he caused Rigdon to be tried before the " High Council " at Nauvoo. Rigdon sent word that he was sick, and could not come, but the trial went on, and of course it could have but one ending. The result was—as the Mormon papers at the time reported—that : " Elder Young arose and delivered Sidney Rigdon over to the buffetings of Satan, for a thousand years, in the name of the Lord ; and all the people said, Amen."

Poor Sidney ! He tried to set up a church for himself, and a good many people followed him, but the attempt was a failure. He is now a very old man, and cannot live long, but he still believes in the truth of Mormonism, as established by Joseph Smith.

Brigham's next step was to declare that the government of the Church was now vested in the Twelve, of whom he was the head. Later still he contrived, by selecting a time when nearly all of the Apostles would be promoted or in some way gratified by a change in the organisation of the Church, to get himself elected President of the Church, in the place of Joseph, with the two Apostles next under him as his associates, under the name of " counsellors ;" and they together formed the First Presidency. Thus Brigham became in name, as well as in fact, the head of the Mormon Church.

Every year, Brother Brigham, in common with all the other officers of the Church, is duly re-elected ; I need hardly say that the re-election is a matter of course—an opposition candidate would stand but a poor chance of success.

Brigham Young is an uneducated man. For that, of course, he is not deserving of blame, but his opposition to education in others and to all that is intellectual and elevating does him little credit. Only a very few years ago he with his two " Counsellors,"—Heber C. Kimball and Jedediah M. Grant, who were both spoken of as model Saints,—held forth in the Tabernacle, in the most unmeasured language, against schools and scholastic acquirements of every description. They were all three untaught men, and like all persons of small mind who have not themselves received any education, they hated and affected to despise those who had. Thoughtful men, although they may never have enjoyed the advantages of literary culture, never fail to see the great power that it is, either for good or evil; and in most cases they try to secure for their children the blessing of which they themselves have been denied. But the Mormon leaders, while they ridiculed and affected to despise men of education, were shrewd enough to see that if schools were established and the children of the Saints permitted to attend them, the bonds of superstition would certainly be shaken and the fabric of Mormonism undermined. They, consequently, discouraged every attempt at self-improvement, and taught the people to aspire to nothing higher for their children than the rudiments of reading, writing, and arithmetic for the boys, and a knowledge of household, dairy, and farm work for the girls.

Before the "Reformation" a few young men anxious to improve their minds, organised what they called the "Literary and Musical Society." They gave pleasant social entertainments to their friends at which they gave recitations, read essays, poems, and other literary productions, varying the programme with selections of music. The authorities looked upon the whole proceeding with disfavor, and soon broke up the society. Not content with this, and in order to show their contempt, they humiliated the members in every possible way, even publicly pointing them out to ridicule, and appointing a good many of them to be doorkeepers in the Tabernacle. Brigham Young, who it is said, never in his life read a book, could not understand that they could find any pleasure in intellectual amusements, and accused them of pride, conceit, and even wickedness. Among the Church leaders it is even now common to speak of any one who has any literary acquirements as "having the big head," and being "next door to apostasy."

Recently greater efforts to obtain a good education for their children have been made by the more intelligent among the Saints, and the Gentiles in Utah have established some very excellent schools. A library and reading-room have also been opened, and the latter has been well attended by the young

men, both Mormons and Gentiles.   Brigham himself has with
his usual inconsistency even gone so far as to give to his own
children those advantages which he selfishly denied to his
poorer brethren.

Of the Prophet's moral character, the less said the better.
He has been remorseless and cruel in his enmities, and he has
connived at and even suggested, if nothing more, some of the
most atrocious crimes that have ever been perpetrated on the
face of the earth.   In business matters, in the payment of
money—to use a popular phrase—his word is as good as his
bond, but in the accumulation of wealth he has evinced an
amount of dishonesty which can scarcely be credited.   Brigham always meets his obligations, and pays his debts, and gets
a lawful receipt :—the prophetic business could not otherwise
be carried on; but the way in which he has obtained his
wealth would put to the blush the most dishonest member of
any "ring" in New York, or elsewhere.   When he attended
his first Conference, he says he had to borrow certain masculine garments and a pair of boots before he could put in
an appearance.   Now it would be difficult to estimate the
value of his property.   He has taken up large tracts of land
all over the Territory, he has the uncontrolled and unquestioned command of all the tithing and contributions of the
Saints, and from gifts and confiscations, and innumerable other
sources, his revenue pours in.   It was once rumored that he
had eighteen or twenty millions of dollars in the Bank of England; but Brigham said that the report was not true.   "The
Church," he added, had a little money invested abroad.   The
difference between "The Church" and the individual Brigham
Young has yet to be determined.

In the year 1852 the "Prophet of the Lord" found that he
had borrowed an inconveniently large sum from the funds of
the Church.   He is "Trustee in Trust" and, of course, legally
responsible; but he never renders an account of his steward-
ship, and no one ever asks him for it.   His sense of honesty
was, however, so strong that he resolved to have his account
balanced, and he went down to the Tithing-Office for that

17

purpose. There he found that his indebtedness amounted to two hundred thousand dollars, and he proceeded to pay it after his own fashion:—the clerk was instructed to place to his credit the same amount "*for services rendered.*" In 1867, he owed *very nearly one million dollars*, which he had borrowed from the same fund, and he balanced his account in the same way. His contract for the Pacific Railroad is said to have yielded him a quarter of a million, and his other contracts and mining speculations, purchases *and thefts* of lands, houses, &c., have been very profitable. The expenses of such a family as Brother Brigham's must be something enormous, but the contributions which by honest and dishonest means he has levied have been so large that he must still be one of the wealthiest men in the States.

Brigham is not a generous man. He has given occasionally, as for instance at the time of the Chicago fire, when he presented a thousand dollars for the sufferers, but even then his motive was evident—the affairs of "Deseret" were under discussion in Congress. Without the certainty of a profitable return, Brigham never gave a cent. The story of his sordid avarice and his contemptible meanness in the accumulation of money would fill a volume.

Morally and physically the Prophet is a great coward. When he and other Church leaders were arrested a year or two ago, charged with the very gravest crimes, the effect upon the Prophet was most distressing. He had solemnly sworn in the Tabernacle that he would shoot the man who attempted to arrest him; but when Judge McKean opened court and placed him under arrest he swallowed his threats and played the coward's part. Before this the world has seen wretches who were notorious for their cruelty and tyranny, and who were also remarkable for their cowardice. For many years he has imitated royalty and has had a strong body-guard to keep watch and ward around his person every night. No man has less cause to apprehend personal violence than Brother Brigham, but the voice of conscience, which, as the poet says, makes cowards of us all, suggests his fears.

No one, probably, ever possessed and lost greater opportunities of doing good and leaving behind him an enviable record than Brother Brigham. In him the Saints, from the smallest to the greatest, placed implicit trust, and it was in his power to mould them at his will. The spiritual and temporal welfare of the people was in his hands. The ability to elevate them socially, mentally, and morally was his. A great trust was committed to his charge. But he has basely betrayed that sacred trust, and has not only left undone what he should have performed, but he has been guilty of the most grievous wrong-doing. He has set at nought all morality with his horrible and debasing teachings respecting a "blood-atonement"—in other words, the *duty* of assassination. He has outraged decency and riven asunder the most sacred social and domestic ties by his shameless introduction of Polygamy. He has sacrilegiously defiled the temple of God, by teaching his followers to worship Adam as their divinity, and has robbed Christ of his birthright by proclaiming that men are the only saviours of their wives and that in respect to women the sacrifice of our Lord was of no direct avail. In a word—both by his preaching and his practice he has set an example so bad as to be utterly without parallel in this civilised age. Kings and emperors there are who hold in slavery the persons of men : hierarchs there are who hold in bondage the souls of the deluded. But the despot meddles not with the eternal welfare of his subject, nor does he pollute the sacred precincts of the hearth and home ; and the false priest is not permitted to meddle with temporal affairs. But the Mormon despot—Brigham Young—has played the tyrant in both spiritual and worldly matters,—has meddled with the person, the property, and the lives and the liberty of his dupes ; and has at the same time debased and enslaved their souls.

But let it not be supposed that I write this hastily, or without due consideration. People outside of Utah may be deceived, as indeed they frequently are, by representations made in ignorance of what Mormonism and the Prophet really are.   But the Gentiles long resident in Utah, the Apostates, and even the Mormon people themselves, if only they would tell the truth, could testify to the truthfulness of the picture which I have drawn of Brother Brigham.

A better people—aside from their religion—than the believing Mormons when they emigrated to Utah, it would be difficult to find.   Their fault was in their faith.   They were honest, sober, industrious, and ready to sacrifice everything to what they considered religious duty.   I cannot think of them and of the implicit confidence which they placed in Brigham, without wondering at his folly in throwing away the noble opportunity, which was once within his grasp, of establishing a happy and contented people.   Instead of this he has gathered wealth to himself and family ; out of the poverty of his followers he has amassed enormous riches, and with the power to leave behind him a name as one of the benefactors of the human race, he has set the worst example which despot or false prophet ever presented to the world.

CHAPTER XX.

THE wives of Brigham Young have always been subjects of interest to Gentiles who visited Zion; and having spoken of their husband, I think it is only fair that I should say a few words about them.

For many years I have known personally all the Prophet's wives who reside in Salt Lake City, and I wish to speak of them with kindness and respect. They are women whom any one would esteem—conscientious, good, earnest women ; faithful, true-hearted wives, who have devoted their lives to the carrying out of what they believe is the revealed will of God.

When I first knew Brother Brigham, poor man, he had *only* sixteen living with him in Salt Lake City; and even now he has no more than nineteen! Perhaps I ought to say eighteen, since Eliza-Ann has run away from him and left the poor old gentleman desolate and forlorn. The three whom he took after I came to Utah, were Amelia Folsom, Mary Van Cott Cobb, and Eliza-Ann. But the reader will perhaps be interested in hearing about them all, and so I will state the names and order of the ladies as they at present stand—according to the date of their marriage; making mention of the proxy wives last of all, for the sake of convenience and without reference to date. Of course Brother Brigham has *had* many more than nineteen wives, but the following are the living ladies: others are dead or have strayed away, no one knew whither, and perhaps, as Brother Heber once said to me, nobody cared.

Allow me to introduce the Mrs. Young.

MRS. MARY ANN ANGELL YOUNG.
[Number One.]

First in order is Mrs. Mary Ann Angell Young, but she is not the first wife that Brother Brigham ever had. Once upon a time, Brother Brigham was a Methodist; but after listening to the preaching of the Mormon Missionaries he became a vile apostate—as he loves to call those who leave his present faith—and he forsook Methodism. In those days, before he apostatised, and long before he ever dreamed of Polygamy, he had but *one* wife—one only! It must seem strange to the Prophet to look back to that period of solitary existence. His second wife was Mrs. Angell Young; and I call her his first wife because she is the first of those living now. As she was married to him after the death of his first wife, she is, of course, his legal wife, and would be recognised as such in any civilised country. She is a very fine-looking old lady and very much devoted to her unfaithful lord and master, firmly believing in his divine mission. She lives by herself and is seldom troubled with a visit from her affectionate spouse.

Once in a while Brigham brings her out to a party when he has invited any Gentiles, just for appearance sake. Quite a number of persons in Utah believe that she is dead, so very little is seen and known of her. She lives in the White House—Brigham's first residence in Salt Lake City—and is much thought of by those who do know her. Her children are greatly attached to her, and show her a great deal of attention, making up in this way, to a certain extent, for her husband's neglect ; her three sons, Joseph A., Brigham—who it is expected will succeed his father as President of the Church—and John W., as well as her two daughters, Alice and Luna, are all in Polygamy. Each of the sons has three wives ; and each of the daughters has a half-sister as a partner in her husband's affections. Brigham has not the slightest objection to giving two of his daughters to the same husband.

LUCY DECKER SEELY YOUNG.
[Number Two.]

Lucy Decker Seely Young was his first wife in Polygamy. Her former husband was a Mr. Seely. She is short and stout, a very excellent mother and a devoted wife. Her son, Brigham Heber, is now one of the cadets at West Point. The sending of this young man to West Point to be educated, when it was noticed in the public papers, excited some little interest, and the faith of many of the good Mormons was very much shaken by it. They had believed that Brigham really meant what he taught when he told the people not to allow their children to associate with the Gentiles, as it would cause them to lose "the spirit." But they were still further shocked when they learned that several other sons of Brigham were to go to the Eastern States to be educated. They have yet to learn that the Prophet does not intend them to do as he does but rather as he tells them. My own opinion is that Brother Brigham has advocated one course of conduct for the people while he pursued another himself.

CLARA DECKER YOUNG.
[Number Three.]

Clara Decker Young is the third wife. She is a sister of Lucy Seely, and like her is short and stout, but otherwise good-looking. She is more than twenty years younger than her lord, with whom she was once quite a favorite, but like many others, she has " had her day "—to use Brigham's own expression—and is now, as a matter of course, neglected.

HARRIET COOK YOUNG.
[Number Four.]

' Harriet Cook Young, is tall, with light hair and blue eyes, and is an intelligent but not at all a refined woman. She is said to have given a great deal of trouble to Brother Brigham, of whom she has frequently said very hard things. In times past she had the reputation of being a good deal more than a match for her husband when she had any cause of offence against him, but in her quiet moments she is a very sincere Mormon. She has only one son—Oscar Young—now about twenty-five years of age. When he was born, Brigham kindly announced to her that because she was not obedient she should have no more children, and during more than a quarter of a century he has kept his word. Why she has remained with him so long is a mystery, for she makes no secret of her feelings towards him.

LUCY BIGELOW YOUNG.
[Number Five.]

Lucy Bigelow Young is quite a fine-looking woman—tall and fair, and still quite young. She has three pretty daughters. Brigham has recently sent her to live in southern Utah.

MRS. TWISS YOUNG.
[Number Six.]

Mrs. Twiss Young has no children, but she is a very good housewife, and Brigham appreciates her accordingly, and has given her the position of housekeeper in the Lion House. Women have two great privileges in the Mormon Church— they may ask a man to marry them, if they chance to fancy him, and if they don't like him afterwards they are able to obtain a divorce for the moderate sum of ten dollars, which sum the husband is expected to pay. Mrs. Twiss exercised the first privilege in reference to Brother Brigham, but has not yet availed herself of the last. There are other ladies who thought it would be a great honor to be called the wives of the Prophet, and they have requested him to allow them to be called by his name. This he has done, but he has never troubled them with his society.

MARTHA BOWKER YOUNG.
[Number Seven.]

Martha Bowker Young is a quiet little body, with piercing dark eyes, and very retiring. ' Brother Brigham acts towards her as if he had quite forgotten that he had ever married her, and she lives in all the loneliness of married spinster-hood.

HARRIET BARNEY SEAGERS YOUNG.
[Number Eight.]

Harriet Barney Seagers Young, the eighth wife, is a tall, fine-looking woman. She was another man's wife when Brigham made love to her. It is not supposed to be the correct thing for a Saint to court his neighbor's wife, but the Prophet did so in the case of Harriet Barney, and in several other cases too. Harriet was married to a respectable young Mormon gentleman, but after she had lived with him some time and had borne three children to him, the Prophet persuaded her to join his ranks, and she did so, believing that the word of the Prophet was the revelation of the Lord to her, but she has since had bitter cause to repent of her folly. To a Gentile mind such an infatuation must appear very strange, but the Mormon people personally understand the powerful influence which their religion exercises over them, and to them there is nothing very singular in all this.

ELIZA BURGESS YOUNG.
[Number Nine.]

Eliza Burgess Young is the only English wife that Brigham has. She fell in love with the Prophet, wanted him to marry her, and even offered to wait, like Jacob, for seven years if she might be his at last. So she served in the family of her lord for the appointed time, and he finally took her to wife as a recompense for her faithfulness. She has added one son to the Prophet's kingdom.

SUSAN SNIVELY YOUNG.
[Number Ten.]

The tenth wife on my list is Susan Snively Young. She is a German woman—smart, active, and industrious. She has no children, but has been quite a help-meet to her husband in making butter and cheese, in which she excels. Smart Mormons have always had an eye to business, and while living up to their privileges have not invariably sought for wives who were only fair and pleasant to look upon, but have frequently taken them for their own intrinsic worth:—one as a good dairymaid, another as a good cook, a third as a good laundress, and a fourth as a lady to grace the parlor—perhaps even two or three of this last kind, if the Saint were wealthy. There is a good deal of practical wisdom in this. Brother Brigham has gathered of all sorts into his net, and has then sorted them out, placing each lady in the place where he considered she would be most useful and profitable to himself.

MARGARET PIERCE YOUNG.
[Number Eleven.]

Margaret Pierce Young is very lady-like, tall, and genteel. She has the appearance of being very unhappy, and it is certain that she has been very much neglected, but not more so than many of the other wives. She has one son.

EMMELINE FREE YOUNG.
[Number Twelve.]

When first I went to Utah, Emmeline Free Young was the reigning favorite, and she was really the handsomest of Brigham's wives—tall and graceful, with curling hair, beautiful eyes, and fair complexion. Brigham was as fond of her, at the time, as a man of his nature, with such a low estimate of woman, could be. But a younger, though not a handsomer, rival soon captivated his fickle heart, and he left poor Emmeline to mourn in sorrow. She has never been herself since then, and probably never will be—she is a broken-hearted woman. She is the mother of quite a numerous family, and doubtless, as she had been the favorite for so long a time, she had come to believe that her husband would never seek another love. But, if this was so, she sadly miscalculated Brigham, for when his licentious fancy was attracted to another object of affection he cast off Emmeline as ruthlessly as he would an old garment. What decent person could refrain from loathing such a man ! How often has my heart gone out in sympathy towards that poor, wrecked woman whom he had forsaken ; what a pity I deemed it that so much love should be wasted upon a creature who could never understand or appreciate it. And yet Emmeline's fate has been no worse than that of the others ; but I was more with her, and saw how keenly she suffered, and I sympathised with her when her sorrows brought her nearly to the point of death.

AMELIA FOLSOM YOUNG.
[Number Thirteen.]

Amelia Folsom Young is now the favorite, and it is supposed that she will continue to be so, for at last poor Brother Brigham has found a woman of whom he stands in dread. It is doubtful whether he loves her, but nobody in Zion doubts that he fears her. It is said that the Prophet has confided so many of his secrets to Amelia that he is obliged to submit to her tyranny, for fear of her leaving him, and exposing some of his little ways which would not bear the light. Be that as it may, it is generally believed that after all his matrimonial alliances he has at last found his *master* in the person of Amelia. Even good Saints—friends of the Prophet—secretly enjoy the idea of him being at last brought under petticoat government, for it is believed that Brigham used unfair means to obtain her, and that at last he only gained his object by deluding her into the belief that the Lord had revealed to him that it was her duty to become his wife. One thing is very certain—he was as crazy over her as a silly boy over his first love, much to the disgust of his more sober brethren who felt rather ashamed of the folly of their leader. At the theatre a seat was reserved for her at his side, and in the ball-room the same special attention was shown to her. He would open the ball, and, after dancing with each of his other wives who might be present—simply for appearance sake—the remainder of the evening was devoted to her. For all that, his inconstant heart could not remain faithful to her, and old habits and feelings, to all appearance, have come over him again, and he has gone astray.

Julia Dean, the actress, was the first to draw him from Amelia's side, and it would have been a sorry day for Amelia if Julia had favored the Prophet's suit. Then the charms of Mary Van Cott touched his sensitive heart, to say nothing of Eliza-Ann, his last but yet not his best-beloved.

With all this experience, and the constant evidences of the fickleness of Brother Brigham's heart before her eyes, there is no wonder that poor Amelia feels compelled to hold tight the reins, now that they are in her own hands, for, if it is not much to be known as Brigham's wife, it is a great deal to be known as his favorite. As for the future—it is whispered that Brother Brigham has lately been "setting his house in order," and in the ordinary course of nature, Amelia is almost certain to outlive for many years her aged lord, she therefore can afford to wait for the good time coming. But Amelia knows that she would sink into oblivion if he were to cast her off for another before his death.

AMELIA FOLSOM YOUNG, "ELIZA ANN,"

BRIGHAMS FAVORITE WIFE.

BRIGHAMS NINETEENTH WIFE.

MISS ELIZA R. SNOW

MRS. JOHN W. YOUNG

BROTHER BRIGHAMS LAST BABY.

MORMON POETESS AND HIGH PRIESTESS

WIFE OF BRIGHAMS APOSTATE SON

THE LADIES' SIDE OF MORMONISM.

MARY VAN COTT COBB YOUNG.
[Number Fourteen.]

Mary Van Cott Cobb—who became Brigham's wife after his marriage to Amelia—is a very handsome woman, about twenty-eight years of age. She is tall, slender, and graceful, and h.-s been married to the Prophet about six years. At first he appeared to be very devoted to her, but Amelia soon put a stop to that. Nevertheless, she has since her marriage presented a little daughter to her lord, greatly to the annoyance of Amelia, who has no children, and who is reported to have said some naughty things about the matter, which was very wrong of her, for Mary Van Cott is known by every one to be beyond reproach or suspicion. She is said to be very unhappy, and though Brigham has provided her with a fine house and every comfort, yet she seldom sees him—not perhaps more than once in three months, or so—though it is generally believed that his spirit is willing, but Amelia won't allow it.

ELIZA-ANN WEBB DEE YOUNG.
[Number Fifteen.]

Eliza-Ann Webb Dee Young, whose separation from Brigham Young has attracted so much public attention has told her own story in her own words which, as it forms an interesting page in the biography of the Prophet, I shall now present, exactly as it was written, to the reader :

I was living on my father's farm in Little Cottonwood, when, in the summer of 1867, Brigham Young informed my father that he wanted me for a wife. Brigham, with a number of the Apostles and Elders from this city, was visiting Cottonwood on a Sunday and held two meetings for preaching. It was at the close of the forenoon service on that occasion that he walked up to me and said "Had I not better accompany you home." I said, "Certainly, if you wish to." On the way to my father's house Brigham asked me if I had had any proposals of marriage since I had obtained a divorce from my first husband. I answered him, "Yes, that I had had several proposals." He then asked if there was any one of them that I wished to accept. I said, "No," on which he said that he would like to give me a little advice. He advised me not to wait to marry a person whom I loved, but to marry some good man whom I could respect and look up to and receive good counsel from.

I thanked him for his counsel, and as my home was so near to the place of meeting, the conversation abruptly terminated. I thought nothing further of it. His brother Joseph and George Q. Cannon joined us at the dinner table, and while there Brigham and the others remarked how youthful I had grown since I had got out of my former troubles. As I had much improved in every way I did not regard his observations as any intended compliment or any indication of what afterwards I learned to be passing in his mind.

At the close of the afternoon service he went up to my father, took him aside and talked for at least two hours to him about me, and told him how that he had watched me from my infancy, saw me grow up to womanhood, had always loved me and intended to marry me, but having taken Amelia just after the law was passed in Congress prohibiting polygamy, he feared to take another wife soon after, lest it should make trouble, or he would have taken me then. My marriage with a young man was unlooked-for to him, and when he was made acquainted with it he did not just like to stop it, he said, and so he let it go on, but always hoped that the time would come when he would have me.

He wanted father and mother to use all their influence with me, as it would be the best thing I could do. He asked father if a good house, well furnished, and $1,000 a year pocket money would be enough for me, and added that if it was not enough I should have more. Father answered that he thought it would be sufficient.

Brigham stood two hours or more with father and kept the whole of the carriages that conveyed the party standing waiting till after sundown, and little did I think that I was "the object of interest."

When father came home he told mother by herself ; then they told me. I cannot describe my feelings ; I was frightened. The thought of it was a perfect horror. I thought father had gone crazy, and I would not believe his statement for hours. When I realised that it was a fact I could do nothing but cry.

The idea of an old man, sixty-seven years of age, the husband of about twenty wives living, asking me, at twenty-two, to be added to the number filled me with the utmost abhorrence, and when I saw that my parents were under his influence and sustained his proposition, I was ready to die in despair. Oh ! the horrible hours that I spent in crying and moaning, no tongue can picture.

When father saw that I took it so badly he told me that I would not be forced into it, but if I could bring my feelings to it and accept Brigham it would be pleasing to him, and mother favored it in the same way.

About a month after this I was in the city with an intimate lady friend, and as we were walking near to Brigham's house he came to the gate and waited for our arrival. When I saw him I thought that I would get up courage to tell him that I would not marry him, but I could not say it. That peculiar influence that he throws over everybody when he has a purpose to effect completely overcame me. He did not allude to the subject at all. I shook hands and passed on.

He became very kind to my parents, and saw father frequently. He sent for me to come to the city on several occasions and met me at my father's city residence, and talked to me about marriage ; told me how pure his feelings were, and that his only motive was to do me good, save me in the kingdom and make me a queen. All that had no effect upon me; it only disgusted me the more, and the fear that I dared not resist him never left me. This continued for nearly a year. My eldest brother had had some business transactions with Brigham and one of his sons, which resulted in trouble and ultimately in financial injury to my brother. Brigham had been very angry with him and threatened to cut him off from the Church. I heard of those threats, and believing at that time in Mormonism, I heard them with deep sorrow, and confess that, in hopes of turning Brigham's anger away from my brother, I began to entertain the thought that I would yield to his request. I argued as many inexperienced persons do, that as I had had a sorrowful life and my heart was crushed, my future life was nothing, and if I could sacrifice myself for my brother's interest and please my parents, I would at last submit.

Finally, Brigham named the marriage day and informed me, through my father, that what I required in preparation for my marriage he would furnish ; but I would accept nothing. A day before my marriage he brought me three dress patterns—one silk and two merino—and handed to me a purse with a $50 bill.

On the —— April, 1868, I was married to him in the Endowment House by Heber C. Kimball, his First Counsellor. My father and mother were present, with others. Brigham's brother Joseph also took to himself a wife at the same time. After the ceremony I walked over with him to the conference, and in the evening I returned to my father's house and remained there for a month.

For the first few months I had considerable of his attention ; his visits were frequent ; after that his business cares so occupied him, he said, that he could only call about once in three months. After that he came " just as it happened."

When I was married he wanted my mother to live with me in the city, and a year from the marriage he sent us to take charge of his farm, where we remained till last August, and I removed again into the city. While I was at the farm he came very seldom to see me, and oftentimes while he would visit and look round at the farm he never came into the house. I had caused him no trouble ; indeed, he had said I was the best wife he had, for I had never given him a cross word or look. But for that good temper I take no credit, for my silence was all through fear. I never loved him and never said to him that I loved him. I looked upon him as a heartless despot.

From the very beginning of my married association with Brigham Young his manner of providing for me was of the meanest character. I had to come up, even from the farm, four miles distant, to the commissary of his family, and was glad when I could get five pounds of sugar, one-quarter of a pound of tea, a bar of soap and a pound of candles. That I would get about once a month. About a year ago I complained to him that I had not sugar enough and he allowed me what I required.

When I returned to the city he furnished me a house in a very ordinary way and I continued to live in the best manner I could. But it was the same stingy way. When a beef was killed I got some fresh meat ; but I was frequently months without seeing it.

Tired with this manner of existence, I asked his permission to keep boarders, with the view of aiding myself and procuring for one of my sons a musical instrument, as he was passionately fond of music. The permission was granted, and I kept boarders from last March. My house was small, and the business was not very lucrative. I consequently went to him, six weeks ago, and asked him to aid me—to give me some assistance to make life tolerable. He seemed angry, and complained that he had so many expenses and that he wanted me to keep myself—to take the money that I had saved to buy an organ for my son and keep myself and family with it. I got a stove out of him, but that was all. During the last year I only obtained from him two calico dresses. This interview made me sick and I was in bed for a week, with heart sickness. One of the boarders—who was a lawyer—and his wife, asked what ailed me, and I told the story of my troubles and inquired if there was no redress. He said that he thought that there was and he would consult with other lawyers and see what could be done. During all my sickness, while I was his wife, he showed the utmost indifference. He would hear what I had to say, but make almost no answer. Last fall I was attacked with pleurisy, and I managed to get to his office to see him to tell him how ill I was and that I needed some few things. He appeared to comprehend something and finally called "John," the commissary for the family, and told him to get me two bits worth of fresh meat. He has not been inside my house for nearly a year.

While I was feeling bad I read Mrs. Stenhouse's book, and that showed me things in a clearer light than I had seen them before.

I knew every word was true from my own sad experience, and it encouraged me to leave the hateful polygamic life, and I am glad that I have done it.

About five weeks ago I got very weak. I don't know what was the matter with me—probably general debility from grief and mental suffering. My boarders, seeing my condition, aided me freely and were very kind to me.

I resolved to leave his house, packed up my clothes and instructed an auctioneer two weeks ago to take away the furniture and sell it, as a part of it was my own, and I thought I was entitled to the rest. The suit commenced has been instituted by my attorneys, who have every confidence that I can obtain alimony ; but whether I do or not I think the world should know Brigham Young as he is, and my story is a page of his biography.

This is the story of Eliza-Ann—told in her own words. She is the only wife whom Brigham has not supported ; but she has been allowed to keep Gentile boarders. I suppose Brother Young had *some* reason when he made this exception.

"MISS" ELIZA R. SNOW.

[Number Sixteen.]

"Miss" Eliza R. Snow I mention here as I have not followed the order of date. She and the three ladies, whose names I shall presently give, are the proxy wives of Brigham, living with him. Eliza-Ann, who has become notorious of

late, is popularly known as his *nineteenth* wife. She *is* his
nineteenth living wife and the last-wedded, according to date;
but, if the deceased wives were taken into consideration, she
might perhaps be about the thirtieth. In this list I have put
all the living wives who are sealed to Brigham "for eternity,"
first; and thus I count Eliza-Ann number fifteen; but had I
placed the proxy wives,—who are only Brigham's "for time,"
in the list, she would, of course, be the nineteenth. The
newspapers which have written her into notoriety know nothing of "proxy" and "spiritual" wives. All are alike to them.
Eliza Roxy Snow, is always spoken of among the Saints as
Miss Eliza R. Snow. I have already mentioned her, and need
therefore only add that Eliza is the high-priestess and poet-
general of the Church; she is highly thought of by the Saints,
and the year before last was one of a company of Mormon
missionaries who visited the Holy Land, for the purpose of
consecrating it to the Lord. Last summer she travelled
through the settlements in Utah, urging the women to enter
into the "Celestial Order." She is only a proxy wife to Brigham, and will belong to Joseph Smith in the resurrection.

ZINA D. HUNTINGTON JACOBS YOUNG.
[Number Seventeen.]

Zina D. Huntington Jacobs Young is another proxy wife,
and a widow of the Prophet Joseph. She, too, will have to be
handed over in the day of reckoning. She has one grown up
daughter, of whom I shall presently speak under rather interesting circumstances.

EMILY PARTRIDGE YOUNG.
[Number Eighteen.]

Emily Partridge Young is a tall, dark-eyed, handsome
woman, and she also is a "proxy" wife—a relict of Joseph.
When Joseph died, Brigham told his wives that they were at
liberty to choose whom they would for husbands; and some
of them showed their appreciation of his generosity by choosing him himself. Thus it was that Emily Partridge became

18

Brigham's wife. The Prophet has dealt kindly to his brother Joséph Smith, through her, for she has quite a family of children to be handed over with her. She was young and handsome when the Prophet died, but perhaps it would be wrong to suppose that that had anything to do with Brigham's generosity to his brother, for it is generally believed that he took all those wives of Joseph, from pure principle.

AUGUSTA COBB YOUNG.
[Number Nineteen.]

Augusta Cobb Young is a very fine-looking woman and must have been quite handsome in her youthful days. As I before stated, she formerly. lived in Boston, but hearing Brigham preach, she fell in love with him, abandoned her home, children, and husband, and, taking her youngest child with her, went to Salt Lake City, and was married to the Prophet. It was she who, when Brigham began to neglect her, wanted to be sealed to Christ, but was ultimately added to the kingdom of Joseph Smith.

Now these are the Prophet's wives—his real, living wives— nineteen in all. How many spiritual wives he has had it would be impossible to say. Probably he himself does not know their number. Lately, I believe, he has been making his will, and, if so, I suppose he has "taken count of all." He has besides in various parts of Utah many other wives, who are all more or less provided for, but they arè of little account, and he seldom or never sees them. The nineteen whom I have named form his family at home, as I may say—are all under his own roof, or at least they live in Salt Lake City, and are known to every one as his wives. The number of his children it would be very difficult to estimate. I can count up by name between forty and fifty, and I think the Prophet's *living* children are rather under the latter figure. His family has however been much diminished by death, though since I went to Utah this has not been the case so much as I believe it was formerly. One Mormon writer—a very reliable and trustworthy man—says that the children that the Prophet has

lost would fill a fair-sized graveyard.   This very probably may
be true, as in the early days of the settlement in Utah, privation and the lack of proper medical attendance must have
constantly proved fatal to the young children of the Saints.
But it was before my time, and therefore I cannot speak from
personal experience.

A Mormon gentleman one day told me a very funny story
in reference to the Prophet and his little family.   He said that
he had just had occasion to call in at a store in Main street, to
make some purchases, when Brigham himself came in and
entered into conversation with him.   A smart-looking, clever
little boy entered the store a few minutes after and handed a
note to the proprietor.   Brother Brigham seemed to be greatly
interested in the child, and asked him several questions in a
playful way.   Turning at length to my informant he said:
" That's a nice boy, Brother ———.   Whose child is it?"   This
was a very awkward question, for the gentleman was aware
that the child was one of Brigham's own.   He did not like to
tell him so, so he replied indirectly, " He's one of Mrs. . . . . .
Young's children, President."   The Prophet looked somewhat
amused, but did not utter a word in reply.

I give this story only for what it is worth and no more.
The gentleman who told it doubtless expected to be believed ;
but knowing the Prophet and his family, as I do, I consider
the statement exaggerated, to say the least.   It is a heavy
responsibility to have five and forty children—most of them
girls, too—without being accused of forgetting their person-
ality altogether.

In his habits and mode of living, Brigham Young is very
simple, or at least was so until recently.   When I first knew
him he dressed in plain, homespun, homemade, and every
article about his person and his houses, was as plain and
unostentatious as could possibly be.   But the importation of
Gentiles and Gentile goods, since the opening of the railway,
has worked a great change.   His wives who once carried simplicity of dress almost to the verge of dowdyism, have now
acquired a taste for Eastern fashions, and I think if Brigham

were a younger man and were likely to live another ten years he would find that wives were more expensive luxuries now than they were in the era of "dug-outs" and sun-bonnets.

The Prophet's first home in Utah was a little cottage which is now known as the White House.—The same house, I believe, which was valued at sixty thousand dollars, and which Brother Tenant supposed he bought:—a more scandalous and barefaced robbery never was perpetrated.

This on the hill-side, north of the Eagle Gate, and is now the residence of his first wife, Mrs. Angell Young. The Bee-Hive House is the official residence of Brother Brigham. There he used to reign supreme as "Governor" Young; and thence he now issues secular and ecclesiastical edicts to all who acknowledge his sway. There is one lady resident in this house—Mrs. Lucy Decker Young—and no one else is permitted to intrude upon its privacy. Here the prophet has his own private bedroom, and here he breakfasts when he has been at home over night.

The Lion House is what ought to be the home of the Prophet, for here nearly all his wives reside. He has, however, many other houses in the city. On the basement floor, the dining-room, kitchen, pantry, and other general offices. The first floor is divided by a long passage with doors on each side. On the right hand, about half a dozen wives with small families find accommodation. On the left, at the entrance, is the parlor, and the other rooms on that side are occupied by mothers with larger families, and ladies who have a little more than ordinary attention. The upper floor is divided into twenty square bedrooms.

There is no extravagance in the furniture or apparel of these wives, but they are comfortable and are kept neat and clean. Again and again, the Prophet has declared that the ten-dollar fees which are obtained from the divorces provide his wives with pin-money. I do not believe a word of this, as the amount thus obtained is far more than the avaricious soul of the Prophet would allow to pass out of his hands for feminine vanities. But I know of another source of income which is open to the wives. They are allowed all the fruit—peaches especially—which they or their children, can gather or dry. This, in fact, is pretty nearly their only "pin-money:" their "lord" is not a generous man, and they have to make the most of trifles.

The Prophet usually dines in the Lion House at three in the afternoon. Mrs. Twiss Young, as I mentioned before, acts the part of housekeeper, and she acts it well. At three punctually the bell rings and the mothers with their children move down to the dining room. They are all seated at a very long table which is lengthened by turning round at the end of the room. Each mother has her children around her. Brigham sits at the head of the table, with his favorite—when at home—*vis-a-vis*, or on his left, and if a visitor is present he sits at the Prophet's right hand. The repast is frugal but ample, for Brigham is a sober and exceedingly economical man. This is the first time he sees his family. In the evening at seven o'clock the bell again rings, and the mothers and the children again fill the sides and end of the parlor. When they are all seated, the patriarch enters, takes his seat at the table and chats quietly with those who chance to go in with him to prayers. When all the members of the family are assembled, the door is closed. All kneel down and the Prophet prays, invoking special blessings upon Zion and "the kingdom." This is the last that his family see of him for the day, unless they have occasion to seek him privately.

With his family Brother Brigham is said to be kind ; but it is supposed to be more the awe which his position as Prophet inspires, than the love which they bear him as a man which renders him successful in managing them. At the same time, that sweet familiarity is destroyed which should exist between husband and wife, father and children. With such a number of wives, he cannot possibly wait upon them in visiting, and in the ball-room, and other places of amusement. With the exception of his reigning favorite, whoever for the time she may happen to be, no one expects his attentions. At 'the theatre a full number of seats are reserved, and his wives attend, or remain at home, as they please. They sit in the body of the parquètte, among the rest of the people; but one of the two proscenium boxes is reserved for him, and beside him is a chair for the favorite Amelia.

When he goes to the ball, the same special attention is shown. He dances first with the favorite, and, if half a dozen more of his wives have accompanied them, he will dance with each of them once in the course of the evening; but with the favorite he dances as frequently as any youth in the ball-room with his first maiden love. The Apostles and leading men of the community, who dance attendance on him and desire his favor, are sure to seek the pleasure of her hand and place her in the same cotillion with Brigham, who is thus able all the evening to enjoy her company.

Some of the Apostles and Elders look with pain upon this boyishness of the Prophet, and deplore it. Many of them are attached to their first wives, and have shown them consideration and attention which has not always pleased Brother Brigham. I have heard more than one of them express a wish that the Prophet had been a little more attentive to his own first wife. It is only fair to Amelia—the reigning favorite—to state that she has always been kind and respectful to Mrs. Angell Young.

Up to within the last few years the community heard nothing of the Prophet's family but what was strictly decorous and creditable. If there was any wrong-doing it must have been very effectually hidden from the knowledge of outside observers. His wives are kind and faithful mothers, seeking to live their religion and ambitious to increase the glory of their Lord. I know them all personally—some of them intimately; and, while I have heard from some, with heavy hearts, of their difficulties in bearing "*the* cross" which all Mormon women have to sustain, they have tried, I know, to be submissive, and I think it due to them that I should make this present recognition of their goodness of disposition and purity of soul.

CHAPTER XXI.

THE ORIGIN OF "THE REFORMATION":—EXTRAORDINARY DOINGS OF THE SAINTS.

FROM time to time, in the course of this narrative, I have had occasion to allude to a certain period of extraordinary fanatical excitement among the Saints in Utah,—a period which was there popularly termed "The Reformation;" and I think that a brief sketch of the terrible sayings and doings of that time, and the causes which led to them, may be interesting to the reader and may help to explain much which to a Gentile must otherwise be very obscure.

The popular idea of Mormonism is that the peculiar feature which distinguishes it from all other Christian sects is Polygamy. To a certain extent this is, of course, true; but it is only a partial statement of the truth. If Polygamy were to be relinquished, it would still be found that Mormonism had really very little in common with other sects, and very much that was completely antagonistic to them.

The confession of faith published by Joseph Smith during his life-time would certainly deceive an uninitiated person ; and it was in consequence of the ambiguity of that very document that so many unsuspecting persons were from the beginning of Mormonism led astray by the teachings of the Missionaries. The convert was told that the Mormon faith proclaimed the existence of one true God, but he was not told that Father Adam was that deity, and that He is "like a well-to-do farmer." He was told that Christ was the Son of God, but he was not taught that the Virgin Mary was "the lawful wife of God the Father," and that "He intended after the resurrection to take her again, as one of His own wives, to raise up immortal spirits in eternity. He was told of faith in a Saviour, he was not told that men were the only saviours of their wives, and that unless a woman pleased her husband and was obedient and was saved *by him*, she could not be saved at all. He was told that the Saints believed in the Holy Ghost, but he was not told that "The Holy Ghost is a man ; he is one of the sons of our Father and our God. . . You think our Father and our God is not a lively, sociable, and cheerful man ; He is one of the most lively men that ever lived!"

And yet, although such fearful and shocking blasphemy was, of course, hidden from the convert whom it was desirable to impress with the idea that Mormonism was only a development of Christianity, it was openly taught in the sermons in the Tabernacle before thousands of people, and inculcated in the writing of the highest authorities. The passages, which I have just quoted, were preached in public, were taken down in short-hand, were revised under the superintendence of Brigham Young or one of the chief leaders, were then printed, and published in Salt Lake City, and afterwards reprinted in another form.

The verbal repetition of such blasphemy as this would be simply painful and disgusting to any right-minded person. I shall therefore endeavor to give an idea of some of these outrageous doctrines without entering too closely into details. Should the reader, however, wish to search and see for himself, I refer him to the *Journals of Discourses*, the files of the Church papers, and the publications of the Mormon writers generally.

One of the first innovations upon the received faith of ordinary Christians was the doctrine of Polytheism. There can be no doubt that, even in Joseph's time, that doctrine was taught, although, as in the case of Polygamy, all knowledge of it was kept from every one but the initiated—the "strong men" who could be entrusted with the inner secrets of the Church leaders. That such a doctrine, however, was beginning, even then, to form part of the faith of the Saints, may be seen in the following lines upon the occasion of the Prophet's murder:

> "Unchanged in death, with a *Saviour's* love,
> · He pleads their cause in the courts above.
> "His home's in the sky, *he dwells with the Gods*,
> Far from the furious rage of mobs!
>
> .   .   .   .
>
> "He died! he died for those he loved;
> *He reigns! He reigns* in the realms above."

Many other instances, even stronger than this, could easily be given.

The Mormon idea of the other world, while in some respects it differed from the teachings of certain modern "Spiritualists" was not altogether dissimilar. The soul was said to be immortal, and it had three stages of existence. The first was purely spiritual—the state of the soul *before* it came into this world. Spirits in that condition were not perfect, they must first take a fleshly body, and pass through the trials of life, before they could attain to the highest state of existence. Hence it was a solemn duty, as well as their highest privilege, for men to practice Polygamy:—their duty, as by this means, and by this alone, the yet imperfect souls now waiting to come into this world could ever hope to be admitted into the "Celestial Kingdom;"—and a privilege,—as all the souls whom they thus assisted to emigrate would form their own "Kingdoms" in eternity, over which as kings and priests they would reign for ever and ever

The second stage of the soul's existence is the mortal; with which we all are sadly well acquainted. The third is the condition subsequent to the Resurrection, when they believe the flesh and bones will form the raised body, but the blood will not be there; for the blood is the principle of corrupt life, and therefore another spirit supplies its place in heaven. That Christ partook of some broiled fish and part of a honeycomb is evident from Holy Scripture:—the Mormons therefore teach that heaven will be very much the same as earth, only considerably improved. We shall not marry there or be given in marriage; hence it is necessary for us to marry here, and to marry as much as we can, for then in heaven a man will take the wives whom he married on earth, or who have been sealed to him by proxy; they will be his queens, and their children will be his subjects. We shall eat, and drink, and feast, and spend a happy time generally. We shall henceforth never die—hence we shall ourselves be gods!

It was in the preëxistent state, the Mormons teach, that the work of salvation was first planned—but not after the fashion believed by all Christians. A grand celestial council was held, at which all the Sons of God appeared. Michael, the father of all, presided, and stated that he proposed to create a new world, of which he proceeded to give some details. His first-begotten then arose, and made a speech, in which he proposed that Michael, his father, should go down to the world, when created, with Eve, his mother, and do there much after the fashion of what is related of our first parents in the book of Genesis; he himself would descend some thousands of years subsequently, and would lead his erring brethren back, and save them *from* their sins. Lucifer, the second son, then stood forth and unfolded *his* plan. Jealous of the popularity of his elder brother, he proposed to save men *in* their sins.

Great discussion ensued, in which the unnumbered family of heaven divided into three parties,—one under each of the two elder sons, and the third standing neutral. After a terrible conflict, Lucifer, the second son was defeated, and, with all his followers, was driven out of heaven. They descended into the abyss, where they founded the infernal kingdom, of which Lucifer became the chief :—he was henceforth known as the Devil. Adam created his world, and carried out his part of the plan ; and in due time the eldest son, who conquered in heaven, took upon˙ him the form of flesh, dwelt among men, and was known as their Redeemer. The spirits who stood neutral during the fight subsequently took upon them forms of flesh, entering into the children˛of Ham, and were known as Negroes. Therefore it is, that although the American Indians and all other races are eligible for the Mormon priesthood, the negro alone can never attain to that high dignity.

It is only natural, amidst all this confusion of ideas, to ask, Who then is the real Originator of created things ?

In the eternity of matter, the Mormons have from the first believed ; but they have supposed that the formation of worlds and systems had definite dates, although they are unknown to us. Far away in the immensity of space is "KOLOB"—the great and glorious sun of suns, the abode of the First Principle of Godhead of which we can form any conception. Around that Sun, countless other systems revolve, of which ours is one. That Sun itself may be only one of many other systems whose origin and existence is lost in inconceivable space, and concerning which we can form no just realisation while in this finite state. From the First Source in " KOLOB" other gods have proceeded in precisely the same way as genealogies and "family-trees" have been continued on earth. Each new Patriarchal " god" has formed his own earth out of the aggregation of matter ; and over that earth he reigns.

On the 9th of April, 1852, Brigham Young publicly announced that—

" When our father Adam came into the Garden of Eden, he came into it with a celestial body, and brought Eve, one of his wives, with him. He helped to make and organise this world. He is Michael the Archangel, the Ancient of

Days, about whom holy men have written and spoken.   He is our ' Father and our God,' and the only god with whom we have to do."

This public declaration gave great offence and led to the apostacy of many.   Nevertheless Brigham Young thinks that just as Adam came down to Eden and subsequently became a god, in like manner he also himself will attain to the godhead.   Heber C. Kimball, zealous to go a step further declared that Brigham *was* " God," and that he, Kimball, stood towards him in the same relation as the Third Person in the Blessed Trinity does towards the First.

It will hence be seen that subordination is one of the first principles of the Mormon faith, and this even in the Church organisation of the Saints has been distinctively shown.   For the purposes for which it exists the Mormon hierarchy could not be surpassed.   Of the Priesthood there are two orders— the Melchisedec and the Aaronic ; of which the former ranks first and highest.   The lowest rank in the Church is the " Deacon ; " he looks after the places of meeting, takes up collections, and attends to other similar duties.   Next comes the " Teacher " ;—he visits the Saints and takes note of their standing—and reports the same:—weakness of faith or backwardness in paying tithing is never overlooked by him.   After him is the "Priest," and above him is the Elder whose office it is to preach, baptize and lay on hands.   All these belong to the order of the Aaronic—or the Levitical priesthood. "Bishops" are simply Church officers having local jurisdiction.

The lowest grade in the Melchisedec Priesthood is the " Elder."   He administers in all the ordinances of the Church. Above him there is no higher rank as respects the priesthood, but in respect to office there are various gradations, as, for example, the " High Priests," the " Seventies," and "Bishops" who occupy positions of authority, although both go on mission, and also the Apostles.   The "Apostles" were chosen in imitation of the "Twelve" appointed by Christ ; and in the same way the "Seventies," in imitation of the *seventy* disciples sent forth to preach and work miracles.   They claim rank next to the Twelve.   The "Quorum of the Apostles" is presided over by the eldest of their number; the "Quorums of Seventies" are each composed of seventy Elders with a "President" and six "Counsellors." The number of "quorums" is unlimited; and over them all collectively is another president and six counsellors.

The highest authority in the Church is the "First Presidency"—the three members of which at present are Brigham Young, George A. Smith, and Daniel H. Wells,—who are said to represent on earth the three Persons of the Blessed Trinity!

As, from "President" Young down to the most illiterate "Elder," every one is supposed to be specially inspired, and to be immediately guided by the gift of the Holy Ghost, education is utterly unnecessary to the members of the Mormon Priesthood; in fact it has always been looked upon as an impediment to its possessor. *Obedience* is considered the highest qualification, and it was the strict enforcement of obedience on the part of the ordinary people and the lower grades of the Priesthood towards the higher that alone could have made possible that state of affairs which existed during the "Reformation." Hence also it is that Brigham Young and the leaders are rightly held responsible for the deeds of violence and fanaticism which their followers may perpetrate; for it is well known that *no* Mormon, in a matter of grave importance, would dare to act upon his own responsibility and without he felt sure that what he did would meet with the approbation of those in authority.

There is another class of Church-officer which I had very nearly forgotten—the Patriarchs. The chief of these is called "The Presiding Patriarch *over* the Church"; the rest are " Patriarchs *in* the Church." The office of these dignitaries is to bless the people and to be paid for their blessings. The price of good blessings is variable. Not long ago, when money was scarce and payments were made in produce, two dollars was considered reasonable; and if several were wanted for the same family, a reduction was made. Hyrum Smith, the original Prophet's eldest brother, was the first Patriarch; and to him succeeded "Uncle John," as he was popularly called—the eldest brother of Brigham ;—the present Patriarch is the son of Hyrum ; still a young man, who obtained his office by inheritance—and this, I believe, is about the only office in the Church which Brother Brigham has permitted the Smith family to inherit or enjoy.

Odd as it may seem, some of the people have quite a passion for these "blessings." I knew one old Frenchwoman who was said, like the woman in the parable, in respect to the physicians, to have "spent all of her living upon them." I met her one day with a flannel-petticoat under her arm, which she was going to sell. Upon enquiry she frankly told me that she had given her last cent and had sold every scrap of any value which she possessed, and very nearly all her clothes, in order to obtain "blessings," and as she did not understand English she was now going to sell her old petticoat—the very last article of any value which she now possessed—to pay an old dame, who knew a little English, for her services in translating the "blessings." She was in a state of great sorrow at the thought that now her supply of blessings would be stopped—she would have to do without.

The Patriarchs, however, at no time possessed any particular personal or official weight, and from them never proceeded any of those strange doctrines which excited the people to violence and bloodshed. In a religious sense this outrageous fanaticism was all originated in the first place in Missouri by some of the more prominent men, such as Sidney Rigdon, Dr. Avard, David Patten, and others, doubtless with the connivance of the Prophet Joseph, not long after the organisation of the Church; and subsequently by the extreme and preposterous doctrines constantly inculcated by Brigham Young and some of the leading Elders, among whom Jedediah M. Grant and Heber C. Kimball were the most conspicuous. In a political sense it was the natural result of the peculiar position of the Saints in Missouri, Ohio, and Illinois, and of the ridiculous threats of Brigham Young against the Federal Government, after the exodus of the Mormons to Salt Lake Valley, together with the idea which had become popular among the people, that a temporal "kingdom" was to be set up among the Rocky Mountains, and that Christ should personally reign and rule there.

The idea of reviving the old Jewish polity was always uppermost in the minds of the first teachers. Hence they revived the Priesthood and High-priesthood in their various forms ; a magnificent temple was built in Nauvoo, just as another temple is now being erected at Salt Lake City ; and so far did they go that it was even determined that the ancient sacrifices should eventually be restored. At the same time, while the minds of the Mormons, newly-converted and fired with zeal, were bent upon founding the Kingdom of the Saints on earth, the people of Missouri, among whom they dwelt, heard that even in social life the customs of the Jews were to be introduced, and that Polygamy was to be practiced. Husbands and brothers trembled for their wives and sisters, and the hatred to the new religion was increased when it was observed that the Mormons in every political movement held all together and voted as one man, thus exercising an influence which no ordinary religious sect could have possessed or wielded ; this, the discipline of the hierarchy, to which I have already referred, enabled them to do.

Ill-feeling was shown on both sides; in a thousand petty ways at first, with more serious results presently. The Mormons were accused of circulating large quantities of base coin, of cheating and defrauding the Gentiles, as they called everyone—even Jews—who rejected the new religion, and of even being guilty of darker crimes ;—which last charge, however, was at first only hinted at. On the other hand, the Mormons accused their enemies of every possible villainy of which men and women could be guilty. The real fact would appear to be that both the Mormons and their enemies were at that time guilty of much wrong-doing against each other, while, at the same time, much that was alleged on both sides was utterly groundless, and only originated in the natural jealousy which Western pioneers— rough-and-ready frontiers-men, such as the people of those parts then were—would naturally feel when enlisted in two parties, animated by religious and political hatred against each other.

Now came whisperings of still more atrocious deeds. It was alleged that, among the Mormons, a secret body of men had been chosen, who were enrolled, under the most frightful oaths, to avenge every wrong which might be perpetrated against the Saints. This band was said to have originated with Sidney Rigdon and Dr. Sampson Avard, and, as I have somewhere else mentioned, Thomas B. Marsh and Hyde the present chief of the Apostles both made affidavit that such was the case, and that the band was sworn to commit the most shocking acts of vengeance,—and surely Marsh and Hyde ought to know. Various names were chosen for this "death society." First the members were called Daughters of Zion [*from* Micah iv. 13.] But as it sounded rather ridiculous to speak of bearded ruffians as ' daughters,' that name was abandoned, and the title "Avenging Angels" substituted; and that, with some other names then temporarily used, were subsequently dropped for the name "Danites" [*from* Genesis xlix. 17,] which has since been retained;—not by the Mormons, for they have ever denied the existence of any such band, but by the Gentiles.

It matters very little what the name of such a society might be, so long as it existed at all ; and that it does, and has, existed in *some* form cannot reasonably be denied. There probably is not at the present time any formally enrolled society, but it is quite certain that for many years past if "The Church" had only dropped a hint that any man's blood ought to be shed, that man would have had a very short tenure of his life. Even Brigham himself said publicly:

"If men come here and do not behave themselves, they will not only find the Danites, whom they talk so much about, biting the horses' heels, but the scoundrels will find something biting *their* heels. In my plain remarks I simply call things by their own names."

It is beyond a doubt that, notwithstanding all the social changes and improvements of late years, the secret police of

Salt Lake City are in matters of crime, as well as *in fact*, though not perhaps nominally, the successors of the original " death society ;"—many of its members are known to have committed grievous crimes and to have repeatedly dyed their hands in blood. The shocking deeds that every now and then are divulged to the world are all of their doing, and no resident of Salt Lake City, whether Mormon or Gentile, although he might prudently decline to state his opinions, would in his mind question the fact that it is fear of consequences, and only because the Saints are " on their good behavior " in the sight of the Federal Government, that the hands of these wretches are withheld from a continuance of their old enormities.

As might be supposed, the establishment of a secret band of men professedly ready at a moment to steal, to shed blood, or commit any crime at the command of their leaders created great excitement in the whole State of Missouri, and especially in the vicinity of the Mormon Settlements.

Like the Ishmaelites of old, the hands of the Saints were against every man, and every man's hand was against them. They were taught that they were " a chosen nation, a royal priesthood, a peculiar people"—the " Sword of the Lord and of Gideon" was to be theirs ; they were to go forth conquering and to conquer; and the Gentiles were to be trodden down beneath their feet.

As might be expected, trouble immediately arose; the people of Missouri outraged the Mormons, and the Mormons in return outraged them. Murders, thefts, and the most shameful atrocities were of daily occurrence, and the history of those terrible doings would fill a good-sized volume. Suffice it to say, that the excitement continued and increased, reprisals being made on both sides ; finally the mob was triumphant, and after committing many fearful excesses it was organised into a militia—the leading men in authority declaring that the Mormons must either leave the State or else they must be extirpated by the sword.

Notwithstanding all this, the Mormons, at all times an industrious people, were in one sense successful and prosper-

19

ous ; the morality, however, of some of their leading men was
to say the least very questionable. It was openly argued that
the silver and gold were the Lord's, and so were the cattle on
a thousand hills. The Scripture says that God has given his
people all things richly to enjoy. The Saints were the people
of God :—He had given *them* all the wealth and substance of
the earth, and therefore it was no sin for them to help themselves—they were but taking their own. To over-reach or
defraud their enemies was facetiously called by the Mormons
"milking the Gentiles."

Their city called Nauvoo—The Beautiful,—a name given
by the Prophet Joseph and supposed to be of celestial origin,
was well laid out and well built, a costly Temple was nearly
complete, and the leaders, at least, began to show signs
of wealth and prosperity. This however was but the lull
before the storm. Writs upon various charges against Joseph
and the leading Elders had always been floating about, and
the serving of some of the later ones had only been prevented
by technical difficulties or the personal fears of the Sheriff.
To enter Nauvoo for the purpose of arresting the Prophet was
like bearding the lion in his den ; for by this time one of the
best-equipped and best-drilled militia regiments under the
name of the Nauvoo Legion had been organised, and Joseph
had been elected Lieutenant-General. The regiment consisted solely of well-tried Mormons who were devotedly
attached to their leader ; besides which, the whole of the
population of the city was at his call at a moment's notice.

Into the city of the Saints, as far as was possible to prevent
it, no Gentile was allowed to intrude. It was at risk of life
and property that any one ventured. One oddly original
mode of driving out the devoted stranger is worthy of mention
—it was called "*whittling* a man out of the town !" Opposite the victim's door a number of men and overgrown boys
would take up their quarters—each armed with a stout stick
of wood and a huge knife. No sooner did the Gentile appear
than the whole horde gathered in a circle round him. Not a
word was uttered, but each man grasping firmly his stick in

his left hand, pointed its other end to within a few inches of the victim's face, while with the knife in his right hand he sliced a shaving out of the wood in such a way as to bring the point of the knife almost against the face of the unfortunate man. Wherever he turned they attended him, always preserving the strictest silence, and never actually touching him. The intolerable sensation caused by the "whittling" of this strange body-guard—who were in attendance day and night—and the unpleasantness of seeing half a score of sharp knives flashing perpetually within an inch of his nose generally subdued the strongest-minded Gentile—few could endure it for more than a day or so at the utmost : they were glad to leave —" *Whittled out* of the town !"

The evil day, however, at last came. The Prophet, fearing arrest, fled, but was persuaded to return and deliver himself up. The charge against him was one for which reasonable bail could be taken : bail was offered, accepted, and the prisoners discharged. Before leaving court, however, the Prophet and his brother Hyrum, the Patriarch, were arrested upon a trumped-up charge of treason—a charge for which it was impossible that bail should be taken ; they were therefore committed to custody in Carthage jail, under solemn promise from Governor Ford of Illinois that the State should be answerable for their personal protection. The same day, however, a mob of over one hundred men, assisted, it is said, by the militia who were left in charge, burst into the jail and assassinated the Prophet and his brother.

As might be supposed this outrage by no means weakened the Mormon cause—their Prophet was now a martyr, and his name more powerful after death than it could possibly have been had he lived. It was, however, clearer than ever that nothing could now reconcile the people of Illinois to the Mormons, and the latter seriously began to think of leaving that State in a body as they had formerly left Missouri.

The terrible doings of those times I have no idea of relating just now—I simply allude to them in order that the reader may understand how, in the excitement produced in that border-warfare, it was possible for such strange events as afterwards transpired in Utah to originate. I may simply add, that the Temple being completed, and the first "Endowments" given there, the people gathered up what little property they could rescue from the mob, and under the guidance of Brigham Young, and amidst privations, sufferings, and outrages of the most painful character, left the city which they had founded in Illinois and set out for the Rocky Mountains, where, beside the Great Salt Lake, they founded their modern Zion.

Free now from the violence of mobs and Gentile enmity, it might have been supposed that the hatred which had so long been part of the Mormon faith would háve died a natural death. The contrary, however, was the case. The Mexican war was then raging, and, *en route* to the Rocky Mountains, the Mormons had received a proposal from the Federal Government that they should supply a regiment, upon highly advantageous conditions, to join the United States troops which were then operating in California. This suggestion was kindly made, for it was thought that the Mormon regiment thus raised would in reality be only marching their own way in going to California, and that the outfits, pay, arms, &c., which were to be theirs, after the year for which they were enrolled had expired, would be of essential service to them. It was like paying men liberally for making a journey for their own benefit.

Notwithstanding all this, Brigham Young and the leaders represented the transaction in quite another light, and the people were taught that an engagement, into which they had entered of their own free will, and from which they had derived substantial advantages, was an act of heartless cruelty and despotic tyranny on the part of the Government. This feeling was fostered, until at length the Saints as a body regarded themselves as a wronged and outraged people, and considered every Gentile—in fact the whole nation as their natural enemies. This was perhaps all the more singular, since, after the vast tract of country, of which Utah forms a part, had, at the end of the war, been wrested from Mexico, Brigham Young had been appointed by President Millard Fillmore the first Governor and Indian Agent of the territory ; he was therefore in Federal pay, and bound, as long as he retained office, to support the Government, or at the very least not to stir up disaffection.

Trouble soon arose between Governor Young and the Mormons on one side and the Judges and United States courts and officials on the other. Once an armed mob burst into the Supreme Court, and forced the Judge then sitting to adjourn ; at another time a *bonfire* was made of the books and papers of the District Courts ; then a Judge on the bench was threatened with personal outrage ; and subsequently a *posse* summoned by legal (!) process "encamped" for a whole fortnight over against another *posse* summoned without legal process, the two bodies burning with bitter hatred and breathing out threatenings and slaughter. Such a state of affairs could not, of course, last long. On the one side the wildest statements were publicly made against the Government ; threats which uttered by a little band of pioneers against a mighty nation were perfectly ridiculous, stirred up the hearts of the Saints. On the other hand it was pretty certain that Federal troops would have to be sent out to Utah to preserve the peace of the Territory. The Federal Government was nevertheless defied, abused, and derided, and the people, thoroughly blinded by their fanaticism, did not for a moment doubt that should Governor Young "declare war" the United States troops would vanish before the "Armies" of the Saints like chaff upon the threshing-floor. So absurd does all this appear that I should really hardly venture to repeat it were it not that every one in Utah—Mormon and Gentile—knows that I am really understating facts rather than otherwise.

Now came a crisis in Mormon history, for which all these wild sayings and unlawful doings had been so long paving the way :—" THE REFORMATION" was destined to be the crowning point of Saintly folly and Saintly sin.

CHAPTER XXII.

THE "REIGN OF TERROR" IN UTAH:—THE REFORMATION OF THE SAINTS.

Days of Trouble in the Valley—Shedding Innocent Blood—What is Murder?
About Killing a Cat—Better than Their Faith—Cutting Throats for Love—
The Deeds of the Apostle "Jeddy"—The Celebrated Mule—The Saints
Accused—Missionaries Called Home—Their Consciences Accuse Them!—
The Blood-Atonement—What was Said in the Tabernacle—Terrible Doctrines
Taught—Brigham a "God"!—Fearful Blasphemy of Brigham Young—The
Shedding of Blood—"Righteously Murdered—The Principles of Eternity—
Deeds of Darkness—A "Saint" Murders His Wife—A Terrible Story—How
Children Were Married—A Petticoat on a Fence-Pole—A Scarcity of Un-
married Girls—Obeying "Counsel"—Propositions of Marriage—A Trifling
Mistake—Stubborn Facts and Figures—The Most Fearful Deed of All.

THE people were now thoroughly excited. Their religious
antipathy, their political hatred—two of the most powerful passions which move individuals or bodies of men—had
been appealed to, and both in public and private they had
been stirred up to a pitch of frenzy which it is hardly possible
at the present time to comprehend.

There were whisperings now of a most fearful doctrine,
calculated not only to strike terror into the hearts of those
whose faith was weakening, but even to shock with a sense
of horror those who only heard of it from afar—I mean the
doctrine of the BLOOD ATONEMENT.

The Saints had all along been taught to distinguish between
murder and the shedding of innocent blood—the former being

spoken of as a crime for which atonement might be made, but for the latter there was no repentance on earth—it was an unpardonable sin. They were also taught to distinguish carefully between sins which might be forgiven, and sins for which pardon was impossible. Now the difference between murder and shedding innocent blood is this :—the latter is the crime of killing a Saint, which can never be forgiven, but by the death of the transgressor ; but the former is of quite a different character. To murder a Gentile may sometimes be inexpedient, or perhaps even to a certain extent wrong, but it is seldom, if ever, a crime, and never an unpardonable sin.

A friend of mine was in a state of apostacy. The Bishop went to her to expostulate, and told her that if he were her husband he would get rid of her and take away her children as well—he would not on any account live with her.

"Perhaps," she said, "you would not allow me to live at all ? "

" Certainly not," he replied. " I would think about as much of killing you or any other miserable Apostate as I would about killing a cat. If Brigham Young were to tell me to put you to death I would do it with the greatest of pleasure ;— and it would be for your good, too."

Thus, when the famous Revelation on Polygamy says that a man cannot be pardoned for shedding innocent blood, it does not mean that he cannot be pardoned for murdering a Gentile or an Apostate ; for that, under some circumstances, might even be meritorious ; but that the murder of a Saint by one of the brethren cannot under *any* circumstances be for- given on earth, and that his only chance of forgiveness lies in his own blood being shed as an "atonement."

Certain sins cannot be forgiven here on earth—Shedding innocent blood, divulging the secrets of the Endowment House—marital unfaithfulness on the part of the wife— Apostacy ;—these are unpardonable. All other crimes which Gentiles abhor may become even virtues, if done in the cause of the Church. I do not, of course, mean to say that the mass of the Mormon people act up to such atrocious doctrines ; for although, when among themselves, they would admit that the theory was correct, the better instincts of their nature keep them from even putting that theory into practice. But what I do mean to say is, that such doctrines have, over and over again, been distinctly taught in the plainest words in the public hearing of thousands; that they have been printed and re-printed by authority; that they *have* been practiced, and the very highest of the Mormon leaders have applauded; and that, even at the present moment, these doctrines form part of the dogmas of the Church. It is this day a matter of fact, and not a matter of question, that if any Mormon Apostate were to commit any of the unpardonable sins which I have men-tioned, and if he or she were to be assassinated by a private individual, all zealous Mormons—all the leaders.—would maintain that not only was the deed justifiable but even meritorious!

This may seem bad enough, but it is not the worst. The doctrine of the "Blood Atonement" is that the murder of an Apostate is *a deed of love !* If a Saint sees another leave the Church, or if even he only believes that his brother's faith is weakening and that he will apostatise before long, he knows that the soul of his unbelieving brother will be lost if he dies in such a state, and that only by his blood being shed is there any chance of forgiveness for him; it is therefore the kindest action that he can perform toward him to shed his blood—the doing so is a deed of truest love. The nearer, the dearer, the more tenderly loved the sinner is, the greater the affection shown by the shedder of blood—the action is no longer mur-der or the shedding of innocent blood, for the taint of apostacy takes away its innocence—it is making atonement, not a crime; it is an act of mercy, therefore meritorious.

These were the terrible teachings which the "Reformation" brought to light:—they had been whispered before among the elect, and had been acted upon by the "Avenging Angels," but before this they had never been publicly and intelligibly explained.

As I before said, the Saints had been excited to a condition of frenzy and were ready to engage in any fanatical folly, but the way in which the spark was applied to the powder was as ridiculous as its results were terrible.

Jedediah M. Grant, an enthusiast of the wildest kind; a man without education or mental discipline of any description; one of the First Presidency and high in authority among the Saints, had occasion to attend a meeting which was held at Kaysville, a place about twenty-five miles distant from Salt Lake City, and he invited some of the Elders to meet him there to take part in the proceedings. To one of these, "Jeddy" as he was familiarly called, obligingly lent a mule; he himself did not accompany the party but went on before. These Elders were pretty well mounted and one of them being a good horseman made the rest keep up with him. In consequence of this when they arrived at Kaysville the beasts were heated and tired. The Apostle "Jeddy" watched them but said nothing.

Up to a certain point, the meeting passed off pleasantly enough—the Elders present were "good at testimony" and strong in exhorting their hearers to faithfulness. Jeddy was the last speaker. He began in his usual way, but presently warmed up until he became quite excited and then proceeded to accuse every one present of all sorts of wrong-doing. The Elders who had preceded him came in for their full share; he denounced them for their inconsistency and hypocrisy, and bitterly upbraided them for running his mule and their own beasts in such a manner. The Bishop of the place and his counsellors he accused of inactivity and carelessness; and he called loudly upon every one present to repent and do their first works; threatening them with the speedy judgments of Heaven.

All this was well enough if it had stopped there, for it might have been taken for just what it was—an ebulition of temper on the part of "Jeddy" who was naturally vexed that his mule had been over-heated. But like many other manias and epidemics, this Mormon movement began with a most insignificant trifle, and the spirit of fiery denunciation became perfectly contagious. Another meeting was held in the course of a few weeks, and then the mutual accusations of those who were present became, if possible, more bitter than before; the "Saints" were denounced as the vilest of sinners and they were all commanded to be re-baptized. Accordingly, after the meeting, although it was night and the weather was cold, a considerable number were immersed by the Elders, and Jeddy himself was so enthusiastically engaged in the performance that he remained in the water so long that he got a thorough chill and contracted the disease of which he died.

Sunday after Sunday similar scenes were repeated in the Tabernacle, until, had it not been painful, the whole affair would have been ludicrous in the extreme. Every one had strayed from the path of duty, and the fact was announced in the strongest terms. People were called upon by name to publicly confess their sins, and many were then and there pointed out and accused of crimes of which they were entirely guiltless but which they dared not deny. In the midst of all this, the duty of implicit obedience to the Priesthood and the payment of tithes was loudly insisted upon.

Then Missionaries were sent out all over the territory armed with the full authority of the Priesthood and also a catechism which, on account of its obscene character, has since been bought up so successfully by Brigham that it is doubtful if there is a copy in existence. The Mormons have a curious way of appointing Missionaries. If a man is weak in the faith, a depraved bad man, or even a youth with wild tendencies and inclined to sow his wild oats a little too luxuriantly, he is sent on his travels to preach the Gospel:—nothing strengthens a man's faith, it is thought, more than having to defend it from the opposition of unbelievers, and the enforced good example which the Missionary is obliged to set will, it is said, produce a salutary effect upon the exuberance of youth or the depravity of more mature years. In the present instance many of the Missionaries thus sent forth were known to be as immoral as they were grossly ignorant.

There was one terrible meeting at which Brigham himself

was put to the blush. Men of note were there—no one was present who did not belong to the Priesthood. "Jeddy" held forth, and Heber and Brigham were strong upon the occasion. In the midst of the proceedings, Brother Brigham, full of confidence, in the plainest words called upon all who could not plead guiltless of certain crimes to stand up. Three-fourths of those present immediately arose. Utterly shocked, the Prophet entered into explanations; but self-convicted these three-fourths of his hearers stood conscientiously firm. Even Brigham saw the necessity of taking some stringent measures. The Saints were told that if they were re-baptized their sins would be washed away and they could then say they were not guilty of the crimes suggested in the catechism. Subsequently the catechism itself was, as I said, bought up and burnt.

The burden of every sermon was unquestioning obedience, repentance, payment of tithing, and above all the taking of more wives. The Missionaries, without the slightest ceremony, would visit the houses of respectable Saints, examine them out of the abominable catechism, and question husbands and wives in the presence of their children about even their very thoughts, in a manner, and upon subjects, which would amply have justified their being hung up to the nearest tree—Lynch law was in fact too good for such atrocities. Wicked ideas, the utterance of which would have called forth a blush even if heard from the lips of a drunken rowdy in a pot-house, were suggested and explained to young children; while it would have been literally at the risk of life for their parents to have expostulated:—to do so would have shown want of faith, and want of faith would have justified some fanatical scoundrel in using his knife or his pistol for the loving purpose of cutting off his brother's soul from earth in order to save it in heaven !

Meanwhile, Jedediah did not for a moment cease his exhortations, the work must be done thoroughly: the Blood-Atonement must not be forgotten. On one occasion, in the Tabernacle, this crazy fanatic said:—

"I would advise some of you men here to go to President Young, and confess your sins, and ask him to take you outside the city and have your blood shed to atone for your sins."

. . . .

"There are men and women that I would advise to go to the President imme- diately, and ask him to appoint a committee to attend to their case; and then let a place be selected, and let that committee shed their blood. . . . .

"I would ask how many covenant-breakers there are in this city and in this kingdom? I believe that there are a great many; and if they are covenant- breakers, we need a place designated where we can shed their blood."

. . . .

"We have been trying long enough with this people, and I go in for letting the sword of the Almighty be unsheathed, not only in word but *in deed.*"

Lest he should be mistaken he said :

"What ought this meek people who keep the commandments of God do unto them ? 'Why,' says one, 'they ought to pray *the Lord* to kill them.' I want to know if you would wish the Lord to come down and do all your dirty work? . . . . When a man prays for a thing, he ought to be willing to perform it himself. . . . . Putting to death the transgressors would exhibit the law of God, *no matter by whom it was done.*"

Heber C. Kimball, the "model Saint," after a speech to the same effect, in which, as usual, he made use of the most dis- gusting language, added :

"Joseph Smith was God to the inhabitants of the earth when he was among us, and Brigham is God now !"

But more shocking than any other was the language of Brigham Young himself. On the 21st of September, 1856, in a discourse delivered in the Bowery, Great Salt Lake City, and afterwards re-printed by authority in the Journals of Dis- courses, Vol. IV., pp. 53-4, he said :

"The time is coming when justice will be laid to the line and righteousness to the plummet ; when we shall take the old broadsword, and ask, 'Are you for God ?' and if you are not heartily on the Lord's side, *you will be hewn down !*"

. . . .

"There are sins that men commit for which they cannot receive forgiveness in this world or in that which is to come ; and if they had their eyes opened to see their true condition, they would be perfectly willing to have their blood spilt upon the ground, that the smoke thereof might ascend to Heaven as an offering for their sins, and the smoking incense would atone for their sins ; whereas, if such is not the case, they will stick to them and remain with them in the spirit world.

"I know, when you hear my brethren telling about cutting people off from the earth, that you consider it is strong doctrine ; but it is to save them, not to destroy them. . . . .

"I do know that there are sins committed of such a nature that, if the people did understand the doctrine of salvation, they would tremble because of their situation. And, furthermore, I know that there are transgressors who, if they knew themselves, and the only condition upon which they can obtain forgiveness, would beg of their brethren to shed their blood, that the smoke thereof might ascend to God as an offering to appease the wrath that is kindled against them, and that the law might have its course. I will say, further, I have had men come to me and offer their lives to atone for their sins.

" It is true that the blood of the Son of God was shed for sins through the fall and those committed by men, yet men can commit sins which it can never remit. As 't was in ancient days, so it is in our day ; and though the principles are taught publicly from this stand, still the people do not understand them ; yet the law is precisely the same. There are sins that can be atoned for by an offering upon an altar, as in ancient days ; and there are sins that the blood of a lamb, of a calf, or of turtle doves cannot remit, but *they must be atoned for by the blood of the man.*"

One would have supposed that even Brigham had now reached the culminating point of horror and blasphemy. But no ;—a month or so later he even surpassed himself when in a Tabernacle sermon he said :

"When will we love our neighbors as ourselves? In the first place, Jesus said that no man hateth his own flesh. It is admitted by all that every person loves himself. Now if we do rightly love ourselves we want to be saved, and continue to exist, we want to go into the kingdom where we can enjoy eternity, and see no more sorrow nor death. This is the desire of every person who believes in God. Now take a person in this congregation who has knowledge with regard to being saved in the kingdom of our God and our Father, and being exalted, one who knows and understands the principles of eternal life, and sees the beauties and excellency of the eternities before him compared with the vain and foolish things of the world, and suppose that he is overtaken in a gross fault, that he has committed a sin that he knows will deprive him of that exaltation which he desires, and that he cannot attain to it without the shedding of his blood, and also knows that by having his blood shed he will atone for that sin and be saved and exalted with the gods, is there a man or a woman in this house but would say, 'Shed my blood that I might be saved and exalted with the gods?'

" All mankind love themselves : and let those principles but be known by an individual, and *he would* be glad to have his blood shed. This would be loving ourselves even unto an eternal exaltation. Will you love your brothers or sisters likewise when they have a sin that cannot be atoned for without the shedding of their blood ? Will you love that man or woman well enough to shed their blood? *That is what Jesus Christ meant.* He never told a man or woman to love their enemies in their wickedness, never. He never meant any such thing ; His language is left as it is for those to read who have the spirit to discern between truth and error ; it was so left for those who can discern the things of God. Jesus Christ never meant that we should love a wicked man in his wickedness.

"I could refer you to plenty of instances where men have been righteously slain in

order to atone for their sins. I have seen scores and hundreds of people for whom there would have been a chance (in the last resurrection there will be) if their lives had been taken and their blood spilled on the ground as a smoking incense to the Almighty, but who are now angels to the devil, until our elder brother, Jesus Christ, raises them up and conquers death, hell, and the grave.

"I have known a great many men who have left this Church, for whom there is no chance whatever for exaltation, but if their blood had been spilled it would have been better for them.

"The wickedness and ignorance of the nations forbid this principle being in full force, but the time will come when the law of God will be in full force. This is loving our neighbor as ourselves; if he needs help, *help him;* if he wants salvation, and it is necessary to spill his blood on the earth in order that he may be saved, *spill it.*

"Any of you who understand the principles of eternity, if you have sinned a sin requiring the shedding of blood, except the sin unto death, should not be satisfied or rest until your blood should be spilled, that you might gain that salvation you desire. That is the way to love mankind. . . . Light and darkness cannot dwell together, and so it is with the kingdom of God.

"Now, brethren and sisters, will you live your religion? How many hundreds of times have I asked that question? Will the Latter-Day Saints live their religion?"

And so, according to Brigham Young, their Prophet, this was the religion of the Saints! And the people acted up to the "religion" thus taught: and the story is so terrible that one dare not even whisper all its details.

It is no secret that all this was understood *literally.* The wife of one Elder, when he was absent on a mission, acted unfaithfully towards him. Her husband took counsel of the authorities, and was reminded that the shedding of her blood alone could save her. He returned and told her, but she asked for time, which was readily granted. One day, in a moment of affection, when she was seated on his knee, he reminded her of her doom, and suggested that now when their hearts were full of love was a suitable time for carrying it into execution. She acquiesced, and *out of love* he cut her throat from ear to ear.

In many instances the outrages committed against persons who were known to be innocent were so revolting that no woman—nay, even no right-minded man—would venture to more than just allude to them. *A few* however, and only a few, and they *by no means the worst*, of the milder cases, I will just mention.

There was the murder of the Aikin party—six persons—
who were killed on their way to California. The same year a
man named Yates was killed under atrocious circumstances ;
and Franklin McNeil who had sued Brigham for false impris-
onment and who was killed at his hotel door. There was
Sergeant Pike, and there was Arnold and Drown. There
was Price and William Bryan at Fairfield ; there was Almon
Babbitt, and Brassfield, and Dr. Robinson ; there was also
James Cowdy and his wife and child, and Margetts and his
wife ; and many another, too,—to say nothing of that frightful
murder at the Mountain Meadows.

Besides these there is good reason to think that Lieutenant
Gunnison and his party were also victims, although it was
said that they were shot by " Indians." The Potter and Parrish
murders were notorious ; Forbes, and Jones and his mother,
might be added to the same list ; the dumb boy, Andrew
Bernard ; a woman killed by her own husband ; Morris the
rival Prophet, and Banks, and four women who belonged to
their party ; Isaac Potter, and Charles Wilson, and John
Walker. These are but a few. The death list is too long for
me to venture to give it.

One instance I can give from my own personal knowledge.
A sister who occasionally does a little work at my house on
one occasion said to me : " Mrs. Stenhouse, when first I came
to this country I lived in the southern portion of Utah. One
day I saw a woman running across the fields towards our
house, pale and trembling. When she came in she looked
round her as if she were frightened, and she asked if any one
besides our own family were present. On being assured that
there was no one present whom she might fear, she said :—
' Two men came to our house late last night and asked to see
my husband, who had already retired. He was in bed, but
they insisted that he must get úp as they had a message from
"the authorities" for him. When they saw him they requested him to go with them to attend, they said, to some
Church business. I became very much alarmed, for my poor
husband had been known to speak rather freely of late of

some of the measures of the Church, but he tried to reassure me and finally left the house with the two men. In about an hour after they came back bearing between them his lifeless body. They laid him upon the bed, and then one of them pulled aside the curtain which constituted our only cupboard, and took therefrom a bake-kettle and stood it beside the bed, in order to catch the blood that was flowing from a fearful wound in his throat. They then left the house telling me to make as little noise about it as possible or they might serve me in the same way. The men were masked, and I cannot tell who they are, but I spent a fearful night with my poor dead husband.'" This sister added: "Sister Stenhouse, in those more fearful times we dared not speak to each other about such things for fear of spies."

These were all well-known and notorious instances. I say nothing of those of whose fate nothing—not even a whisper —was ever heard; and I say nothing of the frightful "cuttings off" *before* the Reformation and in recent years.

Gentile men and women were *killed*, for hatred; and *that* "killing" was no murder, for theirs was not innocent blood. Apostates, and Saints of doubtful faith, and those who were obnoxious, *had their blood shed*—all *for love*—and that "cutting off" was also no murder, because to secure their salvation by cutting their throats was an act of mercy. Can it be possible that men should thus act and say—and *believe*—that Jesus, the gentle and merciful Saviour, commanded it when He said: "Thou shalt love thy neighbor as thyself?"

All through this Reign of Terror, marrying and giving in marriage was the order of the day. It mattered not if a man was seventy years of age, according to Brother Brigham he was still a boy—"the brethren are all boys until they are a hundred years old"—and some young girl of sixteen, fifteen, or even younger would be "counselled"—that is, *commanded* —to marry him. She might even have a sister no older than herself, and then as likely as not he would take the two to wife, and very probably both on the same day. The girls were told that to marry a young man was not a safe thing, for young men were not tried—it was better to marry a well-tested patriarch and then their chances of "exaltation" in the kingdom of heaven were sure and certain. In this way the life-long happiness of many a girl—little more than a child—was blighted for ever. At the time of which I speak, every unmarried woman, or girl who could by the utmost stretch of possibility be thought old enough to marry, was forced to find a husband, or a husband was immediately found for her, and without any regard to her wishes was forced upon her. Young men, and even boys, were forced, not only into marriage, but even Polygamy, and none dared resist. The marrying mania, in fact, was universal and irresistible—every one *must* marry or be given in marriage. So evidently was this the case that women in jest said that, if one were to hang a petticoat upon a fence-pole, half a dozen men would flock at once to marry it! Absurd as this may seem it was not very far from the truth. Young men and maidens, old men and children, widows, virgins, and youths—in fact every one whether married or unmarried, it mattered not, was "counselled"—commanded—to marry.

There is above fanaticism a stronger law which, despite every effort of the deluded victim, *will* occasionally make itself heard—the voice of Nature. Even during that strange time in which every Saint seemed to have gone stark crazy mad, the frightful anomaly of men of fifty, sixty, and even seventy marrying mere children—girls of fourteen, and even thirteen, —forced itself upon the attention of some of the leaders. The question arose—an odd question to Gentile ears—" At what age is a girl old enough to marry?" Considerable discussion ensued, and even in the Tabernacle the subject was taken up. The voice of authority, however, eventually answered the matter, but not in the way that any ordinary civilised person would expect.

In those times, unmarried girls were very scarce—in the settlements it was difficult to find any at all. Not infrequently it happened that a brother was "counselled" to marry, but could not obey, as there was no unmarried woman in the place

20

where he lived. In that case he generally paid a visit to
Salt Lake City. But business at the Endowment House
nevertheless was pretty lively ; in fact so much so that it was
deemed necessary to set apart certain days for the various
Settlements. Once, when the "Provo day" was fast approaching, two old brethren from that town who had been counselled
to enlarge their families, but who had been unsuccessful in
finding partners, began to despair of being able to obey "the
word of the Lord !" The day before that appointed for the
Endowments and Celestial Marriage arrived, and they were as
far from success as ever. Being neighbors, the two old
gentlemen met and mingled their griefs, and considered what
might be done. It then occurred to them that there was a
certain brother who had two daughters, respectively *twelve*
and *fourteen* years of age, and they resolved to call upon him
about these children. As might be supposed, the father at
first refused them, giving as a reason that the girls were too
young. The old men explained that if they could not marry
the children it was impossible for them to "obey counsel,"
and the father then agreed. The next morning the marriage
ceremony was performed in the Endowment House. One of
these wretches was sixty years of age, and the other a few
years younger. The father of the children was about forty.
I am really afraid that the reader will think that I exaggerate
or misrepresent facts. I wish it were so, for the case is so
outrageously atrocious ; but I am sorry to say that scores
and hundreds of instances similar to this, which occurred
during the Reformation, might be given.

Not long before this infamous transaction, one of these men
looking round in search of a wife, learned that a young English girl was stopping at the house of a certain brother in the
neighborhood. He immediately visited that brother, and said
he should like to be made acquainted with the girl. It happened that the young sister in question had recently been
married, but of that the ancient brother was of course ignorant, and his friend at whose house the lady was stopping,
being fond of a little practical joke at times, did not inform

him of the fact. The would-be lover in a business-like way at once began with his wooing; spoke to the young lady about the Revelation ; of the " counsel " he had received ; of his desire to obey ; and finally offered her his hand and heart—at least as much of the latter as remained. He expatiated upon his prospects and possessions :—he had a small house and a large lot, a good farm, a few cows, a yoke of oxen, and a wagon, —another wife was a trifle which he felt himself well able to keep. The sister listened in silence and seemed a little bashful. At last she said that about such a serious matter she must have a little time for consideration, and asked for a week's thinking-time.

Delighted with his success the gentleman withdrew; but before the end of the week he found out that the lady was married, he saw her husband, he saw the friend at whose house the lady was stopping ; and over the matter he made a considerable fuss.

There are before me as I write, letters, papers, documents of various sorts relative to marriage and the matrimonial affairs of the Saints, at the time of which I speak, that I wish the reader could peep at. I would not like him to read them —in fact, I dared not read them all myself, for some of them are so shameful that the mere knowledge of having read them through would make any right-minded person blush. Taking more wives was the order of the day—*how*, was of little matter.

The work of " Reformation " was in full progress; the people were excited to frenzy ; the Federal troops were expected ; men were marrying and maidens were given in marriage ; every one in Utah was looking forward to the time when the prophecies of Joseph, the Seer, should be fulfilled. and the Son of Man should come :—and then, when one would have supposed that every man would have wished that his hands should be pure, was perpetrated a deed which is unparalleled in modern civilised times—a deed at which angels and men have stood aghast with horror.

CHAPTER XXIII.

THE MOUNTAIN MEADOWS' MASSACRE :—"I WILL REPAY, SAITH THE LORD."

The Train from Arkansas—The Story of a Friend—How an Apostle Merited Death—Mormon Hospitality?—How Justice Slumbered—That Sinner, McLean—Weary and Footsore—What the Governor of the Territory Did not Do—The Story of a Frightful Sin—A Weary Journey—" Without a Morsel of Bread "—Christian-like Indians—Empty Wagons—Military Murderers—Corn, but no Mercy—A Regular Military Call—Pursuing the Pilgrims— The Muster-Call—The Little Children Not to be Killed—The Infamous John D. Lee—The Flag of Truce—" The State of Deseret "—A Deed of Fearful Treachery—Surrounded by " Indians !"—The Emigrants Besieged—Dying for Want of Water—Without Bread—The Mountain Meadows—Atrocious Mormon Villainy—The White Flag—The "Indians" Again—The Mormon Story of the Massacre—Treachery—The " *White* " Indians—Mormon Perfidity— How the Emigrants Were Betrayed—Marching to Death—A Few Children Saved—The Spoil—The Murder of Many Men—The End of a Terrible Story.

I FEEL myself utterly inadequate to tell the story of the Mountain Meadows' Massacre—it is so shocking, so fiend-like. And yet it must be told.

While the work of " Reformation " was going on, and when the United States troops were constantly expected in the Valley of the Great Salt Lake, a large train of emigrants passed through Utah on its way to California. The train consisted of one hundred and twenty or one hundred and thirty persons, and they came chiefly from Arkansas. They were people from the country districts, sober, hard-working, plain folks, but well-to-do and, taken all in all, about as respectable a band of emigrants as ever passed through Salt Lake City.

Nothing worthy of any particular note occurred to them until they reached the Valley—that was the point from which they started towards death.

My old friend Eli B. Kelsey travelled with them from Fort Bridger to Salt Lake City, and he spoke of them in the highest terms. If I remember rightly he said that the train was divided into two parts—the first a rough-and-ready set of men —regular frontier pioneers; the other a picked community, the members of which were all more or less connected by family ties. They travelled along in the most orderly fashion, without hurry or confusion. On Sunday they rested, and one of their number who had been a Methodist preacher conducted divine service. All went well until they reached Salt Lake City, where they expected to be able to refit and replenish their stock of provisions ; but it was there that they first discovered that feeling of enmity which finally resulted in their destruction.

Now it so happened that the minds of the Saints in Salt Lake City were at that time strongly prejudiced against the people of Arkansas, and for a most unsaintly reason. The Apostle Parley P. Pratt, who was one of the earliest converts to Mormonism, and who so ably defended his adopted creed with his pen and from the platform, had not very long before been sojourning in Arkansas and had there run away with another man's wife. This was only a trifle for an "Apostle" to do, and the husband—Mr. McLean—might have known it. But he was a most inconsiderate man and was actually offended with the amorous Apostle for what he had done. He pursued him and killed him, for in those rough parts it was considered that the Apostle did wrong in marrying the man's wife. Nobody, however, took any notice of the matter or brought the murderer to trial. The Mormon people, of course, took the side of the Apostle Parley P. Pratt. Sensitive themselves to the highest degree concerning their wives and daughters, they considered McLean a sinner for doing just exactly what any Saint would have certainly done. Their opinion, however, would have been a matter of consequence only to themselves, had not such fatal consequences resulted from it. Reasoning without reason, they argued that McLean was the enemy of every Mormon, and every Mormon was the enemy of McLean;—McLean was protected in Arkansas therefore every man from Arkansas was an enemy of the Mormons;—an enemy ought to be cut off—therefore it was the duty of every Mormon to "cut off"—if he could—every Arkansas man.

This appears to have been the tone of thought which actuated the minds of the leaders of the people at the time when this emigrant train arrived in the City.

Weary and footsore they encamped by the Jordan River, trusting there to recruit themselves and their teams, and to replenish their stock of provisions. The harvest in Utah that year had been abundant, and there was nothing to hinder them from obtaining a speedy and full supply. Brigham Young was then Governor of Utah Territory, Commander-in-Chief of the Militia, and Indian Agent as well:—he was therefore responsible for all that took place within his jurisdiction. It was his duty to protect all law-abiding persons who either resided in or travelled through the country. The emigrants, so far from being protected, were ordered to break up their camp and move on; and it is said that written instructions were sent on before them, directing the people in the settlements through which they would have to pass to have no dealings with them. This, considering their need of provisions, was much the same as condemning them to certain death.

Compelled to travel on, they pursued their journey slowly towards Los Angeles. At American Fork they wished to trade off some of their worn-out stock and to purchase fresh, —they also desired to obtain provisions. There was abundance of everything from the farm and from the field, for God had very greatly blessed the land that year; but they could obtain nothing. They passed on, and went through Battle Creek, Provo, Springville, Spanish Fork, Payson, Salt Creek and Fillmore, and their reception was still the same,—the word of the Mormon Pontiff had gone forth, and no man dared to hold communion or to trade with them. Now and then, some Mormon, weak in the faith or braver or more fond of money than his fellows, would steal into the camp, in the darkness of the night, bearing with him just what he was able to carry; but beyond this they could procure nothing. Their only hope now lay in the chance of holding out until they could push through to some Gentile settlement where the word of the priestly Governor of Utah was not law. Through fifteen different Mormon settlements did they pass, without being able to purchase a morsel of bread. With empty wagons and on short allowance, they pushed on until they reached Corn Creek, where, for the first time in saintly Utah, they met a friendly greeting *from the Indians* and purchased from them thirty bushels of corn, of which they stood very greatly in need.

At Beaver they were again repulsed, and at Parowan they were not permitted to enter the town—they were forced to leave the public highway and pass round the west side of the fort wall. They encamped by the stream, and tried, as before, to obtain food and fresh cattle, but again to no purpose. The reason why they were refused admission into the town was probably because the militia was there assembled under Colonel Wm. H. Dame—which militia afterwards assisted in their destruction, for which preparations were even now made.

They made their way to Cedar City, the most populous of all the towns of Southern Utah. Here they were allowed to purchase fifty bushels of tithing wheat and to have it ground at the mill of that infamous scoundrel John D. Lee, upon whose memory will rest the eternal curses of all who have ever heard his name. It was, however, no act of mercy—the supplying of this corn. The sellers of it knew well enough even then that it would return to them again in the course of a few days. After all, they had but forty days' rations to carry them on to San Bernardino, in California—a journey of about seventy days. Scanty kindness—miserable generosity! —fifty bushels of corn for a seventy-days' journey, for men, women, and young children, and at least one little one to be born on the road.

They remained· in Cedar City only one day, and so jaded were their teams that it took them three days to travel thence to Iron Creek—a distance of twenty miles; and two days were occupied in journeying fifteen miles—the distance between Iron Creek and the Meadows.

The morning after they left Iron Creek, the Mormon militia followed them in pursuit, intending, it is supposed, to assault them at Clara Crossing. That this was no private outburst, and that, on the contrary, it was done by authority, is evident from sworn testimony to the effect that the assembling of those troops was the result of "*a regular military call from the superior officers to the subordinate officers and privates of the regiment. . . Said regiment was duly ordered to muster, armed and equipped as the law directs, and prepared for field operations.*" A regular military council was held at Parowan, at which were present President Isaac C. Haight, the Mormon High-Priest of Southern Utah, Colonel Dame, Major John D. Lee, and the Apostle George A. Smith.

No military council, whether of the militia or the ordinary troops of the line, would dare to determine upon such an important matter as the cutting off of an emigrant train of one hundred and thirty persons without receiving permission from superior authority. Brigham Young was in this case the superior authority—he was the Commander-in-Chief of the Militia:—the inference is obvious. I do not, of course, say that he gave the order for this accursed deed, but that it was his business to bring the criminals to justice no one can doubt or deny.

The regiment which started from Cedar City under the command of Major John D. Lee, the sub-agent for Indian affairs in Southern Utah, was accompanied by baggage-wagons and the other paraphernalia of war, excepting only heavy artillery, which in this case would have been useless. But, at the same time, a large body of the Piede Indians had been invited to accompany them.

An order came from head-quarters to cut off the entire company except the little children. The emigrants were utterly unprepared, and the first onslaught found them defenceless. Accustomed, however, to border warfare, they immediately corralled their wagons and prepared for a siege— their great misfortune was that they had not any water.

Major John D. Lee, finding the emigrants resolute, sent to Cedar City and Washington City for re-inforcements, which duly arrived.

The next morning, Major John D. Lee assembled his troops, including the auxiliaries which he had summoned, about half a mile from the intrenchment of the fated emigrants, and then and there informed them, with all the coolness which such an infamous scoundrel alone could muster, that the whole company was to be killed, and only the little children who were too young to remember anything were to be spared.

The unfortunate emigrants did not know who their foes were. They saw Indians, or men who were so colored that they looked like Indians, and they saw others who were more than strangers to them, but they had no clue to the cause of their detention. To them all was mystery. That Indians should attack them was quite within the bounds of probability, although there was at that time no cause for such an outrage; but that such an attack should be persistent, and should be carried on under the peculiar circumstances in question, was, to say the least, highly improbable.

A flag of truce was sent down to the unfortunate emigrants: but wherefore a flag of truce?—wherefore any conditions of warfare? and wherefore should the militia regiment be militant against them? No answer can be returned to these questions without disclosing secret scenes of sin and shameful iniquity at the mention of which even the souls of fiend might stand aghast.

A message was sent to the emigrant camp—a message not of Christian love and help, but such as might be sent from one foeman to another. A flag of truce was sent, and with it

a message to the effect that, if the emigrants chose to lay down
their arms and surrender themselves to the militia, their lives
should be spared. Consider the atrocity of this. Here was a
company of harmless emigrants, against whom not even the
slightest wrong-doing had been suggested. Yet, unquestioned,
unaccused, innocent of all wrong-doing, the authorised and
duly constituted militia of Utah Territory—a Territory claiming even then to be admitted into the Union as the State of
"*Deseret*"—was encamped against those unoffending citizens,
with the cruel, the iniquitous purpose of cutting them off.

Who could rightly tell a story so fearful as this? The
emigrant train—men, women, and children fainting and famishing for want of bread and meat. In their pockets was
money wherewith the necessaries of life might have been
bought, and the generous hand of the Almighty had that year
been open so wide and had scattered those necessaries so liberally that nothing but the wickedness of man towards his
fellow could have created a dearth. But so it was that darkness and the fear of death—a fearful death even at the door—
was all those poor emigrants had standing before their eyes.
What right had the Mormon militia to be pursuing, to be
hanging about the skirts of any body of emigrants. Their
very presence was in itself unauthorised—criminal. The
emigrants supposed that they were surrounded by Indians and
expected the cruellest treatment in case of resistance—not
death, but the outrage and shocking atrocities of savages.
They did not know that the red men who threatened their
lives and the lives of their helpless wives and infants were
brought together at that spot for that same purpose by the
counsel of Mormon authorities. They did not know that so
many of the appearing red-skins were only painted devils, mocks
of humanity, wretches who under the mask of a red-skin's color
were eager to perpetrate the foulest of offences—scoundrels a
thousand times damned in the opinion of men and by the
decree of God.

Day after day went by, and the poor creatures began to
despair—who can wonder? The brave men cared little for

their own lives; but there was something fearful in the thought that their darling ones would be scalped, and torn in pieces, and brutally outraged! Who can wonder that they resolved to sell life as dearly as they possibly could? They might at least die in defence of those they loved.

So day followed day. The agony of the unhappy men and women who were thus besieged and were in daily, hourly peril of the most frightful of all deaths can be imagined—not told. Meanwhile, what were those atrocious scoundrels doing who were lying in wait for their blood? Some of them were tricked out as Indians; some were in their own proper dresses; and, moreover, real Utes were there. The unhappy victims could not possibly escape—there was time for the murderers to do their work leisurely. Between chance shots, which were intended to, and did, carry death with them, they amused themselves with "pitching horse-shoe quoits:"—such heartlessness is almost beyond conception.

In terrible need of water, they thought that even the Indians who they supposed were their assailants might possibly respect a token of truce; so they dressed two little girls in white and sent them down to the well. But the fiends—the Mormon militia—shot them down. In the day of doom, the blood of those babes will testify more heavily against Major John D. Lee and Isaac C. Haight, and Colonel Dame, and George A. Smith, and the other wretch who plotted and contrived that fearful iniquity, than any of the base and cowardly crimes which have for years and years blackened their contemptible and miserable souls.

They could not possibly advance. Their corn would not last long. They were famishing for water. How long they could hold out was evidently only a matter of time. Had the train consisted only of men, they might certainly, if with loss, have cut their way through their besiegers and escaped; but with wives and children, and others bound to them by the tenderest ties, such a thing was impossible. They looked and waited. Savage Indians they supposed were their only enemies. Coldly, strangely as they had been treated at the

Mormon settlements, they never for a moment supposed that white men could be in league against them or could meditate their destruction.

Up in the meadows—in the distance—there was a white dusty cloud as if of some person or persons approaching:— the hearts of the emigrants leaped for joy. Was help coming at last? It was evident that a wagon was coming near, and the wagon was filled with armed men;—here was hope. After all the misery of that waitful watching, they were overjoyed, and shouted aloud with gladness, and sprang with open arms to welcome their visitors. Little did they suppose that the fiends who then came down, with pale faces and the manners of white men, were the same as those who, painted and decked out like Indians, had been leaguered about their camp with murderous intentions for so many days.

The wagon came near, and was found to be filled with armed men. Surely now, the unhappy emigrants thought, sub- stantial help had come—the authorities of Utah in the neighborhood, whether Gentile or Mormon, had come out in the cause of civilisation and humanity, and succor was at hand.

A white flag was waved from the wagon as an emblem of peace, and in order that the emigrants might know that it was white men and not the red demons of the hills who approached. They did not, indeed, know that these themselves were the monsters who had wronged them all this time and who were even now compassing their death.

Inside that wagon was President Haight, the infamous Mormon Bishop John D. Lee, and other authorities of the Church in Southern Utah. They professed to the emigrants that they came upon the friendly errand of standing between them and the Indians. They said that the Indians had taken offence at something that the emigrants had done, that they were thirsting for their blood, but that they—the Mormon offi- cials—were on good terms with them and had influence, and would use their good offices in the cause of mercy and of peace. After some discussion they left with the pro- fessed view of conciliating the Indians. Then they returned and said that the Indians had agreed, that if the emigrants marched back to Salt Lake City their lives should be spared ; but that they must leave everything behind them in their camp, even including the common weapons of defence which every Western man carries about his person. The Mormon officials then solemnly undertook to bring an armed force and to guard the emigrants safely back again to the Settlements.

The emigrants were not cowards, and would doubtless have preferred to cut their way through to the South, but they could not leave their wives and little ones, and any terms, however disadvantageous, were better than leaving those they loved to the tender mercy of those wretches.

This agreement being made, the Mormon officials retired, and after a short time again returned with thirty or forty armed men. Then the emigrants were marched out—the women and children in the front, and the men following, while the Mormon guard followed in the rear. When they had marched in this way about a mile and had arrived at the place where the Indians were hid in the bushes on each side of the road, the signal was given for the slaughter. So taken by surprise were the emigrants, and so implicitly had they confided in these murderers that they offered no resistance. The Mormon Militia—their guard—immediately opened fire upon them from the rear, while the Indians, and Mormons disguised as Indians, who were hidden among the bushes, rushed out upon them, shooting them down with guns and bows and arrows, and cutting some of the men's throats with knives. The women and children, shrieking with mortal terror, scattered and fled, some trying to hide in the bushes. Two young girls actually did escape for about a quarter of a mile when they were overtaken and butchered under circumstances of the greatest brutality. The son of John D. Lee endeavored to protect one poor girl who clung to him for help ; but his father, tearing her from him by violence, blew out her brains. Another unhappy girl is said to have kneeled to this same monster Lee, entreating him to spare her life. He dragged her into the bushes, stripped her naked, and cut her throat from ear to ear, after she had suffered worse at his hands than death itself. About half an hour was probably occupied in the butchery, and every soul of that company was cut off, excepting only a few little children who were supposed to be too young to understand or remember what had taken place. The unfortunate victims were then stripped, without reference to age or sex, and then left to rot upon the field. There they remained until torn and dismembered by the wolves, when it was then thought prudent to conceal such as lay nearest to the road. An eye-witness subsequently visiting the spot said :—

The scene of the massacre, even at this late day, was horrible to look upon. Women's hair in detached locks and in masses hung to the sage bushes and was strewn over the ground in many places. Parts of little children's dresses and of female costume dangled from the shrubbery, or lay scattered about, and among these, here and there on every hand, for at least a mile in the direction of the road, by two miles east and west, there gleamed, bleached white by the weather, the skulls and other bones of those who had suffered. A glance into the wagon, when all these had been collected, revealed a sight which never can be forgotten.

The remains were subsequently gathered together by Major Carleton, the United States Commissioner, who erected over them a large cairn of stones, surmounted by a cross of red cedar, with an inscription thereon : " *Vengeance is mine : I will repay, saith the Lord;*" and on a stone beneath were engraved the words :—

" Here 120 men, women, and children were massacred in cold blood, early in September, 1857. They were from Arkansas."

It is said that this monument was subsequently destroyed by order of Brigham Young, when he visited that part of the Territory.

The little children, while their parents were being butchered, had clung about their murderer's knees entreating mercy, but none of them finding it save those who were little more than infants. Their fears and cries the night after the murder are said to have been heart-rending. One little babe, just beginning to walk, was shot through the arm. Another little girl

SCENE OF THE MOUNTAIN MEADOWS' MASSACRE.

"Vengeance is Mine, I will repay—saith the Lord."

was shot through the ear, and the clothes of most of them were saturated with their mothers' blood.   They were distributed among the people of the settlements, and when finally the Government took them under the protection of the nation, the people among whom these little ones lived actually charged for their boarding.   Two of them are said to have uttered some words from which it was presumed that their intelligence was in advance of their years.   They were taken out quietly and—*buried!* This happened some time after the massacre.

Most of the property of the emigrants was sold by *public auction* in Cedar City :—the Indians got most of the flour and ammunition, and the Mormons the more valuable articles. They jested over it and called it " Spoil taken at the siege of Sevastopol."   There is legal proof that the clothing stripped from the corpses, blood-stained, riddled by the bullets, and with shreds of flesh attached to it, was placed in the cellar of the tithing office, where it lay about three weeks, when it was privately sold.   The cellar is said to have smelt of it for years. Long after this time, jewelry torn from the mangled bodies of the unfortunate women was publicly worn in Salt Lake City, and every one knew whence it came.   A tithing of it all is reported upon very conclusive evidence to have been laid at the feet of Brigham Young.

This is the story—most imperfectly told—for I dare not sketch its foulest details,—of the Mountain Meadows Massacre.   Brigham Young, who was at the time Governor of the Territory and also Indian Agent, made no report of the matter.   Let that fact of itself speak for his innocence or guilt.   Would any other governor or agent in another Territory have been thus silent ?   John D. Lee, and Dame, and Haight, and the other wretches have never been brought to trial or cut off from the Church, although their monstrous crime has never been a secret, nor have any endeavors been made to conceal it.

This fearful deed was one of the unavoidable results of the teachings of the Mormon leaders during the Reformation. There were crimes then perpetrated in secret which will never be known until the Day of Doom; and there were horrors which have been known and recorded, but for which no one has been brought to trial or has suffered inconvenience. There are men in Salt Lake City, who walk about unblushingly in broad daylight, but who are known to be murderers, and whose hands have been again and again dyed with blood under circumstances of the most atrocious cruelty.

There was one cruel murder—but by no means the worst—which came under my own personal observation, and which I have alluded to elsewhere—the murder of Dr. John King Robinson in Salt Lake City—which attracted more than ordinary attention. This gentleman was a physician of good standing, who came out as assistant-surgeon with the United States army, and afterwards began to practice in Salt Lake City. He was known as a man of unimpeachable moral character, and there are to this day hundreds of responsible people who would testify to his fair fame and rectitude; although he had by some means incurred the dislike of many of the Mormon leaders. He formed the idea of taking possession of some warm springs on the north of the city, and proposed to erect there baths, an hospital, etc. A small wooden shanty was erected for the purpose of holding possession, but the city authorities claimed the spring, and, after some very unpleasant proceedings, the matter was referred to the law courts, and Judge Titus decided against the doctor.

After this verdict had been rendered, Dr. Robinson seems to have acted very prudently, and to have remained in-doors as much as possible during the succeeding days. Between eleven and twelve o'clock on the night of the third day, however, after the family had retired to rest, a man called at the house, and stating that his brother had broken his leg by a fall from a mule and was suffering very much, he, after some earnest persuasion, induced the doctor to accompany him. Anxious as he might be to remain in-doors at such a time, no professional man would refuse to perform an act of mercy. He accordingly went. At a distance of about a couple of hundred steps from the house he was struck over the head with some sharp instrument, and immediately after shot through the brain. His wife, a young girl, to whom he had only been married a very short time, heard the report of the pistol, and witnesses saw men fleeing from the spot. The police were sent for, and the body was carried to Independence Hall, and afterwards to the victim's house. The Mayor of the city was not informed of the murder until ten o'clock the next day, and the chief-of-police who was sitting round the fire with his men when news of the murder arrived, went to bed immediately and did not visit the scene of the outrage for three days.

The following Sunday, Brigham Young, in the Tabernacle, publicly suggested that the doctor had probably been murdered by some of the soldiers from Camp Douglas, who were dissatisfied with his treatment when they were under his hands, or else that he had fallen in some gambling transaction—both of which statements, however, were known by every one present to be utterly false. No one was ever punished for this cruel murder. This murder did not occur during the Reformation, but it was the natural result of the teachings of those times.

I simply mention these facts without any comment of my own. Let the reader form his own conclusion. More of these frightful stories I do not care to relate; and I should not even have presented these to the notice of the reader had it not been impossible otherwise to give any suitable idea of that terrible "Reformation." The Gentile army came in. The Union Pacific Railroad was opened. Changes and chances altered all that had been, and brought into being that which might be, and that which finally really was. Instead of looking to the events of three or four thousand years ago, men began to act up to things which were—to think and act in the present, not to dream of the past. The day has gone by—but not far—when the perpetration openly of such deeds was possible; but it is still boasted that when "*Deseret*" becomes a State the "Saints" will " shew still greater Zeal *for the Lord!*"

21

CHAPTER XXIV.

WAYS AND WORKS OF THE SAINTS:—THE PROPHET'S MIL-LINERY BILL.

Life in Zion—Introduced to Brother Heber—"Have you got the Blues!"—A wife's trials: Counselled to take Another Wife—The Tabernacle Sermons—The Crowning Glory of a Man—Spiritual Food—"Filled with the Devil"—Face to Face with Polygamy—Winter in Salt Lake City—A New Position—I Produce My Treasures—My "Talkative Friend"—Comforting Visitors—"I don't like Crying Women—Afraid of Opposition—Paid in Salt Chips and Whetstones—Creating a Business—"Something Like Home"—A Bonnet for Brigham's Favorite Wife—Running up a Little Bill—How the *Honest* Prophet Paid It—Has He any Conscience?—My Whole Fortune Gone.

WHEN I arrived in Utah I found that nearly all the Elders with whom I had formerly been acquainted had more than one wife there. Many of these brethren called to see me, and kindly insisted that I should visit their families; but this I felt was almost an impossibility.

My whole nature rebelled at the thought of visiting where there were several wives; for, in defiance of all the teaching that I had listened to and the tyranny to which we had sub-mitted, human nature would assert itself, and my womanly in-stincts revolted against the system. I could not endure the thought of visiting those families in company with my husband. I thought that perhaps sometimes I might venture *alone*; but, Oh, not with him,—no, not with him. It was bad enough and humiliating enough for me to witness by myself the degrada-tion of my sex; but to do so in the presence of my husband was more than I could calmly contemplate. I knew that I should not be able to control myself, and might probably say some very unpleasant things, which I should afterwards regret; for I so thoroughly loathed even the idea of Polygomy at that time that I was filled with a desire to let every one know and understand just what my feelings were on that subject.

I had left New York against my will, although I had not openly rebelled. I had never reproached my husband about it, for I felt that his lot was irrevocably cast with the Mormons: I knew that when I married him, and it was of no use now for me to repine. I must go on to the end—there was no help for me. The journey across the Plains, and all the discoveries which I had made, had not tended to soothe my rebellious heart, and I am not quite sure that I did not sow by the way a little discontent among the sisters. The idea, however, that such was the case did not, I must admit, fill me with much repentance. To my husband I had said very little, but I think he would bear me witness that what I did say was said effectively. Now when I was brought face to face with practical Polygamy and could observe it in its most repulsive phases, I hated it more than ever.

One day, not long after our arrival, as we were taking a walk together, I saw across the road a man gesticulating after an eccentric fashion and beckoning to us. Mr. Stenhouse said: "that is Brother Heber C. Kimball;" and I looked again with interest to see what that celebrated Apostle was like. I had both heard and read a great deal about Brother Heber, and what I had learned was not at all of a character to impress me favorably—he had been so severe in his denunciation of every woman who dared to oppose Polygamy. On the present occasion his conduct was, I thought, anything but gentlemanly; and when we crossed the road to him,—which on account of his position in the Church—next to Brigham himself—we, of course, were compelled to do,—my face must have betrayed my feelings I am sure, for almost his first words after shaking hands were: "Have you got the blues?"

My answer was ready in a moment—"I have had nothing else ever since I came here."

"Well," he replied, "It is time that you should get rid of them, and I am going to talk to you some day soon, for I rather like your looks."

I did not like *his* looks much, however, nor was I at all pleased with his manner. I do not say that I was altogether without blame in feeling thus, for I was prejudiced. Of course I was prejudiced. From the first moment when I heard that Polygamy was a doctrine of the Church, I was predisposed to be dissatisfied with everything :—I was henceforth not myself, for the terrible apprehension of my own fate in the "Celestial Order" had changed my whole nature, and that change of itself was a great source of grief to me. I keenly realised that I was no longer the light-hearted pleasant companion to my husband that I had been, and many a time and oft I wished for his sake that I could die, for I felt that I never could be happy in Mormonism again.

How many times have I knelt by my husband's couch when he was unconscious of it, and have wept bitter tears of sorrow, earnestly praying to the Lord to subdue my rebellious heart, and, if it were necessary, rather than I should be a continual annoyance to my husband whom I loved with all my soul, that every particle of love in my heart should be withered, so that I might perchance, if without love, be able at least to do my duty. I fully realised that in Polygamy there could be no real love; and while my affections were still placed upon my husband, it was torture to live in a community where I was compelled to listen to the "counsels" which were given to him, day after day, regardless of my presence, to take another wife. I was too proud to notice any ordinary allusion that was made to the subject before me; but when the conversation was turned in that direction by those who professed to be sincere friends and to entertain a kindly interest in my welfare, I was compelled to listen and reply.

In my unhappy condition, I thought that perhaps I might derive some consolation from the sermons in the Tabernacle— something that might shed a softer light upon my rugged pathway. But instead of obtaining consolation, I heard that which aroused every feeling of my soul to rebellion and kindled again within me the indignation which I had been so long struggling to conquer.   I heard that woman was an inferior being, designed by the Lord for the especial glory and exaltation of man, that she was a creature that should feel herself honored if he would only make her the mother of his children — a creature who if very obedient and faithful through all the trials and tribulations in life, might some day be rewarded by becoming one of her husband's queens, but should even then shine only by virtue of the reflected light derived from the glory of her spouse and lord.   He was to be her "saviour," for he was all in all to her; and it was through him alone and at his will that she could obtain salvation.   We were informed that man was the crowning glory of creation, for whom all things — woman included — were brought into being; and that the chief object of woman's existence was to help man to his great destiny.

Not a sentence; indeed, not a word did we ever hear as to the possibility of womanly perfection and exaltation in her own right; and not only so, but, as if this were not enough to crush all ambition out of our souls, we were instructed in some new views of marriage.   The great object of marriage, we were told, was the increase of children.   Those diviner objects — the companionship of soul; the devotion of a refined and pure affection; the indissoluble union of two existences — were never presented to the yearning hearts of those poor women who listened to the miserable harangues of the Tabernacle: such aspirations had nothing to do with the hard, cruel facts of their life in Polygamy.

And this I found was how the women of Utah were spiritually sustained.   Seldom, indeed, was taught anything better, but frequently much that was worse.   If Nature, asserting its right to a full return of love, should manifest itself and inspire some of these poor wives to rebel against the lives which they were compelled to lead in Polygamy, then it would be said, in the language of the Tabernacle, that the women were "filled with the devil," and that unless they repented speedily, they

would "apostatise and go to hell;"—an assurance which was
scarcely necessary, for many of those poor souls were enduring as much as if they were there already.   Or if some woman
was found objecting to Polygamy on account of its crushing
and degrading effects upon women generally, then, as I just
said, she was told in the coarse language of Brigham Young
himself that "such women had no business to complain; it
was quite enough honor for them to be permitted to bear
children to God's holy Priesthood."

I found, therefore, that the sermons in the Tabernacle were
not calculated to help me much spiritually.   I had neither
friend nor counsellor on earth to whom I could turn for help—
my God alone remained to me.   But, ah, how different were
my ideas of God then, from those which I entertained before
and since.   Once I could look upon the beauties of nature
and the varied experiences of human life, and while my soul
was lifted up with devotion and gratitude, I could see the loving hand of my Heavenly Father in everything around me.
Now there was neither light nor beauty before my eyes—all
was dark and dreary; there was nothing to draw away my
heart from such sad thoughts as these.   It was painfully clear
to my understanding, then as now, that in Mormonism woman
was to lose her personal identity.   All that Christianity had
done to elevate her was to be ruthlessly set aside and trampled
under foot, and she was instantly to return to the position
which she occupied in the darkest ages of the world's
existence.

I had at that time the daily and hourly cares of a family
devolving upon me, and had not therefore much leisure to
spend in visiting my friends even if I had desired to do so.
Notwithstanding that, however, I had abundant opportunities
of observation; and thus my experience of Mormonism and
Polygamy in Utah is much the same as that of any Mormon
woman of ordinary sense; I only tell what others could relate if
they had the inclination to do so.   It was not possible for me to
live in Salt Lake City without being brought face to face with
Polygamy in some shape or other every day of my life.   Had

it been otherwise, and if remaining at home would have kept it from my view, I probably never should have had the courage to enter a house where it was practiced. To those who know nothing of that degrading system this may seem rather an exaggeration of feeling; and yet, even at that early day, I had seen so much of the folly and weakness of the Mormon brethren, both in London and New York, before we went to Utah, and had witnessed so many evil results of their teachings, that it was with the greatest difficulty that I could control my feelings sufficiently to call upon any family where there was more than one wife. And yet what I knew then was nothing in comparison to what I afterwards witnessed— yes, that I myself endured.

During the winter, although I visited very little, I attended a good many parties at the Social Hall; but I did so more from a wish to be agreeable to my husband than from any pleasure that they afforded me, for life had lost its charm to me, and I was not happy. How many times have I gazed wistfully at those lofty mountains which surrounded the city, and felt that they were indeed my prison walls. How bitterly have I realised that I should never be able to go beyond them. But in a new country, with a family to provide for, a mother has not much time to waste in.pir ing, even if it be for liberty itself, and I would willingly draw the veil over that portion of my life.

As my husband had been on mission for so many years and had spent all his time in the service of the Church, with the exception of a few brief months before we left New York— when he was engaged on the staff of the New York *Herald*— I naturally enough thought that when we reached Zion his occupation would be gone. There would be no need of preaching to the Saints: on the contrary they would be able to teach us; and we should have to find out what we could do in this new country to support ourselves and our children. In this I was not mistaken.

Now among the "absolutely necessary" things which I had brought with me from New York, were about three hundred

dollars' worth of millinery goods, which I had secreted among
our other properties, thinking that they would very probably
come in useful to the fair daughters of Zion—notwithstanding that the Elders had told me of fiery sermons delivered by
the Prophet himself condemning all feminine display, and that
the sisters would scorn to wear Gentile fashions. I knew my
own sex too well to believe that all this was strictly true, and
I felt certain that I should find, even among the Saints, some
weak sisters who would appreciate my thoughtfulness in
bringing such articles for their use. I had also noticed that
the American Elders themselves would frequently enquire
where they could buy the best gloves and the prettiest ribbons
and laces, and that looked a little suspicious.

Quite a number of such articles, therefore, found their way
into my list of "absolute necessaries," and I know that my
husband was secretly quite at a loss to know what had become
of a certain sum of money which he was aware I had obtained from the sale of some of our things in New York.
But my foresight in this instance was very useful to us when
we arrived in Zion.

One day when Mr. Stenhouse was absent seeking employment, I thought I would make a display of my treasures and
surprise him on his return. Accordingly, with the assistance of our faithful domestic, whom I had brought with me
across the Plains, and who had also lived with me in Switzerland, we contrived to place two or three planks in such a way
as to make a rough table on which to display the goods. I
had been secretly at work for about two weeks, trimming the
bonnets and hats, and making a number of head-dresses, such
as were worn in New York when we left; and, although
we had been three months on the Plains, and quite a month
in Utah, yet those bonnets and head-dresses were of the very
latest style to the ladies of Salt Lake City.

My Swiss girl was quite a carpenter, and when my temporary table was arranged, I placed a pretty-looking cloth over
it to hide its defects, and then began to arrange the various
articles. I found that I had a much finer assortment than I

had imagined, for I had bought them at different times, and had packed them away hurriedly, lest Mr. Stenhouse or some of the other Elders—for there were generally one or two in the house—should object to my taking them. When my table was filled, and I found that I had still more to display, I was very much pleased, for I saw in my hats and bonnets, flour, meat, and potatoes for my children, and I felt hopeful, for one of the sisters had assured me that I should be certain to sell them. The next thing to do was to advertise my stock. After some reflection, I remembered another of the sisters, who was quite a good talker, and who felt very kindly towards me. I had known her in England—she had been in Utah about three years, and her husband had by that time been blessed with two other wives. She used to say that she had no patience with a set of grumbling women who did not know what was good for them. I do not think that the blessed-ness enjoyed by her husband was shared by the two wives, for more forlorn-looking women I never saw. My husband, however, told me that this was none of my business, and I believed him, of course, after the fashion of all good wives.

But to return. This good sister, besides being an excellent talker, had really nothing else to do besides visiting her neighbors, for the other wives now took entire charge of all the household duties. So I made her a present of a new bonnet, as I knew that then in two days my goods would be quite sufficiently advertised ; and in this I was not mistaken.

Almost the first visitors who called to see me were a lady and her daughter. I talked freely to her and answered her enquiries, and she told me that she herself had had some experience in the business. "In Salt Lake City," she said, "I think you will not be able to sell those goods; they are too fashionable for the people here, and there is no encouragement given to any one in this business. I am afraid you will be disappointed."

I believed every word she said, and felt all my airy, hopeful castles begin to crumble away. Before she left, however, she very kindly offered to purchase all my goods at a low figure

and thus relieve me of the anxiety and trouble of selling them.
But I had had a little experience in the world,—although probably I appeared to her somewhat innocent,—and I thought
that if she could sell them, there was a chance at least that I
also might be able to do so.   At-any-rate, I resolved to try,
and I told her so when she left me with many kind wishes for
my success.   But what she had said during her visit had
chilled my enthusiasm, and I pictured all my pretty newly-
made articles becoming soiled and faded, with no one to buy
them; while the little ones, barefooted—like so many children
in Utah then—were running about crying for bread which I
could not buy them.   I felt bad, and—if I must confess it—I
sat down and had a good cry.

Just at that moment I heard a knock at the door, and
hastily drying my eyes, I opened it, and there stood my talkative friend.

"Stop crying!" she exclaimed, "What is the matter, my
dear?   Oh *do* stop crying.   I don't like crying women: we
see so many of them among the Saints of God that it is really
a shame and a disgrace.   Tell me what is the matter?
Has your husband got another wife, or are you afraid that
he won't be able to get one?   Come, tell me!"

All this was uttered in a breath, and without the possibility
of my putting in a word by way of reply or remonstrance.   At
last I told her that I had just had a visit from one of the
sisters and her daughter, whom I described.

"I know," she said, "I met her as I was coming here.   Do
you know who she is?"

"No," I replied, "I do not think she told me her name; she
simply came to look at the goods."

"And did she tell you that they would sell well, and
that they are the best investment that you could have
made?"

"Quite the contrary," I said, "She discouraged me so much
that I could not help shedding tears."

"Well now," she answered, "that was Mrs. C . . . . ., one
of our milliners here; and you suppose she was going to en-

courage you to set up an opposition shop, do you? If you do, why, you've got something yet to learn." Indeed I felt that I had got a great deal to learn.

"Now *I* have come to tell you quite a different story," she said, "This very afternoon you will have at least a dozen ladies here; and ladies, too, who have got the money to pay for what they have, and who won't pay you in salt chips and whetstones."

" Do they ever pay in such things ?" I enquired.

"Why certainly they do. That is the kind of pay that the good Saints generally expect their poor brethren and sisters to be satisfied with, and to feed their hungry children upon. But I say that this is wrong. Not that I want to set myself up as a judge in Zion, or that I should criticise the actions of the brethren—God forbid! But when I see the rich brethren grinding the faces of the poor in that way, why, I say that it is wrong. But you must not take any such pay as that. You may not always get money, but you can at least get flour, potatoes, and molasses. Now, I tell you that you are going to sell every article that you have got, and I shall take pleasure in recommending you and talking about it. Why, I've been to about two score people already ;—but, there! I see your husband coming, and I must go!" My husband, indeed, *was* there. He was not very fond of my talkative friend, and passed her by with a polite salutation only ; but when he saw what I had been doing the light dawned upon his mind—he no longer wondered what had become of the dollars in New York, and—astonished at my success—he congratulated me upon the good use to which I had put them.

After this interview I felt quite encouraged, and I very soon found that my friend's predictions were correct. I had no difficulty in selling, and I created quite a little business, although we lived a considerable distance from Main Street. And what with my efforts, and some employment which my husband obtained, we contrived to get through our first winter in Salt Lake City.

But I anticipate.

One day my husband informed me that there was a house about to be vacated shortly, and that Brigham Young had told him we had better take it. It was pleasantly situated near the Tabernacle, and, as houses then were, it was quite a desirable residence. We had it thoroughly cleaned, and then moved in. When I arrived in the evening I found that Mr. Stenhouse, with the assistance of our faithful Swiss girl, had arranged everything as the goods arrived from the other house ; and the place looked so clean, and there was such a bright fire burning that I felt that we now had really something like a home, and my heart was filled with gratitude.

Soon after our establishment in our new home, Brigham sent for me and asked me to make a handsome bonnet for his then favorite wife Emmeline. He left it entirely to my taste ; I was to make just what I pleased, so that it suited her and gave satisfaction.

I made my bonnet ; and when I presented it, Brigham Young was so pleased that he immediately gave me an order to make one for each of his wives. I was very much pleased at this, for we needed furniture and many other necessaries very badly, and I thought that this would enable me to get them. I expected, of course, that my account would be paid in money, for I did not suppose that the Prophet of the Lord would offer me chips or whetstones :—he could afford to pay cash, and, of course, would do so. He had furnished me with some material out of his own store—for Brigham Young had a dry-goods' and grocery store of his own at that time—and I was to furnish the remainder. It was very little indeed that he supplied, and therefore my account was likely to amount to a considerable sum, for almost every wife had at least one bonnet which she wished made over with new trimmings, besides the new one.

I worked constantly for three weeks, with the assistance of two girls, to each of whom I paid six dollars a week besides board. This was a difficult thing for me to do at that time in Utah, for money was seldom seen there then ; but I was rejoicing in the prospect of the comfortable new furniture which I should have when it was all done. Furniture at that time was very expensive; there was nothing better than white pine articles—stained or painted. The commonest kind of wooden rocking-chair cost fifteen dollars, and common painted wooden chairs were six dollars a piece, with everything else in proportion. This being our first winter, we had not been able to get much, and I thought I would devote the proceeds of the work I was doing for Brigham to fitting up the house a little; and, with what I earned from my other customers, I contrived to pay my help, so as to have all the rest clear.

All was completed, and great satisfaction expressed at the result of my labors. So I asked my husband to present my account and, if possible, get it settled—it amounted to about two hundred and seventy-five dollars, although I had dealt very liberally with the Prophet, and had charged for the goods but little more than they cost me. When he returned, I hastened to meet him, for I had partly selected the furniture and I wanted to go and purchase it. But I was like poor Perrette, the milkmaid, who counted her chickens a little too soon; for Mr. Stenhouse told me that Brother Brigham had given orders that the amount should be credited to us *for tithing!* What a shock this was to me; for that sum, small as it may appear, was my whole fortune at the time, and it was gone at one sweep! "Can it be possible," I said, "that he can be so mean as that? Where can his conscience be? or has he any; to deprive me of my hard earnings in this way. He shall not do it—I will *make* him pay me."

My indignation was so great that I did not reflect how imprudent I was to talk thus of the Prophet of the Lord; but my husband said: "What can you *do?* You cannot help yourself. You can *do* nothing but submit. Let us try to forget it; or, if not, it will perhaps be a lesson to us." But I did not forget it and never could, although I tried very hard; and when many months had passed, and I no longer suffered from the effects of my loss, I still remembered it—and I always *shall* remember the way in which Brigham paid for his wives' bonnets.

CHAPTER XXV.

MYSTERIES OF THE ENDOWMENT HOUSE:—FEARFUL OATHS AND SECRET CEREMONIES.

Saintly Privileges—The Origin of the Endowments—The Fraternity of the Saints—Story of the Mysteries—Shocking Doings in Days Gone By—Whisperings of Terrible Deeds—How the Mormons Mind Their Own Business—The Temple Garments—Inside the Endowment House—The Book of Life—Our Robes and Our Oil Bottles—The Washings and Anointings—The High-Priestess—Invoking Blessings—The Mysterious Garment—A New Name—The Garden of Eden—An Extraordinary Representation—The Duplicate of the Devil—The First Degree—Terrible and Revengeful Oaths—The Punishment of the Apostate—Pains and Penalties of Betrayal—Grips and Passwords—The Mysterious Mark—Singular Apostolic Sermon—The Second Degree—Secret and Significant Signs—Behind the Veil—The Third Degree—Celestial Matrimony—Eight Hours of "Mystery"—I Justify Myself.

NOT many weeks after our arrival in Salt Lake City, my husband told me that we might now enjoy the privilege of going through the Endowment House.

This was intended as a great favor to us, on the part of the authorities, for most people have to wait a long while before receiving their Endowments; but my husband's influence and position in the Church was, I presume, the reason why we were admitted so soon.

Now, I had heard so much of the Endowments and the Endowment House that I quite dreaded to pass through this ordeal. The idea of the whole ceremony was, that thereby we should receive the special grace of God; be united—man and woman—making one perfect creature; receive our inheritance as children of God; and, in fact, be made partakers of the plenitude of every blessing.

All this sounds very well as a statement, but it is only the statement which would be made from the ideal Mormon standpoint. I had heard other things about the Endowments which did not present such a favorable impression, and although I do not wish to record all the absurd stories which were, and are, current among the Gentiles, I think it only right that I should state what my own views were before we received our privileges.

Joseph Smith, the Prophet, and very many of his early associates belonged to the ancient and honorable order of Freemasons. When he was initiated into the mysteries of that society, and what position he attained therein, I do not know; but one thing is certain, that when he, under the influence of his own peculiar religious fanaticism, endeavored to engraft upon Freemasonry some of the leading ideas of the new religion, he and those connected with him were publicly disavowed by the lodges in the West. I cannot without some trouble give here any documentary evidence, but I may be permitted, perhaps, to state that I have myself seen newspapers of that period—and the West then was a very primitive country—which contained formal official declarations duly signed by respectable persons, stating that Joseph Smith and others were no longer to be considered in fellowship with any of the Western lodges.

The idea of a bond of brotherhood—secret and indissoluble —seems ever to have been present in Joseph's mind. Whether the germ of this idea was derived from Masonry, or not, is of little moment. Gentlemen who certainly ought to know have assured me that such a notion was altogether ridiculous; but of that, as a lady, I am, of course, not competent to judge. It is, however, quite clear that the clannish or fraternal spirit among the Mormons has always pre-eminently distinguished them, and is just as noticeable at the present day as it was in Joseph's time.

It has always been commonly reported, and to a great extent believed, that the mysteries of the Endowment House were only a sort of imitation—burlesque, it might be—of the rites of Masonry; but I need hardly say that this statement when examined by the light of facts is altogether ungrounded and absurd, as the reader will presently perceive. Still, the notion that some deeply mysterious ceremony was celebrated by the initiated has always possessed a charm to Gentile as well as Mormon minds, and the most extravagant statements have been made in reference to the Endowment House;—in fact, to such an extent has this been the case, that most, if not all, of the Saints who have passed through the House have looked forward to the period of their initiation as a most impressive and painful ordeal, and the influence of this feeling I myself fully realised.

I knew well that no marriage was considered binding unless it had been celebrated in that place. I knew that the Saints, however long they might have been wedded, were under the necessity of being reunited there before they could be considered lawfully married and their children legitimate. According to the highest Mormon Authority no marriage is valid unless the ceremony is performed in the Temple. The Temple is not yet built, and as Joseph, the Prophet said, "No fellow can be damned for doing the best he knows how," the Saints meanwhile do "the next best thing," and are married in the Endowment House. I knew that there and then the faithful were said to be "endowed" with their heavenly inheritance. I saw how *absolutely needful* it was that my husband and myself should become partakers of those mysteries; but I was influenced by the strange stories which I had heard of unhallowed and shameful doings in that same Endowment House, and consequently I feared to enter in.

My fears were not, however, altogether groundless or visionary. It has been whispered—falsely perhaps—that in that Endowment House scenes have been enacted so fearful that words would falter on the lips of those who told the tale concerning them. I have *heard* of such things from men of integrity and honor; but they were not eye-witnesses of what they related, and they could not, or would not, give me their authorities. One thing I am certain of;—if such horrible deeds were ever perpetrated within those walls there remains no *living* witness to testify of them. The lips of who alone could tell the whole truth are sealed in silence which the trump of doom alone shall break.

When I refer the reader to what I have already spoken of the Blood-Atonement, and of the "Reformation," I think that that plain statement of facts renders it clear to any ordinary intelligence, that, if in the Endowment House no such deeds of darkness were ever perpetrated, it was not because such things were contrary to the spirit of Mormonism as taught by Brigham Young and the Apostles, nor was it because such things had never been done with the full approbation of the leaders of the Church, but on account of some accidental reason, into which it is needless to enquire.

It was, of course, no fear of any personal violence or any painful disclosures in that respect that made me reluctant to receive my Endowments, for at that time I was by profession apparently a good Mormon ;—if I had my doubts and misgivings, I had them in common with nine-tenths of the Mormon women, and had therefore nothing to fear. The true cause of my reluctance was of a more delicate and personal nature. I had been informed that, if I refused to go, my husband could not go alone, he would be compelled to take another wife and go with her. This was not all. I found that it was quite common for the Elders to take a second wife when they took their first Endowments, and thus, as they coarsely expressed it, "kill two birds with one stone." Moreover, I had heard of men who feared to introduce Polygamy into their households, presenting to their wives, while going through the House, a young girl as their intended bride, feeling sure that the wife would not dare to make a scene before the Assembly. How could I know that my husband also had not such an idea in his mind? True, I trusted him implicitly, and did not believe it possible that he could deceive me. But had not men who

22

were universally known for their integrity and honor acted in the same way to *their* wives; and with so many evidences of the best and most honest natures being corrupted by the unrighteous teachings of their religion, could I be blamed for doubting him whom I loved best? Wives out of Utah doubt their own husbands, and very frequently have the best of reasons for doing so, but what woman, other than a Mormon, ever lived in constant dread that her husband, who she knew was devotedly attached to her, would do to her the cruellest wrong that man can inflict and woman can endure, for the sake of his religion and in the holy Saviour's name?

My mind was agitated by conflicting thoughts. Sometimes fear and apprehension, sometimes indignation and hatred would make me feel perfectly reckless. Then love to my husband, and thoughts of our little ones calmed my troubled mind, and I was tranquil, until excited by some injury which I witnessed, when once more brooding over the cruel wrongs which, in God's name, had been inflicted upon the women of Utah, my anger would revive again.

There was also another reason why I particularly objected to passing through the Endowment House. I had been told many strange and revolting stories about the ceremonies which were there performed, for it is said that in the Nauvoo Temple the most disgraceful things were done. About what was done at Nauvoo I can say nothing, as it was before my time, but still it is only fair to say, that people who in every other relation in life I should have deemed most reliable and trustworthy were my informants respecting those strange stories. Of the Endowments in Utah I can, of course, speak more positively, as I myself passed through them; and I wish to say most distinctly that, although the initiation of the Saints into "The Kingdom," appears now to my mind as a piece of the most ridiculous absurdity, there was nevertheless nothing in it indecent or immoral;—of which the reader himself shall presently be the judge.

It is an invariable rule among the Mormons, as I have before intimated, for every man or woman to mind his or her own business, and nothing else. In this respect they certainly present a good example to the Gentile world. Thus it was, that until I myself went through the Endowments, I was totally ignorant of what they were; although, of course, so many people with whom I had daily intercourse could so easily have enlightened me if they had been thus minded. With apostates, I, of course, had nothing to do; and, had it been otherwise, it is most probable that they would have been so much ashamed of the folly of the whole performance that they would not have spoken explicitly about it. Besides this, every Mormon's mouth was closed by the oath of that same Endowment House—the penalty of breaking which was death—a penalty which no one doubted would be sternly enforced. Thus, totally in the dark, and remembering only the strange stories told about "washings" and "anointings" and an imitation of the Garden of Eden, with Adam and Eve clothed in their own innocence alone, it can be no wonder that any modest woman should wish to evade all participation in such scenes.

I spoke to my husband about it, and he tried to reassure me, but what he said had rather a contrary effect.

Before we left England, when speaking of these ceremonies, my husband told me that they were simply a privilege and a matter of choice. But what a choice! I might go or refuse to go; but, if I refused, he must—if he went through it all—take another wife in my place—and, as I knew, there would be no difficulty in finding one. I should in consequence be known as a rebellious woman; annoyance and indignity would be heaped upon me; while within my own home I should be compelled to occupy the position of second wife—as the one who is married first in the Endowment House is considered the first wife and has the control of everything. My husband told me that now he was most anxious to go:—he had already been notified three times that such was his privilege, and there were, he said, good reasons why we ought gladly to accept the opportunity. It was an honor, he said, for which many people had waited for years.

My husband reminded me that we had been married by a

Gentile and while living among Gentiles, and that—as I said before—our marriage was not valid, and our children were not legitimate. Only those children of ours who were born *after* the ceremony in the Endowment House would be legitimate,—the others were outcasts from the " Kingdom " unless we adopted them *after* our initiation, and thus made them heirs. In any case, poor children! they could never be considered the *real* heirs—they could only be " heirs by adoption."

So I agreed to go, trying to persuade myself that it was a sacred duty; for although my faith in Mormonism had been roughly shaken, I still believed that its origin was divine.

As we had been but a few weeks in Utah we had not prepared our " Temple garments," not thinking that we should be called upon so soon to go through. We had therefore to borrow, as most people do, for the occasion.

The Temple robe, which is a long, loose, flowing garment, made of white linen or bleached muslin, and reaching to the ancle, had been placed upon us just before we took the oaths. It was gathered to a band about twelve inches long, which rested on the right shoulder, passed across the breast, and came together under the left arm, and was then fastened by a linen belt. This leaves the left arm entirely free. The veil consists of a large square of Swiss muslin, gathered in one corner so as to form a sort of cap to fit the head; the remainder falls down as a veil. The men wear the same kind of under garment as the women, and their robes are the same, but their head-dress is a round piece of linen drawn up with a string and a bow in front, something after the fashion of a Scotch cap. All good Mormons, after they have received their first Endowments, get whole suits of Temple robes made on purpose for them so that they may be ready for use at any time when they are needed. All marriages in the Endowment House are performed in these robes, and in them all Saints who have received their Endowments are buried. Besides our robes we were instructed to take with us a bottle of the best olive oil.

At seven o'clock in the morning of the day appointed, we

presented ourselves at the door of the Endowment House, and were admitted by Brother Lyon, the Mormon poet. Everything within was beautifully neat and clean, and a solemn silence pervaded the whole place. The only sound that could be heard was the splashing of water, but whence the sound proceeded we could not see. In spite of myself, a feeling of dread and uncertainty respecting what I had to go through would steal over my mind, and I earnestly wished that the day was over.

We waited patiently for a little while, and presently a man entered and seated himself at a table placed there for that purpose, upon which was a large book. He opened the book, and then calling each person in turn, he took their names and ages and the names of their fathers and mothers, and carefully entered each particular in the book. Our bottles of oil were then taken from us, and we were supposed to be ready for the ceremony.

First we were told to take off our shoes and leave them in the ante-room, and then to take up our bundles and pass into another room beyond. This was a large bath-room which was divided down the middle by a curtain of heavy material placed there for the purpose of separating the men from the women. Here my husband left me—he going to the men's and I to the women's division. In the bath-room were two or three large bathing tubs supplied by streams of hot and cold water. We were as much concealed from the men as if we had been in an entirely separate room, and everything was very quiet and orderly.

Miss Eliza R. Snow, the poetess, and a Mrs. Whitney, were the officiating attendants on that occasion. The former conducted me to one of the bathing tubs, and placing me in it, she proceeded to wash me from the crown of my head to the soles of my feet. As she did this she repeated various formulas to the effect that I was now washed clean from the blood of this generation and should never, if I remained faithful, be partaker in the plagues and miseries which were about to come upon the earth. When I had thus been washed clean, she wiped me dry, and then taking a large horn filled with the olive oil which we had brought, she anointed me. The oil was poured from the horn by Mrs. Whitney into the hand of Eliza Snow, who then applied it to me. The horn was said to be the horn of plenty which, like the widow's cruse of oil, would never fail as long as the ordinance should continue to be administered. In addition to the crown of my head, my eyes, ears and mouth were also anointed ; my eyes that they might be quick to see, my ears that they might be apt at hearing, and my mouth that I might with wisdom speak the words of eternal life. She also anointed my feet, that they might be swift to run in the ways of the Lord. I was then given a certain garment to put on.

Now this garment is one peculiar to the Mormon people. It is made so as to envelop the whole body and it is worn night and day. I was told that after having once put it on, I must never wholly take it off before putting on another, but that I should change one half at a time, and that if I did so I should be protected from disease and even from death itself; for the bullet of an enemy would not penetrate that garment, and that from it even the dagger's point should be turned aside. It has been said that the Prophet Joseph carelessly left off this peculiar garment on the day of his death, and that had he not done so the rifles of his assassins would have been harmless against him.

When thus arrayed, I proceeded to put on a white night-dress and skirt, stockings, and white linen shoes. A new name was then whispered into my ear, which I was told I must never mention to any living soul except my husband in the Endowment House. This name was taken from the Bible, and I was given to understand that it would be the name whereby I should be admitted into the celestial kingdom. This was of course very gratifying. A circumstance, however, occurred which took from me all the pride which might have been mine in the possession of a new name. There was among our number a deaf woman ; Mrs. Whitney had to tell her her name once or twice over, loud enough for me to hear, and thus I found that her new name, as well as mine, was Sarah. To make the matter worse, another sister whispered : " Why that is my name too." This entirely dispelled any enthusiasm which otherwise I might have felt. I could well understand that I might yet become a Sarah in Israel, but if we all were Sarahs, there would not be much distinction or honor in being called by that name. As a matter of course I supposed that the men would all become Abrahams.

Our washing and anointed being now over, we were ready for the initiation—there were about fifteen couples in all.

A voice from behind the curtain asked Miss Snow if we were ready, and was answered in the affirmative. We were then arranged in a row, the curtain was drawn aside, and we stood face to face with the men who had, of course, on their side of the curtain been put through the same ordeal. I felt dreadfully nervous, for I did not know what was coming next, and I could not quite dismiss from my mind the stories that I had heard about these mysteries. But in spite of my nervousness, curiosity was strong in me at that moment—as it was, I suppose, in the others ; for, as soon as the curtain was drawn aside, we all cast our eyes in the direction of the men. They, as might be expected, were looking in our direction, and when I beheld them, I must say that my sympathies were drawn out towards the poor creatures. However little vanity or personal pride they possessed, they must have felt it unpleasant to have to appear in the presence of ladies in such a dress—or rather *un*dress ; and notwithstanding the solemn meaning of the ceremony, there was just the ghost of a smile upon our faces as we looked at each other and dropped our eyes again. To any one who did not feel as we did the religious nature of the initiation, the scene must have appeared perfectly ludicrous. In fact, some of us felt it so. One sister, just as the curtain was drawn up and we came in full view of our lords, cried out: "Oh dear, oh dear, where shall I go? What shall I do?" This, as may be supposed, caused a laugh which was, of course, immediately suppressed.

We could see how the men looked, but of our own appearance we could not so easily judge. Certainly, we must nave looked anything but handsome in our white garments and with the oil trickling down our faces and into our eyes, making them smart and look red. There was nothing, however, for us to do but to submit quietly and make the best of it we could. Ashamed as I was, I thought I might venture to look at my husband—there could be no harm in that;—but when I saw his demure-looking countenance and his efforts to keep his clothing in order, I thought I should be compelled to laugh outright, for I could see that his thoughts were more occupied about his personal appearance than with the solemnity of the occasion. The men were all dressed in the same kind of garment as the women:—drawers and shirt all in one—very much like those which are used for children to sleep in—and over that an ordinary white shirt, such as men always wear;—that, with socks and white linen shoes, completed their toilet.

Clad after this interesting fashion, we sat opposite to each other for several minutes, and then my husband and myself were instructed to come forward and kneel at the altar while all the rest remained standing. It is the custom thus to select two persons, and we were either picked out by chance, or it might be, as my husband was thought a good deal of by the authorities, that they considered he would feel honored by the preference.

Suddenly a voice was heard speaking to some one, who also replied. This voice from the unseen was supposed to be the voice of Elohim in conversation with Jehovah, and the words that were used were much the same as those contained in the first chapter of the book of Genesis describing the creation of the world. Finally, Jehovah and Elohim declare their intention to come down and visit the earth. This they do, and pronounce all that they behold very good; but they declare that it is necessary that one of a higher order of intelligence than the brute creation should be placed in the world to govern and control all else.

Michael the Archangel is now called, and he is placed upon

the earth under the name of Adam, and power is given him over all the beasts of the field, the fowls of the air, and the fishes of the sea. Moreover the fruits of the earth are all given to him for his sustenance and pleasure, but he is strictly charged, as in Bible-story, not to eat of one particular tree which stands in the midst of the garden. This tree is represented by a small real evergreen, and a few bunches of dried raisins are hung upon it as fruit.

It is now discovered that it is not good for man to be alone; Elohim and Jehovah, therefore, hold another conversation upon that subject, and they finally determine to give a companion to Adam. They, therefore, cause a deep sleep to fall upon Michael—or Adam as he is now called—and they prepare to operate upon him. Here we were all instructed to assume the attitude of deep sleep by dropping our heads upon our breasts. Elohim and Jehovah then came down and go through the motions of removing a rib from the side of the sleeper, which said rib appears immediately upon the scene in the person of Eliza R. Snow. Elohim and Jehovah are generally represented by two of the Twelve Apostles. When Brigham is present he plays a prominent part.

And now the devil makes his appearance in the person of W. W. Phelps. Phelps used always to personate the devil in the endowments, and the *rôle* suited him admirably. He is dead now, but whether it has made any difference in his *status*, I cannot tell, nor do I know who has succeeded him in his office. The devil wears a very tight-fitting suit of black muslin, with knee breeches and black stockings and slippers. This dress had all the appearance of a theatrical costume, and the man himself looked as much like one might imagine the devil would look, as he possibly could. He began by trying to scrape acquaintance with Eve, whom he meets while taking a walk in the garden. The innocent, unsuspecting woman is fascinated by his attentions. Father Adam—who seems to have had a touch of the Mormon about him—perhaps was not the most attentive of husbands; or he may have fallen into the same error into which many of his sons have fallen since

—neglecting to pay the same attentions after marriage as he was wont to before—and left his young wife to the mercy of the tempter. However that may be, Satan and Eve are soon discovered in conversation together, and Eve appears to be particularly pleased with Satan. At length he offers her some of the fruit of the forbidden tree, and after some little demur she accepts it and eats thereof.

Then the devil leaves her, Adam makes his appearance, and Eve persuades him also to eat of the fruit of the tree. After this they make a dumb show of perceiving their condition, and an apron of white linen is produced, on which are sewn pieces of green silk, in imitation of fig leaves, and in these they both attire themselves.

Then all the brethren and sisters produced similar aprons which they had brought with them on purpose, and these they put on, as Adam and Eve had already done. Elohim now appeared again, and called Adam ; but Adam was afraid, and hid himself in the garden with Eve. The curse was now pronounced upon the serpent—the devil—who reäppears upon his hands and knees, making a hissing noise as one might suppose a serpent would do. We were then all driven out of the Garden of Eden, into another room which represented the world ;—and this ended the " First Degree."

We were now supposed to be out in the world, earning our daily bread by the sweat of our brows, and we were informed that although we had been driven out from the presence of the Lord, yet a plan of salvation would be devised for us, by which we should be enabled to return to our first estate. We were to wait patiently until this plan should be disclosed to us.

There was here such a mixture of persons and events that I could not exactly follow the idea that was intended to be conveyed,—if there was any idea at all. Men representing the ancient prophets entered, and gave instructions to the people to prepare themselves for the first coming of our Saviour upon earth. Then we were taught certain pass-words and grips ; and then we were all arranged in a circle. The women covered their faces with their veils, and we all kneeled down, and, with our right hands uplifted towards heaven, we* took the solemn oath of obedience and secrecy. We swore that by every means in our power we would seek to avenge the death of Joseph Smith, the Prophet, upon the Gentiles who had caused his murder, and that we would teach our children to do so ;—we swore, that without murmur or questioning, we would implicitly obey the commands of the priesthood in everything ;—we swore that we would not commit adultery— which was explained to mean the taking of wives without the permission of the holy Priesthood ;—and we swore that we would never, under any circumstances, reveal that which transpired in the Endowment House.

The penalty for breaking this oath, which was worded in the most startling and impressive way, was then explained to us.—The throat of the traitor was to be cut from ear to ear ; his heart and tongue were to be cut out ; and his bowels were—while he was yet living—to be torn from him. In the world to come, everlasting damnation would be his portion.

Let not the reader think that this was merely an imaginary penalty, or that it was expressed merely for the purpose of frightening the weak-minded, for I have already shown that punishments quite as horrible as that have been deliberately meted out to the Apostate, the Gentile, and the suspected Saint by the Mormon Priesthood. The innocent blood which cries for vengeance against Brigham Young and some of the leaders of the Church is sufficient to weigh the purest spirit which stands before the throne of God down to the nethermost abysses of hell.

After these fearful oaths had been taken, with due solemnity, we were instructed in the various signs representing those dreadful penalties ; and we were also given a "grip" peculiar to this degree.

---

* I myself made a movement with my hand—for I believed that my life was at stake and I dared not do otherwise. The words of the oath I did not utter. [See explanation at the end of the chapter.]

We were next entertained by a long address from the Apostle Heber C. Kimball. Never in my life—except from Brigham Young—had I listened to such disgusting language, and I trust I never shall be compelled to listen to anything like it again. Brother Kimball always used to pride himself upon using "plain" language, but that day I think he surpassed himself; he seemed to take quite a pleasure in saying anything which could make us blush. The subject of which he discoursed was the married life in the "Celestial Order;" he also laid great stress upon the necessity of our keeping silence concerning all that we had witnessed in the Endowment House—even husbands to their wives, and wives to their husbands were not to utter a single word. With the sermon ended our "Second Degree."

We were now taken to another room for the purpose of passing through the "Third Degree" of the Order of the Melchisedec Priesthood. When we were all arranged on one side against the wall, a number of individuals entered who were supposed to represent the ministers of every denomination and religion upon the face of the earth. The devil also makes his appearance again. The ministers set forth the various claims of their respective creeds,—each one striving to show that his is the purest and the best,—but the devil sows division and hatred among them, and a good deal of confusion ensues.

Then came in personages representing Peter, James, and John, the Apostles, and they commanded ministers, devil, and all, to depart. They then appeared to organise a new Church in which the true principles of the Gospel were to be taught; our Temple robes were also all changed from the right shoulder to the left, indicating that we were now in the true Church, and that we were to be absolutely and in every way dependent upon the priesthood. Another grip was then given to us, and thus we received the third degree of the Order of Melchisedec Priesthood. In that room was a division made of bleached muslin; in the division a door and in the door a hole, with a lap of muslin over it, through which to pass the hand. Whoever was on the other side could see us, but we could not see them. The men first approached this door. A person representing the Apostle Peter appeared at the opening and demanded who was there. He was told that some one desired to enter. Hands came through the opening in the muslin curtain, and mysterious fingers cut a mark on the left breast of the men's shirts—one mark also over the abdomen, and one over the right knee—which marks the women religiously imitated upon their own garments when they got home. The applicant was then told to put his hand through the opening, and give the last grip belonging to the "Third Degree," and mention his new name. He was then permitted to enter. This was called "going behind the veil." When the men were all admitted, the women were suffered to approach, and were passed through by their own husbands. When a woman has no husband she is passed through by one of the brethren, and to those who are not going to be married or sealed for eternity here the ceremonies end.

Now, as I before stated, according to Mormon ideas, we had never before been legally married. It was therefore necessary that we should now pass through that ceremony. We accordingly were conducted to a desk where our names were entered and we were then passed into another room. In that room was a long, low altar, covered with red velvet, and an arm chair placed at one end of it, in which sat Brigham Young. My husband knelt at one side of the altar and I at the other, with our hands clasped above it in the last grip which had been given to us. Then the ordinary formula of marriage was gone through with, and we were informed that we were sealed for time and for eternity.

Thus we passed through the mysteries of the Endowment House, and at three o'clock in the afternoon we found ourselves at liberty to return home. The various ceremonies had occupied eight hours.

When we reached home, my husband said : "Well, what do you think of the Endowments ?" But I did not dare to answer him truthfully at that time. Had I done so, I should have told him that I was ashamed and disgusted. Never in all my life did I suffer such humiliation as I did that day; for the whole time I was under the impression that those who officiated looked upon us as a set of silly dupes, and I felt annoyed to think that I dared not tell them so. So I told my husband that I would rather not speak about it, and we never have spoken of it to this day. What were his own feelings about the matter, I do not know, for Mormon wives are taught never to pry into their husband's feelings or meddle with their actions. But notwithstanding all my feelings in reference to the Endowments, so foolish was I, that when I afterwards heard the brethren and sisters talking about the happiness which they had experienced while going through, and saying how privileged we ought to feel at being in Zion among the Saints of God, secure in His Kingdom where we could bring up our children in the fear of the Lord, I began again to think that the fault was all in myself, and that it was I who was wrong and not the Endowments. I wondered how, with such a rebellious heart, I should ever get salvation, and I mourned to think that I had not accepted everything with the simplicity of a child.

Some time after our initiation I met the Apostle Heber C. Kimball, and he asked me how I felt upon the occasion. I frankly told him all, but added that I regretted feeling so. He said: "I shall see if you cannot go through again; it is not just the thing, but I shall try and make the opportunity." Nothing more, however, was said about it. But that which troubled me most was the fact that while the oaths were being administered, I dropped my hand and inwardly vowed that I would never subscribe to such things, and at the same time my heart was filled with bitter opposition. This, although I did it involuntarily—my better nature rising within me and overcoming my superstition—I thought at the time was sinful. I now, however, rejoice that such was the case; for not having actually vowed to keep secret those abominable oaths, I can say, without any cavil or equivocation, that I have broken no promise and betrayed no trust by the discoveries which I have just made.

I wish distinctly to make this statement. Others have more or less divulged the oaths of the Endowment House, and have excused themselves with much doubtful sophistry. I NEVER *really took the oaths, although present, and therefore no one can charge me with treachery.*

At a later date, some of the sisters kindly suggested that the spirit of the Evil One had entered into me at that time. But this was at least a very inconsistent statement, for the Mormons believe that no evil spirit can enter into the Endowment House.

Of one thing I am certain—I was then indeed a miserable slave, with no one to stretch forth a kindly hand and strike away the fetters of my mental degradation and lead me forth into light and liberty.

CHAPTER XXVI.

SECRETS OF SAINTLY SPOUSES:—A VISIT FROM MY TALK-
ATIVE FRIEND.

NOT long after I had received my Endowments my talkative friend, of whom I have already spoken, came to see
me and to offer her congratulations. She was quite enthusiastic upon the subject, spoke of the honor which had been conferred upon us, and promised to call frequently to "build me
up." She was particularly anxious to learn whether I did not
feel much better and happier now.

On that point I could say little, for to have answered her
truthfully would have provoked discussion, into which I did
not care to enter. I knew, too, that anything I said to her
would soon be known to everyone else. So I told her that I
was feeling well enough.

" 'Well enough !' " she said, "Is that how you feel ? Come

now, I thought you would have got over all that when you had
been through your Endowments. You remind me of what
Brother Brigham says,—We have so many whining women in
Zion that it is quite a reproach. I do hope that you are not
going to become one of them. Let me give you a bit of
advice : The wisest thing you can do is to look out for another
wife for your husband, and get him to marry her."

" Oh My !" I said, " What are you talking about ? You
surely cannot be in earnest."

" I never was more earnest in my life," she answered.
If you had persuaded your husband to take another wife when
you went through your Endowments you would have got
over all your troubles at one time. The anticipation is ten
times worse than the reality."

" I do not see it in that light," I said. " My own opinion is
that my troubles in that case would only then have begun. I
do not think that you yourself are really happy."

" Oh, nonsense !" she exclaimed. " Why you can see how
happy I am. My husband has two other wives, besides myself,
and a more comfortable family could not be."

" You never told me," I said, " how your husband managed
to get those wives. I should like to hear."

" My husband managed ! Why *he* did not manage at all ;
it was I who arranged everything for him, and I'll tell you
how it was done.

" During the Reformation," she continued, " you, of course,
know the men were constantly urged to take more wives ;
but my husband was rather backward, and used to tell me
there was plenty of time and not the slightest occasion for
him to be in a hurry. I had my own opinion of the matter
and did not agree with him, for you see I was afraid that
after all, he would pick up some young girl or other and fall
in love with her, and all my plans would be disarranged. It
is you know much the best for the first wife to look out for
some girl who will look up to her and respect her, but not love
her husband too much, and then they are likely to get on
well together. If the first wife selects the other wives, it has

23

the effect of showing them that the husband thinks much of her judgment and is willing to abide by it, and that they will have to do the same. This, of course, is as it should be. ·But if she lets her husband choose his own wife, he is almost certain to take a fancy to some one whom the first wife does not like at all, and consequently her authority is undermined. The first wife ought to keep all the power in her own hands."

"Well," I said, "I should not care much, I think, who ruled in my home if another wife was there."

"You think so now," she replied, "but when you get used to Polygamy you will feel quite otherwise. People get used to it—the women as well as the men—and then they leave off fretting and become less selfish. But I was going to tell you how I managed my husband.

"I was very anxious, as I told you, to find another wife for him, and I took into consideration all the suitable girls I knew. There was some objection to almost every one. Some were too pretty and I knew I should detest them; and others were not good-looking, and those my husband could not bear. So I waited patiently, but did not give up the hope of succeeding eventually. At last I met with a girl who I thought would do. She was certainly not bad-looking, but she was very young and I thought I should be able to manage her. The name of this girl was Alice Maynard; she was a neighbor of ours, and one of a large family. She seemed to me to be a quiet, modest little creature, and I knew that she had to work hard and received very little in return. In fact, she led at home a life of drudgery, and even her very clothing bore witness to the poverty of the family. Her mother had often told me that she felt badly for Alice, for Mr. Maynard had three other wives and it was more than he could do to support them all properly

"I called one day upon Mrs. Maynard to broach the matter to her. She received me very kindly and entered into my views at once. She was anxious, she said, for Alice to get married, for then she would be better off. I asked her how she would like her to marry my husband, and told her that we were very comfortably off, as you know we are, and that my husband owned his house and lot and was doing a very good business, and, of course, ought to take another wife. Would she agree to my proposal and let me mention Alice to him ?

" She said, she herself, had no objection, but that perhaps my husband might not like Alice, or Alice might not like him.

" I felt indignant at the idea that any girl should hesitate to marry *my* husband, and I told Sister Maynard that there could not possibly be any hesitation on Alice's part. ' I'm sure I have no objection,' she said, ' if Alice has none. I should only be too happy to see my child in a more comfortable home.'

" Well then, we'll consider the matter settled, I said, and asked if I could see Alice ; so her mother called her in, and I proposed to her for my husband. You can guess, perhaps, how astonished I was when she actually laughed in my face and said she should like to consider the matter ! I did not, however, show her what I thought, but assented to what she said, and invited her to come and take tea with us.

" My husband had often told me, when I was teasing him about taking another wife, that he would willingly marry *any* girl I might choose for him ; and I felt pleased at this for it showed confidence in my judgment. So when he came in, later in the day, I told him I had found a wife for him at last, and that I knew he would like her. ' Why, Ann,' he said, ' I do believe you are going crazy over the wife question ; but if you are I do not want you to drive me crazy also. I really thought this was too bad, after all my trouble for him ; but nevertheless I was resolved that the marriage should take place.

" Three days after that, in accordance with my invitation, Alice came to take tea with us, and I fixed her up to look nice. When she was ready, I took her into the parlor to introduce her to my husband who was sitting there reading. Henry, I said, this is Miss Maynard—the young lady of whom I spoke to you the other day. He looked up from his paper, and, to my astonishment, said, ' Why, Alice, my girl, how do you do ? How are mother and father ? '

"What; I said, do you know Alice, Henry?

"'Certainly I do,' he answered, 'Alice and I have met many times before this, haven't we, Alice?'

"'Yes, sir,' she said, and, oh, *so* demurely. Why, Sister Stenhouse, I began to think that I had actually been deceived, and that while I had innocently supposed that I had found out the girl myself, it was the very one upon whom my husband had had his eye for a long while past. I watched them, however, very narrowly, for I was determined that if my husband had really taken a fancy for the girl he should never have her."

"Why, that would have facilitated matters, would it not?" I said.

"Do you think," she replied, "that I would have allowed them to marry, if they loved each other? No, indeed! The Saints marry from principle and not from love, as Brother Brigham has often told us. I hope you believe me, dear, when I say that I'm not at all a jealous woman, but if my husband dared to fall in love with a girl and to hide it from me, I could not stand it I am sure. No! *principle* is the only thing,—there can be no love in Polygamy. If a man loved his wife do you think he could have the heart to pain her by taking another? On the other hand, it is because of the love which still remains in their hearts, and which they weary themselves to crush out, that so many of the first wives are miserable. But I was going to tell you about Alice. I was mistaken in thinking that my husband had been paying her any attentions. It appeared that he was acquainted with her father and mother, and that at their house he had frequently seen the child Alice, but never supposed she was the Miss Maynard of whom I had spoken. But now they had come together at last he took to her kindly and she to him, and really I sometimes almost thought that they wished to ignore me altogether.

"I did not let them waste much time fussing with one another, but they got on very rapidly, nevertheless; and before I had had time to arrange matters properly, my husband told me that *to please me* he was going to marry Alice. Only fancy me being pleased at him marrying Alice! Why, it wasn't to please myself that I introduced the child to him, but simply because, if he *must* have another wife, it was certainly best for me to choose one whom I could manage. However, they were married not long after, and really I think I never was more disgusted in my life than I was on that occasion. I was not jealous, but I do think he might have paid her a little less attention. In fact I quite regretted, when it was too late, that I had ever brought them together.

"The Mormon men always do make themselves silly over their new wives, and I did not expect my husband to be an exception to the rule; but I was perfectly astonished at the change that took place in Alice. Instead of the quiet, modest girl she used to be, she put on all sorts of airs, and treated me as if I were of not the slightest consequence. I couldn't stand that, and I resolved, if it were only to take the pride out of her, I would get my husband to marry another wife still. He wouldn't object, I knew, for he takes life very easily and he has a great respect for my opinion. Besides which, he is quite well enough off to support three wives, and as a matter of duty, if nothing else, he ought to do so. That would soon bring Miss Alice to a proper state of mind, and she needed something of the sort, for, do you know, she had actually made that silly husband of mine think that she ought to be treated with the same consideration as myself."

"Well but," I said, "if the principle of Polygamy is of God, it is only just that all the wives should be treated alike. If my husband were to marry another woman, much as it would pain me, I should certainly treat her as an equal."

"Then," she replied, "if you do so you will find that the first wives will have nothing to do with you. You will find, when you come to be better acquainted with the people here, that the first wives do not waste much love over the polygamic wives; and, of course, as a rule, the polygamic wives detest the first wives. Then the plural wives get together and talk all manner of evil about the first wives, who do pretty much the same in respect to them. It is only natural that they should do so.

"But I was going to tell you," she continued, "how I selected the third wife. There was an emigrant-train expected in every day; and you know, when the emigrants arrive, all those women who want wives for their husbands, and all those men who want to choose for themselves, go down to the camping-ground, and if they see a girl who takes their fancy, they ask her if she has got a place to go to, and if she has not they offer to receive her themselves. There are hundreds of young girls who arrive here without any one to look after them, and who are only too glad to accept a home for the winter. Now this was exactly what I did. I went down to the camp and looked round for myself, and at last my eyes rested upon a young woman of about thirty or thirty-five years of age, who I thought would be a more suitable wife for my husband than that giggling chit that I chose for him at first. I decided at once that she would do, so I went up to her and asked her if she had any friends. She said she had a brother living in the City; but when I explained to her how we were situated and said that I should like her to come and stay with us till she could look round a little for herself, she agreed at once. Now—I thought—Miss Alice, we shall see whether you are going to have things all your own way any longer!

"I told her, however, as well as my husband, that I had brought home a sister to stay with us awhile, and they received her very kindly, and she soon made herself very useful and agreeable to us all. The Bishop came and talked to my husband, and he made no difficulty at all in acceding to my wishes, and before long he made our visitor—wife, number three; and Alice, as a matter of course, lost a good deal of her influence over him. For my own part, I am much more comfortable. The two plural wives do nearly all the work, and I have little else to do than superintend the household and enjoy myself. My husband is one of those quiet sort of men who never interfere with domestic affairs, and I have matters pretty much my own way now. The only thing that annoys me is his fondness for Alice who makes herself appear most amiable *to him*, deceitful thing! I can't break him of that, but I often tell him that he will find her out some day. He tells me that he looks upon her as a child and feels like a father towards her; no woman, he says, can ever have his love but me. That sounds all very well, but as for believing it, that is quite another thing:—I keep my eye on them and watch them well."

"But," I said, "it appears to me that it would have been far better if you had never given him another wife at all. You would have been saved from annoyance, and the privacy of your home would not have been disturbed. I am the more surprised, as your husband did not himself desire it."

"When you understand better the order of the kingdom, you will not speak in that way," she said. "Do you suppose that I should be satisfied to be the wife of a man who could not exalt me in the celestial kingdom—a man with only one wife? Why I have often told my husband that if he did not get other wives I would leave him. It is necessary for a man to have two wives at least if he would enter into the celestial kingdom. That is why I have been so anxious to get wives for my husband. At the same time there is no necessity for him to fall in love and act in a silly way over them. The only way in such a case is to set one to watch the other, and then they are pretty certain to keep the old man straight. You think, perhaps, that I don't feel all this, but you must not be deceived by appearances. I try to do the will of Heaven with a smile on my face; and the brethren have often told me that if the other sisters were more like me they would not have so much difficulty in establishing Polygamy. But, dear me, Sister Stenhouse, what a long talk we've had! I'll come and see you soon again, but I must hasten away now, for my husband will be home to supper by this time."

So she left me wondering over her strange story of a woman's experience in supplying her own husband with wives.

CHAPTER XXVII.

SPRING opened bright and beautiful, and I began to feel more at home in Zion and more contented with my position. I do not, however, mean that I was satisfied with Polygamy or that I contemplated calmly the prospect of my husband taking a plurality of wives ; but that I had begun to adapt myself to the manners and customs of the Saints, and had already formed many of those pleasant intimacies which lend such a charm to life.

My talkative friend was a constant visitor at our house ; and her strange views of life and of that all-absorbing subject —the management of man under the plural wife system— together with her lively conversation and unceasing flow of spirits, made her visits acceptable ; and she often banished from my mind thoughts which, if unchecked, would have made

my life unbearable. Her husband, too, poor creature, sometimes followed in her train, and on one occasion she actually
brought Alice with her that I might see what sort of a girl
she was. I found her quite good-looking, intelligent, and as
pleasant a little body as one could wish to know ; but at the
same time I detected in the expression of her features—lively
and self-reliant as she was—too many traces of that look of
subdued sadness which casts a cloud over the countenance of
every woman living in Polygamy.

Other friends, besides, I had, too numerous to mention—
friends whom I had known in England, with whom I had
wept over the horrors of Polygamy when it was first announced ; and dear Swiss friends, not a few, who had come
to Zion before us and were now quite settled and at home.

Two faces I longed to see, but of their owners I could at
first get no tidings. Poor, dear Madame Bailiff—my old Swiss
friend, who in past days had shown me so many kindnesses
and whom I had so tenderly loved—where was she ? Somewhere, I knew, in Zion, but not in Salt Lake City ; and to the
chapter of accidents, I felt that I must leave it, whether I ever
saw her again or not. And there, too, was Mary Burton, with
all her sweet, winning ways—she whom I had known as a
child ; whose early womanhood had been darkened by apprehensions of that accursed abomination—Polygamy ; who had
suffered that terrible martyrdom upon the Plains ; who, for
aught I knew, might at that very time need most my sympathy
and sisterly love—Oh, where was she ? Poor Mary ! Might
it not be, that worn out with the fearful sufferings which she
had endured, she had gone to that peaceful rest which she had
so vainly sought on earth ? I had asked every one who came
across my path, who was likely to know, whether they could
give me any information as to where she was ; but I could
learn nothing more than that, not long after their arrival, she
and her husband had left the city and had gone to one of the
Settlements in Southern Utah. I had, therefore, to wait in
uncertainty for any chance which might accidentally bring us
again together.

I was very glad that the winter was over, for we had had rather a rough time during our first few months in Salt Lake City, and the various associations of our life had tended rather to strengthen than to relieve my apprehensions respecting the future. The ball season, which, of course, I cannot pass by in silence, had been a source of annoyance, and, I may say, disgust to me. I had seen so much that was unpleasant at those balls ; and although what I witnessed did not then affect me personally, yet it was painful to see others suffer, and to hear poor women, whose hearts were crushed and broken, tell to each other in whispers the sorrow which had blighted their existence.

Dancing was always very popular among the Saints, and the leading men among them have wisely fostered a taste for it. When the people first went out to Utah, as may be supposed, life was hard and amusements were few. The Mormons, as a body, are examples of industry and diligence.; to them labor is one of the cardinal virtues ; and like all other pioneers they found plenty of employment for their energies. Houses had to be built, land prepared for cultivation, the commonest necessaries of life to be manufactured or raised ; and busy hands were perpetually engaged in a thousand useful industries. But when the day was over, and the dust of toil was washed from the careful brow, it was but natural that the need of a little recreation should be felt.

So in very early days Brigham built a theatre, and a very fair amount of histrionic talent was developed among the Saints. The Social Hall, in which were held balls, public entertainments, and other amusements, was used for histrionic performances before the theatre was built. Brigham owned the theatre. Money was to be made out of it ; and the chance of making money Brother Brigham never permitted to slip through his fingers. Brigham's eyes were sharp enough to see that a theatre would be to him a source of profit, but he did not look far enough. That theatre,—under the immediate direction of the Prophet ; with his own daughters acting in it ; with the plays which were performed under his own censorship—has been one of the many causes which have perceptibly, although perhaps indirectly, shaken the hold which Mormonism had upon many a woman's mind.

A man would probably witness the performance of a play and return from the theatre with no other thought than the remembrance of an hour's amusement. But not so a woman. To her the play suggested something more, and her daughters would share her thoughts. Daily and hourly, it might be, the effects of Polygamy would be brought under their notice as a matter affecting themselves personally. They might be firm in the faith, but the observant instincts of their sex could never be wholly crushed. They would notice the neglect which wives endured even from good husbands; they would see a man leaving the wife of his youth, the mother of his children, and careless of the cruel wrong he did her, leave her in lonely sorrow while he was spending his time in love-making with some young girl who might have been his daughter. They would see a wife crushing out from her heart the holiest impulses which God had implanted there, striving to destroy all affection for him whose dearest treasure that affection should have been, because, indeed, Polygamy could not exist with love. They would see, and know, and themselves personally feel, the degradation and misery of the " *Celestial* Order of Marriage"; and that to them would be the practical picture of life.

But in the theatre—short-sighted Brigham, to allow it to be so!—another picture would be presented for their consideration,—a picture, it might be, ideal in its details and surroundings, but true to the letter in the lesson which it conveyed and the thoughts which it suggested. The disgusting, the brutalising cruelties of Polygamy were never represented on the stage. Thoughts so coarse, so sensual, could never inspire the true poet's pen. No; the tale of love as the poet tells it, is all that is refined, and chaste, and delicate, and pure —the commingling of two souls, the unison of two loving hearts, the hopes, the aspirations, the tender joyful sorrows of two fond natures—of *two alone!* Such is the picture presented as the ideal of the beautiful and of the good. Then, too, the delicate attentions of the devoted lover—his happiness even in the shadow of a smile from *her*,—the lofty pedestal upon which to his imagination *she* stands, a queen and peerless ;—or the confiding love of the heroine of the story—blushingly confessing to herself that there is *one* heart on earth which is all her own and in which none but herself can ever rule or reign.

The Mormon women are not devoid of common sense, nor are they destitute of those quick perceptions which under all circumstances distinguish their sex. They see on the stage representations of the happiness attendant upon love and marriage, such as God ordained, and such as finds a response in every heart ; and they compare such pleasant pictures with what they know and have witnessed of Polygamy, and they draw painful inferences therefrom. Their faith may be proof against apostasy, but the impression left upon their minds produces its effect notwithstanding.

Another institution was the dance Brigham and the leaders knew that it would never do to leave the people without amusements of some kind, and thus the balls and social gatherings were originated. The idea of Prophets, Apostles, High-Priests, and Patriarchs attending a ball and joining in a dance must appear grotesquely incongruous to the Gentile mind ; but out among the Mormons it is quite the thing ; and to the men those balls and parties were very pleasant.

I do not think that many of the Mormon women enjoyed the ball season, and I know to some of them it was the most painful part of their lives. It is a cruel thing for a woman anywhere to know that her husband's affections are divided, that she is not his only love, and that his heart is no longer all her own. But far worse is the lot of the wife in Utah. She has to see and be present when the love-making is going on, when her husband is flirting and saying soft nonsense, or looking unutterable things at silly girls who are young enough to be her daughters ;—nay, her own daughters and her husband's may actually be older than the damsel he is courting for his second wife! Such an outrage upon the holiest feelings of womanhood would not for a moment be tolerated in any civilised community; but among the Saints women 'are taught that this is but one part of that cross which we all have got to bear. Cross-bearing is all very well, and I do not doubt that sorrow and trial have a sanctifying influence upon the soul, but by all means let us have a fair division of the burden. It is not just that the heaviest end of the beam should be placed on poor, weak woman's shoulders, and that her "lord" should even find pleasure in that cross which weighs her to the dust and crushes out from her weary soul the last sparks of love, and happiness, and hope! How sweetly did the men preach patience and submission to the will of Heaven. I wonder where their own patience and submission would have been had matters been reversed and their wives had been taught that it was their privilege and a religious duty to court, and flirt with and marry men younger and handsomer than their husbands!

The brethren never forget what Brother Brigham once said about the Mormon men being all boys under a hundred years of age, and they do not neglect their privileges. Here in the ball-room you may see men of three-score years and even older joining in the dance with girls of sixteen and even younger— making love to them, flirting with them, marrying them. Age or plain looks are nothing with such men; the girls are taught that they can exalt them to greater honor and happiness in heaven than young and untried men could, and that they ought to feel honored by receiving tender attentions from the chosen servants of the Lord. One wife, or even half-a-dozen, if they chance to have so many, of course will not stand in the way. The husband is the lord and master, and a woman's wishes count for nought.

In the ball-room the company of the first wives and, in fact, of many of the plural wives,—once worshipped, but who "had had their day"—was not so much sought as that of young and interesting maidens; and after having stood up with their husbands in the first dance, as a matter of form, many of those forlorn wives might be seen sitting along the sides of the hall, keeping each other company and talking over their sorrows. We used to call these poor ladies "the wall-flowers." Sitting there watchful, noting all that their husbands did or said, those poor women were in themselves a touching protest against the cruelty of the system, such as none but a Mormon heart could have resisted.

But for that horrible system, these balls and parties would, of course, have been extremely pleasant. With the feeling of fraternity which exists among the Saints, such gatherings ought only to be a source of pleasure; but Polygamy blighted everything, and it is with feelings almost of hatred that I recall some of those occasions. How many an aching heart has there felt weary—felt so weary as to long for death. No change of feature might betray the mental struggle, but the bitterness of the soul was all the same. And I have seen wives there whose husbands paid them marked attentions, so that the girls to whom they were making love might notice their devotion and draw favorable auguries for the future in case they married *them*. And the wife has known all this, and has valued her husband's attentions accordingly. And yet the poor deluded women persuade themselves that this system is right and in accordance with the revealed will of God; and they think that the evil—poor creatures!—is in their own hearts and that they deserve to suffer.

The Mormon men sometimes would be rather surprised, I think, if they could hear what their wives say of them at those balls. I have seen very obedient wives so goaded to anger by the conduct of their husbands that they have said very bitter things indeed; and what was not spoken, was felt, I know, by every wife in whose nature the last traces of womanly feeling had not been altogether crushed out.

At one of those balls the Apostle Heber C. Kimball came up to me and said in his jesting way that he would introduce me to his *wife*. He brought up five or six ladies of various ages, one after the other, and said: "There now, I think I'll quit now, for I'm afraid you're not too strong in the faith."

"Are these all you have got?" I asked.

"Oh dear no," he said, "I have a few more at home, and about fifty scattered over the earth somewhere; but I've never seen them since they were sealed to me in Nauvoo, and I hope I never shall again."

Heber was called the model Saint!"

But the ball season passed, and the spring came on and our prospects began to brighten. My husband not only found remunerative employment for his pen in Salt Lake City, but was also engaged as special correspondent to the New York *Herald*, and several of the California papers.

One morning, a countryman, roughly dressed and looking the picture of care, called at our house and asked to see Mr. Stenhouse. I gazed at him for a moment, for I thought there was something familiar in the sound of his voice. He looked at me and I at once recognised him—it was Monsieur Baliff himself, in whose house we had lived in Switzerland. But, oh, how changed he was! Once a refined, handsome, gentlemanly man; now a mere wreck of his former self—careworn, rough-looking, poorly clad. He and his family had been in Utah six years, and had suffered all the ills that poverty can induce:— the change which was wrought in him was so great, that for some moments I was so overcome by my feelings that I could not utter a word. In the few short years which had elapsed since I saw him in his own bright and happy home, he had become quite an old man. I hardly dared to ask about his wife, for I feared what his answer might be; but after a little while he told me that she had sent her love and would like to see me whenever I could find an opportunity to call upon her. They lived some miles from the City, but I told him that I would not fail to visit them whenever it was possible for me to do so.

I talked a long while with Monsieur Baliff, and was much interested in what he told me. He made no complaints; he had still firm faith in Mormonism, and said that if the brethren had not dealt fairly by him they would be answerable to God for what they had done. "Besides," he added, "I do not blame

them so much, for they are Americans and would not be happy
if they did not get the advantage in some way."

I was anxious to ask him if he had been induced to take
another wife, as he had been in Utah during the "Reformation," and I did not see how it was possible for him to have
escaped ; but while I was thinking how I might put the question delicately, he saved me the trouble by himself telling me
that he had married the young servant girl whom his wife had
taken from Switzerland with her. This information was quite
a shock to me, for I well knew the proud spirit of his wife and
I could realise what anguish this second marriage must have
caused her ; I did not, however, like to question him on the
subject. So I turned the conversation into another channel,
and when he went away I sent kind messages to Madame
Baliff, saying that I would seize the very first opportunity of
hearing from her own lips the story of all they had gone through.

Here again I found the trail of that monster—Polygamy.
This time in the home of my dearest friend. From the moment when she and I had mingled our tears together, in Switzerland, over that abomination, life had been to me one long,
weary, sickening battle with my own heart, one futile attempt
to fully convince myself that Polygamy was right and that I
was wrong. I certainly did believe, or thought that I believed,
the doctrine was true. But at times Nature prevailed in the
struggle, and womanly indignation and anger rose in arms
against Faith. These feelings were, however, at once and unhesitatingly subdued ; Faith returned triumphant and I was
again convinced that the Revelation *must* have been the will
of the Lord, and that my duty was to submit but not to question. In moments of comparative self-control I had even tried,
as a Missionary's wife, to justify it to others, but only to witness an outburst of sorrow and anger, and to feel still more
the weakness of my position. That had been my own experience; but how had the time passed with my dear old
friend ? She must, no doubt, have been as greatly disappointed
as I was when she came to Zion and saw things as they really
were, and not as they had been represented to us.

My own eyes had certainly been opened not a little since my arrival. Instead of finding the people enjoying the comforts and blessings of life, which we had been taught were strewn around them in profuse abundance, we found among all but the leading families the greatest poverty and privation. The majority of the people were living in little log or adobe houses, of one or at the utmost two rooms, of most primitive construction, and without the slightest convenience of any description. Their food was bread and molasses, and it might be an occasional morsel of meat; but many of them scarcely even indulged in the latter or in any article of grocery, for months at a time. Their floors and walls were bare, and their clothing poor and scanty; and yet, destitute as they were of all the comforts and conveniences of life, they were conscientiously endeavoring like good Saints to practice Polygamy, because, as they believed, the Lord had commanded it.

In respect to education they were in even a worse position. Books, pictures, and periodicals of any kind there were none, with the exception of that dreary organ of the Church, the "*Deseret News*,"—the soporific influence of which some wicked Apostate has likened to a dose of Winslow's soothing syrup;—Brigham Young, himself an illiterate man, and the leading Elders frowned upon every attempt to raise the intellectual *status* of the people; and so little encouragement was given that no one could afford to keep school. The consequence was that the boys and girls grew up with little more education than their own sense of necessity taught them to acquire for themselves, and it was not until very recently that any suitable efforts were made to supply trained teachers and to open schools in which a thorough education could be afforded.

I have already mentioned the sermons in the Tabernacle, and observed how little calculated they were to elevate the character or cultivate the minds of the people. I have before me as I write a choice morsel extracted from one of the sermons of Heber C. Kimball, which I think I must give for the reader's benefit.

24

Fancy an "Apostle!" thus addressing a large and mixed congregation of men, women, and children :

"Here are some edicated men jest under my nose. They come here and they think they know more than I do, and then they git the big head, and it swells and swells until it gits like the old woman's squash—you go to touch it and it goes ker-smash ; and when you look for the man, why he aint thar. They're jest like so many pots in a furnace—yer know I've been a potter in my time— almighty thin and almighty big; and when they're sot up the heat makes 'em smoke a little, and then they collapse and tumble in, and they aint no whar."

This was Heber's style in general. Next to making modest people blush, nothing pleased him better than to annoy or ridicule any one who had the smallest pretensions to education ; and yet naturally Heber was a kind-hearted man. Brigham's style is very little better, and the substance of his discourses quite as bad. I will give a very favorable specimen taken from a sermon on Polygamy, delivered some years ago, touched up and corrected, and published in the official organ, the *Deseret News :*

"Men will say—'My wife though a most excellent woman has not seen a happy day since I took my second wife.' 'No, not a happy day for a year, says one ; and another has not seen a happy day for five years.

"I am going to set every woman at liberty, and say to them, Now go your way—my women with the rest; go your way. And my wives have got to do one of two things ; either round up their shoulders to endure the afflictions of this world and live their religion, or they must leave ; for I will not have them about me. I will go into heaven alone rather than have them scratching and fighting around me. I will set all at liberty. 'What, first wife too!' Yes, I will liberate you all. I know there is no cessation to the everlasting whinings of many of the women in this territory ; I am satisfied that this is the case ; and if the women will turn from the commandments of God, and continue to despise the Order of Heaven, I will pray that the curse of the Almighty may be close to their heels and that it may be following them all the day long. And those that enter into it (the celestial order) and are faithful, I will promise them that they shall be queens in heaven and rulers to all eternity.

"Now if any of you will deny the plurality of wives, and continue to do so, I promise that you will be damned."

This was sweet language for a Prophet and a Saint to utter, and yet it is not half so coarse or improper as some whole sermons that I have listened to from the lips of Brother Brigham and the other leaders of the Church.

The Apostle Orson Pratt is the only one who has dared, in

the presence of Brigham, to say that education was a proper thing, and that there were many books which would be of good service to the Saints, if they obtained and studied them. On one occasion, Brigham arose in ire, and said:

"The Professor has told you that there are many books in the world, and I tell you that there are many people there. He says there is something in all these books; I say each of those persons has got a name. It would do you just as much good to learn those somebodies' names as it would to read those books. Five minutes revelation would teach me more truth than all this pack of non-sense that I should have packed away in my unlucky brains from books."

But the Prophet has changed with the times, and there are now in Utah very good schools, both Mormon and Gentile, but none of them are *free*-schools. Bishop Taylor once said in a public lecture that they were "destructive to the best interests of the community;"—and the Bishop's "lord" in the Lion-House is exactly of the same opinion, for he has repeatedly declared that "there *shall be no* 'free-schools' within his Saintly 'Kingdom' on earth." Nevertheless, Brother Brigham and his "*Infallible* Priesthood" are at last beginning to discover that although the night of ignorance and superstition may hate the clear daylight of truth and knowledge, when the great Ruler of All commands the light to come forth, it is not in the power of man, with all his boasting, to forbid the sun to shine upon the dark places of the earth.

Balls, parties, and the theatre provided amusement for the people in Salt Lake City itself; but in the Settlements there was little else in the shape of recreation than idle gossip or the harangues of the Tabernacle. In the city, of course, this has all been changed of late years, but in the Settlements of Utah there is the same lack of civilisation as there was fifteen or twenty years ago.

At the time when we went to Utah, Mormon society was slowly recovering from that terrible marrying mania which had set in during the "Reformation," and a season of divorce was the result.

The authorities at that time—as I have already observed—had urged every person, without distinction, into Polygamy.

Men and women had been forced to marry one another without any respect to affection or fitness, and the result was that hundreds of marriages were entered into which made those who contracted them miserable for life, but the consequences of which they could not avoid. At the same time not a few were divorced almost immediately after they were married, and these things were a matter of daily occurrence. Brigham Young, with his eye perpetually on the dollar, finding that his marrying scheme, like many other of his "divine" plans, was a failure, saw at once that quite a nice little sum might be realised by charging a fee for divorces. Nothing was charged for marrying; but if the people insisted on having divorces—why, the best, and certainly the most profitable, thing was to make them pay for them. When we first went to Utah, the Prophet was doing quite a flourishing business in that line. Any one could get a divorce for ten dollars ; and Brigham publicly in the Tabernacle jested about it and said that the money thus obtained came in very conveniently as pin-money for his wives—though I doubt if they ever received a dollar of it. He added, that so far as "eternity" was concerned, these divorces were not worth the paper they were written on,—the people had married for eternity, and in eternity they would have to live together, whether they liked it or not. He says the same to-day ; but still he sells his divorces and gathers in the ten dollars.

All this is an anomaly, although the people do not appear to see it. While, more than any other community, they profess to regard marriage as a sacred institution, they marry and are divorced in a more careless fashion than the people of any civilised country. I could mention instances which would be really ludicrous were they not so shocking.

I know a young woman in Salt Lake City, who is not over twenty-one years of age. She is a very pretty girl and has engaged quite extensively in the divorce business, for she now lives with her fourth husband. She was in my employment after she left her third, and I had an opportunity of studying her character. I noticed that she was frequently visited by a

certain young man who seemed to make himself very agreeable to her, and feeling a great deal of interest in her—for
she had left her father and mother in England, when a mere
child, in order to gather to Zion under the paternal care of
one of the Elders—I asked her why the young man came so
often to see her.

"He is my intended husband," she replied.

"Why," I said, quite astonished, "you have only just been
separated from your last husband, and after so much ill-treatment I should have thought you would have been afraid of
trying another—at-any-rate, so soon as this."

"You're wrong there," she replied, in quite a serious, earnest
way, "I am determined to marry until I get the right one, even
if I have to do so a dozen times. Don't you think I am
right?" This really seemed so shocking that I did not know
what to say.

The most absurd point in all this was, that of her three
former husbands, one was a Gentile, and two were Mormons.
The Gentile, of course, would have no chance in the world to
come, but to each of the two Mormons she was sealed *for
eternity*. Now if Brigham's divorces are of no force in the
next world, and if his marriages are binding, what will this
young woman do between her two Mormon husbands—to say
nothing of the two other Gentile ones, who "do not count!"—
for the Mormons, though they are so generous to themselves
in the matter of wives, will not allow a woman to have a couple
of husbands, either here or in eternity.

What nonsense is all this: what blasphemy to ascribe it to
"the Lord!" How different I found the Mormon "lord" from
that great and glorious Being—source of all goodness, holiness, and truth—to whom in the days of my childhood I had
looked up and adored! The "lord" of whom they so flip-
pantly spoke, was not the same with Him to whom things in
heaven and earth do bow, by whom, and in whom, are all things.
He never blighted the heart of woman, or cursed her with a
perpetual curse; but to Him, since I escaped from the cruel
thraldom which once blighted my existence, day by day my

soul goes out in love and gratitude.   Would that I could infuse into the worn and weary hearts of the women of Utah the knowledge, that God has given freely to *all* His creatures—to woman as well as man—no cruel law to torture their souls, no wretched "Revelation" to embitter their lives, but a Gospel of peace, and gentleness, and love, which makes perfect those who walk therein.

CHAPTER XXVIII.

WHAT WOMEN SUFFER IN POLYGAMY:—THE STORY OF MARY BURTON.

ONE bright summer morning, about six months after our arrival in Salt Lake City, I was sitting in the work-room busy with my girls, when a light tap was heard at the door, and the next instant a lady entered, and coming straight up to me was about to kiss me.

I started back a step, held out my hand, looked her full in the face, and in a moment we were in each other's arms. It was my old friend Mary Burton!

I could with difficulty find words to express my astonishment when I recognised her, so greatly was she changed in every respect. From the very first, whenever we met after a long separation, I had noticed a more than ordinary alteration

She buried her face in her hands and sobbed again.

"Mary dear," I said, "Don't talk like that—he cannot have ceased to love you, I am sure; he used to almost worship you, dear."

"It is because I know that he did once, that drives me crazy. You do not know what I feel, what I have to bear!"

I did not utter a word—my own sorrows were hidden in my own heart—The heart knoweth its bitterness, and a stranger intermeddleth not in the matter. "You have been through the Endowments?" she asked. "So have I. We went through, Sister Stenhouse, about three months after we came to Utah, and never since then have I known a moment's peace. I do not know what they said to my husband, but whatever it was, it produced a great effect upon his mind, and changed him altogether—he has been an altered man from that very time. I have no doubt that they told him that it was his duty to take another wife, and they would say that no promise made to me before our marriage is binding if it comes in opposition to our religion. You know how devoted he is, how firm his faith is. Why, I do believe that he would obey counsel even if it broke his heart and cost him his life. Did they say anything to you or *your* husband, dear?"

"Certainly they did, Mary—we have heard it daily and hourly, and my husband is constantly being counselled about it. I am wretched, Mary, you know I must be; I feel just as you do, but how can we help ourselves?"

"No, we cannot help ourselves—there is no hope;" she said; "but it is a cruel wrong. You know well enough how determined I was never to marry a man who would take another wife. When I thought that Elder Shrewsbury might be influenced by his religion, I made him go to the Apostle and get counsel, and then he solemnly vowed to me that he *never* would enter into Polygamy without my consent—which, of course, was the same as saying that he never would do so at all. Until we went through our Endowments, he never even hinted at such a thing. But they spoke to him then; and one day after he had been having a long consultation with the Bishop, he came and spoke to me. He was not unkind in the least. In fact he seemed to be as much pained at all mention of the subject as I was. He said that the Bishop had been urging him to live up to his privileges, and had explained to him how great a loss in the celestial world it would be, both to him and to me, if he did not take more wives. He was told that now while he was young was the time, and that I would soon get over any pain that I might suffer. Yes, they actually said so. Fancy tearing out the very affections of one's heart and blasting every hope and happiness in life, and then saying that I should soon "get used to it!" I tell you, Sister Stenhouse, a true woman *never* can "get used" to this hideous system. If the hearts of some are dead and cold, it is a curse to them and a curse to their husbands and their children; and if a wife seems careless or callous, as the case may be, it is because love for her husband has first died out in her heart. She feels no jealousy because she has no love; but if a woman has but a spark of love for her husband she will hate with a deadly hatred any other woman whom that husband loves."

"But what did Elder Shrewsbury say when they told him to enter into Polygamy?" I enquired.

"At first he told them it was utterly impossible," she replied, "and he mentioned his promise to me, and said we were very happy together, and that he wished for nothing more. But they knew his weakness and that he would do anything for his religion, and they urged him on that point. It was even a sin against me they said, for if he had no more than one wife he could never exalt me in the Celestial Kingdom,—that I ought to be treated like a child—a very dear, but spoilt child,—and if I refused what was for my own and my husband's benefit and everlasting welfare, he ought to act up to what he knew was right, and leave the consequences with the Lord, who would order all things for the best. My husband told me all this very sadly at first, but I could see that it had an effect upon his mind. They saw it, too, and did not let the subject drop. Every day they spoke to him of it, and at last he gave way— for *my* sake, he said! This was the cruellest wrong of all.

Then one day he told me very firmly and very coldly, as if he had steeled his heart to do so, that he had made up his mind to take another wife."

"What!" I exclaimed, "After the solemn oath he swore never to do such a thing? Why, I could not have believed it of Elder Shrewsbury!"

" I reminded him of his promise," she said, "but he told me that the Revelation justified him in breaking it; that it said in the second clause that 'All covenants, contracts, and oaths not sealed by him who is appointed on earth to hold this power in the last days are of no force after the resurrection'; that for this cause we had been married again for eternity, and that now he was free from his oath. I knelt down before him, and I wept and prayed as if for life itself—I entreated him, if no more, to wait and put off all thoughts of another marriage for a few months, until he had time to consider the matter carefully. He had already thoroughly thought it over, he said, and could not go back now, for the Bishop had chosen a wife for him and had arranged everything. He even told me who it was—a young girl named Wilbur, about fourteen years of age—a mere child. I prayed him if he would be so wicked as to perjure himself and wrong me so foully, at least not to add to his sin by injuring a poor innocent child. He was very indignant with me for that, said that he was doing the child the greatest good he possibly could by marrying her; that he was ensuring her salvation as well as mine; and that he expected to receive the blessing of God."

" Mary," I said, " this system is a fearful curse."

" Curse!" she exclaimed, " Curse is a heavenly word to apply to such a system. Why there is nothing in hell so hateful, so vile, so detestable. It is blight and ruin to everything that is fair and good—I never pass a day but I curse with the bitterest hatred the men who devised it. Women *can* hate bitterly when they choose; but I hate *them* more than ever woman hated before."

" Hush! Hush, dear," I said, " You mustn't talk so, Mary!"

" I mustn't *talk* it perhaps—it's dangerous, I know ;—but I may *think* it. There is not a true-hearted woman in Utah who does not feel as I do this day. Do you think that when they have ruined all our hopes for time and for eternity we shall love them still? Here, but for this wretched system, I should have been a happy wife and mother, and now see what I am—husband, child, all lost—all lost!"

"Is the child dead, Mary?" I asked, very gently, for I feared to pain her.

"Yes dear," she replied, "in fact I believe it never lived—the one I was thinking of. I was ill, very ill indeed, after what my husband had told me. They thought I should die, and I think he was sorry, for he became very kind and tender to me, but that only made me feel worse. Then my child was born, but I never saw it, for I was unconscious for more than a week after, and then they told me that it was not alive, but my husband would never speak to me about it. As I grew better, his cold, stern manner returned, and then at last he married that girl Wilbur, and since then he has married two more, for he is doing very well in business. I think that all his love for me has gone. At first he thought of marrying again because it was a religious principle; and as it was the time of the Reformation he did not dare to refuse; but now his heart is grown hard and cold. You see a change in me, Sister Stenhouse, but I think you'd see a greater change in him. I know, of course, that I used to look at him with the eyes of love, and of course did not see him as other people did; but that is not the only change—it isn't in his face alone; his whole nature seems altered. It quite pains me sometimes to see it."

" Do you feel any happier now—any calmer, Mary?"

"Yes," she said, "Yes, and no. I do not love him as I used to—how could I? But when I look into my heart I find, if I tell you the truth, that a little love *does* remain there. If only I could *quite* cease to love him I think I should be happy; but when I pet and play with my little girl—for we have had one child since that dreadful time—some of my love for him comes back again, and I sit down and have a good cry. Sometimes that isn't enough to calm me and I shut the door and walk up and down the room and swear ;—there, don't look so horrified, Sister Stenhouse! I cannot help it; if I did not give way to my feelings now and then I should die outright ;—and sometimes I break a few things,—but he never knows it, and it does me good. We came into the city yesterday on a visit, and we shall stay for a few days. He brought me, I believe, as a matter of form; but I found out where you lived, and I came to see you. You never answered my letter and I did not know whether you had left New York yet. I really *am* glad to see you, Sister Stenhouse. And it is true that Brother Stenhouse has not taken another wife yet ? "

" Not yet," I said, " But, as I told you, he has been spoken to about it, and I cannot tell what he may do. As you say, Mary, the Mormon women have not much to make them happy."

I took her in then to get some refreshments, and I asked her to stay for the day. She said that she had a message which some one had left for Elder Shrewsbury ; that she would go and leave it, as it was of some importance, and that she would come back again.

In about an hour she returned, and somehow, although I had intended to talk of quite another subject, we got back to our common grievance again. I do not wonder at this for it was the perpetual theme of all our thoughts. Queen Mary, of unpleasant memory, is said to have fretted over the loss of the town of Calais until she believed that after her death that name would be found written upon her heart ; and I really do think, were such a thing possible, the word 'Polygamy' would be found indelibly engraved upon the heart of many a wretched wife in Utah.

Mary gave me a great deal of information. In that she was quite herself, as I knew her in by-gone days. Nothing escaped her observation. She sat down with me and told me all her troubles and I need hardly say how deeply I sympathised with her. So I tried to comfort her, and spoke about her child, but even respecting that poor little thing she felt no hope. "Why when it grows up, she said, it will be as miserable as I am—I

can see no prospect of happiness in the future for it." We
agreed that the only way whereby we might prevent our children from experiencing sorrow and misery similar to our own,
was to teach them from the very first that Polygamy was the
natural and proper, as well as the revealed, order of marriage—
in fact to "bring them up" in the system. What a miserable
resource was this for a mother who loved her children!

"One thing, Mary," I said, referring to her own personal experience in Polygamy—"one thing I do not quite understand.
You, of course, had made your husband specially promise before you married him that he would never take another wife,
and he was therefore bound, as a man, by every moral obligation, not to do so. But other women have not been situated
as you were, and they have exacted no promises from their
husbands. Yet it always seemed to me that your doing so
was quite superfluous, for you must be aware, Mary, that the
Revelation says that before a man can take a second wife he
must have the full consent of the first. The Elders in Europe
used to make a great deal of that point, as you may remember, for they said that this provision took from the Revelation
any harshness or injustice which it might otherwise appear to
show. I know many women who submitted on this account, for they argued that if their permission was necessary,
they could always, by refusing, save themselves from any
further trouble. Now if that was so, how came *your* husband
to take another wife against your will? I say *your* husband,
because I should have no difficulty in many other cases. I
have been repeatedly told that husbands never troubled themselves about the Revelation when they wanted another wife,
unless it was to silence the first wife with it, if she rebelled.
But I always regarded Elder Shrewsbury as a conscientious
man, and I firmly believed that he would never willingly give
you a moment's pain. When he made that promise to you, he
had the Revelation before him, and had also the Apostle to go
to if he needed the 'Word of the Lord.' He was therefore
bound by that promise, notwithstanding anything that the
Revelation might say to the contrary; and even had he made

no promise, the Revelation was on your side. We are told that every woman must first give her consent."

"That is all very true, Sister Stenhouse," she said, "to a certain extent. The theory is as you say, but you have not heard the whole. I know the Revelation pretty nearly by heart and so I can tell you exactly what it does say. The first wife is said to hold the keys of this power, by which is meant that she can refuse. But then it goes on to say that when her husband has taught her the law of the Priesthood—that is Polygamy—"*she shall believe* or *she shall be destroyed*, saith the Lord your God, for I will destroy her." You see there is no loophole of escape for the woman. Her husband is to teach her the law and she *shall* believe; and if she does not—and of course people have no power to make themselves believe what they please—she is to be destroyed, and God will destroy her! Do you know, Sister Stenhouse, there are stories whispered here of women who *did* refuse and who stood in their husband's way, and it is said that the Priesthood did not wait for the Lord to destroy, but carried out the law themselves.

"My dear Mary, we really must not talk in this way," I said—"it's quite wicked. My husband would never forgive me if he knew what we have been talking about. He says that all these stories are untrue, and that they are all exaggerations or fabrications of the Apostates who wish to bring scandal on our religion."

"I do not wish to shake your faith, Sister Stenhouse, but my own is pretty well gone," she replied. "Of course I never speak to my husband about these things, nor do I dare to talk to any one else ; but I feel it quite a relief to see you and to be able to say what I think, for I know I can confide in you. But we have wandered sadly from your question. You were talking about the first wife giving her consent ?"

"Yes," I said, "and you were about to tell me whether it was really and practically necessary in every instance. You have been here longer and have seen more than I have."

"The wife's consent is by no means necessary, Sister Stenhouse. It may be asked sometimes as a mere matter of form, and, of course, in the Endowment House, when she gives the other wives to her husband, she may be said to give her consent to his marrying them. It is nothing but a piece of folly to talk about women having the power to withhold their consent, and it is simply an insult and a mockery for their husbands to ask it; they well know before they ask that their wives dare not refuse to give it. But it enables them to boast to the Gentiles that they do not take other wives until their first wife gave her consent. This is what is meant by 'the liberty of the Gospel,' I suppose, about which Brother Brigham talks so much. But every one knows perfectly well that this is all a farce, and that he would take other wives all the same however stoutly the first wife might refuse. She would only make herself miserable. even if she got off as well as that. The idea really is that in Polygamy there are four who must give their consent: Brigham Young must first receive a revelation from the Lord stating that he approves of the proposed marriage. Then the first wife's permission must be obtained. Then the consent of her parents. And, last of all, the girl herself is to be asked.

"This all sounds very fair," she continued, "but in practice it is quite otherwise. Without President Young's consent there can be no marriage at all ; but if it is the will of Brigham, the refusal of the first wife and the parents and the girl herself do not for a moment signify."

"But did your husband, Mary, act in this way?"

"Well, not quite. He told me that if I refused it would make not the slightest difference ; and as I believed him, I, of course, went, and did not make a scene. It would have only made matters worse. Some of the older sisters came round and talked me over, and explained and insisted, and "labored" with me as they called it, until I hardly knew what to think or do—my mind was quite unsettled. Eliza R. Snow is quite great at that sort of work. When my husband took his other two wives, he did not consult me at all, but simply told me that on a certain day I must go with him to the Endowment House. We went, and he married two sisters on the same day, but it did not do him much good. They are handsome girls, but have very bad tempers and we often have a very unpleasant time. The second wife, poor child, suffered most when he married the other two. She did not seem to like me very much at first, which was quite natural, but when the other two were brought home she seemed quite to cling to me, and I have, strange to say, taken quite a fancy to her. In all our disputes she always sides with me, and in return I always stand up for her, as a matter of course. I am getting used to this wretched life ; I have stifled all my love ; and I am sorry to say that sometimes I almost hate every one around me, including my husband. Now and then the old longing for some one to love, for some one to confide in, comes over me. I felt like that this morning when I came here, and that is what made me act so badly."

"Say nothing of that, Mary ;" I replied. " I wish you would stay with me while you are in the City."

" No," she said, " We shall be here for a day or two, but I do not think my husband would like me to stay here altogether. He knows that you are aware of his attachment to me once and his promises in the old times, and very likely he would be a little ashamed to meet you. He'll make business an excuse, and in fact he is busy all the day. So I'll come round alone as much as I can, and we'll have a good talk again."

I saw her to the door, and then she turned and said, " I'll come again and see you, Sister Stenhouse, before we leave the city. I know you think me very wicked ; but, there ; don't be shocked, dear !—I'm not so very bad, after all."

Thus saying, she kissed me, laughed with the ghost of her former merry ways when first I knew her, and said good-night. I watched her till she was lost in the darkness, and then I closed the door, saying to myself, with a sigh, "Ah me ! can this be the Mary that once I knew ?"

CHAPTER XXIX.

HOW MARRIAGES ARE MADE IN UTAH—A NEW WIFE FOUND FOR MY HUSBAND.

My Old Friend Madame Baliff—Painful Reverses of Fortune—Shameful "Counsel" during the "Reformation"—A Choice of Two Evils—Reminiscences of a Happier Life—A Message from Brigham Young—A Serious Trust —An Interesting Case—Suffering for the Faith—My Talkative Friend Again —I Receive Strange Congratulations—An Inquisitive Lady—A Lady who Could "Build-Up" a Rebellious Wife—The Apostle Heber C. Kimball Pays Me a Special Visit—"Plenty of Wives Around the Town"—A Morning drive with the "Model Saint"—A Lesson on Children's Dresses—Good "Counsel" Thrown Away—Heber Suggests a Wife for my Husband—How Love is Developed in Mormon Wives—"The Finest Thing in the World"—The Shadow of Coming Evil.

NOT long after this, I was enabled to visit my Swiss friend, Madame Baliff. Ever since her husband had called upon me in Salt Lake City, I had watched anxiously for an opportunity of seeing her, for I felt much interested in learning how time had passed with her since we parted in Geneva.

I found her in a little log-cabin of two rooms, with bare walls, bare floor, and miserably furnished ; and in this wretched abode Poverty and Polygamy had wrecked the life of my poor friend, whom I had known under such different circumstances. Here, together with their five children, lived also the second wife, with *her* two children. It was with difficulty that I could recognise in the poor, careworn, broken-spirited, and ill-clad woman who stood before me, the once gay, light-hearted, happy, and elegantly-dressed lady whom I had known in Switzerland. Mormonism had in. her case utterly blighted her existence. It seemed to me hardly possible that so great a change should have been wrought in her in such a few years as had elapsed since last I saw her. What suffering she must have endured, I thought, what mental agony, what physical pain, to write those wrinkled lines of care upon her once handsome face ; and, Ah! what a pang I felt at the remembrance that I myself had been instrumental in leading her into Mormonism and Polygamy. Self-reproach I did not feel, but sorrow I did. I had thought to lead her into the way of holiness and heavenly peace by winning her to the religion of the Saints, but that which I in my enthusiasm had believed would be the greatest blessing which one poor mortal could communicate to another, had turned to a curse, and instead of the happy wife and mother which she once had been, she had become a victim to that faith which in its very existence is an insult to womanhood.

In temper and disposition she was, however, just the same ; her affectionate nature was unchanged. No doubt she read in my features the painful surprise which I experienced in witnessing her altered circumstances ; but she met me with not a single word of reproach for my being the cause of her leaving her own dear country. I should not have blamed her had she hated me, though she knew, of course, that I had wronged her innocently.

She told me of the difficulties which they had had to contend with after their arrival in Utah, and how they had been compelled to part with almost everything they had, in order to provide bread for their children. When they left London, they took with them several handsome carpets, china, glass, and a large quantity of silver ware, besides bedding and clothing of every description, for they were well-to-do in the world, and had quite enough for themselves, after they had liberally assisted the poorer Saints to emigrate. Upon their arrival in

Utah, the husband—good man that he was—was willing to come down to the level of his brethren and to go farming among them. A brother who knew him in his own country, and imagined, I suppose, that he could afford to lose, sold him a farm that he himself had become disgusted with, though, of course, he did not say so, and when my inexperienced friend, Monsieur Baliff, found that nothing could be done with it, he supposed that the land was good enough but that he himself was not competent to work it. No one ventured to hint that he had been cheated, as it was one of the Church authorities who had sold him the land. After spending upon it all that he possessed, he was finally compelled to abandon it. They were now very much straightened in circumstances, and my poor friend told me that she had frequently been compelled— as they were entirely destitute of money—to take a silver spoon or fork to the butcher's market to trade with, and there they drove a hard bargain with her, and she obtained next to nothing in exchange for her silver. Her crystal and plate now grace the table of a certain rich man in Utah. Every article they possessed went in this way at a most ruinous sacrifice, until nothing remained, and then the husband was forced to engage in manual labor, while the poor wife employed herself in whatever feminine work she could obtain ; they receiving in return just what people chose to pay them. In the midst of their troubles the husband was " counselled " to take another wife.

" But why did he not refuse to do so ?" I asked.

" If you had been here during the Reformation you would not ask me such a question as that. Sister Stenhouse, you ought to thank God that you were not here then. There were shocking things done at that time, and the men were all crazy about marrying. They married every woman who was single, and even little girls who had scarcely reached their teens ; it was a time of terror, and no one dared to rebel."

She then told me that her husband had been, as one might say, compelled to marry a young Swiss girl whom they had brought out to Utah with them as a domestic. This girl had been a very faithful servant and Madame Baliff had become very much attached to her. During the Reformation the Bishop visited them and "counselled" Monsieur Baliff to take a second wife. The girl was also "counselled" to marry, and when she said that she did not know of any one to whom she would like to be married, the Bishop told her that he himself would find a suitable man.

"My husband told me what the Bishop had urged him to do," said Madame Baliff, "and we talked the matter over in a practical way. We knew that the girl would be forced to marry somebody, and that then she would have to leave us, which would put us to the very greatest inconvenience, for situated as we were we could hardly get on without her assistance. At the same time, he also would be compelled to obey counsel, and we came to the conclusion that as there was no way of evading the difficulty altogether, it would be better for him to marry the girl than to bring a stranger into the house. So he asked her, and she accepted him, and they were married. She is a good girl and tries to do her best, but it is a great trial to me, and one which I trust you may never be called upon to bear. My husband is as kind and gentle a man as ever lived, and he has done all he could to keep me from feeling unhappy ; had it been otherwise I dare not think what I should have done—I believe I should have gone mad or died. In our household arrangements, of course it made very little difference, but it was inexpressibly painful to me, and though I suppose I shall remain a Mormon till the day of my death I have learned to hate Mormonism."

Poor Madame Baliff! Hers was a life of privation and sorrow, of late years. Happy as woman could be in her youthful days, she little dreamed what Providence had in store for her ere her earthly course had run. With a faithful and devoted husband ; with a charming little family growing up around her ; with all that could make life fair and beautiful. But that accursed thing—Polygamy—came and poisoned all her happiness, and blighted all her hopes ; and when, but a few months ago, worn out and weary of life, she left behind her all her sorrows and all her misery, I could not weep that she had gone to a better land beyond the veil, but I thanked God that at last, poor soul, her days of trial were for ever over and she had entered into her eternal rest.

One day Brother Brigham sent me word that he wished to see me.

I went to him, and he told me that he wanted me to become acquainted with a certain young girl in whom he took a great interest. She was the daughter, by his first wife, of Jedediah M. Grant, the famous Apostle of the "Reformation"—her name was Carrie, and she was now an orphan. Brother Brigham wished me to have her with me every day, for she was not "feeling well," he said, and he thought I might do her some good. This "not feeling well" I afterwards discovered meant that she was almost ready to apostatize. If she desired it, I was to teach her my business; not that she needed to follow any profession, for, as President Young explained, she had a good home; but her mind needed occupation, and he did not care how she employed her time, so long as she was with me every day and could be made to "feel well."

I listened to all that Brother Brigham said, and accepted the trust in good faith—not only to please him, but because the girl was an orphan, and my heart went out towards her even before I had seen her.

Before I returned home, I called at the house where Carrie was stopping, and arranged that she should come every day to see me, under pretext of learning the business. Now it so happened that we each conceived a liking to the other the very first moment we met; we made friends together at once, and she wanted to begin coming to me the very next day. She was a sweet-looking and intelligent girl, fair but fragile, and with a peculiar expression of melancholy sadness dwelling upon her features, which gave her a painfully inter-esting appearance. I never, before or since, met with a young girl who habitually looked so unhappy; and I thought that perhaps physical weakness might be the cause, for it was evident that in constitution she was extremely delicate—I almost feared consumptive.

The first day we spent together she told me that her parents had been among the pioneers to Utah, that her only sister had died on the Plains, and that she had lost her mother soon after they had arrived in Salt Lake City. As the only remaining child of her mother, she had been a great pet with her father, but he too had died about four years previous to the time of which I speak, and she had never been happy since. "I often long to die," she said, "that I might join my mother and father; no one loves me here, and I have nothing to live for." Her father had married four wives after her mother's death, and they were all very kind to her, but she did not feel that she had a home. She told me, that about six months before she came to me, she had started to go east, to her mother's friends, for they had frequently written to her urging her to come to them, and that when she was about two weeks' journey from Salt Lake City, Brigham Young sent after her, and she was brought back. "But," she said, "I shall never be happy here, Sister Stenhouse, I know I never shall; and why should they not let me leave and go to my relatives?"

I knew very well that it was of no use for her to try to get away, for we had no railroad then, and escape was almost impossible. I therefore tried to make her more cheerful, and told her that a girl as young as she was—for she was scarcely seventeen—had much to live for. But her unhappiness had become almost a settled melancholy and she seemed to be interested in nothing. Besides which, the task I attempted was all the more difficult as I was not at all happy myself.

One day the conversation happened to turn upon Polygamy, and in a moment I saw that all her trouble arose from that miserable doctrine, and from that alone. We had not exchanged many words upon the subject when she exclaimed: "Oh, how I hate Polygamy! God forgive me; but I cannot help it, Sister Stenhouse! I *do* hate it; and yet I believe that it is true." Poor child! I understood her too well, for her position was exactly mine;—from that moment we were fast friends.

Here was the child of one of the greatest fanatics that Mormonism has ever known, one of the wildest advocates of the " Celestial Order of Marriage," perfectly loathing the system ; and yet, poor girl, believing it firmly, and believing too that she could not obtain salvation unless she entered into it. How I pitied and loved that poor girl!—and yet what strength or consolation could I offer her, being myself as painfully situated as she was. Our mutual sorrow united us still more closely in loving companionship. I had rarely met among the Mormon girls with one so thoughtful and observing, so kind and gentle. She had not been with me many weeks before she had entwined herself so completely round my heart that I was lonely when she stayed away and I tried to keep her with me altogether. I tried in every way to make her feel at home when at my house ; and noticing her delicate health, and thinking that she did not always get those little things to tempt her appetite which an invalid should always have, I found out many trifles which I believed would please her, and always tried to get them for her. She seemed to think much of these little attentions, and I have always believed that she loved me very dearly.

Some of my neighbors began to whisper pretty plainly to me that Brother Brigham had an object in view in asking me to interest myself in Carrie's welfare. They told me they believed that my husband, if he had not already been counselled to marry her, would be before long. Knowing, as I did, Carrie's aversion to Polygamy, these suggestions did not trouble me very much ; but I begged my informants not to speak of the matter in my young friend's presence as it would only disturb and annoy her. I was the more anxious on this point as her health had by that time began very perceptibly to improve, and sometimes she seemed to be almost joyous and light-hearted. Sometimes she would sew, and sometimes she read or played with the children, of whom she was very fond, and I always allowed her to do just as she pleased.

One day my talkative friend called to see me. She had not been near the house for several months, and I think, at her last visit, she must have taken offence at my telling her that I thought she had not acted wisely in procuring wives for her husband. She had, however, now an object in coming which I soon discovered.

She was shown in, and as soon as she was fairly seated, I observed that, while talking to me, she was inquisitively scrutinizing Carrie's face, as if trying to discover her character or read her thoughts. Suddenly—she did everything impulsively—she interrupted the conversation, saying: "Sister Stenhouse, I want to speak to you privately." I asked her to come with me into the next room, and she did so, but before I had time to close the door, she exclaimed: "Allow me to congratulate you: you have done very wisely!"

"Congratulate me upon what?" I asked.

"Upon the excellent choice you have made for your husband," she replied; "I knew very well you would ponder over my good counsel and seek another wife for Brother Stenhouse, and I am certain that my example and my faith and prayers have helped you, for I have asked the Lord to strengthen you to do just what you are doing."

"Doing!" I said, "What am I doing? I really don't understand what you mean."

"Oh nonsense!" she exclaimed, "But *I* understand, if you don't. You wish to keep it a secret, I suppose, until the happy event takes place. And you are quite right in that, for there are so many busybodies here, and they do interfere so much in their neighbors' affairs that it isn't pleasant. But, of course you needn't fear *me*—*I* shouldn't think of breathing one single word of the matter, unless you wished me to do so."

"I'm really at a loss to know what you mean," I said, very much annoyed with her.

"Oh," she said, "If you think that I am interfering, I will not say another word, for I should very much dislike to be considered meddlesome. But you know, my dear Sister Sten-

MY TALKATIVE FRIEND.

house, the great interest I have always felt concerning you; from the very first when I knew you in England I always prophesied great things of you, but I was a little afraid when I saw your opposition to Polygamy, and I cannot tell how happy I felt when I heard yesterday that you had found a wife—and a good wife too—for your husband.

"I find a wife for my husband!" I exclaimed. "That I never would. I dislike Polygamy far too much to do so. No; if he ever wants another wife, I shall never help him to find her—he'll have to get her himself. Besides which, I don't believe he does think of ever taking more wives."

I believed what I said. During our residence in Utah, my fears had calmed down, for my husband very seldom mentioned Polygamy in my presence, unless the brethren or sisters introduced the subject. I naturally concluded that, now he had seen so much of the practical results of the doctrine, he, like myself, had become disgusted with it. But my talkative friend, of course, knew nothing of my thoughts. "Who is that young girl, then, that I saw just now?" she asked; "Is not that Miss Grant?" I replied that it was.

"Well," said she, "I was told that you had asked her to marry your husband."

"There is no truth in the report," I said, "I am sure that she has never thought of such a thing, nor have I, nor has my husband; and I would not have such a thing spoken of for the world."

"Well," she replied, "I am really quite disappointed. You have a splendid opportunity, and I do believe that that was what Brother Brigham meant when he asked you to see after her. In fact, I was told that it was his only motive, all along."

"Then Brother Brigham will soon find out his mistake, I can assure you," I answered, "for I never will ask her; and, moreover, if I thought for a moment that she would ever wish such a thing, much as I love her, I should then hate her."

"My dear Sister," she said, "how do you expect ever to get salvation? I suppose you think that is none of my business, and that I should leave you in the hands of the Lord. But before I go, let me ask you to see Eliza Snow as soon as you have an opportunity. She will build you up, and do you a world of good."

I told her I needed no "building up;" all I wanted was that my husband and myself should be left alone, and that people should not meddle with our affairs.

She apologised for what she had said, and we returned to the sitting-room, and she asked me to introduce her to Miss Grant. I did so, although I feared that in some way or other she would be the means of interrupting the pleasant relationship which had hitherto existed between us.

After she had gone, her conversation troubled me a great deal. What did it all mean? Had the busybodies been trying to bring about an alliance between my husband and Carrie? Had Brigham Young been working all along to this end? However it might be, I resolved that, at least, Carrie should know nothing of the matter from me.

One morning, the Apostle Heber C. Kimball called in his carriage. It was very early, being only about seven o'clock. Mr. Stenhouse went out to see him, but in his blunt way he said : " I do not want you, I want Sister Fanny to take a ride with me." My husband brought him into the house and he told me he wanted to have a talk with me, " You must not fix up," he said, " or I won't ride with you. Come along in your wrapper and slippers, and just put on your sunbonnet."

I told him that I never went out in a sunbonnet. "Well then, do it for the first time," he said.

I suggested that I had had no breakfast, and asked him if he would wait and have some with us.

" No," said he, " I have plenty of wives around this town, and we will find breakfast somewhere." So I started just as I was, and he told the driver—who, I think, was one of his own sons—to call round and see " the folks "—meaning his wives. Then, turning to me, he said : " You never looked prettier, Sister Fanny, you ought always to wear a sunbonnet, but you like dress a great deal too much—you will keep your husband poor—and then how will he be able to carry out the commands

of God? Did you ever think of that? Then, again, you dress
your children too much; it must take pretty well all your
time to make their clothes; and, see, what it must cost. Now,
I'm going to give you some good advice. Do what my folks
do. I tell them to make a linsey dress for each of the children, in the spring, and let them wear it all the summer, and
then, when the winter comes, it will be so full of grease and
dirt that it will be sure to keep them warm. Now I'm sure
you won't consent to do that with *your* children, so it is good
counsel thrown away." I knew well enough that Brother Heber was only jesting, for apparently he provided very well for
his family, although he allowed them no luxuries. He went on
to say: " But that isn't what I wanted to speak to you about ;
I had something else to say. When is your husband going to
marry Miss Grant? That girl has got to be looked after by
some good man and woman, and I think that you and Brother
Stenhouse would do first-class. What do you think ?"

" I should not like my husband to marry her," I said.

" And why not, Sister Fanny?" he asked.

" Because I myself love her," I replied.

" Why that is the very reason why he ought to do it the
sooner," he said, " and you would continue to love her, and
love her all the better, too, when she belonged to your husband, and when you saw how much *he* loved her." He laughed
outright as he said this, and told me not to look so solemn.
" Why," he said, " it's the finest thing in the world to develop
love in the women ; a man never gets so much attention in his
life as when he has got several wives all trying their best to
please him."

" That may be," I said, " but who is to pay attention to their
wives ?"

" Things have been all upside down in the world, Sister
Fanny," he answered, " and the Priesthood is going to set them
all in order. It is the women's place to minister to the men,
and the men, in return, will save them in the Kingdom, if
they are good girls."

By this time we had driven round several of his fields in the lower part of the City, and at last we stopped at the house of one of his wives. She very kindly prepared breakfast for us; after which we called to see two or three other wives, and then returned home. On the way back, he tried to get me to promise that I would persuade my husband to marry Miss Grant. This I positively refused to do, although it would have been dangerous for me not to acquiesce had it not been that Brother Heber was attached to me and allowed me to say what I liked against Polygamy, laughing at me and telling me to "hold on" when I became too much in earnest.

This constant reference to Carrie began to trouble me seriously, although, so far, I had not yet spoken about it either to her or to my husband, and did not intend to. I felt sure that Carrie, poor child, was perfectly innocent; she had refused to go to several parties with us, and had otherwise declined to accompany my husband, and I believed that I had no cause for uneasiness.

Thus time passed, and more than a year flew by, and Carrie still remained with me. Lately I thought that her manner was changed and that she was a good deal altered. I noticed that she was shy when in the presence of my husband, and that she rather avoided him. For a long time I had not suspected that anything was wrong between them, and the knowledge that Carrie was troubled, and that my husband was the cause, came upon me suddenly. She began by staying away for several days at a time, and at last she told me that she was going away for a while to visit a friend in the country. She looked so unhappy that I felt sure that all was not right, and begged her not to go, but she would not listen to me. It was necessary for her to go, she stated, and would say no more. She bade me good-bye, and for two months I heard nothing of her, supposing that she was in the country, and then I was surprised to learn that she was visiting with a friend in another part of the city, and that she was very ill indeed. I immediately went to call upon her, and she was much pleased to see me, and then I discovered that she had not been in the country at all, but had been there in the City with her friend.

I could not at the time understand her conduct, but as she, in common with most other delicate people, was rather capricious, I allowed it to pass without any comment. She told me that as soon as she felt a little better she would come and see me, but she never came, and I was somewhat offended at her supposed neglect, and thought that before I visited her again I would wait and see whether she first came up to our house.

All this time, a friend of Carrie's was in the habit of looking in very frequently upon some trifling errand or other, and I noticed that she always waited for the return of my husband, and then made some excuse to go out with him, and they had long conversations together. There was some mystery, I clearly perceived, and as a wife and a woman I determined that it was my duty to find out what that mystery was.

CHAPTER XXX.

TAKING A SECOND WIFE :—THE EXPERIENCE OF THE FIRST.

A Mysterious Errand—Going a Courting—Silence and Obedience, a Wife's Duty—Kept in the Dark—Mistaken Kindness—The Conflict Between Faith and Reason—A "Rebellious Woman"—My Poor Friend Carrie—Women Advocating Polygamy—Finding a Wife for My Husband—The Poor Victim —An Unusually Loving Husband—A Consultation with Brother Brigham— The Curse of a Whole Life—The *Fiat* of the Prophet—The Penalties of Disobedience—"I Can Only Consent"—A Message from Eliza R. Snow— The Bad Logic of the Poetess—An Unwilling Sacrifice—An Unalterable Decision.

I DID not presume to ask my husband what it was that he had to talk about with Carrie's friend, but I instinctively felt what it might be, and I was so much troubled in mind that I thought I would never go to see her again.

By that time I had learned, as every Mormon wife does learn, never to ask questions. The wife of a Saint never dares to ask her husband whither he is going or when he will return. She is not expected to know or care what business her husband may have on hand when he leaves home in the evening, after making a most elaborate toilet, with frequent admiration of himself in the mirror. If the poor wife feels that she *must* say something, to give vent to her overwrought feelings, she simply asks in a conscious, guilty way, when he will be home again ; wishing too often in her secret heart that he might say—Never. Her duty is to be silent and unobservant ; and though some poor women have, when their outraged feelings were overcharged, inadvertently betrayed curiosity respecting the movements of the absent ones, they have soon been sternly taught their duty, and those loving husbands have given them good cause to repent of their inquisitiveness.

And who can blame these disconsolate, lonely women if thus they feel? Their religion alone is to blame. It has been the destruction of that sweet confidence which should exist between husband and wife, and it has divided hearts and interests which should inseparably have been for ever one. This, slowly but no less painfully, I was beginning to understand. However earnestly I might try to combat the idea, my life was wretched with the one continual fear of what I might see or hear of my husband. I tried to drive away such thoughts, and I called to mind all the acts of kindness and devotion which he had shown whose love my heart held dear. Sometimes, arguing with myself, I said: No, *my* husband will not deceive *me* ; no matter what other men may do or be with their wives, *my* husband will be frank and true with me.

So I thought then; but I was destined to realise in my own experience how utterly impossible it is for any man, no matter how honest and truthful he may naturally be, to practice Polygamy without becoming a hypocrite ; and the more he loves his wife, the greater hypocrite he will become, trying to deceive her with the foolish notion that half his cruelty is done in attempting to " spare her feelings."

Up to this time I had been able, with some effort, to banish those doubts which would, against my will, intrude upon my mind. I had schooled myself to believe, that when it was really necessary, my husband would frankly and freely speak to me about that subject which was ever uppermost in my heart, and I knew my own nature sufficiently well to feel sure that I could grapple with any difficulty, if once I looked it boldly in the face. All that I feared was deception on my husband's part. That, I felt, would be more than I could

26

endure. In the whole course of our married life hitherto, I had never known him to deceive me, and even now, although influenced by the counsel of the Elders, he thought of bringing to our home another wife, I well knew that he sympathised with me ; for he knew the deep, deep sorrow that the dread alone of Polygamy had for years brought to my heart, and he might well be apprehensive of what the practical reality would be. At a later period, I knew that he fell into that error, common among Mormon men, of keeping "it" from their wives until all was settled. This was not the kind of treatment calculated to inspire me with confidence ; it may suit some natures, but I doubt even that. Men frequently imagine that they understand a woman's nature better than she does herself, and acting upon this belief, and full of good intentions, they err most fatally.

My husband thought that he was acting kindly to me when he said nothing of all that transpired between him and Carrie ; but when I saw the visits of Carrie's lady-friend so frequently repeated, I began to suspect the truth and was much troubled. I was, however, too proud to question him on the subject, at the risk of getting an evasive answer, and it was evident that the two persons most intimately interested in the matter intended that I should be kept in the dark. I saw through all this and it did not tend either to restore my peace of mind or to make me more pleasant in my intercourse with Carrie or my husband. In their conduct I could see nothing but deception, however good their intentions might be, and I felt that they were treating me as a child. The thought was very painful to me, and it was only with a great effort that I suppressed it.

In fact, I dared not think ; but when doubts and fears crowded themselves upon my mind, so that I was compelled to give them utterance, I would lock myself in my room or wander away to some lonely spot and there vent my feelings in indignant words. At other times I did think over the wrongs which Polygamy inflicted, until my feelings were almost beyond endurance ; then in those moments of anguish

I would prostrate myself in humility and repentance before the Lord, and would plead for strength to endure and submit to His will. Then again, I would pace the room, my soul filled with rebellion, and heartfelt curses against a system which had so withered and blighted all my life and had taken for ever the sunshine out of my existence. For ever! Ah! how those words lingered in my thoughts; how they chilled my heart, and left me utterly without hope; for we were told that eternity would be but a repetition of this life on earth. Polygamy, we were taught, was to be practiced in eternity; it was to be the "Celestial Order of Heaven"; it was an eternal law. But if it was so loathsome now, how should I ever become reconciled to, and happy in, it? Then too we were told by the Elders that we should have no other heaven than that which we began on earth, and I was at a loss to conjecture what sort of a heaven mine would be. It may appear strange that such absurdities should ever seriously have found a place in my mind; but when one at starting accepts a system as true—however absurd that system may be—and learns to regard all that is connected with it as beyond the shadow of a doubt—after years of discipline, the mind is ready to receive almost anything that may be offered to it from the same source. In my own case, I was so convinced that, however reason might object, all that we were taught was true, that I was utterly without hope, and would have felt happy could I have believed that death was annihilation. Of earthly happiness I had given up all expectation.

These painful feelings, of course, had a marked effect upon my daily life. I grew weary, and my health failed, I became thin, and my features were marked with care and anxiety. When people came to see me, I said little to them and their very presence I felt irksome. Mechanically I went through the daily routine of duty, but my heart was in nothing that I did. I dared not even trust myself to speak to any one, for fear of becoming the subject of conversation and attracting the attention of the authorities, which was not at all desirable, for the position of a "rebellious woman" in those days was anything but pleasant. I stood alone. Upon my husband I looked with suspicion ; my children were too young to understand me ; Carrie, whom I had taken to my heart, to whom I had confided my sorrows, whose own welfare had been so dear to me, had, as I thought, turned against me, like an adder, and there was no one in whom I could trust. It seemed to me too cruel for Carrie to treat me so, and yet I could not doubt that she was acting unfaithfully towards me.

Surrounded by my children, living under the same roof with my husband, my heart was, nevertheless, filled with a sense of utter loneliness and desolation. There was no one in whom I could confide, to whom I might tell my sorrows, and from whose counsel or strength I might derive comfort. I dared not even go and lay my griefs before God, for I had been led to believe that all my suffering was caused by an arbitrary decree which He willed to be enforced. How false a notion of that loving heavenly Father whose tender care is so manifestly shown in his gentle dealings with the weakest of His creatures!

It was now about six months since Carrie left my house, and I was under the impression that all that time certain well-intentioned sisters had been doing all they could to bring about a marriage between her and my husband. Her health, however, was so bad that sometimes for weeks together she did not leave her room. At the time, of course, I knew nothing of this, but I afterwards heard of it. When I called upon her, which I did when I found that she was too ill to come to see me, I thought she was greatly changed in her manner, but when I thought of her lonely position my heart warmed towards her and I forgot all my suspicions. Certainly, I wanted to ask her one plain question relative to my husband, but my pride would not allow me to speak to her on that subject unless she first mentioned it to me. One day I thought that she was about to make a confession. Talking indifferently of ordinary matters, she suddenly said, "I am surprised you ever wish to see me;" but when I asked her why, expecting that she would now explain what had so long troubled me, she answered evasively, and nothing more was said.

I shall always believe that I myself was not the only person interested at that time about Carrie's feelings. There are some of the sisters who—strange as it may seem—spend their lives in promoting the practice of Polygamy. When once these good sisters have set their hearts to get a man a second wife, they do not let a trifle discourage them ; if they do not succeed with one girl, they try with another, and it is seldom that they fail of meeting with their reward.

In Carrie, at this time, they found a subject of peculiar interest. If her failing health put an end, for a time, to all thoughts of her own marriage, that was no reason why my husband should not select a second wife elsewhere. Poor victim ! He, of course, had no pleasure or interest in the matter ; his religion alone compelled him ; he suffered as much as I did ! To look round on all the young and pretty girls he knew ; to select one and pay his court to her, was painful enough I dare venture to assert ; but he seemed to bear it very well indeed, and the " Revelation " appeared to agree with him nicely.

With Carrie's absence from our house, the rumors about her which had troubled me so much somewhat subsided. Nothing could silence the secret apprehension which continually held my soul in dread ; but the fear of my young friend's influence once removed, I was comparatively at peace. It was, however, but the lull before the storm. I soon learned that in losing Carrie I did not lose Polygamy, and from about that time I can date my husband's desire to sustain his brethren in the performance of their duty and his wish to act as they did, especially in reference to the " Celestial Order of Heaven." Just at that time the " Morrill Bill " for the suppression of Polygamy was presented to Congress, and all true Mormons were made to feel that it was their duty to stand by their leader ; and though, in itself, they might see nothing desirable in Polygamy, yet, if they had not already multiplied wives, it was their duty to do so without any delay.

Ever watchful as I was, I noticed little changes in my husband, which under ordinary circumstances would have escaped my observation. By this time one all-absorbing idea had taken possession of my mind, and my husband's thoughts, I believe, were turned in the same direction—only our wishes did not exactly coincide. Polygamy was the thought common to both, but upon its desirability we entertained dissimilar views.

A man with Polygamy upon his mind was then a creature which I did not understand, and which I had not fully studied. Some years later, when I had a little more experience in Mormonism, I discovered several never-failing signs by which one might know when a man wished to take another wife. He would suddenly awaken to a sense of his duties ; he would have serious misgivings as to whether the Lord would pardon his neglect in not living up to his privileges ; he would become very religious, and would attend to his meetings—his " testimony meetings," singing meetings, and all sorts of other " meetings," which seemed just then to be very numerous, and in various other ways he would show his anxiety to live up to his religion. He would thus be frequently absent from home, which, of course, he deeply regrets, as he loves so dearly the society of his wife and children. The wife, perhaps, poor simple soul !—thinks that he is becoming unusually loving and affectionate, for he used not, at one time, to express much sorrow at leaving her alone for a few hours ; and she thinks how happy she ought to feel that such a change has come over her husband, although, to be sure, he was always as good as most of the other Mormon men.

My husband was a good and consistent Mormon, and very much like the rest of his brethren in these matters ; and the brethren, knowing themselves how he felt, sympathised with him, and urged him on, and, by every means in their power, aided him in his noble attempts to carry out " the commands of God !"

One evening, when he came home, he seemed preöccupied as if some matter of importance were troubling his mind.

This set me thinking, too. I saw that he wanted to say something to me, and I waited patiently. " I am going to the ball," he presently remarked, "and I am going alone, for Brother Brigham wishes me to meet him there." I knew at once what was passing in his mind and dared not question him. He went and saw Brigham. What passed between them, I do not know, but when my husband returned he intimated to me that it had been arranged that he should take another wife.

The idea that some day another wife would be added to our household was ever present in my mind, but somehow, when the fact was placed before me in so many unmistakeable words, my heart sank within me, and I shrank from the realisation that *our* home was at last to be desecrated by the foul presence of Polygamy. The very effort which my husband made to break the news gently to me made my heart more rebellious.

What intelligence *could* be more terrible to an affectionate wife, the mother of a family, than this. In my girlhood, as the reader knows, I had forsaken all for the sake of my husband and his religion. We had toiled together and suffered together. For fifteen long years our interests and our affections had been one and inseparable. Nothing, but the fear of Polygamy, had ever come between my husband and myself; —but for that horrible apprehension, and the unhappy feeling which it occasioned, no wedded pair could have been more truly united than my husband and myself, but *that*, certainly— that only—*had* cast a shadow over the bliss of our domestic life. Our little ones—a mutual care—had grown up around us ; they had occupied all our thoughts and all our attention, and in them our own love seemed to be renewed. They were now, at least the elder ones, fast ripening into manhood and womanhood and gave promise that they would be the glory and blessing of our old age. Our home was never disturbed by any of those petty dissentions and divided interests which make so many families unhappy. When in the evening we gathered round our peaceful fireside, in the pleasant interchange of thought, in intelligent conversation, and domestic amusements, and in little loving courtesies, we realised, as far as could be realised in this imperfect state, the meaning of that household expression—"a little heaven upon earth." In a word ;—while God had abundantly blessed us in basket and in store,—my husband's tender affection had ever been to me the same as it was on our marriage-day ; my heart, with all the true deep love which a woman can feel, had found its only happiness in him ; while our children, bound to each of us alike by the fondest ties, formed a family, which for unostentatious, but true, affection, and for unity of thought and aim, could not anywhere have been surpassed.

But now all this was to be changed. Let a Gentile mother think how she would feel if she heard her children talk of "Father taking *another wife !*" Let her think what it would be if another woman—however good and pure she might be —were brought home to take her place in the family circle, to divide with her her husband's affections, to come, after years of undivided love, between herself and him who had so long been all in all to her ! And yet, all this I felt, and, oh, much, *much* more than I could ever express ; for who can tell in words the deepest bitterness which the heart too sadly feels ?

Everything around me changed. Every one I met reminded me of the miserable idea which had taken possession of my thoughts. All that before had seemed so bright and beautiful now revolted me, and my soul itself seemed filled with unavailing and unnatural hatred. I hated Mormonism, I hated the Revelation. I hated myself, and I hated my husband. All that had been influenced by, or in contact with, the detested and accursed thing I utterly abhorred. My woman's soul within me made me feel that I should gladly stand aloof from that degrading horror, and shake even from my clothes the touch of any one, or anything, that had been polluted by any connection with it.

Almost fainting, now that the truth came home to me in all its startling reality, I asked my husband when he proposed to take his second wife.

"Immediately," he replied, "that is to say, as soon as I can."

We were silent for some time. My mind was troubled. Had I been able to consider the whole affair as an outrage upon humanity in general, and an insult to my sex in particular, I should have replied with scorn and defiance. Had I implicitly believed in the divinity of the Revelation I should have bowed my head in meek submission. But I did neither of these. The feelings of my heart naturally led me to hate with a most perfect hatred the very mention of the word Polygamy, while at the same time I still believed, or tried to make myself believe, that the Revelation was from God, and must therefore be obeyed. Such was the strange and contradictory position in which I was placed.

I tried to reason with myself. My husband and the Elders had taught me that the fault was not in Mormonism but in my early Gentile training; and I believed them, and thought that all the inconsistencies which I had heard of, or seen, in Brigham Young and the other prominent men, should be attributed to the weakness of human nature; and not to the system. Still, doubts would suggest themselves; only, however, to be immediately suppressed, for it was by slow degrees that the truth dawned upon my mind. It was only natural that I should hesitate. I was a wife and a mother, and I could not consult my own wishes or desires. It was my duty, I knew, to do what was right, at whatever cost to my own feelings, and I dared not think of open rebellion. Had I then rebelled, I must have renounced all that in life I held dearest—husband, children, all. I knew my husband's devotion to the faith and that he would not hesitate to make any sacrifice for it. He would even glory in giving up what men hold dearest, for the sake of the Church, and we had both been taught that whosoever forsook husband or wife for the sake of the Church, it should be accounted to them for righteousness. I saw around me daily and hourly the effects of this teaching upon the unfortunate wives and children, but I nevertheless strove—how painfully none but myself could tell—to banish from my mind

every doubt, and to esteem the natural questioning of my heart
a sin.

"Are you not satisfied that it is right for me to take another
wife ?" my husband asked.

"I have never yet really doubted that the Revelation was
from God," I replied, "for I cannot believe that any man would
be so blasphemous and wicked as to set forth such a revelation in God's name, unless he received it as he said he did.   If
it is from God, of course you are right to obey it; but if I
were to consult my own feelings I would never consent to live
in Polygamy.   I would rather risk salvation, and tell the Lord
that He had placed upon me a burden heavier than I was able
to bear, and that I regarded Him as a hard taskmaster.   But
when the salvation of my husband and children, to say nothing of my own, is at stake, my wishes and happiness go for
nothing, and I can only consent."

From that moment, I felt like a condemned criminal for
whom there was not a shadow of hope or a chance of escape.
Could I possibly have looked upon the sacred obligations of
marriage as lightly as Mormonism taught me to regard them,
I believe I should have broken every tie and risked the consequences.   But I had vowed to be faithful unto death, and if
this second marriage was for my husband's welfare, and for the
salvation of us and of our children, I resolved to make the
effort to subdue my rebellious heart, or die in the attempt.
For the first time in my life, I thanked God that I was not a
man, and that the salvation of my family did not depend upon
me; for if fifty revelations had commanded it I could not have
taken the responsibility of withering one loving, trusting
heart.   I felt that if such laws were given to us, our woman's
nature ought to have been adapted to them, so that submission
to them might be as much a pleasure to us as it was to the
men, and that we might at least feel that we were justly dealt
with.

Not long after this, my husband brought me a message
from Eliza R. Snow.   She wanted me to take tea with her and
he urged me to accept the invitation.   I did not want to go,

for I knew too well her object in sending for me. She had been talking with my husband about me, I felt sure, and that was how she came to send the message by him. I went, however, and, as I anticipated, she wanted to talk with me about Polygamy, and to try to convince me that it was for our best interests that my husband should take another wife, and that it was quite time he did so.

I told her that he was not yet in a position to do so. "We have quite a family," I said, "and I think he should at least be allowed to wait until he has accumulated a little before he embarrasses himself with new responsibilities."

"And where would the kingdom of God be," she asked, "if we had all talked in this way? Let your husband take more wives, and let them help him, and you will feel blessed in keeping the commands of God."

"There would be no good in my husband taking another wife," I said, "while I feel as I do now. To be acceptable to .the Lord, a sacrifice should be made willingly and in a proper spirit, and I do not think that under present circumstances it is proper for him to do this thing."

"Let him be the judge of that," she replied; "do not seek to control him; he alone is responsible, and therefore let him do as he thinks best."

"But," I said, "he himself does not want another wife yet." But I spoke with hesitation, for my heart misgave me.

"You are mistaken;" she answered, "your husband is a very good man and desires to live his religion, and it is a great grief to him to know that you feel as you do, and you really must try to overcome your opposition. If you had a loaf of bread to make, and you made it, and it was pronounced good, do you think it would be of the slightest consequence what feelings agitated your mind while you were making it, so long as it was well made? So it is with the Lord. He does not care with what feelings you give your husband another wife, so long as you do so."

This was a miserable attempt at reasoning, to say nothing of its falsity; and notwithstanding all she said, I still felt that no blessing would even attend an unwilling sacrifice, and I told her so. She spoke to me very kindly, however, and tried to encourage me, and suggested that Carrie would be a very proper person for my husband to marry. I had now no longer any doubt in my mind that it had been all "arranged," and that opposition on my part would be all in vain. I was indignant at this, for I believed that, as the Revelation itself said, I— the first wife—ought first to have been consulted. This, however, I subsequently found was as false as the system itself. I believed that I was the victim of a conspiracy, and I did not intend to submit without giving them some trouble.

I returned home, pondering over what had been said to me; with a feeling of intense weariness oppressing my heart. I did not know what to think. It appeared to me that every one had determined that Carrie should be my husband's second wife, and I now believed, with my talkative friend, that Brigham Young had certainly intended it from the beginning. I felt that I would rather that he should marry almost any one else than her; for I felt certain that I should hate any woman whom he might marry, no matter how much I might have loved her before.

But my mind was soon relieved of its trouble respecting poor Carrie, for, as I before mentioned, her failing health forbade all thoughts of marriage, and my husband, after a short time, never spoke to me about her. The real cause of my distress, however, was by no means removed—it was determined, without appeal, that my husband should, notwithstanding any impediment to the contrary, take another wife, whoever that chosen one might be,—my apprehensions, therefore, were not removed, they were only turned in another direction.

CHAPTER XXXI.

TRIALS—THE SECOND WIFE CHOSEN—SHADOWS OF LIFE.

A List of Eligible Young Ladies—Making a Selection—Asking the First Wife's Consent—My Husband's Bride Elect—Watching a Husband's Wooing—"Her Little Day of Triumph"—Another Victim to the *Heavenly* "Order"—The Important Claims of Love—Reminiscences of a First Love—Submissive to the Faith—A Man Cannot Love Two at One Time—A Very Youthful Bride—A "Very Painful Task"—A Long Courtship—Bearing the Cross—A Visit from my Husband's Bride-Elect—Belinda—Carrie Grant's Illness—Divulging a Secret—"Love me one day Longer"—The Approach of Death—A Strange Promise for a Wife to Give—I Choose a Wife for My Husband—Carrie's Last Hours—"It is Better So"—A Sacred Pledge—My Last Visit to Carrie—A Sad Farewell.

T HE next day my husband proposed several young girls for my consideration, but I felt that it was of very little consequence to me upon whom his choice might fall.

It is a custom among the Mormon married men—those at least who make any pretensions to doing what is right and who wish to spare the feelings of their wives as much as the degrading system will allow—to make it appear as if the second wife were chosen by the first, and they go through the form of consulting with her as to who shall be selected. The husband will mention the names of several eligible young ladies, among whom is sure to be the one upon whom he has already set his affections. If the wife should try to make herself agreeable by suggesting one or another of these young ladies, some objection is sure to be raised. One is too thought-less; the relations of another are not quite so agreeable as they might be; and the temper of a third is said to be not very good. In this way, one after another is taken off the list, until only one remains—the bright particular star of whom all along the husband has been thinking,—and if the wife should make any objections to *this* one, the husband, of course, has a ready answer. In most cases her extreme youth is an excuse for everything; she will have plenty of time to learn, and will be the more ready to be taught.

When once they have obtained the reluctant consent of their wives, it is astonishing how bright and cheerful these Mormon husbands become. Notwithstanding all that they have said to the contrary, it is evident that Polygamy is no trial to *their* faith. They say that it is as great a cross to them as it is to their wives, but somehow or other they take very kindly to it.

It was soon settled who should be the honored maiden to whom my husband should pay his addresses. Her name was Belinda, and she was the daughter of the Apostle Parley P. Pratt, whom I have already mentioned as coming to an untimely end in Arkansas. I, of course, was not expected to ask any questions or evince any curiosity respecting the girl or my husband's relations towards her. I had given my consent, I had acted my part, or at least all the part that was expected of me; I had fulfilled my duty as a Mormon first wife when I agreed to another wife being taken, and, henceforth, all that transpired was—so the Elders would have said—no business of mine.

Mormon domestic matters are to the Gentile looker-on a perfect mystery. No one outside of Mormonism can realise the position of a wife, in her husband's own house, waiting for him to bring home to her another wife. But the Mormon women understand and *feel* it all. They know what it is to watch the course of a husband's courtship and note how he progresses with his wooing; and they could, if they dared, tell the painful feelings that rankle in their breasts at such a time.

Nor is the new wife much happier. The girl against whom the first wife now feels so bitterly, will, in all probability, some day be as unhappy as *she* is now. In due course of time, when the wooing is over and the maiden is won, she will be brought home, and will have her little day of triumph until her lord and master deems it necessary to add another "jewel" to his crown, and then *her* heart will be rent, as the first wife's was, and another crushed and degraded victim will be added to that list of suffering women who have become martyrs to this *heavenly* order of marriage!

Intent on his wooing, the husband is, of course, particularly attentive to his personal appearance, and spares no pains to render himself attractive to the young lady whose affections he proposes to win. Business, and domestic duties, of course, give place to the more important claims of love, and everything must be sacrificed upon the altar of that blind divinity. The wife sees all this, but she is not expected to feel. She remembers the time when her husband used to find his greatest pleasure in paying *to her* those little endearing attentions which love demands, and finds its reward in rendering. She remembers the time when he vowed at the altar to be faithful until death, and how often afterwards he has reiterated that vow and declared that no other woman should ever win from him a thought that would be disloyal to her.

It is impossible for any man to act justly—to say nothing of acting with affection—towards his wife while his thoughts and wishes are wandering towards a younger rival. Words are uttered, which in themselves perhaps are trifling, but which, under the circumstances, have a meaning bitterly cruel; and little things are done which, like the worm at the root, gnaw the heart itself and embitter the whole existence. Women whose minds were said to be strong, have written and spoken much of late years in an endeavor to unsex themselves. That men and women should be morally and socially equal, no right-minded person can for a moment doubt, but a woman never was and never will be a man. In sentiment and feeling, her mind is utterly the reverse of masculine, and no man, however refined or sensitive he may be, can ever fully understand a woman's heart. A man may be faithfully and devotedly attached to his wife, but she can never be to him what he is to her. Every thought and affection of her soul is centred in him. He is the life of her own existence. In her eyes he is all that is noble and good and true. He is her idol, her love, her all. Horribly then, Ah, a thousand times horribly and cruelly do they sin against the holiest principles of human nature, who crush with coldness and unkindness those warm and tender sentiments of affection which in her heart a woman cherishes towards her husband. How often have I mourned in secret some careless word, or cold, indifferent look which my truant husband has thoughtlessly bestowed upon me when leaving the house to visit his intended bride—words, which, to him, had no particular meaning, perhaps, but which pierced my heart :—I knew too well that he *could not* love two at once. It was evident which way his thoughts were wandering, although he, like the rest of his brethren, assured me that principle and religion—and no other motive—attracted him so often to the side of his more youthful and, of course, more pleasing companion.

My husband's intended certainly was very young—almost too young for a bride she would have been considered in any other community—and I must in fairness allow that she was very handsome. It is of the utmost importance that a Mormon girl should marry young. Women everywhere are never anxious to grow old, but among the Mormons age is especially dreaded by the women, for when years have robbed them of their personal attractions, in most cases they lose all hold upon their husband's affections and find themselves obliged to give place to prettier and more youthful rivals. A woman's position in the world to come, as I have before mentioned, depends, so the elders say, very much upon the number of children she has borne in this ; it is, therefore, a consideration of the very first importance that she should marry as early in life as possible, and this obligation is never for a moment overlooked by the refined and pure-minded Mormon men.

And now began the "painful task" of wooing the young lady. My husband told me that it was "a very painful duty," and as an obedient wife I felt bound to believe him. It was, of course, no pleasure to him to pay his addresses to an interesting young girl; it was no anxiety to be with her which made him hasten away to the damsel's house of an evening. Oh dear no! it was pure principle, love for the kingdom of God, and "a very *painful* task!" He seemed, however, to bear it remarkably well, and manifested a zeal which was perfectly astonishing to me considering the circumstances. In fact, I felt it my duty to restrain him a little for the sake of his health, for he seemed so anxious to perform his "task" properly that he could scarcely spare time to take his meals; but regardless of his own feelings he did not pay much attention to my suggestions.

But deeply as I sympathised with my husband, there were times when I felt that mine was indeed no imaginary sorrow, and that nothing could lull the storm that had gathered in my breast. The affliction which I had so long dreaded was now right at my door, and the most painful feelings agitated my mind. Sometimes I shut myself up in my own room and tried to reason with myself; then I would kneel, and pray, and weep with passionate emotion; and again I would pace the floor, my heart overflowing with anger and indignation. I never, at that time, knew what it was to be happy, for I felt that I was a burden and hindrance to my husband and I longed to die. I had loved him so devotedly that I could not even now cast him from my heart, and though I felt bitterly my position, I believed that he would not willingly wound me and that he was acting from the purest of motives. But it was all in vain. I could not change my nature, and my heart would rebel.

The courtship was continued for months, and the end seemed as far off as ever; for on account of the youthfulness of the bride elect my husband wished the marriage indefinitely postponed. It would be impossible for me to tell the thousand annoyances and indignities to which I was forced to submit— trials which might appear too trifling even to name, but which

27

to a wife, under such circumstances, were crosses which she found it hard enough to bear. My husband knew nothing of these things, and, had he done so, it is more than probable that he would have considered it weakness in me to be troubled about matters of such small consequence—little actions and foolish words which he would have said I ought to have treated with contempt. It was easy to say that, but not so easy to do. Let any wife picture to herself how she would feel, if after schooling her heart to submission, after realising that she was no longer to be first and dearest in her husband's affections, she were to be constantly hearing the friends and relations of the young girl to whom her husband was engaged boasting of his devotion to her and openly expressing their belief that he had never loved before! How would any wife be pleased if, whenever her husband's intended received a valuable present from him, she were particularly informed of the fact, and a thousand little aggravating details were added to make her, if possible, more miserable. I do not know how such things would appear to a man's mind if matters were reversed and the wife took a couple of husbands to her heart, but I have noticed that "the lords of creation" are generally—and, no doubt, justly—sensitive enough, even if they only suspect their wives of engaging in a trifling flirtation; and I know that, however silly she may be considered for doing so, a woman in her heart feels all these things.

A woman can nerve herself to endure almost anything, and outwardly she may conceal her feelings, but there are limits beyond which endurance is not possible. A chance meeting with the girl who has superseded her in her husband's love; or worse still, should she chance to surprise the affectionate couple *tête à tête*, is sufficient to dispel all her good resolutions and to destroy that tranquility of mind which she finds it so difficult to preserve. She becomes sick at heart, nervous and entirely unfitted for her duties. I have frequently heard Mormon women say that, notwithstanding their husbands had been for many years polygamists, they could never see the other wives without a feeling of anger and indignation arising in their hearts. I know that in my own case I never became reconciled to the system.

My husband was called away to the Eastern States upon business, and his marriage was postponed, as I have already mentioned, to give the bride an opportunity of growing a little older first. I thought that the present would be a good time to show her some little attentions, which I believed it was my duty to do. The idea of coming in contact with her was certainly not at all pleasant, but I felt that it was only right for me to act in a friendly manner towards her, however painful it might be. She was the cause of much sorrow to me, but I could not blame her, for she had been born and brought up in the system, and, of course, supposed it true; but, for all that, it is utterly impossible for any woman to think complacently of another who is weaning from her her husband's affections, however innocent that other may be of intentional wrong.

Belinda was a very nice girl and, under other circumstances, I believe I should have liked her very much. I looked upon her as little more than a child, and my husband has frequently told me that he also regarded her in that light, but to me it was of small consequence that he thought of her as a child, so long as he acted towards her as a woman. Now that he was away from home there was no danger that she would meet him, so I invited her in a friendly way to call upon me. She came, and I had one or two other ladies present, for I was not like my husband in that particular—*I* had no anxiety to be alone with her. My effort to cultivate a friendly feeling towards her was not very successful. There was a coldness and restraint on both sides which we could not overcome, and I felt not a little relief when the evening was over. Subsequently I renewed the attempt, but to no purpose; her very presence in my house and among my children seemed in itself an insult to me.

It was not strange that I should feel thus. Think what the feelings of any wife would be under such circumstances. A family of children was growing up around me. Anxious for their future welfare, I surrounded them with the best influences which I could command, and my constant effort was to train them so that they should blush at everything that was not honorable and upright. I had daughters of my own—one of them quite growing up into womanhood. Had my husband been a Gentile, and had he gone astray, his wrong-doing would not have been introduced into my home itself, nor would it have been a subject of conversation among my children. But under Mormonism how was I situated? Why, I was compelled to drain the cup of degradation to its very dregs—the sanctity of my home itself was invaded, and I felt ashamed to think that I—wife and mother as I was—was entertaining *my husband's affianced "wife"* (!)—a child no older than my own eldest girl; and before long she would be brought home in my presence and among my children! Oh, detestable and unnatural desecration of the sanctity of home! Oh brutalising and immoral burlesque upon religious faith! How could I ever have deluded myself into the idea that such a profanation of all that is good could by any possibility be right, that such an outrage upon decency and propriety, such a violation of the laws of reason and religion could be pleasing in the sight of an all-pure God?

During my husband's absence, my poor friend Carrie Grant had been daily growing worse in health. I had once asked my husband if there was any truth in the rumors that I had heard of his attachment to her, but he had assured me that there was no foundation for them. Subsequently I learned from Carrie's own lips that this was not exactly true. She said he had deceived me for the sake of sparing my feelings, but I did not appreciate such kindness. Mormonism is full of deceptions. Men deceive their wives, and in return the wives deceive their husbands; and it is all for the sake of the kingdom of God.

Poor Carrie! Her's was a short and unhappy life—even her little dream of love was overclouded by disappointment. She was now constantly confined to her room, and whenever it was possible I used to call upon her, and attempted to make her feel more happy and cheerful. She used to ask me to talk with her about Mormonism. "You know," she said, "that I have never known any other religion, and I believe that this is right though it does not make me happy. My father loved Mormonism so much that I feel it *must* be right; the fault is in my own evil nature that does not bend to the will of Heaven."

One day she said to me: "I am getting worse, Sister Stenhouse, and I am glad of it, for I shall die. I am of no good here—there is nothing for me to do; if I lived, I should only cause trouble; it is better as it is."

"Carrie," I said, "You must not talk like that. You are still very young and probably will live for many years, and you do not know what future may lie before you."

"Do not blame me too much," she replied, for I am not the only unhappy girl in the city. I know many girls who are very miserable. Married women think that they are the only ones who suffer, while we girls know that nowhere upon the face of the earth can be found such an unhappy set as we are. Why did Brigham Young keep me from going to my friends in the East? I should have been happier then—I should have felt better. But now I want to die, and I am weary waiting for death."

In this melancholy mood I found her one day when she appeared particularly sad. She had been ill then about ten months; but her loving blue eyes were just as bright as ever, and I could see very little change in her, except that she was not able now to leave her couch without assistance, and she spoke as if it fatigued her very much. It was quite impossible to arouse her from the state of melancholy into which she had fallen, and it seemed to me that she could not last long. I offered to take her to my house, and said I would nurse her there and take care of her; but she said she was very kindly treated by her father's family and did not wish to change. She seemed to cling to me as if she could not bear that I should leave her, and she told me she had something on her mind that troubled her; she wanted to have a long talk with me about it, but not that day, she said. I went home that evening with tears in my eyes.

As the end was fast approaching, she one day said: "I want
to tell you now, Sister Stenhouse, what I spoke of before, if
you are willing to listen and will not be angry with anything
I say. Remember, I am dying, or I never would speak to you
as I am going to."

I told her of my great love for her, and that nothing that
she could say would change that love.

"You do not know what I want to ask you, or you would
not say so," she replied; "and I so dread to lose your love that
I am afraid to tell you what is in my mind. But you know
that I am dying and you will not be very hard with me."

She was then silent for some time, as if too much fatigued
to continue the conversation. "No: I cannot tell you to-day,"
she said at last, "I want you to love me one day longer."

I urged her not to doubt that my love towards her could
never change, and told her that it was better for her to speak
at once and relieve her mind. She took my hand, and looked
long and tenderly at me, and then she said: "I will tell you
all, and if your love can stand that test, then indeed you *do*
love me."

I encouraged her, and she began: "Would you hate me if I
told you that I loved your husband?"

"No," I replied, "I would not hate you, Carrie." I said no
more, for it seemed to me that it would be wrong of me to tell
her of my suspicions and all that I had suffered at the thought
that my husband had conceived an affection for her.

"Can you possibly answer me as calmly as that?" she said;
"I thought that the very mention of such a thing would almost
kill you, for I saw how much you loved your husband, and, Ah,
how I have suffered at the thought of telling you. But that
is not all I wanted to say, or I need never have spoken to you
at all. I wanted to ask you to do me one last kindness, and
then I think I shall die happy. You know that we have been
taught that Polygamy is absolutely necessary to salvation, and
if I were to die without being sealed to some man I could not
possibly enter the celestial kingdom. My friends wish me to
be sealed to one of the authorities of the Church, but I can-

not bear the idea of being sealed to a man whom I do not love. I love your husband, and I want you to promise that I shall be sealed to him. If I had thought that I should recover, I never would have let you know this, for I would not live to give you sorrow. But, when I am gone, will you kneel by your husband's side in the Endowment House, and be married to him for me? Will it pain you much to do that for me, Sister Stenhouse?"

I felt so strangely as I listened to all this that I could not utter a single word, and she continued: "We shall then be together in eternity, and I am happy at the thought of that, for I think I love you even better than I love him. And then I believe we shall have overcome all our earthly feelings and shall be prepared to live that celestial law, and perhaps we may prefer it, for no doubt we shall know no unhappiness there."

The exertion of talking seemed to be too much for her, and she remained silent for some time. I felt ashamed that I had allowed my feelings to influence me at such a moment, for while she had been speaking I had allowed my thoughts to travel back over the past year, and, now that she admitted her love for my husband, very many circumstances came painfully to my recollection and confirmed all that she said. I resolved, however, not to question her, but to allow her to tell me just what she pleased. So I knelt down by her side and whispered into her ear a solemn promise that I would do all that she desired. Poor girl: how I felt for her! When I had given her this pledge, she appeared much relieved and told me freely all that had passed between my husband and herself, and she said she had left my house simply because she could not endure to cause me any sorrow. I told her of my husband's contemplated marriage with Belinda Pratt, and she appeared a good deal troubled at it. "Let me be second," she said, "for then I shall feel that I am nearer to you, and I want you always to think that, when you die, if I have the power, I shall be the first to meet you and take you by the hand."

Thus we talked together for a long time, and it was with

painful interest that I listened to what she said. It was a
singular interview;—a wife receiving from a young girl the
confession that she loved her husband; that he had fully
returned her affection, and had even talked with her about
marriage: the girl requesting the wife to be married for her
to her own husband, and the wife, full of tender love towards
the girl, freely giving her a promise that she would do so. In
my sorrow at parting from her, and the great affection that I
felt towards her, all feelings of jealousy were utterly forgotten.
Before I left I said: "Carrie, whether you live or die, you shall
be married to my husband, if he ever enters into Polygamy;
and I say this although I do not doubt that he will do so, and
at the same time I think that you will live."

I really believed that she might recover; for now this burden was off her mind, I thought she would have strength to
subdue her sickness, and at first it seemed as if this would
really be the case. The next day she appeared so much
better that her friends all became hopeful, and when I told
her that I had written to my husband and had told him, that
since he had made up his mind to go into Polygamy, I wished
him to marry her, she appeared so happy and showed her joy
in so many innocent ways that I could not be angry.

"How do you think he will feel," she said, "when he gets
your letter?—Do I look pretty well to-day? And do you
think that if I continue to get better I shall have regained my
looks before he comes home."

"Oh," I said, humoring her, "You will look quite pretty by
the time he returns, I shall be really jealous of you."

In an instant the thought of how much all mention of her
in connection with my husband must be painful to me, occurred
to her mind, and she begged me to forgive her for her carelessness. "No," said she, "I will try never to give you pain,
and you must always love me."

For some days this improvement in her appearance continued, and I thought, and hoped, that we should soon have
her round again. I really wished her to live now, for if it
was absolutely necessary that Mr. Stenhouse *must* practice

Polygamy, I would prefer that, rather than any other woman, he should marry her, for I felt that she would understand me as no one else could.

Thus, after all, I really had selected a second wife for my husband!

But the change in poor Carrie's looks was altogether deceptive. News came to me one morning that she was very much worse, and I hastened to see her. As I entered the room, her eyes brightened, and she said: "I'm glad that you have come, Sister Stenhouse, for I feel that I am going soon. Then, after a pause, she added, holding up her hands—"Do you know what that means?" The finger nails were turning blue.

"That means death," she said; "and it is better so." After this we conversed together for some time upon various topics of special interest to her in the position in which she then was, and presently she said, as if asking a question,— "You will keep your promise, I know."

"Carrie," I answered, "if there is anything that I can say or do that will make you feel more certain that I will keep my promise, if I live to do so, tell me, and I will do it."

"I am afraid," she said, "that, after all, he never loved me. He pitied my lonely situation and was so kind and good to me that I learned to love him, and those meddlesome sisters tried to get him to marry me, but I would not be false to you. Then we both thought it was best not to tell you, as it would make you grieve, although it never could take place. Even now, had I not known that I was dying, I never would have told you. But you will not love me less when you think of me after I am gone?"

I told her that my affection for her would never change, and I talked with her, and tried to soothe her dying moments, and to make her feel less lonely; and thus the morning passed away. In the afternoon she was silent and apparently unconscious, and before another day dawned she had passed away to her rest.

CHAPTER XXXII.

MARRIAGE FOR THE DEAD—ENTERING INTO POLYGAMY—
THE NEW WIFE.

Memories of My Poor Friend Carrie—The Last Untroubled Sleep—Her Hopes and Mine—Alone in the Night—A Mysterious " Presence "—"I Plainly Saw Carrie Leaning Over Me"—The Wedding-Ring—"The 'Presence' in the Room Was Gone"—Troubled About the Ring—Beside the Coffin of My Dead Friend—I Place the Ring on Her Finger—My Husband's Gift for Carrie—"He Considered it was Only a Dream"—Waiting for the Event—The Saddest Day of My Life—My Husband's Second Marriage—I Give Away the Bride!—Fulfilling My Promise—I Am Married to My Husband for Carrie—Brigham's Decree : The Claims of the Living and the Dead—Married for Eternity—The Bride and Bridegroom—After the Wedding—Loneliness and Grief—A Night of Darkness and Sorrow.

THE following evening I went round again to the house, to gaze once more at the form of my dear friend.   She was lying in her coffin, dressed for the grave, and I looked at her long and tenderly as she rested sleeping there.   Her features were peaceful and natural as if in slumber ; an expression of calm tranquility hovered around her countenance, and in the repose of death she seemed almost happy.   Poor girl ! her life had been short indeed, and she had known but little pleasure, but I believed that she was now beyond the reach of earthly sorrow and earthly disappointment, happy in that land where suffering and tears are all unknown.   " There shall be no night there," the Lord of that other life had said.   Sorrow and sighing shall flee away from that bright and glorious land ;

and the grief and pain which on earth are the portion of so many tried and weary hearts, shall find no entrance into that eternal rest which our Father in heaven has prepared for us beyond the floods of death.

Oh, better far, I thought, it is that thus she should pass away. True, she has seen but little of life, and has not tasted many of its joys ; but, as a compensation, how much has she been spared. She was so gentle and so sensitive, so unfit to battle with the stern realities of existence, that I felt she had gained rather than lost in being taken away in the morning of her life. Those anxieties, trials, and cares, which are more or less the portion of every one of us, would never weary her now ; and, especially, she was for ever beyond the reach of those painful thoughts and feelings which are the lot of the Mormon women alone. Certainly, she thought, as also did I, that in that other, future life, after the resurrection, we should live together a life much like that which we lived on earth, only more glorious and happy. We could not marry or be given in marriage in the world to come ; but those who had been united on earth for eternity, whether personally or by proxy, would, in heaven, lead a married life together and fulfil all the duties and obligations of that position. Carrie believed firmly, that if I were sealed to my husband for her, she would be his second wife in heaven ; and the reason why I had promised to be married for her before my husband was united to other wives was, that by so doing, she would rank before all the rest. I, as first wife, would be queen in my husband's kingdom, if I continued faithful and very obedient : Carrie, as second wife, would rank next to me ; and the others who might afterwards be added would be placed according to the date of their marriage. We none of us doubted that all this was true ; and the thought that by her marriage with my husband she would be sure of " exaltation " in the celestial kingdom had comforted the last hours of my poor friend.

I was musing sadly over these things as I returned home that evening, resolved that nothing on my part should be left undone which might ensure her future happiness, and I presume that in my mind her death, and the promise which I had made, were the all-absorbing thoughts. Certain it is that a little incident occurred to me, which produced a vivid impression upon my mind, then and for a long time after. I believed that I was visited by my departed friend.

Now, I was not naturally superstitious, and I would not, on any account, have the reader think that I was a believer in the very extraordinary claims of modern Spiritualism. At the time of which I speak, I knew absolutely nothing of the "manifestations" and "communications" received at *séances* —I had, in fact, been so isolated, and was so ignorant of the doings of the world in general, that I had never even heard of such things. I certainly did not believe that apparitions of the dead returned to trouble us with communications of any kind; but, nevertheless, I was that night convinced that Carrie's spirit stood beside me, and spoke to me, just as in life she might herself have done. Even now, after the lapse of several years, I hardly know what to think of the matter, for it made such a powerful impression on my mind. Probably it was all a dream—a vivid and life-like dream, but nothing more. The reader will remember that at the time I was in a very delicate condition of health, my mind was quite unsettled with trouble and anxiety, and for some time past my thoughts had been constantly fixed upon poor Carrie and her sad fate. These circumstances combined might perhaps have shaped my ideas and raised up before me that strange vision. To me, however, at the time, it had all the force of reality; and while I leave it to the reader's common-sense to determine what really were the facts of the case, I think I should not be justified in altogether omitting an incident so singular, which, at such a critical period of my life, so strongly affected me.

I was sitting alone in my room, and reading, when suddenly I felt as if some one had opened the door and entered, and I looked round to see who it was. I felt a "Presence," if I may so speak, but I saw no one. So, thinking that I was nervous, and resolved to control my feelings, I took up my book again and tried to interest myself in it. A few minutes elapsed, and then I was startled again, for I felt sure that some one was leaning over me, and I seemed almost to hear them breathe.

Quite certain now that the events of the preceding day had unsettled my mind, I laid aside my book and prepared to retire for the night. But still I could not get rid of that feeling which we all experience when some one is near us whom we cannot see but of whose presence we are instinctively aware. After disrobing, I lay down and began to read until I was sleepy; I then turned down the light, without entirely extinguishing it, when, immediately after, the " Presence" seemed to stand beside my bed, and I lost all power over myself. I was not, I believed, asleep, but at the same time I did not seem to be perfectly awake. But the " Presence " was now no longer invisible—I plainly saw Carrie leaning over me.

" Is that you, Carrie ?" I said.

" Yes," she answered, or seemed to answer, " I want something from you." Then pointing to a gold ring upon my finger—not my wedding ring, though it was *a* wedding ring —she said : " I want you to give me that ring."

" You shall have it," I answered ; and she then bent over me and kissed my cheek. I distinctly felt the coldness of her lips as she touched me ; and in another instant she was gone.

I was wide awake, but trembling, and covered with a cold perspiration, for I felt certain that Carrie's spirit had been with me, and now that she had spoken to me I felt that the " Presence" in the room was gone. I could sleep no more, although all fear had left me, and I lay awake for hours thinking over the matter and trying to explain it away.

In the morning, I persuaded myself that it was all a dream or the effects of a disturbed imagination ; but as I had promised—whether dreaming or awake it mattered little—to give her the ring, I resolved to keep my word and put it on her finger secretly as she lay in her coffin. With that intention I went to the house, some time before the funeral was appointed to take place, but, as there was constantly some one in the room, I felt ashamed to carry out my purpose, lest they should think me silly to do such a thing.

As the time approached when they should carry her to the grave, I became so troubled about the ring that I could not rest, so I went into another room where one of Brigham Young's wives, and a plural wife of Carrie's father, were talking together; and I told them of my dream; for so I called the vision of my dead friend, although it seemed to me reality.

They urged me to lose no time but to go instantly and put the ring on the finger of the corpse. "If you do not," they said, "You will never feel happy; she will never rest, but will be sure to come back to reproach you." So I went and did as they said. Without any one noticing me, I stood beside the casket, and raised the beautiful hand which looked so pure and wax-like, but oh, so cold!—and I placed the ring on the wedding finger, and then covered it with the other hand. Then again, beside the dead body of my friend, I vowed to be faithful to the promise that I had made to her; and after that I felt at peace.

Not long subsequently to this, my husband returned home. The following morning he took from his pocket a very beautiful ring which he presented to me, asking me to wear it for his sake. Directly after, he held up another—a plain gold ring—and asked me if I knew who that was for. I thought that I knew, for, as he was soon to be married to Miss Pratt, I supposed it was for her. My pride, however, would not allow me to say so. I therefore simply replied that I did not know, feeling, at the same time, very much inclined to add, "You had better give this one with it, whoever it is for;" for I thought it unkind of him to show Belinda's ring to me.

I was silent, however, and he then said: "This one I bought for Carrie when I received your letter."

"Then I shall have to wear it now," I said; and then I told him all that I have just related, but I think he considered it was only a dream or the fancy of a troubled imagination.

I now expected very soon to be called upon to undergo the most painful ordeal that any wife can be required to pass through : I was to give my husband another wife—such is the sacrifice demanded of every Mormon woman.

The thought of doing this was worse than death to me. I felt injured, humiliated and degraded by it, and yet I still tried to believe that it was the will of God, and must therefore be right. To me, this outrage upon all the purest feelings of womanhood seemed more like the will of men—men of the basest and most unholy passions. It was repulsive to me in whatever form it was presented, but still I reproached my own rebellious heart for feeling so, for I had been told that the ways of the Lord were past finding out, and however unlike Him this Revelation might appear, we Mormon women had been taught that it was our duty to bend our wills and to suffer in unquestioning and uncomplaining silence.

As the time approached, I felt like a condemned criminal awaiting the day of execution. A sense of apprehension, a dread of coming evil, was ever present to my mind, and everything appeared to me through the medium of my griefs. To a certain extent, my husband also suffered, for it would be impossible, I think, for any man to see his wife suffering so intensely without feeling for her, and I sometimes believed that his sympathy for me was so great, that, if he had dared, he would even then have refused to obey the counsel of the Priesthood.

Then, too, he had a little trouble of his own, for he began to realise that this innovation upon the sanctity of our home would make a great change in his future—his freedom would be gone.

However gratifying it may be to a man's feelings to know that there is no limit to his privileges, and that he is always at liberty—no matter how many wives he may already possess—to fall in love with every pretty girl he meets, and marry her

if she consents ; yet every intelligent man must be conscious
that it can be no easy matter to keep peace between many
wives in one house, and that, if he wishes to act rightly by all,
he must train himself to be scrupulously just, never showing
any partiality in look or deed, or even by a word. There are
many such men among the Mormons. They are conscientious and good men, who try to live their religion, but who at
the same time desire to act kindly towards their wives. My
husband began to realise the great responsibility that he was
about to take upon himself, and seeing his thoughtful and
troubled look, I tried to hide my own feelings ; for every true
wife knows that nothing so powerfully arouses a woman to
struggle with her own sorrows as the knowledge that her husband is unhappy.

The dreaded day at length arrived, the day which for so
long, and with such painful forebodings, I had anticipated. I
had spent a very wakeful and unhappy night, and felt very
sick and nervous, for I was about to become a mother, and my
health was anything but strong. I hardly felt as if I should
have courage to go through that day. I was, however, compelled to nerve myself to the task, and I began to make my
preparations for going to the Endowment House. The only
thing that gave me strength was the thought that my husband
had consented that I should go through the ceremony of being
married to him that day for Carrie ; for even then I supposed
that those who would be married in heaven must first be married on earth, and that, too, by those who had received authority from on high.

Ever since I had first embraced Mormonism I had been
entirely cut off from Gentile society, although living in the
Gentile world. Abroad, and also when in New York, the
cares of a family kept me very much at home, and the continual state of apprehension in which I was, rendered me
averse to visiting among friends. Thus it was that I never
conversed freely with any one who could have informed me
truthfully of the origin of Mormonism, and consequently I
brooded over my religion as a melancholy fact ; but, though

with moments of weakness and wavering, I never thoroughly doubted its divine origin. The terrible sacrifice which was about to be required of me, might, I thought, be painful to make, but it was no less the will of God. I must submit, whatever the effort might cost me.

The morning was bright and lovely—a morning calculated to inspire happy hopes and pleasant feelings; but to me it brought nothing but fear and trembling. Even the innocent prattle of my children annoyed me, and they not knowing how deeply I was suffering looked at me with wonder in their eyes. Oh, I thought, surely my husband will at length comprehend the greatness of the love I bear him; surely he will now appreciate the sacrifice I make for his sake and for my religion. Even now, if I did not know that he believes this doctrine to be true, and he would feel condemned if, through any opposition of mine, he were not allowed to practice it, I would at the last moment dash this bitter cup from my lips and take my chance of the consequences in a future state!

Utterly cast down and broken-hearted, I felt almost as if the Lord himself had forsaken me, and there was no one to whom I could look for aid. I could not go to my husband in that hour for sympathy; for I well knew that his thoughts must be with his intended bride, and that my sorrows would only trouble him at a time when he must desire to be at peace. Besides which, I was too proud to plead for love at a shrine that I felt should rightfully be all my own. And then, too, I knew not but what he might tell *her* of my feelings; and it would be too great a humiliation for me should she think me jealous of the position which she now occupied, and her influence over my husband.

With such feelings I went to the Endowment House. There at the altar I was to give proof of my obedience and of my faith in my religion, by placing the hand of the new wife in that of my husband. The thought was almost madness. To have followed my husband to the grave would have been a terrible blow to me; but to live to see him the husband of another woman was something that seemed to me beyond en-

28

durance. Notwithstanding every effort of faith, doubts would arise, and in bitterest anguish I thought—this is more like the work of cruel man than of God. Why should man have this power over woman, and she so helpless? Surely a just and impartial God can have nothing to do with this! There was a darkness before my eyes, and struggle as I might, I could see no ray of light. No glimmering of hope.

First, my husband was married to Miss Pratt; and then to me for Carrie. Thus I fulfilled my pledge to my departed friend. Later in the day, I placed the ring which my husband had bought for her upon my finger, instead of the one which I had put on her wedding-finger in the coffin. I shall always wear it in remembrance of her, although among the Mormons at that time wedding-rings were never thought of, and to this day are only used by the more educated and refined who cling to Gentile customs. I had found before going to the Endowment House that I could not have Carrie sealed to my husband next to me, for Belinda had objected, and her mother had appealed to Brigham Young about it. They told me that he had said that the living had claims before the dead, although my own feelings would have led me to think otherwise. Brigham Young performed the ceremony. He sat at the end of the altar and we three knelt down—my husband on one side and Miss Pratt and myself on the other. Speaking to me, Brigham Young asked: "Are you willing to give this woman to your husband to be his lawful wife for time and for all eternity? If you are you will signify it by placing her right hand within the right hand of your husband."

I did so; but what words can describe my feelings! The anguish of a whole lifetime was crowded into that one single moment. The painful meaning of those words, "for all eternity" withered my soul, and the unending contract which my husband had made with another woman was practically a divorce from me. I had now laid everything upon the altar of sacrifice, for I had given away my husband. What more could the Lord require of me that I was not prepared to do?

I was bewildered and almost beside myself, and yet I had

to hide my feelings. Hope was for ever banished from my life. To whom could I look for sympathy among those who were around me? They were most of them men who had ruthlessly wrecked the lives and lacerated the hearts of hundreds of women before my turn came, and the sight of an unhappy wife was so common in their experience that it was more likely to awaken their anger than their pity. I felt this instinctively, and I resolved that they should never know how much my poor heart was torn. My husband, it is true, was there. *My* husband! Was he not now the husband of another woman, and, therefore, no longer belonging to me. I knew that I never could overcome my early teaching sufficiently to *feel* that this was right, though, such was my wretched fanaticism, that I mentally and verbally assented to it. I felt that now I stood alone—our union was severed. There could never be any copartnership between that other wife and myself—no, never. Salvation or no salvation, it was impossible that I could ever love her. From that day I began to hide all my sorrows from my husband, and it was but very seldom that I uttered a word of discontent, and when I expressed what I felt, it was in anger ; but never in sorrow, seeking sympathy.

I remember when we returned home—that home which had now lost its charm, for the young wife was to live there—my husband said to me : "You have been very brave, but it is not so hard to bear, after all, is it?" I had hidden my feelings so well that he really thought that I was indifferent. But during the remainder of the day how I watched their looks and noticed every word! To me their tender tones were daggers, piercing my heart and filling me with a desire to revenge myself upon the father of my children. Oh, what fanatics we Mormon women have been ever to have believed for a single moment that a just and loving Father and God would have given a command that in almost every instance has produced such fearful results upon those who should have been happy wives and mothers, and consequently upon their children. Indeed, even then it made me feel that there was no justice in heaven, if this love which is the best part of woman's nature—this

love that we had always believed was a part of divinity itself
—this principle, without which there would be nothing worth
living for—if this had been made our greatest curse, and the
woman who showed herself most actuated by this gentle influence was to be the greatest victim.

I felt that day that if I could not get away by myself alone,
and give expression to my overcharged feelings, I should certainly lose my reason. I was utterly miserable. It was only
in the dead of night, in my own chamber, that I gave way to
the terrible anguish that was consuming me. God and my
own soul can alone bear witness to what I suffered in that
time of woe. That night was to me such as even the most
God-forsaken might pray never to know ; and morning dawned
without my having for a moment closed my eyes.

CHAPTER XXXIII.

DOMESTIC ARRANGEMENTS OF THE SAINTS:—POLYGAMY FROM A WOMAN'S STANDPOINT.

A First Wife's Experience in Polygamy—"Getting Used to it"—The Doings and Devices of Polygamic Wives—How Mormon Men Deceive and are Deceived—Feminine Drill-Sergeants—The Ladies who advocate Polygamy !—A Present for Brother Brigham—Getting up a Petition—How Signatures are Procured—Inscribing the Names of the Dead as Voters—Cruel efforts of Hopeless Women—A Mormon idea of a Husband's Duty—The Domestic Arrangements of the Saints—A Man with Six Wives—How he Divides his Time—A Crafty Proceeding—The Reward of Generosity—Primitive Habitations—Polygamy in the Rough—The Discarded Wife in the Wagon-Box—" Build up the Kingdom ! "—Four Wives and their Children in One Room—Advantages of a Large House—Wealthy Polygamists—Married to Two Sisters—Marrying a Step-Daughter—Managing a Husband—The Influence of Good Cookery—Wives in Various Settlements—The Case Reversed : A icture.

I WAS now to realise personally in my own home life what Polygamy actually was. Hitherto I had observed how other women suffered and how other men treated their wives ; but now the painful reality had come to my own door, and I was to experience the effects of the system upon myself, and instead of noting the conduct of other men I should be able to observe the change which Polygamy might work in my own husband.

How little do the Mormon men know what it is in the truest sense to have *a* wife, though they have so many " wives " after their own fashion. Almost imperceptibly to the husband, and even to the wife herself, a barrier rises between them from the very day that he marries another woman. It matters not how much she believes in the doctrine of plural marriage, or how willing she may be to submit to it; the fact remains the same. The estrangement begins by her trying to hide from him all her secret sorrows; for she feels that what has been done cannot be undone now, and she says, " I cannot change it; neither would I if I could, because it is the will of God, and I must bear it; besides, what good will it do to worry my husband with all my feelings? He cannot help me; and is he not another woman's husband?" Then comes, perhaps, the painful thought, " I have no longer any desire to confide in him." Or it may be that she detects some familiarity between her husband and the other wife; and she feels bitterly towards both, for strive as she may, human nature cannot be altogether crushed out.

Before long the wife begins to feel her husband's presence itself become irksome to her—even his touch makes her shudder. She strives to hide all this; but, oh, with what anguish of soul! She may keep up an appearance of tranquility, and when spoken to about plural marriage may lead people to believe that she is happy, and even her own husband may think that she has become "used to it;" but women never "get used to it" until they have in a great measure, or perhaps entirely, lost their love for their husbands.

This was a mistake that my own husband made in respect to me. He realised, I know—as much as the generality of men ever can realise of a woman's feelings—that I was suffering intensely, and he tried in every way to make my burden lighter. But, like his brethren, he thought that, because he was getting used to it, I was also. I can truly say I never did get used to it, and never could.

That was a time of great misery to me, much as I tried to control my feelings. Day by day I strove to hide from my heart even the knowledge of my own unhappiness, and when I could no longer endure, I would lock myself in my room and give vent to the anguish that was consuming me. I realised, however, that this continual conflict of feeling was unfitting me for my duties. Everything was becoming a trial to me. I could not bear to be spoken to; the prattle of my children that had always been so dear to me, was now discordant to my feelings; and all their little questionings were irksome. I determined that this should no longer be the case; I would battle with my own heart; I would henceforth devote my whole life—worthless as that life appeared to have become—to the welfare of my little ones. This was a conclusion that hundreds of wretched Mormon wives have arrived at, and when this is the case there is some hope for them. But many give way to despair, and go down broken-hearted to their graves.

How much of true affection do the Mormon husbands lose! A man may have a dozen wives; but from them all combined he will not receive as much real love and devotion as he would from one alone, if he made her feel that she had his undivided affection and confidence. How terribly these men deceive themselves! When peace, or rather quiet, reigns in their homes, they think that the Spirit of God is there. But it is not so. It is a calm not like the gentle silence of sleep, but as the painful stillness of death—the death of the heart's best affection and all that is worth calling love. All *true* love has fled, and indifference has taken its place. The very children feel it. What do they, what can they, care about their father, whom they so seldom see? Of course, as in everything else, there are exceptions to the rule; but I am speaking now of Polygamists in general. .

Some wives, afraid of creating a prejudice against themselves and of being forsaken altogether, deceive their husbands, and make them believe that they are satisfied. It must be admitted that, in acting thus, these wives are not always actuated by a fear of losing the society or love of their husbands, for, in Polygamy, love dies a natural death; but it is galling to a woman's pride to have it said that she has been cast off for another. Then, too—and some women would consider this the most important reason of all—the best provision is usually made for the home where the husband stops most frequently; and the wife, if not for her own sake, at least for her children's, will be anxious to have a well-provided house. This is only natural. The "divine" plan has always been worked out in a very human way.

When a man has several wives, there is, of course, no necessity for him to stay with an unhappy or mopish one, as he can always find a more pleasant reception elsewhere. Men who can really believe that women are satisfied and happy under such a system must be entirely ignorant of human nature. And yet I have known many gentlemen from Utah who, when asked how the Mormon women submitted to Polygamy, have answered: "Oh, very well. They are perfectly happy, for they look upon it as a religious duty, and are satisfied and contented with it."

How false is all this! What an incorrect idea does it give of the wives of Utah! Some of these very men, to my certain knowledge, know better than this, and have had a very different experience in their own families. I have in my mind a prominent man from Salt Lake City, who told a reporter of the New York *Herald* how happily his own wives lived together, while every one at home knows that they could not well be more miserable, for *his* wives do not wear the mask. I could name many other families in which it is just the same.

There is a class of women in Utah who act as a sort of drill-sergeants to the other women; these form what is called "The Female Relief Society;" they take the lead among the Mormon women, get up memorials to Congress against anti-Polygamic bills, and otherwise spend their time in advancing the interests of the "Celestial Order." To the good brethren these ladies are invaluable helpers when they desire to add to the number of their wives; and going from house to house to gather contributions for the Society, they have ample opportunities for discovering the feelings of those who are rebellious, and giving a great deal of "counsel" which frequently produces very painful results. The members of this Relief Society—even the poorest—are, without exception, expected to contribute to its funds—if it be only a skein of yarn or a spool of thread. They make their visits fortnightly, and gather in contributions with such success that in more than one ward they have been able to build a fine store, have filled it with goods, and have had a surplus in hand, which was duly handed over as a present to Brother Brigham. Brother Brigham is always ready and willing to receive gifts, whether large or small. There was an instance of this which fell under my own observation, and which, though I was still in the Church, annoyed me very greatly. An old lady applied to me for sewing, and, as I was in need of some one, I employed her. She suffered a good deal from asthma, and finally became so bad that it was with the greatest difficulty that she could even walk. She told me frequently that a cup of tea was "*such* a comfort to her;" but she would not allow herself that luxury, as she was resolved to put by all that it might have cost her for tea, and sugar, and other little luxuries, and make a present of the money to Brother Brigham. I learned subsequently that she did save up as much as $20, which, in the presence of witnesses, she presented to the Prophet—and *he actually took it!* I was told that in a sermon delivered at Ogden, a short time after, he gave the poor woman great credit for having performed a good deed, and recommended others to go and do likewise!

It is difficult to discover how the poor are benefited by the Relief Society, and yet it was ostensibly for their welfare and assistance that the Society was called into existence. I know of many instances where poor persons have applied for help, which has either been refused them, or else has been offered in such a way that it could not be accepted.

It must not be supposed that all the Mormon women who belong to the Relief Society are as great admirers of Brother Brigham as the ancient dame of whom I have just spoken. Some belong to it because they cannot help themselves. One of these very sisters once told me that when they got up the ladies' petition to Mrs. Grant, praying her to use her influence with the President in favor of Mormon husbands practicing Polygamy, they did not give themselves the trouble to call upon all the ladies who belonged to the Society, but took their names from the books, without even obtaining permission first. Another lady told me that when they came to her house to get the signature of herself and daughters, they asked her if she had any dead daughters, as, if she had, it was just as proper to sign for them as for the living, for they would be certain to believe in Polygamy now they were in heaven, whatever might have been their condition on earth. This is the way in which elections are conducted, and memorials and petitions are got up in Utah.

Moreover, it must not be imagined that those who are most zealous in signing petitions and forcing them upon their sisters, are necessarily the greatest believers in the " Celestial Order." No; in not a few of these women are seen some of the worst effects of the system. One of these very ladies told me that she had "seen enough of old Brigham and Polygamy in this world, she hoped she would never set eyes on him in the next." And yet this lady was very highly spoken of for her zeal in getting up the petition in favor of Polygamy. These are the women who, finding their own happiness wrecked, are not satisfied until they have dragged every other woman they meet with into the same snare. They appear to have no mercy upon their own sex, and when persuasive words fail to soften the " rebellious " wife they will repeat to her that portion of the "Revelation" which says that the wife who refuses consent shall be destroyed; and thus they work upon her fears and her devotion to her religion. It is painful to see women so hopeless themselves that they find a satisfaction in making others equally miserable.

An utter disregard to the feelings or happiness of individuals is one of the distinguishing features of Mormonism. Polygamy hardens the hearts of both men and women towards those whom they should love most tenderly; what wonder then that the less sacred ties of friendship and common humanity should be disregarded? "Do I not furnish you with breadstuffs?" the wealthy Bishop or Apostle has often said to a neglected wife, "what more do you want?" She had perhaps complained of neglect, but his coarse nature could not comprehend that her soul craved its daily food as much as her body—that a true-hearted wife needs the love and companionship of her husband; and that she ought to feel that he is living for her and for her children, just as faithfully as she is living for him.

Any idea of mutual obligation between husbands and wives has, I believe, never entered the mind of Brigham Young and the leaders who most nearly imitate him. He himself has forsaken wife after wife, giving them no love, no companionship; nay, scarcely even a thought. They have gone out of his life as completely as if they had never possessed the slightest interest in his eyes. He has, however, continued to give them "breadstuffs," clothing and shelter, which he could so well afford; but it was for appearance sake, and certainly not for love.

When a man has more than one wife, his affections must of necessity be divided; he really has no home in the truest sense of the word; his houses are simply boarding-places. Should he have all his wives in one house, as is often the case, they are then all slaves to the system, each one is watching the others—and they know it—trying to discover something that can be secretly told to the husband to draw away his affections from the rest. What more miserable position could be imagined?

There is, however, no fixed principle regulating Mormon men in the management of their families—every one is at liberty to do as he thinks best, and scarcely two families are governed alike. When Salt Lake City was first settled, the people had to live as best they could, and a man was glad to get even one roof under which he and all his wives might be sheltered. Now, when the husband is wealthy he generally provides separate homes for his wives. Some wealthy men, however, still have all their wives and families together.

I have in my mind, as I write, a very prominent Mormon, who has half a dozen wives; and he divides his time among them after this fashion. The first week he stays with the first wife; the next week he is with the second; then he goes back

to the first.   The fourth week he passes with the third wife;
then he returns for another week to the first.   And thus he
continues to give one week to the first wife, and the next to
one of the other five in turn, until he has blessed them all
with his presence.   Now, it would at a casual glance appear
that this first wife has by far the largest share of her husband's society; but if the truth must be told, it must be
admitted that the husband is not quite so generous as he
appears.   The last wife of this good man is a young and pretty
girl, and she lives with the first wife, and thus his devotion to
the latter is rewarded by the presence of the former.   Each
of the other wives has one week of his society and attentions
in every eleven—about five weeks apiece of companionship
with their husband in the course of a whole year.   Other men
with the same number of wives pass constantly between one
house and another; they can never be found when wanted;
their lives are one eternal round, and they may be said to have
no real abiding place.

In every settlement in Utah, long, low-roofed houses may
be seen with a row of doors and windows alternating.   Even
in Salt Lake City, much as it has changed of late years, such
houses may still be found.   To every door and window there
is, of course, a wife; and the furniture of her room consists
of a bed, three chairs, and a table.   Then, if the man is a very
devout Mormon and wishes to increase his kingdom by adding
another wife to the inhabitants of the long many-doored house,
a wagon-box is so arranged as to form a sleeping apartment
for the new comer; or, what is more likely, one of the old
wives is put into the wagon-box, and the new one takes her
place.

A house with two wings is rather a favorite style with those
men, who, to silence their conscience and the priesthood, con-
clude to take " just *one* extra wife," and no more.   The wives,
with their children, occupy, respectively, each a wing ; and the
entrance-door opens into a parlor, which serves as a recep-
tion-room for both families.   The husband in this case spends
a week on one side of the house and a week on the other,

alternately ; and thus, by an impartial division of his attentions, he preserves peace in his family. A man who is comfortably off can, of course, arrange his domestic affairs so as to avoid, as far as is possible, the inconveniences of the system, but a poor man is forced to submit to circumstances. Many men have entered into Polygamy, with two, three, and even four wives, all, with their children, living together under one roof —in one room—in the most disgraceful and barbarous manner ; but even for this the leaders were really more to blame than the poor deluded men themselves ; for the command to "Build up the Kingdom !—build up the Kingdom !" —in other words, take many wives and raise up large families —has been so constantly and imperatively insisted upon that good sense and propriety have at last been entirely overlooked.

In a very large house, with many wives, there is greater safety and peace for the husband than in a small house with only two wives. When there are only two apartments, the husband, if not in one is supposed to be in the other, and the neglected wife frequently expresses her opinion of her rival in the opposite room in very powerful language. Scenes may be witnessed in such households which are too shocking to disclose. Brigham Young was conscious of this when he said he "would stand no more fighting and scratching around him"; and yet, in the face of all this, he dares to tell the people that this is the "Order of *Celestial* Marriage." With many wives living together in a large house there are many advantages. The whereabouts of the husband is not so easily discovered, and the unhappy or jealous wife is at a loss to know upon whom to vent her ire. On this account even men with small means prefer to have three wives instead of two, as each wife, not knowing which of the other two she ought to hate the most, divides her jealousy. It takes, however, a wise man to know how to live in Polygamy, so as to balance all the conflicting interests and obtain a little peace, if happiness is out of the question.

Where the husband is a rich man and has abundant wealth

wherewith to supply the wants of his numerous wives and
children, and to furnish all the necessary accommodation that
a growing family demands, much of the jealousy and ill-feeling inseparable from Polygamy can, to a certain extent, be
avoided. But when poor men, as I myself have witnessed,
live with several wives and a whole army of children, huddled together in a miserable room or two, it is painful and
inconvenient in the extreme. And yet such is frequently the
case. I know one man, otherwise very respectable, who lives
with three wives and eleven children in two wretched rooms
no better than a stable, and they think that in this they are
pleasing God.

Some men have entered into Polygamy so poor and unprovided for that their dwelling consisted of just one sitting room
and one sleeping apartment, for the two wives together with
the husband ; and it is quite a common thing to see two or
even three wives living together in one very small house. A
family was pointed out to me, which consisted of two wives,
one son about sixteen years of age, a daughter of fifteen, and
numerous other younger children ; and all lived together in
two small rooms and a shed.

It would be quite impossible, with any regard to propriety,
to relate all the horrible results of this disgraceful system. It
has debased the minds, and degraded the lives, of good and
honest men and women, while those who naturally had a tendency towards evil have become a hundred times worse. Marriages have been contracted between the nearest relatives ;
and old men tottering on the brink of the grave have been
united to little girls scarcely in their teens ; while unnatural
alliances of every description, which in any other community
would be regarded with disgust and abhorrence, are here
entered into in the name of God, and under the sanction
of a " Revelation " supposed to proceed from the pure and
holy Saviour.

I was much shocked and disgusted when first I went to
Utah, to find a man whom under other circumstances I had
known in London, living with two sisters whom he had mar-

ried in the manner I have just described, and, strange as it may appear, it was not with them a matter of necessity. When I knew the husband in Europe, I considered him a man of education and refinement, but I certainly was mistaken, for no man whose nature was at all sensitive would have lived as he did. His wives, too, who had been considered highly respectable English girls, were not ashamed of their degraded position—they professed to believe in bringing the world back to its primitive purity and innocence.

It is quite a common thing in Utah for a man to marry two and even three sisters. I was well acquainted with one man who married his half-sister; and I know several who have married mother and daughter. I know also another man who married a widow with several children; and when one of the girls had grown into her teens he insisted on marrying her also, having first by some means won her affections. The mother, however, was much opposed to this marriage, and finally gave up her husband entirely to her daughter; and to this very day the daughter bears children to her step-father, living as wife in the same house with her mother!

In another instance, a well-known man in Salt Lake City, who has several wives and married daughters, married a young girl of fifteen years of age whom his wife had adopted and brought up as her own.

Men who do such things as these have no excuse in their religion. It is pretended that the Mormon Prophet received a Revelation sanctioning Polygamy, but no one ever supposed that it was therefore necessary for persons so near akin in blood to marry; when such disgraceful alliances have taken place they have been the result of the brutal passions of men, and cannot be charged directly to their religion. Their religion is to blame for debasing their minds and destroying in them those pure feelings which would have rebelled against these shameful marriages; but their religion only enjoined them to marry many wives; it never taught them to select those wives from their own households.

The women, in Polygamy, as might be expected, have all

along had to bear the heaviest part of the burden. It is painful to see how some of them will strive to maintain a hold upon their husband's affections. They may, perhaps, feel bitterly their lonely and neglected position, and they may detest the system, but they try, nevertheless, to make their homes as pleasant and attractive as possible. Some do this for one reason, some for another; but in most instances the chief motive is a desire to draw away the husband from the other wives;—not that they particularly wish for his company or his love, but they like to show their power over him. I know some of these Mormon men whose wives " manage " them in this way. They think not a little of themselves, and believe that they are indeed the lords of creation, and can have everything their own way; while, all the time, they are perfect objects of ridicule to every one who knows them, on account of the way they are " managed " by their wives. Such men fancy that they govern absolutely in their households, and with head erect they will boastfully say to their neighbors, " See how I manage *my women*"—little thinking that it is the women who are " managing" them.

Other good women make their homes pleasant from a sincere desire that their husbands should be happy, and will study the most rigid economy while living alone, so as to save out of their frequently poor allowance sufficient to entertain the husband well when it comes to their turn to receive a visit from him. Many a woman has thus earned the flattering opinion of her husband for economy, and it has very materially strengthened her influence over him. I knew a lady, who by a little management of this sort so pleased her spouse that he placed her at the head of his household, and the other wives had to go to her for everything. This was all the glory she had ever dreamed of or desired.

Women of years and experience act thus; but young and thoughtless wives frequently try an opposite experiment, and when their husbands come to see them they are always poor, always needy—they never have enough of anything. This attempt to excite sympathy is seldom or never so successful as the other plan. The pleasant home and smiling welcome are more attractive to the Mormon husband than the complaints of a dissatisfied wife. Many a good Saint, although, of course, he would scorn to acknowledge it, is well known to make his principal home with the wife who is the best cook, notwithstanding that affection may not run in the same direction ; but when the wife who sets the best table is also the wife best beloved, the husband is a happy man indeed.

Quite a number of the leading Mormons have wives in the various settlements ; and this is very convenient to them if they have to travel much. If the wives are old and experienced, as wives who are sent into the country generally are, they can then look after and manage a farm ; and if they have growing boys, the farm can be worked upon a very economical plan. The younger wives in the city can be supplied from them with all the butter, cheese, vegetables, &c., that they require. It takes considerable shrewdness to manage women in such a way as to turn all their abilities to good account and to make them profitable. American men, I have always found, were most successful in this experiment ; the English, as a general rule, are not smart enough, though I have known instances where smart Englishmen with several wives have so arranged as to live entirely without working themselves. They managed matters to perfection ; getting all the labor that was possible out of those unhappy women, and in return breaking their hearts with unkindness and neglect.

Mormon men say, " Do not the Gentiles do just as bad ?"

No ; they do not ! There are bad men everywhere, and, as every one knows, there are among the Gentiles men whose cruelty to their wives could not be surpassed. But those men do not attempt to hide their sins under the mantle of religion ; they do not crucify their wives in the name of God. Bad men among the Gentiles support a woman—whether wife or not—so long as they care anything about her ; and do the Mormon men do anything more ? Hundreds of discarded wives in Utah could bear me witness that when they grew old, or their husbands grew tired of them, they cast them off

29

quite as ruthlessly and with as little compunction as any unprincipled Gentile man ever discarded a mistress who no longer had any place in his affections. In one respect certainly the Mormon men bear off the palm for cruelty; for *they* add insult to injury. The sins of wicked Gentiles are hidden from their wives; but the Mormon men flaunt their sins in their wives' faces, and in the faces of their grown-up sons and daughters, and style their iniquity "The Celestial Order of Heaven!"

Let me ask the good brethren who read this, to act for once impartially, and try to put themselves in a woman's place; and let me for their benefit draw a little picture for them to contemplate.

It is evening, and the family are all assembled in their pleasant home—a home made happy by the kind and thoughtful care of a loving father. Peace and tranquility dwell in every heart, and the father is happy in being surrounded by his children, to whom he is fondly attached. He listens to the prattle of the little ones, or the music and songs of the elder children; and for a time he is forgetful of everything save the happiness of the hour.

Suddenly his wife—the mother of his children—whom he dearly loves, rises from her seat beside the fire and retires to her own apartment. There she arranges her toilet with irreproachable care, sees that every straying curl is in its place, and gives every touch to her appearance which she thinks is likely to render her attractive in the eyes of a man. She now descends the stairs, ready to leave the home of this, her first husband, for she is going to see her second husband, or some young man to whom she has taken a fancy, and who she thinks would be suitable for a third. She kisses her children good-bye, and is about to take an affectionate farewell of their father when she suddenly discovers that he is not looking happy. "What is the matter now?" she says; "Is not your home a pleasant one; have I not taken pains to train your children in a proper manner; and have I not remained an hour longer than usual with you? What folly it is for you to

PUTTING HIMSELF IN HER PLACE.

be moping in this way : this is not the way to live our religion, if we expect to get the blessing of God. You know
very well it is very painful for me to leave you and my
children ; but we must be obedient to the commands of God,
and I owe attentions to my other husband as well as to
you ! "

Can any man be supposed who would for a moment endure
such an outrage upon decency and common-sense—such a
violation of all that is sacred in the human heart ? And yet
this is only reversing the case ; and just as any Mormon man
can suppose he would feel, if the wife he loved were to act in
the way I have described, so do Mormon wives feel—only as
much more acutely, as women are more sensitive in their
affections than men. I remember painfully the bitterness of
soul which I experienced when there was only one wife
besides myself ; and thousands of women in Utah could bear
witness, if they would, to the hopeless misery which the
system causes, and the desolate void which it creates in the
heart of every thoughtful and affectionate wife.

CHAPTER XXXIV.

LIGHTS AND SHADOWS OF POLYGAMY :—MARRIAGE AND BAPTISM FOR THE DEAD.

Domestic Difficulties—Husband and Lover—How Brother Brigham Treats His Wives—Polygamy in Poverty—Obedience the Crowning Virtue—How Women Feel and Act in Polygamy—A First Wife's Trials—The Young Second Wife—Home Life in Polygamy—The Husband Displays His "Jewels"—Our Worldly Prosperity—The First Daily Paper in Utah—Whisperings of Murder—Not in the Confidence of "The Church"—Brigham's Inconsistencies—Mr. Stenhouse Refuses a Contract—How Brother Brigham "Jumps at an Offer"—How He Makes His Money—I Remind My Husband of Certain Things—Another Visit from My Talkative Friend—Baptism for the Dead—Baptized for Queen Anne—A Strange Description of Paradise—Napoleon and Washington Mormon Elders—Queen Elizabeth Enters into Polygamy—Becoming Proxy for Henry VIII.—The Wife of the Thief on the Cross—Waiting for Queen Fanny!

MY life was now one continued series of deceptions, as was also that of my husband, and we began habitually to wear the mask when in each other's presence. It cannot be otherwise in Polygamy. To avoid wounding the feelings of the first wife, the husband, if he cares for her, affects an indifference for the second wife which he does not really feel; and the first wife is not deceived by it, for she knows he is only acting a part, and that as soon as her eyes are off him he will be transformed into the most ardent lover.

If affectionate before and demonstrative in his love towards his wife and children, he has to suppress it all now, lest he should arouse jealousy in the heart of the other wife and be thought partial. He can never now manifest a husband's or a father's love ; hence his own nature becomes cramped, and the affections of his heart are dwarfed. His children grow up ignorant of what he really is, and, although he is living in the same house with them, it might truthfully be said that they do not know what it is to have a father. Consequently, their love for him is very limited ; they know nothing of those spontaneous effusions of tenderness which link the heart of the child to its parent ; and themselves, in their own experience, ignorant of that domestic happiness which in childhood is the charm of home, and, in fact, never knowing what a home should be, when they, in their turn, marry and have children of their own, they set up another of those cold and soulless homes with which Polygamy is cursed.

But let me lift the curtain and give an illustration from the family of Brigham Young himself. In that family I have seen the practical working of the plural-wife system exemplified under its most favorable aspect. I have conversed with Brigham's wives as a sister in the same faith, and I know how they feel ; but I am compelled to confess that, notwithstanding all the order and system which characterise the Prophet's household, and the fact that his wives are, on account of his great wealth, free from the troubles and inconveniences entailed by Polygamy in poverty, and although they are, taken collectively, as amiable and good women as any in Utah—their lives are unhappy and they themselves are miserable. They have never known the meaning of domestic happiness, and though to the casual observer they may appear contented with their lot, secretly they mourn over the constant struggle in their hearts between the system and their own womanly nature. Even the most favored of them lead cold, mechanical lives ; joy and affection they have never known. Many of them have been cast off for years, and all are neglected except the favorite of the hour.

The Mormon leaders teach that a woman's exaltation in

heaven depends upon the number of her children, and yet Brigham has wives who might be mothers of large families, but whom he has neglected for years. They are called the wives of Brigham Young, and they live under the same roof with him; but they have no real husband, and their children no father in the dear sense of that word as ordinary Christians understand it. They know nothing of the sweet familiarity, the loving interchange of thought and feeling which belongs to true married life. Once a day they are honored by the presence of their lord and master at their table; and this privilege is, of course, only enjoyed by those who live in the same house with him,—those who live in other houses very seldom see him more frequently than once in two or three months. They bask in the sunshine of his presence for about half an hour in the evening when the family assembles in the Lion House for prayer. But in the theatre, the Tabernacle, and the ball-room, the majority of them only see and worship him at a distance. They are but pensioners upon his bounty; all their individuality is destroyed, and they are completely lost in him. They have no position in society— he is the only person ever seen or talked of. People in Salt Lake City neither know nor care any more about Mrs. Young the first or the nineteenth than they do about the wives of any other Saint. In their home life they have to bear all the bitterness and heartburnings which, patient, pious women as they are, the silly and licentious favoritism of their "husband" for the last new wife, whoever she may be, always produces. I think that no man in Utah so recklessly wounds the feelings of his wives in this respect, or acts as if he thought it was a woman's duty to crush every feeling and bring herself to submit without a question to her husband's will, as does Brigham Young. And yet his wives, whose withered and blighted existence is a reproach to humanity, are very good specimens of what the *Celestial* Order of Matrimony can produce. What, under less favorable conditions, Polygamy is, I leave the reader to imagine.

Let us look at the family life in some of the country

settlements where the husband—without any order or system in his nature, and without the means or even the idea of providing for the comfort of his family—is seeking in his coarse way to imitate Brother Brigham and to work out his own idea of Celestial Marriage. There we shall find the same repression of all womanly feeling, the absence of any sanctifying or refining influence, while at the same time the hard lot of the wives is unrelieved by even the solitary recreations and the personal comforts of Brigham Young's wives. This is the condition of many a poor, weary wife in Utah.

These are the women who Brigham Young has said should be "damned" if they murmured or rebelled. What hope is there for them or for their children? Between the two extremes—Polygamy as it exists in the Prophet's household, and as it is in the homes of poor Mormons in the Settlements—the celestial order of marriage can be found under all conceivable circumstances of poverty and wealth, ignorance and culture. It had been told us frequently and emphatically that the "privilege" of Polygamy was reserved for those who had demonstrated their purity by a life of goodness ; and the idea that it was denied to the wicked and licentious was very reassuring to the minds of many. But we soon discovered that if only a man was obedient to the Priesthood, his moral character had little or nothing to do with his obtaining more wives. Assassins and inebriates like Porter Rockwell, and even murderers like Bill Hickman and John D. Lee, and other wretches, had as many wives, and even more, than some of the best men in the community. It is, I believe, true that John D. Lee had several wives sealed to him after it was known that he had taken such an atrocious part in the Mountain Meadows' Massacre.

It is a fact that Polygamy among the Mormons has been entered into by people of every kind, under all circumstances, and from every conceivable motive—from the basest to the purest. But its effect has invariably been to develope the weaker side of human nature. At the same time, like other institutions which for religious purposes have suppressed true

manly and womanly instincts, it has in exceptional cases produced much that was noble and generous.   Many faithful first
wives, seeing in the practice of the celestial order the prospec-
tive glory of their husbands, have borne the heavy burden of
life patiently and uncomplainingly, and even, while daily suffering that which was worse than death, have sought to be kind
and loving to those very women, who under a false belief have
invaded the sanctuary of their rights and stolen from them
that which they held most dear.   While I know of very many
polygamic wives who have sacrificed themselves continually,
receiving the most meagre show of love and attention, hoping
and striving to harmonise matters ; on the other hand I could
tell of many first wives who have urged their husbands into
Polygamy, merely that the plural wives might become the
household drudges while they themselves took their ease and
pleasure.   Then, again, there are polygamic wives who have
taken the power into their own hands, grasping every comfort
and monopolising every attention, while the first wife pined
away unnoticed and crushed with domestic cares.   With men,
too, there was the same variety.   Some have delayed entering
into Polygamy for years, and then they have taken every precaution to avoid giving pain to their first wives ; while others,
on the contrary, have been perfectly indifferent as to what
pain they caused their wives, relentlessly trampling under their
feet every sentiment of delicacy and affection.

In my own case, my husband did all he could to spare my
feelings as much as possible ; but it was, nevertheless, a hard
task for me to subdue my own heart, and I found that all that
I had anticipated in imagination was nothing compared with
the realisation.   Feelings of degradation, disgust, and humiliation filled my heart constantly and without ceasing.   From the
day of my husband's second marriage, I could never look upon
him with pleasure—he was no longer *my* husband, and I now
felt no desire to confide in him.   Even the very sight of him
filled my rebellious soul with the bitterest feelings, although, at
the same time, I knew and felt that he tried in every way to
smooth my rugged pathway.

Strange as it may at first appear, had it been otherwise my burden would have been lighter, for, if he had treated me with cruelty and neglect, I should have withdrawn all affection from him and would have cast him out of my heart for ever. It is a painful thing for a wife to think thus of the father of her children.

It may have been wrong, perhaps, but I confess that for my husband's intended bride I felt such a detestation that I could not endure her presence, although I knew that she was not to blame. I believed that I should not have felt it so much if she had been a little older; but to have a mere child placed on a level with me, and to be compelled to treat her with all the respect due to a wife, was so terribly humiliating to me that at times I thought that I could not endure it another day. She, of course, expected to be treated with all the consideration which is proper to a wife, and to be consulted in everything by my husband, as a wife should be. She was not, however, competent to undertake any household duties or wifely cares, and was herself an additional responsibility to me. Young and inexperienced as she was, she had everything to learn; but, at the same time, she stood so much upon her dignity that it was anything but a pleasant task to teach her. It, of course, devolved upon me to instruct her in everything, and I found it anything but a congenial task. I soon began to look upon her simply as a boarder, and expected nothing more from her than I should if she had really been such.

She took very kindly to this position, and would spend her days in her own room, reading and otherwise amusing herself, and, of course, was always pleasant and well-dressed to receive her husband. But this did not suit *me*. In fact I do not know what would have suited me at that time, for I was disposed to be displeased with everything. And yet a visitor to our house would, I have no doubt, have said, How very pleasantly those two wives get along together. This has been said of scores of women in Utah by casual observers—Gentiles who thought they "understood" the system. How little do they know the aching void and the bitter hatred which exists in the hearts of those wives—the detestation which they have of one another. How little can they know, when everything is so carefully hidden, even from their husbands. It is a shameful thing that women—faithful wives and mothers—should be placed in such a position.

How many times during the day have I been compelled to leave everything and rush to my chamber, and there on my bended knees supplicate for strength to endure, thinking all the time that, in ordaining this Revelation, God had given us a burden greater than we could bear.

Then, in the evening, when we were assembled together in our cosy parlor, as we were wont to be, all traces that remained of the terrible struggle which I had endured were a sad countenance and perhaps the deepening lines upon my brow, which contrasted unpleasantly with the bright and cheerful face of the young wife, and made my husband feel that I was getting very sour in my disposition, as, indeed, was probably the case.

I was totally ashamed of these thoughts, at times, and felt that it was very wrong of me to feel so unkindly towards this young girl, whose only offence against me was that she had acted up to the religious teachings that had been instilled into her mind from infancy. I reminded myself that, for aught I knew, my own dear child might be placed in a similar position; and then how should I feel? How prophetic this fear proved eventually, the reader will presently see.

Such thoughts as these would soften my heart towards the young wife, and although she probably never dreamed that I had felt unkindly towards her, yet, to silence my conscience, I would strive in every possible way to show her some kind attention. I could but feel and know that she was a good but inexperienced girl; and I am bound to say that both she and my husband tried to conduct themselves in such a way as to give me as little offence as possible. Situated as I was, however, nothing escaped my observation, and I felt most keenly. Had I been treated with the cruelty and neglect which has fallen to the lot of so many unfortunate women in Utah, I should probably have been in my grave to-day, or in that

Asylum, which has been provided by the Church—situated on a lonely hill at a sufficient distance from the city, so that the cries of the unhappy, ill-treated, insane women should not be heard.

Things and actions, which at another time I should have considered too trifling to notice, had now a painful significance to me. On one occasion, not long after the wedding, my husband asked me to take a walk with him, and I consented. Among the Mormons it is a custom to take their wives out together very frequently. Their object, I presume, is to display the "jewels" in their crowns before the eyes of their less fortunate brethren. I had resolved that I would never submit to this—if my husband would not take me out alone I would stay at home. On the occasion I mention, when I came out of my room ready dressed, I found him and his wife, Belinda, waiting and chatting pleasantly together and looking unutterable love at each other. At least, so I thought, and I felt greatly insulted and annoyed, and told them I did not wish to go. I carefully avoided showing any outbursts of temper before the young lady which I thought would be undignified, for I desired at least that she should respect me, though I did not want her love. If I had expected that they would urge me to accompany them, I should have been greatly mistaken, for my refusal appeared to be just what they wanted. They tripped off together as light-hearted and happy as children, while I remained rooted to the spot, tearing my pocket handkerchief to pieces, and wishing I could do the same with them.

I used sometimes to wonder whether it would be the same in the Mormon heaven, where this Celestial Order of Marriage is expected to be carried out in all its fullness, and I felt troubled for myself. These dreadful feelings would, I believed, be the ruin of my soul, and I thought it was impossible for me to obtain salvation until I had entirely subdued them, and that I had not power yet to do. I had, however, so concealed what I felt that my husband believed that I was becoming used to this new life, which I am happy to say I never did. Sometimes I felt that it was useless for me to fight against the will of Heaven, if this indeed was a divine law, and as yet I dared not take upon myself to say it was not, although in my secret heart I had at last begun sometimes to question in earnest. My poor, benighted soul was looking anxiously at that time for a ray of light to guide my faltering footsteps. I did not wholly believe, but I dared not rebel, for fear of drawing down the wrath of an offended God upon my innocent children and upon my husband, who I was firmly convinced was actuated by a sincere desire to do the will of Heaven.

There were, however, sometimes, little things which did not quite harmonise in my mind. I remember once saying to my husband, when he was telling me that nothing but a firm belief in the divinity of the Revelation would induce him to take another wife and that he would do so from principle alone, that I thought, if that were the case, an older and more plain-looking woman would do quite as well, and that he could dispense with so much courting. "You are compelled to wear dresses," he replied, "but you do not allow those dresses to occupy all your thoughts. Nevertheless, you take some pleasure in selecting them, and you desire that they should be pretty and look well. So it is with men seeking wives."

This mode of putting the case was, I have no doubt, very convincing to my husband's mind, and, at the moment, I could not answer him. But calmer thought would have told me that while wearing and choosing dresses was by every right-minded person considered perfectly legitimate, taking other wives was by no means regarded in that light. The wrong was not so much in the way the thing was done as in doing it at all and under any circumstances. Logically speaking, the argument was good enough, but the premises were utterly unsound.

Day after day my rebellious soul was agitated by the same troubled feelings. There was no rest for me—nothing upon which I could stay my mind. My husband was painfully aware that there was a coldness and restraint existing between his young wife and myself, and I know that he was grieved by it, for he had tried in every way to create a friendly feeling between us. I felt, however, that it was utterly impossible that I could ever be affectionate towards his other wife, much as I might strive. I would do my duty, but I could not love her, or, in fact, him either for that matter, when he was associated with her. I regret to be obliged to confess such a truth, but from that time, and as long as I remained in Mormonism, the sentiment that was uppermost in my mind was an utter detestation of the whole system. I despised myself for being the abject slave that I was. Why could I not have the moral courage to set everything at defiance—Revelation and all—and free myself from the bondage that enthralled me?

I know this day scores of women in Utah who think and feel exactly as I did then, who suffer wrongs against which their hearts daily and hourly rebel, but who, like me, dread to cast aside the yoke of the oppressor.

At that time, in respect to pecuniary matters we were very comfortably off. Almost immediately after our arrival in Utah, Mr. Stenhouse had found employment on the staff of the *Deseret News*. Before long, he obtained the appointment of Postmaster for Salt Lake City, and before his marriage with Miss Pratt, he had started the *Telegraph*—the first daily paper that was ever published in Utah. From the beginning it had been remarkably successful, for Brigham had counselled the people to sustain it, knowing very well that he himself would in return be supported by my husband. Brigham had no more devoted follower than Mr. Stenhouse was then, for the scales had not yet fallen from his eyes, and he believed the Prophet was really what he claimed to be—a faithful servant of God. True, we had frequently talked together of his very mean actions; but my too generous, or perhaps too credulous, husband had attributed all that to the weakness of his human nature, and would not believe that it affected his priesthood. He therefore sustained him strongly and consistently before the public; not for gain, for he had given too many instances of his devotion to be suspected of that; but I may say from pure attachment, for I know too well that at that time he was almost ready to lay down his life for the sake of his religion.

The *Telegraph* soon became the leading journal in Utah,

and in a little while we were surrounded by every comfort and
luxury which at that time could be procured in Salt Lake City.
No family in the Territory was better provided for than was
ours, not excepting Brigham Young's. I had always believed
that if my husband were left alone, untrammelled by the
Church, to make his own way, he would do so successfully. In
this I was not mistaken. We now owned a fine dwelling-
house, a valuable city lot and house, where the paper was
printed, and also another very desirable lot, near to Brigham
Young's residence. This last lot was my own ; it was very
beautifully situated, and we expended on it upwards of three
thousand dollars. Everything that my husband undertook at
that time seemed to prosper—not excepting his love affairs.

Just then a great deal was whispered privately about certain
murders which had been committed, all knowledge of which
was strenuously denied by the authorities. When any case
was so notorious that it could not possibly be altogether
hushed up, we were told that the murdered persons were dangerous people and had been killed in self-defence by those
whom they in the first instance had attacked.

My husband, like hundreds of others, was never in the confidence of the Church authorities in these matters. He believed
firmly in the divine mission of Joseph Smith, and shut his
eyes to the actions of Brigham Young, thinking that he alone
would be responsible to the Lord for his misdeeds. When I
drew his attention to the inconsistency of Brigham's conduct,
as on more than one occasion I did, he said we had enough to
do to look at home and see that we ourselves did what was
right. This, of course, was true, but I thought, nevertheless,
that a little more consistency on Brigham's part would not be
amiss.

I recollect a gentleman named Cook, for whose memory I
entertain the most sincere respect, wishing my husband to
take a contract to furnish grain for the Overland Mail Company, and how he urged him to do so for the benefit of his
family. Not long before that, however, Brigham had denounced in the Tabernacle all those who took contracts or

who had any dealings with the Gentiles in any way whatsoever. One merchant in particular he singled out, and before
the whole congregation, showered upon him all his wrath—
going so far as to call him a thief, and saying that he " would
apostatise and go to hell." Yet Brigham to-day is associated in
business with that same man !

Another gentleman, a Mr. Street, who constructed the first
telegraph line from California to Salt Lake City, acted a very
friendly part towards my husband, and wished to advance his
interests. He one day came to me and said, " Mrs. Stenhouse,
let me beg of you to use all your influence with your husband, and, if necessary, even insist upon his taking this contract which I have offered him. He is doing wrong to his
family by refusing, for he would make twenty thousand dollars, with very little trouble. I have urged him until I am
tired, and unless you insist he will refuse from fear of doing
wrong, after all that Brigham Young has said upon that subject ; though I told him that Brigham would take it himself
and jump at it, if I were to offer it to him."

I had urged my husband before, and I felt certain that he
would not listen to my counsel. The contract *was* offered to
Brigham Young, and he *did* jump at it, and made his thousands
out of it. Even at that time I could not see why it would be
a sin for my husband to make the money, any more than for
Brigham to do so. But this inconsistency was observable in
everything. Many of the farmers' wives have frequently
told me that their husbands had been called to account
severely for taking their provisions to Camp Douglas to sell to
the Gentiles, while at the same time they had seen many of
Brigham's own teams there with produce

I felt it my duty to keep such things always before my
husband's eyes ; but he was what is vulgarly called a " hard-
shell " Mormon and it took a great many raps to crack the
shell and let in a little light. He, of course, would deny this ;
but wives, I think, are not generally mistaken in such matters.
I never neglected any opportunity, and when once I perceived
the slightest signs of weakness, I went to work with a will,

until I got him to admit frankly that he was dissatisfied with
many things. But for all that, he still held to the belief that
Mormonism was true, whatever Brigham might be. To get
him to admit that Brigham was not right was a great deal, and
it gave me hope for the future. I tried hard to enlighten his
understanding, but made very little progress. The difficulty,
I believe, was that Mormonism possesses charms for the men
that it never has for the women. I firmly believe that they
willingly close their eyes to that which it does not suit them
to see. However that may be, notwithstanding all my
efforts, my husband still continued to sustain Brigham, and
worse still, before long he began to evince an earnest desire to
sustain one of Brigham's daughters also—of which I shall say
more presently.

My talkative friend called one day to speak of a very serious
subject.

"I have come, Sister Stenhouse," she said, "to talk to you
about a matter of great importance, but I don't want to
offend you, and you must promise beforehand to forgive me."

I readily promised, and she added: "I thought I should find
you very unhappy, Sister Stenhouse, about poor, dear Carrie
Grant, and I think if you are so you deserve it, but I don't like
you to be miserable, and so I came to comfort you."

"But, Sister Ann," I said, "I don't want to be comforted
in the way you seem to mean. I have been very sad indeed
at losing Carrie, but you know I did everything I could
for her, poor girl, and I have nothing to blame myself for."

"Nothing to blame yourself for?" she exclaimed. "Why,
Sister Stenhouse, you have everything to blame yourself for.
If poor Carrie has less glory it is all your fault."

"How so?" I said.

"Why," she answered, "if you had not held back and expressed your dislike, Carrie would have married your husband,
and would most likely have been alive now. She would have
had *her* family, and would have added to your husband's glory;
while now, although she is your husband's wife, she has no

children, and, of course, must have less glory in the Kingdom."

"Well, Sister Ann," I said, "I never thought of it in that
light. I loved Carrie very much, and I tried to make her love
me. It was not until almost the last that I knew of her love
for my husband ; but if I had known before, I am sure my
own heart would have rebelled against my husband taking
another wife. I did, however, ask him to marry her, and
after she was dead I was married to him for her."

"That's all very well, Sister Stenhouse," she replied, " but
for all that, I think you have committed a great wrong against
that poor orphan girl. You ought to be thankful that at last
you were able to repair a little of the mischief which you did.
I don't want to vex you, but I am really sorry that you had
such an antipathy to your husband having Carrie. However,
I suppose now he has really got another wife you are r t so
much set against Polygamy. You must find it quite a blessing to have Miss Pratt—I beg pardon, I mean Mrs. Stenhouse,
number two—with you now."

I did not answer her, for I had my own opinion about the
matter. She went on without hesitation : "Well, you must
not be vexed with me, dear ; I say it all for your good, you
know ; but I do wish you felt a little more as I do about these
matters. Why, do you know, I have been trying to show
my faith and zeal in every possible way ever since we
came to Utah. It was only last week I was baptized for
Queen Anne."

"Queen Anne!" I exclaimed. "What can you possibly
mean ? "

" Exactly what I say, Sister Stenhouse—I was baptized for
Queen Anne, and if you like I'll tell you all about it. It is
only just what every one else has been doing, only they were
baptized for other people. I don't think you've ever thought
much of this, and so I'll explain myself. You see, Sister
Stenhouse, the Elders teach us that the whole world is lying
in darkness and sin, and has been so, ever since the apostolic
gifts were lost ages ago. Now there is no salvation outside

30

the Church, and you may remember that Christ Himself went
and preached to the miserable souls in Paradise."

"In Paradise?" I said, "why I thought that was a happy
place."

"Oh, no, Sister Stenhouse," she said, "not very happy. The
souls of those who have not heard the Gospel, and have not
been baptized, go there, and it's a sort of prison for them until
they are brought out again through the kindness of some
believer. The thief on the cross went there, and Christ went
there and preached to the spirits in prison, and when the
Elders die they go on mission to Paradise and preach to them
also. All your people and my people, our fathers, and mothers, and grandfathers, and so on, right up to the apostolic
times, are waiting in Paradise with millions and millions of
souls to be released and be admitted into the Celestial Kingdom. All the good brethren and sisters have been doing their
best to get out their relations and friends, and I know many
of them who have sent over to England and have spent large
sums of money in tracing their pedigrees and genealogies, in
order to find out the right names and to be baptized as proxies for the dead who owned those names. I have been baptized
for a good many of my own relations, and I mean to be baptized for scores more; and many of the brethren, too, have
been married as proxies for their own friends, and for distinguished people besides, so that they might be admitted into
the celestial kingdom and raise up patriarchal families of their
own. The poor souls, if they were released from Paradise by
a proxy baptism, could not, of course, have been married in
heaven, as there is no giving in marriage there; so some one
was married for them as proxy to some one else, and now they
can begin to establish their own celestial kingdoms."

"And have you been proxy in this way, Sister Ann?" I asked.

"No, and yes," she replied, "I haven't yet been proxy in
marriage for any one, but I was proxy in baptism. When we
were children I remember we used to have some rhymes about
Queen Anne, and as it was my own name I always thought a
great deal of her. It seemed to me that it would be very nice,

and at the same time very charitable, if I were to help her out
of Paradise—It quite struck my fancy, for it was no small
thing to have a real queen thankful to you for so much. So I
went and was baptized for her, and now she is out of Paradise
and has entered the Celestial Kingdom. But that isn't all.
There was my old friend, George Wilford, who heard all about
the matter, for I see him frequently, and he at once said that
he would be baptized for Prince George of Denmark, Queen
Anne's husband, and he means to do so, and, after that, we'll be
married by proxy for them here on earth, and then they'll both
be happy."

' "Why, Sister Ann, what a droll idea," I said.

"Sister Stenhouse," she replied, quite seriously, "It's very
wrong of you to talk so. Some of the best Saints have stood
proxy in this way. There was one lady who stood proxy for
the Empress Josephine, and her son stood for Napoleon, and
some one else for Washington. Queen Elisabeth, too, has
been baptized by proxy. And now Napoleon and Washington
are both Mormon Elders, and I suppose some one will be
married for Queen Elizabeth, and she'll enter into Polygamy.
Do you know, Sister Stenhouse, there was one brother who
out of pure kindness said he would be baptized for the thief
on the cross, for he supposed that no one else would take pity
on him, and a sister who was present said she would be baptized for his wife, if Brother Brigham thought he ever had
one. I've been persuading my Henry to be baptized for Henry
the Eighth, for I'm sure he needed baptism for the remission
of sins; and he—I mean *my* Henry—has promised me to do
so ; but he says that he means to ask Brother Brigham first
before he is married for him—if ever he is—as King Henry
was almost a polygamist in his way, and my husband thinks
there is not much need to be married for him at all."

"I can't help being amused," I said. "Of course I have
often heard of being baptized for the dead, and I know the
Elders say that St. Paul spoke of it in one of his epistles, but
I never thought of it in *that* light; I always thought we should
have to wait till the Temple was finished."

"That's true, Sister Stenhouse;" she replied,—"all the marriages of all the Saints—of every one, in fact, on the face of the earth—ought to be solemnized in the Temple here in Salt Lake City, and every one ought to receive their Endowments in it; but as it is not yet finished, the Lord permits us to be married, and everything else, in the Endowment House. But you know yourself that there's a Record kept, and that when the Temple is finished, the ceremony will be all gone through with again. I've heard it said that many of the Elders and their wives will live there, and that day and night perpetually the ceremonies will be going on. You ought to be baptized, however, *now* for as many relations as you can think of."

"I think I shall wait, Sister Ann," I said, "until I can find a Queen Fanny, and then I'll be baptized for her."

She did not like me saying this, for she evidently thought I was jesting. I was not jesting, however, but I felt greatly amused, for this peculiar doctrine of the Saints had never struck me in such an odd light before. Sister Ann was shocked at the way in which I viewed her strange stories, but "I'll come again in the course of a day or two, Sister Stenhouse," she said, "and put you all straight."

CHAPTER XXXV.

FESTIVITIES AND SOCIAL GATHERINGS OF THE SAINTS :—
THE PROPHET'S WHISKEY SHOP, AND DRY-GOODS STORE.

An Absent Husband's "Kingdom"—A Suggestion—A Pleasant Time for a
Wife—"The Old Woman is Full of the Devil"—What I heard at the Pic-
Nics—A "Bishop" and his Four Wives—Quite a Spectacle:—The "Woman
in White!"—The "Peg" that God Made for Brigham's Hat—Dancing among
the Saints—How Balls and Social Parties are Conducted—A Man Disgraced by
Following his Wife—Sad Fate of a Swedish Lady—Life in a "Dug-Out"—
Another Phase of *Celestial* Marriage!—A Wronged Wife who Poisoned Her-
self—An Apostle's *Five* Wives!—Doing a Kindness for a Dead Uncle—
Marrying four Wives on the Same Day—The Fish Brought in by Brother
Brigham's Net—A Slumbering Conscience—The Prophet's Theatre—The
"Word of Wisdom"—Brigham Young's Whiskey-making Establishment—
The "Revelation" and the Five-gallon Keg—Why Brigham sells bad Whis-
key—The Dry-Goods Store of "the Prophet of the Lord."

THE more I saw of the practical working of the system in
Utah, the more did I learn to detest Polygamy; for
although I hesitated to reject Mormonism altogether, I could
not for a moment believe that many things of which I heard,
and many which came beneath my own observation, could
under any circumstances be considered right.

About that time, I made the acquaintance of a sister whom
I shall call Mrs. W——. Her husband was on mission and

had left his family without any suitable provision. She herself was a remarkably neat and lady-like woman; but she appeared to be delicate in health, and spoke with so much languor and despondency that, directly I saw her, I was led to suspect that her house also was haunted by that spectre—Polygamy.

She complained of poverty, and told me that her courage was really failing; for, after she had striven so hard to provide a home for her children, her husband had taken a young wife, who seemed to think she had as much right in the sister's house as the sister had herself. "She does not assist in the least towards getting a living," she said, "and we have been left entirely unprovided for, as the Church takes no care of the Missionaries' wives. What is the use of slaving as I do to prolong such a life as mine? My husband is coming home soon, and he is sure to bring one or two girls with him. They all do so."

During our conversation, she told me that some of the dignitaries of the Church had intimated to her that the wives of Missionaries who were obliged to be absent for several years had duties to perform which ought not to be neglected. It devolved upon them to see that their husband's "kingdom" did not suffer during their absence, and that if she herself were more complying in this respect, her pathway would be rendered smoother. I had heard it hinted before that such abominable suggestions had been thrown out, but this was the first time that I had met with any one to whom they had personally been made. There are bad men in every community, and the Saints are no exception. It is but fair to state that the great mass of the Mormon people would be as truly horrified at such doctrines and practices as any Gentile man or woman could be.

The constant anxiety of this lady, of whom I have been speaking, was such that she often threatened to poison herself and thus put an end to her misery. Her husband began to pay his addresses to a young English girl who came in with the hand-carts, and he made as great a simpleton of himself as it is possible for a man to do when he is in love. He was scarcely ever at home; and often of an evening the wife would see the young girl walking towards the house waiting for her—the wife's—husband, and on two occasions the girl threw a little stone at the window to indicate that she was there. The poor wife never dared to say a word against Polygamy in the presence of her husband. When she felt so utterly miserable that she could no longer contain herself, and ventured a word of remonstrance at his cruel neglect of her and her five little ones, he would tell her—quoting the brutal language of Brother Brigham—that "she had had her day, and that it was nothing but right that his future wife should now have some attentions paid her. She must round up her shoulders and submit to the cross which we all have to bear!"

One day he brought the young girl home to tea without saying a single word previously to his wife about it, and it was as much as she could do to be civil to the girl. She mastered her feelings, however, sufficiently to treat her properly; but during the evening she had her temper tried to the uttermost. Her husband sat all the time beside the girl, talking in an under-tone, and toying with her curls. At last the wife's feelings were worked up beyond endurance, and she told her husband that, if he did not instantly desist, she would leave the house. "You can go when you please," he said, "there are plenty more women in the world, I guess. I suppose you are jealous that you are not getting the same attention yourself."

Then he turned to the girl and said, "Come, let us take a walk; the old woman is full of the devil—she will get better after awhile."

To say nothing of the man himself, what can be thought of a girl who would marry a man who treated his wife in this manner in her presence? And yet many Mormon girls think that such men have simply been unfortunate in their first choice of a wife, and will never treat *them* so.

This was another home, the happiness of which I saw wrecked. In England, that poor wife had been gay and happy, and her husband was as faithful and attentive to her as a husband should be. Now, utterly broken-hearted, without any interest in this world, and without hope for that which is to come, she was going to her grave, forsaken by man and, as she poor woman also thought, forsaken by her God.

Often at parties and at pic-nics I met with unhappy wives who unfolded their griefs to me, and some of the things which they related were of a very painful nature. There were instances of downright brutality and cruelty which would not admit of repetition. There were also hundreds of cases in which wives suffered, not so much by any one particular act of wrong, as by innumerable daily and hourly trials, which came upon them at all times, and made existence itself a curse to them.

I remember once, at a pic-nic party, meeting with several first wives whom I had known before I came to Utah, and the stories which they told me were really shocking. At those parties, which, of course, were intended for pleasure and amusement, there was much that was painful in the conversation of the women among themselves, but which would never have been noticed by a stranger. Pic-nics are generally understood to be held in the open air, and in the country ; but we used to call the ward-parties which were held in the Social Hall by that name. The Social Hall was built for this and similar purposes, and was provided with a kitchen and other necessary offices, for the preparation of suppers and other refreshments. It was in this building that plays were acted before the theatre was erected.

The pic-nic parties are quite an institution. Rich and poor, young and old, babies and all, assembled at them to have "a good time." They take their own "pic-nic" with them, set their own tables, make their own tea and coffee, and nurse their own babies. On the occasion to which I allude we went rather early, and thus I had an opportunity of watching the arrivals. Some of them presented a very amusing appearance. There was the Bishop of the ward and all his wives. Two of his boys went in front of him, carrying a very large clothes basket full of "pic-nic," as the eatables were called. Then, straggling after him, came four women and a bevy of noisy children. The wives were all dressed in grey linsey skirts, blue muslin sacques, and green sunbonnets. When they took off their bonnets I found that they all wore wreaths of roses or some other flowers. On entering, I found that quite a number had already assembled and were sitting bolt upright along the sides of the hall, as whist as mice—the women on one side, and the men on the other. At the further end of the hall I saw an old lady sitting whom I recognised as one of my neighbors. She struck me as looking so strangely that I went over to see what was the matter with her. She was pleased to see me, asked me how I thought she looked, and said that this was the first party she had attended since she came to the Valley. She had supposed that it was absolutely necessary for her to wear something white, and had therefore arrayed herself in a white night-dress which answered the purpose of a loose sacque. Sacques and skirts were all the rage at that time. She had on also a little white muslin nightcap, and altogether she looked very neat and clean, but certainly not fit for a party. I did not, of course, like to tell her so, but I felt sorry to see her dressed in that style.

Brigham Young was there, and kept his hat on all the time, as was his custom ; and Heber C. Kimball sat during the evening with a red pocket-handkerchief thrown over his head, while the Apostle George A. Smith, a cousin of Joseph, the originator of Mormonism, had a similar article thrown carelessly round his neck. Heber once said publicly in the Tabernacle, when speaking of the wearing of hats, and the proper degree of respect which ought to be shown to the Prophet : " I never feel as though I wanted to wear my 'at when Brigham is present. I consider that the master should wear his 'at, or 'ang it on the peg that God made for it, which is his 'ead, of course." All these things, however, have been changed since Brigham came under the gentle control of Amelia.

On the occasion of which I speak, Heber came up the Hall, soon after we entered, with five or six of his wives following him. The wives always follow the husband. In fact, every-

thing that is done, whether in word or deed, impresses one
with the conviction that the Mormons are determined to make
the women feel and fully understand that they are inferior
beings. Even in the dance the man takes the lead. In all
the *classes* and promenades he precedes his wives and all
other women. In a special council, held in Salt Lake City,
Brigham Young once said : " For a man to follow a woman is,
in the sight of Heaven, disgraceful to the name of a man."
They have a curious kind of dance in Salt Lake City, called a
double cotillion, in which one man dances with two women.
This is done in order to accommodate those who have many
wives. On entering the hall, a number is given to each man,
and he is not expected to dance until his number is called.
When that is done, they come like a streak across the hall to
the ladies' side, to get partners; and when the dance is ended
they conduct them back to their seats, and then all retire as
they came, with the exception of a few love-sick swains who
are reckless enough to break through this rule, in order to
enjoy the society of their lady-loves between the dances.

It is only old and hardened Saints, however, who will venture to set at defiance long established regulations and endure
the scrutinizing gaze of the brethren on the opposite side of
the hall. All this has a very unsociable and stiff appearance to those who attend one of these parties for the first
time.

At the particular pic-nic of which I speak, I met a Swedish
lady whom I had known in New York. She had come out to
Utah, believing fully all that had been told her of that new
Zion. She was not very young or good-looking when she
arrived, but she had a good deal of money, and consequently
was much troubled with offers of marriage. Finally she consented to become a second wife ; but she very soon discovered that her husband thought more of her money than he
did of herself. He gave her no peace until he got it all into his
own hands, and then he neglected her utterly ; scarcely ever
even coming to see her.

This poor woman, quite deserted by her husband, was

obliged to live in what they call in Utah a "dug-out." A "dug-out" is a large cellar, or hole, excavated in the ground, just like the place formed in digging the foundation for a house. It generally is only one fair-sized room, roofed in on the top with boards, and with a few steps in front by which to descend. Sometimes in such a place a man lives with a couple of wives and a host of children, and this is one phase of the order of " *Celestial* Marriage."

The Swedish lady, of whom I speak, had been well brought up in her own country and was well educated ; she could, however, speak but little English, and therefore found it very difficult to find employment, after the good brother had relieved her of her property. So she worked in the fields, or did anything else which she could get to do. She lived a wretched sort of life, and, finally, poisoned herself ; but no one seemed to care much about it, for very little attention is paid to the death of a woman in Utah, unless she is a favorite wife. No one troubles himself to make any investigations in such a case: —the woman was neither young nor handsome, and she might just as well die as live !

The visitor to Utah is only allowed to see the holiday, outside manners of the people. If he thinks he sees more, he is in most cases, deceived. But any one who really knows the great mass of the Mormon wives as they really are, would confess that a more weary, worn, and dejected set of women could nowhere be found.

How could it possibly be otherwise ? The whole system is radically wrong. How could men act properly to their wives when they marry as many as three, four, five, and six in one single day ? Such things have actually been done, absurdly impossible as it may seem. There was the Apostle Franklin D. Richards, of whom I have previously had occasion to speak. He married *five* wives. George Grant—the brother of Jedediah M. Grant, the Apostle of the Utah " Reformation "— married *four* women at one time. They owned some very fine property, and ill-tempered people said that Brother Grant had an eye principally to that. But he, good soul, would tell you that he did it altogether from principle. They all do, and I presume they ought to know best.

When Franklin D. Richards married the five or six widows of his uncle, Dr. Richards, some people said that he was actuated by the same motive ; but his friends said that his only wish was to be a father to the fatherless and a husband to the widow! Brigham is always very willing that any of the brethren should marry the widows of deceased Apostles or other dignitaries ; but as for their property, that is quite another thing. He himself always has an eye to that, and whenever it is possible, the net of the Prophet draws into its meshes all that is valuable, whether small or great.

As for Brother Brigham's own iniquities, it would take a book much larger than this present volume to tell them all. He lives, in fact, and has lived, for years, in a condition of such constant antagonism to all right and honorable principles, that I really believe that at last he hardly knows when he is doing wrong. He does not like his actions to be scrutinized, and he has always taken special pains to prevent the people from intermingling with the Gentiles, who he feared might excite in them a spirit of inquiry.

When the United States army went to Utah, in 1857, one half of the old Tabernacle was appropriated to the sisters, and the other half to the brethren. The centre of the new Tabernacle is now devoted exclusively to the sisters, and no husband or brother is permitted to sit near them. This is done for the purpose of avoiding the slightest opportunity for any Gentile to converse with them ; for the Mormons, as a rule, have not the slightest confidence in their wives, and are very jealous of them. I suppose this is natural, and that the men, knowing their own frailty, judge their wives from their own stand-point of morality. Brigham Young is the most distrustful of them all. He not only guarded the women in the Tabernacle, but when the theatre was built, he arranged so that it would be impossible for Gentiles to mix with the families of the Saints. The Mormon families occupied the parquette, and the Gentiles had the first circle. The poor among the Saints are, of course, regarded as the common herd, at all times, except when a collection is required, and then they are solemnly reminded that they are a sanctified and peculiar people. It is not therefore necessary that any trouble should be bestowed upon them, and no effort is made to preserve them, in the theatre, from contamination with the Gentiles. Gentiles and Mormons sit together in the second and third circles, and no one is expected to take any notice of it, as the theatre is Brigham's own property.

If the theatre had been owned or conducted by any one else than Brother Brigham, it would have been a sin for the Mormons to have mingled in it with the Gentiles. The people would have been " counselled " to remain at home, if they could not sit by themselves exclusively. But the fact that Brigham is the owner of the theatre does away with any sinfulness in the people attending it and sitting side by side with the Gentiles.

In the same way, when Brigham made whiskey, the whiskey was sanctified. Joseph Smith gave a " revelation " which he called " The Word of Wisdom," enjoining those who among the Saints would be most saintly, never to touch any kind of strong drink ; not even tea or coffee, or anything warm. This revelation, as I before mentioned, we ourselves followed while on mission, as, in fact, did all the members of the Church in Europe. It was only when we saw the American Apostles and Elders—more fond of creature comforts than obeying the commands of the Prophet—that we thought it was needless for us abstain any longer ; and accordingly followed their example, and ceased to deny ourselves many of those things which are generally considered to be among the necessaries of life. The Saints in Europe were not backward in imitating the Apostolic example ; and thus the " Word of Wisdom " has fallen into disuse.

This I do not think was a matter to be regretted ; for originally this revelation was, I believe, given not for the promotion of sobriety, but simply to get the people to save their money; so as to bring in more to the coffers of the Church.

Its disuse enabled many a poor soul—old men and sick women to whom a cup of warm tea or coffee was the greatest comfort of their lives—to partake of those beverages without fear of committing sin against the "Word" of the Lord.

Whether Brother Joseph himself kept his "Word of Wisdom" may very well be doubted, for his own son, Alexander, says, "There are those who say that the Revelation [on Polygamy] was received over a five-gallon keg of whiskey." Certain it is that Brother Brigham, seeing that even among the Saints every one did not care to keep this "Word of Wisdom," turned the weakness of the people to profitable account.

A certain Mr. Howard set up a whiskey-making establishment in Salt Lake City, and was doing a very good business in that line ; but Brother Brigham declared that no more should be made, and Mr. Howard was told to go on a mission to preach the Gospel. Soon after he left, the establishment was again running, and a great quantity of whiskey was sold ; but as it was dispensed at a store surmounted by an imitation of the All-seeing Eye, over the inscription, "Holiness unto the Lord"—the sign of Zion's Coöperative Institution—nothing was thought of the matter. The nature of the whiskey was, of course, changed. Some said, however, that it was not changed for the better, and that Brother Brigham's whiskey was much inferior to Brother Howard's, and much weaker. Probably, Brother Brigham thought that strong drinks were not good for the people, and made the whiskey weaker out of pure love to them.

Many young Mormon boys, otherwise respectably brought up, have been ruined by the too free sale of whiskey by the Church. I know one young man, in Utah, who told me that this had been the case with himself and several others. He always silenced his conscience by saying that he had never tasted anything but what was made at Brother Brigham's establishment and sold at one of the Church stores. Finally, seeing the inconsistency of these things, he turned away from Mormonism, Brigham, and whiskey, all at the same time, and then became a respectable and steady young man.

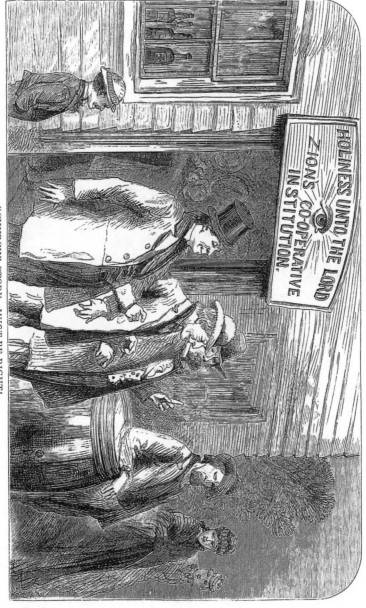

"CHURCH" STORE—*MUST BE RIGHT!*

When we went to Salt Lake, the Saints were not permitted to keep Gentile boarders. If they did so they lost their standing in the Church. Those who persisted in doing so created great scandal, and were themselves attacked without mercy in the Tabernacle sermons. They were told that intercourse in any shape with the Gentiles would cause them to lose the spirit, and they were, therefore, warned against it. Since then, however, so greatly have matters changed, that two of Brigham Young's own wives have taken in Gentile boarders; and more than one of his daughters have taken in Gentile sewing in order to provide a little extra pocket money for themselves— money which they spent in what their father calls "wretched Gentile fashions."

While the Prophet himself, and Daniel H. Wells, his counsellor, the Mayor of Salt Lake City, have made themselves conspicuous in denouncing everything that was not Mormon, some of their wives, and also their own sons and daughters, are at this moment aping every Gentile who comes within sight, and have done their very best to dress according to the very latest Gentile style. The people, when they see Brigham and his family themselves leading the way, think that there can be no great sin in following; and the more so as they are able to purchase all the finery that their hearts can desire at the dry-goods store of "the Prophet of the Lord!"

CHAPTER XXXVI.

MY DAUGHTER BECOMES THE FOURTH WIFE OF BRIGHAM YOUNG'S SON.—THE SECOND ENDOWMENTS.

Learning More of the Inner Life—The Mistakes of Newspaper Correspondents in Utah—Looking through Mormon Spectacles—Kept in the Dark—The Second Wife Begins Housekeeping—Getting Rid of *Her!*—My Clara's Lover—Joseph A. Young—The Engagement—Waiting for "Something" to Turn Up—Asking Permission to Go East—How Mormon Girls are Deceived and Deceive Themselves—Brother Brigham "Counsels" Brother Stenhouse—The Wedding Day Fixed—The Marriage Ceremony in the Endowment-House—Brother Brigham Officiates—Married for Time and for All Eternity—The Fourth Wife of a Polygamist—A Mother's Sorrow—We Receive our Second Endowments—"*Our*" Husband Anointed King and Priest—Belinda and Myself made Queens and Priestesses—A Little Stranger : The Second Wife's Baby—"The Conclusion of the Whole Matter."

AFTER I had consented, and in reality had given my husband a second wife, my *status* in Mormon polygamic society was very considerably improved. First wives who lived in, and firmly believed, this "Order of Celestial Marriage," tried in every way to make me feel that I was one with them ; and those who had not much faith felt more kindly towards me, because I had been caught in the same snare with themselves.

Every polygamic wife—whether first, second, third, or tenth—no matter how much or how little she may believe in "Celestial Marriage" ; no matter how refined or how coarse and degraded her nature may chance to be; cannot help feeling that her position is inferior to that of a monogamic wife. On this account, many of the Mormon women are never satisfied until they have drawn every woman of their acquaintance down to their own level. The influence of this supposed "Revelation" is by no means elevating or refining.

I was now upon an equal footing with other first wives. They had, therefore, no hesitation in confiding to me their griefs; and situated as I was, I had abundant opportunities of hearing stories of cruelty, wrong, and suffering, under the "Celestial" system—many of them so utterly revolting that I would not dream of relating them again. Polygamy among the Mormons is so involved in disgusting and disgraceful details, that a modest woman would not dare to relate all she knew. In this book I have endeavored to be true to my title and to "*tell all*," as far as such a thing was possible. But there are thousands of horrible incidents, too degrading for mention, which form part and parcel of the system of Polygamy, but which no woman who had any respect for herself would think of putting upon paper.

Previous to the time when my husband took his second wife, although I had learned too much, I had to a certain extent been kept in the dark respecting some of the vile and loathsome practices of Polygamy; but after that, by slow degrees, I was thoroughly initiated into the system.

Visitors to Utah would perhaps notice in the faces of the Mormon wives a dull, careworn, weary expression, altogether the reverse of that contented look which is seen among "Gentile" women. But those very women would never disclose to the stranger the depth of that sorrow which is wearing away their lives. Some few, indeed, have been led to speak of their troubles; but they have afterwards found that the very persons in whom they confided most, distorted and exaggerated every word that they had uttered, for the sake of making a good story for the press. In many cases, the names of those who were thoughtless enough to expose their sorrows, together with little personal matters which should never have

31

been made public, were put into print; and when the matter came before the Church authorities—as in course of time it was certain to do—there was a great deal of trouble and unpleasantness. Women, consequently, as a rule, tell nothing; and book-makers and people connected with the press, while they give to the world astonishing stories of what they have heard know really nothing of the truth. When a smart man, or a man connected with the press, comes to Utah, the Church authorities take him in hand at once. He is carried here and there, and treated with the utmost deference; a pair of Mormon spectacles is placed by Brigham, or one of his numerous factotums, upon the visitor's eyes, and through them he looks at all that transpires. Then comes a glowing account in the papers, or else apocryphal stories appear in the visitor's last new book; and unsophisticated people, who innocently suppose that all that is in print must be true, begin to think that the stories of the evil-doing of the Prophet, which from time to time have crept out, were only scandalous reports, and that Brigham Young—like Somebody else who shall be nameless!—was, after all, not quite so black as he has been painted.

The intelligent Saints, however, are not thus deceived. They may hold to Mormonism, and may regard Brigham in his priestly capacity as a Prophet; but they are not blind to his sins. I could, from my own personal knowledge, mention the names of men in whom Brigham Young has the fullest confidence and who are in daily communication with him. Their faith, in most instances, has really fled, although in name they are still "Saints;" they bow the knee before the Prophet's throne, but in their hearts they despise him; for years of intercourse with him have taught them what he really is.

This is, however, carefully hidden from the outer world. A gentleman, who had for five years resided in Salt Lake City, said to me a few months ago: "Mrs. Stenhouse, when I had been here about three weeks I thought that I knew enough of Mormonism to write a book; when I had been here three months I began to think that I did not know quite as much; and now, after five years, I have come to the conclusion that I

really know nothing at all. I have lived in a Mormon family
for the past year, but that has not increased my knowledge.
They are constantly upon their guard. They treat me kindly,
but they never let me know any thing."

This, I believe, has been the experience of nearly all the
Gentiles resident in Salt Lake City. Gentlemen had no
chance of learning anything, and the opportunities of ladies
were only a trifle better.

Up to this time I had said very little to my children about
my doubts and fears. With the exception of my daughter
Clara, they were all too young. Clara was just budding into
womanhood and day by day gave promise of more beauty and
interest in her future life. I dreaded to cast a cloud across
her way by telling her of my own apprehensions in respect to
Polygamy. If that were the "Order" of "Heaven," she would
certainly have to live in it; and in any case it was the "order" of
Brigham Young, and my child could not escape from it, for no
one, unless at peril of life, could flee from Zion, in those days.
I kept, therefore, from my daughter all my own troubles, feeling that she herself would soon enough have trials of her own.
She saw how much I suffered, and no doubt knew the cause;
and, although she could not fully enter into my feelings, her
companionship was a great consolation to me, and I loved her
all the more because I felt that my own heart was widowed.
How often I prayed that she might be spared such a life as
that which I lived.

We had lived together in Polygamy about a year, when my
husband told me that his young wife desired to have a home
of her own, and that he intended to provide her with one.
This was very pleasant intelligence to me; for the sight of that
other wife constantly before my eyes—sitting at my table, in the
midst of my family, walking in the garden with my husband in
the evening, or *tête-à-tête* with him in the parlor—was more
than I could bear. I began to feel, whether justly or not, that
my presence was a restraint to them, and that they felt
annoyed when I was with them. This feeling was so strong
with me that I constantly avoided them, and I finally concluded

to spend the evenings in my own room with my children, for then, being out of their presence, I should perhaps be at peace. All this time I hoped that my husband would urge me to come back again to the parlor, and several times he did so, but I thought that I was *de trop*, and remained in my room. He thought that I was making myself quite disagreeable, and such probably was the case, for no wife could be pleasant or happy, situated as I was.

This, however, was all changed when my husband established a second home. I did not mind being deprived of his society so long as I could get rid of *her*. Personally I had no ill feeling towards her, for she had always treated me with respect; the only reason why I hated her was because she was his wife; even her presence was painful to me, and when she was near me I hardly felt able to breathe.

Just at that time, the marriage of my daughter Clara first began to be talked about seriously. One day my husband being out driving with Joseph A. Young, the eldest son of the Prophet, the subject was discussed between them, and Joseph A. made a proposition of marriage. This, to me, was the cause of considerable uneasiness, as Joseph A. was a polygamist, and at first I altogether refused to listen to the suggestion. At that time Clara was not fifteen years of age, and not only did I consider her altogether two young to think of marriage, but I was shocked at the bare idea of her becoming a polygamic wife. I almost hated Joseph for asking for her.

Personally I had no objection to Clara's lover. I had known him for several years. He was an intelligent, generous-hearted, and handsome man, of very good standing among the Saints, and wealthy. As a friend, I valued and esteemed him; but that he, a polygamist, should wish to marry my darling daughter was very repugnant to my feelings. Clara was then growing old enough to understand my more serious thoughts and sentiments, and her companionship was very precious to me. The thought of her marrying into Polygamy was to my mind almost as painful as the thought of her death would have been.

My husband agreed with me that she was too young to

marry; but on that point *he* could not offer any great objection, as his own wife although very womanly in appearance was but very little older in years. I told Joseph A. of my reluctance to the proposed marriage and he fully entered into my feelings. I could not absolutely refuse him, but I wished to gain time. Every day found me more and more weak in the faith, and I thought that, if I could only postpone my Clara's marriage for a few years, something might transpire which would relieve me of my difficulty.

Joseph promised to wait just as long as we thought proper, if only we would allow him to speak to Clara and explain to her the sentiments with which he regarded her. In this he acted in a way very unlike the Mormon men generally, and I respected him accordingly. I promised him that I would not influence my daughter, but would let her decide for herself. This, after much careful consideration, I came to the conclusion was all that I could do. My mind at that time was in a very troubled state. Day by day my doubts respecting the plural wife system became stronger and stronger, and I felt that before very long some great change *must* take place, both in my faith and in my life. At the same time, outward circumstances gave no promise of any such change. My husband gave no signs of apostasy, and, as a Saint, I knew he would never think of undertaking anything without the permission of Brother Brigham. We did not even dare to leave the city without consulting the Prophet. In times, then very recent, it was at the risk, and sometimes, indeed, at the sacrifice, of life, that any one left Salt Lake Valley without permission; and even at the present moment no good Saint who values his standing in the Church would dream of going East without first obtaining the approval of Brigham Young. I could not, therefore, at the time of which I write, foresee the great changes which have since taken place. To refuse my daughter to the Prophet's son, would, I knew, be utterly useless. By partial submission I might gain some advantages; and the longer I postponed the marriage, the greater chance there was that "something" might turn up, which we all

more or less look for when we are placed in circumstances
which admit of the exercise of very little choice or effort.

My only objection against Joseph A. was, as I just stated,
that he was a polygamist ; but so long as we remained in the
Church I could not openly allege this in opposition to the
proposed marriage.   If my Clara married a single man, there
was every chance, if not an absolute certainty, that after a
while he would take another wife, or wives.   This had been
the case with other girls with whom my child was acquainted.
They had married single men, trusting that their influence
over them would be sufficient to retain their affections ever to
themselves alone ; but they had soon reason to see how groundless their expectations and hopes had been.   If, on the other
hand, I gave my daughter to a polygamist, there was certainly
no reason why Joseph A. should be refused.   I felt surrounded
on every side by difficulties, and out of them all I endeavored
to choose the least.

One day my husband told me that Brigham Young had seriously spoken to him about the matter, and had " counselled "
him to let the marriage take place at once, saying that my
Clara was quite old enough.   After this, objection on my part
would have been utterly unavailing.   Everything was settled
at the *fiat* of Brigham ; and the feelings and judgment of a
father and mother in respect to their own daughter were, of
course, of not the slightest consequence.

The wedding-day was therefore fixed, when the sweet flower
of my own quiet garden was to be transplanted to another
home.

We went to the Endowment House—my husband, myself,
and our daughter, together with some friends of the family.
There we met with Joseph A. Young, the expectant bridegroom ; his father, Brigham Young ; Joseph A.'s first wife—
Mary Young ; and several of the brethren.   The bride and
bridegroom, and the bridegroom's first wife, were all dressed
in their Temple robes.   We then entered a small room where
the altar, of which I have already spoken, is placed.   At the
end of the altar, Brigham was seated in a large arm-chair

covered with crimson velvet. The altar was also crimson.
Brigham officiated. Joseph A.'s first wife, Mary Young, knelt
in front of the long crimson altar; and my daughter Clara
knelt beside her on a sort of faldstool or ledge, arranged for
that purpose. Behind the altar, knelt Joseph A. Brigham
said : " Joseph, are you willing to take Clara Stenhouse to be
your lawful and wedded wife for time and for all eternity?"
Joseph answered, " Yes." Then Joseph's first wife was told
to place the right hand of my daughter in the right hand of
her husband, in token that she was willing; and then Clara
was questioned, as Joseph had been. When she replied in the
affirmative, Brigham said, " I pronounce you man and wife in
the name of the Lord. Amen." They were now married;
and Brigham Young, Joseph A.'s first wife, and a few other
friends came home to the wedding breakfast, after which my
daughter went to her own pleasant home.

Thus my worst fears were realised—my own daughter had
become a polygamic wife—she was the fourth wife of her husband, Joseph A. Young.

It is a source of sorrow to any mother who really loves her
children to lose them, even if it be for their own good and
happiness ; but in my own case there were reasons why I felt
the loss of my daughter more than I should have done under
ordinary circumstances. I felt quite desolate without her ; for
when left all alone, when my husband took his second wife,
and when I had no one else to turn to, my little daughter had
entwined herself about my heart in a thousand sweet .and
loving ways. She knew how great an influence music had
over me, and how much I loved to hear her play and sing ;
and when she saw how sad my heart was, or caught me in
tears, she would go to her piano, and lure me to her side by
some sweet song which she knew was dear to my memory.
But, with her went all that love and gentleness which in my
time of deepest trouble sustained me and kept me from absolute despair.

I have often wondered whether Joseph ever realised how
great, how dear, a gift I bestowed upon him when I gave him

my little Clara. But in saying this I do not mean to cast the shadow of a doubt upon his true-heartedness and love towards her. He was always kind and thoughtful, considering her comfort in everything; and although they have now been married seven years, he has never changed, but is the same to her as on the first day of their marriage. A good, kind, and gentle husband he has ever been, anticipating her every wish, tenderly and carefully guarding her from even a painful thought. My only regret has been that he is a polygamist, and she a polygamic wife.

Not long after this, my husband one day told me that a select few had been chosen to receive their Second Endowments, and that we were to be honored with the same privilege. This I was told was one of the highest honors that could be conferred upon us, as the Second Endowments had never been given to any one since the Mormons left Nauvoo.

The glory of this privilege I did not myself, however, feel; and, notwithstanding any respect which might be intended by our names being added to the list of chosen ones, I refused to see the slightest good in the whole affair. I am afraid I was naturally perverse,—or was it that the light was now beginning to dawn more clearly upon my mind? I know not. But I raised every possible objection, feeling, though I did, that all opposition on my part was useless. I knew that I should have to go, but I felt a dismal satisfaction in letting every one know how much I hated the system.

Our second wife;—I say " *our*," because I had been taught that my husband and myself were indissolubly one, even in the matter of taking wives ;—" our " second wife seemed the happiest of us all when the day arrived, and I believe she considered that we were very highly favored. After preparing our Temple robes, we started for the Endowment House. The reluctance which I felt caused me to lag behind, and I was *gently* reminded several times that I was making myself very disagreeable. I did not, however, feel much remorse, for my husband had still one good, obedient wife walking at his

POLYGAMY IN LOW LIFE:—THE POOR MAN'S FAMILY.

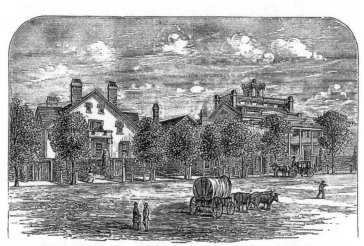

POLYGAMY IN HIGH LIFE:—THE "PROPHET'S" MANSION.

side, who I knew would sympathise with him ; and that, as every one is aware, is more than falls to the lot of every man.

When we reached the Endowment House, we ladies were shown into one room and *our* husband into another. We then proceeded to array ourselves in our robes, caps, and aprons— the same as when we received our first Endowments—and when all was ready we were ushered into another room by one of the brethren, who was also dressed in his Temple robes. There we met *our* husband and several other brethren, all dressed in the same way. We sat down, and oil was then poured upon the head of *our* husband, by two of the brethren —Daniel H. Wells, and another—and he was then ordained a King and Priest to all eternity. After that, we two wives were anointed in like manner, and ordained Queens and Priestesses, to reign and rule with *our* husband over his kingdom in the celestial world.

Had I ever solaced myself with the notion, which some Mormon women entertain, that first wives are queens over all the rest, I should have been sadly disappointed when I heard "*our*" second wife ordained to the same high office as myself. As it was, however, my faith was so small that I should have been quite contented had they consecrated her alone queen for Eternity, so long as they would have allowed me to rule and reign by myself in my own home for Time.

The ceremony did not last long ; but it all appeared to me such folly that I was anxious to leave the place, and though I dared not say so, I was truly ashamed to be seen coming out of the House. While going through these Endowments I was filled with a thorough contempt for everybody and everything around me, and I suppose that my feelings were visible upon my countenance, for, after leaving the House, I remember the Apostle John Taylor asking me if I did not feel well, and I told him as plainly as I dared what really was the matter. He spoke to me very kindly, and tried to re-assure me, but the scales were now falling from my eyes, and all his arguments availed nothing.

Notwithstanding all this, I was not ready yet to cast off the yoke, and a few months after our Second Endowments I again gave evidence of my faith. An event occurred in the other branch of my husband's family which produced a strong impression upon my mind—a little daughter was presented to him by his second wife. I was, of course, expected to go and visit the young mother and child, and I thought I could never bring my mind to do that.

It would be impossible for me to define my feelings at that time ;—loathing and hatred for him and for her, and even for the poor innocent babe, on the one side ; and, on the other, thoughts of what I considered was my duty towards God, my husband, and his other lawful wife. I was bewildered.—My heart said, Do not go ; but my conscience said, It is your duty to treat her kindly, for she believes she has done you no wrong. Then I thought—She is a young mother, and without you frowning upon her, sorrow will come swiftly enough to her door.

I saw that my husband was troubled as to what my feelings might be, although he had not had courage to tell me himself of the interesting event. He was afraid of paining me and sent a lady friend with the intelligence. I spoke to him myself and told him that I would go and see Belinda and her child. He thanked me and said, "God bless you for that." Then I went to see her ; but I was thankful when the visit was over, and although I went again many times, and tried my very best to treat her kindly and even affectionately, I could never get over the painful feelings which agitated my mind when in her presence.

CHAPTER XXXVII.

REALITIES OF POLYGAMIC LIFE:—ORSON PRATT : THE STORY
OF HIS YOUNG ENGLISH WIFE.

Peculiar Position of Plural Wives—The Troubles of a Pretty Young Welsh Girl
—The Story of Orson Pratt and His Young Wife—The "Champion of
Polygamy "—The Wife of an Apostle—Leaving a Mother and her Babes to
Starve—The Neglected Wife—Destitute and Forsaken—Attacked by Fever
—The Wretched Wife Loses her Senses—She Wanders Forth Upon the
Prairie with her Babes—The Good Deeds of Brother Kelsey and his Wife
—They Clothe and Feed the Poor Wife—The " Philosopher " and his dying
Wife—He Takes Matters Comfortably—" It is Too Late, Orson ; Too Late !"
Another Victim to Polygamy—How a Wife's Rocking-chair was Stolen—
How a Good Brother Whipped His Little Wife—Whence Come the Elders'
Wives—Dupes from the Old World—" Gone East !"—His other " Home "—
The Advent of Three Little Babies—Why I Blame those Men.

I DO not think that Polygamic wives feel the anomalies and
cruelties of the " Celestial Order " half so keenly as the first
wives, or they would never enter into it.

The position of the plural wives—second, third, fourth, or
twentieth, it matters not—is but a mockery, after all ; and in
many respects they are more to be pitied than the first wives.
The first wives have known, if only for a little while, a husband's love and care ; but that has never been felt by the
second wives. They are, in fact, in many respects little
better than slaves ; and if they are sensitive girls, their position must be extremely painful, for they must realise at all
times that they are receiving the attentions of another

woman's husband; and in many instances they are even afraid to be seen speaking to their husband for fear of bringing down the wrath of the first wife upon their heads. Others, who are not so sensitive, assert their own rights and are defiant.

I am well acquainted with a pretty young Welsh girl who was a second wife. Her husband had converted her to Mormonism while he was on a mission to Europe, and, when they reached Salt Lake, he married her. I saw her first two years after her marriage, when one day she came to me in the greatest distress. She asked me if I would give her some employment, and, greatly surprised at the request, I asked her how she came to need anything to do, as I knew her husband could well afford to support her.

" I have left my husband," she answered, "for I could stand no longer the ill-treatment that I received. I endured it until, as you see, my health is failing and I am broken-hearted. The creature I married has no manhood in him. He has allowed me to be treated like a slave, and has himself half-starved me and has acted towards me with the greatest inhumanity. When I married him," she said, " I was willing to make myself useful in the family, and I did so. But one thing after another was given me to do until I became a regular drudge—they would not have dared to treat a hired girl in the way they treated me. I was put into a miserable little back room, and was never allowed to see any of my friends ; I had to work early and late. When at last my position would not admit of my working quite so much, they punished me with all sorts of petty unkindnesses, and nearly starved me, giving me only a little flour or a few potatoes every day.

"At last," she continued, "I went to Brother Brigham to know what I should do. He sent for my husband and talked to him a long time, and he promised to do better if I would go back with him. Brother Brigham counselled me to do so, and try him again ; and I went. Soon after that, my babe was born, and then they treated me with worse unkindness."

"Who do you mean by *they* ?" I asked.

"I mean my husband and his wife," she replied; "They did not seem to look upon me as a wife at all, and, even in the coldest mornings and immediately after my child was born, they used to make me get up first and light fires and pre- pare breakfast and begin work generally, and I was only too glad if I escaped with a little fault-finding. I stood it as long as I could, because Brother Brigham had counselled me to do so ; but now I have left them again and do not mean to return." This was the story of one poor girl's troubles.

Now the man who did this is a good Mormon in good standing in the Church to-day. He is employed by the authorities and his poor young wife is now working for the Gentiles—a much happier woman, if her face speaks truly, since her separation, although she has to support herself and child. She, like hundreds of other young girls, came to Utah without friend or relative, and this is how a good brother "took care" of her.

But I must be permitted to relate a still more painful story —the story of a poor innocent girl allured from her happy home in England by one of the most distinguished of the Mormon Apostles ; brought over by him to Utah as his wife, and there suffered to die in misery and neglect.

The Apostle Orson Pratt, who is called among the Saints "The Champion of Polygamy,"—a man who has devoted his life to Mormonism, and whose writings have done more than the labors of all the other Apostles to win converts to Poly- gamy ; a man who on more than one occasion has boldly stood up against many of the absurdities and blasphemies of Brig- ham Young ; a man upon whom, on account of his independ- ence, Brigham has frowned, and who has consequently never attained to the wealth of his more obsequious brethren ; a man who in all the ordinary affairs of life would command the respect of every one around him.—This was the man who per- petrated the atrocious villainy which I am about to relate ; and much against my own personal inclinations I feel compelled to tell the story, as it shows how shockingly this debasing system can pervert an otherwise upright mind.

Orson Pratt married the young girl of whom I speak, in Liverpool, by special dispensation from Brigham Young, and her parents—themselves devout Mormons—thought that their daughter was highly honored in becoming the wife of an Apostle. She was very pretty and attractive, and for a time he paid great attention to her, and brought her over to Utah as his bride. Arrived there he utterly neglected her, and she experienced all the horrors of polygamic life.

The Apostle was living in Salt Lake City. He had left his young wife and her children in Tooele—a place about forty miles distant. There they lived in a wretched little log-cabin, the young mother supporting her little ones as best she could. When her last child was born she was suffering all the miseries of poverty, dependent entirely upon the charity of her neighbors. At the time when most she needed the gentle sympathy of her husband's love that husband never came to see her.

One morning there was literally nothing in the house for herself and her children, who, knowing nothing of their mother's sufferings, cried to her for bread.

The poor mother quieted them with a promise that they should soon have something to eat, and then she went and begged a few potatoes from a neighbor ; and upon these they subsisted for three days. She then took her children with her, for they were too young to be left alone—her babe was only three weeks old—and she went round to see if she could get work of any kind to do. In this she was not successful ; and at length, worn out by continual anxiety and privation, and heart-broken by the neglect which she had experienced, she sank beneath a fever which promised very soon to prove fatal.

For some time the neighbors nursed her ; but they, of course, had their own families to attend to, and could not give her quite all their time, and thus occasionally she was left alone. One evening, when such was the case, she got up in a state of delirium, and barefooted, and almost destitute of clothing, took her children, and wandered forth with them into the snow. The good people of Tooele went out over the prairie, anxious to find and bring back the poor maniac, but for a long time their search was in vain. At last, not knowing whither she went, she wandered to the house of Brother Eli B. Kelsey—a "vile apostate" as Brigham Young would call him; but known to every one else, Saint, Apostate, or Gentile, as one of the best and kindest-hearted men that ever lived. In Brother Kelsey's house, she and her little ones were kindly received by him and his good wife—from whose lips I first heard this painful story—and their wants attended to. They were clothed and fed, and were then carried back to the log-cabin which they called their home.

Next day the Mormon Bishop of Tooele assembled the people, and money was collected and sent to Salt Lake City, to Orson Pratt, begging him to come immediately, if he wished to see his wife alive. But the Apostle did not come. At that time he was actually engaged in taking another bride, and he wanted to hear nothing of his dying wife.

Then the good Bishop sent a young man, who rode all night, to compel him immediately to take the coach for Tooele—the young man paying his fare so that he might have no excuse. Then, at last, he came.

Arrived at the little town where his poor wife lay dying, Orson conducted himself like the philosopher he professes to be. Before him stood the hovel, within which were his deserted little ones—wailing, as if sensible of the great loss of a mother's care which they would soon have to sustain;—and there, on her dying bed, was that poor wife and mother tossing in wild delirium. But he, the cause of all that woe, passed by that wretched hovel and its death-scene to the comfortable home of a well-to-do brother, at whose house he first obtained his supper, and then calmly returning, entered the place where his wife was lying, and for a moment surveyed the scene. Then he quietly remarked to one of the sisters present: "She has a good deal of fever."

Another sister who stood by, impulsively exclaimed, "Good God!—Brother Pratt, this is more than fever—she is dying."

"Oh dear, no, sister;" he calmly replied, "she will recover."

It was evident, however, to all but Orson that his wife *was* dying, and that no earthly power could save her.

The next day she was still raving, and it was told me that in her wild frenzy she even attempted to strangle her babe. Orson essayed to hold her, but she caught his gold chain and snapped it in two. His touch and the sight of the chain recalled her for a moment to her senses, and she said reproachfully— "You are puffed up with pride, Orson, with your gold chain and rings, while you leave me and my babes to starve. Poor little lambs! where are they?"

For a moment the yearning of a mother's heart for her children conquered the fever that tortured her mind, and she listened to her husband's attempted words of comfort, as he said, "I am with you now Eliza, and I will take care of you."

Steadily, for a moment, she looked up into his face, and, with tears in her eyes, said mournfully: "It is *too late*, Orson—It is *too late!*"

These were the last sane words which she uttered in this life, although she still lingered on insensible.

The next morning, the Apostle Pratt resolved to leave for Salt Lake City and his young bride. The Bishop, however, called a council and summoned him to remain until his wife was dead. Nevertheless he did not wish to stay, and, being an Apostle, he overruled the council. At the last moment before his intended departure, one of the sisters said: "Brother Pratt, should she die, what shall we do with her?"

"Oh, she won't die," he replied.

"But should she," the sister urged.

"Then bury her with her children," he answered.

After much solicitation, he was prevailed upon to remain for a few hours, and the next morning his wife died. The language of her last moments, as she raved and tossed in mad delirium, showed how terrible had been her mental agony, and how much she had suffered from this frightful system.

DESPAIR!

But one might easily fill a large volume with stories quite as cruel as this. It is simply absurd to expect that it should be otherwise. Men and women can train and discipline their minds, they can crush out the affections of their hearts if they will; but no effort of man can change man's nature entirely or root out altogether humanity from the soul. Women may endure, as that poor woman did whose story I have just related, but they never can get perfectly adapted to the system of "Celestial Marriage." The nearer they approach to its requirements, the further they recede from all that is held good and noble in womanhood, and as for the men, they are brutalised by every effort which they make to conform with it.

During the summer, about three years ago, a young-looking woman, very shabbily dressed, came frequently to my house with heavy baskets of fruit which she entreated me to buy. One day she said: "You do not remember me, Sister Stenhouse, I think, and I do not wonder for I am so changed. I have to work very hard now, for all I have to live upon is what I can make by selling fruit, or any little work that I can get my neighbors to give me to do; and if my husband could prevent even that I believe he would. I am obliged to gather my fruit at night and hide it from him, and that is why I urged you so to buy, for I never know when I may meet him."

I was very much surprised at this, as her husband, I knew, was getting a good salary, and appeared to be a most gentlemanly man. His first wife, I was aware, had left him—it was said, on account of cruelty and neglect—and he had married this one just after her arrival from England. I had every reason to believe that she had been a good wife to him, and a mother to his motherless children; but he had taken another wife since he married her and had cruelly neglected this poor woman, leaving her his first wife's children to take care of. She said that he was again paying his addresses to another still, and she expected that he would soon marry her. And yet this woman [his second wife] told me that all he had left for her and the children to live upon was a sack of bran and

32

about fifty pounds of corn meal. Everything else had been taken to the third wife, even to the best articles of furniture.

She said: "One evening I had been sitting in the porch in my rocking-chair, when he came in and remained about an hour. As soon as he left, I went out to bring in the chair, and was just in time to see him carrying it off;—I knew where he was going with it." I saw this poor woman frequently, and bought her fruit often when I did not need it, for it grieved me to see her carrying such heavy loads in her then delicate situation. After a time I lost sight of her, and then I heard that she was dead. One day her own daughter,—for she was a widow when she married this man,—came to me before leaving the city. "I am going away to some friends," she said, "for I will never live near that man—he killed my mother; he kicked her so severely that she never recovered, and when her child was born, they both died from the effects of the blows which she had received—and I hate him."

Nothing was ever done to this man—his wife was his own property. He is still regarded as a good Mormon; and when he went to Washington, about two years ago, he took with him letters of recommendation from the leading men in the Church, and the Washington papers spoke of him as being a very gentlemanly and intelligent man. I would give his name, but that I hardly think it would be fair to single him out from his brethren, of so many of whom I could tell just as shameful stories. My Mormon friends, however, will know very well of whom I speak.

Another first wife of one of the Mormon authorities told me how her husband whipped her because she would not consent to his stripping *their* home of everything that was either useful or handsome in order to furnish a house for his second wife. Finally he shut her up while he took her entire parlor furniture away. She was a fragile little woman and perfectly helpless when in the power of a strong man, and therefore was forced to submit, as there was no appeal to law in Utah.

It is a very difficult thing for a woman after listening, day

after day, to such tales of woe and misery, and knowing them
to be true, to retain much respect for a polygamist, whoever
he may be. For my own part I regard them all with such
feelings of loathing—for I cannot forget my own sufferings—
that I can hardly speak civilly *of* them, and would prefer never
to speak *to* them. I know scores of ladies—married ladies—
Mormon ladies, who in secret feel and speak just as I do upon
this subject.

For many years past, the American Elders have derived a
rich harvest from Britain, and Scandinavia. After the introduction of Polygamy, an Elder was seldom known to return
from mission without bringing with him one, two, and sometimes three young girls, or else arranging in some way for
their emigration. The Missionaries, however, preferred, whenever it was possible, to bring the girls with them, for if they
trusted them to the care of a brother returning before or after,
he very frequently turned traitor, and carried off the prize
himself.

The Elders were not permitted to marry these extra wives
while on, or returning from, a mission, unless they had special
permission from Brigham Young. But quite a number of the
poor weak brethren were so impulsive and so anxious to be
married, that they could not wait for the ceremonies of the
Endowment House. One conscientious Swiss brother, named
Loba, who could find no one willing to take the responsibility
of marrying him while crossing the Plains, said that as he was
an Elder he could just as well marry himself, and be under no
obligation to anybody; and he did so. He had fallen in love
with a little miss—a mere child, about one quarter of his own
age.

Many men have married wives, and have brought them
home, before their first wives knew even that they were in
love. They had not had courage to introduce the subject, but
believed that when the wife found that it was done and could
not be undone, she would see the uselessness of feeling badly,
and would soon get over it. But no wife who has been thus
treated ever did "get over it." What can a man know of

woman's nature who would dare to act thus towards her, and think that she would become reconciled to such treatment?

What strange ideas the Mormon men must have of woman's nature if they believe that women can submit to such treatment as this and still love them! What folly to think even of love! Can they not discover, if by nothing else, by the changed manner, the almost cold indifference, of those who were once gushing over with affection, whose winning and endearing ways captivated their hearts—that *something* must be wrong—that love has ceased to exist in the hearts of their wives, and that a cold, stern sense of duty and religious obligation has taken its place?

It would be very wrong for me to say that there are no men who try to be just in the practice of Polygamy, for I know many who try their very best to act impartially to all their wives, but this is not really the result of their religion about which some of these men appear to care very little. I feel sure that if they are good men, notwithstanding the evil effects of Mormonism upon them, they would have been much better men without it.

On the other hand, I have known men who, before they became Mormons, were reputed good husbands and fathers, but who afterwards became cold and harsh in their natures, cruel to their wives, and neglectful to their children,—it seemed as if they thought of nothing else but courting the girls and taking more wives, altogether regardless as to whether they could support them or not.

Some of the Elders, finding that they might not marry plural wives before they reached Utah, have bound the foreign girls by solemn vows and covenants to marry them when they arrived in Salt Lake Valley; and the poor girls, believing, that because these men were Missionaries, all they said and did *must* be right, have often—in fact, in almost every instance—to their own great injury, kept their "covenants" and married the men to whom they were vowed. I have known personally and intimately several sisters who have in this way ruined their prospects and blighted the hopes of their whole lives, and sadder stories than theirs could not be told.

My husband had again left Salt Lake City, and had gone to "the States,"—as we then called "going East;" for it was such a long journey that we felt ourselves altogether out of the pale of civilisation. I felt, therefore, comparatively free; for I could now, whenever I desired to do so, walk out, or visit a friend, without the constant dread of meeting him and his wife. It always humiliated me to see them together, although I believed that it was perfectly right that my husband should show attentions to his other wife. It was not *now* jealousy that I felt—the day of jealous feeling was long past;—I felt disgusted, and I was humbled at the sight of them. At one time, for nearly six months I remained at home, never going further than my own garden,—simply for the reason that I feared to meet *her* in the presence of any of my friends— particularly any of my Gentile friends ; or worse still, with *him*. I felt sure that, had we met, I should have tried to avoid them or have passed them by unnoticed, which would, of course, have been an insult, and would have caused re- marks from strangers, and ill feeling, which, of all things, I felt most anxious to avoid.

There is no privacy in a polygamic family where the wives live together, and very little indeed when they live in sepa- rate houses ; for each wife finds pleasure in telling all the little weaknesses of the other wives to her own "particular friends,"—and those "particular friends," in turn tell *their* "particular friends," until in due course it becomes known to some kind-hearted busybody who considers it her duty to go to the wife whose foibles have thus been bandied about from one to the other, and tell her "how shamefully she has been slandered." Then it is the poor husband's turn to hear the whole burden of trouble,—never, of course, exaggerated in the least,—and he is expected to make peace, if he can, among his numerous wives.

Perhaps all this fuss has been caused by the husband

himself—he never intending it, all the time. Not unlikely he gave a new dress or some article of wearing apparel to one wife or her children, and the others have noticed it. It may be that, perhaps, he did not think that the others needed it, and probably they did not ; but that does not matter in the least. Jealous wives do not stop to consider such a trifle as that. The poor man is told that he must be just and fair to all, and when he gives a dress to one, he must give dresses to the others also, whether he can afford it and they need it, or not.

These wives are lynx-eyed, and each one notices every article of clothing that the others wear ; and, no matter how economical one wife may be, or how extravagant another, the careful one must never look better dressed than her less saving rival, or the husband will certainly be blamed for favoritism.

After living in Polygamy and observing all these things, I came to the conclusion that the men who tried to act justly were, after all, greatly to be pitied ; and I had no doubt in my mind that many of them would only be too happy to be mono-gamic husbands once again. At one time I believed this of my own husband. He appeared to be annoyed when "duty" compelled him to leave my home and family circle, and go to his other "home." I half fancied that he had at last come to think that Polygamy was a most unnatural condition of affairs, and that he would be very glad if it were not compulsory. Of course, I drew my own conclusions, but I by and by found that they were somewhat premature.

I had supposed that, possibly, his young wife was not so attractive to him now as she had been ; and this I must confess, did not grieve me very much. But, notwithstanding all that, so great had been my fanaticism, that I had still re-maining sufficient faith in the unholy practice to make me feel that if we expected ever to get a blessing from heaven through compliance with the "celestial" command, it was neces-sary that my husband should be just to his other wife and treat her kindly and considerately.

As I said before, from the moment when he first selected another wife, his society lost every charm for me, and therefore I was not so very generous, after all, when I urged him to spend as much time as he possibly could with Belinda. I felt that if I had lost everything in this life for Polygamy ; and if Polygamy, after all, by any chance, might turn out true ; I might as well strive to get a little glory in the next world. But, after all, it was but a poor soulless attempt, and so miserable did I feel that I frequently wished that I could be completely annihilated after death.

My husband's cares were also increasing, for his young wife had already presented him with three daughters. I presume, if at any time she was cross at his long absences, the children were influenced by her spirit, and when my husband did visit her, his reception was probably either too warm or too cool, and, in any case, more lively than suited his quiet tastes. He assured me that he never spoke an unkind word to her, but would listen to all she had to say in a meek and quiet spirit, feeling all the time that she was young and inexperienced. This no doubt was all very well, but what woman can bear to see a man listening quietly to all she has to say, when she herself is in anything but a calm state of mind? We like men to *feel* what we say.

I have known many husbands in Polygamy who made it a practice not to say anything to their wives when they were recounting their wrongs, but preferred to get up and leave without a word—showing them no sympathy whatever, but teaching them, with all that cold indifference which in time chills the most loving heart and silences the voice of affection for ever, what their position *really* was.

I have also heard husbands say : " I provide my wife with all she needs or can wish for, and surely she cannot suppose that I will allow her or any other woman to dictate to me as to what I shall do with myself or how I shall spend my time. I shall follow in the footsteps of Brother Brigham, and go where I please, and stay as long as I please, and come back when it suits me."

The Mormon men are very much to blame in this respect. They take young innocent girls from the warm and happy influence of home, and after a few brief weeks of devotion, they leave them in the cold atmosphere of the world, to battle single-handed with new cares and new duties, to bear sickness and solitude with what courage they may, and thus, disconsolate and alone, go their way into the tangled mazes of life. This the Mormon husbands do, without a thought of the solemn vows they break and the heavy responsibilities which they evade; for they never for one moment reflect, that if there is incompatibility, it results in most instances from the fact that they have acted worse than foolishly in choosing girls so young and inexperienced that they could not possibly be fit companions for men who might in point of age have been their fathers, and even then have had a very fair margin of years to spare.

CHAPTER XXXVIII.

"OUR" HUSBAND'S *FIANCÉE*—A SECOND WIFE'S SORROWS—STEPS TOWARDS APOSTACY.

A Little Misapprehension—My Husband's Kingdom—The chosen Maiden—The Prophet's daughter, Zina—Reviewing a Lady-Love—A Strange Consultation—The Accepted Lover—Love of no ordinary Kind—"Something very Beautiful "—" He never loved Before "—Progressive Affection—Why Zina pitied Us—" Our Husband ! "—Sorrows of a Second Wife : Belinda in Trouble—A Pleasant "Duty ! "—The Flirting in the Prophet's Parlor—Wavering Faith—The "Revelation " Criticised—Homœopathic Religion—The Book of Mormon *condemns* Polygamy !—A very Questionable " Prophet "—Belinda's Bereavement—Accused of Favoring the Gentiles—Lover's Quarrels —A Long Courtship—" If one girl wont, another will ! "—Steps towards Apostacy.

A T one time, as I have already stated, I had almost begun to think that my husband had seen enough of the discomforts and heartlessness of polygamic life, and that his eyes were looking back wishfully to the time when, as the old Scotch ballad says :

> " One loving heart was all his own,
> But there as king he reigned supreme."

My faith in my own acuteness and perception was, however, very considerably shaken when one day he told me that he thought it was about time for him to think of taking another wife. I suppose he expected that I should express some astonishment or offer objections, for he proceeded to give me excellent reasons for what he was about to do.—His greatly improved circumstances; his desire to sustain his brethren; and, above all, the necessity that he should "build up a kingdom!"

There was no gainsaying all this. The Lord had certainly very greatly blessed him in basket and in store; it was, moreover, praiseworthy in him to wish to sustain his brethren; and nobody could deny that he ought to have a "kingdom!" To crown all, the young lady whom he proposed to honor this time could not possibly be objected to by any loyal Saint, for she was of the seed royal of the modern Israel—a daughter of the high-priestly house of Brigham Young!

I suppose, if I had been a right-minded woman, I should have felt the great glory that there was in this proposed alliance. But, in point of fact, such is the perversity of human nature, I did not feel at all pleased, although I could say nothing in objection. I had had some slight suspicion that my husband's eyes, to say nothing of his heart, had lately been inclined to wander in a certain direction, for he had become so particularly regular in his attendance at the theatre. I mentioned the matter to him once or twice, but he answered, that as an editor it was a matter of necessity for him to attend, and that he ought to be there always. This I might, perhaps, have believed, had it not been that it was now several years since his paper was first established, and hitherto his personal attendance at every representation had not been considered absolutely indispensable—reporters had been able to do all that was necessary.

His proposal to marry this young lady, now it was openly stated, shed light upon many things which had before appeared to me rather obscure. Her name was Zina, and she was the daughter of Mrs. Zina D. Huntington Jacobs, whom I have already mentioned as one of the Prophet's wives. She was one of the actresses in the theatre—for many of Brigham's daughters at that time took part in the representations—and I had frequently observed very pretty little notices of her in the Salt Lake *Daily Telegraph*. Sometimes it had occurred to me that these notices were not quite merited, for other actresses in the same play had really appeared more proficient; but that, of course, was only my own private opinion. Somehow or other, my husband's opinion seemed always to clash with mine whenever there was a lady in the question; and in this case I had again and again differed from him in opinion concerning this same young lady, long before I suspected that he had a more than friendly interest in her.

Strange as it would have appeared to any one unused to the ways and works of Mormon Polygamy, my husband consulted me about the matter; and it was agreed that he should propose to the lady in question. I offered little objection, except mentioning that I thought he would have quite as well fulfilled the commands of God if he had taken an older and plainer-looking wife. These things are generally fully determined before any mention of the matter is made to the first wife, and opposition on her part is seldom of any avail. Besides which, I did not much care now how many wives my husband took,—he might as well have twenty, as the one too many which he already had,—his marriage to another could not possibly make me feel any worse, provided I was not compelled to associate with *her*. I had resolved that I would never live on familiar terms with his other wives—not because I might disrespect or dislike them personally, but because I could not overcome the purer and better teachings of my early life.

My husband in due form proposed, and was accepted; and it was soon rumored abroad that he was going to marry one of the "President's" daughters,—Brigham is always spoken of as "President" Young among the Saints. In the course of a day or two they were formally "engaged," and a more loving couple could not possibly have been found. The young lady herself afterwards told me that *their* love was of no ordinary kind; and I'm sure I did not doubt her word. But consider how pleasant such intelligence must have been to a wife!

Zina's friends who wished to cheer me up and make me happy, told me that my husband's love for her was perfectly engrossing, they "thought he could never have really loved before"—there was something very beautiful in their loves!" I need hardly say that I saw these things in quite another light. Of course, when I saw the letters which were constantly passing to and fro,—brought to my house by persons who evidently knew they were bearers of missives of love,—and when I witnessed their effect upon my husband, and saw such anxiety evinced that *I* should not see them, I did not for a moment doubt their affectionate devotion to each other, but I must admit that to me there was very little "beauty" in it.

The young lady, I believe, regarded my husband's second wife and myself with a great deal of sympathy; for she thought that, however affectionate he might have been to us, *she* was his first *real* love. It is a most astonishing fact, that if a Mormon man has ten, fifteen, or even twenty wives, he will be certain, when courting the twenty-first, to make her believe that "he never really loved before;" and then, if afterwards he took a twenty-second, you may be quite sure that she too would be persuaded, or would persuade herself, into a belief in the very same statement. With the last wife, it is always an article of faith that *she* is the husband's first and only love. It is a curious question :—If a man of many wives starts with as much love for his first wife as ordinary one-wifed men have for theirs, and goes on increasing his love with each additional wife, so that he can always say to the last that "he never really loved before ;" how much love will he have when he gets to the tenth or the twentieth? At that rate, Brigham, who in the course of his life has had—say, thirty wives, must have a "30-love" power of affection for the last. The extent of his devotion must be something utterly astounding ; by this time the old man must be a perfect Vesuvius of love!

Zina pitied us, I know, when she realised that *we* could never know the great depth of *our* husband's love for her. She spoke and acted as if this were how she felt ; and I have no doubt that she intended, after her marriage with *our* husband, to treat us with great kindness and consideration, as a sort of recompense for what we never had truly known, and never could know *now*—*our* husband's love! This was very kind, certainly, but I fear it was not at all appreciated by Belinda or myself.

As is almost always the case when the husband takes a third wife, a better state of feeling was brought about between my own husband's second wife and myself. Belinda no longer centred all her jealousy in me, and I, of course, had to divide mine. She now, to a certain extent, began to realise what I had suffered when my husband courted her; she felt badly, and I really did sympathise with her when I remembered how young she was and that she was the mother of three little children. She had her moiety of a husband, it is true; but, like all other polygamic wives, that was her misfortune rather than her comfort or strength. Many a wife would be happier were she a widow; in fact, widows are the happiest class of women in Utah, for they realise that it is far better to have a dead sorrow than a living one.

Now, our husband always maintained that he was not in love with Miss Zina, but that in making love to her he was acting entirely from principle. So all the brethren say; and I have never yet heard of any one of them ever confessing— except, of course, to the maiden herself—that he was in love. To the maiden herself he says, not only that, but a great deal more. But if our husband, at the time of which I speak, was not in love, the saints forbid that I should ever see him in that condition! I am sure when I heard his *fiancée* speaking of their devotion to each other, and of the fond attachment of her heart to him (for she felt no delicacy in speaking to me— his wife—about such matters,) I came to the conclusion that I had never known what it was to really love, and that my nature was too crude and unrefined to understand the mysteries of the tender passion. There was no love in the case, *our* husband repeatedly told us—all pure duty!—There are some men, especially among the Mormons, and at certain times, who find this kind of "duty" quite a pleasure.

Long courtships had become quite fashionable among the brethren in Salt Lake City, and I dreaded a long courtship more than anything else, for there is so much that is humiliating, and I might even say disgusting, to a wife when her husband is engaged in love-making to another woman, that I hoped, as much as possible, to be spared passing through such an ordeal a second time.

As the accepted lover and affianced husband of Brother Brigham's daughter, *our* husband was, of course, constantly in attendance at the Prophet's house. But he was not the only good brother who spent his evenings in Brigham Young's parlor ; for it was then—and I suppose it is to-day—a regular rendezvous for middle-aged and young men, and even boys ; and there the Prophet's little girls, as well as those who were grown or growing up, obtained an excellent training in the art of flirting and courting.

It has always been said among the Saints that Brigham's girls and the daughters of Daniel H. Wells were the boldest and least retiring maidens to be found in Salt Lake City, and that they presumed greatly upon their imaginary high position ; which position nobody but themselves cared anything about. It is well known that the very people upon whom they look down are those who rightly should receive their warmest gratitude and respect, on account of the more than liberal support which they have given to their father, even to the detriment of their own children. But too much must not be expected of young girls brought up in Polygamy.

When first I heard that my husband had set his affections upon one of these girls, I felt convinced that he could not have made a very wise choice. Men are never very wise in such matters, but when they are influenced by the peculiar motives which actuate the Mormon men they become doubly silly ; and I could not help dreading that the mere fact of my husband having selected a daughter of the Prophet as his future wife would bring trouble upon us all. What shape that trouble would take, I could form no conjecture, but I felt sure that a change of some sort was fast approaching. My faith was almost gone—I felt the degrading position in which the " Celestial " system placed me and my children, and it seemed to me that I could no longer endure it. My children I could not, and would not, leave, but it was impossible for me to continue to live as I had been living—nor would I think of

bringing up my children any longer to believe and live a religion which had so cruelly blighted all my own life. It was for
them that I feared now,—I felt that for their sake I must
break away from this horrible system.

My own life, I thought, was not worth caring for, but the
idea of my little girls growing up and following in my
footsteps and enduring as I had endured, was more than I
could bear. Something must be done to save them from
such a fate.

About this time I procured a copy of the " Revelation on
Celestial Marriage," and read it through carefully and calmly,
from beginning to end. The reader may, perhaps, remember
that when a copy of it was first given to me, in Switzerland, years before, I was so angry and indignant that when
I had got only partly through it I cast it from me in disgust
as an outrage upon all that was good and true. From that
time, although I had heard portions of it quoted and read, I
had never perused it as a whole. On two occasions, at least,
my friend Mary Burton was very near reading it through with
me, and had we done so, I have not the slightest doubt that
my eyes would have been opened to the absurdity and wickedness of the whole system, and years of wretchedness would
have been spared me.

Such, however, was not the case. It was not until I had
almost drained the cup of sorrow and degradation that, at last,
I found an antidote in the deadly thing itself which had been
the source of all my unhappiness. I was acting upon the
homœopathic principle—" *similia similibus curantur*,"—and
using a dose of poison to cure a disease caused by that
poison ;—but if the reader has perused the " Revelation " I
think he will admit that it was a pretty big dose for any
woman to swallow.

As I read, I saw plainly *from the wording of the document* that if ever it was given to Joseph Smith—no matter by
whom, it was given *long after* he had *practiced* Polygamy—or
something as bad—and to sanction what he had already done.
I had read in the Book of Mormon :

"David and Solomon truly had many wives and concubines, *which thing was an abomination before me saith the Lord.* . . . . . . Hearken to the Word of the Lord : for there shall not any man among you have, save it be one wife ; and concubines he shall have none." [*Book of Mormon,* p. 118.]

In the Book of the Covenants, given through Joseph Smith, and held sacred by every Saint, I had read :

"Thou shalt love thy *wife* with all thy heart, and cleave unto *her* and *none* else." [*Book of Covenants,* p. 124.]

And yet when I turned to the "Revelation" I found in the very first clause :

Verily, thus saith the Lord unto my servant Joseph, that inasmuch as you have enquired at my hand, to know and understand wherein I, the Lord, JUSTIFIED [!] my servants Abraham, Isaac and Jacob, as also Moses, David and Solomon, my servants, as touching the principle and doctrine of their having many wives and concubines," &c.

What could I possibly think of a "Prophet" who, after having the law laid down so clearly, and being told so distinctly that the doings of David and Solomon were an "abomination," and that a man should have *but one wife,* should enquire of the Lord how he "*justified*" the very things which He had just declared were "an abomination" unto him ?— Then, too, what blasphemy to represent God as one day giving a "Revelation" declaring a thing sinful, and the next day "justifying" it! I felt perfectly humiliated with myself that I had never before had the courage to look the matter calmly in the face and discover, as I must have discovered, had I only used my unaided reason, the shameful imposture which had been palmed upon us. I now made careful enquiry, and it was soon clear to me that evidence was not wanting to prove that the doctrine of plural marriages originated in the licentious hearts of Joseph Smith and those associated with him. When once I was convinced of that, the whole fabric of my religion crumbled before my eyes ; and from that time I can hardly say that I had faith in anything that had been taught me.

My husband's second wife was also very unhappy now. She, too, after the general rule, had flattered herself that *she* was " his first and only love," and it was not pleasant to have her dream of happiness dispelled ; but now that another " jewel " was to be added to *our* husband's crown she could no longer deceive herself. She little knew, poor girl, when she married, that a Mormon's heart is like a honeycomb— there is always a vacant cell wherein another may nestle.

Real trouble, too, she had.—One of her children was taken very sick, and after a severe illness died. I remained with her night and day, and did what I could for the poor child. Had it been possible for me to have felt a greater loathing and detestation for that vile system of Polygamy, that feeling would have been conceived while I watched at the bed-side of my husband's dying child. It was there that I vowed that no Polygamist should ever marry another daughter of mine, and resolved that to my dying day my voice should be raised against the unholy and unnatural teachings of the Mormon Priesthood. I looked at that lonely young mother, who in her hour of trial ought to have had *all* her husband's sympathy, *all* his attention, to support her ; but who, instead, knew that, however kind he might be to her, he was contemplating a new marriage, and his thoughts must of necessity be more or less with his purposed bride. All unkind feeling was banished from my heart—I forgot that she was my husband's wife, and remembered only that, like myself, she was a suffering woman, a victim to a false faith ; and I felt very deeply for her in her time of sorrow and bereavement.

My husband, at this time, had been a member of the Mormon Church for twenty-five years. He had lectured, preached, written and published, in Great Britain, Switzerland, and the United States, in support of the Mormon faith. He had been a most earnest and consistent member of the Church, and devotedly attached to Brigham Young. This attachment to Brother Brigham he shared in common with all the staunchest of his brethren ; for while the members of the Church retain unshaken confidence in the new revelation, they naturally acquire a great regard for the Prophet, and render him un-

33

questioning obedience. I believe that my husband would willingly have laid down his life, if by so doing he could have shielded Brigham Young from harm or have been of essential service to him.

But causes were now in operation which, by and by, detached him from the Church, and made it possible for me also to leave the Mormon faith. Hitherto, for my children's sake, I dared not leave the Church without my husband, and I therefore anxiously watched for anything which might rescue him from the bondage in which he was held.

As proprietor of a daily paper, his business had frequently called him to the Eastern States for several months at a time, and I observed that after those visits his editorials took a more liberal turn. My Mormon friends frequently said to me, " Brother Stenhouse is doing himself no good by his constant association with the Gentiles ;" and subsequently, when we did apostatise, our secession from the Church was attributed to contaminating Gentile influences.

Then, too, we had frequent visits from strangers passing through Salt Lake City. I saw, with pleasure, that this intercourse with the outside world was gradually undermining my husband's confidence in the teachings of the Elders, and it gave me courage to hope that, after all, the day of liberty might dawn at last. Feeling as I did thus, it will not surprise the reader that I regarded with more and more distrust the proposed marriage of my husband to Brother Brigham's daughter ; for I felt that then he would be deeper than ever in the toils of the Priesthood, and I sometimes almost believed that it was my duty to use every influence in my power to prevent it.

Putting my own feelings out of the question, it is probable that I might have done this simply for his own good ; for I doubted not that some day the scales must fall from his eyes, and then he would be thankful that I had prevented the marriage. Our paths by this time had certainly diverged far asunder, and my husband had another wife and family ; but I believed that he was sincere, though sadly mistaken, or I should not have felt so kindly towards him as I did.

At other times, and observing his devotion, I almost myself began to think that perhaps the nonsense that I had heard was, after all, true, and that this girl *was* the only one he had really loved ; and, if so, of course he ought to marry her. In fact, so divided was my attention that I hardly knew what to think; I therefore resolved to act according to circumstances.

Brigham Young, in one of his sermons, says that: "The first thing manifested in the case of apostacy was the idea that the Prophet was liable to make a mistake : when a man believes that, he has taken the first step towards apostacy ; he need only take one step more, and he is out of the Church." This was spoken of Joseph and his Saints, but it suits just as well Brigham and his: I knew very well that my husband had taken the first step, and I sincerely hoped that he might soon take the second. For my own part, I had for some time, not only believed that a Prophet *might* be mistaken, but, as Brother Heber would say, I *knew* it.

My husband and his bride elect, like all other lovers, had frequent little quarrels—I suppose for the purpose of making up again, and being then all the more ardent in their affection. But they now had a disagreement which lasted longer than all that had gone before; although I suppose that neither of them had, at that time, the slightest idea how it was going to end. They had been courting for fifteen months at least, and after so much devotion on the part of my husband, and so much fervent affection on the part of the young lady, it really did seem too bad that so large an amount of love should be thrown away. It was hard that after such a long strain upon their religious and devotional feelings—for they were both very pious lovers—all their labor of love should come to nought. Things had certainly taken a twist, for I know well enough that at one time they both firmly believed that their marriage was preördained in heaven, and that they were as completely one in feeling as mortals ever could be. The mother, too, who was a very pious woman, once told my husband that she had had a vision in which it was revealed to her that they were destined for each other in the eternal worlds:—the lovers of

course firmly believed her. But, for all that, the estrangement still continued, and my husband was constantly making
it wider by the articles which appeared in his paper, until at
last certain of the sisters whispered that the heart of the lady
had been attracted towards some brighter luminary.

Long courtships often end disastrously; but when I heard
rumors of the lady's presumed faithlessness, it seemed to me
hardly fair, for the day had been fixed for the marriage and
the wedding-dress actually made. Of course I sympathised
with my husband.—Would any wife like to see her husband
disappointed in his love-affairs with another woman, I wonder?

While under these natural feelings of indignation, I one
day told Brigham Young, that I thought, after all the courting
that had been done—and it was not a trifle—they certainly
ought to be married. He said he was willing enough himself,
if they wished it; but girls, he said, often changed their minds,
and as they could have but one husband, it was only fair that
their wishes should be consulted. "If Zina has really changed
her mind," he added, "I have plenty of other daughters, and
they have all got to be married, let him take one of them,—if
one won't, another will!" The reader will see the liberal ideas
which Brother Brigham entertains on the subject of marriage.

It may, perhaps, seem rather strange that I should be anxious
to have them marry; but, after all that I had seen and endured
in Polygamy, can it be wondered at that I should no longer
regard the father of my children as my own husband? Had
I thought him a bad man, or had he acted as I know
many of the good brethren do act; had he brought home girl
after girl with the hope of alluring one or more of them into
Polygamy, or had he been utterly reckless of my feelings, I
might perhaps have been able to cast him from my heart
without a single regret. But I really believed that he was
acting consistently with the teachings of his religion, and if I
felt degraded by the life I lived, it was not his fault—it was
the fault of the system. I therefore felt that if things came
to the worst, and if I were driven to extremities, and forced
to separate from him, I should like to know that he had a wife

whom he loved. I felt certain that there was now but little love between him and his second wife, and that some day a separation was sure to take place. The idea of divorce was so repugnant to my feelings that it was only in moments when grief overpowered me, and my heart was wrung with anguish, and I felt utterly reckless, that I for one moment thought of anything like it. Even then I only entertained the idea of a separate life—not divorce. That last resource of the unhappy wife was, however, spared me; and, looking back, I thank God that in His all-wise providence He so shaped my life at that time that my husband and myself, no longer disunited by that disgrace to civilisation and Christianity—Polygamy—can now rejoice together that that last step was never taken, and that no false creed or superstition can ever again divide our interests or our hopes.

Nevertheless, it was strange that the words of my talkative friend should be again verified, and that a second time I should be found persuading my husband to take another wife!

CHAPTER XXXIX.

SOME CURIOUS COURTSHIPS—BRIGHAM RUINS OUR FOR-
TUNES—BELINDA DIVORCES "OUR" HUSBAND.

Some Curious Courtships—"The Nicest ole 'oman in the Country!"—"Bespoke"
Wives—Marrying in Haste—A Woman with Nine Husbands—A Difficult
Question—The Autocrat of Utah—Reminding a Husband—Accused of Favor-
ing the Gentiles—The "Subjugation of Women"—The *Daily Telegraph* in
Trouble—Removing to Ogden—Brigham Young Resolves to Ruin Us—A
Crafty Prophet—The Ruin of Our Fortunes—"It Makes Me a Free Man!"
"Our" Husband's Divorce—"Take Care of That Paper"—Inside the
Prophet's Office—Signing the Document—A Curious Bill of Divorce—Be-
linda—Forming a Resolution—A Sacrifice Worth Making.

THE reader will see that, setting aside the fact that my
husband was already married, there was nothing in his
courtships to distinguish them from those of lovers among the
Gentiles.

But all courtships in Utah are not carried on in this fashion.
Some of the brethren entirely omit the love-making part, and
with them to take a new wife is simply to make a bargain.
The better the Saint, the less, as a rule, does he seem to care
about the feelings of the woman whom he makes his wife.
My husband, however, was still leavened with the fashions of
the old world and the days of his youth, and like some of the

other brethren of good standing in Salt Lake City, he fell into Gentile ways instead of keeping to the true style of Mormon courtship.

I heard of one American Elder who went to the young lady upon whom he had fixed his choice, and without a word of preliminary discourse of an affectionate nature, said: "I've twenty head o' stock, fifty acres o' good land; got a good log-house, an' *the nicest ole 'oman in the country !* — Now, sis, will you have me ?" Whether the fair damsel was dazzled by this alluring picture or not, I am not quite certain, but one would suppose that she *ought* to have been.

Now, to balance the Yankee, it is only fair that I should tell you of a certain Englishman who lived in Cache Valley, about a hundred miles from Salt Lake, and who was very anxious to find a second wife. He could not get one in the place where he lived, as the girls were all either married, or, as the Mormons say, "bespoke;" so he came to Salt Lake City as a last desperate resort. To the first unmarried girl to whom he was introduced, without a moment's hesitation he proposed in the following abrupt fashion:

"Say, sis! My bishop told me to take a week's holiday, and come down here and get a wife. Now, if you don't mind going back with me, I shall start to-morrow morning."

The next morning, at seven o'clock, the young lady was to be seen standing by the Englishman's wagon with a sunbonnet on her head and a bundle under her arm. They went to the Endowment House, got sealed for all eternity, and started for home. Hundreds of girls in Utah have been won "for all eternity" with just as little trouble. They must have been girls of *rather* more than average mortal intelligence, if in the time taken to form their decision they could tell from the little they know of the men who had proposed to them, that they would be willing to live with them "for time ;" but to make a bargain for "eternity" with so little ground to rest upon, certainly does seem a little rash.

The Mormons, of all people, with their peculiar notions respecting the eternity of the marriage contract, should be careful whom they marry. But, to tell the truth, they are the most careless.

There is living in Utah, to-day, a woman whom I know, who has been sealed "for all eternity" to no less than nine husbands; and if the divorces which she has obtained are, as Brother Brigham says, not worth the paper upon which they are written, she will be likely to have some trouble when she meets them all in another world. I know of several others who have been sealed to four, five, or six husbands! One of Brigham's own sisters was the wife of several husbands after this fashion. How all these matters can be set right it is difficult to determine, but somebody will have work to do.

Mormonism had been, to my husband, everything. It had for years grown with his growth, until it had become a part of himself. Doubts had occasionally crept into his mind, it is true, but it required time to effect a change. The measures adopted by Brigham Young in the spring of 1869, for the purpose of controlling the commerce of Utah, as well as the property and faith of the people, caused great discontent. The teachings of the Tabernacle were wild and arrogant, and Brigham assumed that it was his right to dictate in everything, "even," he said, "to the setting up of a stocking or the ribbons which a woman should wear." Many of the people, when they heard these words and witnessed the fanaticism created thereby, were aroused to opposition, but Brigham only became more fierce in his denunciations and more harsh in his measures.

I could plainly see that all this had the, to me, much desired effect of alienating my husband from Mormonism, and I never allowed an opportunity of strengthening the impression thus produced to pass unimproved. The articles in his paper showed the condition of his mind, and brought down upon him the wrath of Brigham. At this also I rejoiced, and did not fail to make him feel that he ought to resent the Prophet's interference. Brigham felt too certain of the submission of his slave, and accused Mr. Stenhouse of having published favorable notices of Gentile stores, also of having their advertisements in his paper, and otherwise aiding and abetting the wicked Gentiles,—all which accusations my husband began to feel was an infringement upon his own private personal rights as a citizen and a man. One circumstance followed another, and I could plainly see that his confidence in Brigham's inspiration was slowly but surely dwindling away, and that the day which I had so long anxiously watched for was breaking at last. Notwithstanding this, however, there was one bond which still united him by no weak tie to the Church—he was a Polygamist. The contemplated marriage between him and Brigham's daughter could, I believed, never now take place; but even allowing that, he still had another wife; and now that I had entirely lost faith in Mormonism generally, and the "Celestial Order of Marriage" in particular, I resolved that I would no longer have a partner in my husband's affections—as if he were a "joint-stock concern!"—I would have the whole of a husband, or none. I had not yet, however, sufficient courage to speak to him of my feelings.

I can imagine I see some strong-minded woman smile at the idea of a wife wanting courage to speak to her husband. But such women never knew what Mormonism is. Had they been born Gentiles, they would probably never have entered the Mormon Church; had they been born in the Church they would have been what John Stuart Mill calls "subjugated." John Stuart Mill considered the "Subjugation of Women" among the Gentiles a hard thing, and he wrote a pamphlet and "expressed his mind" about it. But I fancy, if he could have known the iron cruelty of Mormon Polygamy; if he could have seen how the hearts of women are crushed and ground down by the "Celestial" Order among the Saints, until not a spark of womanhood remains in them; if he could have seen the "Subjugation of Women" in Utah, he would have considered *their* case a thousand times harder than that of their Gentile sisters and would never have ceased writing pamphlets or "expressing his mind."

One Sunday evening, Mr. Stenhouse, when he came home,

said to me: "Brother Brigham has given me a mission; he wishes me to go to Ogden and publish my paper there."

This was very unexpected news; but with the vividness of lightning, a glimpse of what the Prophet intended by such a strange proposition flashed across my mind. " He wishes to ruin us!" I exclaimed; " You surely will not go!"

Now Brigham, of course, knew that my husband's paper had a large circulation in Utah Territory as well as in Salt Lake City, and that his business was in a most prosperous condition; he knew also that to do aught that might impair or destroy that business, would be to bring misery and disaster upon all who were dependent upon it for their daily bread. And yet, for all that, he told my husband to break up his establishment, or in his own words, to "pull up root and branch," and go to a place where the people were so miserably poor that it was impossible to make a newspaper successful among them.

In all this the crafty Prophet no doubt acted wisely. The *Daily Telegraph* would in all probability become a power in the Territory, and he feared that in a short time it would emancipate itself from his control. Brother Brigham has none of the far-seeing perception of the eagle—that perception which has enabled great men to forecast coming events, and thus, to a great extent, mould them when they came. His is more the cunning, crafty eye peculiar to cats, which are blinded when the pure light from heaven falls upon them, but are very quick indeed to perceive the very smallest thing which transpires in holes and dark places within their own contracted little circle of vision. No man can be sharper or more quick-sighted than Brigham in his own circle and within range of his own mental powers; but his circle is limited, and beyond it his mental powers never soared.

I do not doubt that, long before this time, he had noted that my husband was weakening in the faith; but he had waited for his opportunity, and now he considered that it had come. We knew very well that this was the way in which he had always acted towards those whom he feared or doubted:

—when he saw them growing weak in the faith he ruined them, or did the best he could to that effect, before they finally left the Church. I urged my husband to resist this arbitrary decree on the part of the Prophet, and represented strongly the misery which would result from his failure, and the utter impossibility of success. But I soon found that, though he doubted Brigham, his faith in Mormonism was by no means all gone—he, like many another, feared that in disobeying Brigham, perhaps, after all, he might be resisting God. He could see the wrong-doing of the Prophet, and felt that his conduct was unworthy of one who pretended to such great things; but he regarded this as the weakness of the Prophet's humanity, at the same time believing that in matters of religion he might be divinely inspired. He was still under the influence of the past—he could not yet break asunder the yoke, and bid defiance to Brigham and the Priesthood. He told me that now was the time for him to prove his obedience, cost what it might; and all the brethren urged him to submit, saying that the Lord would overrule everything for his good.

Believing this, he broke up his establishment at Salt Lake City, and went, as "counselled," to Ogden. There he remained for several months, during which time he was losing money every day. Finding at last that he could stand it no longer, he asked Brigham Young's permission to return and recommence his paper in Salt Lake City, for no one then dared stir a foot without permission. This was granted, for Brigham had now accomplished his purpose. But some of our friends told me that the teachers, when making their weekly visits, were telling the people not to take in Brother Stenhouse's paper again, if he came back to Salt Lake City, for he was apostatising, and they must not sustain an Apostate. Now, I thought, my husband will believe that I was right in my judgment of Brigham's motives.

My own family and that of the second wife, did not accompany my husband to Ogden; he was therefore quite at home when he returned, but the expense of transferring his business

from one place to another was perfectly ruinous. He had
not only purchased valuable property, as I before mentioned,
in the City, but he had also realised quite a comfortable little
fortune by the success of his paper; but now the property
had to be mortgaged, and his fortune was, of course, utterly
insufficient for these heavy daily losses. Just then, the severe
illness of my eldest son, in San Francisco, made it necessary
that we should leave immediately to attend him, for we had
received intelligence that he was not at all likely to recover.
As it was my own son who was sick, my husband had very
naturally determined that I should accompany him; but this
brought on such a severe fit of jealousy on the part of his
young wife, who already was by no means too happy, that
when we returned, after my son's recovery, she threatened to
obtain a divorce. My husband told me of this, but I had so
frequently heard such threats from wives who were unhappy
or neglected that I thought little about it.

One day, not long after our return, I was quite surprised to
see Mr. Stenhouse and Joseph A. Young drive up to the
door, looking as if something of great importance had just
transpired. Mr. Stenhouse jumped out of his buggy and
hurriedly gave me a letter, as I thought,—at the same time
saying, "Take great care of this for it makes me a free man
again." Saying this, he left the house, jumped into the buggy
again, and was gone, while I stood holding the paper, wondering what it all could mean.

My husband had told me to "take care" of the paper. He
neither said "read it" or "don't read it," and, of course, I was
not in the least curious. The envelope was not sealed, so I
made up my mind that, though he had not said so, he must
have wished me to read what was inside, and at any rate I resolved to risk doing so. To my astonishment I found that the
document which he said set him free, was nothing else than
a bill of divorce between him and his young wife. It appeared
afterwards that she had been to Brother Brigham, had told
him of her grievances, and had asked for a divorce.

Now when the wife of any man who is of good standing in

the Church, and whom Brigham wishes to honor, comes to him for a divorce, he generally sends for the husband *first*, tells him about it, and they talk it over together. The husband is counselled to "make the matter up," and a compromise is effected. In the case of my husband, Brigham acted otherwise. The clerk had been directed to make out the papers, which the second wife signed, and, as far as she was concerned, her marriage was dissolved. My husband was then notified that he was wanted at the Prophet's office, and he had a very shrewd guess as to what the nature of the business was for which his presence was desired. He waited till the afternoon when he knew that Brigham would be absent, and then as he was driving out with Joseph A., the Prophet's son, he drew up before the office and asked Joseph to accompany him inside in order to witness a little business which he had to transact. Joseph agreed; but when he found what the business really was, he strongly urged my husband not to sign the papers, or, at least, to take time and consult with President Young first. Mr. Stenhouse, however, never for a moment doubted that Brigham had expected by this hasty move to bring him to his feet, and he would not therefore yield. So, asking the clerk for the papers, he signed them, and Joseph also signed them as a witness—the other witness was David Mackenzie, Brigham's clerk. Belinda had already affixed her name. Ten dollars were then handed over as the usual fee; My husband took one copy of the "bill of divorce," the wife had a right to a second copy, and the third was deposited in the archives of Zion. My husband had then, as we have seen, hastened home to tell me that he was "a free man:"—and yet these two had been "sealed" to each other at the altar in the Endowment House *"for all eternity !"*

This is the way that divorces are granted in Utah:—there is not the slightest difficulty about them, if only Brother Brigham is willing. The reader would, perhaps, be interested in seeing one of these terrible documents. I therefore append a true, perfect, and exact copy of my husband's own bill of divorce. It is a *fac simile*—type, signatures, and all. This is

a specimen of an orthodox divorce among the *bon ton* in Salt
Lake City.   Out in the Settlements they do things in a much
more primitive style, and some of their documents are rather
amusing.   The following is a correct copy of a Mormon divorce bill taken from the records of Beaver City :—

March 8th 1871

To whomsoever it may concern

This is to certify that in the beginning of 1869 when I gave a bill of divorce
to Sarah Ann Lowry I gave to her for the good of her four children the following property viz A parcel of land of about nine acres enclosed all around with a
house of two rooms and one cow and heifer

WILLIAM C RITTER

I could, if space permitted, give many others equally interesting.

I cannot say that I was much grieved at the sight of my husband's divorce.   At the same time, long training in the school of
trouble had hardened my heart and rendered me almost indifferent, and I cannot say that I very greatly rejoiced.   Nature
adapts us morally, as well as physically, to the positions which
we have to occupy in life.   The hand of him who labors much
becomes hard, and the unshodden foot grows horny, and the
heart which at first is tender and, like the æolian harp, ready
to answer to the slightest passing breath, by and by, beneath
the rough hand of trial and the world, becomes callous and
stony, and the roughest storms and the sweetest pleasures
alike seem to make little impression upon it.

Thus it was with me when I received that paper.   A few
years before, a reliable assurance that my husband would never
enter into Polygamy would have been to me the realisation of
my best earthly wishes.   But now my heart was almost dead,
and I felt as if I hardly cared one way or the other.   If I felt
thus, who had still all my darling children around me, who
had never missed one dear little face from the fireside or from
the table ; what must have been endured by those mothers
who not only gave away their husbands to other wives, but
who lost child after child, until, bereft of all they loved on
earth, they could but, like Rachael, sit down in ashes and
mourn for the dead ?

DUPLICATE.

Know all Persons by these Presents:—That we the undersigned _Patriai B McEntire_ and _Belinda Stenhouse_ _____ his Wife, before her marriage to him _Belinda Pratt_ do hereby mutually **Covenant, Promise** and **Agree** to **DISSOLVE** all the relations which have hitherto existed between us as HUSBAND AND WIFE, and to keep ourselves **Separate** and **Apart** from each other, from this time forth.

In Witness Whereof We have hereunto set our hands at _Salt Lake City_ this _25_ day of _November_ A. D. 18 _69_

Signed in the Presence of

Joseph Young Jr
_Wm. H. S._

P. B. McEntire

Belinda Stenhouse

But the more I thought over what had happened, the more doubtful I felt as to what the result would be. That there would be some great change in our life, I felt assured ; but to me the change was coming almost too late. Then, too, the young wife who in her hasty anger had obtained the divorce.— I felt that her happiness must surely be gone, and I could not bear the thought that my peace should be purchased with the sorrows of another. Brother Brigham's part in the matter was also ever present in my mind. That he had resolved to bring ruin upon my husband I did not now for a moment doubt. But if a weak woman's efforts could in any way assist in thwarting his designs, I fully resolved that he never should have the satisfaction of seeing those designs successful. I would stand by my husband, I would work for, and assist, him, and would give not even a passing thought to what I might have suffered, or remember that he had ever loved others better than myself. I would be to him now the true wife that before God I had vowed to be, for worse as well as for better; and however I myself might have been wronged, I would, for my part, endeavor faithfully to perform my whole duty to my husband and to God.

After I had formed this mental resolution, and had begun to realise our new position, I felt as if awakening from a long dream of many years ;—I was released from the clutches of that frightful nightmare—Polygamy ; and I could once more take my place beside my husband as his wife. I knew that he would have much to contend against, and would need all the moral support that I could accord to him. Brigham's efforts in respect to my husband's paper had been far too successful, and although it was still carried on, fresh difficulties sprang up every day. My husband had been deceived by Brigham's oily manner and plausible way ; but to others his intention in sending him away was no secret. A man, named Bull, who is now and was also at that time, employed in the *Deseret News* office, said that no one but Mr. Stenhouse had ever been deceived by what the Prophet had done—it was commonly reported that Brigham intended to ruin my husband, and that

34

when he prophesied that the paper in Ogden should be a great success, he was himself perfectly aware that it was utterly impossible that such should be the case.

Whether Brigham was the deceiver or the deceived, I do not wish to say. Men who consider themselves inspired, and go on day by day uttering all sorts of nonsense and blasphemy, and giving impertinent and mischievous advice in the " name of the Lord,"·at last become thoroughly impervious to reason, and daily and hourly deceive themselves. I hope, for his own sake, it was so with Brigham, for I would rather believe him a self-made fool than a downright knave ; and in many of his transactions—perhaps I ought almost to say *all*—it is clear to every one that he is either one or the other. Of one thing I am certain,—I was fully contented that we should lose all, if only my husband were taken, once and for ever, clean out of the meshes of Mormonism. We might have to make a terrible sacrifice, but to me it was a sacrifice well worth the making.

CHAPTER XL.

MARY BURTON—LIFE'S JOURNEY ENDED · REST AT LAST.

Sent for in Haste—"Sister Mary had taken Poison"—Mary's Troubles—Elder Shrewsbury's Wives—Removing to Salt Lake City—Domestic Life without Love—A Wife's Despair—A Divided Household—Seeking Sympathy—The forsaken Wife—The change which Polygamy produced in a Husband—Comforting a heartbroken Wife—Dark thoughts—Waiting for the End—Mary attempts to destroy Herself—A Painful Story—Heartless conduct of Elder Shrewsbury—A Wife's Curse—Shadows of the Night—Broken-Hearted—The Little Medicine Chest—A fatal Potion—Elder Shrewsbury visits his dying Wife—"What a Curse was there!"—With my dying Friend—Life's Journey Ended—Rest at last.

IT was about this time that one morning, very early, before I was well up, a young girl came to the house in a great hurry, asking to speak to me without a moment's delay.

I threw a wrapper round me, and went out at once to see her. She said she came from the house of Sister Mary Burton, and begged me to come directly and see her, for Mary had taken poison and it was thought she was dying.

Now, I have been so much engaged of late in telling my own sorrows, that Mary Burton has quite dropped out of my story. But it must not be supposed that all that time I saw nothing of my poor friend. On the contrary, I had seen her much more frequently of late than I used to when I first came to Salt Lake City. When I last spoke of her it was when she was about to return to Southern Utah, where she and her husband then resided. It was evident to me from her conversation, as it must have been to the reader, that her faith in Mormonism had even then entirely gone, that she felt her husband's neglect and unkindness most keenly, and that she had become a miserable, broken-hearted woman. It was very painful to contrast what she now was with what she had been when I first knew her, and then to think what a happy wife and mother she might have been if the spectre of Mormonism had not crossed her path.

Mary and her husband, Elder Shrewsbury, left the Settlements about a year after the time I last mentioned her, and took up their abode in Salt Lake City. Elder Shrewsbury had prospered exceedingly, and when he came to Salt Lake he brought with him, besides Mary, his second wife, Ellen, who, as we before noticed, had become very much attached to her. The other three wives and their children were left at the farm in Southern Utah. He would probably have brought them all with him, had there been in the City a house large enough to hold them all. As it was, he purchased a good lot about half a mile from where we resided, with a comfortable house upon it ; and there his first and second wives lived together. This was the man who had solemnly sworn before God, that *he* would *never* practice Polygamy ! But I doubt if Elder Shrewsbury, with his comfortable house in the City, his farm and lands in the South, his fast increasing property, and his many wives, felt truly the hundredth part of the happiness which he would have experienced in the devotion of *one* faithful heart, even had it been in the midst of poverty and care. He, however, poor infatuated man, did not think thus ; he was actually even now courting a young girl of about seventeen years of age, who the two wives daily expected would be brought home to aid in building up their husband's " Kingdom." I do not think Mary cared much about this. It was the taking of the first plural wife that was her great sorrow. After that, her love for her husband weakened, until it altogether died out, and she did not care how many wives he took.

Mary's high spirit was always urging her into rebellion. In married life both husband and wife give way to each other in a thousand little things, of no consequence in themselves, but quite sufficient, without the presence of love, to sow the seeds of discord. But when love has fled, and the husband looks upon his wife—the companion of his youth, the mother of his children—not as the partner of his whole life and the sharer of all his joys and sorrows, but as a person whose presence is a reproach to him and who is an inconvenience rather than otherwise ;—and when the wife regards her husband as one whom formerly she loved with true devotion, but who has cruelly broken her heart and trampled upon her feelings, and who is nothing to her now but a tyrant whose very presence is painful to her,—can there then be any forbearance, any of those gentle kindnesses, any of those loving forgivenesses, any of those mutual tendernesses and sweet confidences which constitute the charm of married life, and make it what the Apostle said it was—a type of the sacred union between Christ and His people in heaven.

In giving up Mormonism, my unhappy friend gave up, as too many have done, faith in all else. She had lived, as she thought, a life of religion ; and when she found what a terrible mockery of all that is holy that so-called religion was, she cast it aside, thinking that all religion was vain. She did not see that she would have acted just as wisely in rejecting all food because she chanced to partake of some that was poisoned ; she did not see that, although the broken reed on which she rested was unable to yield her any true support, nevertheless the everlasting foundations of Eternal Truth which God Himself has laid can *never* be removed ; and that though creeds and systems may fail and pass away, only to give place to·others equally unsatisfactory, yet those divine verities are established for ever, are beyond the reach of earthly vicissitudes, and know nothing of time or change.

Utterly miserable and sick at heart, Mary cared not whether she lived or died. There was nothing to bind her to life, and beyond the life of this world she was altogether without hope. A more wretched existence it is scarcely possible to imagine.

While they were still in the Settlements, she treated the other wives with the greatest contempt, sitting by them at the table or passing them in the house without vouchsafing a look or a word. Her husband, as might be expected, avoided her whenever it was possible, and the other wives returned her coldness and disdain, and in turn annoyed her as much as they could when they were not too busy looking after one another. It would be impossible to picture a house more divided against itself than was that of Elder Shrewsbury.

When the two wives, Ellen and Mary, lived together with their husband in Salt Lake City, Mary, of course, had no opportunity of showing her hatred and contempt for the Polygamic wives. But towards her husband she evinced a cold disdain, as if he were now nothing at all to her—as if her very heart itself had been withered. For Ellen, who since Elder Shrewsbury had taken his other wives had clung to her with a child-like affection, and to her own little girl alone, she showed that deep and constant love which she had once lavished upon such an unworthy object.

She used to come to me and tell me all her griefs ; and in a passion of rage and tears she would hurl defiance at Mormonism and curse bitterly the system that had wrecked her life. Then I would soothe her, and speak calmly to her, and try to place matters in their best light; and she would sit and listen in a painful state of apathy as if she cared for none of these things. Presently she would rise and go, and then, perhaps, I would not see her for weeks together, unless I chanced to call upon her at her own house. Sometimes, for days and even weeks at a time, she would shut herself up in her room and refuse to see her husband or any one else, except her little girl, who slept in the same room with her, and who at such times used to bring in what food they wanted ; for in these melancholy fits she would not even let the servants come near her.

There was a little table near the window, and from the case-ment of the window could be seen in the far distance the lofty ranges of the Wahsatch Mountains. And sitting at that table, gazing from that window, with her cheek resting upon her hand, Mary would watch the whole day long as if entranced in some ecstatic vision. Her little girl—a child of winning ways, bashful to an extreme and very pretty, but, though so young, with a look of wistful sadness upon her childish face—had become accustomed to her mother's ways ; and when one of these long spells of melancholy came upon her, she would either steal out quietly and wander away for a long walk all by herself—for she never played with the other children in her father's house—or else, as was more frequently the case, she would sit down on the ground near her mother and silently amuse herself with a book or some childish toy.

To my mind there was something inexpressibly painful in all this. When Mary did not come to see me, I would call round at her husband's house, and try to draw her out from her melancholy seclusion. It was very seldom that I saw Elder Shrewsbury, and I cannot say that I wished to do so. He had, as his wife told me, undergone a complete change since I knew him in England.—The open look, the upright bearing, the earnestness of speech, which then characterised him, were now gone for ever. He was still a handsome man, rather portly, and evidently well to do in the world ; but there were lines about his eyes which ought not to have been seen in the face of a man of his years ; and his lips, without uttering a word, told their own story. I could remember watching those lips—rather full and voluptuous even then—in the old days when Polygamy was unknown and Mormonism came upon us in all its freshness and stirred our very souls to their utmost depths.—Then they seemed instinct with the thought and intellect of the man, and their very expression conveyed a meaning almost as eloquent as the words which proceeded from them. Now they were listless and heavy ; and if any expression hovered around them still, it was an expression of sensuality and selfishness. Was it, I sometimes asked myself, Polygamy that ruined that man ; or was there in his nature—hidden of course in early days—that which led him to Polygamy, and which, had there been no Mormonism, would have developed itself in some other degrading way?

Heartbroken and wretched, weary of life, and yet with no hopeful assurance of life beyond the grave, poor Mary lived on year after year, while those who seemed to dance in the very sunshine of existence were cut off like the summer flowers in the harvest-field. Lately, however, I thought I saw symptoms of a change. The pitcher may be taken often to the fountain, but it will be broken at last, and this poor, weak body of ours, wonderful as its powers of endurance are, cannot last for ever. With a mind at ease and happy, we can bid defiance to many of the ills which flesh is heir to, but when the mind is troubled, and the heart is weary, and the flesh also is weak, the thread of life is ready at any moment to be snapped asunder.

I saw this clearly in the case of my poor friend. Every time she came to see me, or I called at her house, I noticed that she was perceptibly growing thinner and thinner; her eye seemed brighter, and there was always a flush upon her cheek, which would have been beautiful had it not been for the seal of melancholy which was stamped upon every feature. But the brightness of the eye, and the flush upon the cheek, were not symbols of health, but the imprint of the finger of death.

She did not know this. Though she longed to die, she little thought that death was so near her. Sometimes she would talk almost happily of the old by-gone days; then she would sit brooding over her griefs; and then again she would talk anxiously about the future of her little daughter. I had seen other wives as wretched as poor Mary was,—aye, more so, for they had abject, grinding poverty superadded to all their woes;—but, more than for any other I felt for my poor friend, and exerted myself to the uttermost to comfort her. In this I had been to a certain extent successful. She would appear for a time a little more cheerful, but it was not long before she relapsed into her habitual melancholy way.

That which troubled me most of late, in my intercourse with Mary, was the fact that she was always talking about *death*. This certainly was no matter of surprise to me, but it was very painful. Over and over again she would discuss the question—whether under *any* circumstances suicide could be justified, and whether if any one, in absolute despair were to take away their own life, God would ever pardon them.

I would never enter into such subjects as these, for I considered that such conversation showed a morbid condition of mind, could not possibly be of any good to either of us, and would only suggest harmful thoughts. But again and again Mary reverted to the subject, and I really at last began to grow quite anxious about her.

It was not, therefore, with surprise that I received the summons that morning. I did not wait to ask any questions about the poisoning, but hastened to the bedside of my unfortunate friend, trusting that I might yet be in time to render some assistance.

I found her lying on the bed, partly dressed, and, as it seemed to me at first, asleep. There was, at the bedside, and bending over her, the second wife, who was in as much trouble as if the sufferer had been her own sister. The poor girl had been weeping, and was evidently very much distressed. There was also present in the room another sister, whom I recognised as a friend of Mary's. The little daughter of the unfortunate woman was there as well. One person, whom every one would naturally have expected to see at the bedside of a dying wife under such circumstances, was conspicuous by his absence,—I mean, of course, Elder Shrewsbury himself.

I sat down on the bed, beside poor Mary, and took her hand in mine. It was cold but damp, and her breathing was somewhat heavy. She was still unconscious. I asked the pretty pale-faced girl—the second wife—who was bending over her, how it had all happened, and whether they had had a doctor.

"Oh, yes," she said, sobbing all the time, "we sent for the doctor, and he has only just gone. He said he had done all he could, and that we could let her sleep on now."

She then told me what had taken place. It appeared that the night before, Elder Shrewsbury had gone up into Mary's room to speak to her about a matter of some importance. Although living in the same house she had not seen him for several weeks, and the mere fact of being in his presence agitated her. He told her he had come to talk about her child —little Mary, called Mary after her mother. For some reason or other, which nobody then seemed to understand, Elder Shrewsbury had taken a fancy that the child should be separated from her mother; he wanted to send her to stay with his other family in the Settlements, and it was for this purpose he came to see Mary that night. It certainly did seem the refinement of cruelty to separate the child from her poor mother, who would thus have become, as one might say, doubly widowed; and I am strongly inclined to question whether Elder Shrewsbury's motives were of the purest kind. It is, however, only just to state, that subsequently, when speaking to a friend about the matter, he said that he had long noticed in his wife what he considered were incipient symptoms of madness, and he thought that his duty towards the child imperatively demanded that he should immediately take her away from her mother. He added—as was indeed true—that his other wives in the South would have taken the greatest care of her.

Mary was furious when the proposal was made to her. She bitterly upbraided her husband for all his cruelty and neglect, she cursed him for his perfidy, and she vowed that nothing but death should separate her from her little girl.

Elder Shrewsbury trembled at the anger of his poor forsaken wife, and he crept out of her room and downstairs. But Mary could not be appeased. She went to the room of the second wife—the only creature in the house, besides her little girl with whom she sometimes condescended to hold intercourse—and there she acted in a very wild and extrav-

"AND IT SHALL COME TO PASS THAT AT EVENTIDE THERE SHALL BE LIGHT."

`agant way. It was with great difficulty that she was at last persuaded to lie down and take a little rest. She would not go to her own room; so Ellen—the second wife—persuaded her to remain with her all the night. She lay down, but did not sleep. She muttered strange things, and by and by sat up in the bed and spoke as if people were present whom she had known years and years ago. Ellen was frightened; but out of love to Mary, and not wishing that others should see her in that crazy condition, she did not call for help, thinking that presently she would fall asleep and in the morning all would be right. But the long night passed away, and just before day-break Ellen fell into a sort of fitful slumber. It would seem that just then poor Mary discovered for the first time that she was not sleeping in her own room, and that her little daughter was not with her. Distracted as her mind was, she probably thought that they had stolen the child away, and went in search of her.

She found her way to her own room, and then what happened no one, of course, could tell. She must have seen that her child was safe; and it is not unlikely that, reassured on that point, she felt that she needed rest, and thought that it would be best to take some sedative to produce the sleep which she believed would restore her to herself again. She had in her room a little leather medicine-chest—a very useful article for any one travelling, or to keep in the house—and to that she must have had resort. Certain it is, that when, an hour later, Ellen awoke and went to see what had become of her husband's first wife, she found the little medicine-chest open upon the bureau, Mary lying upon the bed, apparently asleep, and a faint sickly smell, which one better versed in such things would have known was the smell of opium, pervading the whole room.

Ellen began to scream and call for help, and one of the women about the house, who was up at that early hour, came to see what was the matter. She, upon hearing what Ellen said, rushed downstairs shrieking for assistance. Fortunately for every one, Elder Shrewsbury, who had just risen, was

standing in the hall-way below. He took hold of the noisy
woman and asked her what was the matter, and after hearing
all she had to say he sent her to attend to her domestic duties,
with a strict injunction to say nothing to a living soul about
what she had seen or heard.

Elder Shrewsbury then went up to Mary's room, and there
he learned that all that the silly woman had just said to him
was quite true. He, however, betrayed no emotion. Very
calmly he put the stopper back into the laudanum bottle, then
looked at his watch and hesitated, all the while that pale-
faced Ellen was looking anxiously at him, wanting to know
what she could *do*. After a few moments of indecision, Elder
Shrewsbury turned to Ellen and said, "Yes; go for the
doctor."

Ellen flew upon her mission.

Meanwhile, Elder Shrewsbury looked towards the bed
where poor Mary lay—Mary, for whose love he had perjured
his soul—Mary who never would have been his had he not
given that sacred promise, the breaking of which made him
an outlaw from heaven and a thing to be despised of men.
He looked for one single moment at his poor wife as she lay
there, and then he turned upon his heel and went out of the
room. For the wealth of all the world I would not feel as
that man felt, if the thoughts which then crowded upon his
brain were what, for the sake of our common humanity, I
trust they were. The remembrance of the life which his folly
or fanaticism—it matters little which—had blasted; the
thought of that solemn vow which he had taken to love her
only and for ever; the sight of that dear one to whom he
had once plighted his troth, now desolate, forsaken, almost
maniac in her wretchedness.—Oh God! what a curse was
there for any man's soul to bear !

The physician, when he came, administered an emetic and
made them walk the patient about the room. Ellen and
the friend of Mary who was present volunteered for this
service. They supported her, one on each side, and paced
her round and round the room, thus compelling her to exer-

tion; and from time to time they made her swallow doses of strong coffee, in which a little brandy had been mixed. When, at length, signs of returning consciousness were apparent, the physician left, promising to call again in the course of the morning.

It was then that some one present thought of sending for me, and I arrived not long after the physician had gone. I was the only person, outside the family, beside the friend whom I have mentioned, who knew of any thing that had taken place—so careful were they that the matter should not get abroad; and I should certainly not have been summoned had it not been for the close intimacy which existed between Mary and myself, which made us more like sisters than friends. The reader must not, however, suppose that in relating this I am even now betraying a trust; for my friends in Utah know as well as I do that so many unhappy wives have in their desperation been driven to attempt self-destruction, that having no clue in the name, which solely out of love for my poor friend, I have all through this narrative given her, they will not know who to fix upon as the person to whom I allude.* There is, however, *one* still living—*he* will know—let his own conscience be his accuser.

In about half an hour's time, Mary began to recognise those who were around her, but she did not seem disposed to speak. She opened her eyes and looked dreamily at me for a long time, but the slight pressure of my hand was her only recognition of my presence. I bent down over her and whispered a few assuring words in her ear, and for a moment a faint, weary smile lighted up her thin, pale face. It was not like the sweet smiles of the by-gone days which used to suffuse her whole countenance with sunshine—it was but the very ghost of a smile. Presently she sank into a gentle slumber; but I still sat by her on the bed, holding her hand in mine, and I

* Besides poor Mary's family, in *every* other instance [with the solitary exception of Sister Ann—my "talkative friend"—who is still living and is so well known in Salt Lake City,] I have been as scrupulous in giving *real* names as I have been in stating only facts which I had either witnessed or knew beyond question were true.

remained there for two or three hours. Then, after seeing that every thing was at hand which she could possibly want if she awoke, and assured by Ellen that she would not leave her until she was able to sit up, I left for my own home.

At the bottom of the stairs, in the hall-way, I was confronted by Elder Shrewsbury himself. This surprised me, as hitherto he had most sedulously avoided coming in contact with me. He gave me one searching glance, as if to read my thoughts, and then said :. " Sister Stenhouse, this is a most unhappy affair, but say nothing about it—no good can come of talking of such matters."

I assured him that for Mary's sake—not for his—I would not speak of what had transpired; but when he held out his hand for me to shake I affected not to see it, but wished him good-morning, and left the house.

*   *   *   *   *   *   *

For some time she said nothing to me about the sad event which had so greatly troubled us, and when at length she hesitatingly alluded to it, I was much relieved to find that the taking of the deadly drug was on her part wholly accidental. It was as I from the first suspected—for I knew and loved my dear friend too well to wrong her even by a thought. Cruelly as she had suffered, wretched and miserable as she was, bitterly as she felt, the instincts of her heart were too true and her nature too noble to allow of her seeking oblivion from her troubles in voluntary and premeditated death, as I have known was the case with many wretched Mormon wives. She had only thought to take an opiate to soothe the feverish excitement which had almost bereft her of reason, and, in the weak and enfeebled condition in which she was, the draught had been too powerful for her. Guiltless as she was, she dreaded that others might impute wrong motives to her in what she had done; and even to me she spoke of her sickness painfully and with hesitation.

After this, I called day after day upon my poor friend, until she was sufficiently recovered to walk about and even to get out of doors a little. The story of the unhappy attempt which she was supposed to have made upon her life, by some means, however, got rumored abroad, and she heard of it. She said nothing at the time, but I believe it preyed upon her mind. Weak and failing in health, as she long had been, the shock which her system had received was too much for her, and it was evident to every one who saw her that her earthly trials would soon be ended. She sank gradually, and life ebbed from her gently and without pain. A few days before she died, she sent for me, and I spent several hours with her. I might say that they were happy hours; for the near prospect of death seemed to have dispelled all those gloomy fears of the future life, which had for so many years troubled her soul; and she now looked forward with peaceful resignation to her approaching change. Death came at last to her when she was sleeping, and she passed away tranquilly and without a sigh. I almost rejoiced when I heard that at last her weary journey was over and she was at rest. She had been ever very dear to me, and I loved her with the fondest affection. But I shall never think of her without bitter feelings towards that unholy system which brought her to an untimely grave; for she of all others was one of the fairest flowers which were ever blighted by Mormonism and Polygamy.

CHAPTER XLI.

MY HUSBAND DISFELLOWSHIPPED—WE APOSTATISE—
BRUTAL OUTRAGE UPON MY HUSBAND AND MYSELF.

A Crisis—Effects of Superstition and Blind Obedience—Questioning Brother
Brigham's Authority—The Faithful are "Counselled" Against My Husband
—The School of the Prophets—Arbitrary Measures—My Husband is Dis-
fellowshipped—"I *Will* Be Free!"—The Breaking of Bonds—The Day of
Liberty—Asking to be "Cut Off" from the Church—A Brutal Outrage
Upon My Husband and Myself—The Secret Police—Who Were the Guilty?—
How the Bodies of Murdered Men are "Discovered!"—The Fate of Apos-
tates—Carrying Out the Teachings of Brigham—Who *Ought* to be Blamed—
What an Ill-Treated Wife Told Me—Brigham's Explanation—He Accuses
Belinda's Brothers—How Crimes Are Explained Away—Why Brigham
Withdrew an Offered Reward—What People Dared Not Say.

NOTWITHSTANDING all my own personal troubles
and the difficulties which surrounded us, the loss of my
dear friend affected me very deeply. And yet her story is
the same as might be told of hundreds of other English girls
who have been lured from their happy homes and have died
broken-hearted and neglected in Utah.

Now came that change in our life which I had so long
hoped for, but which had always seemed to me so very far
distant. We had been tossed by many a storm, but the
violence of this last gale was such that it forced us clean out
of the sea of Mormonism, and landed us high and dry upon
the firm ground of apostacy.

My husband had been so long engaged in the defence of

Mormonism that it had become almost a part of himself ;—its doctrines and observances seemed to him beyond a question, its weak and doubtful points were ignored, and implicit obedience to the behests of the Priesthood was with him an article of faith. When therefore I heard him, with others, talking over some of the questionable teachings of the Church, criticising Brigham's counsellings, 'doubting some of his measures, and speaking of him as they would of any of the other brethren, I was satisfied that his days of faith were numbered. The point that I had all along been aiming at was to get him to think for himself, for hitherto he had been a mere tool in the hands of the Priesthood. Long years of submission and receiving as divine inspiration all that a "Prophet" is pleased to say, necessarily benumbs the soul and withers its life, until unconsciously the victim becomes an abject slave. And this is the position to-day of many otherwise well-informed and intelligent people in the Mormon Church—they are mere automata.

About the time when my husband returned with his paper to Salt Lake City, the *Utah Magazine*, a liberal journal just struggling into existence, began to call in question some of Brigham's measures, and the editors, who were all men of some mark in the Mormon Church, presumed to hint that the people had rights and privileges as well as the Priesthood. This was done in a very quiet, unobtrusive way, but it was, nevertheless, pronounced rebellion and apostacy. My husband's paper was silent upon the subject; and, in consequence, he was suspected of being in league with the enemy. This was another good reason why the people should be "counselled" not to take in the *Telegraph*. Although he was not yet sufficiently advanced in thought to give much direct aid to the questioners of Brigham's authority, I saw with pleasure that he did not wish to oppose them ; the tone of his paper was evidently changing, and the articles which appeared from time to time gave serious offence to Brigham Young. This, however, was not all his wrong-doing ;—he had of late been neglectful in his attendance at the "School of the Prophets"

35

—a meeting which was then held every Saturday for the benefit of the Elders, but which has now for a time been discontinued, on account of some of the brethren turning traitor and revealing all that was said.

Together with the editors of the *Utah Magazine*, Mr. Stenhouse and one or two others were summoned to appear at the School on the following Saturday, to give their reasons for previous non-attendance. This they had all along anticipated, and were therefore not surprised at the summons, but they hardly expected that Brigham would act so precipitately; for, without waiting to hear their reasons, he disfellowshipped them all for irregular attendance.

Brigham's assumption of the right to disfellowship men from the Church because of irregular attendance at the School was a stretch of authority which startled my husband: "What will he not do next?" he said. "To submit would be to acknowledge him absolute, and me a slave. There is but one alternative now—slavery or freedom. Cost me what it may, I *will* be free!"

Those who have never been enslaved by a superstitious faith which mentally and bodily enthrals its devotees, as Mormonism does, can form no idea of the joy, the happiness, which is experienced when, after years of spiritual servitude, the shackles are burst asunder and the slave is "FREE!" There is pleasure even in the thought itself that one is free—free to think and free to act, free to worship according to the dictates of one's own conscience, and free to speak one's own opinions and sentiments, without the constant fear that some spy is listening to every word and that the consequences may be far from pleasant!

In August of the same year, my husband sent a respectful and kindly letter to the Bishop of our Ward, stating that he had no faith in Brigham's claim to an "Infallible Priesthood," and that he considered that he ought to be cut off from the Church. I added a postscript, stating that I wished to share my husband's fate—little thinking that within three days my request would be answered in a too literal manner.

A little after ten o'clock, on the Saturday night succeeding our withdrawal from the Church, we were returning home together. The night was very dark, and as our residence is in the suburbs of the City, north of the Temple block, and the road very quiet, the walk was a very lonely one and perhaps not altogether too safe. We had gone about a third of the way, when we suddenly saw four men come out from under some trees at a little distance from us. In the gloom of the night we could only see them very indistinctly, and could not distinguish who they were. They separated; and two of them came forward and stumbled up against us, and two passed on beside us. For a moment I thought that they were intoxicated, but it was soon clear that they were acting from design. As soon as they approached, they seized hold of my husband's arms, one on each side, and held him firmly, thus rendering him almost powerless. They were all masked, for it was supposed that thus we should not be able to discover their identity, and that if by any chance an investigation should subsequently be made into the doings of that night it would not be possible for any one to witness against them.

I am inclined to think that these wretches, when they planned the attack, had not calculated upon my being present with my husband, and I imagine that when they saw me with him they supposed I should scream and run away, after the manner of many women. In this, however, they were mistaken. I still clung to my husband's arm, but with my left hand caught hold of one of the ruffians by the collar of his coat; for I apprehended the worst, well knowing of what atrocities these men were capable. It is no secret that the police of Salt Lake City—for it is the police who there commit murders and other inhuman outrages—treat with the greatest brutality all the unhappy Gentiles and Apostates whose misfortune it is to fall into their power. This also is the wretched effects of the fanatical teaching of the Church. These men believe that Utah is Zion—the "Kingdom of God," and that citizens of the United States are but intruders upon this holy ground; that they ought to be driven out and despoiled of everything, and even murdered if opportunity offers. They make no secret of these feelings towards the Gentiles, and towards Apostate Mormons it is shown, if possible, in a somewhat stronger manner.

The movements of the two men who held my husband were somewhat impeded by my clinging to his arm, and they seemed to hesitate for a moment. The other two, who stood a few feet distant from us, also hesitated. One óf the men who held my husband said to them, "Brethren, do your duty." We recognised his voice at once as that of a certain policeman— a young man whom we had known in England when a child, and with whose family we had been upon the most friendly terms.

In an instant I saw them raise their arms, as if taking aim, and for one brief second I thought that our end had now surely come, and that we, like so many obnoxious persons before us, were about to be murdered for the great sin of apostacy. This, I firmly believe, would have been my husband's fate, if I had not chanced to be with him or had I run away;—they would probably have beaten him to death;—they, who I have every reason 'to believe were two of the regular and two of the special policemen;—and then, the next morning, they would have "discovered" the body, and it would have been said that he had been murdered by Gentiles or Apostates in a personal quarrel or a street brawl. My presence somewhat disarranged their plans, and it was that probably which caused the two men to hesitate, not knowing what would be considered their "duty" under present circumstances.

A much less noble fate than assassination was reserved for us. The wretches, although otherwise well armed, were not hold-´ing revolvers in their hands as I at first supposed. They were furnished with huge garden-syringes charged with the most disgusting filth, in the preparation of which they took especial pains. So kindred to their own base natures was such an act that I doubt not they found it quite a labor of love. The moment the syringes were pointed at us, my husband, thinking a shot was coming, moved his head, and thus to a certain

extent escaped the full force of the discharge. I, however. was
not so fortunate. My hair, bonnet, face, clothes, person—
every inch of my body, every shred that I wore—were in an
instant saturated, and my husband and myself stood there
reeking from head to foot.

The villains, when they had perpetrated this disgusting and
brutal outrage, turned and fled. We ran after them for some
little distance, but we had no arms and nothing with which
to defend ourselves; in fact we pursued them instinctively
rather than with any idea of overtaking them. There was
another man standing a little distance off in the direction in
which they were running, and we could not tell how many
might be concealed:—the place, too, was dark and lonely, for
they had gone behind the Temple block—a fit corner for murderers to skulk in; a convenient spot for the commission of
any unholy deed. I was burning with indignation, and longed
to revenge myself upon the brutal cowards who had assaulted
us. In my anger I called upon them to come and kill us outright, for I would have preferred death to such an indignity.
I almost wonder that they did not take me at my word and
return and finish their foul work, for they have long acted
upon the principle that "dead men tell no tales."

There were, at that time, in Utah, a great many special or
secret police who were always ready for any dirty, brutal, or
murderous work. Just near our home in Salt Lake City, there
is one miserable old fellow who has not yet been called to
account for his numerous crimes and villainies. In his younger
days he was one of these secret police, and, to judge from his
language, his only regret now is that he is no longer fit for
active service. He has often told a neighbor of mine, who he
believes is a good Mormon, that nothing would give him more
pleasure than to serve my husband and myself as he thinks
we deserve—simply because we have dared to oppose Mormonism. The wife of one of the men whom we had suspected,
not long after came to see me and told me that she did not
doubt that her husband had been engaged in the affair, for she
had accused him of it and he had not denied it. It seems

perhaps strange that any wife should act thus, but this poor woman had a great regard for me, but none at all for her husband who treated her most brutally.

I shall never forget that night. I declared that henceforth I would tear from my heart every association—every memory—every affection, which still remained to bind me to Mormonism—not one solitary link should be left. Henceforth I would be the declared and open enemy of the Priesthood. To the utmost of my power—weak though I might be—I would arouse the women of Utah to a sense of the wrongs which they endured; I would proclaim to the world the disgrace which Mormonism is to the great American nation, the foul blot that it is upon Christianity and the civilisation of the age!

I do not blame the mass of the Mormon people that such outrages as this can be perpetrated in their midst,—I blame the Priesthood, and I blame the leaders and their teachings. I know the honest hearts of the Mormon community at large, and that as a body they revolted at the atrocious wrong that had been done to us. Although no one who valued their standing in the Church dared openly express what they felt, hundreds did so in private; while the whole Gentile community was aroused and indignant, and letters came from all parts of the country, and visitors daily called upon me to express their sympathy.

My son-in-law, Joseph A. Young, on the night of the attack offered a reward to the chief of the police, for the apprehension of the ruffians; but we knew well enough they would never be discovered. A few Gentile friends also offered a reward of five hundred dollars for any evidence that might lead to their identification, but nothing, of course, was elicited. The Mormon paper, in order to divert attention from the guilty parties, insinuated that the outrage had been provoked by some family difficulty, and suggested that the brothers of my husband's second, and now divorced, wife were the offenders. This I knew was utterly false, for they were respectable young men who would have scorned such an action, and between them and my husband not the slightest ill feeling existed. I therefore sent a letter to Belinda, telling her what had been said and asking her to write to me stating that it was all untrue. I felt sure that she would willingly comply with my request, and I proposed, as I informed her, to publish her reply, and thus exonerate her brothers from all blame.

A lady who was present when Belinda received the note, told me that she asked her mother, who was also there at the time, what she should do about it, and that her mother said—"You had better take the letter to Brother Brigham, and do whatever he counsels you to do." She did so, and Brother Brigham told her to pay no attention to it. Brigham did not care whether her brothers or any one else were disgraced, or who was made the scapegoat, so that the vile minions of the Priesthood might escape undetected.

The suggestion that a personal difficulty or a family matter had provoked the outrage was by no means a new one. In the same way the "Indians" had been credited with many a deed of blood when Apostates fleeing from Zion were found murdered and horribly mangled in the Cañons or on the Plains. The same course also was adopted when Dr. Robinson, of whom I have already spoken, was assassinated. On the following Sunday, in the Tabernacle, Brigham Young suggested that the doctor had met his death in a gambling quarrel, and that some man whom he had personally wronged had dealt the fatal blow. But every one in Salt Lake City—whether Mormon or Gentile, Brigham Young included—knew that Dr. Robinson was innocent of any gambling predilections, and was the last man to make a personal enemy. Then Brigham offered a reward of five hundred dollars for the discovery of the murderers; but subsequently, when several of the brethren had been arrested, charged with that very crime, and indictments against them had been found by the Grand Jury, he withdrew his offer lest, as he said, some evil-minded person might commit perjury for the sake of the reward!

It was the same with ourselves. Every one could conjecture with tolerable accuracy who it was that had planned the outrage, but the reward which was offered was, as we well

knew it would be, all in vain.   Good Mormons did not dare to
express their thoughts ; but we all knew that the outrage was
the direct result of the teachings of the Tabernacle, and that
although the authorities might not, and probably did not,
directly command it, they connived at it, and never took the
first step towards the discovery of the wretched scoundrels
who perpetrated the deed.

CHAPTER XLII.

NOT long after our separation from the Mormon Church, I
received another visit from my talkative friend.

As according to her custom she was making a preliminary
"fuss" at the door before entering, I heard her voice, and was
at a loss to conjecture whether she came for the purpose of
lamenting my apostacy and entreating my immediate return
to the bosom of the Church, or to condole with me concerning the brutal outrage to which we had been subjected. In
both suppositions I was, however, mistaken—she came to talk
about her own woes.

"You'll be surprised, my dear Sister Stenhouse," she said,
"to see me looking so utterly miserable. I'm sure I must
look the picture of despair, and I feel it. You don't know

what I've been suffering, and how shamefully I have been used."

"You look very well I think, but I'm sorry to hear you have met with any difficulty," said I, when she stopped for a moment to take breath.

"Oh, you may say so," she replied, "but you know you don't think so in your heart. Why, I did not even stop to put on my bonnet straight," she said, stealing a look at the glass, "and I ran all the way here, for I felt as if I should die if I could not pour my sorrows into the bosom of some faithful-hearted friend. Oh! I have been treated shamefully, and I feel it the more as you know what a reserved woman I am and how seldom it is that I open my lips about family matters, even to my dearest friends!"

"Well, but," I said, "what really is the matter? You have not yet told me what your trouble is."

"Sister Stenhouse," she said, "you have had a few little vexations in the course of your life, I know, but they are nothing to compare to the frightful indignities that I have suffered in the course of the last few days. I never thought I should come to this! I hate every man in the place, and I detest my husband most of all, and I loathe his wives, and I execrate Brother Brig—"

"Why, Sister Ann, what can have happened?" I exclaimed, interrupting her.

"Happened!" she cried, starting from her chair in indignation, "I tell you, Sister Stenhouse, nothing has '*happened*'— nothing was done by chance—he did it all with his eyes open and against my advice—I tell you he did it *on purpose!*"

"Did *what?*" I asked, "and *who* was it that did it?" But by this time I had begun to form a shrewd guess as to *who* the culprit was.

"Why, he married that wretched little shrimp of a girl, with blue eyes, and red hair, and a die-away, lackadaisical manner— it was *he*—my husband, Henry—he married her this very day, and I tell you he did it on purpose!"

"I'm sorry that it annoys you," I said, "but really I am surprised after all you have said to me that you should care if he had taken half-a-dozen wives, to say nothing of the one he married this morning, and who you say is only a very little one.

"It doesn't matter the size, Sister Stenhouse," she said, "but the color of the eyes and the shade of the hair matters a great deal. If that miserable little minx had had black hair or green eyes I daresay Henry would not have cared two straws about her, unless he had done it out of sheer perversity, for all men are made of the same contrary stuff. But he dotes on blue eyes; I heard him myself tell her so one day, when I was listening to them through the crack of the door, and they didn't know I was so near. But my wounded feelings would not suffer me to remain silent, and I bounced in, and, said I,—Henry, how dare you talk such outrageous nonsense to that child in my presence?

"'But I didn't know you were present,' he said.

"I tell you," said I, "I'm quite disgusted with you; a man with three wives—and *me* one of them—to go talking twaddle to a little chattering hussy like that, with her cat's eyes and her red hair!"

"'Golden hair, my dear,' he said, 'Charlotte's hair is golden.'

"I say *red !*—it's straight, staring *red*—as red as red can be, I told him; and then we had a regular fight over it. I don't mean that we came to blows, but we had some hot words, and he went out and left us two alone. Then that young hussy was impudent, and I don't know how it was, but, somehow, when we left off our conversation I found some of Charlotte's red hair between my fingers; and there"—she said, innocently, holding out quite a respectable sized tuft of auburn hair,— "there; I put it to you, Sister Stenhouse, *is* that red, or is it not?"

I was about to reply; but, without waiting an instant, she dashed the stolen locks to the ground, and said—"I daresay Sister Stenhouse, you think me a little hasty, and yet among my friends I've always been quite proverbial for the calmness and evenness of my temper; but I've been tried very much

lately, and—if only you would not keep interrupting me, dear !—
if you'd just allow *me* to say a word or two in my turn !—I'd
tell you something that would open your eyes to the ingratitude and wickedness of men. I don't wonder that you have
left the Church ; I am thinking of doing so myself, and you
won't wonder at it when you hear what I've got to say. What
do you say to *my* leaving the Church ? Won't people be
astonished ? But I declare, Sister Stenhouse, I *do* seriously
mean to leave the Church as soon as I get my new bonnet—"

"Why your new bonnet ?" I asked in surprise.

"Because, dear, I shall become an object of interest. All
the sisters will have their eyes upon me, and even Gentiles
will say—There's a lady who had the courage to leave the
Mormon Church and quit an ungrateful husband who was not
worthy of her. And you know, Sister Stenhouse, it would not
do to have people looking at me and talking about me before I
got my new bonnet."

This was a rather amusing reason for delay in changing
one's religion, but it was quite characteristic of my friend. So
I humored her a little and tried to get her to explain how it
all came about:

"Oh yes," she said, "I ought to have told you that before, but
I was so angry at what had just happened that I forgot everything else. The fact is, my husband is *a man*, and there's no
calculating what a man will do. Women, you know, are proverbial for the constancy of their affections and their slowness
in changing their minds—you know when you're talking to a
woman that she *is* a woman, and you know exactly what to do
with her ; but with a man it's quite different. You can't calculate a man—you can't fathom him. When you've been
thinking one way and another, and at last begin to fancy you
know what to do, why then, a man—if it's him you've got to
do with—will turn just round, and while you've been making
everything smooth for him to do one thing, he'll go and do
exactly the opposite. I know what men are by this time, and
I speak from experience.

"It was just so with Henry and this girl. He has gone

quite against the grain with me, and I feel it all the more because he used to be so quiet and anxious to do exactly what I
wanted.   But he doesn't care a fig now whether I'm pleased
or not—he only thinks about this red-headed girl.   In fact he's
quite crazy about her, and if there's any sin in apostacy, you
may remember that it was he who drove me into it."

"That seems hardly fair," I said, "for you knew all along
that it was his privilege to take more wives."

"That's very true," she exclaimed, "it *is* his privilege to
take wives, but it's *my* privilege to choose them for him.   I'm
a good Mormon and I don't mind how many wives my husband takes, if he'll only act reasonably about getting them.
But, Sister Stenhouse, I do *not* want a parcel of girls about the
house.   I'm so far from wishing to usurp authority, that, as I
told Henry, I would not mind if his wives were even a little
older than me, but I won't have them younger.   It makes
Henry look so silly.   Why, to see him with that girl Charlotte,
now, who isn't more than half my own age—No ; I don't mean
that, I mean she's slightly younger than I am—you might
really almost imagine that he thought more of her than he
does of me.   I know he doesn't, for he has told me so, but
any one to see them together would get quite a wrong impression."

"When did he marry Charlotte?" I asked.   "You spoke so
hastily, Sister Ann, that I did not quite understand you."

"When ?   Why he married her this morning, as I thought
I told you—he has only just done it.—He said he was anxious
to be in a quiet state of mind to-day, so I gave him a piece of
my mind, and he was so astonished at the pointed way in
which I explained to him what a fool he'd been making of
himself that he quite showed it in his face.   The fact is, Sister
Stenhouse, he has lately become rather more than I could
manage.   About six months ago he seemed, I thought, to be
getting a little inattentive to his last wife, so I thought it was
quite time for me to see about finding him another.   So I
looked round, but didn't for some time meet with a suitable
person.   At last I found a very nice young woman, thirty-five

or forty years of age, who I thought would do. She was nice and tall—a little taller than Henry himself, but that didn't matter for she was stout in proportion. Henry would have it that she didn't look straight with her two eyes, but that was all nonsense. She was a nice, motherly woman, with a deep bass voice which sounds so well in large, fat women ; but though she wasn't what you would call handsome, she certainly wasn't plain. My reason in choosing her was that I thought she would do nicely for the housework and could look after the children, for I was forced to stay at home so much that it was quite injuring my health."

" A very good reason," I said.

" So I thought, dear," she replied ; "but I could not bring Henry to see it in that light. Whenever I spoke to him about her he said she was old enough to be his grandmother, and squinted. At last I got quite tired out, for I could never get him to call upon her, and when she came to the house he hardly said a word to her; so I got her to come and stay with us, for then I thought Henry would become accustomed to her presence. But he took to holding his tongue at meal times—the only times when we all met together—and it was as much as I could do to keep up the conversation, for you know I am naturally very taciturn. Then he suddenly took to attending all the Church meetings, and it was astonishing how many he discovered it was his duty to attend, he seemed to be absent almost every evening. The mystery to me was, what could have made him so pious all of a sudden—he seemed altogether too good—You can understand, Sister Stenhouse, that had there been any young girl at the meetings, to whom he had taken a fancy, it would have been useless for them to try to throw dust in *my* eyes—you know that *I'm* not likely to be deceived?"

I said that I did know it, and she continued:—

"There was one of the brethren—a near neighbor of ours, who, between ourselves, I think rather admires me, for he said once quite publicly that I beat every one he knew in conversation, and if that's not a compliment, I don't know what is:—

well, this brother I got to watch my husband. I told him that I did not want him to act as a spy upon his movements, as that would have been very mean. I only wanted him to watch carefully all that he said and did at the meetings and to notice who he spoke to, and if it was a meeting where women were admitted, to be doubly watchful, and especially to notice how he looked when he talked with any one. You see, Sister, I agree with you that it is quite right for us to look closely after our husbands, although, of course, I would be the last one to encourage a system of *espionage*."

I ventured to suggest that I had not expressed any opinion at all about watching our husbands, and said I believed there were not half-a-dozen women in Salt Lake City who would dare to think of such a thing.

"Well, never mind all that, Sister Stenhouse," she said, "If you did not have that opinion you might have had it, and it comes to much the same thing. I used to see the good brother I spoke of very frequently—in fact, almost every day—and the first question I always asked was—Did my husband come to meeting last night? As often as not he said he didn't know for he hadn't been himself, and after a month or more I had learned nothing, except that my husband was never seen with a lady at any of the meetings. This was all very well; but so certain was I that all his dressing and titivation was not done for nothing, and that he wouldn't be so pious without expecting to get something in return—for he is a very good and sensible man in all religious matters—that I resolved to take the whole affair in hand myself, and ferret out the mystery, if there really was one. The very next night he went out as usual, and I, having dressed myself in readiness, followed him. But we hadn't gone two minutes walk before I met the brother I just mentioned, and, of course, I was compelled to stop and tell him all about it; and, by the time we left off, my husband was out of sight and it was no good looking after him. Some people, when they begin to talk, you never know when they'll end, and this good brother is one of them—you can't edge in a word.

"Well, you see, now I was out it seemed a pity to go home
without calling upon some one; so I went round to Sister
Ellis. They told me she was out and I was just going away
when, lo and behold, who should I see but my dear Henry
marching down the street in the direction of the theatre with
a red-headed girl hanging on his arm. Oh, said I to myself,
that's the kind of Church-meeting you go to my dear, is it?
They were so busy with one another—I never saw Henry
look worse or more stupid in my life—that they didn't see me
at all. I did not cross over to them, for I felt too much com-
passion for their folly to wish to interrupt them then. Go on,
my dears, I thought; make the most of your opportunity for
I'll answer that *one* of you won't go to the theatre again for
some time. I wasn't the least bit jealous—jealousy is a sentiment that could never dwell in *my* bosom—but I *did* hate
the sight of that odious girl, and I resolved to take my husband
in hand immediately."

"Well Sister," I said, "I should have thought that his finding
a wife for himself would have saved you a world of trouble."

"Oh dear no, Sister Stenhouse," she replied, "it was trouble
I did not want to be saved. Men have no business, in my
opinion, to choose their own wives, after the first. I know the
men do do it, one and all; but it's a shameful stretch of authority.
I should like to know whether it is not of much more consequence to me what wife my husband has than it is to him?
However, I resolved that my husband should never marry the
red-headed girl, and the very next morning I told him so, and
what do you think the inhuman creature said? 'You've been
persuading me all these years,' he said, 'to take another wife,
although I've already got three, and now I've begun to do so
you blame me. I think I've as good a right as any one to say
who I'll marry and who I won't.' Did you ever hear of such
ingratitude? Would you hear of such a thing from *your*
husband, Sister Stenhouse?"

I told her that with Mormonism my husband had given up
Polygamy; and she continued:

"Well, I tried to bring him to reason, but it was of no use.

And then I told him that the girl should never set foot inside the house while I was in it. This was a very unfortunate speech, for I do believe that up to that time he wanted as much as possible to keep the girl out of my way; but the moment I said that, to show his dignity I suppose, he declared that she should come to tea with us that very afternoon, and he would go and fetch her; and he did so. I wouldn't go down to tea at first, though both the other wives were there and he sent up for me, but my pride would not allow me to stoop. At last I got tired of being all alone, and as it occurred to me that perhaps they might be enjoying themselves without me, I resolved to go down and see if I could not do something to annoy them. Down I went, and Henry, all smiling, introduced the girl to me as 'Sister Charlotte,' talking of her as if he had known her for years. Was it not shameful?"

"It must have been very awkward for you," I said.

"It was indeed, Sister Stenhouse, and I soon made it awkward for *them;* I assure you, after I joined them, there was not a soul present who had a moment's comfort till that girl went away. My husband, however, took her home, and from that very day he seemed resolved to have the upper hand. He never for a moment would listen to a word I said about the girl; he brought her in every evening and took her to the theatre constantly, and paid her ten times more attention than he ever paid me. I wasn't jealous, Sister Stenhouse; no one—as I said before—could ever suspect me of jealousy, but I *did* hate that girl. If he had not loved her, I can't say whether I myself might not have liked her. But the very fact of him loving her makes me detest her, but its only a little proper pride on my part—I'm not in the least jealous, Oh dear no!"

"Of course not," I said.

"I don't know about that," she said, "I've borne enough from those two to drive fifty women crazy with jealousy, and things went on from bad to worse, until the other day when, as I told you, we had that little unpleasantness. My husband

36

when he came back was downright angry, and made use of shocking language, and told me that, if he could not have peace in the house, he would have me board out by myself in some other part of the city. He said that I had scratched Charlotte's face and torn out her hair; but that was quite untrue, as I told him; and as for the hair which fell out, it was all an accident. He said that Charlotte did not like such accidents and that he would not put up with it. He was very cross and disagreeable all the rest of the day and made me quite miserable and broken hearted, and the next day, to wind it all up, he told me that he and Charlotte had arranged the day of the wedding. I stormed and raved, for I had fully resolved that, marry whom he might, he should never marry a girl if he *really* loved her or if I had not chosen her. But it was of no use—I was forced to go over with him to the Endowment House to give him that detestable little vixen. I tell you, Sister Stenhouse, I hate her; and oh, oh, dear what *shall* I do now my husband has fallen in love with her!"

Here, to my infinite astonishment, she rose from her seat and rushed about the room, wringing her hands and exclaiming, "Oh dear! Oh dear!" She then threw herself right down on the couch and actually burst into tears, crying out "Oh dear, what shall I do with my Henry and that girl!"

I raised her up and tried to comfort her as well as I could, but she was a very awkward woman to deal with under such circumstances. The more gently I spoke to her, the more violent did she become, and the louder were her lamentations. She forgot that she had been the cause of her husband taking any plural wives at all, and she upbraided him as the source of all her woes. One moment she would denounce him as a heartless wretch: then she would go into fits of maudlin sympathy over him, declaring that her Henry was the dearest man alive until "that horrid red-headed girl" led him astray. "Oh dear, dear Sister Stenhouse," she exclaimed as she threw both her arms round my neck and covered me with tears—"never do as I have done—*never* get a wife for your husband again, or he'll learn to do it for himself. And, oh, Sister Stenhouse let us kneel down and ask the Lord to strengthen us in this hour of tribulation; and, oh," she added piteously, "I should take it such a very great favor, Sister, if you wouldn't mind trimming that bonnet for me—you've got such taste!"

I assured her that I would trim the bonnet or do anything else that would help to assuage her grief. So she had her cry out and then she went on talking. She stopped and had some lunch, and still she talked; and at last when a little girl came round with a message from her husband saying that she was wanted at home, she left me in the middle of a long speech in which she was explaining the steps which she meant to take to bring her Henry "to reason," and to compel him to obtain a divorce from "that red-headed hussy."

The same evening she came again. This time she brought with her the bonnet and the materials for trimming it, and I promised her that she should have but a little while to wait; for she said she was overflowing with anxiety to quit the Mormon Church, and she felt convinced that that could not properly be done by any one wearing an old or dowdy bonnet. She had had a warm time with the bride and bridegroom, and seemed quite cheerful at the thought that she had thoroughly spoilt the happiness of their wedding-day, for she had left them both with ruffled tempers and in the worst of humors. After that she was almost always with me until the bonnet was finished, which was not until a couple of days later, for I was delayed by some more important matters which unexpectedly engaged my attention; and when she went away she was as lavish with her thanks and praises as she was with her promises respecting the mighty things which she was going to do, and the bright example she would become to the women of Utah.

I did not see her for several weeks, and then I accidentally met her in the street, and asked her why she had not called upon me lately. She was wearing the new bonnet, but I had heard nothing about her apostacy.

"Oh, Sister Stenhouse," she said, "I'm delighted to see you! You've been constantly in my thoughts, but I've been so hard

at work—Oh, *so* busy, that I really had not time for anything
—not even to apostatise."

"How was that?" I asked.

"Oh," she replied, "when I thought over the matter I saw
very clearly that it wouldn't do to render myself conspicuous
with this old dress. The bonnet's very nice and I want to
thank you, dear, for the trimming; but I must wait till I get
that silk dress which Henry says I really shall have soon.
I'm not so very sure though whether he would give me the
dress if I were to apostatise, so I'd better wait and get it first.
Then, too, you see I've had my hands full. If you want to
make a man slight one woman and get tired of her, there's
nothing like putting a nicer woman than her in his way. So
I reconsidered the matter and resolved, cost what it might,
I'd get another wife for my husband right away. I don't care
now whether she's old or young, ugly or pretty, so long as she
cuts out that detestable red-headed girl. I've run all over the
town and rushed about here and there, all for his sake, though
he'll never be grateful for it; and now at last, do you know,
dear, I really do think I've got the girl I want. She's all dark
—dark hair, dark eyes, dark complexion. If he marries her,
as I mean him to do, she'll lead him a fine life, notwithstanding all her winning ways. I wouldn't stand in *his* shoes when
she's his wife; but I know *I* shall be able to manage her, for I
have a deeper insight into character than he has, and a better
command of temper. She'll teach Miss Charlotte to keep her
place, and she'll make Henry mind too. It'll do him good;—
I've done it all out of love to him, not a spark of jealousy or
ill feeling, as you are well aware."

The idea of setting one wife against another, in order to
keep the peace, would appear in the case of my talkative
friend to have been successful; for, sure enough, six months
after the time of which I have just spoken, her Henry did
marry the dark beauty, and she and her auburn predecessor
presented an interesting contrast when they chanced to appear
in the street together in the company of their husband. There
did not seem to be much love lost between them.

Successful in her plans, and having, as she said, now brought her Henry to reason, my talkative friend gave up all idea of leaving the Church, and when I last saw her she said "I'm busy now looking after a likely girl, for I do think a man in my Henry's position ought to live his religion and have *at least seven wives!*—seven, you know, is such a very lucky number."

CHAPTER XLIII.

AFTER WE LEFT THE CHURCH—INTERESTING FACTS AND FIGURES—THE MORMONISM AND MORMONS OF TO-DAY.

After We Left the Church—Beginning Life Afresh—The Coldness of Our Former Friends—Disposing of the Daily Telegraph—How Fuller Flourished: Ran a Paper and Ran Away—Our New Position—My Husband Goes East—Effects of the "New Movement"—"Zion's Co-operative Mercantile Institution"—Brigham's Store—"Country-folks Seeking After a Sign"—An Old Lady's Stock in the "Coöp"—A Pound and a half of Nails!—The "Order of Enoch"—The Crowning Swindle!—The Very Vilest Slavery of All—How Reporters and Visitors are Fooled by Brigham—The Ladies' Petitions—Legalising the Marriage of Children!—The Franchise Conferred on Mormon Women—How Unanimously they Vote!—The Ballot Farce in Utah—How they Allowed the Mules to Vote!—Finery *versus* Faith—The Position in Utah To-day—The Apostacy of Brother Brigham's Son—Some Singular Statistics—Undoing the Past.

> "The world was all before them where to choose
> Their place of rest : with Providence their guide,
> They hand in hand with trembling steps and slow,
> Through Eden took their solitary way."
>
> *Paradise Lost.*

WHEN we left the Mormon Church, we were not quite as badly off as were our first parents when they began life, although in some respects we certainly resembled them. The world was all before us, and it was necessary that we also should choose a place of rest; but it was by no means an Eden from which we were dismissed,—or, rather, had dismissed ourselves,—and in the matter of experience in the thorny ways of that world in which we were about to begin afresh the battle of existence, we certainly had the advantage over the exiles from Paradise.

The crisis of our own lives had now arrived;—the act of sending in our resignation as members of the Church cut us off from all the associations of the past and all the friendships and pleasant intimacies of so many years;—a great gulf divided our by-gone life from the unknown future which lay before us.

My husband was now made painfully aware that it was altogether useless for him to attempt to carry on his paper, for his subscribers, as I before stated, had been "counselled" to discontinue taking it in. The *Daily Telegraph* had had a very large circulation, but as there was very little money in the Territory, the yearly subscriptions were mostly paid at harvest time, and many of them in grain. At the time, therefore, when the paper was finally given up, the Mormon people, as the book-keeper in Ogden informed me, owed about twenty thousand dollars; but when it was discovered that we were "Apostates," the majority of them considered that they were released from all obligations on that score, and my husband being an easy, generous-minded man, most of them evaded payment. The idea that, because we had left the Church, no Saint was bound to pay us any debts which they might happen at the time to owe, was the natural result of the teachings of the Tabernacle. Apostates are delivered over to "the buffetings of Satan," and the Saints consider it is *their* duty to begin in this world their master's work of castigation. Any ill turn that can be done to an Apostate is consequently a good action in the opinion of the Mormons, and they neglect no opportunity of showing that these are the sentiments which influence them.

Although we had now left the Mormon Church, never to return, my husband could not at once shake off entirely that influence which had so long held him captive. His thoughts and belief, his hopes and ambitions, had for a quarter of a century all pointed in one direction, and the very idea of rebellion on his part against the authority of the Priesthood, would, but a very little while before the time of which I speak, have been considered by him an utter impossibility. It was impossible, in a few short months only, to undo the work of five-and-twenty years—the best years of his life. He could no longer remain in the Church or conscientiously support Brigham Young; but he had not outgrown Mormonism sufficiently to enable him to throw off the yoke entirely and make his paper an opponent of Brigham and his faith. Could he have done so, I think it is highly probable that the *Telegraph* might yet have been saved, for I know that many of the more influential of the Gentiles would have aided him materially in such a course. As it was, nothing remained but to give it up with the best grace he could.

Two offers in reference to the paper were received by Mr. Stenhouse, and it remained for him to decide which he would accept. One of them came from a Gentile, who proposed to run it in opposition to Brigham Young, and the other came from a certain Mr. Fuller, who had for some time been my husband's travelling agent, and was a very intimate friend of John W. Young, Brigham's youngest son by his first wife. We knew that this Mr. Fuller had nothing beyond his salary, but, as the friend of Brigham's son, we thought that probably it was the Prophet's wish that he should have this paper and we believed that he was simply buying it for the Church. My husband argued that, although he could no longer unite with the Mormons, he could at least refrain from doing them any injury; he therefore concluded that, rather than let the paper go into the hands of an avowed enemy, he would sell it to Mr. Fuller, who, on account of his friendship for the Prophet's family, would, he presumed, try to be just to the people.

This, no doubt, was very conscientious and just, although, of course, no Mormon would give my husband credit for entertaining such sentiments. For my own part, I naturally wished him to accept the offer that would pay him best, which was that made by the Gentile. He could not, however, bring his mind to do this. The paper, therefore, was sold to Mr. Fuller, who ran it for a few months and then himself ran away, leaving behind him debts enough to swallow up everything. Thus ended the *Telegraph* under that name, but destined, however, to rise again as the *Salt Lake Herald*—a paper devoted to the interests of Brigham and the Priesthood. To my husband it was an utter loss, but it was hardly fair that his conscientious conduct should meet with such an ill return.

It was now necessary that some steps should be taken to provide for our family. The reader may, perhaps, remember that when we first arrived in Salt Lake City, as I stated, I myself engaged in business until my husband was able to find some suitable and profitable employment. When the *Telegraph*, however, was established and proved such a great success, and we were in a position of affluence, I considered—the pressure of necessity being removed—that I should do well to resign my own business connection and employ my time more profitably in domestic affairs. This was a great relief to me, for I always felt considerable repugnance to mixing with the world in the way of business, while among my children and attending to their wants and interests I found myself in my own legitimate sphere. But there was now no alternative. All interest in the *Telegraph* had been resigned; my husband's property had been wasted in an attempt to keep it up, and he had nothing now to depend upon. Something must be done, and I resolved that I would not be backward in bearing my full share of the burden.

It was only natural that we should feel very much unsettled in mind by the great change which had taken place in our position, for it is no easy matter to cut asunder the ties and associations of a life-time. Any one suddenly changing his religious faith would, to a certain extent, feel and understand what I mean in this respect. But in reference to any ordinary religion, the person forsaking it would probably experience comparatively little alteration in his every-day life. In Mormonism it is very different, especially to any one who has occupied a prominent position among the Saints. To resign our religion was to revolutionize our lives. Every thing was changed : the friends of years would look coldly on us and avoid us ; persons whom we had before shunned as Gentiles or Apostates would be the only individuals who would regard us with favor ;—our entire position in the midst of a most exclusive community was completely reversed ; in a word, we ourselves were now " Apostates ! "

Thinking to turn the current of his thoughts, and believing that change would be beneficial to him, I suggested to my husband that he should pay a visit to the Eastern States. In New York I believed he could find employment which would help to divert his thoughts from Mormon affairs and, at the same time, would be profitable to him in other respects. My suggestion was acted upon, and my husband set out East, while I prepared to engage again in the same business which I had formerly conducted so successfully.

Now, for the first time since I embraced Mormonism, I mixed freely with Gentiles and those who had left the Church, and it was not long before I found that this intercourse with the outer world produced a marked and decided effect upon my mind. My views were enlarged and my thoughts became more liberal in their tone. My husband's letters showed me that a similar change was taking place in him.

We were not the only Apostates from the Church at that time. The New Movement, as the reaction against the tyranny of Brigham Young was called, was then in progress ; and the minds of all intelligent Saints were led to reflect upon the unheard-of claims of Brigham's "Infallible" Priesthood. At this time the Prophet endeavored to rivet still more firmly the fetters. which bound his deluded followers, by establishing "Zion's Coöperative Mercantile Institution" and reviving the "Order of Enoch."

The Coöperative Institution was announced as a joint-stock concern, established under the pretence that it would be a benefit to the working classes, and all the members of the Church were invited to purchase shares, which were sold at twenty-five dollars each. The statement so often made by Brigham and repeated by strangers, to the effect that the exorbitant prices charged by Gentile merchants necessitated the establishment of such an institution was, as every Mormon knows, only a pretence, and a very shallow one, too ; for the Walker Brothers and other merchants had, for many years, supplied goods to Mormons and Gentiles alike, at what, under the circumstances, were reasonable and just prices; for the railway not then being constructed, and every article of commerce being of necessity carried across the Plains—a distance of over a thousand miles—by horse-teams, prices were, of course, very high, and would, if this circumstance were not taken into consideration, appear extortionate. In fact, subsequently, the "Coöperative" stores, which had started with high rates, under the belief that every rival would be crushed, were compelled to lower their prices to those of the Walker Brothers, or, in spite of their faith, the Mormons would have forsaken Brigham's Institution for the sake of their pockets. Many, in fact, did secretly go to Gentile stores, but they were watched by the police and reported to the teachers.

That large Mormon store, in which Brigham Young had such a heavy interest, was to become the parent establishment, the fountain-head from which temporal blessings, in the shape of cheap goods of every description, were to flow unto the people. Each Ward was to have its own store, and there the Saints of that Ward were expected to deal exclusively, and, as the teachers said, "keep off Main street where the Gentile stores were located." These Ward-stores purchased their goods from the parent store where nothing was sold by wholesale.

All the lesser Mormon Merchants were "counselled" to sell out their stock to the Church, for just what the Church chose to offer them, or dispose of it otherwise as best they could, and then they might go farming, or on mission, or anything else—but sell out they must, for they were plainly told that they would not be allowed to carry on business in opposition to the new Institution.

Now, instead of benefitting the poorer Saints, by supplying goods to them at a small advance upon cost prices, as was at first proclaimed to be the object of the "Co-op"—as the Institution was briefly and familiarly called—the reverse was the case, for competition was altogether banished. All the trade of the Gentile merchants—with one or two exceptions—was forcibly taken from them, for the people were not to trade in any store without first looking to see if the sign of the Institution—a picture of "The All-seeing Eye," and the words "Holiness unto the Lord"—were over the door-way. How often I have seen groups of country people straggling along, with their heads thrown back and their eyes straining aloft in eager quest of that sign, although perhaps their purchases would only amount to a few yards of ribbon or a paper of pins!

No one can predict what the Church—otherwise Brigham—will do, if money should chance to tempt him. In this case, the parent Coöperative store turned, as I might say, traitor to the Ward-stores—its own children—for no sooner had they all been established, and had bought up all the old stock from the parent store, than it was whispered abroad that the latter was about to open in the retail line with a splendid stock of new goods—to suit the Gentiles, of course; for the Saints were not allowed to trade outside of their own Ward-stores, where they were expected to buy up all the old goods. In fact, in order to gain Gentile trade and fill the pockets of Brigham and the leading Elders who really constituted the Institution (and do so still), the same prices were asked at the parent store as had been charged the poor, confiding stock-holders of the Ward-stores at wholesale. This, of course, caused great dissatisfaction, and many of the Saints rebelled, declaring they would go where they pleased to spend their money, when they had any to spend. The Ward-stores, in consequence, were obliged, at great loss, to lower their prices, and many were utterly ruined. Others which had more capital tided over the difficulty, and learned a lesson concerning the honesty of the Church leaders which it is to be hoped did them good

As an example of the way in which matters were managed, I may instance a very old and infirm woman who was one of their victims. She came to me one day and said, "Sister Stenhouse, will you buy out my stock in the Coöperative store? Our store has failed, and I have my twenty-five dollars' worth in my basket. I pitied her and asked her to let me see her stock, and thereupon she brought out *a pound and a half of nails!* I *did* buy out her stock, for I thought that the nails might be handy to have in the house, although I did not give her twenty-five dollars for them. Another person—a Frenchman, whom I knew—bought a share, and when he saw certain ruin looming over his Ward-store, he went to the headquarters and purchased twenty-five dollars' worth of goods, and having got them all secured, laid down his shareholders' receipt in payment and beat a hasty retreat. He was a fortunate man and acted prudently, but Alas! for the poor souls who ventured all their little savings in these Church "Institutions" and then were left to poverty and starvation.

The "Order of Enoch" is the crowning swindle of all. Its victims, under a legal form, make over to the Church every cent of which they may be possessed, even to the very clothes upon their backs, and place themselves—their whole life and being—entirely at the command of "The Church." They do, in fact, *literally* make themselves slaves, only their slavery is infinitely worse and more debasing than the bondage of the Negro, for *they* give soul and mind, as well as body and goods, utterly, absolutely, and for ever, into the iron grasp of the Mormon Priesthood. This "Order of Enoch" is quite a favorite institution with Brigham Young, who has lately been preaching it up throughout Utah; and many hundred fanatical and deluded Saints have at his instigation *given*—not sold, for they receive nothing in return—themselves into this abject slavery. And yet these are the institutions which "unprejudiced" newspaper reporters and editors, when they visit Utah, and are, according to the fixed and ordinary custom of Brigham, treated and toadied to until, poor dupes, they think that the favors they receive are simply marks of the appre-

ciation of the Mormons for their own conceited or deluded
selves personally, and not part and parcel of his system:—
these, I say, are the institutions which such visitors laud to
the skies when they speak of the Prophet's generosity, his
open-heartedness, his patriarchal benevolence, and his other
saintly virtues.

When we left the Church, these institutions were attracting
a good deal of attention among the Saints. The "Coöperative" still flourishes, and the "Order of Enoch" has within the
last few weeks been gathering into its net, not tens, but
hundreds of dupes.

About this time, also, it was that the Mormon women, under
the auspices of Eliza R. Snow and the Female Relief Society,
got up that petition to Mrs. Grant, to which I have referred
in another place, begging her to use her influence with the
President in favor of a toleration of Polygamy. The names
to that petition were affixed without any reference to propriety
or right. Hundreds of names were copied from the books of
the Society without any permission being obtained, or even
asked, of their owners. It was then, as I before stated, that
the names of the dead were actually added as subscribers to
the petition, and in one case, when a lady mentioned that her
dead daughter had never belonged to the Church, as she died
before her mother heard of Mormonism, she was told that her
daughter would now, of course, have found out that Polygamy
was the true order of domestic life in heaven, and that she
would certainly be willing to subscribe if she could return to
earth. Her name was, therefore, added without any further
ceremony, although she had been dead a good many years.

In January, 1872, a counter-petition was got up by the
Gentile and Apostate ladies. It set forth the cruel bondage
which Polygamy inflicts upon women; spoke of the heartless
conduct of the Mormon leaders, and of the murders and other
foul crimes which had been committed by them or at their
instigation; showed that, should Utah become a State, under
the name of *Deseret*,—which has ever been the ambition of
Brigham Young,—there would be no protection for life or

property; stated that the authorities themselves had declared that when statehood was. conferred, Gentiles and Apostates would have good cause to tremble; and, finally, prayed the National Government to stretch forth its long arm of power for the defence and protection of honest and law-abiding citizens. This petition was signed by four hundred and forty ladies of Utah, most of them members of the Mormon Church, whose *real* names were all fairly and openly *affixed by their own selves*. It was presented to the Senate by the Hon. Schuyler Colfax—then Vice-President; was read, discussed, and ordered to be printed. As might be supposed, it excited a great deal of angry discussion on the part of the Church authorities; and the following Sundays the names of those who had signed were read out in the Tabernacle, and *strong* remarks made upon their conduct, in order to intimidate them and prevent others from following their example. The consequence was that many of their husbands and sons were threatened with loss of employment, and they were thus forced to retract.

That same year, a bill was brought into the Territorial Legislature, providing that *boys of fifteen years of age and girls of twelve might legally contract marriage*, with the consent of their parents or guardians! In stating this disgraceful fact, I feel certain that the reader who has never lived among the Saints and is not versed in Utah affairs will think that I must be mistaken in what I say. It is, however, I am sorry to say, only too true, and the records of the Legislature will bear me witness. The fact was stated in the *New York Herald* of January 27, 1872.

It will be a matter of interest to the advocates of women's suffrage to learn that Brigham Young conferred the franchise upon the Mormon ladies. This, at first, appears to be a very liberal measure; but let not the innocent reader be deceived thereby. The opening of the mines and the great influx of Gentiles, consequent upon the completion of the Union Pacific Railroad, proved very clearly to Brigham that the day *might* come when the Gentiles would have an equality, if not a majority, of votes, and in that day the slavish despotism of the Mormon Priesthood would be overthrown. The time, certainly, was very far off, but it was wise to provide for contingencies. So a bill was brought in conferring upon women the privilege of voting. No Mormon woman would for a moment ever dream of voting otherwise than she was directed by her husband, and no man would think of voting except as he was "counselled" by the Priesthood. Thus, a man with half a dozen wives would now have half a dozen votes, and Brother Brigham, instead of having only his own single vote, would have nineteen for his nineteen wives, to say nothing of his daughters and the whole army of spiritual wives which he might produce. I have often seen one solitary man driving into the City a whole wagon-load of women of all ages and sizes—they were going to the poll, and their votes would be *one!* It is very easy to see how in this way the influence of the Priesthood has been extended, and women themselves have been made the instruments for rivetting still more firmly their own fetters. But it is by no means easy to see that women in Utah have derived any benefit from being permitted to vote.

Voting among the Saints has always been carried on in a very free and easy manner. One gentleman—an English convert—not long since told me that when he had been less than two months in the States, and, of course, was not naturalised, and had no rights as a citizen, he was "counselled" by the Mormon leaders to give in his vote; he did so, and, in obedience to instructions received, he gave in also his wife's vote and the vote of their little baby girl—an infant of only a few months old—although that was before the voting of *women* was legalised.

Others have voted two or three times, so as to make sure that the Church should not lose their interest. And this very common practice of the same persons voting over and over again renders all statistics given by Mormon authority utterly untrustworthy. Besides which, the voting-tickets are all numbered, and the voters' names carefully registered in a book, so that the Priesthood can tell at a moment's notice on which

side, or for whom, a man has cast his vote. In this way the
ballot in Utah becomes a most ridiculous farce, instead of a
means for obtaining unbiassed and uninfluenced elections.
Anxious to obtain admission into the Union as a State, it is
the interest of Brigham Young and the leaders to swell the
numbers of the population by every means in their power.
For this they have strained every nerve to bring over converts
from abroad, and with the same object—to "build up the kingdom"—they have forced Polygamy upon the people. The most
unscrupulous measures have been resorted to, and it is even
said that on one occasion when a goodly show of names was
needed, not only were the names of the dead and of relations
and converts who had never been in the country at all, added
as subscribers to the document, but that they actually Christened their mules—conferring upon them the names of men,
and then made *them* vote also!

Notwithstanding the vigilance of the Priesthood, many
young Mormon ladies have preferred Gentile husbands, and
some of them have left the Territory; but they have been
invariably traduced and scandalised, and whenever the rumor
of misfortune occurring to any of them reached Salt Lake
City, it was retailed with undisguised gratification, as a sweet
morsel, by the Priesthood. Some Mormon mothers, hating
the idea of their daughters marrying polygamists, have encouraged the addresses of Gentiles, and were only too glad to have
their children marry out of Mormonism. Such mothers, of
course, are apostate in heart, although nominally they may not
have left the Church.

The extravagancies of modern dress render it every year
more and more difficult for men of moderate means to support
many wives. Fashion is proving a deadly foe to Polygamy,
and the feminine taste for finery is in Utah helping to bring
about some really good practical results. There is now a
pleasing change noticeable in the plural marriages in Salt
Lake City. There are not nearly so many marriages of this
kind among the actual citizens as there were three or four
years ago. The opening of the mines and the construction of

37

the railroad brought so many strangers among us that it was impossible to withstand their influence. Many of our young Mormon maidens have been beguiled into matrimony by these wicked Gentiles, against whom Brother Brigham has so often warned us; and not only so, but many good Saints have apparently come to the conclusion that though Polygamy was so absolutely necessary to their own salvation, it is not by any means essential to the salvation of their daughters. Thus, some of them have given their daughters to the sons of strangers, to become in due time mothers of a race of wicked Gentiles, and if one might judge from their conversation they do not appear to regret it very much.

The dislike of the women to Polygamy has increased, especially in Salt Lake City, although in the Settlements fanaticism is as rampant as ever, and the "Celestial" system is the order of the day. Young Mormon girls are disgusted when they hear young men and even boys talking of their "privileges," boasting how many wives they mean to take, and how they will take two on the same day in order to preserve peace. Girls of the slightest feeling or intelligence resent all this and the more refined regard these little would-be Polygamists, and all they say, with intense loathing and contempt. To Gentile girls such insults are of course unknown, and the Mormon girls, when they have the opportunity of mixing with the outside world, are not slow to discover that while, if they marry among people of their own faith, they will never occupy their proper position in society, if they become Gentile wives they will be the cherished companions and equals of the men to whom they are united. Sensitive girls will say that they would rather have a little less glory in the world to come and have a little more comfort in this.

Then, too, the married women compare the condition of the Gentile wives with their own, and the comparison is by no means in favor of Polygamy. A polygamic wife who is one of many and only sees her husband occasionally, and that as a favor, cannot well visit a Gentile wife in her own home without drawing a comparison by no means in favor of Mormonism. Many Mormon wives have thus become unhappy ; and hence the most strenuous exertions are made on the part of the leaders to prevent as far as possible all intercourse between the Saints and the outside world. Notwithstanding this, a leading attorney in Salt Lake City told me, that during the year succeeding our abandonment of Mormonism, more than one hundred first wives called upon him proposing to enter suit for divorce and alimony, and this represents but a small proportion of those who would sacrifice almost anything if only they could escape from Polygamy.

Left to itself, Mormonism would long ago have perished, so great has been the number of Apostates. But England and Scandinavia furnish yearly a multitude of dupes, who come over every summer by thousands to aid in carrying on the imposture. These, with the people in the Settlements, who are purposely kept in ignorance, slavery, and poverty, perpetuate Polygamy in Utah.

John W. Young, the Prophet's son, to whom I have already alluded, became disgusted with Polygamy and abandoned it. Therefore, according to his father's teaching, he cannot now enter into the " Celestial Kingdom." But Brigham Young says that he, as the successor of Joseph Smith, holds the " Keys of the Kingdom," and he probably thinks that he will be able to shuffle his son John W. in, in a quiet way. For my own part I do not suppose that Brigham Young believes one word of the nonsense he teaches to the people—he is far too shrewd for that ! A certain Utah official once said to my husband, " Brigham has got the best thing in America, and he means to hold on to it." *That* is about the sum and substance of Brigham's religion.

About eight years ago, John W.—who is a handsome, gentlemanly young man—married a Miss Lucy Canfield, of Ogden—it was said, in obedience to the " counsel " of his father. Two years subsequently he married Miss Clara Jones, whose father when living had occupied a prominent position in the Church. This lady also, it was stated, he married in obedience to a command of the Prophet, who had been known to say that he wished one of his sons to marry her and that, if they did not, he would marry her himself. Brigham has often told men to marry certain women, and they have felt bound to obey, believing, probably, as Mormon men generally do, that it makes very little difference, after all, who they married, as they have got to have a certain number of wives in order to enter the " Celestial Kingdom," and among them all they will be sure to find one whom they can love. Mormon men are not very different from other men; for although they tell their numerous wives quite another story, they can truly love but one woman at a time. Some good Saints, I doubt not, do really believe to the contrary, but love thus divided is not worthy of the name. In this respect men resemble women,—no woman can love two men at the same time.

The two young girls, the wives of John W. Young, of course, each in turn, believed that she was the beloved one; but subsequently they discovered how greatly they had been mistaken, for John W. had not yet met with his "affinity." In the course of time, however, the fair one appeared who was to enslave his heart, and John W. submitted without a murmur.

Mrs. Lucy Canfield Young, the first wife, had cousins living in Philadelphia, and as John W. was returning from England, where he had been on mission, at the request of his wife he called to see them, and there he met with his fate in the person of Miss Lizzie Canfield—one of his wife's cousins. He immediately fell deeply in love with this young lady and requested her to go with him to Salt Lake City to visit his wife. She agreed, and, with her sister, accompanied him, and before they arrived at the termination of their journey she had promised to marry him. She had no faith in Mormonism, but every thing was forgotten in love.

After their marriage, Miss Canfield—now Mrs. John W. Young, number three—became very unhappy, for she felt deeply her degraded position, and though she dearly loved her husband, would have left him had she not felt that such a step would render him perfectly miserable, for it was evident that he cared nothing at all for his other two wives. They, poor girls, were also destined to become victims to this disgraceful system—abandoned in their youth, and one of them the mother of two or three children.

The first wife—Lucy Canfield Young—perceiving that her husband no longer cared for her, with true womanly dignity withdrew from his husbandly care, obtained a divorce, and became "Miss" Lucy Canfield again.

Mrs. Clara Jones Young could not so easily bring her mind to leave the father of her children, but still hopes that her truant husband will return to his unhappy wife, from whom he has not yet been divorced, although he no longer lives with her. In this, however, she is mistaken;—John W. will never return to her, for he is completely disgusted with his father's pet scheme of "Celestial" marriage, and, undoubtedly, would be formally separated from his second wife, were it not that, according to Mormon law, the wife alone has the privilege of applying for a divorce. He is, in fact, at heart a "vile Apostate," as his father calls seceders from the Church; for no one can possibly be a good Mormon without believing with all his soul in Polygamy. Take Polygamy and the Endowments from Mormonism, and there is nothing left to distinguish that faith from any other of the absurd religions which have from time to time been advocated by fanatical men.

John W. Young, notwithstanding the apostate spirit which has fallen upon him, has lately been appointed to preside over the Saints at St. George, in Southern Utah, and I sincerely trust that he will lead all those good Saints, over whom he is sent to preside, to think as he does respecting plural marriage, and that his wife may do her best to create in the minds of the unhappy and degraded sisters around her a desire for that higher social position, that perfect equality with man, which is the inalienable right of every woman.

It is very fortunate for John W. Young that he is the son of his father; for if he had been any other man's son, and had abandoned Polygamy, he would never have been appointed to preside over the Saints in St. George, or anywhere else. But Brigham is all-powerful in Mormondom ; it is he who controls the affairs of the "Kingdom"; and if he chooses to allow an Apostate son not only to pass muster but to be accounted worthy to rule among the Saints, who shall gainsay it? Brigham has a bitter hatred of Apostates and apostacy. The very name—"Apostate"—is the most cruel arrow in his quiver. And yet the very man, who if Brigham's own precedent were followed, ought to succeed him—Orson Hyde, the President of the Twelve Apostles, was once an Apostate, in Missouri, and a very cowardly one at that. Brigham himself, little as he perhaps imagines it, is the. Prince of Apostatès. He became an Apostate Methodist when he left Methodism and joined the Mormons, and certainly he is now an Apostate from Mormonism as Joseph Smith first taught it. The change from Methodism to Mormonism, as it was first presented to the world, was nothing near so great as the departure which Brigham has made from the original faith of the Saints. There have been many Apostates from the teachings of Joseph in early days, but, of all Apostates, Brother Brigham is the chief.

It may, perhaps, surprise the reader to learn that in polygamous Utah, notwithstanding the constant importation of young girls from abroad, there are two thousand and fifty-six more males than females. In four counties only are the females in excess of the males. In Salt Lake County, which includes Salt Lake City, there are two hundred and ninety-nine more females than males ; in Cache County there are ninety-three more ; in Iron County there are thirty-one ; and in San Pete there are two hundred and thirty-eight more females than males. In all the other seventeen counties, the males are in excess of the females. In many instances the sexes are singularly balanced ; as, for instance, in Washington County, where there are fifteen hundred and thirty-two males and exactly the same number of females. Weber County has an excess of three hundred and thirty-six males ; Piute has sixty-nine males to thirteen females, and in Sevier County there are nineteen unfortunate males who are not blessed with the presence of a single female! These figures I obtained from the Census Bureau at Washington. They speak for themselves, and clearly demonstrate that, as far as Utah is concerned, instead of Polygamy being a necessity on account of the preponderance of the female sex, the facts are exactly the reverse; and if some men have two, four, six, eight or ten wives, for every wife they take some other man is forced to remain single. Considering the multiplicity of wives among the more pious Saints, and the large number of miners who, of course, are either unmarried or have not brought their wives with them to Utah, it is quite evident that there must be a good many single men in Utah.

But before closing my narrative, I must add a few words relative to myself. After my husband had been in New York for some months, it became necessary on account of business that I should join him there. I did so, and found him busy upon a history of Mormonism which he had for some years contemplated writing, and for which he had collected a large amount of valuable facts and statistics from the Historian's Office in Salt Lake City. While still a Mormon he had proposed to vindicate the Saints and justify their leaders, but now that his eyes were open to the degrading superstition and cruel bondage of the system, he was determined, as far as he had ability to do so, to expose the corruption and tyranny of the Priesthood. I heartily coincided with him, and encouraged him with wifely commendations.

At that time, I had no idea of becoming myself an author, and it was not until the close of that same year, when I paid a second visit to New York, that I first seriously entertained the idea of appearing before the public. I was induced to write a little volume which I thought would expose some of the cruel wrongs which Mormon Polygamy inflicts upon deluded, helpless women. My work was very kindly received and extensively circulated, but it was, I must confess, only a very imperfect and brief sketch. In this present volume I have endeavored to supply the deficiencies of the former, and in a

truthful, if imperfect, sketch of my own life and my own experience in, and observations of, the workings of the polygamic system, I have endeavored to give my readers a just idea
of what Polygamy and Mormonism really are.

With the exception of the little literary efforts which I have
made from time to time to expose through the press the iniquity
of the " Celestial Order of Marriage," no event of more than personal and private interest has, since I left the Mormon Church,
interrupted the even tenor of my life.   Last year, however, I
was able to deal another blow—weak, it might be, but still it
was a blow—directed at that false system against which I have
sworn eternal enmity.   I lectured upon Mormon Polygamy in
Washington, and Boston, and other large cities, and attempted
in my humble way to attract the attention of the Gentile
world to the iniquities of that terrible superstition which, in
Utah, has degraded womanhood and wrecked the happiness of
thousands of my deluded sisters.   I met with sympathy everywhere, and then, as now, I resolved that efforts like these I
would never relax until, if God spared my life, I should see
the last stone in the fabric of Mormonism overturned and Mormon Polygamy counted among the sins and follies of the past.

His literary work accomplished, my husband returned to
Salt Lake City.   Looking back over the past, our Missionary
life and our faith in Brighamism seems like a dream, so difficult is it for us to realise that we ever submitted our souls to
the slavery of the Priesthood or placed any credence in that
mass of folly, superstition, and licentiousness, known as Mormonism.   During all his efforts to obey counsel and build up
a " kingdom," my husband, I know, never ceased to love me.
For the misery which he then, in—as I firmly believe—his
conscientious endeavors to live his religion, inflicted upon me,
I have long ago freely and fully forgiven him.   I think that
during all that time he never ceased to entertain the fondest
affection for me ; and, if he was foolishly confiding in those
who he believed were divinely authorised and speaking by inspiration, can I blame him when I remember that I myself
was actuated by the same faith?

It was impossible to obliterate utterly the education and influences of a whole life's experience. That wall of partition—Polygamy—which separated my husband from me for so many years, is now for ever broken down. But the effects of Mormonism will, no doubt, though unconsciously to ourselves, tinge the whole of our future life. We can never forget the past. The mournful sympathy which, according to the poet, the Peri at the gate of Paradise expressed over the sins and sorrows of humanity, might, with a slight variation, be applied to our own lives :—

> "Poor race of men, said the pitying spirit,
> Dearly ye pay for your primal fall ;
> Some traces of Eden ye still inherit,
> But the trail of the serpent is over them all."

The terrible effects of our religion will, I know, follow us to our graves ; but that temporary alienation has, I think, like the quarrels of lovers, only made us still dearer to each other; and now, happy in our family circle, and with our children growing up around us, untainted by the fearful superstition which embittered and wasted their parents' lives, we feel that in them is our greatest blessing, and thank God that we have lived to see the day when our greatest ambition is, by every effort which lies within our reach, to aid in undoing that work which we spent the best years of our life in endeavoring to perform.

L' ENVOI.

In the preceding pages I have endeavored to present to the reader the story of my life's experience in Mormonism and Polygamy, and to place before him a truthful picture of the doctrines and practices of the Saints.

Much has already been written on this subject—much that is in accordance with facts, and much that is exaggerated and false. Hitherto, with but one exception*—that of a lady who wrote very many years ago, and who in her writings, so mixed up fiction with what was true, that it was difficult to determine where the one ended and the other began—no woman who *really* was a Mormon and lived in Polygamy ever wrote the history of her own personal experience. Books have been published, and narratives have appeared in the magazines and journals, purporting to be written by Mormon wives; it is, however, perhaps, unnecessary for me to state that, notwithstanding such narratives may be imposed upon the Gentile world as genuine, that they were written by persons outside the Mormon faith would in a moment be detected by any intelligent Saint who took the trouble to peruse them.

Two objects influenced my mind when I first proposed to write this volume. In the first place, I earnestly desired to stir up my Mormon sisters to a just sense of their own position. I longed to make them feel, as I do, the cruel degrada-

---

*Mrs. Ettie V. Smith.

tion, the humiliating tyranny, which Polygamy inflicts. I wanted to arouse them to a sense of their own Womanhood, and a just appreciation of those Rights and Duties which, as women, God has conferred upon them. I was anxious that they should understand and know the inconsistency and folly of that superstitious faith by which they have been so egregiously deluded; that they might learn to hate and loathe the falsely-named "Celestial" system of marriage; and rising in honest indignation and disgust against the tyranny of the oppressor, break asunder the yoke of bondage, cast from them for ever the moral, religious, and social fetters wherewith they are bound, and, walking in the light of truth, assert their perfect equality with their sons, their husbands, their fathers, and their brethren, and henceforth claim and occupy that position which God assigned them, and which *by right* is theirs!

In the second place, I was anxious to enlist for them the sympathy of the Gentile world. Most strenuous efforts have been made, large sums of money have been spent, and secret intrigues, as well as open and honorable negotiations, have been carried on for the purpose of obtaining admission for Utah into the Union, under the title of *The State of Deseret*. The name "Deseret" itself is taken from the Book of Mormon, and is said to signify in the celestial tongue a honey-bee; wherefore it is that the escutcheon of Utah Territory is a bee-hive; and to grant that name "Deseret" alone would be a concession to Mormon superstition. Out here in the Valley of the Great Salt Lake we are perfectly well aware that, with Utah once admitted as a State, it would be almost impossible for Gentiles to live peaceably and safely among the Mormons; and of this fact their leading men and their official organs have repeatedly boasted. With Utah as a State, and Brigham Young once more Governor, the enslavement of the people to the Priesthood would be complete, and the cruel bondage of Polygamy would be rivetted a thousand times more firmly upon the unfortunate women. I was anxious, therefore, to attract the attention of Congress and the Nation at large to these facts; that thus, when Mormon bills and

Mormon petitions, replete with falsified statistics, and perverted, and—in many instances—utterly untrue, statements, are presented to the National Legislature, neither the representatives of the Nation nor the Nation itself may be deceived thereby. These were the two objects which I proposed to myself in writing my own experience as a wife and mother among the Mormons, and I trust to some extent at least I have realised them.

I have told my story simply, but truthfully, and, as far as was possible, I have endeavored to TELL IT ALL. Some facts I have had occasion to relate, so horrible and repulsive, that a person unused to Mormonism and unversed in Mormon doctrine and Mormon practice would find dificulty in giving credence to such things—and yet, Alas! they are *all too true!* It is only right that I should add, that in the conduct and publicly expressed opinions of Brigham Young and many of the leaders, there have been such disgusting atrocities and such impure statements that for the sake of decency and propriety I dared not even mention them. For this *suppressio veri* I feel assured the reader will not blame me. In all that I have said I have most scrupulously kept to *the very letter of the truth*— I have neither exaggerated nor concealed, and in every respect my great endeavor has been to act with the strictest impartiality and justice.

Mine, in one sense, is the story of a wasted life. From the day when I linked my destiny with that of a Mormon Missionary Elder, to the time when, after long weary years of trial and endurance, I abjured the faith of the modern Saints, I suffered a constant martyrdom. Poverty, self-denial, and suffering, I gloried in, when I believed myself the humble instrument in the hands of the Almighty for proclaiming the "Fulness of the Gospel" to those who were walking in the darkness of unbelief. The trials of a Missionary life were to me a pleasure. I bore with gladness the cross, believing that hereafter I should exchange it for the glories of an eternal crown ; and I think, even now, I should never have wearied of that life of devotion, so great was my faith in my religion, had the leaders of the Church remained steadfast to that simple Gospel creed which we were at first taught was the Evangel of the Latter-Day Dispensation. But when Polygamy—that accursed thing! that offspring of deceit and licentiousness!— came across our path, darkening the way and blighting the affections, the hopes, the whole life, of every true woman among the Saints ; when Polygamy came, casting its foul stain over all that was holy, crushing out from our hearts all that was good, and pure, and heaven-born, degrading our woman-hood and embittering existence itself; when its dark shadow, like the gloom of the deadly Upas, brought death of the soul and the withering of the heart's true love to all who came within its influence ;—then my faith began to waver, my zeal to wax cold, and in anticipation, and subsequently in realisa-tion, of the cruel wrong which that system could inflict upon the affections and life of a wife and mother, I endured daily a trial of my faith—a moral and spiritual martyrdom, such as I trust my readers may never experience.

Not a day passed but what more and more evidence of the wickedness of the system, and its cruel debasement of woman's nature, was brought beneath my observation. Whatever came in contact with it, whoever fell beneath its influence, was the subject of immediate loss ;—men, women, and children alike suffered from its effects. The innocence of childhood was sullied by its contamination ; girlhood and youth were degraded and disgraced ; the fair, sweet dreams of virgin purity were marred by its presence ; the ideal of love—pure, faithful, holy, heavenly, which God himself has implanted in the heart, was rudely trampled upon, and perverted, and destroyed ; the lives of wives and mothers were but the record of outrage, cruelty, and wrong, or else the deadening and blasting of every holy impulse·and every tender emotion ; while men themselves were brutalised and debased ;—the husband became the lord, and frequently the tyrant and the despot ; and the wife was either the toy of the hour, or the drudge who looked after the children—but never the cherished companion, the help-meet of the man. Such was the influence of Polygamy—such the results of the " Celestial Order of Marriage!"

Contrary to the laws of the land; contrary to the holiest sentiments of the heart; contrary to the divine teachings of Heaven, that system still exists! It is a disgrace to the National Government; it is a reproach to Civilisation; it is a blot upon the fair escutcheon of the World's Greatest Republic!

And yet visitors will come from Utah, and will tell you that the Mormon women are happy in Polygamy, for it is a part of their religion. Never; until new hearts and new natures are given to the women of Utah, and all that is womanly, and pure, and sacred, is crushed out from their souls, can one single woman be truly happy in Polygamy! They may *say* so publicly, they may, for their religion's sake, *tell strangers* that thus it is; but listen to them when they are alone among themselves; read, if you can, their hearts, and mark the bitterness which they try to stifle there; nay, see upon their very features the handwriting which bears witness against their assertion that they are happy and which proclaims to the world the sorrow which they vainly try to hide!

I send forth this little book with many earnest prayers and many heartfelt aspirations that my Mormon sisters may be benefitted thereby. Out of the evil which man originates, God alone can produce good; and I trust that my feeble attempt to portray the cruel wrong which Polygamy inflicts upon the Women of Utah may excite the sympathy of every man and woman whose influence may avail to hasten that time when this relic of ancient barbarism may be utterly rooted out before the advancing civilisation of the age.

The night—the gloomy night of superstition—cannot last for ever. Already there are signs of the coming dawn. The time, I trust and pray, will not long be delayed when the veil shall be removed from the eyes of the enslaved men and women of our modern Zion, and they shall cast aside for ever the yoke of the Priesthood. I trust that I shall yet live to see the day when the Mormon wives and mothers shall awake to a sense of their position and responsibilities, shall understand that God never required that their womanhood should be degraded, their love crushed out, and the holiest instincts of their nature perverted; I trust to see them assert their inalienable rights—their womanly prerogatives—their very birthright itself; I trust to see them shake off the slavery of that cruel superstition which has so long held them captive; I trust to see them take their places side by side with Gentile matrons—the honored wives and mothers of the men of Utah; I trust to see that dark shadow banished from their features, banished from their hearts, banished from their lives, —I trust to see them FREE!

Full of love for them—my sisters, my friends, the companions of my life hitherto, whose religion was once my own, whose hopes and joys I have shared, whose sorrows and trials have been also mine — with hopeful prayer I lay down my pen and present my labors to the world. And if my humble efforts shall have conduced, even in the smallest degree, to keep one sister from entering into this sinful "Order"; if they shall have aroused the Women of Utah to investigate the foundations of their faith, to calmly and impartially consider the iniquities of the system of Polygamy, to renounce the man-made slavery of the "Celestial Order"; if I shall be found to have awakened in the minds of thinking men and women a hatred for the licentious doctrine which enslaves the wives and daughters of the Saints; if I have to any extent enlisted active, practical sympathy in their behalf— I shall feel that my endeavors have been abundantly rewarded and that my labors have not been bestowed in vain.

CPSIA information can be obtained
at www.ICGtesting.com
Printed in the USA
JSHW021920060223
37371JS00001B/4

9 781429 01902